1991

John Dewey

The Collected Works, 1882–1953

GENERAL EDITOR, JO ANN BOYDSTON

Index

EDITED BY ANNE S. SHARPE

ASSOCIATE EDITOR, HARRIET FURST SIMON

ASSISTANT EDITOR, BARBARA LEVINE

Southern Illinois University Press

Carbondale and Edwardsville

Manufactured in the United States of America

Editorial expenses for this edition have been met in part by grants from the Editions Program of the National Endowment for the Humanities, an independent Federal agency, and from the John Dewey Foundation. Publishing expenses have been met in part by a grant from the John Dewey Foundation.

Library of Congress Cataloging-in-Publication Data

Index to the collected works of John Dewey, 1882–1953 / edited by Anne S. Sharpe; associate editor, Harriet Furst Simon; assistant editor, Barbara Levine.
p. cm.
1. Dewey, John, 1859–1952—Dictionaries, indexes, etc.
I. Sharpe, Anne S. II. Simon, Harriet Furst. III. Levine, Barbara.
B945.D45Z85 1991 90-20120
016.191—dc20 CIP
ISBN 0-8093-1728-1

The paper used in this publication meets the minimum requirements of American National Standard for Information Sciences—Permanence of Paper for Printed Library Materials, ANSI Z39.48-1984. ♾

Contents

Preface vii

Contents of The Collected Works of John Dewey 1

The Early Works, 1882–1898 1

The Middle Works, 1899–1924 7

The Later Works, 1925–1953 25

Title Index to The Collected Works 53

Subject Index to The Collected Works 101

Preface

This cumulative index to the thirty-seven volumes of The Collected Works of John Dewey, 1882–1953, includes a Collected Works Contents, Title Index, and Subject Index. In the Title Index and the Subject Index, abbreviations are used to indicate the three series in which The Collected Works appear: **E**: *The Early Works, 1882–1898* (five volumes); **M**: *The Middle Works, 1899–1924* (fifteen volumes); and **L**: *The Later Works, 1925–1953* (seventeen volumes). Entries are keyed to the series abbreviations and volume numbers within that series; series and volume numbers appear in bold type and page numbers in regular type: for example, **E5**: 202; **M2**: 53; **L15**: 192.

The Collected Works Contents incorporates all the tables of contents of the individual volumes. This list provides a chronological, volume-by-volume overview of all items in the *Early Works, Middle Works,* and *Later Works.* The individual items that were republished in the collective books *Essays in Experimental Logic; The Influence of Darwin on Philosophy and Other Essays in Contemporary Thought; Impressions of Soviet Russia and the Revolutionary World, Mexico—China—Turkey; Philosophy and Civilization;* and *Problems of Men* appear at the date of original separate publication.

The Title Index lists alphabetically by shortened titles and by key words all items in The Collected Works. Articles republished in the collective books listed above are also grouped under the titles of those books. All titles that have a key noun in common are indented under the main entry for that noun in the following order: first, titles in which the key word has been inverted for indexing; second, titles in which the key word is followed by a conjunction or preposition; and third, titles in which the key word is used as an adjective. When the initial modifier in the subentry refers to more than one title, it is followed by a colon; otherwise, it is followed by a comma. For example:

Activity, **M6**: 361
  Good of, **M14**: 193
  Growth in, **L11**: 243
  and the Training of Thought, **M6**: 304; **L8**: 281
  Movement, **L9**: 169

or

Education, **M6**: 425
  Aims in, **M9**: 107
  Elementary: Aim of History in, **M1**: 104; Federal
    Aid to, **M10**: 125; Psychology of, **M1**: 67
  Public, on Trial, **M10**: 173

This order is similar to the format used in Milton Halsey Thomas's *John Dewey: A Centennial Bibliography* (Chicago: University of Chicago Press, 1962).

The Subject Index includes all information in the original volume indexes. This index expands that information by adding the authors of introductions to each volume, authors and titles of books Dewey reviewed or introduced, authors of appendix items, and relevant details from the source notes. In main entries, first-name initials have been supplied for all authors with identical surnames; in subentries, initials appear only when identical surnames might be confused. In addition to general cross-references, Dewey's own cross-references in the index to *Logic: The Theory of Inquiry* have been retained, keyed here to the *Later Works* publication of *Logic*: **L12**.

In the Subject Index, three formal changes from the individual volume indexes have been made. First, throughout the seventy-one years covered by The Collected Works, Dewey's spelling of several words varied; individual volume indexes reflect those spelling variations, as, for example, "aesthetic / esthetic," "scepticism / skepticism," and "subject matter / subject-matter / subjectmatter." Such variant spellings have been regularized in this index to a single form that will therefore differ at times from the forms found in the separate volumes. Second, extensive subentries in individual volume indexes have been, where possible, consolidated under more inclusive terms. Third, separate references to a subject on three or more consecutive pages that were originally indexed "34, 35, 36, 37" have been indexed "34–37."

The cumulative Subject Index to The Collected Works of John Dewey, 1882–1953, was created with the help of CINDEX, a series of programs designed by David R. Chesnutt and written by Jean W. Mustain at the University of South Carolina; CINDEX played a crucial role in preparing this index.

However, taking the work beyond CINDEX proved to be an undertaking of greater complexity than could be foreseen; simply entering the data from thirty-seven individual indexes—created by a number of editors with different approaches to indexing terms and concepts and published over a period of twenty-one years—into the computer and letting the computer program sort the data could not result in a coherent cumulative index.

In brief, the process of preparing the Subject Index entailed the following steps: the printed indexes from each of the thirty-seven volumes of The Collected Works were entered into a data file in CINDEX structured file format and proofread against the original indexes. Preliminary editing of the structured file indexes involved checking cross-listings and ambiguous entries. The separate structured files were then merged on the Southern Illinois University at Carbondale mainframe computer. The merged index data were further edited and checked, main entries and subentries that varied from volume to volume were regularized, and another merged index was produced. At each stage, the Center for Dewey Studies staff edited the merged indexes to consolidate duplicate entries, simplify extensive subentries, reorganize information, and design answers to questions that arose during the editing. Finally, all three editors edited and corrected the data for a last resorting and incorporation of editorial changes.

Throughout this entire process of preparing, organizing, inputting data, merging, sorting, editing, revising, checking, further revising, and proofreading each step, we have had extremely able and valuable help from a number of persons. Both David Chesnutt, editor of *The Papers of Henry Laurens*, and Charles T. Cullen, president and librarian of the Newberry Library (formerly editor of *The Papers of Thomas Jefferson*), offered encouragement and advice based on their own extensive experience in using CINDEX. Clarence Boykins at Southern Illinois University Computing Affairs provided important assistance in writing necessary modifications in the programs that made it possible to merge the large amount of data involved. The Dewey Center secretaries, Diane Meierkort and Janice Danley, have been constant, reliable editorial assistants.

Contents
The Collected Works of John Dewey, 1882–1953

The Early Works of John Dewey, 1882–1898

1: 1882–1888

Introduction by Lewis E. Hahn, xxiii

ESSAYS

The Metaphysical Assumptions of Materialism, 3
The Pantheism of Spinoza, 9
Knowledge and the Relativity of Feeling, 19
Kant and Philosophic Method, 34
The New Psychology, 48
The Obligation to Knowledge of God, 61
Education and the Health of Women, 64
Health and Sex in Higher Education, 69
Psychology in High-Schools from the Standpoint of the College, 81
The Place of Religious Emotion, 90
Soul and Body, 93
Inventory of Philosophy Taught in American Colleges, 116
The Psychological Standpoint, 122
Psychology as Philosophic Method, 144
"Illusory Psychology," 168
Knowledge as Idealization, 176
Professor Ladd's *Elements of Physiological Psychology*, 194
Ethics and Physical Science, 205
The Ethics of Democracy, 227

Leibniz's New Essays Concerning the Human Understanding, 251
Preface, 253
1. The Man, 255
2. The Sources of His Philosophy, 268
3. The Problem, and Its Solution, 284
4. Locke and Leibniz—Innate Ideas, 299

5. Sensation and Experience, 313
6. The Impulses and the Will, 327
7. Matter and Its Relation to Spirit, 342
8. Material Phenomena and Their Reality, 355
9. Some Fundamental Conceptions, 373
10. The Nature and Extent of Knowledge, 384
11. The Theology of Leibniz, 403
12. Criticism and Conclusion, 414

2: 1887

Introduction by Herbert W. Schneider, xxiii

PSYCHOLOGY

Preface, 3
Note to the Second Edition, 5
Note to the Third Edition, 5
1. Science and Method of Psychology, 7
2. Mind and Its Modes of Activity, 18

Part One: Knowledge, 29
3. Elements of Knowledge, 29
4. Processes of Knowledge, 75
5. Stages of Knowledge: Perception, 137
6. Stages of Knowledge: Memory, 154
7. Stages of Knowledge: Imagination, 168
8. Stages of Knowledge: Thinking, 177
9. Stages of Knowledge: Intuition, 204

Part Two: Feeling, 215
10. Introduction to Feeling, 215
11. Sensuous Feeling, 218
12. Formal Feeling, 228
13. Development of Qualitative Feelings, 239
14. Intellectual Feelings, 256
15. Aesthetic Feeling, 267
16. Personal Feeling, 281

Part Three: The Will, 299
17. Sensuous Impulses, 299
18. Development of Volition, 309
19. Physical Control, 321
20. Prudential Control, 332
21. Moral Control, 342

22. Will as the Source of Ideals and of Their Realization, 357

3: 1889–1892

Introduction by S. Morris Eames, xxi

ESSAYS

The Late Professor Morris, 3
The Philosophy of Thomas Hill Green, 14
The Lesson of Contemporary French Literature, 36
Galton's Statistical Methods, 43
Ethics in the University of Michigan, 48
A College Course: What Should I Expect from It? 51
On Some Current Conceptions of the Term "Self," 56
Is Logic a Dualistic Science? 75
The Logic of Verification, 83
Philosophy in American Universities: The University of Michigan, 90
Moral Theory and Practice, 93
Poetry and Philosophy, 110
The Present Position of Logical Theory, 125
How Do Concepts Arise from Percepts? 142
Lectures *vs.* Recitations: A Symposium, 147
The Scholastic and the Speculator, 148
Green's Theory of the Moral Motive, 155
Two Phases of Renan's Life, 174

REVIEWS

Review of Edward Caird's *The Critical Philosophy of Immanuel Kant*, 180
Review of John P. Mahaffy and John H. Bernard's *Kant's Critical Philosophy for English Readers*, 184
Review of J. E. Erdmann's *A History of Philosophy*, 185
Review of J. MacBride Sterrett's *Studies in Hegel's Philosophy of Religion*, 187
Review of J. H. Baker's *Elementary Psychology*, 190
Review of Francis Howe Johnson's *What Is Reality?* 192
Review of the Rev. A. J. Church's *The Story of the Odyssey*, 193

The Angle of Reflection, 195

Introduction to Philosophy: Syllabus of Course 5, 211

Outlines of a Critical Theory of Ethics, 237
Preface, 239
Introduction, 241

Part One: Fundamental Ethical Notions, 249
1. The Good, 249
2. The Idea of Obligation, 328
3. The Idea of Freedom, 340

Part Two: The Ethical World, 345

Part Three: The Moral Life of the Individual, 353
1. The Formation and Growth of Ideals, 354
2. The Moral Struggle or the Realizing of Ideals, 372
3. Realized Morality or the Virtues, 382
Conclusion, 386

4: 1893–1894

Introduction by Wayne A. R. Leys, xiii

ESSAYS

Christianity and Democracy, 3
Renan's Loss of Faith in Science, 11
The Superstition of Necessity, 19
Anthropology and Law, 37
Self-Realization as the Moral Ideal, 42
Teaching Ethics in the High School, 54
Why Study Philosophy? 62
The Psychology of Infant Language, 66
Austin's Theory of Sovereignty, 70
The Ego as Cause, 91
Reconstruction, 96
The Chaos in Moral Training, 106
Fred Newton Scott, 119
Intuitionalism, 123
Moral Philosophy, 132
The Theory of Emotion, 152

REVIEWS

Review of Bernard Bosanquet's *A History of Aesthetic*, 189
Review of Josiah Royce's "On Certain Psychological Aspects of Moral Training" and "The Knowledge of Good and Evil" and Georg

Simmel's "Moral Deficiencies as Determining Intellectual Functions," 197
Review of Lester Frank Ward's *The Psychic Factors of Civilization;* Benjamin Kidd's *Social Evolution;* George Burton Adams's *Civilization during the Middle Ages;* and Robert Flint's *History of the Philosophy of History*, 200
Review of James Bonar's *Philosophy and Political Economy in Some of Their Historical Relations*, 214

The Study of Ethics: A Syllabus, 219
Prefatory Note, 221

Part One, 223
1. Nature of Ethical Theory, 223
2. The Factors of Moral Conduct: The Agent and His Sphere of Action, 228

Part Two: Psychological Ethics, 235
3. A General Analysis of Conduct, 235
4. The Moral Consciousness, 240
5. Moral Approbation, Value and Standard, 247
6. Reflective Approbation, or Conscience, 292
7. Obligation, 311
8. Freedom and Responsibility, 337
9. Virtue and the Virtues, 351

APPENDIXES

1. The Relation of Philosophy to Theology, 365
2. Comments on Cheating, 369
3. Ethics and Politics, 371

5: 1895–1898

Introduction by William R. McKenzie, xiii

ESSAYS

The Significance of the Problem of Knowledge, 3
The Metaphysical Method in Ethics, 25
Evolution and Ethics, 34
Ethical Principles Underlying Education, 54
My Pedagogic Creed, 84
The Reflex Arc Concept in Psychology, 96
Interest in Relation to Training of the Will, 111
The Psychology of Effort, 151

The Psychological Aspect of the School Curriculum, 164
Some Remarks on the Psychology of Number, 177
Imagination and Expression, 192
The Aesthetic Element in Education, 202
Results of Child-Study Applied to Education, 204
The Kindergarten and Child-Study, 207
Criticisms Wise and Otherwise on Modern Child-Study, 209
The Interpretation Side of Child-Study, 211
Plan of Organization of the University Primary School, 223
A Pedagogical Experiment, 244
Interpretation of the Culture-Epoch Theory, 247
The Primary-Education Fetich, 254
The Influence of the High School upon Educational Methods, 270
Pedagogy as a University Discipline, 281
Educational Ethics: Syllabus of a Course of Six Lecture-Studies, 291
Educational Psychology: Syllabus of a Course of Twelve Lecture-Studies, 303
Pedagogy IB 19: Philosophy of Education, 1898–1899—Winter Quarter, 328

REVIEWS

The Philosophic Renascence in America. Review of Paul Deussen's *The Elements of Metaphysics;* F. Max Müller's *Three Lectures on the Vedanta Philosophy;* David J. Hill's *Genetic Philosophy; Hegel's Philosophy of Mind,* translated by William Wallace; Herbert Nichols and William E. Parsons's *Our Notions of Number and Space;* Théodule Ribot's *The Diseases of the Will;* Charles Van Norden's *The Psychic Factor;* Alexander T. Ormond's *Basal Concepts in Philosophy;* and Paul Carus's *A Primer of Philosophy*, 342
Review of *Johnson's Universal Cyclopaedia,* vols. I–V, 347
Review of Sophie Bryant's *Studies in Character* and John Watson's *Hedonistic Theories from Aristippus to Spencer*, 350
Review of Levi L. Conant's *The Number Concept*, 355
Review of H. M. Stanley's *Studies in the Evolutionary Psychology of Feeling*, 358
Review of James Sully's *Studies of Childhood*, 367
Review of William Torrey Harris's *Psychologic Foundations of Education*, 372
Review of James Mark Baldwin's *Social and Ethical Interpretations in Mental Development* [*Philosophical Review*], 385
Rejoinder to Baldwin's Social Interpretations: A Reply, 399
Review of James Mark Baldwin's *Social and Ethical Interpretations in Mental Development* [*New World*], 402

MISCELLANY

Letter to the Editor of the *Chicago Evening Post*, 423
Psychology of Number, 424
On the Study of History in the Schools, 429
The Sense of Solidity, 430

APPENDIXES

1. The Need for a Laboratory School, 433
2. The University School, 436
3. Letter and Statement on Organization of Work in a Department of Pedagogy, 442
4. Report of the Committee on a Detailed Plan for a Report on Elementary Education, 448

The Middle Works of John Dewey, 1899–1924

1: 1899–1901

Introduction by Joe R. Burnett, ix

The School and Society, 1
Publisher's Note, 3
Author's Note, 3
Author's Note to Second Edition, 4
1. The School and Social Progress, 5
2. The School and the Life of the Child, 21
3. Waste in Education, 39
4. Three Years of the University Elementary School, 57
5. The Psychology of Elementary Education, 67
6. Froebel's Educational Principles, 81
7. The Psychology of Occupations, 92
8. The Development of Attention, 97
9. The Aim of History in Elementary Education, 104

ESSAYS

"Consciousness" and Experience, 113
Psychology and Social Practice, 131
Some Stages of Logical Thought, 151
Principles of Mental Development as Illustrated in Early Infancy, 175
Mental Development, 192

Group IV. Historical Development of Inventions and Occupations, 222
General Introduction to Groups V and VI, 225
The Place of Manual Training in the Elementary Course of Study, 230

REVIEW

Review of Josiah Royce's *The World and the Individual*. Gifford Lectures, First Series: The Four Historical Conceptions of Being, 241

The Educational Situation, 257
Prefatory Word, 259
1. As Concerns the Elementary School, 260
2. As Concerns Secondary Education, 283
3. As Concerns the College, 300

MISCELLANY

The University Elementary School, 317
Comment on William James's *Principles of Psychology*, 321

2: 1902–1903

Introduction by Sidney Hook, ix

ESSAYS

The Evolutionary Method as Applied to Morality
I. Its Scientific Necessity, 3
II. Its Significance for Conduct, 20
Interpretation of Savage Mind, 39
Academic Freedom, 53
The University of Chicago School of Education, 67
Bulletin of Information: The University of Chicago School of Education, 72
The School as Social Centre, 80

MISCELLANY

In Remembrance, Francis W. Parker, 97
In Memoriam: Colonel Francis Wayland Parker, 98
Discussion of "What Our Schools Owe to Child Study" by Theodore B. Noss, 102

Memorandum to President Harper on Coeducation, 105
Letter to A. K. Parker on Coeducation, 108

REVIEWS

Review of Lightner Witmer's *Analytical Psychology*, 119
Review of Josiah Royce's *The World and the Individual*. Second Series: Nature, Man, and the Moral Order, 120

Contributions to *Dictionary of Philosophy and Psychology*, 139

The Child and the Curriculum, 271

Studies in Logical Theory, 293
Preface, 295
1. The Relationship of Thought and Its Subject-Matter, 298
2. The Antecedents and Stimuli of Thinking, 316
3. Data and Meanings, 337
4. The Objects of Thought, 351
5. [On Mill and Whewell], 368

3: 1903–1906

Introduction by Darnell Rucker, ix

ESSAYS

Logical Conditions of a Scientific Treatment of Morality, 3
Ethics, 40
Psychological Method in Ethics, 59
Notes upon Logical Topics, 62
Philosophy and American National Life, 73
The Terms "Conscious" and "Consciousness," 79
Beliefs and Existences [Beliefs and Realities], 83
Reality as Experience, 101
The Experimental Theory of Knowledge, 107
Experience and Objective Idealism, 128
The St. Louis Congress of the Arts and Sciences, 145
Rejoinder to Münsterberg, 151
The Realism of Pragmatism, 153
The Postulate of Immediate Empiricism, 158
Immediate Empiricism, 168
The Knowledge Experience and Its Relationships, 171

The Knowledge Experience Again, 178
Emerson—The Philosopher of Democracy, 184
The Philosophical Work of Herbert Spencer, 193
Religious Education as Conditioned by Modern Psychology and Pedagogy, 210
The Psychological and the Logical in Teaching Geometry, 216
Democracy in Education, 229
Education, Direct and Indirect, 240
The Relation of Theory to Practice in Education, 249
Significance of the School of Education, 273
Culture and Industry in Education, 285
Remarks on "Shortening the Years of Elementary Schooling" by Frank Louis Soldan, 294
Introduction to Irving W. King's *The Psychology of Child Development*, 299

REVIEWS

Review of Katharine Elizabeth Dopp's *The Place of Industries in Elementary Education*, 307
Review of W. R. Benedict's *World Views and Their Ethical Implications*, 310
Review of F. C. S. Schiller's *Humanism*, 312
Review of George Santayana's *The Life of Reason*, vols. 1–2, 319

MISCELLANY

Introduction of the Orator, 325
The Organization and Curricula of the [University of Chicago] College of Education, 327
The School of Education, 342
Method of the Recitation, 347

4: 1907–1909

Introduction by Lewis E. Hahn, ix

ESSAYS

The Influence of Darwinism on Philosophy, 3
Nature and Its Good: A Conversation, 15
Intelligence and Morals, 31
The Intellectualist Criterion for Truth, 50
The Dilemma of the Intellectualist Theory of Truth, 76

The Control of Ideas by Facts, 78
The Logical Character of Ideas, 91
What Pragmatism Means by Practical, 98
Discussion on Realism and Idealism, 116
Discussion on the "Concept of a Sensation," 118
Pure Experience and Reality: A Disclaimer, 120
Does Reality Possess Practical Character? 125
A Reply to Professor McGilvary's Questions (1912), 143
Objects, Data, and Existences: A Reply to Professor McGilvary, 146
Address to National Negro Conference, 156
Education as a University Study, 158
Religion and Our Schools, 165
The Bearings of Pragmatism upon Education, 178
History for the Educator, 192
The Purpose and Organization of Physics Teaching in Secondary Schools, 198
Teaching That Does Not Educate, 201
The Moral Significance of the Common School Studies, 205

REVIEWS

Review of *Studies in Philosophy and Psychology* by former students of Charles Edward Garman, 217
Review of George Santayana's *The Life of Reason*, 5 vols., 229
Review of A. Sidgwick and Eleanor M. Sidgwick's *Henry Sidgwick*, 242
Review of Albert Schinz's *Anti-pragmatisme*, 245

Syllabus: The Pragmatic Movement of Contemporary Thought, 251

Moral Principles in Education, 265
1. The Moral Purpose of the School, 267
2. The Moral Training Given by the School Community, 269
3. The Moral Training from Methods of Instruction, 275
4. The Social Nature of the Course of Study, 279
5. The Psychological Aspect of Moral Education, 286

5: 1908

Introduction by Charles L. Stevenson, ix

ETHICS

Preface, 3
1. Introduction, 7

Part I: The Beginnings and Growth of Morality, 21
2. Early Group Life, 23
3. The Rationalizing and Socializing Agencies in Early Society, 41
4. Group Morality—Customs or Mores, 54
5. From Custom to Conscience; From Group Morality to Personal Morality, 74
6. The Hebrew Moral Development, 89
7. The Moral Development of the Greeks, 106
8. The Modern Period, 134
9. A General Comparison of Customary and Reflective Morality, 160

Part II: Theory of the Moral Life, 185
10. The Moral Situation, 187
11. Problems of Moral Theory, 197
12. Types of Moral Theory, 207
13. Conduct and Character, 221
14. Happiness and Conduct: The Good and Desire, 241
15. Happiness and Social Ends, 261
16. The Place of Reason in the Moral Life: Moral Knowledge, 278
17. The Place of Duty in the Moral Life: Subjection to Authority, 305
18. The Place of Self in the Moral Life, 328
19. The Virtues, 359

Part III: The World of Action, 381
20. Social Organization and the Individual, 383
21. Civil Society and the Political State, 404
22. The Ethics of the Economic Life, 435
23. Some Principles in the Economic Order, 460
24. Unsettled Problems in the Economic Order, 468
25. Unsettled Problems in the Economic Order (Continued), 480
26. The Family, 510

6: 1910–1911

Introduction by H. S. Thayer and V. T. Thayer, ix

ESSAYS

A Short Catechism concerning Truth, 3
The Problem of Truth, 12
Science as Subject-Matter and as Method, 69
Valid Knowledge and the "Subjectivity of Experience," 80

Some Implications of Anti-Intellectualism, 86
William James [*Independent*], 91
William James [*Journal of Philosophy*], 98
Brief Studies in Realism, 103
Maeterlinck's Philosophy of Life, 123
The Study of Philosophy, 136
The Short-Cut to Realism Examined, 138
Rejoinder to Dr. Spaulding, 143
Joint Discussion with Articles of Agreement and Disagreement: Professor Dewey and Dr. Spaulding, 146
A Symposium on Woman's Suffrage [Statement], 153
Is Co-Education Injurious to Girls? 155

REVIEW

Review of Hugo Münsterberg's *The Eternal Values*, 167

MISCELLANY

Syllabus of Six Lectures on "Aspects of the Pragmatic Movement of Modern Philosophy," 175

How We Think, 177
Preface, 179

Part One: The Problem of Training Thought, 181
1. What Is Thought? 182
2. The Need for Training Thought, 192
3. Natural Resources in the Training of Thought, 204
4. School Conditions and the Training of Thought, 216
5. The Means and End of Mental Training: The Psychological and the Logical, 224

Part Two: Logical Considerations, 233
6. The Analysis of a Complete Act of Thought, 234
7. Systematic Inference: Induction and Deduction, 242
8. Judgment: The Interpretation of Facts, 259
9. Meaning: Or Conceptions and Understanding, 271
10. Concrete and Abstract Thinking, 286
11. Empirical and Scientific Thinking, 293

Part Three: The Training of Thought, 303
12. Activity and the Training of Thought, 304
13. Language and the Training of Thought, 314
14. Observation and Information in the Training of Mind, 328

15. The Recitation and the Training of Thought, 338
16. Some General Conclusions, 348

Contributions to *A Cyclopedia of Education*, vols. 1 and 2, 357

7: 1912–1914

Introduction by Ralph Ross, ix

ESSAYS

Perception and Organic Action, 3
What Are States of Mind? 31
The Problem of Values, 44
Psychological Doctrine and Philosophical Teaching, 47
Nature and Reason in Law, 56
A Reply to Professor Royce's Critique of Instrumentalism, 64
In Response to Professor McGilvary, 79
Should Michigan Have Vocational Education under "Unit" or "Dual" Control? 85
A Policy of Industrial Education, 93
Some Dangers in the Present Movement for Industrial Education, 98
Industrial Education and Democracy, 104
Cut-and-Try School Methods, 106
Professional Spirit among Teachers, 109
Education from a Social Perspective, 113

REVIEWS

A Trenchant Attack on Logic. Review of F. C. S. Schiller's *Formal Logic: A Scientific and Social Problem*, 131
Review of Hugh S. R. Elliot's *Modern Science and the Illusions of Professor Bergson*, 135
Modern Psychologists. Review of G. Stanley Hall's *Founders of Modern Psychology*, 137
Review of William James's *Essays in Radical Empiricism*, 142
Statement on Max Eastman's *The Enjoyment of Poetry*, 149

Interest and Effort in Education, 151

MISCELLANY

Introduction to *A Contribution to a Bibliography of Henri Bergson*, 201

Introduction to *Directory of the Trades and Occupations Taught at the Day and Evening Schools in Greater New York*, 205

Contributions to *A Cyclopedia of Education*, vols. 3, 4, and 5, 209

REPORTS OF DEWEY'S ADDRESSES

Reasoning in Early Childhood, 369
Lectures to the Federation for Child Study, 377
Professor Dewey's Report on the Fairhope [Alabama] Experiment in Organic Education, 387
The Psychology of Social Behavior, 390
Professor for Suffrage, 409

8: 1915

Introduction by Sidney Hook, ix

ESSAYS

The Subject-Matter of Metaphysical Inquiry, 3
The Logic of Judgments of Practice, 14
The Existence of the World as a Logical Problem, 83
Introductory Address to the American Association of University Professors, 98
Annual Address of the President to the American Association of University Professors, 104
Faculty Share in University Control, 109
Industrial Education—A Wrong Kind, 117
Splitting Up the School System, 123
State or City Control of Schools? 128

German Philosophy and Politics, 135
Preface, 137
1. German Philosophy: The Two Worlds, 139
2. German Moral and Political Philosophy, 161
3. The Germanic Philosophy of History, 183

Schools of To-Morrow, 205
Preface, 207
1. Education as Natural Development, 211
2. An Experiment in Education as Natural Development, 222
3. Four Factors in Natural Growth, 236
4. The Reorganization of the Curriculum, 248

5. Play, 275
6. Freedom and Individuality, 294
7. The Relation of the School to the Community, 314
8. The School as a Social Settlement, 339
9. Industry and Educational Readjustment, 353
10. Education through Industry, 365
11. Democracy and Education, 388

MISCELLANY

Professorial Freedom, 407
The Situation at the University of Utah, 409
Education vs. Trade-Training: Reply to David Snedden, 411
Letter to William Bagley and the Editorial Staff of *School and Home Education*, 414
Reply to Charles P. Megan's "Parochial School Education," 416
Reply to William Ernest Hocking's "Political Philosophy in Germany," 418
The One-World of Hitler's National Socialism, 421

9: 1916

Introduction by Sidney Hook, ix

DEMOCRACY AND EDUCATION

Preface, 3
1. Education as a Necessity of Life, 4
2. Education as a Social Function, 14
3. Education as Direction, 28
4. Education as Growth, 46
5. Preparation, Unfolding, and Formal Discipline, 59
6. Education as Conservative and Progressive, 75
7. The Democratic Conception in Education, 87
8. Aims in Education, 107
9. Natural Development and Social Efficiency as Aims, 118
10. Interest and Discipline, 131
11. Experience and Thinking, 146
12. Thinking in Education, 159
13. The Nature of Method, 171
14. The Nature of Subject Matter, 188
15. Play and Work in the Curriculum, 202
16. The Significance of Geography and History, 215
17. Science in the Course of Study, 227

18. Educational Values, 240
19. Labor and Leisure, 259
20. Intellectual and Practical Studies, 271
21. Physical and Social Studies: Naturalism and Humanism, 286
22. The Individual and the World, 300
23. Vocational Aspects of Education, 316
24. Philosophy of Education, 331
25. Theories of Knowledge, 343
26. Theories of Morals, 356

10: 1916–1917

Introduction by Lewis E. Hahn, ix

ESSAYS

The Need for a Recovery of Philosophy, 3
The Concept of the Neutral in Recent Epistemology, 49
The Need for Social Psychology, 53
Duality and Dualism, 64
Spencer and Bergson, 67
The Pragmatism of Peirce, 71
Voluntarism in the Roycean Philosophy, 79
Logical Objects, 89
Concerning Novelties in Logic: A Reply to Mr. Robinson, 98
George Sylvester Morris: An Estimate, 109
Current Tendencies in Education, 116
Experiment in Education, 121
Federal Aid to Elementary Education, 125
Method in Science Teaching, 130
The Need of an Industrial Education in an Industrial Democracy, 137
Learning to Earn: The Place of Vocational Education in a Comprehensive Scheme of Public Education, 144
The Modern Trend toward Vocational Education in Its Effect upon the Professional and Non-Professional Studies of the University, 151
Democracy and Loyalty in the Schools, 158
The Case of the Professor and the Public Interest, 164
Professional Organization of Teachers, 168
Public Education on Trial, 173
Our Educational Ideal in Wartime, 178
Universal Service as Education, 183
The Schools and Social Preparedness, 191
American Education and Culture, 196
Nationalizing Education, 202

Force, Violence and Law, 211
On Understanding the Mind of Germany, 216
Progress, 234
Force and Coercion, 244
The Hughes Campaign, 252
In a Time of National Hesitation, 256
Conscience and Compulsion, 260
The Future of Pacifism, 265
What America Will Fight For, 271
Conscription of Thought, 276
Fiat Justitia, Ruat Coelum, 281
The Principle of Nationality, 285
In Explanation of Our Lapse, 292
Enlistment for the Farm, 296

REVIEWS

Vocational Education. Review of John A. Lapp and Carl H. Mote's *Learning to Earn*, 303
The Tragedy of the German Soul. Review of George Santayana's *Egotism in German Philosophy*, 305
H. G. Wells, Theological Assembler. Review of H. G. Wells's *God the Invisible King*, 310
War Activities for Civilians. Review of *National Service Handbook*, 315

MISCELLANY

Prefatory Note to *Essays in Experimental Logic*, 319
Introduction to *Essays in Experimental Logic*, 320
An Added Note as to the "Practical" in *Essays in Experimental Logic*, 366
Ill Advised, 370
American Association of University Professors, 371
Announcement from Committee on University Ethics, American Association of University Professors, 373
Report of Committee on University Ethics, American Association of University Professors, 374
Universal Military Training, 377

REPORT

Organization in American Education, 397

11: 1918–1919

Introduction by Oscar Handlin and Lilian Handlin, ix

ESSAYS

The Objects of Valuation, 3
Concerning Alleged Immediate Knowledge of Mind, 10
The Motivation of Hobbes's Political Philosophy, 18
Philosophy and Democracy, 41
Education and Social Direction, 54
Vocational Education in the Light of the World War, 58
America in the World, 70
Internal Social Reorganization after the War, 73
A New Social Science, 87
Political Science as a Recluse, 93
What Are We Fighting For? 98
The Cult of Irrationality, 107
The Post-War Mind, 112
The New Paternalism, 117
Morals and the Conduct of States, 122
The Approach to a League of Nations, 127
The League of Nations and the New Diplomacy, 131
The Fourteen Points and the League of Nations, 135
A League of Nations and Economic Freedom, 139
Theodore Roosevelt, 143
Japan and America, 150
Liberalism in Japan, 156
On the Two Sides of the Eastern Sea, 174
The Discrediting of Idealism, 180
The Student Revolt in China, 186
The International Duel in China, 192
Militarism in China, 199
Transforming the Mind of China, 205
Chinese National Sentiment, 215
The American Opportunity in China, 228
Our Share in Drugging China, 235
Autocracy under Cover, 241
Preliminary Confidential Memorandum on Polish Conditions, 248
Second Preliminary Confidential Memorandum on Polish Conditions, 255
Confidential Report of Conditions among the Poles in the United States, 259

REVIEWS

Creative Industry. Review of Helen Marot's *Creative Impulse in Industry*, 333
Review of Robert Mark Wenley's *The Life and Work of George Sylvester Morris*, 336

MISCELLANY

Syllabus of Eight Lectures on "Problems of Philosophic Reconstruction," 341
Introductory Word to F. Matthias Alexander's *Man's Supreme Inheritance*, 350
Reply to a Reviewer [Randolph Bourne], 353

12: 1920

Introduction by Ralph Ross, ix

ESSAYS

Our National Dilemma, 3
Freedom of Thought and Work, 8
Americanism and Localism, 12
How Reaction Helps, 17
The Sequel of the Student Revolt, 22
Shantung, As Seen from Within, 28
The New Leaven in Chinese Politics, 41
What Holds China Back, 51
China's Nightmare, 60
A Political Upheaval in China, 65
Industrial China, 71

Reconstruction in Philosophy, 77
Prefatory Note, 79
1. Changing Conceptions of Philosophy, 80
2. Some Historical Factors in Philosophical Reconstruction, 95
3. The Scientific Factor in Reconstruction of Philosophy, 110
4. Changed Conceptions of Experience and Reason, 124
5. Changed Conceptions of the Ideal and the Real, 139
6. The Significance of Logical Reconstruction, 156
7. Reconstruction in Moral Conceptions, 172
8. Reconstruction as Affecting Social Philosophy, 187

LECTURES

Three Contemporary Philosophers: William James, Henri Bergson, and Bertrand Russell, 205

MISCELLANY

Bolshevism in China: Service Report, 253
Introduction to 1948 Reprint of *Reconstruction in Philosophy*, 256

13: 1921–1922

Introduction by Ralph Ross, ix

ESSAYS

Valuation and Experimental Knowledge, 3
Knowledge and Speech Reaction, 29
Realism without Monism or Dualism, 40
An Analysis of Reflective Thought, 61
Is China a Nation? 72
The Far Eastern Deadlock, 79
The Consortium in China, 86
Old China and New, 93
New Culture in China, 108
Hinterlands in China, 121
Divided China, 127
Shantung Again, 139
The Tenth Anniversary of the Republic of China, 147
Federalism in China, 149
China and Disarmament, 156
A Parting of the Ways for America, 159
The Issues at Washington, 173
Shrewd Tactics Are Shown in Chinese Plea, 191
Four Principles for China, 194
Underground Burrows, 197
Angles of Shantung Question, 201
The Conference and a Happy Ending, 204
Chinese Resignations, 209
Three Results of Treaty, 212
A Few Second Thoughts on Four-Power Pact, 213
As the Chinese Think, 217
America and Chinese Education, 228

The Siberian Republic, 233
The Far Eastern Republic: Siberia and Japan, 240
Racial Prejudice and Friction, 242
Public Opinion in Japan, 255
Some Factors in Mutual National Understanding, 262
Education by Henry Adams, 272
Events and Meanings, 276
Industry and Motives, 281
Classicism as an Evangel, 286
Mediocrity and Individuality, 289
Individuality, Equality and Superiority, 295
The American Intellectual Frontier, 301
Pragmatic America, 306
Social Absolutism, 311
Education as a Religion, 317
Education as Engineering, 323
Education as Politics, 329

REVIEWS

Review of Walter Lippmann's *Public Opinion*, 337
Review of Charles Hitchcock Sherrill's *Prime Ministers and Presidents* and Frazier Hunt's *The Rising Temper of the East*, 345

Syllabus: Types of Philosophic Thought, 349

Contribution to *Encyclopaedia and Dictionary of Education*, 397

MISCELLANY

Rejoinder to Dora W. Black's "American Policy in China," 409
Foreword to Salmon O. Levinson's *Outlawry of War*, 411
First Introduction to Scudder Klyce's *Universe*, 412
Reply to "Liberalism and Irrationalism," 421

REPORT OF INTERVIEW WITH DEWEY

Report by Charles W. Wood, 425

14: 1922

Introduction by Murray G. Murphey, ix

HUMAN NATURE AND CONDUCT

Preface, 3
Introduction, 4

Part I: The Place of Habit in Conduct, 13
1. Habits as Social Functions, 15
2. Habits and Will, 21
3. Character and Conduct, 33
4. Custom and Habit, 43
5. Custom and Morality, 54
6. Habit and Social Psychology, 60

Part II: The Place of Impulse in Conduct, 63
7. Impulses and Change of Habits, 65
8. Plasticity of Impulse, 69
9. Changing Human Nature, 76
10. Impulse and Conflict of Habits, 88
11. Classification of Instincts, 92
12. No Separate Instincts, 104
13. Impulse and Thought, 117

Part III: The Place of Intelligence in Conduct, 119
14. Habit and Intelligence, 121
15. The Psychology of Thinking, 127
16. The Nature of Deliberation, 132
17. Deliberation and Calculation, 139
18. The Uniqueness of Good, 146
19. The Nature of Aims, 154
20. The Nature of Principles, 164
21. Desire and Intelligence, 171
22. The Present and Future, 182

Part IV: Conclusion, 191
23. The Good of Activity, 193
24. Morals Are Human, 204
25. What Is Freedom? 209
26. Morality Is Social, 216

Foreword to the 1930 Modern Library Edition, 228

15: 1923–1924

Introduction by Carl Cohen, ix

ESSAYS

Fundamentals, 3
Kant after Two Hundred Years, 8
Tradition, Metaphysics, and Morals, 14
Values, Liking, and Thought, 20
Some Comments on Philosophical Discussion, 27
A Sick World, 42
Science, Belief and the Public, 47
Ethics and International Relations, 53
Logical Method and Law, 65
Shall We Join the League? 78
Reply to Lovejoy's "Shall We Join the League of Nations?" 83
Shall the United States Join the World Court? 87
Political Combination or Legal Cooperation? 105
If War Were Outlawed, 110
What Outlawry of War Is Not, 115
War and a Code of Law, 122
Secularizing a Theocracy, 128
Angora, the New, 134
The Turkish Tragedy, 139
Foreign Schools in Turkey, 144
The School as a Means of Developing a Social Consciousness and Social Ideals in Children, 150
Social Purposes in Education, 158
Individuality in Education, 170
The Classroom Teacher, 180
"What Is a School For?" 190
Culture and Professionalism in Education, 193
Making Education a Student Affair, 198
The Prospects of the Liberal College, 200
The Liberal College and Its Enemies, 205

REVIEWS

China and the West. Review of Bertrand Russell's *The Problem of China*, 215
Review of George Santayana's *Scepticism and Animal Faith*, 219
Review of C. K. Ogden and I. A. Richards's *The Meaning of Meaning*, 223
Review of Charles S. Peirce's *Chance, Love, and Logic*, 226

Syllabus: Social Institutions and the Study of Morals, 229

Report and Recommendation upon Turkish Education, 273

MISCELLANY

Preliminary Report on Turkish Education, 301
Introduction to F. Matthias Alexander's *Constructive Conscious Control of the Individual*, 308
In Behalf of Culture, 316
Dewey Aids La Follette, 317
Statement on Scholasticism, 318

The Later Works of John Dewey, 1925–1953

1: 1925

Introduction by Sidney Hook, vii

EXPERIENCE AND NATURE

Preface, 3
1. Experience and Philosophic Method, 10
2. Existence as Precarious and as Stable, 42
3. Nature, Ends and Histories, 69
4. Nature, Means and Knowledge, 100
5. Nature, Communication and Meaning, 132
6. Nature, Mind and the Subject, 162
7. Nature, Life and Body-Mind, 191
8. Existence, Ideas and Consciousness, 226
9. Experience, Nature and Art, 266
10. Existence, Value and Criticism, 295

The Unfinished Introduction, 329
Experience and Philosophic Method, 365

2: 1925–1927

Introduction by James Gouinlock, ix

ESSAYS

The Development of American Pragmatism, 3
Corporate Personality, 22
A Naturalistic Theory of Sense-Perception, 44
Individuality and Experience, 55
Events and the Future, 62

The Meaning of Value, 69
Value, Objective Reference and Criticism, 78
The Ethics of Animal Experimentation, 98
Affective Thought, 104
Art in Education—and Education in Art, 111
What Is the Matter with Teaching? 116
The "Socratic Dialogues" of Plato, 124
Substance, Power and Quality in Locke, 141
William James in Nineteen Twenty-Six, 158
Bishop Brown: A Fundamental Modernist, 163
America's Responsibility, 167
America and the Far East, 173
Highly Colored White Lies, 176
Is China a Nation or a Market? 181
We Should Deal with China as Nation to Nation, 185
The Problem of Turkey, 189
Church and State in Mexico, 194
Mexico's Educational Renaissance, 199
From a Mexican Notebook, 206

REVIEWS

Practical Democracy. Review of Walter Lippmann's *The Phantom Public*, 213
The Changing Intellectual Climate. Review of Alfred North Whitehead's *Science and the Modern World*, 221
A Key to the New World. Review of Bertrand Russell's *Education and the Good Life*, 226
Review of Graham Wallas's *The Art of Thought*, 231

The Public and Its Problems, 235
Prefatory Note, 237
1. Search for the Public, 238
2. Discovery of the State, 259
3. The Democratic State, 282
4. The Eclipse of the Public, 304
5. Search for the Great Community, 325
6. The Problem of Method, 351

MISCELLANY

1946 Introduction to *The Public and Its Problems*, 375
Dedication Address of the Barnes Foundation, 382

Literature or Mathematics? Comment on Raymond Weeks's *Boys' Own Arithmetic*, 386
Foreword to William James Durant's *The Story of Philosophy*, 387
An International Symposium on Scholasticism, 388

3: 1927–1928

Introduction by David Sidorsky, ix

ESSAYS

Philosophy and Civilization, 3
Anthropology and Ethics, 11
Body and Mind, 25
The Inclusive Philosophic Idea, 41
Appearing and Appearance, 55
"Half-Hearted Naturalism," 73
Meaning and Existence, 82
Philosophies of Freedom, 92
Philosophy, 115
A Critique of American Civilization, 133
The Pragmatic Acquiescence, 145
The Fruits of Nationalism, 152
Imperialism Is Easy, 158
"As an Example to Other Nations," 163
Rejoinder to James T. Shotwell, 168
Outlawing Peace by Discussing War, 173
Justice Holmes and the Liberal Mind, 177
Why I Am for Smith, 184
Psychology and Justice, 186
China and the Powers: II. Intervention a Challenge to Nationalism, 196
The Real Chinese Crisis, 199
Impressions of Soviet Russia:
I. Leningrad Gives the Clue, 203
II. A Country in a State of Flux, 208
III. A New World in the Making, 215
IV. What Are the Russian Schools Doing? 224
V. New Schools for a New Era, 233
VI. The Great Experiment and the Future, 242
The Direction of Education, 251
Progressive Education and the Science of Education, 257

Why I Am a Member of the Teachers Union, 269
Bankruptcy of Modern Education, 276
The Manufacturers' Association and the Public Schools, 280

REVIEWS

Philosophy as a Fine Art. Review of George Santayana's *The Realm of Essence*, 287
Philosophy's Search for a Satisfying Vision of Reality. Review of Alfred Hoernlé's *Idealism as a Philosophy* and Bernard Bosanquet's *Science and Philosophy and Other Essays*, 294
The Integration of a Moving World. Review of Edmund Noble's *Purposive Evolution: The Link between Science and Religion*, 299
Science, Folk-lore and Control of Folk-ways. Review of C. E. Ayres's *Science: The False Messiah*, 305
Things, Thought, Conversation. Review of Scott Buchanan's *Possibility* and Mortimer Adler's *Dialectic*, 311
The Way to Think. Review of Ernest Dimnet's *The Art of Thinking*, 316
Politics and Human Beings. Review of William Ernest Hocking's *Man and the State* and G. E. G. Catlin's *The Science and Method of Politics*, 318
Review of Robert H. Lowie's *The Origin of the State*, 324
Review of Carleton Kemp Allen's *Law in the Making*, 326
Brave Gospel. Review of Mary H. Lewis's *An Adventure with Children*, 330

MISCELLANY

Foreword in Paul Radin's *Primitive Man as Philosopher*, 335
Introductory Word in Sidney Hook's *The Metaphysics of Pragmatism*, 338
Introductory Note in Joseph Kinmont Hart's *Inside Experience*, 342
Introduction to Roswell P. Barnes's *Militarizing Our Youth*, 346
Afterword in Charles Clayton Morrison's *The Outlawry of War*, 348
An Appreciation of Henry George, 359
A Tribute to Morris Raphael Cohen, 361
To the Chinese Friends in the United States, 364

4: 1929

Introduction by Stephen Toulmin, vii

THE QUEST FOR CERTAINTY: A STUDY OF THE RELATION OF KNOWLEDGE AND ACTION

1. Escape from Peril, 3
2. Philosophy's Search for the Immutable, 21
3. Conflict of Authorities, 40
4. The Art of Acceptance and the Art of Control, 60
5. Ideas at Work, 87
6. The Play of Ideas, 112
7. The Seat of Intellectual Authority, 136
8. The Naturalization of Intelligence, 156
9. The Supremacy of Method, 178
10. The Construction of Good, 203
11. The Copernican Revolution, 229

Syllabus for the Gifford Lectureship in Natural Theology, 251

5: 1929–1930

Introduction by Paul Kurtz, xi

The Sources of a Science of Education, 1

Individualism, Old and New, 41

Prefatory Note, 43

1. The House Divided against Itself, 45
2. "America"—By Formula, 50
3. The United States, Incorporated, 58
4. The Lost Individual, 66
5. Toward a New Individualism, 77
6. Capitalistic or Public Socialism? 90
7. The Crisis in Culture, 99
8. Individuality in Our Day, 111

Construction and Criticism, 125

ESSAYS

From Absolutism to Experimentalism, 147
Philosophy, 161
James Marsh and American Philosophy, 178
The Sphere of Application of the Excluded Middle, 197
The Applicability of Logic to Existence, 203
In Reply to Some Criticisms, 210
Conduct and Experience, 218

Psychology and Work, 236
Qualitative Thought, 243
What Humanism Means to Me, 263
What I Believe, 267
Three Independent Factors in Morals, 279
Philosophy and Education, 289
General Principles of Educational Articulation, 299
Our Illiteracy Problem, 311
How Much Freedom in New Schools? 319
The Duties and Responsibilities of the Teaching Profession, 326
Freedom in Workers' Education, 331
Labor Politics and Labor Education, 338
What Do Liberals Want? 346
Apostles of World Unity: XVII—Salmon O. Levinson, 349
Religion in the Soviet Union: II—An Interpretation of the Conflict, 355
Social Change and Its Human Direction, 363

REVIEWS

The School and Society. Review of George S. Counts's *School and Society in Chicago*, 371
An Organic Universe. Review of Alfred North Whitehead's *Process and Reality*, 375
The Course of Modern History. Review of Harry Elmer Barnes's *World Politics in Modern Civilization*, 382

MISCELLANY

Dr. Dewey and Mr. Woll by Matthew Woll, 387
Reply to Woll, 389
The Sportsmanship Brotherhood by Daniel Chase, 390
Mr. Woll as a Communist-Catcher, 392
Letter to University of Michigan School of Education, 393
Juvenile Reading, 394
Understanding and Prejudice, 396
Foreword to Helen Edna Davis's *Tolstoy and Nietzsche*, 398
Foreword to Eastern Commercial Teachers' Association First Yearbook, *Foundation of Commercial Education*, 401
Introduction to Henry Evelyn Bliss's *The Organization of Knowledge and the System of the Sciences*, 404
Introduction to Maurice Hindus's *Humanity Uprooted*, 407
Foreword to Fischel Schneersohn's *Studies in Psycho-Expedition*, 410
Introduction to *Training for Group Experience*, edited by Alfred Dwight Sheffield, 412

Censorship, 417
In Response, 418
Tribute to James H. Tufts, 424

REPORTS

Lobby Inquiry Opens Tomorrow, 429
Attacks Wage Disparity, 431
Child Relief Steps Urged on Congress, 432
Asks Federal Fund to Aid Unemployed, 434
Asks Hoover to Act on Unemployment, 436
Puts Needs of Idle at Two Billions, 439
People's Lobby Hits Sugar Loan to Cuba, 440
John Dewey Assails the Major Parties, 442
Dewey Supports Vladeck, 443
Dewey Asks Norris to Lead New Party, 444
Dewey for Farm Backing, 447

6: 1931–1932

Introduction by Sidney Ratner, xi

ESSAYS

Context and Thought, 3
George Herbert Mead as I Knew Him, 22
Human Nature, 29
Politics and Culture, 40
Science and Society [Address], 49
Science and Society [*Philosophy and Civilization*], 53
Social Science and Social Control, 64
The Collapse of a Romance, 69
The Way Out of Educational Confusion, 75
American Education Past and Future, 90
Monastery, Bargain Counter, or Laboratory in Education? 99
Appreciation and Cultivation, 112
Political Interference in Higher Education and Research, 118
The Economic Situation: A Challenge to Education, 123
The Schools and the White House Conference, 131
Dewey Describes Child's New World, 137
Discussion of "Freedom, in Relation to Culture, Social Planning, and Leadership," 142
Education and Birth Control, 146

"The Irrepressible Conflict," 149
The Jobless—A Job for All of Us, 153
The Need for a New Party: I. The Present Crisis; II. The Breakdown of the Old Order; III. Who Might Make a New Party?; IV. Policies for a New Party, 156
Is There Hope for Politics? 182
Peace—by Pact or Covenant? 190
Are Sanctions Necessary to International Organization? No, 196
Address to the National Association for the Advancement of Colored People, 224
The Place of Minor Parties in the American Scene and Their Relation to the Present Situation, 231
Democracy Joins the Unemployed, 239
Prospects for a Third Party, 246
After the Election—What? 253

REVIEWS

College Sons—and Parents. Review of Christian Gauss's *Life in College*, 259
"Surpassing America." Review of Sherwood Eddy's *The Challenge of Russia;* George S. Counts's *The Soviet Challenge to America;* and William C. White's *These Russians*, 263
Review of Frederick Hallis's *Corporate Personality: A Study in Jurisprudence*, 268
Review of George Herbert Palmer's *The Autobiography of a Philosopher;* Ralph Barton Perry's *A Defence of Philosophy;* and George Santayana's *The Genteel Tradition at Bay*, 271
Charles Sanders Peirce. Review of *Collected Papers of Charles Sanders Peirce*, vol. 1, edited by Charles Hartshorne and Paul Weiss, 273
Marx Inverted. Review of Gerald Heard's *The Emergence of Man*, 278
Self-Saver or Frankenstein? Review of Oswald Spengler's *Man and Technics*, 280
Bending the Twig. Review of Albert Jay Nock's *The Theory of Education in the United States*, 286
Making Soviet Citizens. Review of Thomas Woody's *New Minds: New Men?* and Nicholas Hans's *History of Russian Educational Policy*, 291
The Meiklejohn Experiment. Review of Alexander Meiklejohn's *The Experimental College*, 295
A Philosophy of Scientific Method. Review of Morris R. Cohen's *Reason and Nature: An Essay on the Meaning of Scientific Method*, 299
Reply to Cohen's "Reason, Nature and Professor Dewey," 304

MISCELLANY

Prefatory Remarks in George Herbert Mead's *The Philosophy of the Present*, 307
Introduction to Theodore T. Lafferty's *Studies in Philosophy*, 311
Foreword to Paul H. Douglas's *The Coming of a New Party*, 313
Introduction to F. Matthias Alexander's *The Use of the Self*, 315
Introduction to Jagadish Chandra Chatterji's *India's Outlook on Life*, 321
The People's Lobby, 322
To Replace Judge Cardozo, 323
A Third Party Program, 324
Vladeck and Laidler, 326
Funds for Brookwood Labor College, 327
Help for Brookwood, 328
What Is It All About? 330

PEOPLE'S LOBBY

Urges Tax on Rich to Meet Debts Cut, 337
Urges State-Aid Plan for Work Insurance, 339
Full Warehouses and Empty Stomachs, 341
The President and the Special Session, 345
Secretary Klein Asked Basis for Optimism, 346
Rejoinder to Secretary Klein, 351
Challenge to Progressive Senators to Act for Relief, 355
The Key to Hoover's Keynote Speech, 357
Lobby Challenges Senator Borah's Opposition to Reconsideration of Interallied Debts, 364
President Dewey Opposes Blanket Freight Increase, 368
President Dewey Calls on Hoover to Recognize Government Responsibility for Unemployment, 372
President Dewey Opposes Community Chest Drives for Unemployed, 374
The Federal Government and Unemployment, 377
The Only Way to Stop Hoarding, 379
Church Leaders Ask Church Act on Unemployment, 381
Prosperity Dependent on Building from Bottom Up, 383
Calls Wagner "Keyman" on Unemployment Aid, 384
You Must Act to Get Congress to Act, 386
The Senate Birth Control Bill, 388
Joint Committee on Unemployment Demands Congress Act, 390
Voters Must Demand Congress Tax Wealth Instead of Want, 392
President Dewey Asks Senators to Stay on Guard, 393

Roosevelt Scored on Relief Policy, 395
Get Mayor and Governor to Demand Relief, 397
Introduction [Unemployment Insurance], 399

INTERVIEWS AND REPORTS OF STATEMENTS AND ADDRESSES

Setting New Goals at Seventy, 403
John Dewey Surveys the Nation's Ills, 408
Statements to the Conference on Curriculum for the College of Liberal Arts, 414
A Résumé of Four Lectures on Common Sense, Science and Philosophy, 424
Teachers as Citizens, 433
A Statement by the Executive Committee, 436
Prof. Dewey Is Impressed by Discontent, 438
Dewey Raps Progressives on Parley Eve, 440

7: 1932

Introduction by Abraham Edel and Elizabeth Flower, vii

ETHICS

Preface to the 1932 Edition, 3
Preface to the First Edition, 5
1. Introduction, 9

Part I: The Beginnings and Growth of Morality, 19
2. Early Group Life, 22
3. Basic Activities and Agencies, 39
4. Group Morality—Customs or Mores, 49
5. From Custom to Conscience; From Group Morality to Personal Morality, 68
6. The Hebrew Development, 82
7. The Moral Development of the Greeks, 97
8. The Roman Contribution to the Modern Moral Consciousness, 125
9. Factors and Trends in the Modern Moral Consciousness, 135

Part II: Theory of the Moral Life, 159
10. The Nature of Moral Theory, 162
11. Ends, the Good and Wisdom, 184
12. Right, Duty, and Loyalty, 214
13. Approbation, the Standard and Virtue, 235

14. Moral Judgment and Knowledge, 262
15. The Moral Self, 285

Part III: The World of Action, 311
16. Morals and Social Problems, 314
17. Morals and the Political Order, 340
18. Ethical Problems of the Economic Life, 373
19. Collective Bargaining and the Labor Union, 385
20. Moral Problems of Business, 403
21. Social Control of Business and Industry, 412
22. Toward the Future, 423
23. Marriage and the Family, 438

8: 1933

Introduction by Richard Rorty, ix

CONTRIBUTIONS TO *Encyclopaedia of the Social Sciences*

Logic, 3
Outlawry of War, 13
Philosophy, 19

CONTRIBUTIONS TO *The Educational Frontier*

The Social-Economic Situation and Education, 43
The Underlying Philosophy of Education, 77

How We Think: A Restatement of the Relation of Reflective Thinking to the Educative Process, 105
Preface to the New Edition, 107
Preface to the First Edition, 109

Part One: The Problem of Training Thought, 111
1. What Is Thinking? 113
2. Why Reflective Thinking Must Be an Educational Aim, 125
3. Native Resources in Training Thought, 140
4. School Conditions and the Training of Thought, 156

Part Two: Logical Considerations, 169
5. The Process and Product of Reflective Activity: Psychological Process and Logical Form, 171

6. Examples of Inference and Testing, 187
7. Analysis of Reflective Thinking, 196
8. The Place of Judgment in Reflective Activity, 210
9. Understanding: Ideas and Meanings, 221
10. Understanding: Conception and Definition, 235
11. Systematic Method: Control of Data and Evidence, 248
12. Systematic Method: Control of Reasoning and Concepts, 259
13. Empirical and Scientific Thought, 268

Part Three: The Training of Thought, 279
14. Activity and the Training of Thought, 281
15. From the Concrete to the Abstract, 293
16. Language and the Training of Thought, 301
17. Observation and Information in the Training of Mind, 315
18. The Recitation and the Training of Thought, 326
19. Some General Conclusions, 342

REVIEWS

The Adventure of Persuasion. Review of Alfred North Whitehead's *Adventures of Ideas*, 355
A Challenge to Criticism. Review of Martin Schütze's *Academic Illusions in the Field of Letters and the Arts*, 360
Review of Rexford G. Tugwell's *The Industrial Discipline and the Governmental Arts*, 364

9: 1933–1934

Introduction by Milton R. Konvitz, xi

A Common Faith, 1
1. Religion versus the Religious, 3
2. Faith and Its Object, 21
3. The Human Abode of the Religious Function, 40

ESSAYS

Steps to Economic Recovery, 61
The Future of Radical Political Action, 66
Unity and Progress, 71
Imperative Need: A New Radical Party, 76
What Keeps Funds Away from Purchasers, 81
American Ideals (I): The Theory of Liberty vs. the Fact of Regimentation, 87

Why I Am Not a Communist, 91
The Supreme Intellectual Obligation, 96
A Great American Prophet, 102
Intelligence and Power, 107
The Crisis in Education, 112
Education and Our Present Social Problems, 127
Dewey Outlines Utopian Schools, 136
Shall We Abolish School "Frills"? No, 141
Why Have Progressive Schools? 147
Education for a Changing Social Order, 158
The Activity Movement, 169
Education and the Social Order, 175
Character Training for Youth, 186
The Need for a Philosophy of Education, 194
Can Education Share in Social Reconstruction? 205

REVIEWS

A God or The God? Review of *Is There a God?* by Henry Nelson Wieman, Douglas Clyde Macintosh, and Max Carl Otto, 213
Dr. Dewey Replies, 223
Social Stresses and Strains. Review of *Recent Social Trends in the United States*, 229
Review of *Mr. Justice Brandeis*, edited by Felix Frankfurter, 237
Santayana's Orthodoxy. Review of George Santayana's *Some Turns of Thought in Modern Philosophy*, 240
Acquiescence and Activity in Communism. Review of Theodore B. H. Brameld's *A Philosophic Approach to Communism*, 244

PEOPLE'S LOBBY BULLETIN

Unemployed and Underpaid Consumers Should Not Pay Billion Dollar Subsidy to Speculators, 249
Relief Is Vital, 252
The Banking Crisis, 254
Congress Faces Its Test on Taxation, 256
The Real Test of the "New Deal," 259
Superficial Treatment Must Fail, 261
Inflationary Measures Injure the Masses, 265
Wild Inflation Would Paralyze Nation, 267
Lobby Asks Special Session on Debts, 269
Unemployment Committee Asks Adequate Relief, 271
Farm Processing and Other Consumption Taxes Must Be Repealed, 273

The Next Session and the People's Lobby, 275
President's Policies Help Property Owners Chiefly, 277
New Deal Program Must Be Appraised, 280
A Real Test of the Administration, 282
America's Public Ownership Program, 285
Facing the Era of Realities, 287
No Half-Way House for America, 289

MISCELLANY

Religions and the "Religious," 293
Reply to Edwin Ewart Aubrey and Henry Nelson Wieman in "Is John Dewey a Theist?" 294
Introduction to *Challenge to the New Deal,* edited by Alfred Mitchell Bingham and Selden Rodman, 296
Foreword to George Raymond Geiger's *The Philosophy of Henry George*, 299
Meaning, Assertion and Proposal, 303
To Save the Rand School, 305
The Drive against Hunger, 307
Radio's Influence on the Mind, 309
Preface to the English Edition of *Terror in Cuba*, 310
Statement on Technocracy, 312

REPORTS AND INTERVIEW

On the Grievance Committee's Report, 315
The Report of the Special Grievance Committee of the Teachers Union, 320
New York and the Seabury Investigation, 346
Tomorrow May Be Too Late: Save the Schools Now, 386

10: 1934

Introduction by Abraham Kaplan, vii

ART AS EXPERIENCE

Preface, 7
1. The Live Creature, 9
2. The Live Creature and "Ethereal Things," 26
3. Having an Experience, 42
4. The Act of Expression, 64

5. The Expressive Object, 88
6. Substance and Form, 111
7. The Natural History of Form, 139
8. The Organization of Energies, 167
9. The Common Substance of the Arts, 191
10. The Varied Substance of the Arts, 218
11. The Human Contribution, 250
12. The Challenge to Philosophy, 276
13. Criticism and Perception, 302
14. Art and Civilization, 329

11: 1935–1937

Introduction by John J. McDermott, xi

Liberalism and Social Action, 1
Preface, 3
1. The History of Liberalism, 5
2. The Crisis in Liberalism, 23
3. Renascent Liberalism, 41

ESSAYS

An Empirical Survey of Empiricisms, 69
Mystical Naturalism and Religious Humanism, 84
Peirce's Theory of Quality, 86
Characteristics and Characters: Kinds and Classes, 95
What Are Universals? 105
One Current Religious Problem, 115
General Propositions, Kinds, and Classes, 118
World High Court for Knowledge? 127
Authority and Social Change, 130
Whitehead's Philosophy, 146
Tribute to F. C. S. Schiller, 155
The Teacher and the Public, 158
The Need for Orientation, 162
Education and New Social Ideals, 167
Anniversary Address, 171
The Challenge of Democracy to Education, 181
The Dewey School: Introduction, 191
The Dewey School: Statements, 193

The Dewey School: Appendix 2, The Theory of the Chicago Experiment, 202
Democracy and Educational Administration, 217
Education, the Foundation for Social Organization, 226
What Is Learning? 238
Growth in Activity, 243
Freedom, 247
Socialization of Ground Rent, 256
Future of Liberalism, 258
International Cooperation or International Chaos, 261
Taxation as a Step to Socialization, 265
Government and Children, 268
Our Un-Free Press, 269
Needed—A New Politics, 274
A Liberal Speaks Out for Liberalism, 282
The Future of Liberalism, 289
Democracy Is Radical, 296

THE LEON TROTSKY INQUIRY

Declaration of Purposes by the American Committee for the Defense of Leon Trotsky, 303
Introductory Statement of the Commission of Inquiry, 306
"Truth Is on the March," 310
Summary of Findings, 321
The Moscow Trials, 326
Significance of the Trotsky Inquiry, 330

SOCIAL FRONTIER

The Teacher and His World, 339
The Crucial Role of Intelligence, 342
Toward Administrative Statesmanship, 345
United, We Shall Stand, 348
Youth in a Confused World, 353
Toward a National System of Education, 356
Liberty and Social Control, 360
The Meaning of Liberalism, 364
Liberalism and Equality, 368
Liberalism and Civil Liberties, 372
The Social Significance of Academic Freedom, 376
Henry Linville Pension Fund, 380
Class Struggle and the Democratic Way, 382

Horace Mann Today, 387
Rationality in Education, 391
President Hutchins' Proposals to Remake Higher Education, 397
"The Higher Learning in America," 402
Education and Social Change, 408

REVIEWS

The Founder of Pragmatism. Review of *Collected Papers of Charles Sanders Peirce,* edited by Charles Hartshorne and Paul Weiss, vol. 5, *Pragmatism and Pragmaticism*, 421
Intimations of Mortality. Review of Corliss Lamont's *The Illusion of Immortality*, 425
Bergson on Instinct. Review of Henri Bergson's *The Two Sources of Morality and Religion*, 428
Nature and Humanity. Review of Oliver L. Reiser's *Philosophy and the Concepts of Modern Science*, 432
Review of Alfred M. Bingham's *Insurgent America*, 438
The Jameses. Review of Ralph Barton Perry's *The Thought and Character of William James*, 441
Santayana's Novel. Review of George Santayana's *The Last Puritan*, 446
The Work of George Mead. Review of George H. Mead's *Mind, Self and Society* and *Movements of Thought in the Nineteenth Century*, 450
Religion, Science, and Philosophy. Review of Bertrand Russell's *Religion and Science*, 454
The Philosophy of William James. Review of Ralph Barton Perry's *The Thought and Character of William James*, 464
Charles Sanders Peirce. Review of *Collected Papers of Charles Sanders Peirce,* edited by Charles Hartshorne and Paul Weiss, vols. 1-6, 479
"Either—Or." Review of Zalmen Slesinger's *Education and the Class Struggle*, 485
Subject-Matter in Art. Review of Walter Abell's *Representation and Form*, 487
Liberalism in a Vacuum. Review of Walter Lippmann's *An Inquiry into the Principles of the Good Society*, 489
Review of Stephen Spender's *Forward from Liberalism*, 496

MISCELLANY

Foreword to Albert Coombs Barnes and Violette de Mazia's *The Art of Renoir*, 501

Foreword to Carl Christian Jensen's *Seventy Times Seven*, 506
Foreword to *Education in the Soviet Union,* edited by William Allan Neilson, 509
Introduction to Myrtle Byram McGraw's *Growth: A Study of Johnny and Jimmy*, 510
Foreword to Angelo M. Pellegrini and Brents Stirling's *Argumentation and Public Discussion*, 515
Introduction to Richard Ward Greene Welling's *Self Government and Politics in School*, 516
Introduction to Harry W. Laidler's *Looking Forward, 1937*, 517
Introduction to Harry W. Laidler's *Looking Forward, 1938*, 519
The Educational Function of a Museum of Decorative Arts, 520
How They Are Voting: 2, 526
Aid for the Spanish Government, 527
Younger Men Are Key, 529
Righting an Academic Wrong, 530
The Future of Democracy, 532
Acceptance Speech, 533
The Forward View: A Free Teacher in a Free Society, by John Dewey and Goodwin Watson, 535
An Active, Flexible Personality, by John Dewey, Boyd H. Bode, and William Heard Kilpatrick, 548

REPORTS

Comment on Horace Meyer Kallen's "What Pragmatism Means for the Social Sciences," 563
Panel Discussion: Education Today, 567

12: 1938

Introduction by Ernest Nagel, ix

LOGIC: THE THEORY OF INQUIRY

Preface, 3

Part One: Introduction: The Matrix of Inquiry, 7
1. The Problem of Logical Subject-Matter, 9
2. The Existential Matrix of Inquiry: Biological, 30
3. The Existential Matrix of Inquiry: Cultural, 48
4. Common Sense and Scientific Inquiry, 66
5. The Needed Reform of Logic, 86

Part Two: The Structure of Inquiry and the Construction of Judgments, 103
6. The Pattern of Inquiry, 105
7. The Construction of Judgment, 123
8. Immediate Knowledge: Understanding and Inference, 142
9. Judgments of Practice: Evaluation, 161
10. Affirmation and Negation: Judgment as Requalification, 182
11. The Function of Propositions of Quantity in Judgment, 200
12. Judgment as Spatial-Temporal Determination: Narration-Description, 220
13. The Continuum of Judgment: General Propositions, 244
14. Generic and Universal Propositions, 263

Part Three: Propositions and Terms, 281
15. General Theory of Propositions, 283
16. Propositions Ordered in Sets and Series, 310
17. Formal Functions and Canons, 327
18. Terms or Meanings, 347

Part Four: The Logic of Scientific Method, 367
19. Logic and Natural Science: Form and Matter, 369
20. Mathematical Discourse, 391
21. Scientific Method: Induction and Deduction, 415
22. Scientific Laws—Causation and Sequences, 437
23. Scientific Method and Scientific Subject-Matter, 458
24. Social Inquiry, 481
25. The Logic of Inquiry and Philosophies of Knowledge, 506

13: 1938–1939

Introduction by Steven M. Cahn, ix

Experience and Education, 1
Preface, 3
1. Traditional *vs.* Progressive Education, 5
2. The Need of a Theory of Experience, 11
3. Criteria of Experience, 17
4. Social Control, 31
5. The Nature of Freedom, 39
6. The Meaning of Purpose, 43
7. Progressive Organization of Subject-Matter, 48
8. Experience—The Means and Goal of Education, 61

Freedom and Culture, 63
1. The Problem of Freedom, 65
2. Culture and Human Nature, 80
3. The American Background, 99
4. Totalitarian Economics and Democracy, 116
5. Democracy and Human Nature, 136
6. Science and Free Culture, 156
7. Democracy and America, 173

Theory of Valuation, 189

ESSAYS

The Determination of Ultimate Values or Aims through Antecedent or A Priori Speculation or through Pragmatic or Empirical Inquiry, 255
Unity of Science as a Social Problem, 271
The Relation of Science and Philosophy as the Basis of Education, 281
Does Human Nature Change? 286
Democracy and Education in the World of Today, 294
Education, Democracy, and Socialized Economy, 304
The Economic Basis of the New Society, 309
The Unity of the Human Being, 323
What Is Social Study? 338
To Those Who Aspire to the Profession of Teaching, 342
In Defense of the Mexican Hearings, 347
Means and Ends, 349

MISCELLANY

The Philosophy of the Arts, 357
Foreword to David Lindsay Watson's *Scientists Are Human*, 369

14: 1939–1941

Introduction by R. W. Sleeper, ix

ESSAYS

Experience, Knowledge and Value: A Rejoinder, 3
I Believe, 91
Time and Individuality, 98
My Philosophy of Law, 115

The Philosophy of Whitehead, 123
Nature in Experience, 141
The Vanishing Subject in the Psychology of James, 155
Propositions, Warranted Assertibility, and Truth, 168
The Objectivism-Subjectivism of Modern Philosophy, 189
Presenting Thomas Jefferson, 201
Creative Democracy—The Task Before Us, 224
The Case for Bertrand Russell, 231
Social Realities *versus* Police Court Fictions, 235
The Basis for Hope, 249
The Meaning of the Term: Liberalism, 252
Art as Our Heritage, 255
"Contrary to Human Nature," 258
Address of Welcome to the League for Industrial Democracy, 262
Education: 1800–1939, 266
Higher Learning and War, 273
The Basic Values and Loyalties of Democracy, 275
For a New Education, 278

REVIEWS

Review of Charles A. Beard and Mary R. Beard's *America in Midpassage*, 283
Review of Douglas Clyde Macintosh's *Social Religion*, 286
Review of Max C. Otto's *The Human Enterprise: An Attempt to Relate Philosophy to Daily Life*, 289
The Techniques of Reconstruction. Review of Karl Mannheim's *Man and Society in an Age of Reconstruction*, 293
Review of *The Philosophy of George Santayana,* edited by Paul Arthur Schilpp, 295

ADDRESSES

Message to Friends of the John Dewey Labor Research Fund, 311
Lessons from the War—in Philosophy, 312

MISCELLANY

Introduction to William James's *Talks to Teachers on Psychology*, 337
Introduction to *Problems of Ageing*, 341
Foreword to Elsie Ripley Clapp's *Community Schools in Action*, 351
Foreword to Edwin C. Johnson's *Mars in Civilian Disguise!* 355
Introduction to *The Bertrand Russell Case*, 357
Foreword to *Educational Trends*, 360

Introduction to *American Journal of Economics and Sociology*, 362
"No Matter What Happens—Stay Out," 364
The Committee for Cultural Freedom, 365
"Democratic Ends Need Democratic Methods for Their Realization," 367
Russell as a Moral Issue, 369
Investigating Education, 370
Censorship Not Wanted, 373
Statement on Academic Freedom, 374
Dewey Greets Teachers Union, 375

15: 1942–1948

Introduction by Lewis S. Feuer, xi

ESSAYS

William James and the World Today, 3
William James as Empiricist, 9
The *Principles*, 18
William James' Morals and Julien Benda's, 19
How Is Mind to Be Known? 27
Inquiry and Indeterminateness of Situations, 34
The Ambiguity of "Intrinsic Good," 42
Anti-Naturalism in Extremis, 46
Valuation Judgments and Immediate Quality, 63
Further as to Valuation as Judgment, 73
By Nature and by Art, 84
A Comment on the Foregoing Criticisms, 97
Some Questions about Value, 101
Are Naturalists Materialists? 109
Ethical Subject-Matter and Language, 127
Peirce's Theory of Linguistic Signs, Thought, and Meaning, 141
Prefatory Note to *Problems of Men*, 153
Introduction to *Problems of Men*: The Problems of Men and the Present State of Philosophy, 154
Religion and Morality in a Free Society, 170
The Penning-in of Natural Science, 184
The Revolt against Science, 188
Democratic versus Coercive International Organization: The Realism of Jane Addams, 192
Dualism and the Split Atom, 199
World Anarchy or World Order? 204

The Crisis in Human History, 210
Liberating the Social Scientist, 224
Henry Wallace and the 1948 Elections, 239
American Youth, Beware of Wallace Bearing Gifts, 242
How to Anchor Liberalism, 248
The Democratic Faith and Education, 251
Challenge to Liberal Thought, 261
The Problem of the Liberal Arts College, 276
Implications of S. 2499, 281

REVIEWS

Mission to Moscow Reveals No New Evidence on Soviet Trials. Review of Joseph E. Davies's *Mission to Moscow*, 289
Behind the Iron Bars. Review of David J. Dallin and Boris I. Nicolaevsky's *Forced Labor in Soviet Russia*, 295

FOREWORDS AND INTRODUCTIONS

Foreword to John E. Stoner's *S. O. Levinson and the Pact of Paris*, 301
Introduction to *The Little Red School House*, by Agnes de Lima et al., 303
Foreword to H. Heath Bawden's "Method," 305
Foreword to Eric Williams's *Education in the British West Indies*, 308
Foreword to Earl C. Kelley's *Education for What Is Real*, 310
Introduction to Alexander Dorner's *The Way beyond "Art"—The Work of Herbert Bayer*, 312
Foreword to Henry Schaefer-Simmern's *The Unfolding of Artistic Activity*, 315

TRIBUTES

Tribute to James Hayden Tufts, 321
James Hayden Tufts, 324
Boyd H. Bode: An Appreciation, 326

LETTERS TO THE EDITOR

Rejoinder to Charles W. Morris, 331
Dewey vs. Meiklejohn, 333
Rejoinder to Meiklejohn, 337
Russia's Position, 338
Dr. Dewey on Our Relations with Russia, 342
Several Faults Are Found in *Mission to Moscow* Film, 345
Moscow Film Again Attacked, 351

More on *Mission to Moscow*, 354
The Case of Odell Waller, 356
John Dewey on *The Theory of Economic Progress*, 359
Comment on Bell and Polanyi, 361
Commentary and Liberalism, 362

MISCELLANY

Letter in Introduction to *Don't Be Afraid!* 365
Statement on Jefferson, 366
Why I Selected "Democracy and America," 367
Message to the Chinese People, 369
Message to the Teachers of Perú, 371
Comment on Sidney Hook's *Education for Modern Man*, 372
Comment on *I Want to Be Like Stalin*, 373
George Seldes and "Fact," 375
Man and Mathematics, 376
Appreciation of the Rand School, 378

16: 1949–1952

Introduction by T. Z. Lavine, ix

Knowing and the Known, with Arthur F. Bentley, 1
Preface, 3
Introduction: A Search for Firm Names, 6
1. Vagueness in Logic, 8
2. The Terminological Problem, 46
3. Postulations, 74
4. Interaction and Transaction, 96
5. Transactions as Known and Named, 110
6. Specification, 131
7. The Case of Definition, 154
8. Logic in an Age of Science, 184
9. A Confused "Semiotic," 210
10. Common Sense and Science, 242
11. A Trial Group of Names, 257
12. Summary of Progress Made, 275
Appendix: Dewey's Reply to Albert G. A. Balz, 280

TYPESCRIPTS

What Is It to Be a Linguistic Sign or Name? 297
Values, Valuations, and Social Facts, 310

Importance, Significance, and Meaning, 318
How, What, and *What For* in Social Inquiry, 333

ESSAYS

The Field of "Value," 343
Has Philosophy a Future? 358
Philosophy's Future in Our Scientific Age, 369
Experience and Existence: A Comment, 383
Contribution to "Religion and the Intellectuals," 390
Aesthetic Experience as a Primary Phase and as an Artistic Development, 395
Contribution to *Democracy in a World of Tensions*, 399
Modern Philosophy, 407

17: 1885–1953

Foreword by Jo Ann Boydston, xi
Introduction by Sidney Hook, xvii

ESSAYS

Doctor Martineau's Theory of Morals, 3
The Health of Women and Higher Education, 7
The Revival of the Soul, 10
What Is the Demonstration of Man's Spiritual Nature? 15
The Church and Society, 19
War's Social Results, 21
The Problem of Secondary Education after the War, 26
Impressions from Canton, 29
On Philosophical Synthesis, 35

FOREWORD, INTRODUCTIONS, PREFACES

Preface to *The Influence of Darwin on Philosophy*, 39
Introduction to Percy Hughes's *The Center, Function and Structure of Psychology*, 42
Introduction to *Looking Forward: Discussion Outlines*, 44
Introduction to *Looking Forward, 1933*, 45
Introduction to *Looking Forward, 1934*, 46
Introduction to *Looking Forward, 1935*, 47
Introduction to *Looking Forward, 1936*, 48
Foreword to Philip P. Wiener's *Evolution and the Founders of Pragmatism*, 50

Introduction to Samuel Tenenbaum's *William Heard Kilpatrick*, 52
Preface to Japanese Translation of *Democracy and Education*, 57
Introduction to *Selected Poems of Claude McKay*, 58

ADDRESSES

Commencement Address: San Jose State Normal School, 63
The Educational Principles Involved, 67
Socializing the Schools, 72
The Educational Balance, Efficiency and Thinking, 77
Message to the American Federation of Teachers, 83
John Dewey Responds, 84
Greetings to the Urbana Conference, 88

REVIEWS

Science and the Idea of God. Review of John Fiske's *The Idea of God as Affected by Modern Knowledge*, 93
Review of Sir Frederick Pollock's *Essays in the Law*, 98
Review of Hugo Krabbe's *The Modern Idea of the State*, 101
Review of Roscoe Pound's *Law and Morals: The McNair Lectures*, 105
Review of Mary C. Love's *Human Conduct and the Law*, 108
Review of Abraham Flexner's *Universities: American, English, German*, 110
Review of Charles Edward Merriam's *The Making of Citizens*, 112
Review of T. V. Smith's *The Promise of American Politics*, 115

STATEMENTS

Answer to "Do We Want Rifle Practice in the Public Schools?" 121
Opinion on "Military Training for American School Boys," 122
View on "What the War Means to America," 123
On Military Training in Schools, 124
Letter on *Encyclopaedia of the Social Sciences*, 125
On Immortality, 126
In Defense of Mary Ware Dennett's *The Sex Side of Life*, 127
Report on "Forms of Art Exhibition" at the Pennsylvania Museum of Art, 128
Dewey Hails Editorial on United Command, 130
What Kind of a World Are We Fighting to Create? 131
Endorsement of Dean Alfange, 133
John Dewey Hails the Liberal Party, 134
Comment on "Religion at Harvard," 135

Communists as Teachers, 136
A Statement to the Society, 138
Mr. Acheson's Critics, 140

TRIBUTES

Clarence J. Selby, 145
Clifford Beers, 146
Alvin Johnson, 147
Emily Greene Balch, 149

SYLLABI

Introduction to Philosophy, 153
History of Education, 161
Psychology for Teachers, 187

EDUCATIONAL LECTURES BEFORE BRIGHAM YOUNG ACADEMY

1. How the Mind Learns, 213
2. Social Aspects of Education, 226
3. Imagination, 242
4. Periods of Growth, 255
5. Attention, 269
6. Period of Technic, 284
7. Habit, 298
8. Social Value of Courses, 310
9. Memory and Judgment, 323
10. Some Elements of Character, 336

UNPUBLISHED WRITINGS

The Historical Method in Ethics, 351
Knowledge and Existence, 361
Some Thoughts concerning Religion, 374
Tolstoi's Art, 381
The Meaning and Progress of Morality, 393
Some Connexions of Science and Philosophy, 402
Brief Studies in Realism III, 415
A Working Method in Social Psychology, 422
Problems of Contemporary Philosophy: The Problem of Experience, 429

Methods in Philosophy and the Sciences, 442
Between Two Worlds, 451
The Future of Philosophy, 466
What *Is* Democracy? 471
Education for a New and Better World, 475
Comment on Recent Criticisms of Some Points in Moral and Logical Theory, 480
Pedagogy:—Memorandum, 485
The Russian School System, 487
Child Health and Protection, 511
American Federation of Teachers Statement, 520
John H. Randall's *Our Changing Civilization*, 522
Remarks on Richard Welling's *As the Twig Is Bent*, 523
Memorandum for Mr. Pringle, 524
Tribute to S. J. Woolf, 526
Statement on Retirement of Frank Becker, 527

ADDENDUM: The Value of Historical Christianity, 529

Title Index
The Collected Works of John Dewey, 1882–1953

Series and volume numbers are in boldface type

E: Early Works, 1882–1898
M: Middle Works, 1899–1924
L: Later Works, 1925–1953

Absolutism: Social, **M13**: 311
to Experimentalism, From, **L5**: 147
Abstract: Concrete and, **M6**: 391
From the Concrete to the, **L8**: 293
Abstraction, **M6**: 359
Academic Freedom, **M2**: 53; **M6**: 460
Social Significance of, **L11**: 376
Statement on, **L14**: 374
Academic Wrong, Righting an, **L11**: 530
Acceptance, Art of, and the Art of Control, **L4**: 60
Accommodation, **M6**: 359
Acheson, Dean, Critics of, **L17**: 140
Action, Organic, Perception and, **M7**: 3
Active, Flexible Personality, **L11**: 548
Activity, **M6**: 361
Good of, **M14**: 193
Growth in, **L11**: 243
and the Training of Thought, **M6**: 304; **L8**: 281
Movement, **L9**: 169
Adams, Henry, Education by, **M13**: 272
Adaptation, **M6**: 364
Addams, Jane, Realism of, **L15**: 192
Adjustment, **M6**: 365
Administration, Real Test of the, **L9**: 282
Administrative Statesmanship, Toward, **L11**: 345
Aesthetic Element in Education, **E5**: 202
Aesthetic Experience as a Primary Phase and as an Artistic Development, **L16**: 395
Affective Thought, **L2**: 104
Affirmation and Negation, **L12**: 182
Afterword to
Morrison, Charles Clayton, *The Outlawry of War*, **L3**: 348
Agent and His Sphere of Action, **E4**: 228
Aid for the Spanish Government, **L11**: 527
Aims: Natural Development and Social Efficiency as, **M9**: 118
Nature of, **M14**: 154

Aims (*continued*)
and Ideals of Education, **M13**: 399
in Education, **M9**: 107
Alfange, Dean, Endorsement of, **L17**: 133
Altruism and Egoism, **M6**: 366
Ambiguity of "Intrinsic Good," **L15**: 42
America: Democracy and, **L13**: 173; Why I Selected, **L15**: 367
Higher Learning in, **L11**: 402
Japan and, **M11**: 150
No Half-Way House for, **L9**: 289
Parting of the Ways for, **M13**: 159
Pragmatic, **M13**: 306
What It Will Fight For, **M10**: 271
What War Means to It, **L17**: 123
and Chinese Education, **M13**: 228
and the Far East, **L2**: 173
by Formula, **L5**: 50
in the World, **M11**: 70
American Association of University Professors, **M10**: 371
[Announcement], **M10**: 373
Annual Address of the President to the, **M8**: 104
Introductory Address to the, **M8**: 98
[Report], **M10**: 374
American Background, **L13**: 99
American Civilization, Critique of, **L3**: 133
American Committee for the Defense of Leon Trotsky, Declaration of Purposes by the, **L11**: 303
American Education: Organization in, **M10**: 397
Past and Future, **L6**: 90
and Culture, **M10**: 196
American Federation of Teachers: Message to the, **L17**: 83
Statement, **L17**: 520
American Ideals, **L9**: 87
American Intellectual Frontier, **M13**: 301
Americanism and Localism, **M12**: 12
American National Life, Philosophy and, **M3**: 73
American Opportunity in China, **M11**: 228
American Prophet, Great, **L9**: 102
American Youth, Beware of Wallace Bearing Gifts, **L15**: 242
America's Public Ownership Program, **L9**: 285
America's Responsibility, **L2**: 167
Analogy, **M6**: 369
Analysis and Synthesis, **M6**: 370
Analysis of Reflective Thought, **M13**: 61
Angle of Reflection, **E3**: 195
Angora, the New, **M15**: 134
Animal Experimentation, Ethics of, **L2**: 98
Antecedents and Stimuli of Thinking, **M2**: 316
Anthropology and Ethics, **L3**: 11
Anthropology and Law, **E4**: 37
Anti-Intellectualism, Some Implications of, **M6**: 86
Anti-Naturalism in Extremis, **L15**: 46
Apostles of World Unity: XVII—Salmon O. Levinson, **L5**: 349
Appearance, Empirical Account of. *See* Appearing and Appearance

Appearing and Appearance, **L3**: 55
Appreciation and Cultivation, **L6**: 112
Approbation, the Standard and Virtue, **L7**: 235
Art: By Nature and by, **L15**: 84
Naturalism in, **M2**: 142
and Civilization, **L10**: 329
as Our Heritage, **L14**: 255
in Education, **M6**: 375; and Education in Art, **L2**: 111
Art as Experience, **L10**
Art Exhibition, Forms of, Report on, **L17**: 128
Arts: Common Substance of the, **L10**: 191
Decorative, Educational Function of a Museum of, **L11**: 520
Philosophy of the, **L13**: 357
Varied Substance of the, **L10**: 218
and Sciences, St. Louis Congress of the, **M3**: 145
Atom, Split, Dualism and the, **L15**: 199
Attention, **L17**: 269
Development of, **M1**: 97
Aubrey, Edwin Ewart, and Henry Nelson Wieman, Reply to, **L9**: 294
Austin, John, His Theory of Sovereignty, **E4**: 70
Authorities, Conflict of, **L4**: 40
Authority: Subjection to, **M5**: 305
and Social Change, **L11**: 130
Autocracy under Cover, **M11**: 241
Ayres, C. E., *The Theory of Economic Progress*, Comment on, **L15**: 359
Bagley, William, Letter to, **M8**: 414
Balch, Emily Greene, Tribute to, **L17**: 149
Baldwin, James Mark, Reply to, **E5**: 399
Balz, Albert G. A., Dewey's Reply to, **L16**: 280
Banking Crisis, **L9**: 254
Barnes Foundation, Dedication Address of the, **L2**: 382
Becker, Frank, Statement on Retirement of, **L17**: 527
Beers, Clifford, Tribute to, **L17**: 146
Behavior, Unit of. *See* Reflex Arc Concept in Psychology
Belief, Science, and the Public, **M15**: 47
Beliefs and Existences, **M3**: 83
Beliefs and Realities. *See* Beliefs and Existences
Bell, Daniel, and Karl Polanyi, Comment on, **L15**: 361
Benda, Julien, William James' Morals and His, **L15**: 19
Bergson, Henri, **M12**: 221
and Herbert Spencer, **M10**: 67
Between Two Worlds, **L17**: 451
Birth Control, Education and, **L6**: 146
Birth Control Bill, Senate, **L6**: 388
Black, Dora W., "American Policy in China," Rejoinder to, **M13**: 409
Bode, Boyd H., An Appreciation, **L15**: 326
Body: Soul and, **E1**: 93
and Mind, **L3**: 25
Bolshevism in China, **M12**: 253
Borah, William E., Lobby Challenges His Opposition to Re-

Borah, William E. (*continued*)
consideration of Interallied Debts, **L6**: 364
Bourne, Randolph, Reply to, **M11**: 353
Breakdown of the Old Order, **L6**: 161
Brief Studies in Realism, **M6**: 103
Brief Studies in Realism III, **L17**: 415
Brigham Young Academy, Educational Lectures before, **L17**: 211
Brookwood Labor College:
Funds for, **L6**: 327
Help for, **L6**: 328
Brown, William Montgomery, Fundamental Modernist, **L2**: 163
Butler, Nicholas Murray, Introduction of, **M3**: 325

Calculation, Deliberation and, **M14**: 139
Canton, Impressions from, **L17**: 29
Cardozo, Benjamin Nathan, To Replace, **L6**: 323
Causation, **M6**: 379
and Sequences, **L12**: 437
Censorship, **L5**: 417
Not Wanted, **L14**: 373
Challenge of Democracy to Education, **L11**: 181
Challenge to Liberal Thought, **L15**: 261
Challenge to Philosophy, **L10**: 276
Chaos in Moral Training, **E4**: 106
Character, **M6**: 381
Conduct and, **M5**: 221
Some Elements of, **L17**: 336
and Conduct, **M14**: 33
Training for Youth, **L9**: 186
Characteristics and Characters: Kinds and Classes, **L11**: 95
Chase, Daniel, Reply to, **L5**: 390
Cheating, Comments on, **E4**: 369
Chicago, Board of Education, **E5**: 423
Chicago, University of: Organization and Curricula of Its College of Education, **M3**: 327
Significance of the School of Education, **M3**: 273
Chicago, University of, School of Education, **M2**: 67; **M3**: 342
Bulletin of, **M2**: 72
Chicago Experiment, The Theory of the, **L11**: 202
Child: School and the Life of the, **M1**: 21
and the Curriculum, **M2**: 271
Child Health and Protection, **L17**: 511
Schools and the White House Conference on, **L6**: 131
Childhood, Early, Reasoning in, **M7**: 369
Child Relief Steps Urged on Congress, **L5**: 432
Children, Government and, **L11**: 268
Child's New World, Dewey Describes, **L6**: 137
Child-Study: Criticisms Wise and Otherwise on Modern, **E5**: 209
Interpretation Side of, **E5**: 211
Kindergarten and, **E5**: 207
Lectures to the Federation for, **M7**: 377
Results of, Applied to Education, **E5**: 204
China: American Opportunity in, **M11**: 228
Bolshevism in, **M12**: 253
Consortium in, **M13**: 86
Divided, **M13**: 127

Federalism in, **M13**: 149
Four Principles for, **M13**: 194
Hinterlands in, **M13**: 121
Industrial, **M12**: 71
International Duel in, **M11**: 192
Is It a Nation? **M13**: 72
Is It a Nation or a Market? **L2**: 181
Militarism in, **M11**: 199
New Culture in, **M13**: 108
Old, and New, **M13**: 93
Our Share in Drugging, **M11**: 235
Political Upheaval in, **M12**: 65
Republic of, Tenth Anniversary of the, **M13**: 147
Student Revolt in, **M11**: 186
Transforming the Mind of, **M11**: 205
We Should Deal with It as Nation to Nation, **L2**: 185
What Holds It Back, **M12**: 51
and Disarmament, **M13**: 156
and the Powers, **L3**: 196
China's Nightmare, **M12**: 60
Chinese, As They Think, **M13**: 217
Chinese Crisis, Real, **L3**: 199
Chinese Education, America and, **M13**: 228
Chinese Friends in the United States, To the, **L3**: 364
Chinese National Sentiment, **M11**: 215
Chinese People, Message to the, **L15**: 369
Chinese Plea, Shrewd Tactics Are Shown in, **M13**: 191
Chinese Politics, New Leaven in, **M12**: 41
Chinese Resignations, **M13**: 209
Christianity: Historical, Value of, **L17**: 529
and Democracy, **E4**: 3
Church and Society, **L17**: 19
Church and State in Mexico, **L2**: 194
Church Leaders Ask Church Act on Unemployment, **L6**: 381
Citizens, Teachers as, **L6**: 433
Civilization: Art and, **L10**: 329
Philosophy and, **L3**: 3
Role of Philosophy in the History of. *See* Philosophy and Civilization
Civil Liberties, Liberalism and, **L11**: 372
Civil Society and the Political State, **M5**: 404
Classicism as an Evangel, **M13**: 286
Classroom Teacher, **M15**: 180
Class Struggle and the Democratic Way, **L11**: 382
Coeducation: Is It Injurious to Girls? **M6**: 155
Letter to A. K. Parker on, **M2**: 108
Memorandum to President Harper on, **M2**: 105
Coercion, Force and, **M10**: 244
Cohen, Morris R.: "Reason, Nature and Professor Dewey," Reply to, **L6**: 304
Tribute to, **L3**: 361
Collapse of a Romance, **L6**: 69
College, As Concerns the, **M1**: 300
College, Liberal: Prospects of the, **M15**: 200
and Its Enemies, **M15**: 205
College, Liberal Arts, Problem of the, **L15**: 276
College Course: What Should I Expect from It? **E3**: 51
College of Liberal Arts, Statements to the Conference on Curriculum for the, **L6**: 414

Colleges, American, Inventory of Philosophy Taught in, **E1**: 116
Commentary and Liberalism, **L15**: 362
Committee for Cultural Freedom, **L14**: 365
Common Faith, **L9**: 1
Common Sense, Science and Philosophy, Résumé of Four Lectures on, **L6**: 424
Common Sense and Science, **L16**: 242
Common Sense and Scientific Inquiry, **L12**: 66
Communist, Why I Am Not a, **L9**: 91
Communists as Teachers, **L17**: 136
Community, Relation of the School to the, **M8**: 314
Community Chest Drives for Unemployed, Dewey Opposes, **L6**: 374
Comparison, **M6**: 388
Compulsion, Conscience and, **M10**: 260
Conception, **M6**: 390
  and Definition, **L8**: 235
Conceptions: Some Fundamental, **E1**: 373
  and Understanding, **M6**: 271
Concepts, How Do They Arise from Percepts? **E3**: 142
Concrete and Abstract, **M6**: 391
Concrete to the Abstract, From the, **L8**: 293
Conduct, **M6**: 392
  Character and, **M14**: 33
  General Analysis of, **E4**: 235
  Happiness and, **M5**: 241
  and Character, **M5**: 221
  and Experience, **L5**: 218
Conference [Washington] and a Happy Ending, **M13**: 204
Conference on Education and Philosophy, Greetings to the, **L17**: 88
Conflict, **M6**: 392
  Irrepressible, **L6**: 149
  of Authorities, **L4**: 40
Congress: Child Relief Steps Urged on, **L5**: 432
  Faces Its Test on Taxation, **L9**: 256
  Joint Committee on Unemployment Demands It Act, **L6**: 390
  Voters Must Demand It Tax Wealth Instead of Want, **L6**: 392
  You Must Act to Get It to Act, **L6**: 386
Conscience: Reflective Approbation, or, **E4**: 292
  and Compulsion, **M10**: 260
Conscious and Consciousness, The Terms, **M3**: 79
Consciousness: Moral, **E4**: 240
  and Experience, **M1**: 113
Conscription of Thought, **M10**: 276
Construction and Criticism, **L5**: 125
Consumers, Unemployed and Underpaid, Should Not Pay Billion Dollar Subsidy to Speculators, **L9**: 249
Content, Form and, **M6**: 458
Context and Thought, **L6**: 3
Control, **M6**: 393
  Art of, Art of Acceptance and the, **L4**: 60
  Moral, **E2**: 342
  Physical, **E2**: 321
  Prudential, **E2**: 332

of Data and Evidence, **L8**: 248
of Ideas by Facts, **M4**: 78
of Reasoning and Concepts, **L8**: 259
Copernican Revolution, **L4**: 229
Corporate Legal Personality, Historic Background of. *See* Corporate Personality
Corporate Personality, **L2**: 22
Country in a State of Flux, **L3**: 208
Course of Study, Theory of, **M6**: 395
Courses, Social Value of, **L17**: 310
Creative Democracy—The Task Before Us, **L14**: 224
Crisis: Banking, **L9**: 254
Present, **L6**: 156
in Culture, **L5**: 99
in Education, **L9**: 112
in Human History, **L15**: 210
in Liberalism, **L11**: 23
Criticism: *Construction and,* **L5**: 125
Value, Objective Reference and, **L2**: 78
and Perception, **L10**: 302
Criticisms: In Reply to Some, **L5**: 210
Recent, of Some Points in Moral and Logical Theory, **L17**: 480
Wise and Otherwise on Modern Child-Study, **E5**: 209
Croce, Benedetto, Reply to, **L15**: 97
Cuba, People's Lobby Hits Sugar Loan to, **L5**: 440
Cultivation, Appreciation and, **L6**: 112
Cult of Irrationality, **M11**: 107
Cultural Freedom, Committee for, **L14**: 365
Culture: American Education and, **M10**: 196
Crisis in, **L5**: 99
Free, Science and, **L13**: 156
Freedom and, **L13**: 63
In Behalf of, **M15**: 316
Politics and, **L6**: 40
and Culture Values, **M6**: 404
and Human Nature, **L13**: 80
and Industry in Education, **M3**: 285
and Professionalism in Education, **M15**: 193
Culture-Epoch Theory, **M6**: 408
Interpretation of the, **E5**: 247
Curriculum: Play and Work in the, **M9**: 202
Reorganization of the, **M8**: 248
School, Psychological Aspect of the, **E5**: 164
for the College of Liberal Arts, Conference on, Statements to the, **L6**: 414
Custom, **M6**: 413
and Habit, **M14**: 43
and Morality, **M14**: 54
Cut-and-Try School Methods, **M7**: 106
Cyclopedia of Education, **M6**: 357; **M7**: 207

Darwin, Charles, Influence of, on Philosophy, **M4**: 3
Darwin, Charles, Influence of, on Philosophy and Other Essays in Contemporary Thought, **E5**: 3; **M1**: 113; **M3**: 83, 107, 128, 158; **M4**: 3, 15, 31, 50; **L17**: 39
Data and Evidence, Control of, **L8**: 248
Data and Meanings, **M2**: 337

Debts, People's Lobby Asks Special Session on, **L9**: 269
Debts Cut, Urges Tax on Rich to Meet, **L6**: 337
Deduction, **M6**: 414
Induction and, **M6**: 242; **M7**: 239; **L12**: 415
Definition, **M6**: 415
Case of, **L16**: 154
Conception and, **L8**: 235
Deliberation: Nature of, **M14**: 132
and Calculation, **M14**: 139
Democracy: Basic Values and Loyalties of, **L14**: 275
Challenge of, to Education, **L11**: 181
Christianity and, **E4**: 3
Creative, The Task Before Us, **L14**: 224
Education, and Socialized Economy, **L13**: 304
Ethics of, **E1**: 227
Future of, **L11**: 532
Industrial, Need of an Industrial Education in an, **M10**: 137
Industrial Education and, **M7**: 104
Joins the Unemployed, **L6**: 239
Philosophy and, **M11**: 41
Totalitarian Economics and, **L13**: 116
What Is It? **L17**: 471
and America, **L13**: 173; Why I Selected, **L15**: 367
and Education, **M6**: 417; **M8**: 388; in the World of Today, **L13**: 294
and Educational Administration, **L11**: 217
and Human Nature, **L13**: 136
and Loyalty in the Schools, **M10**: 158
in a World of Tensions, **L16**: 399
in Education, **M3**: 229
Is Radical, **L11**: 296
Democracy and Education, **M9**
Democratic Conception in Education, **M9**: 87
Democratic Ends Need Democratic Methods for Their Realization, **L14**: 367
Democratic Faith and Education, **L15**: 251
Democratic State, **L2**: 282
Democratic Way, Class Struggle and the, **L11**: 382
Demonstration, **M6**: 418
Dennett, Mary Ware, *The Sex Side of Life*, In Defense of, **L17**: 127
Desire: Good and, **M5**: 241
and Intelligence, **M14**: 171
Determination of Ultimate Values or Aims, **L13**: 255
Determinism, **M6**: 419
Development, **M6**: 420
of American Pragmatism, **L2**: 3
Dewey, John, Labor Research Fund, Message to Friends of the, **L14**: 311
Dewey School: Appendix 2, **L11**: 202; Introduction, **L11**: 191; Statements, **L11**: 193
Dialectic, **M6**: 422
Dictionary of Philosophy and Psychology, **M2**: 139
Didactics, **M6**: 423
Dilemma of the Intellectualist Theory of Truth, **M4**: 76
Disarmament, China and, **M13**: 156
Discipline, **M6**: 423
Interest and, **M9**: 131
Discontent, Dewey Is Impressed by, **L6**: 438

Discrediting of Idealism, **M11**: 180
Dualism, **M6**: 424
Duality and, **M10**: 64
Realism without Monism or, **M13**: 40
and the Split Atom, **L15**: 199
Dualistic Science, Is Logic a? **E3**: 75
Duality and Dualism, **M10**: 64
Duties and Responsibilities of the Teaching Profession, **L5**: 326
Duty, Place of, in the Moral Life, **M5**: 305
Dynamic, **M6**: 424

Eastern Sea, On the Two Sides of the, **M11**: 174
Economic Basis of the New Society, **L13**: 309
Economic Freedom, League of Nations and, **M11**: 139
Economic Recovery, Steps to, **L9**: 61
Economic Situation: A Challenge to Education, **L6**: 123
Economy, Socialized, Democracy, Education, and, **L13**: 304
Education, **M6**: 425
Aesthetic Element in, **E5**: 202
Aims and Ideals of, **M13**: 399
Aims in, **M9**: 107
American: Organization in, **M10**: 397; Past and Future, **L6**: 90; and Culture, **M10**: 196
Art in, **M6**: 375; and Education in Art, **L2**: 111
Bearings of Pragmatism upon, **M4**: 178
Can It Share in Social Reconstruction? **L9**: 205
Challenge of Democracy to, **L11**: 181
Crisis in, **L9**: 112
Culture and Industry in, **M3**: 285
Culture and Professionalism in, **M15**: 193
Current Tendencies in, **M10**: 116
Democracy, and Socialized Economy, **L13**: 304
Democracy and, **M6**: 417; **M8**: 388; in the World of Today, **L13**: 294
Democracy in, **M3**: 229
Democratic Conception in, **M9**: 87
Democratic Faith and, **L15**: 251
Direct and Indirect, **M3**: 240
Direction of, **L3**: 251
Economic Situation a Challenge to, **L6**: 123
1800-1939, **L14**: 266
Elementary: Aim of History in, **M1**: 104; Federal Aid to, **M10**: 125; Psychology of, **M1**: 67; Report of the Committee on a Detailed Plan for a Report on, **E5**: 448
End in, **M6**: 436
Ethical Principles Underlying, **E5**: 54
Experiment in, **M6**: 451; **M10**: 121; as Natural Development, **M8**: 222
Experience and, **L13**: 1
For a New, **L14**: 278
Foundation for Social Organization, **L11**: 226
Higher: Health and Sex in, **E1**: 69; Health of Women and, **L17**: 7; President Hutchins' Proposals to Remake, **L11**: 397; and Research, Political Interference in, **L6**: 118

Education (*continued*)
History of (Syllabus), **L17**: 161
Idealism and Realism in, **M7**: 228
Individuality in, **M15**: 170
Interest and Effort in, **M7**: 151
Investigating, **L14**: 370
Liberal, **M7**: 271
Making It a Student Affair, **M15**: 198
Means and Goal of, **L13**: 61
Modern, Bankruptcy of, **L3**: 276
Monastery, Bargain Counter, or Laboratory in? **L6**: 99
Moral Principles in, **M4**: 265
Nationalizing, **M10**: 202
Need for a Philosophy of, **L9**: 194
Organic, Fairhope (Ala.) Experiment in, **M7**: 387
Organization and Curricula of the [University of Chicago] College of, **M3**: 327
Philosophy and, **L5**: 289
Philosophy of, **M7**: 297; **M9**: 331; (Syllabus), **E5**: 328
Primary-, Fetich, **E5**: 254
Progressive, and the Science of Education, **L3**: 257
Public, on Trial, **M10**: 173
Rationality in, **L11**: 391
Relation of Science and Philosophy as the Basis of, **L13**: 281
Relation of Theory to Practice in, **M3**: 249
Results of Child-Study Applied to, **E5**: 204
School of, **M3**: 342
Secondary: As Concerns, **M1**: 283; Problem of, after the War, **L17**: 26
Significance of the School of, **M3**: 273
Social Aspects of, **L17**: 226
Social-Economic Situation and, **L8**: 43
Social Purposes in, **M15**: 158
Sources of a Science of, **L5**: 1
Theory of Infancy in, **M7**: 245
Thinking in, **M9**: 159
Today (Panel Discussion), **L11**: 567
Toward a National System of, **L11**: 356
Traditional vs. Progressive, **L13**: 5
Underlying Philosophy of, **L8**: 77
Universal Service as, **M10**: 183
Vocational Aspects of, **M9**: 316
Waste in, **M1**: 39
and Birth Control, **L6**: 146
and Instruction, **M6**: 434
and New Social Ideals, **L11**: 167
and Our Present Social Problems, **L9**: 127
and Philosophy, Greetings to the Conference on, **L17**: 88
and Social Change, **L11**: 408
and Social Direction, **M11**: 54
and the Health of Women, **E1**: 64
and the Social Order, **L9**: 175
as a Necessity of Life, **M9**: 4
as a Religion, **M13**: 317
as a Social Function, **M9**: 14
as a University Study, **M4**: 158
as Conservative and Progressive, **M9**: 75
as Direction, **M9**: 28
as Engineering, **M13**: 323
as Growth, **M9**: 46
as Natural Development, **M8**: 211
as Politics, **M13**: 329
by Henry Adams, **M13**: 272

for a Changing Social Order, **L9**: 158
for a New and Better World, **L17**: 475
from a Social Perspective, **M7**: 113
through Industry, **M8**: 365
vs. Trade-Training, **M8**: 411
Educational Administration, Democracy and, **L11**: 217
Educational Articulation, General Principles of, **L5**: 299
Educational Balance, Efficiency and Thinking, **L17**: 77
Educational Confusion, Way Out of, **L6**: 75
Educational Ethics (Syllabus), **E5**: 291
Educational Frontier, **L8**: 41
Educational Function of a Museum of Decorative Arts, **L11**: 520
Educational Ideal, Our, in Wartime, **M10**: 178
Educational Lectures before Brigham Young Academy, **L17**: 211
Educational Methods, Influence of the High School upon, **E5**: 270
Educational Principles Involved, **L17**: 67
Educational Psychology (Syllabus), **E5**: 303
Educational Readjustment, Industry and, **M8**: 353
Educational Renaissance, Mexico's, **L2**: 199
Educational Situation, **M1**: 257
Educational Values, **M7**: 362; **M9**: 240
Education Development Act of 1947, Implications of, **L15**: 281
Educator, History for the, **M4**: 192
Efficiency, Educational Balance, and Thinking, **L17**: 77
Effort, **M6**: 434
Psychology of, **E5**: 151
Ego as Cause, **E4**: 91
Egoism, Altruism and, **M6**: 366
Election, After It, What? **L6**: 253
Elementary Course of Study, Place of Manual Training in the, **M1**: 230
Elementary School Record, **M1**: 222, 225
Emerson, Ralph Waldo—Philosopher of Democracy, **M3**: 184
Emotion, Theory of, **E4**: 152
Empirical, Experience and the, **M6**: 445
Empiricism, Immediate, **M3**: 168
Postulate of, **M3**: 158
Empiricisms, Empirical Survey of, **L11**: 69
Encyclopaedia and Dictionary of Education, **M13**: 397
Encyclopaedia of the Social Sciences, **L8**: 1
Encyclopaedia of the Social Sciences, On, **L17**: 125
End in Education, **M6**: 436
Ends: Means and, **L13**: 349
the Good and Wisdom, **L7**: 184
Energies, Organization of, **L10**: 167
Engineering, Education as, **M13**: 323
Enlistment for the Farm, **M10**: 296
Environment and Organism, **M6**: 437
Epistemological Realism. *See* Brief Studies in Realism

Epistemology, **M6**: 440
Concept of the Neutral in Recent, **M10**: 49
Equality: Liberalism and, **L11**: 368
Individuality, and Superiority, **M13**: 295
Escape from Peril, **L4**: 3
Esipov, Boris Petrov, and N. K. Goncharov, *I Want to Be Like Stalin*, Comment on, **L15**: 373
Essays in Experimental Logic (1916), **M1**: 151; **M2**: 298, 316, 337, 351; **M4**: 78, 91, 98; **M6**: 103; **M8**: 14, 83; **M10**: 319, 320, 366
Esthetic. *See* Aesthetic
Ethical Principles Underlying Education, **E5**: 54
Ethical Subject-Matter and Language, **L15**: 127
Ethical Theory, Nature of, **E4**: 223
Ethics (1908), **M5**
Ethics (1932), **L7**
Ethics, **M3**: 40
Anthropology and, **L3**: 11
Educational (Syllabus), **E5**: 291
Evolution and, **E5**: 34
Historical Method in, **L17**: 351
Metaphysical Method in, **E5**: 25
Outlines of a Critical Theory of, **E3**: 237
Psychological Method in, **M3**: 59
Study of (Syllabus), **E4**: 219
Teaching, in the High School, **E4**: 54
and International Relations, **M15**: 53
and Physical Science, **E1**: 205
and Politics, **E4**: 371
in the University of Michigan, **E3**: 48
of Animal Experimentation, **L2**: 98
of Democracy, **E1**: 227
Evaluation, **L12**: 161
Events and Meanings, **M13**: 276
Events and the Future, **L2**: 62
Evidence, **M6**: 442
Evolution, **M6**: 443
and Ethics, **E5**: 34
Evolutionary Method as Applied to Morality, **M2**: 3, 20
Example to Other Nations, As an, **L3**: 163
Excluded Middle, Sphere of Application of the, **L5**: 197
Existence: Applicability of Logic to, **L5**: 203
Ideas and Consciousness, **L1**: 226
Knowledge and, **L17**: 361
Meaning and, **L3**: 82
Value and Criticism, **L1**: 295
as Precarious and as Stable, **L1**: 42
of the World as a Logical Problem, **M8**: 83
Existences: Beliefs and, **M3**: 83
Objects, Data, and, **M4**: 146
Experience, **L13**: 61
Aesthetic, as a Primary Phase and as an Artistic Development, **L16**: 395
Conduct and, **L5**: 218
Consciousness and, **M1**: 113
Criteria of, **L13**: 17
Having an, **L10**: 42
Individuality and, **L2**: 55
Knowledge and Value, **L14**: 3
Nature and Art, **L1**: 266
Nature in, **L14**: 141

Need of a Theory of, **L13**: 11
Problem of, **L17**: 429
Pure, and Reality, **M4**: 120
Reality as, **M3**: 101
Sensation and, **E1**: 313
Valid Knowledge and the Subjectivity of, **M6**: 80
and Objective Idealism, **M3**: 128
and Philosophic Method, **L1**: 10, 365
and Reason, Changed Conceptions of, **M12**: 124
and the Empirical, **M6**: 445
and Thinking, **M9**: 146
Experience and Education, **L13**: 1
Experience and Nature, **L1**
Experiment, Chicago, The Theory of the, **L11**: 202
Experiment, Great, and the Future, **L3**: 242
Experimentalism, From Absolutism to, **L5**: 147
Experimental Theory of Knowledge, **M3**: 107
Experimentation, Logic of, **M6**: 453
Experiment in Education, **M6**: 451; **M10**: 121
as Natural Development, **M8**: 222
Explanation, **M6**: 455
of Our Lapse, **M10**: 292
Expression: Act of, **L10**: 64
Imagination and, **E5**: 192
Expressive Object, **L10**: 88
External Object, **M6**: 457

Fact, **M6**: 457
Facts: Control of Ideas by, **M4**: 78
Interpretation of, **M6**: 259
Faculty Share in University Control, **M8**: 109
Fairhope (Ala.) Experiment in Organic Education, **M7**: 387
Faith and Its Object, **L9**: 21
Far East, America and the, **L2**: 173
Far Eastern Deadlock, **M13**: 79
Far Eastern Republic, **M13**: 240
Farm, Enlistment for the, **M10**: 296
Farm Backing, Dewey for, **L5**: 447
Farm Processing and Other Consumption Taxes Must Be Repealed, **L9**: 273
Federal Aid to Elementary Education, **M10**: 125
Federal Government and Unemployment, **L6**: 377
Federation for Child Study, Lectures to the, **M7**: 377
Feeling: Aesthetic, **E2**: 267
Formal, **E2**: 228
Introduction to, **E2**: 215
Knowledge and the Relativity of, **E1**: 19
Personal, **E2**: 281
Sensuous, **E2**: 218
Feelings: Intellectual, **E2**: 256
Qualitative, Development of, **E2**: 239
Fiat Justitia, Ruat Coelum, **M10**: 281
Fighting For, What Are We? **M11**: 98
Force, Violence and Law, **M10**: 211
Force and Coercion, **M10**: 244
Foreword to
Barnes, Albert C., and Violette de Mazia, *The Art of Renoir*, **L11**: 501
Bawden, H. Heath, "Method," **L15**: 305

Foreword to (*continued*)
Clapp, Elsie Ripley, *Community Schools in Action*, **L14**: 351
Davis, Helen Edna, *Tolstoy and Nietzsche*, **L5**: 398
de Mazia, Violette, and Albert C. Barnes, *The Art of Renoir*, **L11**: 501
Douglas, Paul H., *The Coming of a New Party*, **L6**: 313
Durant, William James, *The Story of Philosophy*, **L2**: 387
Educational Trends, **L14**: 360
Foundation of Commercial Education, **L5**: 401
Geiger, George Raymond, *The Philosophy of Henry George*, **L9**: 299
Jensen, Carl Christian, *Seventy Times Seven*, **L11**: 506
Johnson, Edwin C., *Mars in Civilian Disguise!* **L14**: 355
Kelley, Earl C., *Education for What Is Real*, **L15**: 310
Levinson, Salmon O., *Outlawry of War*, **M13**: 411
Neilson, William Allan, ed., *Education in the Soviet Union*, **L11**: 509
Pellegrini, Angelo M., and Brents Stirling, *Argumentation and Public Discussion*, **L11**: 515
Radin, Paul, *Primitive Man as Philosopher,* **L3**: 335
Schaefer-Simmern, Henry, *The Unfolding of Artistic Activity*, **L15**: 315
Schneersohn, Fischel, *Studies in Psycho-Expedition*, **L5**: 410
Stirling, Brents, and Angelo M. Pellegrini, *Argumentation and Public Discussion*, **L11**: 515
Stoner, John E., *S. O. Levinson and the Pact of Paris*, **L15**: 301
Watson, David Lindsay, *Scientists Are Human*, **L13**: 369
Wiener, Philip P., *Evolution and the Founders of Pragmatism*, **L17**: 50
Williams, Eric, *Education in the British West Indies*, **L15**: 308
Form: Natural History of, **L10**: 139
Substance and, **L10**: 111
and Content, **M6**: 458
and Matter, **L12**: 369
Formal Functions and Canons, **L12**: 327
Four Factors in Natural Growth, **M8**: 236
Four-Power Pact, Few Second Thoughts on, **M13**: 213
Fourteen Points and the League of Nations, **M11**: 135
Freedom, **L11**: 247
Academic, **M2**: 53; **M6**: 460; Social Significance of, **L11**: 376; Statement on, **L14**: 374
Idea of, **E3**: 340
Nature of, **L13**: 39
Philosophies of, **L3**: 92
Problem of, **L13**: 65
Professorial, **M8**: 407
What Is It? **M14**: 209
and Individuality, **M8**: 294
and Responsibility, **E4**: 337
in New Schools, How Much? **L5**: 319
in Relation to Culture, Social Planning, and Leadership, **L6**: 142

in Workers' Education, **L5**: 331
of Thought and Work, **M12**: 8
of Will, **M6**: 464
Freedom and Culture, **L13**: 63
Freight Increase, Dewey Opposes Blanket, **L6**: 368
French Literature, Contemporary, Lesson of, **E3**: 36
Froebel, Friedrich Wilhelm, His Educational Principles, **M1**: 81
Full Warehouses and Empty Stomachs, **L6**: 341
Function, **M6**: 466
Fundamentals, **M15**: 3
Future: Events and the, **L2**: 62
Great Experiment and the, **L3**: 242
Present and, **M14**: 182
of Democracy, **L11**: 532
of Liberalism, **L11**: 258, 289
of Pacifism, **M10**: 265
of Philosophy, **L17**: 466
of Radical Political Action, **L9**: 66

Galton, Francis, His Statistical Methods, **E3**: 43
Generalization, **M7**: 209
General Propositions, **L12**: 244
Kinds, and Classes, **L11**: 118
Geography and History, Significance of, **M9**: 215
Geometry, Psychological and the Logical in Teaching, **M3**: 216
George, Henry, Appreciation of, **L3**: 359
German Philosophy and Politics, **M8**: 135, 421
Germany, On Understanding the Mind of, **M10**: 216
Gifford Lectureship, Syllabus for, **L4**: 251
Goals, Setting New, at Seventy, **L6**: 403
God, Obligation to Knowledge of, **E1**: 61
Goncharov, N. K., and Boris Petrov Esipov, *I Want to Be Like Stalin*, Comment on, **L15**: 373
Good, **E3**: 249
Construction of, **L4**: 203
Intrinsic, Ambiguity of, **L15**: 42
Uniqueness of, **M14**: 146
and Desire, **M5**: 241
Government and Children, **L11**: 268
Great American Prophet, **L9**: 102
Great Community, Search for the, **L2**: 325
Green, Thomas Hill: His Theory of the Moral Motive, **E3**: 155
Philosophy of, **E3**: 14
Ground Rent, Socialization of, **L11**: 256
Growth: Periods of, **L17**: 255
Natural, Four Factors in, **M8**: 236
in Activity, **L11**: 243
Guterman, Norbert, Reply to, **L9**: 293

Habit, **L17**: 298
Custom and, **M14**: 43
and Intelligence, **M14**: 121
and Social Psychology, **M14**: 60
Habits: Impulse and Conflict of, **M14**: 88
Impulses and Change of, **M14**: 65
and Will, **M14**: 21
as Social Functions, **M14**: 15

Half-Hearted Naturalism, **L3**: 73
Happiness and Conduct, **M5**: 241
Happiness and Social Ends, **M5**: 261
Harmony, **M7**: 210
  Pre-established, **M2**: 212
Harper, William Rainey: Memorandum on Pedagogy to, **L17**: 485
  Memorandum to, on Coeducation, **M2**: 105
Harvard, Religion at, **L17**: 135
Hazlitt, Henry, Reply to, **L15**: 359
Health and Sex in Higher Education, **E1**: 69
Health of Women: Education and the, **E1**: 64
  and Higher Education, **L17**: 7
Hedonism, **M7**: 211
Higher Learning and War, **L14**: 273
Higher Learning in America, **L11**: 402
Highly Colored White Lies, **L2**: 176
High School: Influence of the, upon Educational Methods, **E5**: 270
  Teaching Ethics in the, **E4**: 54
Historical Development of Inventions and Occupations, **M1**: 222
Historical Factors in Philosophical Reconstruction, Some, **M12**: 95
Historical Method in Ethics, **L17**: 351
History: Aim of, in Elementary Education, **M1**: 104
  Significance of Geography and, **M9**: 215
  Study of, in the Schools, On the, **E5**: 429
  for the Educator, **M4**: 192
  of Education (Syllabus), **L17**: 161
  of Liberalism, **L11**: 5
Hitler, Adolf, His One-World of National Socialism, **M8**: 421
Hoarding, Only Way to Stop, **L6**: 379
Hobbes, Thomas, Motivation of His Political Philosophy, **M11**: 18
Hocking, William Ernest, "Political Philosophy in Germany," Reply to, **M8**: 418
Holmes, Oliver Wendell, and the Liberal Mind, **L3**: 177
Hook, Sidney, *Education for Modern Man*, Comment on, **L15**: 372
Hoover, Herbert: Asks Him to Act on Unemployment, **L5**: 436
  Dewey Calls on Him to Recognize Government Responsibility for Unemployment, **L6**: 372
  His Policies Help Property Owners Chiefly, **L9**: 277
  Key to His Keynote Speech, **L6**: 357
  and the Special Session, **L6**: 345
Hope, Basis for, **L14**: 249
House Divided against Itself, **L5**: 45
How, What, and *What For* in Social Inquiry, **L16**: 333
How Is Mind to Be Known? **L15**: 27
How Reaction Helps, **M12**: 17
How the Mind Learns, **L17**: 213

How They Are Voting, **L11**: 526
How We Think (1910), **M6**: 177
How We Think (1933), **L8**: 105
Hughes, Charles Evans, His Campaign, **M10**: 252
Human, Morals Are, **M14**: 204
Human Abode of the Religious Function, **L9**: 40
Human Being, Unity of the, **L13**: 323
Human Contribution, **L10**: 250
Human History, Crisis in, **L15**: 210
Humanism: Naturalism and, **M9**: 286
  Religious, Mystical Naturalism and, **L11**: 84
  What It Means to Me, **L5**: 263
  and Naturalism, **M7**: 213
Humanities, **M7**: 218
Human Nature, **L6**: 29
  Changing, **M14**: 76
  Contrary to, **L14**: 258
  Culture and, **L13**: 80
  Democracy and, **L13**: 136
  Does It Change? **L13**: 286
Human Nature and Conduct, **M14**
Hunger, Drive against, **L9**: 307
Hutchins, Robert Maynard, His Proposals to Remake Higher Education, **L11**: 397
Hypothesis, **M7**: 218

I Believe, **L14**: 91
Idea: Inclusive Philosophic, **L3**: 41
  Innate, **M7**: 251
  and Ideation, **M7**: 221
Ideal and the Real, Changed Conceptions of the, **M12**: 139
Idealism, **M7**: 224
  Discrediting of, **M11**: 180
  Objective, Experience and, **M3**: 128
  Realism and, **M4**: 116
  and Realism in Education, **M7**: 228
Ideals: American, **L9**: 87
  Formation and Growth of, **E3**: 354
  Moral Struggle or the Realizing of, **E3**: 372
  Will as the Source of, and of Their Realization, **E2**: 357
Ideas: Control of, by Facts, **M4**: 78
  Logical Character of, **M4**: 91
  Play of, **L4**: 112
  and Meanings, **L8**: 221
  at Work, **L4**: 87
Ill Advised, **M10**: 370
Illiteracy Problem, Our, **L5**: 311
Illusory Psychology, **E1**: 168
Imagination, **E2**: 168; **L17**: 242
  and Expression, **E5**: 192
Imitation, **M7**: 234
Immediate Empiricism, **M3**: 168
  Postulate of, **M3**: 158
Immediate Knowledge, **L12**: 142
  Concerning Alleged, of Mind, **M11**: 10
Immediate Quality, Valuation Judgments and, **L15**: 63
Immortality, On, **L17**: 126
Immutable, Philosophy's Search for the, **L4**: 21
Imperative Need: A New Radical Party, **L9**: 76
Imperialism Is Easy, **L3**: 158
Importance, Significance, and Meaning, **L16**: 318
Impressions of Soviet Russia and the Revolutionary World, Mexico—China—Turkey (1929), **M12**: 71; **M13**: 72;

Impressions of Soviet Russia (continued)
M15: 128, 134, 139; L2: 194, 199, 206; L3: 158, 203, 208, 215, 224, 233, 242
Impulse: Plasticity of, M14: 69
and Conflict of Habits, M14: 88
and Thought, M14: 117
Impulses: Sensuous, E2: 299
and Change of Habits, M14: 65
and the Will, E1: 327
Individual: Social Organization and the, M5: 383
and the World, M9: 300
Individualism, Old and New, L5: 41
Individualism, Toward a New, L5: 77
Individuality, M7: 237
Equality and Superiority, M13: 295
Freedom and, M8: 294
Mediocrity and, M13: 289
Time and, L14: 98
and Experience, L2: 55
in Education, M15: 170
in Our Day, L5: 111
Induction and Deduction, M6: 242; M7: 239; L12: 415
Industrial Education: Need of an, in an Industrial Democracy, M10: 137
Policy of, M7: 93
Some Dangers in the Present Movement for, M7: 98
Wrong Kind, A, M8: 117
and Democracy, M7: 104
Industry: Education through, M8: 365
and Educational Readjustment, M8: 353
and Motives, M13: 281
Infancy, Early, Principles of Mental Development as Illustrated in, M1: 175
Infancy, Theory of, in Education, M7: 245
Infant Language, Psychology of, E4: 66
Inference, M7: 248
Systematic, M6: 242
Understanding and, L12: 142
and Testing, Examples of, L8: 187
Inflation, Wild, Would Paralyze Nation, L9: 267
Inflationary Measures Injure the Masses, L9: 265
Influence of Darwin on Philosophy, M4: 3
Influence of Darwin on Philosophy and Other Essays in Contemporary Thought (1910), E5: 3; M1: 113; M3: 83, 107, 128, 158; M4: 3, 15, 31, 50; L17: 39
Information, M7: 249
Initiative, M7: 251
Innate Idea, M7: 251
Inquiry: Existential Matrix of, L12: 30, 48
Pattern of, L12: 105
and Indeterminateness of Situations, L15: 34
Instincts: Classification of, M14: 92
No Separate, M14: 104
Instruction, Education and, M6: 434
Instrumentalism, Reply to Professor Royce's Critique of, M7: 64
Intellectual and Practical Studies, M9: 271

Intellectual Authority, Seat of, **L4**: 136
Intellectual Frontier, American, **M13**: 301
Intellectualist Criterion for Truth, **M4**: 50
Intellectualist Theory of Truth, Dilemma of the, **M4**: 76
Intellectual Obligation, Supreme, **L9**: 96
Intellectuals, Religion and the, **L16**: 390
Intelligence: Crucial Role of, **L11**: 342
  Desire and, **M14**: 171
  Habit and, **M14**: 121
  Naturalization of, **L4**: 156
  and Morals, **M4**: 31
  and Power, **L9**: 107
Interaction and Transaction, **L16**: 96
Interest, **M7**: 252
  Many-Sided, **M7**: 275
  Public, Case of the Professor and the, **M10**: 164
  and Discipline, **M9**: 131
  in Relation to Training of the Will, **E5**: 111
Interest and Effort in Education, **M7**: 151
International Cooperation or International Chaos, **L11**: 261
International Duel in China, **M11**: 192
International Organization: Are Sanctions Necessary to? **L6**: 196
  Democratic versus Coercive, **L15**: 192
International Relations, Ethics and, **M15**: 53
International Symposium on Scholasticism, **L2**: 388
Interpretation of Savage Mind, **M2**: 39
Introduction, General, to Groups V and VI, **M1**: 225
Introduction to
  Alexander, F. Matthias, *Constructive Conscious Control of the Individual*, **M15**: 308
  —*Man's Supreme Inheritance*, **M11**: 350
  —*The Use of the Self*, **L6**: 315
  American Journal of Economics and Sociology, **L14**: 362
  Barnes, Roswell P., *Militarizing Our Youth*, **L3**: 346
  Benson, Jean, *Looking Forward, 1933*, **L17**: 45
  Bingham, Alfred Mitchell, and Selden Rodman, eds., *Challenge to the New Deal*, **L9**: 296
  Bliss, Henry Evelyn, *The Organization of Knowledge and the System of the Sciences*, **L5**: 404
  Chatterji, Jagadish Chandra, *India's Outlook on Life*, **L6**: 321
  Cowdry, Edmund Vincent, ed., *Problems of Ageing*, **L14**: 341
  Cowles, Edward Spencer, *Don't Be Afraid!* **L15**: 365
  de Lima, Agnes, et al., *The Little Red School House*, **L15**: 303
  Dewey, John, and Horace M. Kallen, eds., *The Bertrand Russell Case*, **L14**: 357
  Directory of the Trades and Occupations Taught at the

Introduction to (*continued*)
Day and Evening Schools in Greater New York, **M7**: 205
Dorner, Alexander, *The Way beyond "Art"—The Work of Herbert Bayer*, **L15**: 312
Eastman, Max, ed., *Selected Poems of Claude McKay*, **L17**: 58
Edwards, Anna Camp, and Katherine Camp Mayhew, *The Dewey School*, **L11**: 191
Hart, Joseph Kinmont, *Inside Experience*, **L3**: 342
Hillyer, Mary W., *Looking Forward, 1934*, **L17**: 46
—*Looking Forward, 1935*, **L17**: 47
—*Looking Forward, 1936*, **L17**: 48
Hindus, Maurice, *Humanity Uprooted*, **L5**: 407
Hook, Sidney, *The Metaphysics of Pragmatism*, **L3**: 338
Hughes, Percy, *The Center, Function and Structure of Psychology*, **L17**: 42
James, William, *Talks to Teachers on Psychology*, **L14**: 337
Kallen, Horace M., and John Dewey, eds., *The Bertrand Russell Case*, **L14**: 357
King, Irving Walter, *The Psychology of Child Development*, **M3**: 299
Klyce, Scudder, *Universe*, **M13**: 412
Lafferty, Theodore T., *Studies in Philosophy*, **L6**: 311
Laidler, Harry W., *Looking Forward, 1937*, **L11**: 517
—*Looking Forward, 1938*, **L11**: 519
League for Industrial Democracy, *Looking Forward: Discussion Outlines*, **L17**: 44
McGraw, Myrtle Byram, *Growth: A Study of Johnny and Jimmy*, **L11**: 510
McKay, Claude, *Selected Poems of Claude McKay*, ed. Max Eastman, **L17**: 58
Mayhew, Katherine Camp, and Anna Camp Edwards, *The Dewey School*, **L11**: 191
Mudge, Isadore Gilbert, ed., *A Contribution to a Bibliography of Henri Bergson*, **M7**: 201
Rodman, Selden, and Alfred Mitchell Bingham, eds., *Challenge to the New Deal*, **L9**: 296
Sheffield, Alfred Dwight, ed., *Training for Group Experience*, **L5**: 412
Tenenbaum, Samuel, *William Heard Kilpatrick*, **L17**: 52
Unemployment Insurance, **L6**: 399
Welling, Richard, *Self Government and Politics in School*, **L11**: 516
Intuition, **E2**: 204; **M7**: 260
Intuitionalism, **E4**: 123
Inventions and Occupations, Historical Development of, **M1**: 222
Investigating Education, **L14**: 370
Irrationality, Cult of, **M11**: 107
Irrepressible Conflict, **L6**: 149
Isolation, **M7**: 261

James, William, **M6**: 91, 98; **M12**: 205

His Morals and Julien Benda's, **L15**: 19
Vanishing Subject in the Psychology of, **L14**: 155
and the World Today, **L15**: 3
as Empiricist, **L15**: 9
in Nineteen Twenty-Six, **L2**: 158
Japan: Liberalism in, **M11**: 156
Public Opinion in, **M13**: 255
Siberia and, **M13**: 240
and America, **M11**: 150
Jefferson, Thomas: Presenting, **L14**: 201
Statement on, **L15**: 366
Jobless—A Job for All of Us, **L6**: 153
John Dewey Labor Research Fund, Message to Friends of the, **L14**: 311
Johnson, Alvin, Tribute to, **L17**: 147
Judgment, **M6**: 259; **M7**: 262
Construction of, **L12**: 123
Continuum of, **L12**: 244
Function of Propositions of Quantity in, **L12**: 200
Further as to Valuation as, **L15**: 73
Its Place in Reflective Activity, **L8**: 210
Memory and, **L17**: 323
as Requalification, **L12**: 182
as Spatial-Temporal Determination, **L12**: 220
Judgments of Practice, **L12**: 161
Logic of, **M8**: 14
Justice, Psychology and, **L3**: 186
Juvenile Reading, **L5**: 394

Kahn, Sholom J., "Experience and Existence in Dewey's Naturalistic Metaphysics," Comment on, **L16**: 383
Kallen, Horace M., "What Pragmatism Means for the Social Sciences," Comment on, **L11**: 563
Kant, Immanuel: after Two Hundred Years, **M15**: 8
and Philosophic Method, **E1**: 34
Kindergarten and Child-Study, **E5**: 207
Kinds, General Propositions, and Classes, **L11**: 118
Kinds and Classes, **L11**: 95
Klein, Julius: Asked Basis for Optimism, **L6**: 346
Rejoinder to, **L6**: 351
Knowing and the Known, **L16**: 1
Knowledge, **M7**: 265
Elements of, **E2**: 29
Experience, and Value, **L14**: 3
Experimental, Valuation and, **M13**: 3
Experimental Theory of, **M3**: 107
Immediate, of Mind, Concerning Alleged, **M11**: 10
Logic of Inquiry and Philosophies of, **L12**: 506
Moral Judgment and, **L7**: 262
Nature and Extent of, **E1**: 384
Processes of, **E2**: 75
Significance of the Problem of, **E5**: 3
Theories of, **M9**: 343
Unification of, **M2**: 261
Valid, and the Subjectivity of Experience, **M6**: 80
World High Court for? **L11**: 127
and Existence, **L17**: 361
and Speech Reaction, **M13**: 29

Knowledge (*continued*)
and the Relativity of Feeling, **E1**: 19
as Idealization, **E1**: 176
Knowledge Experience Again, **M3**: 178
Knowledge Experience and Its Relationships, **M3**: 171

Labor and Leisure, **M9**: 259
Laboratory School, Need for a, **E5**: 433
Labor Politics and Labor Education, **L5**: 338
La Follette, Robert M., Dewey Aids, **M15**: 317
Laidler, Harry W., B. C. Vladeck and, **L6**: 326
Language: Ethical Subject-Matter and, **L15**: 127
and the Training of Thought, **M6**: 314; **L8**: 301
Law, **M7**: 269
Anthropology and, **E4**: 37
Force, Violence and, **M10**: 211
Logical Method and, **M15**: 65
My Philosophy of, **L14**: 115
Nature and Reason in, **M7**: 56
War and a Code of, **M15**: 122
League for Independent Political Action, Statement by the Executive Committee, **L6**: 436
League for Industrial Democracy, Address of Welcome to, **L14**: 262
League of Nations: Approach to a, **M11**: 127
Fourteen Points and the, **M11**: 135
Shall We Join the? **M15**: 78, 83
and Economic Freedom, **M11**: 139
and the New Diplomacy, **M11**: 131
Learning: What Is It? **L11**: 238
to Earn, **M10**: 144
Lectures, Résumé of Four, on Common Sense, Science and Philosophy, **L6**: 424
Lectures vs. Recitations, **E3**: 147
Legal Cooperation, Political Combination or? **M15**: 105
Leibniz, Gottfried Wilhelm: Theology of, **E1**: 403
and John Locke, Their Innate Ideas, **E1**: 299
the Man, **E1**: 255
the Sources of His Philosophy, **E1**: 268
Leibniz's New Essays Concerning the Human Understanding, **E1**: 251
Leisure, Labor and, **M9**: 259
Leningrad Gives the Clue, **L3**: 203
Lessons from the War—in Philosophy, **L14**: 312
Levinson, Salmon O., Apostle of World Unity, **L5**: 349
Liberal Arts, Statements to the Conference on Curriculum for the College of, **L6**: 414
Liberal Arts College, Problem of the, **L15**: 276
Liberal College: Prospects of the, **M15**: 200
and Its Enemies, **M15**: 205
Liberal Education, **M7**: 271
Liberalism: *Commentary* and, **L15**: 362
Crisis in, **L11**: 23
Future of, **L11**: 258, 289
History of, **L11**: 5
How to Anchor It, **L15**: 248
Liberal Speaks Out for, **L11**: 282
Meaning of, **L11**: 364
Meaning of the Term, **L14**: 252

Renascent, **L11**: 41
and Civil Liberties, **L11**: 372
and Equality, **L11**: 368
and Irrationalism, Reply to, **M13**: 421
in Japan, **M11**: 156
Liberalism and Social Action, **L11**: 1
Liberal Party, Dewey Hails the, **L17**: 134
Liberals, What Do They Want? **L5**: 346
Liberal Speaks Out for Liberalism, **L11**: 282
Liberal Thought, Challenge to, **L15**: 261
Liberating the Social Scientist, **L15**: 224
Liberty, Theory of, vs. the Fact of Regimentation, **L9**: 87
Liberty and Social Control, **L11**: 360
Linguistic Sign or Name, What Is It to Be a? **L16**: 297
Linguistic Signs, Thought, and Meaning, Peirce's Theory of, **L15**: 141
Linville, Henry, Pension Fund, **L11**: 380
Live Creature, **L10**: 9
and "Ethereal Things," **L10**: 26
Lobby Inquiry Opens Tomorrow, **L5**: 429
Localism, Americanism and, **M12**: 12
Locke, John: Substance, Power and Quality in, **L2**: 141
and Gottfried Wilhelm Leibniz, Their Innate Ideas, **E1**: 299
Logic, **L8**: 3
Applicability of, to Existence, **L5**: 203
Concerning Novelties in, **M10**: 98
Is It a Dualistic Science? **E3**: 75
Needed Reform of, **L12**: 86
and Natural Science, **L12**: 369
of Inquiry and Philosophies of Knowledge, **L12**: 506
of Judgments of Practice, **M8**: 14
of Verification, **E3**: 83
Logic: The Theory of Inquiry, **L12**
Logical, Psychological and the, **M6**: 224
in Teaching Geometry, **M3**: 216
Logical Character of Ideas, **M4**: 91
Logical Conditions of a Scientific Treatment of Morality, **M3**: 3
Logical Form, Psychological Process and, **L8**: 171
Logical Method and Law, **M15**: 65
Logical Objects, **M10**: 89
Logical Problem, Existence of the World as a, **M8**: 83
Logical Reconstruction, Significance of, **M12**: 156
Logical Subject-Matter, Problem of, **L12**: 9
Logical Theory: Present Position of, **E3**: 125
Studies in, **M2**: 293
Logical Thought, Some Stages of, **M1**: 151
Logical Topics, Notes upon, **M3**: 62
Lost Individual, **L5**: 66
Lovejoy, Arthur O., Reply to, **M15**: 83

McGilvary, Evander Bradley: Reply to His Questions, **M4**: 143, 146
Response to, **M7**: 79

Maeterlinck, Maurice, His Philosophy of Life, **M6**: 123
Man and Mathematics, **L15**: 376
Mann, Horace, Today, **L11**: 387
Manual Training, Place of, in the Elementary Course of Study, **M1**: 230
Manufacturers' Association and the Public Schools, **L3**: 280
Many-Sided Interest, **M7**: 275
Marsh, James, and American Philosophy, **L5**: 178
Martineau, James, His Theory of Morals, **L17**: 3
Materialism, **M7**: 275
  Metaphysical Assumptions of, **E1**: 3
Materialists, Are Naturalists? **L15**: 109
Material Phenomena and Their Reality, **E1**: 355
Mathematical Discourse, **L12**: 391
Mathematics, Man and, **L15**: 376
Matter: Form and, **L12**: 369
  and Its Relation to Spirit, **E1**: 342
Mead, George Herbert, as I Knew Him, **L6**: 22
Meaning, **M6**: 271
  Assertion and Proposal, **L9**: 303
  Importance, Significance, and, **L16**: 318
  and Existence, **L3**: 82
  and Progress of Morality, **L17**: 393
  of Purpose, **L13**: 43
  of Value, **L2**: 69
Meanings: Data and, **M2**: 337
  Events and, **M13**: 276
  Ideas and, **L8**: 221
  Terms or, **L12**: 347
Means and End of Mental Training, **M6**: 224
Means and Ends, **L13**: 349
Mediocrity and Individuality, **M13**: 289
Megan, Charles P., "Parochial School Education," Reply to, **M8**: 416
Meiklejohn, Alexander: Dewey vs., **L15**: 333
  Rejoinder to, **L15**: 337
Memory, **E2**: 154
  and Judgment, **L17**: 323
Men, Younger, Are Key, **L11**: 529
Mental Development, **M1**: 192
  Principles of, as Illustrated in Early Infancy, **M1**: 175
Mental Training, Means and End of, **M6**: 224
Metaphysical Assumptions of Materialism, **E1**: 3
Metaphysical Inquiry, Subject-Matter of, **M8**: 3
Metaphysical Method in Ethics, **E5**: 25
Metaphysics, **M7**: 276
  Tradition, and Morals, **M15**: 14
Method, **M7**: 277
  Nature of, **M9**: 171
  Problem of, **L2**: 351
  Scientific, **M7**: 335; **L12**: 415
  Supremacy of, **L4**: 178
  Working, in Social Psychology, **L17**: 422
  in Science Teaching, **M10**: 130
  of the Recitation, **M3**: 347
Methods in Philosophy and the Sciences, **L17**: 442
Mexican Hearings, In Defense of the, **L13**: 347
Mexican Notebook, From a, **L2**: 206

Mexico, Church and State in, **L2**: 194
Mexico's Educational Renaissance, **L2**: 199
Michigan, Should It Have Vocational Education under "Unit" or "Dual" Control? **M7**: 85
Michigan, University of: Ethics in, **E3**: 48
Philosophy in, **E3**: 90
School of Education, Letter to, **L5**: 393
Michigan Schoolmasters' Club, Anniversary Address, **L11**: 171
Militarism in China, **M11**: 199
Military Training: Universal, **M10**: 377
for American School Boys, **L17**: 122
in Schools, On, **L17**: 124
Mill, John Stuart, and William Whewell, On, **M2**: 368
Mind: Body and, **L3**: 25
Concerning Alleged Immediate Knowledge of, **M11**: 10
How Is It to Be Known? **L15**: 27
How It Learns, **L17**: 213
Observation and Information in the Training of, **M6**: 328; **L8**: 315
Post-War, **M11**: 112
Radio's Influence on the, **L9**: 309
Savage, Interpretation of, **M2**: 39
What Are States of? **M7**: 31
and Its Modes of Activity, **E2**: 18
Mission to Moscow Film: Again Attacked, **L15**: 351
More on, **L15**: 354
Several Faults Are Found in, **L15**: 345
Modern Philosophy, **L16**: 407
Monastery, Bargain Counter, or Laboratory in Education? **L6**: 99
Monism, **M7**: 284
or Dualism, Realism without, **M13**: 40
Moral and Logical Theory, Recent Criticisms of Some Points in, **L17**: 480
Moral Approbation, Value and Standard, **E4**: 247
Moral Conceptions, Reconstruction in, **M12**: 172
Moral Conduct, Factors of, **E4**: 228
Moral Consciousness, **E4**: 240
Moral Control, **E2**: 342
Moral Ideal, Self-Realization as the, **E4**: 42
Morality: Custom and, **M14**: 54
Evolutionary Method as Applied to, **M2**: 3, 20
Logical Conditions of a Scientific Treatment of, **M3**: 3
Meaning and Progress of, **L17**: 393
Realized, or the Virtues, **E3**: 382
Religion and, in a Free Society, **L15**: 170
and Moral Sense, **M7**: 285
Is Social, **M14**: 216
Moral Judgment and Knowledge, **L7**: 262
Moral Knowledge, **M5**: 278
Moral Life: Place of Duty in the, **M5**: 305
Place of Reason in the, **M5**: 278
Place of Self in the, **M5**: 328

Moral Motive, Green's Theory of the, **E3**: 155
Moral Philosophy, **E4**: 132
Moral Principles in Education, **M4**: 265
Morals: Doctor Martineau's Theory of, **L17**: 3
 Intelligence and, **M4**: 31
 Social Institutions and the Study of (Syllabus), **M15**: 229
 Theories of, **M9**: 356
 Three Independent Factors in, **L5**: 279
 Tradition, Metaphysics, and, **M15**: 14
 and the Conduct of States, **M11**: 122
 Are Human, **M14**: 204
Moral Self, **L7**: 285
Moral Significance of the Common School Studies, **M4**: 205
Moral Situation, **M5**: 187
Moral Struggle or the Realizing of Ideals, **E3**: 372
Moral Theory: Nature of, **L7**: 162
 Problems of, **M5**: 197
 Types of, **M5**: 207
 and Practice, **E3**: 93
Moral Training, Chaos in, **E4**: 106
Morris, Charles W., Rejoinder to, **L15**: 331
Morris, George Sylvester: Estimate of, **M10**: 109
 The Late, **E3**: 3
Moscow Film Again Attacked, **L15**: 351
Moscow Trials, **L11**: 326
Motives, Industry and, **M13**: 281
Münsterberg, Hugo, Rejoinder to, **M3**: 151
My Pedagogic Creed, **E5**: 84
Mystical Naturalism and Religious Humanism, **L11**: 84

Naïve Realism *vs.* Presentative Realism. *See* Brief Studies in Realism
Names: Firm, Search for, **L16**: 6
 Trial Group of, **L16**: 257
National Association for the Advancement of Colored People, Address to, **L6**: 224
National Dilemma, Our, **M12**: 3
National Education Association, Acceptance Speech, **L11**: 533
National Hesitation, In a Time of, **M10**: 256
Nationalism, Fruits of, **L3**: 152
Nationality, Principle of, **M10**: 285
Nationalizing Education, **M10**: 202
National Negro Conference, Address to, **M4**: 156
National Socialism, One-World of Hitler's, **M8**: 421
National Society of College Teachers of Education, Statement to, **L17**: 138
National Understanding, Some Factors in Mutual, **M13**: 262
Nations, As an Example to Other, **L3**: 163
Nation's Ills, Dewey Surveys the, **L6**: 408
Native Resources in Training Thought, **L8**: 140
Nativism, **M7**: 286
Natural, **M2**: 141
Natural Development and Social Efficiency as Aims, **M9**: 118
Naturalism, **M2**: 142
 Half-Hearted, **L3**: 73

Humanism and, **M7**: 213
Mystical, and Religious Humanism, **L11**: 84
and Humanism, **M9**: 286
in Art, **M2**: 142
Naturalistic Theory of Sense-Perception, **L2**: 44
Naturalists, Are They Materialists? **L15**: 109
Natural Realism, **M2**: 142
Natural Resources in the Training of Thought, **M6**: 204
Natural Science: Logic and, **L12**: 369
Penning-in of, **L15**: 184
Natural Theology, Syllabus for Gifford Lectureship in, **L4**: 251
Nature, **M2**: 142; **M7**: 287
By, and by Art, **L15**: 84
Communication and Meaning, **L1**: 132
Ends and Histories, **L1**: 69
Life and Body-Mind, **L1**: 191
Means and Knowledge, **L1**: 100
Mind and the Subject, **L1**: 162
Philosophy of, **M2**: 148
and Extent of Knowledge, **E1**: 384
and Its Good, **M4**: 15
and Reason in Law, **M7**: 56
in Experience, **L14**: 141
Necessity, **M2**: 149
Need for a New Party, **L6**: 156
Need for a Philosophy of Education, **L9**: 194
Need for a Recovery of Philosophy, **M10**: 3
Need for Orientation, **L11**: 162
Need for Social Psychology, **M10**: 53
Need of an Industrial Education in an Industrial Democracy, **M10**: 137
Negation, Affirmation and, **L12**: 182
Negro Conference, National, Address to, **M4**: 156
Neo-Criticism, **M2**: 153
Neo-Humanism, **M7**: 290
Neo-Platonism, **M2**: 153
Neo-Pythagoreanism, **M2**: 153
Nescience, **M2**: 153
Neutral, Concept of the, in Recent Epistemology, **M10**: 49
New Deal, Real Test of the, **L9**: 259
New Deal Program Must Be Appraised, **L9**: 280
New Era, New Schools for a, **L3**: 233
New Paternalism, **M11**: 117
New Psychology, **E1**: 48
New World in the Making, **L3**: 215
New York and the Seabury Investigation, **L9**: 346
Nexus, **M2**: 154
Nihilism, **M2**: 154
Nisus, **M2**: 155
Noetic, **M2**: 155
No Matter What Happens—Stay Out, **L14**: 364
Nominalism, **M2**: 156
Non-Being, **M2**: 156
Non-Ego, **M2**: 158
Noology, **M2**: 158
Norm and Normative, **M2**: 159
Norris, George William, Dewey Asks Him to Lead New Party, **L5**: 444
Noss, Theodore B., "What Our Schools Owe to Child Study," Discussion of, **M2**: 102
Noumenon, **M2**: 160
Nous, **M2**: 161
Nullibrists, **M2**: 163

Number, **M2**: 163
Psychology of, **E5**: 424; Some Remarks on the, **E5**: 177

Object, **M2**: 164
Expressive, **L10**: 88
External, **M6**: 457
and Subject, **M7**: 291
Objectivism, **M2**: 165
Objectivism-Subjectivism of Modern Philosophy, **L14**: 189
Objects: Logical, **M10**: 89
of Thought, **M2**: 351
of Valuation, **M11**: 3
Objects, Data, and Existences, **M4**: 146
Obligation, **E4**: 311
Idea of, **E3**: 328
to Knowledge of God, **E1**: 61
Observation and Information in the Training of Mind, **M6**: 328; **L8**: 315
Occamism, **M2**: 165
Occasionalism, **M2**: 165
Occupations, Psychology of, **M1**: 92
One, The, **M2**: 166
Ontological Argument, **M2**: 167
Ontologism, **M2**: 169
Ontology, **M2**: 170
Opinion, **M2**: 172; **M7**: 292
Optimism, **M7**: 292
and Pessimism, **M2**: 174
Organic, **M2**: 177
Organism, **M2**: 178
Environment and, **M6**: 437
Organization of Energies, **L10**: 167
Organization of Work in a Department of Pedagogy, **E5**: 442, 443
Orientation, Need for, **L11**: 162
Outlawing Peace by Discussing War, **L3**: 173
Outlawry of War, **L8**: 13
What It Is Not, **M15**: 115
Outlines of a Critical Theory of Ethics, **E3**: 237
Outness, **M2**: 179
Oversoul, **M2**: 180

Pacifism, Future of, **M10**: 265
Palingenesis, **M2**: 180
Panentheism, **M2**: 180
Panlogism, **M2**: 181
Panpneumatism, **M2**: 181
Panpsychism, **M2**: 181
Pantheism, **M2**: 181; **M7**: 294
of Spinoza, **E1**: 9
Panthelism, **M2**: 185
Parker, A. K., Letter to, on Coeducation, **M2**: 108
Parker, Francis Wayland: In Memoriam, **M2**: 98
In Remembrance, **M2**: 97
Parousia, **M2**: 185
Parties, Major, Dewey Assails the, **L5**: 442
Parties, Minor, Place of, in the American Scene, **L6**: 231
Party, Liberal, Dewey Hails the, **L17**: 134
Party, New: Need for a, **L6**: 156
Policies for a, **L6**: 173
Who Might Make a? **L6**: 167
Party, New Radical, Imperative Need for a, **L9**: 76
Party, Third: Its Program, **L6**: 324
Prospects for a, **L6**: 246
Passion and Passive, **M2**: 185
Paternalism, New, **M11**: 117
Peace, Outlawing, by Discussing War, **L3**: 173
Peace—by Pact or Covenant? **L6**: 190

Pedagogical Experiment, **E5**: 244
Pedagogic Creed, My, **E5**: 84
Pedagogy: Memorandum on, **L17**: 485
as a University Discipline, **E5**: 281
Pedagogy, Department of: Letter on Organization of Work in, **E5**: 442
Plan for Organization of Work in a Fully Equipped, **E5**: 443
Pedantry, **M7**: 294
Peirce, Charles Sanders: His Theory of Linguistic Signs, Thought, and Meaning, **L15**: 141
His Theory of Quality, **L11**: 86
Pragmatism of, **M10**: 71
Pennsylvania Museum of Art, "Forms of Art Exhibition" at, **L17**: 128
People's Lobby, **L6**: 322
Asks Special Session on Debts, **L9**: 269
Hits Sugar Loan to Cuba, **L5**: 440
Next Session and the, **L9**: 275
Perception, **E2**: 137
Criticism and, **L10**: 302
and Organic Action, **M7**: 3
Peril, Escape from, **L4**: 3
Period of Technic, **L17**: 284
Periods of Growth, **L17**: 255
Peripatetics, **M2**: 186
Permanence, **M2**: 187
Perseity, **M2**: 187
Personality, **M7**: 295
Active, Flexible, **L11**: 548
Perú, Teachers of, Message to the, **L15**: 371
Pessimism, **M7**: 296
Optimism and, **M2**: 174
Phase, **M2**: 188
Phenomena, Material, and Their Reality, **E1**: 355
Phenomenalism, **M2**: 188; **M7**: 297
Phenomenology, **M2**: 188
Phenomenon, **M2**: 189
Philosophers, Three Contemporary, **M12**: 205
Philosophical Discussion, Some Comments on, **M15**: 27
Philosophical Reconstruction, Some Historical Factors in, **M12**: 95
Philosophical Synthesis, On, **L17**: 35
Philosophical Teaching, Psychological Doctrine and, **M7**: 47
Philosophic Idea, Inclusive, **L3**: 41
Philosophic Method: Experience and, **L1**: 10, 365
Kant and, **E1**: 34
Psychology as, **E1**: 144
Philosophic Reconstruction, Problems of (Syllabus), **M11**: 341
Philosophic Thought, Types of (Syllabus), **M13**: 349
Philosophies of Freedom, **L3**: 92
Philosophy, **M2**: 190; **L3**: 115; **L5**: 161; **L8**: 19
Challenge to, **L10**: 276
Changing Conceptions of, **M12**: 80
Contemporary, Problems of, **L17**: 429
Future of, **L17**: 466
Has It a Future? **L16**: 358
Introduction to (Syllabus), **E3**: 211; **L17**: 153
Inventory of, Taught in American Colleges, **E1**: 116
Its Role in the History of Civilization. *See* Philosophy and Civilization

Philosophy (*continued*)
Lessons from the War in, **L14**: 312
Modern, **L16**: 407; Aspects of the Pragmatic Movement of (Syllabus), **M6**: 175; Objectivism-Subjectivism of, **L14**: 189
Moral, **E4**: 132
Need for a Recovery of, **M10**: 3
Poetry and, **E3**: 110
Problems of Men and the Present State of, **L15**: 154
Reconstruction in, **M12**: 77, 256
Relation of, to Theology, **E4**: 65
Relation of Science and, as the Basis of Education, **L13**: 281
Scientific Factor in Reconstruction of, **M12**: 110
Some Connexions of Science and, **L17**: 402
Study of, **M6**: 136
Why Study It? **E4**: 62
and American National Life, **M3**: 73
and Civilization, **L3**: 3
and Democracy, **M11**: 41
and Education, **L5**: 289
and the Sciences, Methods in, **L17**: 442
in the University of Michigan, **E3**: 90
of Education, **M7**: 297; **M9**: 331; (Syllabus), **E5**: 328; Underlying, **L8**: 77
of Law, My, **L14**: 115
of the Arts, **L13**: 357
of Thomas Hill Green, **E3**: 14
Philosophy and Civilization (1931), **E5**: 96; **M2**: 39; **M4**: 125; **M7**: 3, 56; **M15**: 65; **L2**: 3, 22, 44, 104; **L3**: 3, 25, 41, 55, 92; **L5**: 218, 243; **L6**: 53
Philosophy and Civilization, **L3**: 3
Philosophy's Future in Our Scientific Age, **L16**: 369
Philosophy's Search for the Immutable, **L4**: 21
Phoronomy, **M2**: 202
Physical and Social Studies, **M9**: 286
Physics Teaching in Secondary Schools, Purpose and Organization of, **M4**: 198
Plan for Organization of Work in a Fully Equipped Department of Pedagogy, **E5**: 443
Plan of Organization of the University Primary School, **E5**: 223
Plato, **M7**: 312
Socratic Dialogues of, **L2**: 124
Play, **M7**: 318; **M8**: 275
and Work in the Curriculum, **M9**: 202
of Ideas, **L4**: 112
Plenum, **M2**: 203
Pleroma, **M2**: 203
Plexus, **M2**: 203
Pluralism, **M2**: 203; **M7**: 324
Plurality, **M2**: 205
Unity and, **M2**: 261
Pneuma, **M2**: 205
Pneumatology, **M2**: 206
Poetry and Philosophy, **E3**: 110
Polanyi, Karl, and Daniel Bell, Comment on, **L15**: 361
Poles in the United States, Confidential Report of Conditions among the, **M11**: 259
Policies for a New Party, **L6**: 173
Polish Conditions: Preliminary Confidential Memorandum on, **M11**: 248

Second Preliminary Confidential Memorandum on, **M11**: 255
Political Action, Radical, Future of, **L9**: 66
Political Combination or Legal Cooperation? **M15**: 105
Political Interference in Higher Education and Research, **L6**: 118
Political Philosophy, Motivation of Hobbes's, **M11**: 18
Political Science as a Recluse, **M11**: 93
Politics: Education as, **M13**: 329
Ethics and, **E4**: 371
Is There Hope for? **L6**: 182
New, Needed, **L11**: 274
and Culture, **L6**: 40
Posit, **M2**: 207
Positive, **M2**: 208
Positivism, **M2**: 208; **M7**: 324
Possibility, Impossibility, and Possible, **M2**: 210
Postulate of Immediate Empiricism, **M3**: 158
Postulations, **L16**: 74
Post-War Mind, **M11**: 112
Power, Intelligence and, **L9**: 107
Practice: Moral Theory and, **E3**: 93
Theory and, **M7**: 354
Pragmatic Acquiescence, **L3**: 145
Pragmatic America, **M13**: 306
Pragmatic Movement of Contemporary Thought (Syllabus), **M4**: 251
Pragmatic Movement of Modern Philosophy, Aspects of the (Syllabus), **M6**: 175
Pragmatism, **M7**: 326
American, Development of, **L2**: 3
Bearings of, upon Education, **M4**: 178
Realism of, **M3**: 153
What It Means by Practical, **M4**: 98
of Peirce, **M10**: 71
Pre-established Harmony, **M2**: 212
Preface to
Dewey, John, *Democracy and Education* (Japanese translation), **L17**: 57
Mead, George Herbert, *The Philosophy of the Present*, **L6**: 307
Terror in Cuba, **L9**: 310
Prejudice: Racial, and Friction, **M13**: 242
Understanding and, **L5**: 396
Preparation, Unfolding, and Formal Discipline, **M9**: 59
Present and Future, **M14**: 182
Presentationism, **M2**: 213
Present Crisis, **L6**: 156
Press, Our Un-Free, **L11**: 269
Primary, Primitive, Primordial, **M2**: 213
Primary-Education Fetich, **E5**: 254
Primum Mobile, **M2**: 213
Principle, **M2**: 214
Principles, Nature of, **M14**: 164
Pringle, Henry Fowles, Memorandum for, **L17**: 524
Problem, **M7**: 330
Terminological, **L16**: 46
and Its Solution, **E1**: 284
of Freedom, **L13**: 65
of Logical Subject-Matter, **L12**: 9
of Method, **L2**: 351
of the Liberal Arts College, **L15**: 276

Problem (*continued*)
of Truth, **M6**: 12
of Values, **M7**: 44
Problems of Contemporary Philosophy: Problem of Experience, **L17**: 429
Problems of Men (1946), **M3**: 3; **L5**: 178; **L11**: 130, 146, 162, 181, 217, 282, 289, 339, 342, 345, 348, 360, 364, 368, 372, 376, 454, 464; **L13**: 281, 286, 294, 338; **L14**: 34, 141, 155, 168, 189; **L15**: 27, 42, 63, 73, 84, 101, 153, 154, 188, 251, 261, 276
Problems of Men and the Present State of Philosophy, **L15**: 154
Problems of Moral Theory, **M5**: 197
Problems of Philosophic Reconstruction (Syllabus), **M11**: 341
Process, **M7**: 331
Professional Organization of Teachers, **M10**: 168
Professional Spirit among Teachers, **M7**: 109
Professor and the Public Interest, Case of the, **M10**: 164
Professorial Freedom, **M8**: 407
Progress, **M7**: 331; **M10**: 234
Unity and, **L9**: 71
Progressive Education and the Science of Education, **L3**: 257
Progressives, Dewey Raps, on Parley Eve, **L6**: 440
Progressive Schools, Why Have Them? **L9**: 147
Progressive Senators, Challenge to, to Act for Relief, **L6**: 355
Property, **M2**: 215
Proposition, **M7**: 333
Propositions: General Theory of, **L12**: 283
Generic and Universal, **L12**: 263
Ordered in Sets and Series, **L12**: 310
Warranted Assertibility, and Truth, **L14**: 168
of Quantity, Their Function in Judgment, **L12**: 200
Prospects for a Third Party, **L6**: 246
Prosperity Dependent on Building from Bottom Up, **L6**: 383
Psychological and the Logical, **M6**: 224
in Teaching Geometry, **M3**: 216
Psychological Aspect of the School Curriculum, **E5**: 164
Psychological Doctrine and Philosophical Teaching, **M7**: 47
Psychological Method in Ethics, **M3**: 59
Psychological Process and Logical Form, **L8**: 171
Psychological Standpoint, **E1**: 122
Psychologism, **M2**: 215
Psychology, **E2**
Psychology: Educational (Syllabus), **E5**: 303
Illusory, **E1**: 168
New, **E1**: 48
Reflex Arc Concept in, **E5**: 96
Science and Method of, **E2**: 7
Social, Working Method in, **L17**: 422
and Justice, **L3**: 186
and Pedagogy, Modern, Religious Education as Conditioned by, **M3**: 210
and Philosophic Method. *See* Consciousness and Experience
and Social Practice, **M1**: 131
and Work, **L5**: 236

as Philosophic Method, **E1**: 144
for Teachers (Syllabus), **L17**: 187
in High-Schools from the Standpoint of the College, **E1**: 81
of Effort, **E5**: 151
of Elementary Education, **M1**: 67
of Infant Language, **E4**: 66
of Number, **E5**: 424; Some Remarks on the, **E5**: 177
of Occupations, **M1**: 92
of Social Behavior, **M7**: 390
of Thinking, **M14**: 127
Public: Eclipse of the, **L2**: 304
Search for the, **L2**: 238
Teacher and the, **L11**: 158
Public and Its Problems, **L2**: 235, 375
Public Education on Trial, **M10**: 173
Public Interest, Case of the Professor and the, **M10**: 164
Public Opinion in Japan, **M13**: 255
Public Ownership Program, America's, **L9**: 285
Purchasers, What Keeps Funds Away from, **L9**: 81
Pure, **M2**: 215
Pure Experience and Reality, **M4**: 120
Purpose, Meaning of, **L13**: 43
Puts Needs of Idle at Two Billions, **L5**: 439

Qualitative Feelings, Development of, **E2**: 239
Qualitative Thought, **L5**: 243
Quality, Peirce's Theory of, **L11**: 86
Quest for Certainty, **L4**
Quietism, **M2**: 216

Racial Prejudice and Friction, **M13**: 242
Radical Party, A New, Imperative Need for, **L9**: 76
Radical Political Action, Future of, **L9**: 66
Radio's Influence on the Mind, **L9**: 309
Rand School: Appreciation of the, **L15**: 378
To Save the, **L9**: 305
Rationalism, **M2**: 216; **M7**: 334
Rationality in Education, **L11**: 391
Reaction, How It Helps, **M12**: 17
Reading, Juvenile, **L5**: 394
Real, Changed Conceptions of the Ideal and the, **M12**: 139
Realism, **M2**: 218
Brief Studies in, **M6**: 103
Brief Studies in, III, **L17**: 415
Epistemological. *See* Brief Studies in Realism
Naïve, *vs.* Presentative Realism. *See* Brief Studies in Realism
Short-Cut to, Examined, **M6**: 138
and Idealism, **M4**: 116
of Pragmatism, **M3**: 153
without Monism or Dualism, **M13**: 40
Realities, Facing the Era of, **L9**: 287
Reality: Does It Possess Practical Character? **M4**: 125
Pure Experience and, **M4**: 120
and the Criterion for the Truth of Ideas. *See* Intellectualist Criterion for Truth
as Experience, **M3**: 101
Reals, **M2**: 223
Reason: Changed Conceptions of Experience and, **M12**: 124

Reason (*continued*)
Place of, in the Moral Life, **M5**: 278
Understanding and, **M2**: 259
Reasoning and Concepts, Control of, **L8**: 259
Reasoning in Early Childhood, **M7**: 369
Recitation: Method of the, **M3**: 347
and the Training of Thought, **M6**: 338; **L8**: 326
Recitations, Lectures vs., **E3**: 147
Reconstruction, **E4**: 96
as Affecting Social Philosophy, **M12**: 187
in Moral Conceptions, **M12**: 172
Reconstruction in Philosophy, **M12**: 77, 256
Reflection, Angle of, **E3**: 195
Reflective Activity: Place of Judgment in, **L8**: 210
Process and Product of, **L8**: 171
Reflective Approbation, or Conscience, **E4**: 292
Reflective Thinking: Analysis of, **L8**: 196
Why It Must Be an Educational Aim, **L8**: 125
Reflective Thought, Analysis of, **M13**: 61
Reflex Arc Concept in Psychology, **E5**: 96
Regimentation, Fact of, Theory of Liberty vs., **L9**: 87
Reify, **M2**: 224
Relation, **M2**: 224
Relationship of Thought and Its Subject-Matter, **M2**: 298
Relief: Challenge to Progressive Senators to Act for, **L6**: 355
Get Mayor and Governor to Demand, **L6**: 397
Unemployment Committee Asks Adequate, **L9**: 271
Is Vital, **L9**: 252
Policy, Roosevelt Scored on, **L6**: 395
Religion: Education as a, **M13**: 317
Some Thoughts concerning, **L17**: 374
and Morality in a Free Society, **L15**: 170
and Our Schools, **M4**: 165
and the Intellectuals, **L16**: 390
at Harvard, **L17**: 135
in the Soviet Union, **L5**: 355
versus the Religious, **L9**: 3
Religions and the "Religious," **L9**: 293
Religious Education as Conditioned by Modern Psychology and Pedagogy, **M3**: 210
Religious Emotion, Place of, **E1**: 90
Religious Function, Human Abode of the, **L9**: 40
Religious Humanism, Mystical Naturalism and, **L11**: 84
Religious Problem, One Current, **L11**: 115
Renan, Ernest: His Loss of Faith in Science, **E4**: 11
Two Phases of His Life, **E3**: 174
Reply to Some Criticisms, **L5**: 210
Response, Stimulus and, **M7**: 346
Response at 70th Birthday Celebration, **L5**: 418
Response at 90th Birthday Celebration, **L17**: 84
Responsibility, Freedom and, **E4**: 337
Review of
Abell, Walter, *Representation and Form*, **L11**: 487

Adams, George Burton, *Civilization during the Middle Ages,* **E4**: 200
Adler, Mortimer, *Dialectic,* **L3**: 311
Allen, Carleton Kemp, *Law in the Making,* **L3**: 326
Ayres, C. E., *Science: The False Messiah,* **L3**: 305
Baker, James Hutchins, *Elementary Psychology,* **E3**: 190
Baldwin, James Mark, *Social and Ethical Interpretations in Mental Development,* **E5**: 385, 402
Barnes, Harry Elmer, *World Politics in Modern Civilization,* **L5**: 382
Beard, Charles A., and Mary R. Beard, *America in Midpassage,* **L14**: 283
Benedict, Wayland Richardson, *World Views and Their Ethical Implications,* **M3**: 310
Bergson, Henri, *The Two Sources of Morality and Religion,* **L11**: 428
Bernard, John H., and John P. Mahaffy, *Kant's Critical Philosophy for English Readers,* **E3**: 184
Bingham, Alfred M., *Insurgent America,* **L11**: 438
Bonar, James, *Philosophy and Political Economy in Some of Their Historical Relations,* **E4**: 214
Bosanquet, Bernard, *A History of Aesthetic,* **E4**: 189
—*Science and Philosophy and Other Essays,* **L3**: 294
Brameld, Theodore B. H., *A Philosophic Approach to Communism,* **L9**: 244
Bryant, Sophie, *Studies in Character,* **E5**: 350
Buchanan, Scott, *Possibility,* **L3**: 311
Caird, Edward, *The Critical Philosophy of Immanuel Kant,* **E3**: 180
Carus, Paul, *A Primer of Philosophy,* **E5**: 342
Catlin, G. E. G., *The Science and Method of Politics,* **L3**: 318
Church, Alfred John, *The Story of the Odyssey,* **E3**: 193
Cohen, Morris R., *Reason and Nature: An Essay on the Meaning of Scientific Method,* **L6**: 299
Conant, Levi L., *The Number Concept,* **E5**: 355
Counts, George S., *School and Society in Chicago,* **L5**: 371
—*The Soviet Challenge to America,* **L6**: 263
Dallin, David J., and Boris I. Nicolaevsky, *Forced Labor in Soviet Russia,* **L15**: 295
Davies, Joseph E., *Mission to Moscow,* **L15**: 289
Deussen, Paul, *The Elements of Metaphysics,* **E5**: 342
Dimnet, Ernest, *The Art of Thinking,* **L3**: 316
Dopp, Katharine Elizabeth, *The Place of Industries in Elementary Education,* **M3**: 307
Eastman, Max, *The Enjoyment of Poetry,* **M7**: 149
Eddy, Sherwood, *The Challenge of Russia,* **L6**: 263
Elliot, Hugh S. R., *Modern Science and the Illusions of Professor Bergson,* **M7**: 135

Review of (*continued*)
Erdmann, Johann Eduard, *A History of Philosophy*, **E3**: 185
Fiske, John, *The Idea of God as Affected by Modern Knowledge*, **L17**: 93
Flexner, Abraham, *Universities: American, English, German*, **L17**: 110
Flint, Robert, *History of the Philosophy of History*, **E4**: 200
Frankfurter, Felix, ed., *Mr. Justice Brandeis*, **L9**: 237
Gauss, Christian, *Life in College*, **L6**: 259
Hall, G. Stanley, *Founders of Modern Psychology*, **M7**: 137
Hallis, Frederick, *Corporate Personality: A Study in Jurisprudence*, **L6**: 268
Hans, Nicholas, *History of Russian Educational Policy*, **L6**: 291
Harris, William Torrey, *Psychologic Foundations of Education*, **E5**: 372
Hartshorne, Charles, and Paul Weiss, eds., *Collected Papers of Charles Sanders Peirce*, vol. 1, **L6**: 273; vol. 5, **L11**: 421; vols. 1-6, **L11**: 479
Heard, Gerald, *The Emergence of Man*, **L6**: 278
Hill, David J., *Genetic Philosophy*, **E5**: 342
Hocking, William Ernest, *Man and the State*, **L3**: 318
Hoernlé, Alfred, *Idealism as a Philosophy*, **L3**: 294
Hunt, Frazier, *The Rising Temper of the East*, **M13**: 345
James, William, *Essays in Radical Empiricism*, **M7**: 142
—*The Principles of Psychology*, **M1**: 321; **L15**: 18
Johnson, Francis Howe, *What Is Reality?* **E3**: 192
Johnson's Universal Cyclopaedia, vols. 1-5, **E5**: 347
Kallen, Horace M., ed., *The Philosophy of William James*, **L2**: 158
Kidd, Benjamin, *Social Evolution*, **E4**: 200
Krabbe, Hugo, *The Modern Idea of the State*, **L17**: 101
Ladd, George T., *Elements of Physiological Psychology*, **E1**: 194
Lamont, Corliss, *The Illusion of Immortality*, **L11**: 425
Lapp, John A., and Carl H. Mote, *Learning to Earn*, **M10**: 303
Lewis, Mary H., *An Adventure with Children*, **L3**: 330
Lippmann, Walter, *An Inquiry into the Principles of the Good Society*, **L11**: 489
—*The Phantom Public*, **L2**: 213
—*Public Opinion*, **M13**: 337
Love, Mary C., *Human Conduct and the Law*, **L17**: 108
Lowie, Robert H., *The Origin of the State*, **L3**: 324
Macintosh, Douglas Clyde, *Social Religion*, **L14**: 286
Macintosh, Douglas Clyde, Henry Nelson Wieman, and Max Carl Otto, *Is There a God?* **L9**: 213, 223
Mahaffy, John P., and John H.

Bernard, *Kant's Critical Philosophy for English Readers,* **E3**: 184
Mannheim, Karl, *Man and Society in an Age of Reconstruction,* **L14**: 293
Marot, Helen, *Creative Impulse in Industry,* **M11**: 333
Mead, George Herbert, *Mind, Self and Society,* **L11**: 450
—*Movements of Thought in the Nineteenth Century,* **L11**: 450
Meiklejohn, Alexander, *The Experimental College,* **L6**: 295
Merriam, Charles Edward, *The Making of Citizens: A Comparative Study of Methods of Civic Training,* **L17**: 112
Mote, Carl H., and John A. Lapp, *Learning to Earn,* **M10**: 303
Müller, F. Max, *Three Lectures on the Vedanta Philosophy,* **E5**: 342
Münsterberg, Hugo, *The Eternal Values,* **M6**: 167
National Service Handbook, **M10**: 315
Nichols, Herbert, and William E. Parsons, *Our Notions of Number and Space,* **E5**: 342
Nicolaevsky, Boris I., and David J. Dallin, *Forced Labor in Soviet Russia,* **L15**: 295
Noble, Edmund, *Purposive Evolution: The Link between Science and Religion,* **L3**: 299
Nock, Albert Jay, *The Theory of Education in the United States,* **L6**: 286
Ogden, C. K., and I. A. Richards, *The Meaning of Meaning,* **M15**: 223
Ormond, Alexander T., *Basal Concepts in Philosophy,* **E5**: 342
Otto, Max Carl, *The Human Enterprise: An Attempt to Relate Philosophy to Daily Life,* **L14**: 289
Otto, Max Carl, Henry Nelson Wieman, and Douglas Clyde Macintosh, *Is There a God?* **L9**: 213, 223
Palmer, George Herbert, *The Autobiography of a Philosopher,* **L6**: 271
Parsons, William E., and Herbert Nichols, *Our Notions of Number and Space,* **E5**: 342
Peirce, Charles Sanders, *Chance, Love, and Logic,* **M15**: 226
—*Collected Papers of Charles Sanders Peirce*, ed. Charles Hartshorne and Paul Weiss, vol. 1, **L6**: 273; vol. 5, **L11**: 421; vols. 1-6, **L11**: 479
Perry, Ralph Barton, *A Defence of Philosophy,* **L6**: 271
—*The Thought and Character of William James*, **L11**: 441, 464
Pollock, Frederick, *Essays in the Law,* **L17**: 98
Pound, Roscoe, *Law and Morals: The McNair Lectures,* **L17**: 105
Randall, John H., Jr., *Our Changing Civilization,* **L17**: 522
Recent Social Trends in the United States, **L9**: 229

Review of (*continued*)
Reiser, Oliver L., *Philosophy and the Concepts of Modern Science*, **L11**: 432
Ribot, Théodule, *The Diseases of the Will*, **E5**: 342
Richards, I. A., and C. K. Ogden, *The Meaning of Meaning*, **M15**: 223
Royce, Josiah, *The World and the Individual*, vol. 1, **M1**: 241; vol. 2, **M2**: 120
—"The Knowledge of Good and Evil," **E4**: 197
—"On Certain Psychological Aspects of Moral Training," **E4**: 197
Russell, Bertrand, *Education and the Good Life*, **L2**: 226
—*The Problem of China*, **M15**: 215
—*Religion and Science*, **L11**: 454
Santayana, George, *Egotism in German Philosophy*, **M10**: 305
—*The Genteel Tradition at Bay*, **L6**: 271
—*The Last Puritan*, **L11**: 446
—*The Life of Reason*, vols. 1-2, **M3**: 319; 5 vols., **M4**: 229
—*The Realm of Essence*, **L3**: 287
—*Scepticism and Animal Faith*, **M15**: 219
—*Some Turns of Thought in Modern Philosophy*, **L9**: 240
Schiller, F. C. S., *Formal Logic: A Scientific and Social Problem*, **M7**: 131
—*Humanism*, **M3**: 312
Schilpp, Paul Arthur, ed., *The Philosophy of George Santayana*, **L14**: 295
Schinz, Albert, *Anti-pragmatisme*, **M4**: 245
Schütze, Martin, *Academic Illusions in the Field of Letters and the Arts*, **L8**: 360
Sherrill, Charles Hitchcock, *Prime Ministers and Presidents*, **M13**: 345
Sidgwick, Arthur, and Eleanor M. Sidgwick, *Henry Sidgwick*, **M4**: 242
Simmel, Georg, "Moral Deficiencies as Determining Intellectual Functions," **E4**: 197
Slesinger, Zalmen, *Education and the Class Struggle*, **L11**: 485
Smith, T. V., *The Promise of American Politics*, **L17**: 115
Spender, Stephen, *Forward from Liberalism*, **L11**: 496
Spengler, Oswald, *Man and Technics*, **L6**: 280
Stanley, Hiram Miner, *Studies in the Evolutionary Psychology of Feeling*, **E5**: 358
Sterrett, James MacBride, *Studies in Hegel's Philosophy of Religion*, **E3**: 187
Studies in Philosophy and Psychology, **M4**: 217
Sully, James, *Studies of Childhood*, **E5**: 367
Tugwell, Rexford G., *The Industrial Discipline and the Governmental Arts*, **L8**: 364
Van Norden, Charles, *The Psychic Factor*, **E5**: 342
Wallace, William, trans., *Hegel's Philosophy of Mind*, **E5**: 342
Wallas, Graham, *The Art of Thought*, **L2**: 231

Ward, Lester Frank, *The Psychic Factors of Civilization,* **E4**: 200
Watson, John, *Hedonistic Theories from Aristippus to Spencer,* **E5**: 350
Weeks, Raymond, *Boys' Own Arithmetic,* **L2**: 386
Weiss, Paul, and Charles Hartshorne, eds., *Collected Papers of Charles Sanders Peirce,* vol. 1, **L6**: 273; vol. 5, **L11**: 421; vols. 1-6, **L11**: 479
Welling, Richard, *As the Twig Is Bent,* **L17**: 523
Wells, H. G., *God the Invisible King,* **M10**: 310
Wenley, Robert Mark, *The Life and Work of George Sylvester Morris,* **M11**: 336
White, William C., *These Russians,* **L6**: 263
Whitehead, Alfred North, *Adventures of Ideas,* **L8**: 355
—*Process and Reality,* **L5**: 375
—*Science and the Modern World,* **L2**: 221
Wieman, Henry Nelson, Douglas Clyde Macintosh, and Max Carl Otto, *Is There a God?* **L9**: 213, 223
Witmer, Lightner, *Analytical Psychology,* **M2**: 119
Woody, Thomas, *New Minds: New Men?* **L6**: 291
Revival of the Soul, **L17**: 10
Revolt against Science, **L15**: 188
Rifle Practice, Do We Want It in the Public Schools? **L17**: 121
Right, Duty, and Loyalty, **L7**: 214
Righting an Academic Wrong, **L11**: 530
Robinson, Daniel Sommer, Reply to, **M10**: 98
Romance, Collapse of a, **L6**: 69
Roosevelt, Franklin D., Scored on Relief Policy, **L6**: 395
Roosevelt, Theodore, **M11**: 143
Royce, Josiah: Reply to His Critique of Instrumentalism, **M7**: 64
Voluntarism in the Philosophy of, **M10**: 79
Russell, Bertrand, **M12**: 235
Case for, **L14**: 231
as a Moral Issue, **L14**: 369
Russia: Country in a State of Flux, **L3**: 208
Dr. Dewey on Our Relations with, **L15**: 342
Great Experiment and the Future, **L3**: 242
Impressions of Soviet. See Impressions of Soviet Russia
New World in the Making, **L3**: 215
Russian Schools, What Are They Doing? **L3**: 224
Russian School System, **L17**: 487
Russia's Position, **L15**: 338

St. Louis Congress of the Arts and Sciences, **M3**: 145
Same and Other, **M2**: 231
Sanctions, Are They Necessary to International Organization? **L6**: 196
San Jose State Normal School (Commencement Address), **L17**: 63
Savage Mind, Interpretation of, **M2**: 39
Scepticism, **M2**: 231
Schema, **M2**: 235
Schematism, **M2**: 235
Schiller, F. C. S., Tribute to, **L11**: 155

Scholastic and the Speculator, **E3**: 148
Scholasticism, **M2**: 236
International Symposium on, **L2**: 388
Statement on, **M15**: 318
School: Elementary, As Concerns the, **M1**: 260
Relation of It to the Community, **M8**: 314
University Primary, Plan of Organization of the, **E5**: 223
What Is It For? **M15**: 190
and Social Progress, **M1**: 5
and the Life of the Child, **M1**: 21
as a Means of Developing a Social Consciousness and Social Ideals in Children, **M15**: 150
as a Social Settlement, **M8**: 339
as Social Centre, **M2**: 80
Conditions and the Training of Thought, **M6**: 216; **L8**: 156
"Frills," Shall We Abolish Them? **L9**: 141
Methods, Cut-and-Try, **M7**: 106
Studies, Common, Moral Significance of the, **M4**: 205
System, Splitting Up the, **M8**: 123
School and Society, **M1**: 1
Schools: Democracy and Loyalty in the, **M10**: 158
Foreign, in Turkey, **M15**: 144
Military Training in, On, **L17**: 124
New: for a New Era, **L3**: 233; How Much Freedom in? **L5**: 319
Public: Manufacturers' Association and the, **L3**: 280; Do We Want Rifle Practice in? **L17**: 121
Religion and Our, **M4**: 165
Save Them Now, **L9**: 386
Secondary, Purpose and Organization of Physics Teaching in, **M4**: 198
Socializing the, **L17**: 72
State or City Control of? **M8**: 128
Study of History in the, On the, **E5**: 429
Utopian, Dewey Outlines, **L9**: 136
and Social Preparedness, **M10**: 191
and the White House Conference on Child Health and Protection, **L6**: 131
Schools of To-Morrow, **M8**: 205
Schopenhauerism, **M2**: 244
Science: Belief and the Public, **M15**: 47
Common Sense and, **L16**: 242
Natural, Penning-in of, **L15**: 184
Physical, Ethics and, **E1**: 205
Renan's Loss of Faith in, **E4**: 11
Revolt against, **L15**: 188
Unity of, as a Social Problem, **L13**: 271
and Free Culture, **L13**: 156
and Method of Psychology, **E2**: 7
and Philosophy: Relation of, as the Basis of Education, **L13**: 281; Some Connexions of, **L17**: 402
and Society: (Address), **L6**: 49; (Philosophy and Civilization), **L6**: 53
as Subject-Matter and as Method, **M6**: 69
in the Course of Study,

M9: 227
Teaching, Method in, **M10**: 130
Sciences, Methods in Philosophy and the, **L17**: 442
Scientific Age, Philosophy's Future in Our, **L16**: 369
Scientific Factor in Reconstruction of Philosophy, **M12**: 110
Scientific Inquiry, Common Sense and, **L12**: 66
Scientific Laws, **L12**: 437
Scientific Method, **M7**: 335; **L12**: 415
and Scientific Subject-Matter, **L12**: 458
Scotism, **M2**: 244
Scott, Fred Newton, **E4**: 119
Seabury, Samuel, Investigation, New York and the, **L9**: 346
Search for Firm Names, **L16**: 6
Secularizing a Theocracy, **M15**: 128
Selby, Clarence J., Tribute to, **L17**: 145
Seldes, George, and "Fact," **L15**: 375
Self, **M7**: 339
Moral, **L7**: 285
Place of, in the Moral Life, **M5**: 328
Some Current Conceptions of the Term, On, **E3**: 56
Self-Consciousness, **M7**: 343
Self-Realization as the Moral Ideal, **E4**: 42
Seligman, Edwin R. A., Letter to, **L17**: 125
Seminal Reasons, **M2**: 244
Senators, Dewey Asks Them to Stay on Guard, **L6**: 393
Sensation: Concept of a, **M4**: 118
and Experience, **E1**: 313
Sensationalism, **M2**: 245; **M7**: 345
Sense of Solidity, **E5**: 430
Sense-Perception, Naturalistic Theory of, **L2**: 44
Sensualism, **M2**: 247
Sequences, Causation and, **L12**: 437
Setting New Goals at Seventy, **L6**: 403
Shantung: As Seen from Within, **M12**: 28
Question, Angles of, **M13**: 201
Shantung Again, **M13**: 139
Short-Cut to Realism Examined, **M6**: 138
Shotwell, James T., Rejoinder to, **L3**: 168
Siberia and Japan, **M13**: 240
Siberian Republic, **M13**: 233
Sick World, **M15**: 42
Significance, Importance, and Meaning, **L16**: 318
Significance of the School of Education, **M3**: 273
Singularism, **M2**: 247
Situations, Inquiry and Indeterminateness of, **L15**: 34
Smith, Alfred E., Why I Am for Him, **L3**: 184
Snedden, David, Reply to, **M8**: 411
Social, Morality Is, **M14**: 216
Social Absolutism, **M13**: 311
Social Action, Liberalism and, **L11**: 1
Social as a Category. *See* Philosophic Idea, Inclusive
Social Aspects of Education, **L17**: 226
Social Behavior, Psychology of, **M7**: 390
Social Change: Authority and, **L11**: 130
Education and, **L11**: 408
and Its Human Direction, **L5**: 363

Social Consciousness and Social Ideals in Children, School as a Means of Developing a, **M15**: 150
Social Control, **L13**: 31
Liberty and, **L11**: 360
Social Direction, Education and, **M11**: 54
Social-Economic Situation and Education, **L8**: 43
Social Ends, Happiness and, **M5**: 261
Social Facts, Values, Valuations, and, **L16**: 310
Social Frontier, **L11**: 337
Social Ideals, New, Education and, **L11**: 167
Social Inquiry, **L12**: 481
How, What, and *What For* in, **L16**: 333
Social Institutions and the Study of Morals (Syllabus), **M15**: 229
Socialism, Capitalistic or Public? **L5**: 90
Socialization: Taxation as a Step to, **L11**: 265
of Ground Rent, **L11**: 256
Socializing the Schools, **L17**: 72
Social Order: Education and the, **L9**: 175
Education for a Changing, **L9**: 158
Social Organization: Education the Foundation for, **L11**: 226
and the Individual, **M5**: 383
Social Perspective, Education from a, **M7**: 113
Social Philosophy, Reconstruction as Affecting, **M12**: 187
Social Practice, Psychology and, **M1**: 131
Social Preparedness, Schools and, **M10**: 191
Social Problem, Unity of Science as a, **L13**: 271
Social Problems, Our Present, Education and, **L9**: 127
Social Progress, School and, **M1**: 5
Social Psychology: Habit and, **M14**: 60
Need for, **M10**: 53
Working Method in, **L17**: 422
Social Purposes in Education, **M15**: 158
Social Realities *versus* Police Court Fictions, **L14**: 235
Social Reconstruction, Can Education Share in? **L9**: 205
Social Reorganization, Internal, after the War, **M11**: 73
Social Results, War's, **L17**: 21
Social Science: New, **M11**: 87
and Social Control, **L6**: 64
Social Scientist, Liberating the, **L15**: 224
Social Settlement, School as a, **M8**: 339
Social Significance of Academic Freedom, **L11**: 376
Social Study, What Is It? **L13**: 338
Social Value of Courses, **L17**: 310
Society: Church and, **L17**: 19
Free: Free Teacher in a, **L11**: 535; Religion and Morality in a, **L15**: 170
New, Economic Basis of the, **L13**: 309
Science and: (Address), **L6**: 49; (*Philosophy and Civilization*), **L6**: 53
Socratic Dialogues of Plato, **L2**: 124
Soldan, Frank Louis, "Shortening the Years of Elementary Schooling," Remarks on, **M3**: 294

Solidity, Sense of, **E5**: 430
Soul: Revival of the, **L17**: 10
and Body, **E1**: 93
Sources of a Science of Education, **L5**: 1
Sovereignty, Austin's Theory of, **E4**: 70
Soviet Union, Religion in the, **L5**: 355
Spanish Government, Aid for the, **L11**: 527
Spaulding, Edward Gleason: Rejoinder to, **M6**: 143
and Professor Dewey, **M6**: 146
Special Session, President and the, **L6**: 345
Specification, **L16**: 131
Speculation, **M2**: 247
Speech Reaction, Knowledge and, **M13**: 29
Spencer, Herbert: Philosophical Work of, **M3**: 193
and Henri Bergson, **M10**: 67
Spinoza, Benedict, Pantheism of, **E1**: 9
Spirit, Matter and Its Relation to, **E1**: 342
Spiritual Nature, What Is the Demonstration of Man's? **L17**: 15
Splitting Up the School System, **M8**: 123
Sportsmanship Brotherhood, **L5**: 390
State: Democratic, **L2**: 282
Discovery of the, **L2**: 259
Political, Civil Society and the, **M5**: 404
or City Control of Schools? **M8**: 128
States, Morals and the Conduct of, **M11**: 122
Statistical Methods, Galton's, **E3**: 43
Statue of Condillac, **M2**: 248
Steps to Economic Recovery, **L9**: 61
Stimulus and Response, **M7**: 346
Student Revolt: Sequel of the, **M12**: 22
in China, **M11**: 186
Studies, Intellectual and Practical, **M9**: 271
Studies in Logical Theory, **M2**: 293
Study of Ethics (Syllabus), **E4**: 219
Subject, **M2**: 248; **M7**: 347
Object and, **M7**: 291
Subjectivism, **M2**: 252
Subject-Matter: Nature of, **M9**: 188
Progressive Organization of, **L13**: 48
of Metaphysical Inquiry, **M8**: 3
Substance, **M2**: 252
and Form, **L10**: 111
Substantiality Theory or Substantialism, **M2**: 253
Suffrage, Professor for, **M7**: 409
Sui Generis, **M2**: 254
Summary of Progress Made, **L16**: 275
Summists, **M2**: 254
Superficial Treatment Must Fail, **L9**: 261
Superstition of Necessity, **E4**: 19
Supreme Intellectual Obligation, **L9**: 96
Syllogism, **M7**: 349
Syncretism, **M2**: 255
Synthesis, Analysis and, **M6**: 370
System, **M2**: 255; **M7**: 351
Systematic Method, **L8**: 248, 259

Tabula Rasa, **M2**: 256
Taxation: Congress Faces Its Test on, **L9**: 256

Taxation (*continued*)
as a Step to Socialization, **L11**: 265
Taxes, Farm Processing and Other Consumption, Must Be Repealed, **L9**: 273
Teacher: Classroom, **M15**: 180
Free, in a Free Society, **L11**: 535
and His World, **L11**: 339
and the Public, **L11**: 158
Teachers: Communists as, **L17**: 136
Professional Organization of, **M10**: 168
Professional Spirit among, **M7**: 109
Psychology for (Syllabus), **L17**: 187
as Citizens, **L6**: 433
Teachers Union: Dewey Greets, **L14**: 375
Grievance Committee's Report, On the, **L9**: 315
Report of the Special Grievance Committee of the, **L9**: 320
Why I Am a Member of the, **L3**: 269
Teaching: To Those Who Aspire to the Profession of, **L13**: 342
What Is the Matter with It? **L2**: 116
Ethics in the High School, **E4**: 54
Geometry, Psychological and the Logical in, **M3**: 216
Profession, Duties and Responsibilities of the, **L5**: 326
Teaching That Does Not Educate, **M4**: 201
Technic, Period of, **L17**: 284
Technocracy, Statement on, **L9**: 312
Term, **M7**: 352
Terminological Problem, **L16**: 46
Terms or Meanings, **L12**: 347
Theism, **M7**: 353
Theocracy, Secularizing a, **M15**: 128
Theology: Relation of Philosophy to, **E4**: 365
Syllabus for Gifford Lectureship in Natural, **L4**: 251
Theory and Practice, **M7**: 354
Theory of Emotion, **E4**: 152
Theory of the Chicago Experiment, **L11**: 202
Theory of Valuation, **L13**: 189
Thinking, **E2**: 177
Antecedents and Stimuli of, **M2**: 316
Concrete and Abstract, **M6**: 286
Educational Balance, Efficiency and, **L17**: 77
Empirical and Scientific, **M6**: 293
Experience and, **M9**: 146
Psychology of, **M14**: 127
What Is It? **L8**: 113
in Education, **M9**: 159
Third Party, Prospects for a, **L6**: 246
Third Party Program, **L6**: 324
Thomism, **M2**: 256
Thought: Affective, **L2**: 104
Analysis of a Complete Act of, **M6**: 234
Conscription of, **M10**: 276
Context and, **L6**: 3
Empirical and Scientific, **L8**: 268
Impulse and, **M14**: 117
Liberal, Challenge to, **L15**: 261
Native Resources in Training, **L8**: 140
Need for Training, **M6**: 192
Objects of, **M2**: 351
Qualitative, **L5**: 243
Training of: Activity and the,

M6: 304; L8: 281; Language and the, M6: 314; L8: 301; Natural Resources in the, M6: 204; Recitation and the, M6: 338; L8: 326; School Conditions and the, M6: 216; L8: 156
Values, Liking, and, M15: 20
What Is It? M6: 182
and Work, Freedom of, M12: 8
Thought and Its Subject-Matter: Antecedent Conditions and Cues of the Thought-Function. *See* Antecedents and Stimuli of Thinking
Content and Object of Thought. *See* Objects of Thought
Datum of Thinking. *See* Data and Meanings
General Problem of Logical Theory. *See* Relationship of Thought and Its Subject-Matter
Relationship of, M2: 298
Time and Individuality, L14: 98
Tolstoi, N. Lyof, Art of, L17: 381
Tomorrow May Be Too Late: Save the Schools Now, L9: 386
Totalitarian Economics and Democracy, L13: 116
Trade-Training, Education vs., M8: 411
Tradition, M7: 356
Metaphysics, and Morals, M15: 14
Transaction, Interaction and, L16: 96
Transactions as Known and Named, L16: 110
Transcendent, M2: 257
Transcendentalism, M2: 258; M7: 357
Transient, M2: 258
Treaty [of Washington], Three Results of, M13: 212
Trial Group of Names, L16: 257
Trotsky, Leon: American Committee for the Defense of, Declaration of Purposes by, L11: 303
Commission of Inquiry: Introductory Statement of the, L11: 306; Summary of Findings of, L11: 321
Inquiry, Significance of the, L11: 330
Truth, M7: 358
Dilemma of the Intellectualist Theory of, M4: 76
Intellectualist Criterion for, M4: 50
Problem of, M6: 12
Propositions, Warranted Assertibility, and, L14: 168
Short Catechism concerning, M6: 3
Is on the March, L11: 310
Tufts, James Hayden, L15: 324
Tribute to, L5: 424; L15: 321
Turkey: Foreign Schools in, M15: 144
Problem of, L2: 189
Turkish Education: Preliminary Report on, M15: 301
Report and Recommendation upon, M15: 273
Turkish Tragedy, M15: 139
Tychism, M2: 259
Types of Philosophic Thought (Syllabus), M13: 349

Ubication, M2: 259
Underground Burrows, M13: 197
Underlying Philosophy of Education, L8: 77
Understanding, L8: 221, 235
Conceptions and, M6: 271

Understanding (*continued*)
and Inference, **L12**: 142
and Prejudice, **L5**: 396
and Reason, **M2**: 259
Unemployed: Asks Federal Fund to Aid, **L5**: 434
Democracy Joins the, **L6**: 239
Dewey Opposes Community Chest Drives for, **L6**: 374
and Underpaid Consumers Should Not Pay Billion Dollar Subsidy to Speculators, **L9**: 249
Unemployment: Asks Hoover to Act on, **L5**: 436
Church Leaders Ask Church Act on, **L6**: 381
Dewey Calls on Hoover to Recognize Government Responsibility for, **L6**: 372
Federal Government and, **L6**: 377
Joint Committee on, Demands Congress Act, **L6**: 390
Aid, Wagner Called "Keyman" on, **L6**: 384
Committee Asks Adequate Relief, **L9**: 271
Unification of Knowledge, **M2**: 261
Unitarianism, **M2**: 261
United, We Shall Stand, **L11**: 348
United Command, Dewey Hails Editorial on, **L17**: 130
United States, Incorporated, **L5**: 58
Unit of Behavior. *See* Reflex Arc Concept in Psychology
Unity and Plurality, **M2**: 261
Unity and Progress, **L9**: 71
Unity of Science as a Social Problem, **L13**: 271
Unity of the Human Being, **L13**: 323
Universal, **M2**: 263; **M7**: 360
Universal Military Training, **M10**: 377
Universal Postulate, **M2**: 265
Universals, What Are They? **L11**: 105
Universal Service as Education, **M10**: 183
Universe, **M2**: 265
University Control, Faculty Share in, **M8**: 109
University Elementary School, **M1**: 317
Three Years of the, **M1**: 57
University Primary School, Plan of Organization of the, **E5**: 223
University School, **E5**: 436
Unknowable, **M2**: 266
Unthinkable, **M2**: 266
Urbana, Ill., Conference, Greetings to, **L17**: 88
Utah, University of, Situation at the, **M8**: 409
Utilitarianism, **M7**: 360
Utopian Schools, Dewey Outlines, **L9**: 136

Vacuum, **M2**: 267
Validity, **M7**: 362
Valuation: Objects of, **M11**: 3
and Experimental Knowledge, **M13**: 3
as Judgment, Further as to, **L15**: 73
Judgments and Immediate Quality, **L15**: 63
Value: Experience, Knowledge and, **L14**: 3
Field of, **L16**: 343
Meaning of, **L2**: 69
Objective Reference and Criticism, **L2**: 78
Some Questions about, **L15**: 101

of Historical Christianity, **L17**: 529
Values: Educational, **M7**: 362; **M9**: 240
Liking, and Thought, **M15**: 20
Problem of, **M7**: 44
Valuations, and Social Facts, **L16**: 310
or Aims, Ultimate, Determination of, **L13**: 255
Virtue and the Virtues, **E4**: 351
Virtues, **M5**: 359
Realized Morality or the, **E3**: 382
Vladeck, Baruch Charney: Dewey Supports, **L5**: 443
and Harry W. Laidler, **L6**: 326
Vocational Aspects of Education, **M9**: 316
Vocational Education: Modern Trend toward, **M10**: 151
Place of, **M10**: 144
in the Light of the World War, **M11**: 58
under "Unit" or "Dual" Control, Should Michigan Have? **M7**: 85
Volition, Development of, **E2**: 309
Voluntarism in the Roycean Philosophy, **M10**: 79
Voters Must Demand Congress Tax Wealth Instead of Want, **L6**: 392
Voting, How They Are, **L11**: 526

Wage Disparity, Attacks, **L5**: 431
Wagner, Robert F., Called "Keyman" on Unemployment Aid, **L6**: 384
Wallace, Henry: American Youth, Beware of Him Bearing Gifts, **L15**: 242
and the 1948 Elections, **L15**: 239
Waller, Odell, Case of, **L15**: 356
War: Higher Learning and, **L14**: 273
If It Were Outlawed, **M15**: 110
Internal Social Reorganization after the, **M11**: 73
Its Social Results, **L17**: 21
Lessons from the, in Philosophy, **L14**: 312
Outlawing Peace by Discussing, **L3**: 173
Outlawry of, **L8**: 13; What It Is Not, **M15**: 115
Problem of Secondary Education after the, **L17**: 26
What It Means to America, **L17**: 123
World, Vocational Education in the Light of the, **M11**: 58
and a Code of Law, **M15**: 122
Warranted Assertibility, Propositions, and Truth, **L14**: 168
Wartime, Our Educational Ideal in, **M10**: 178
Washington, Issues at, **M13**: 173
Washington Conference and a Happy Ending, **M13**: 204
Waste in Education, **M1**: 39
What I Believe, **L5**: 267
What *Is* Democracy? **L17**: 471
What Is It All About? **L6**: 330
What Is Learning? **L11**: 238
Whewell, William, and John Stuart Mill, On, **M2**: 368
Whitehead, Alfred North, Philosophy of, **L11**: 146; **L14**: 123
White House Conference on Child Health and Protection, Schools and the, **L6**: 131
Wieman, Henry Nelson, and Edwin Ewart Aubrey, Reply to, **L9**: 294
Will: Freedom of, **M6**: 464
Habits and, **M14**: 21

Will (*continued*)
  Impulses and the, **E1**: 327
  Interest in Relation to Training of the, **E5**: 111
  as the Source of Ideals and of Their Realization, **E2**: 357
Woll, Matthew: Reply to, **L5**: 389
  as a Communist-Catcher, **L5**: 392
Woman's Suffrage, **M6**: 153
Women: Education and the Health of, **E1**: 64
  Health of, and Higher Education, **L17**: 7
Wood, Charles W., Interview by, **M13**: 425
Woolf, S. J., Tribute to, **L17**: 526
Workers' Education, Freedom in, **L5**: 331
Work Insurance, Urges State-Aid Plan for, **L6**: 339
World, **M2**: 269
  America in the, **M11**: 70
  Individual and the, **M9**: 300
  Sick, **M15**: 42
  What Kind Are We Fighting to Create? **L17**: 131
  Anarchy or World Order? **L15**: 204
  Court, Shall the United States Join the? **M15**: 87
  High Court for Knowledge? **L11**: 127
Worlds, Between Two, **L17**: 451

You Must Act to Get Congress to Act, **L6**: 386
Younger Men Are Key, **L11**: 529
Youth: American, Beware of Wallace Bearing Gifts, **L15**: 242
  Character Training for, **L9**: 186
  in a Confused World, **L11**: 353

Subject Index
The Collected Works of John Dewey, 1882–1953

Series and volume numbers are in boldface type

E: Early Works, 1882–1898
M: Middle Works, 1899–1924
L: Later Works, 1925–1953

Abbey, Edwin Austin, **L10**: 239
Abbott, Grace, **L17**: 517, 573
Abdul Hamid, **M15**: 130, 145
Abelard, Peter
  realism of, **M2**: 221
  on reason and ethics, **M5**: 141
Abell, Walter, **L11**: 487-88
Abercrombie, Lascelles
  on inspiration, **L10**: 72n, 355
  on words, **L10**: 246-47
Aborigine
  customs and attitudes of, **M2**: 42-51
About
  knowledge as, **L12**: 153-54
  double meaning of, **L12**: 167-68, 180, 468
Absentmindedness, **M14**: 121
Absolute, **L12**: 44, 216-17
  relative correlated with, **E1**: 22-26
  Royce on, **M1**: xi, xii, 250, 256
  Bradley on, **M4**: 55-58
  in German philosophy, **M8**: 182, 419
  Fichte on, **M8**: 187
  space and time, **L14**: 105
  ends, **L14**: 121-22
  vs. experimental, **L14**: 317
  unknowableness of, **L17**: 94, 482
Absolute being
  Royce on, **M2**: 128-31, 134-37
Absolute experience, **L1**: 55-57
  Royce on, **M2**: 123-24
Absolute idea
  history as evolution of, **M10**: 224
Absolute idealism, **M7**: xiv, 284; **M9**: 309; **M13**: 478n; **M15**: 337; **L12**: 524-26
Absolute object
  in sensationalist theory, **E1**: 25-29
Absolute rational whole
  Royce on, **M10**: 80
Absolute reality, **M3**: 124; **M12**: 92, 94
Absolute reason, **L13**: 148-49
  Fichte on, **M8**: 188
Absolutes
  of Newton, **L4**: 115, 116, 120

Absolutes (*continued*)
  Barry on, **L4**: 128n
  in formation of values, **L4**: 207, 211
  of physics, **L16**: 61, 346
  in normative theory, **L16**: 338, 453
  restrict inquiry, **L16**: 339, 355, 455
  in politics, **L16**: 362
Absolute spirit, **M8**: 430; **L13**: 148-49
Absolute truth, **M7**: xv
  vs. experience, **L14**: 321-22
Absolute unity
  Fichte on, **M8**: 172
Absolute whole, **M7**: 187
  Hegel and Froebel on, **M9**: 62-65, 73
Absolutism, **M6**: 175; **M7**: 423; **M12**: 135, 189; **L7**: 54; **L13**: 241; **L17**: xxxii
  medieval and modern, **M3**: 90
  related to justice, **M10**: xxxviii, 281-84
  Royce's transition to, **M10**: 84
  Kant and, **M12**: 136
  in method, **L2**: 357-61
  objective or realistic, **L13**: 117, 120
  theological form of, **L13**: 122
  truth in, **L13**: 131, 257
  physical, **L13**: 184
  pragmatic critique of, **L15**: xxvii-xxix, 3-6, 24-26
  moral, **L15**: 58, 59, 172-81, 236, 267-68, 271
  social, **L15**: 162-63
  and fanaticism, **L17**: xxiv
Absolutistic theory, **L16**: 348-49
Absorption, **L8**: 345
Abstinence
  Emerson on, **L7**: 210
Abstract
  transition to, **M6**: 286-92; **L8**: 293-300
  in *Cyclopedia of Education*, **M6**: 391-92
  value of, **L8**: 276-77
  as terminology, **L16**: 93n
Abstract art, **L10**: 99, 156, 256, 316-17
Abstract intellectualism
  related to individualism, **M9**: 307-8
Abstraction, **M12**: 166-67, 179; **M13**: 418; **L1**: 151-52; **L11**: 97-99, 113, 121; **L12**: 25-26, 120, 135, 137-38, 254, 257-58, 302-4, 307, 309, 329, 338, 349-51, 354, 393-94, 400-401, 411-13, 438. *See also* Hypothesis; Universal proposition
  process of, **E2**: 180-81; **E3**: 148-49; **E5**: 261, 383
  feeling as, **E3**: 258
  D. Phillips on, **E5**: 182
  in *Cyclopedia of Education*, **M6**: 359
  in science, **M9**: 233-36; **L4**: 196-97; **L5**: 7-12; **L16**: 252-53
  in Locke's theories, **M9**: 276
  Dewey's use of, **L4**: xii
  in Greek philosophy, **L4**: xiv
  role of, **L4**: 90n; **L16**: 285-86, 292, 361, 446
  transition to, **L4**: 123, 125, 127
  positive phase of, **L4**: 132
  as precondition of method, **L4**: 173-75, 190, 237
  in art, **L10**: 60, 73, 100-101, 127, 214, 220, 264, 289
  and conception, **L12**: 462-64, 468

knowledge involves, **L16**: 14n
of Quine, **L16**: 49-50
levels of, **L16**: 103n
in mathematics, **L16**: 276, 431
Academic art
cause of, **L10**: xxi, 113, 143, 147, 157, 163, 183, 270, 273, 293
praised, **L10**: 315
Academic degrees, **L15**: 278
Academic freedom, **M8**: 102; **L2**: 58-60; **L5**: 331-45; **L9**: 206-7; **L11**: 376-79, 570-72; **L13**: xiii, 9, 24, 52; **L14**: xix, 374, 431
nature of, **M2**: xix, 62-64
restriction of, **M2**: 55-58; **L14**: xix, 374, 431
Harper on, **M2**: 60-61
in *Cyclopedia of Education*, **M6**: 460-64
related to academic tenure, **M8**: 106-8
Dewey on, **M8**: 407-8
at University of Utah, **M8**: 409-10
related to Russell, **L14**: 231, 237, 246, 248, 357-59
Academicians, **L10**: 305
Academic Illusions in the Field of Letters and the Arts (Schütze), **L8**: 360-63; **L10**: 320n, 365
Academic tenure
academic freedom related to, **M8**: 106-8
Academy
as preparatory school, **E5**: 271
Plato's founding of, **M7**: 313
Accident
in history, **M14**: 9, 73, 117
in consequences, **M14**: 36, 38, 143-45, 164-66, 174, 209-12
logical, **L12**: 94-95, 138-41, 201
Accommodation
in *Cyclopedia of Education*, **M6**: 359-61, 365
in habituation, **M9**: 52, 54-56
Accuracy
in language, **L16**: 446
requires attention, **L17**: 304
of visualists, **L17**: 329
Accurate
as name, **L16**: 259
Achan
as example of group morality, **M5**: 23-24, 34, 62, 100; **L7**: 23, 32, 57, 91
Acheson, Dean, **L17**: 140-41, 561, 562
Achievement, **M12**: 191
concept of, **L7**: 203
education related to, **L17**: 72-73
importance of, **L17**: 205
Acknowledgment
as recognition, **L12**: 154-55
Acquaintance, **M8**: 25; **L1**: 248-49
as knowledge, **L12**: 153-55; **L15**: 31
Acquisition, **M14**: 82-84, 99-102
Act
Baldwin on, **E5**: 416
related to judgment, **M3**: 12-20; **M13**: 13, 20-22
moral, as social, **M9**: 367-70
Bain on, **M10**: 108n
related to meaning, **M13**: 63, 384, 395
related to function, **M13**: 70
and language, **M13**: 383
motor-affective, **M15**: 21-22, 339-40
conformity of, **M15**: 347

Act (*continued*)
individual and, **L2**: 247, 249
inseparable from product, **L16**: 155-57, 160
involved in valuing, **L16**: 345, 352
Action, **M12**: 125-26; **L1**: 126, 215, 237, 255, 263, 319; **L4**: 44, 58, 85; **L11**: 212, 501-2; **L15**: xxviii-xxix, 176-77. *See also* Operations, **L12**
reflex, **E1**: 98-100; **L17**: 192-96
purposive, **E1**: 100-103
moral, **E1**: 209-10, 340-41; **E2**: 343-46, 349-56; **E4**: 60
self and, **E1**: 334-37; **E4**: 51n, 204-6; **L7**: 288-90, 292, 306; **L16**: 130, 155, 231-32
as contingent, **E1**: 335-36
ethical, **E2**: 349-52
religious, **E2**: 361
related to knowledge, **E3**: 230-31; **E5**: 21-22; **M7**: 6; **M9**: 340; **M13**: 52; **L3**: 38, 51-52; **L4**: 155, 164, 170-72, 224-26; **L8**: 86-90, 92-94, 97; **L17**: 48, 158
character as motive of, **E3**: 259
in sensori-motor circuit, **E5**: 97
and emotion, **E5**: 324; **L11**: 38, 213, 244
and volitional consciousness, **E5**: 361
Bergson on, **M7**: 3, 15; **M10**: 69-70
consequences of, **M9**: 356, 359, 370; **M12**: 173-74; **L4**: 3-4, 189-91, 210, 219-23, 227; **L12**: 53-60; **L13**: 59, 105, 130, 238, 256-57
as instrumental, **M10**: 45
Spencer on, **M10**: 69-70
Peirce on, **M10**: 74, 77; **L11**: 424
necessities of, **M13**: 49
influences affecting, **M13**: 330; **L4**: 43, 88-89, 120-21, 125-29, 133-35, 211, 230, 249; **L7**: 293, 295-96; **L13**: 43, 45, 94, 100, 108, 129, 161-62, 192, 222, 250, 258, 283; **L17**: 86
direct, **L2**: 255
and freedom, **L3**: xxvii-xxviii, 106-7; **L17**: 384
and behavior, **L3**: 32-33
cultural, **L3**: 36; **L10**: 329, 351; **L12**: 48-65
and choice, **L3**: 97, 101, 104; **L17**: 339
analysis of, **L4**: xiii, xv
realm of, **L4**: 6-7, 18, 21, 24-27, 169, 234
function of, **L4**: 26, 82, 107, 237, 239, 241, 243, 248; **L7**: 240, 294, 316; **L16**: 92, 245, 336
methods of, **L4**: 29, 30
related to values, **L4**: 35-36, 207, 210, 215; **L8**: 91, 102-3
nature of, **L4**: 70, 71, 157-60, 178-87, 190, 195; **L16**: xxviii, 66-68, 98, 140, 328, 332
kinds of, **L4**: 196, 200, 201, 237; **L16**: 101, 112-14
related to philosophy, **L5**: 141-43
public vs. private, **L7**: 336-37
part of esthetic experience, **L10**: xvii, xxvi, 27, 29, 45-47, 51-56, 128, 178, 207, 213, 260-61, 265-68, 273, 281, 283, 294

biological, **L12**: 30-47
as close of inquiry, **L12**: 66-67, 145-47, 166-67, 170-71
pure, **L12**: 78, 92, 95-96, 483-84
general, **L12**: 248-50, 269-70
fair vs. unfair, **L13**: 33-34
rule-of-thumb, **L13**: 131-32
group, **L13**: 206
Bentley on, **L16**: xxiii
as name, **L16**: 71, 259
Maxwell on, **L16**: 100
Osborn on, **L16**: 116n
inner life vs. outward, **L17**: 81
unity as, **L17**: 157
physical basis of mental, **L17**: 190-92
ideo-motor, **L17**: 201, 263, 332
ideal of, **L17**: 396
quality of, **L17**: 410
Action Française, L' (Paris), **L15**: 387-88
Active
in child development, **E5**: 91
Activist party (Polish), **M11**: 265, 275, 298
Activity
and passivity, **E1**: 338; **M9**: 345
as object of desire, **E3**: 254-55; **E4**: 47; **E5**: 439
related to pleasure, **E3**: 256-57
capacity as, **E4**: 46, 49, 50
unconscious, **E4**: 235; **L17**: 154-55
external vs. internal, **E5**: 121; **L9**: 169-71; **L13**: 39-41, 104; **L17**: 156-57, 159
in education, **E5**: 144; **M9**: 207-8; **L9**: 169, 173-74, 179; **L15**: 304
modes of, **E5**: 230-31
of child, **M1**: 210-11, 231; **M6**: 363, 387; **L11**: 193-95, 200, 213, 243-45
in forming judgments, **M3**: 12-13
related to thought, **M6**: 304-13; **M9**: 152-53, 161, 271-75, 356-60; **L8**: 281-92
and observation, **M6**: 329-30; **L8**: 317
in *Cyclopedia of Education*, **M6**: 361-64
unified vs. divided, **M7**: 472
Froebel on, **M8**: 276-77
freeing of, **M9**: 112
extension of meaning of, **M9**: 215-18
imagination in, **M9**: 245-46
in modern theory, **M9**: 275-80
related to environment, **M9**: 283
industrial, as cultural, **M9**: 298
individual vs. group, **M9**: 311
as impulsive, **M14**: 84-86, 110, 144, 155-56, 202
pure, **L4**: 15, 17, 75, 237
organization of, **L8**: 152-54
desire vs. social value in, **L9**: 172-73; **L10**: 330-31
allied with God, **L9**: 432-34, 436
in esthetic experience, **L10**: 66-68, 71, 73, 79, 161, 218, 227, 233, 260, 261, 278, 283-88, 291
distance, **L12**: 35-38
intelligent, **L13**: 45, 57, 59
experimental, **L13**: 131
evoked by signs, **L13**: 198, 200-201
as end, **L13**: 209, 234-36; **L17**: 383, 484
continuity of, **L13**: 244

Activity (*continued*)
artistic, **L15**: 315-17
as name, **L16**: 115n, 259, 381, 439
harmonious vs. wasteful, **L17**: 153
coordination of, **L17**: 153-54
division of, **L17**: 155
unity of, **L17**: 157
learning by physical, **L17**: 217
as test, **L17**: 470
Act of 1857 (Great Britain), **L7**: 446
Acton, John Emerich Edward Dalberg Acton, **L1**: 333-35, 360
Actor, **L10**: 86, 162, 205, 263
role of, **L16**: 101n, 108, 185, 213, 240
as name, **L16**: 104, 114n, 146, 259-60
rejected view of, **L16**: 105, 122, 130
mind as, **L16**: 124
related to action, **L16**: 155, 231-32
hypostatized, **L16**: 156
Actual
vs. ideal, **E3**: 259; **L7**: 13, 120-21; **L17**: 155
Hitler on, **M8**: 430
Hegel on, **L4**: 51
defined, **L4**: 239-48
God as union of ideal and, **L9**: xvi-xvii, 34-36, 435-39
Actuality, **L1**: 109; **L12**: 94n, 111, 138, 182-83, 252, 271, 288, 337-39, 385-88, 396
related to potentiality, **E1**: 319; **L12**: 132, 164, 238, 332, 476; **L16**: 426
related to experience, **L16**: 461
Actualization
vs. potentiality, **L16**: 434-35
Adair v. U.S., **L7**: 395-97
Adams, George B., **E4**: 200, 213
Adams, George Plimpton, **L5**: 147n; **L9**: xiin
Adams, Henry, **M12**: 13; **M13**: 272-74; **L6**: 297; **L10**: 37, 354
Adams, Henry Carter, **M5**: 550
Adams, James Truslow, **L6**: 93
Adams, John, **M13**: 298-99, 303; **L13**: 68, 108, 401; **L14**: 203, 208-10, 218; **L17**: 148
Adamson, Robert, **E1**: xxviii
on psychology, **E1**: 147-48
on definition, **L16**: 163, 168, 181n
Adamson law, **L7**: 400
Adaptation, **M13**: 378; **L11**: 502
in *Cyclopedia of Education*, **M6**: 359, 364-65
related to environment, **M9**: 52
related to religion, **L9**: 11-14
esthetic, **L10**: 119-22, 140, 176
rudiments of social, **L17**: 260
Addams, Jane, **L3**: 273; **L5**: xi, 418, 419, 421; **L6**: 125; **L7**: 315; **L15**: xxiii, 509; **L17**: 517, 573
on group loyalty, **M5**: 136
on peace, **M10**: 266-67; **L15**: 192-98; **L17**: 149
Added determinants, **L12**: 321
Addis, Charles, **M13**: 87
Addition
summative, **L12**: 336-40
Addresses on Fundamental Features of the Present Age (Fichte), **M8**: 180
Addresses to the German Nation (Fichte), **M8**: 174, 181
Adelard of Bath, **L14**: 394
"Adjusting Men to Machines" (D. Bell), **L15**: 225-26, 361

Adjustment
moral sense of, **E3**: 313-14
related to environment, **E5**: 51; **M9**: 51-52; **M10**: 8, 9
in *Cyclopedia of Education*, **M6**: 365-66
James on, **L14**: 165
Adkins v. Children's Hospital, **L7**: 400
Adler, Felix, **E3**: 93; **M6**: xii; **L13**: 295, 402; **L15**: xxix
Adler, Mortimer, **M13**: 391; **L3**: 311, 314-15
Administration
school, **M9**: 104, 171, 368
possibilities of intelligent, **L13**: 313
qualities of good, **L17**: 69-70
of education, **L17**: 71, 179
Administration Group
in Teachers Union, **L9**: 323-26, 335, 336, 342
charges against, **L9**: 326-30
Administrators
qualities for school, **L17**: 71
Adolescence (G. Hall), **L11**: 243
Adolescence, **M6**: 231; **L8**: 185
interest in, **E5**: 311
stages of, **M1**: 215-21
emotions during, **L17**: 345
Adolescence and High School Problems (R. Pringle), **M1**: xvn
Adrian, Edgar, **L13**: 327
Adults
education for, **L9**: 100, 184-85, 191; **L11**: 61, 165, 175, 176, 232, 347, 509, 519, 543; **L17**: 45-47
in utopian schools, **L9**: 136-37
related to child, **L11**: 209, 213
Adventures of Ideas (Whitehead), **L8**: 355-59; **L11**: 147n, 148n, 152n; **L14**: 124-40, 189-90
Adventure with Children, An (M. Lewis), **L3**: 330-31
Aeschylus, **E3**: 118; **E4**: 225; **M5**: 130; **L7**: 97, 101, 121
Aesthetic Experience, The (Buermeyer), **L10**: 321n
Aesthetics. *See* Esthetics
Affection
Kant on, **M5**: 314-16
in child development, **L6**: 141
development of, **L17**: 344-45
"Affective Thought," **L2**: xxi; **L6**: 330, 332, 493, 496, 498
Affectivity
and environment, **L2**: 105, 106
Affecto-motor theory, **M15**: 21-22, 25, 339-40, 343, 348
Affirmation, **L12**: 198. *See also* Agreement, **L12**; Ground, **L12**; Identity, **L12**; Inclusion, **L12**
and assertion, **L12**: 123
nature of, **L12**: 263, 423-24
negation-, **L12**: 427, 459
and judgment, **L14**: 175
AFL. *See* American Federation of Labor
Africa, **L15**: 61, 308
totem group in, **M5**: 26; **L7**: 26
Against Method (Feyerabend), **L8**: xivn
Agassiz, Louis, **E5**: 265; **L17**: 204
Age
as division in primitive societies, **M5**: 36-37; **L7**: 35-36
Ageing
problems of, **L14**: 341-50
Agent
related to valuing, **L16**: 6, 345, 348

Aggregates
and collections, **L12**: 203-4, 208-10, 360-63, 409-10
Agitation
Russian definition of, **L17**: 495
Agnosticism, **E4**: 6; **M13**: 417; **L4**: 154; **L9**: xx, 57
criticized, **E1**: 206-7
in philosophy, **E3**: 125
in science, **E3**: 141
equivalent to nescience, **M2**: 153-54
growth of, **M10**: 24
Agnostic positivism, **M10**: 38
Agreement, **L12**: 184, 263, 428; **L16**: 399
of consequences, **L12**: 25-26, 52-53, 57-60, 477
Agricultural Adjustment Administration (AAA)
on dollar distribution, **L9**: 83-84
on parity prices, **L9**: 84-85
Agricultural instinct
in education, **E5**: 250-51
Agricultural societies, **L14**: 204
Agriculture, **L10**: 152; **L11**: 10, 16, 169, 228, 256, 262; **L13**: 164, 319; **L16**: 405. *See also* Farmers
helps war effort, **M10**: 296-300
methods of, **M11**: 63
in Japan, **M11**: 161-66
in China, **M11**: 216-17
of opium, **M11**: 238
of Poles, **M11**: 285, 294
need for organization in, **L9**: 249
Russian study of, **L17**: 502-3
Agriculture, Department of, **L6**: 361; **L9**: 85
Agriculture Adjustment Act, **L11**: 373
Aid
federal, to education, **L9**: 392-93
Aidos, **L7**: 122
Aids to Reflection (Coleridge), **L5**: 148, 178, 180, 181
Aiken, Henry, **L15**: 127n
"Aim and Progress of Psychology, The" (Kantor), **L16**: 130n
Aims, **L13**: 223. *See also* Ends; Purpose
nature of, **M9**: 107-11
criteria of good, **M9**: 111-13, 182-83
educational, **M9**: 113-17; **M13**: 320, 399-400
vocational, **M9**: 318-21
deliberation about, **M13**: 12
growth as, **M13**: 402, 404
and consequences, **M14**: 155-60, 168-70
development of, **L7**: 185
social, **L13**: 304
unity of, **L13**: 340
importance of, **L17**: 279, 283
Albania, **M15**: 380
Albertus Magnus, Saint, **M2**: 240; **L14**: 394
Alcmaeon of Croton, **M12**: xiii
Alcohol
Russian problem with, **L17**: 506
Alcott, Louisa May, **M7**: 358
Aldrich, Virgil C., **L16**: 210n
Alertness
importance of, **L17**: 280-82
Aleuts
tribal regulation of, **L3**: 13-14
Alexander, F. Matthias, **M14**: 23n, 28n; **L1**: 225n, 229n
on conscious control, **M11**: x, 350-55, 359-60; **L6**: 315-20
contrasted with Coué, **M15**: 45-46

method of, **M15**: 308-15
Alexander, Georgia, **M8**: 208
Alexander, Hartley Burr
on Carus Foundation, **L1**: 393-95
Alexander, Samuel, **M12**: xxx
on rightness, **E4**: 246
on moral progress, **M5**: 385
on poetry, **L10**: 70, 355
Alexander of Hales, **M2**: 240
Alexander the Great, **M8**: 194; **M10**: 237; **L8**: 23; **L15**: 207
Alexandria, Egypt, **L8**: 5, 24, 357, 359
Alexandrian civilization, **L10**: 331
Alfange, Dean, **L17**: 133, 560
Algonquin Indians, **M7**: 400
Alienation, **L15**: 169
All. *See also* Universal proposition, **L12**
ambiguity of term, **L11**: 120-21
meanings of, **L12**: 193-94, 200, 254-58, 296, 325-26
as qualitative, **L12**: 203-4, 207-9
"Alleged New Discovery in Logic, An" (D. Robinson), **M10**: 415-30
Allen, Carleton Kemp, **L3**: 326-29
Allen, Devere, **L6**: 249
Allen, Florence, **L5**: 353; **L8**: 16
Allen, Ira, **L14**: 266
Allies, **M12**: 35, 63, 66; **M15**: 129. *See also* Great Powers
conceptions about, **M11**: xi-xii, 127, 158, 159, 177-79, 365
relation with U.S., **M11**: 107, 182, 229
in WWI, **M11**: 109-10, 129, 230
in Siberia, **M11**: 167
China's relation with, **M11**: 186, 190, 199-202, 229
at peace conference, **M11**: 198
and Polish question, **M11**: 267-302 passim, 316, 320-24, 330, 402
in peacetime, **M15**: 106-7
and World Court, **M15**: 390
Allotment plan
for farmers, **L9**: 249-50
All Our Years (Lovett), **L14**: 431
Allport, Gordon W., **L14**: 5, 15, 38-41
Alogism
Royce's rejection of, **M10**: 80
Alsace-Lorraine, **M11**: 136; **M12**: 60
Alter, Victor, **L15**: 350
Alternation
logical, **L12**: 337-39
Althusius, Johannes, **L2**: 39, 40
Altman, Jules, **L16**: 5
Altruism, **M14**: 92-93, 97, 202
and egoism, **E3**: 285, 307-8
criticism of, **M5**: 347-51
in *Cyclopedia of Education*, **M6**: 366-69
theory of, **L7**: 292-98
dangers of, **L7**: 294, 301, 314-15
Ambition, **L7**: 73
Ambrose, Saint, **L7**: 137
America in Midpassage (C. Beard and M. Beard), **L14**: 283-85
American Association for the Advancement of Science, **M6**: 69n; **M8**: 105; **L6**: 118n
Dewey addresses, **L17**: xvii-xviii
American Association of School Administrators, **L13**: 281n
American Association of Teachers Colleges, **L9**: 158n

American Association of University Professors (AAUP), **M8**: 98-108, 409; **M9**: xiv; **M10**: ix, xxxix, 165, 371-72, 450-52; **L6**: xxii, 120, 122, 503; **L14**: 274; **L15**: xviii
Dewey president of, **M2**: xix
Committee on Academic Freedom and Tenure, **M10**: 370
Committee on University Ethics, **M10**: 373-76
American Association of University Women, **L6**: 342; **L17**: 553
American Bar Association, **M8**: 102
American Chemical Society, **L6**: 120
American Civil Liberties Union, **L9**: 87; **L15**: 356
Dewey in, **M10**: ix, xxxix
American College of Physicians, **L13**: 323n
American Commission plan, **M13**: 129
American Committee for the Defense of Leon Trotsky, **L11**: 310n, 321n. *See also* Commission of Inquiry into the Charges Made against Leon Trotsky in the Moscow Trials
Declaration of Principles of, **L11**: 303-5
function of, **L11**: 306-7, 598-99
criticism of, **L11**: 334
American Committee for the Outlawry of War, **M15**: xiv, 103; **L5**: 352; **L8**: 14, 15, 17
American Commonwealth, The (Bryce), **L11**: 184
American dream, **L11**: 535, 536, 547
American Education Fellowship, **L17**: 88, 558
American Education Past and Future, **L6**: xxii
American Farm Bureau Federation, **L9**: 250, 273
American Federationist, **L5**: 333
American Federation of Labor (AFL), **M10**: 169, 170; **L5**: 317, 331-45, 372, 373, 392; **L6**: 172, 236, 251; **L7**: 429; **L9**: 250, 252; **L11**: 349, 351; **L14**: 375; **L15**: 240, 245; **L17**: 83
and AFT, **L9**: 123-24, 335
and education, **L9**: 124-25, 130n
opposes sales taxes, **L9**: 273
American Federation of Teachers (AFT), **M10**: 168n, 370; **L5**: 331-33, 336; **L6**: 433-35; **L9**: 112, 114; **L11**: 161, 349, 351
Dewey's membership in, **L3**: 269-75
activities of, **L3**: 271-73
solidarity of, **L3**: 279
role of, in improving education, **L9**: 122, 125-26
Dewey on, **L9**: 123-24
and AFL, **L9**: 123-24, 335
and Teachers Union, **L9**: 318, 320n, 329
25th anniversary of, **L14**: 375
goal of, **L17**: 83
revokes local charters, **L17**: 520
communism within, **L17**: 520-21
American Friends of Spanish Democracy, **L11**: 527
American Hebrew, **L5**: 396-97
American Historical Review, **M11**: 314

American Indians. *See* Indians, North American
American Institute of Architects, **L9**: 262
Americanism, **L5**: 330
characteristics of, **L5**: 50-57
European view of, **L5**: 50-52, 101, 109
judicial supremacy of, **L17**: 118
Americanization, **M12**: 12-16
American Journal of Economics and Sociology, **L14**: 362-63
American Labor party, **L17**: 133, 560
American Legion, **L6**: 236; **L11**: 576
American Liberty League, **L9**: 88-89
American Medical Association, **M8**: 102
American Newspaper Guild, **L11**: 352, 604
American Peace Commission (Commission of Inquiry), **M11**: 401-3
American Peace Mobilization, **L15**: 348
American Philosophical Association, **M7**: 44n, 47n; **M10**: 79, 447; **L3**: 41n; **L5**: 210n, 461n, 477n, 487n; **L11**: xxiv, 289n; **L14**: 431; **L15**: 154, 324
Münsterberg lauded at, **M1**: xiii
American Psychological Association, **M3**: 351n; **M7**: 47n
Dewey president of, **M1**: ix, 131n
founding of, **M10**: 53
American Revolution, **L6**: 463; **L7**: 148-50; **L15**: 217, 252
American Road to Culture, The (Counts), **L9**: 177
American Society of Civil Engineers, **L6**: 120
American Sociological Society, **L15**: 225
American Sociology and Pragmatism (J. Lewis and R. Smith), **L6**: xiii
American Teacher, **L9**: 329
American Telephone and Telegraph, **L5**: 59
America's Social Morality (Tufts), **L15**: 322, 325
Ames, Adelbert, Jr., **L15**: xxiii, 310-11, 510
Ames, Edward Scribner, **M5**: ix; **L15**: 321n
Ames, Van Meter, **L6**: 311
Amherst College, **L15**: 324
Amiel, Henri Frédéric, **E4**: 193-94; **M4**: 44, 242
Amity
Bentham on, **M5**: 265-66
Among Cannibals (Lumholtz), **M2**: 46n
Among Congo Cannibals (J. Weeks), **L3**: 82
Amos, **M5**: 91, 96; **L7**: 83, 84, 88
Amoy (Xiamen), China, **L6**: 205
Amsterdam, Netherlands, **L10**: 117, 358
Amusements
rival political interests, **L2**: 321-22
Analogy, logic of
in *Cyclopedia of Education*, **M6**: 369-70
Analogy of Religion, Natural and Revealed, The (J. Butler), **L5**: 147, 150; **L9**: xii, 422
Analysis, **M14**: 128-29; **L4**: 74, 99, 139; **L10**: vii. *See also* Data, **L12**; Elimination, **L12**; Selection, **L12**

Analysis (*continued*)
and synthesis, **E3**: 78-80; **L13**: 56-57
related to thought, **M6**: 266-70; **L8**: 216-20; **L10**: 308-9, 313-17
and scientific method, **M6**: 297-98; **L8**: 272-75
in *Cyclopedia of Education*, **M6**: 370-75
importance of, **L7**: xxxiii; **L17**: 290-91
generalized, **L8**: 242
of Cassirer, **L16**: 115n
Moore on, **L16**: 205-7
in semiotic, **L16**: 232
of activity, **L17**: 156-57
facts as, **L17**: 157, 158
excess of, **L17**: 292
Analysis of Knowledge and Valuation, An (C. Lewis), **L5**: xxix
Analytical Psychology (Witmer), **M2**: 119
Analytic logic, **M10**: 335
Analytic realism, **M8**: 68; **M10**: 90
Analytic-synthetic distinction, **L16**: xxxiii
Analytic Theory of Heat, The (Fourier), **L15**: xvii
Anarchism, **M7**: 419; **M12**: 247; **L2**: 252
Anarchy, **L11**: 459-60; **L15**: 205
and democracy, **L7**: xviii
as threat, **L16**: 399
Anarchy, State, and Utopia (Nozick), **L2**: xxxv
Anatolia, Turkey, **M15**: 134, 137, 139-40, 146, 293
Anaxagoras
on nous, **M2**: 161-62
on vacuum, **M2**: 267
atheism of, **L17**: 182
Anaximenes, **M2**: 205
Ancestors
group importance of, **M5**: 25; **L7**: 26
worship of, **M5**: 35-36; **L7**: 34-35, 56
Anchises, **M5**: 36; **L7**: 34
And, **L12**: 335-38, 438-39
Andersen, Hans Christian, **M8**: 241
Anderson, Benjamin M., Jr., **L6**: 360
Andover Theological Seminary, **L5**: 178
Andronicus of Rhodes, **M2**: 186
Anesthetic
cause of, **L10**: 46, 47, 84, 156, 202, 267
Anfu Club (China), **M12**: 65-69, 255; **M13**: 122, 124, 135, 139, 145
opposes student movement, **M13**: 100
overthrow of, **M13**: 149-50
Anfu party, **L2**: 183
Angell, James Rowland, **M5**: ix; **L5**: xi, 419, 420; **L7**: 430
on moral conduct, **M5**: 14
at University of Chicago, **L16**: xiv
Angell, Norman, **M11**: 182; **L2**: 33n
Angelus (Millet), **L17**: 245
Angelus Silesius, **M2**: 216
Anger, **E4**: 172-73, 183-84; **M14**: 65-66, 106
Anglo-Japanese alliance
renewal of, **M13**: 77, 91, 125-26, 177
meaning of, **M13**: 121
viewpoints toward, **M13**: 177-79, 191, 219
end to, **M13**: 212-15
Angora (Ankara), Turkey, **M15**:

128, 134, 135, 282, 418, 419
compared with Constantinople, **M15**: 136-38
Animal art, **L10**: 317n
"Animal Faith and the Art of Intuition" (S. Lamprecht), **L14**: 306
Animals, **M12**: 81-82, 232-34, 245
training of, **M9**: 16
experimentation with, **L2**: 98-100
responsibility toward, **L2**: 100-102
similar to man, **L10**: 39, 40, 243
behavior of, **L16**: 144, 147, 230n, 321, 325-27, 472-73
as ancestor, **L16**: 412, 414
Animism, **M2**: 181; **M9**: 221; **L1**: 142-43, 243, 262; **L5**: 226, 230; **L14**: 193-94, 383
of primitive mind, **M2**: 43
Animosity
as reason for sanctions, **L6**: 216
Ann Arbor Railroad Co. et al. v. United States et al., **L6**: 371
Anselm, Saint, **M2**: 168-69
Anstruther-Thomson, C., **L10**: 357
Antecedent conditions
affect moral validity, **M2**: xii
fallacy regarding, **M2**: 10-11
positive aspects of, **M2**: 13
Dewey's view of, **M2**: 14-15
Antecedent objects, **L5**: xxvii-xxviii
Antecedents
knowledge as disclosure of, **L4**: 18, 56, 58, 150-54, 157, 160, 164-66, 193, 196, 232, 236
in science, **L4**: 101, 102, 138, 144, 147, 186, 200, 219, 230
determine validity of ideas, **L4**: 110, 116, 117, 132, 133
determine values, **L4**: 206, 211, 217, 219, 240, 242, 246
Anthropocentrism, **L14**: 143
Cohen on Dewey and, **L14**: 380-81
Anthropologist, **L10**: 330
Anthropology (Kant), **L5**: 179
Anthropology, **L1**: 37-43, 118, 287-88; **L6**: xvi, 37-38, 278-79; **L16**: 63n
related to ethics, **L3**: xxiii-xxiv, 11, 14, 16, 19
laws of uniformity in, **L5**: 170-71
related to religion, **L9**: 3
research in, **L13**: 85
cultural, **L13**: 248
and war, **L14**: 320, 330, 431
"Anthropology and Ethics," **L7**: xv
"Anthropology and Law," **L14**: xxii
Anthropomorphism, **L17**: 93
Fiske on, **L17**: 94, 96-97
Anticipation, **L10**: 142-43, 149; **L15**: 37-38
as quality of experience, **M10**: 10
intellectual, **M13**: 53
in knowledge, **M13**: 457, 467, 468
Anti-clerical legislation, **L2**: 194-96
Antigone (Sophocles), **M2**: 145; **L7**: 103, 122
Anti-Imperialist League, **L15**: 22
Anti-intellectualism
pragmatism as, **M6**: 86-90
Dewey accused of, **M9**: xx-xxiv

Anti-Intellectualism in American Life (Hofstadter), **M9**: xx
Antin, Mary, **M10**: 184
"Anti-Naturalism in Extremis," **L15**: xiii
Antinomianism, **L1**: 118
Antinomy, **L13**: 110
Antioch (Antakaya), Turkey, **L8**: 357
Antioch College, **L6**: 419, 503; **L11**: 226n, 567n, 580
Anti-pragmatisme (Schinz), **M4**: 245-49
Anti-pragmatists, **M8**: 48
Antiquity, **M12**: 97-98
Anti-Saloon League, **L6**: 236
Anti-Semitism, **M8**: 188; **L13**: 301; **L15**: 388
  in Poland, **M11**: 262, 264, 278, 280-82, 308
Antisocial nature
  denial of man's, **M9**: 28
  of gangs, **M9**: 91
Antisthenes, **L2**: 125, 128-29
Antithesis
  principle of, **E4**: 165-69
Anti-War Pact
  violations of, **L6**: 450, 467, 470-71, 484
  international obligations under, **L6**: 452, 454, 460, 462, 473, 476
  China and, **L6**: 458
Anwhei faction (China), **M12**: 69-70
Apata, Peru, **L15**: 510
Apathy
  related to moral theory, **M5**: 202
  and politics, **L6**: 182-83, 185, 188
Apologetics, **L9**: 26, 27, 37, 217; **L14**: 326
"Apologia Pro Mente Sua" (Santayana), **L14**: 295; **L15**: 423
Apologists
  purpose of, **L17**: 96
  on Christianity, **L17**: 374
Apology (Plato), **M12**: xii; **L11**: xxvi; **L16**: 471
A posteriori, **M8**: 158
  as philosophical issue, **M10**: 14
  Russell on, **M10**: 93
Apostles Creed, **L2**: 165
Appearance, **L1**: 17, 52, 53, 111-13, 325, 344; **L4**: 19, 24, 247
  separated from philosophy, **M10**: 46
  defined, **L3**: 55-59
  and intellectual significance, **L3**: 60-61
  as sign, **L3**: 62-63, 69-70
  misconstruction of nature of, **L3**: 63-64, 67, 71
  and reality, **L14**: 25, 26, 196-97; **L17**: 367n
Appearance and Reality (F. Bradley), **M1**: 256; **M3**: 171n; **M4**: 54-55; **M7**: xiv
"Appearing and Appearance," **L3**: xix-xx
Appellate Division
  of New York State courts, **L9**: 376-77
Apperception
  theory of, **E2**: 78-82; **E5**: 297
  organs of, **E2**: 112
  dependent on adjustment, **E2**: 123-25
  related to retention, **E2**: 130-33
  and conception, **E2**: 180
  connected with qualitative feeling, **E2**: 239-40
  Herbart's theory of, **M9**: 76

Appetite, **M14**: 7, 110, 188; **L11**: 73
related to energy, **E5**: 129
and action, **L13**: 162
Appliances
in inquiry, **L16**: 327-30
Application, **L1**: 147, 325-26; **L12**: 373-75; **L16**: 91. *See also* Operations, **L12**; Reference, **L12**
in science, **L1**: 119, 128-31
as name, **L16**: 260
processes of, **L16**: 308
Appraisal, **L8**: 220; **L16**: 311
valuation as, **L13**: 195, 209-11, 216, 223-24
related to prizing, **L13**: 212-13
of propositions, **L13**: 222, 237
of means and ends, **L13**: 229
of desires and ends-in-view, **L13**: 233, 238
Appreciation, **M8**: 25; **L1**: 70, 80, 110, 121, 150; **L12**: 176-79. *See also* Consummation, **L12**
related to values, **M7**: 45-46; **L8**: 195
in education, **M9**: 242-58; **L6**: 112-13, 117
Prall on, **M15**: 26, 340, 343
esthetic, **L1**: 159-60, 267-68, 278, 281-82; **L2**: 111-15; **L6**: 40, 45-46, 113; **L10**: 60-61, 181-82, 190, 203, 261, 280, 304
related to criticism, **L1**: 298-300; **L10**: 312, 320, 328
objects of, **L4**: 177, 238
achievement of, **L4**: 209, 214, 236, 241
in thinking, **L8**: 340-41
Apprehension, **M12**: 161-62; **L2**: 74n; **L13**: 194; **L16**: 192
immediate, **L12**: 92-94, 142-60, 168-70, 183, 418-19
realistic, **L12**: 168, 493-94
vs. comprehension, **L14**: 53-54
perceptual and conceptual, **L17**: 416n
Apprenticeship
earliest form of, **M9**: 10
as vocational education, **M9**: 321
Approbation, **E4**: 292-95
in moral theory, **L5**: 285-88; **L7**: 237, 253-55, 259-60, 309
as concept, **L7**: 182, 235
and standards, **L7**: 238-40, 246, 265
utilitarian theory of, **L7**: 242-43
as social, **L7**: 288-89, 302-3
motive of, **L17**: 3
A priori, **M7**: 286, 297; **M8**: 200; **L1**: 148; **L5**: xxviii-xxix, 215, 257n, 471-76; **L12**: xvii, xix, 18, 23, 28, 31, 47, 50, 106, 147, 155, 156, 389, 464, 497-98, 503, 522-24
Kant on, **M8**: 157-60
as philosophical issue, **M10**: 14
related to pragmatism, **M10**: 44
Russell on, **M10**: 93
necessity of, **L17**: 481
Apriorism, **M7**: 459
British empiricism as, **M10**: 48
Aptitude
disclosure of, **L17**: 512-13
Apuleius, Lucius, **M2**: 249
Aquinas, Saint Thomas. *See* Thomas Aquinas, Saint
Arabia
customs of, **M5**: 33; **L7**: 32

Arabs, **L8**: 6
Arbitration
prevents war, **M15**: 124
Arbitration, Permanent Court of. *See* Hague Tribunal
Architectonic, **L10**: 233, 235
Architects, **L10**: 231
Architecture, **E2**: 274-75; **L9**: 262; **L16**: 397
Byzantine and Turkish, **L2**: 191
in Leningrad, **L3**: 215
as expression of purpose, **L7**: 125-26
Roman, **L7**: 126
nature of, **L10**: 13, 36, 37, 58, 111-15, 130, 136, 147, 162-63, 168, 173-74, 180-89, 193, 200, 201, 207-8, 214-17, 222-26, 233-38, 242-45, 258, 270, 272, 300, 303, 321
transmits civilization, **L10**: 331-34, 344-48
Architecture of Humanism, The (G. Scott), **L10**: 133n
Archiv für Rechts- und Sozialphilosophie, **L14**: xxiv
Are Sanctions Necessary to International Organization? (Foreign Policy Assn.), **L6**: 196n, 450n
Argumentation, **M12**: 97, 132-33; **L11**: 515
Argumentation and Public Discussion (Pellegrini and B. Stirling), **L11**: 515
Aristippeans, **L2**: 133
Aristippus, **E5**: 352, 353; **M2**: 245
Aristo, **M2**: 186
Aristocracy, **M12**: 239-40; **L7**: 73; **L13**: 108
and peasantry, **E3**: 178-79
and democracy, **M13**: xii, 297-300; **L13**: 295
in U.S., **M13**: 290
intellectual, **M13**: 290, 297, 302-3
Aristophanes, **L7**: 98; **L17**: 182
Aristotelian logic, **M7**: 352, 438; **M8**: xi, 79; **L5**: 166-67, 244; **L8**: 6-7; **L12**: 49, 85, 130, 387; **L16**: 65, 145, 185
fundamental truths in, **M1**: 162, 164-65; **M2**: 196-97
compared with scientific method, **M1**: 172-74
induction and deduction in, **L12**: xxiv, 416-20
related to modern logic, **L12**: 86-102
definition in, **L12**: 91, 139-40, 239, 357
immutable objects in, **L12**: 133
predication in, **L12**: 139-41, 285
fixed species in, **L12**: 182-83, 260
affirmation and negation in, **L12**: 198
quantity in, **L12**: 201-2
kinds in, **L12**: 252-54
theory of syllogism in, **L12**: 323; **L16**: 270
three canons of, **L12**: 342-45
term in, **L12**: 347
Aristotelian physics, **L16**: 98, 104-5, 371
Aristotle, **E1**: xxxiii; **E3**: 91; **E4**: 130, 171n, 214, 215, 216, 371; **E5**: 141, 212, 213, 400; **M4**: 24; **M5**: 518; **M7**: xxii, 299; **M8**: 174; **M12**: xii, xvii, xxvii, 87, 89, 90, 111; **M15**: 200, 335, 336; **L1**: 53, 55, 58, 96, 162, 166, 178,

192, 335; **L2**: xxiv, 78-79, 86, 128, 241; **L3**: 7, 56; **L4**: xix; **L5**: 157, 230; **L6**: 31; **L7**: 104, 166, 266; **L9**: 240, 241, 243; **L10**: vii; **L11**: xxii, 565; **L13**: 58, 136, 160, 268; **L14**: 109, 123, 140, 193; **L16**: 124; **L17**: 5, 405
on body and soul, **E1**: 112, 114, 115
on matter, **E1**: 166, 348; **M7**: 292
on government, **E1**: 230; **M11**: 27; **L2**: 215, 321
on class system, **E1**: 247-48; **M3**: 286-87; **M4**: 33-34
influence of, **E1**: 257, 272, 280-81, 314, 319, 427; **E4**: 137-38; **M10**: 109-11; **L5**: 184-89; **L6**: 276; **L11**: 401; **L14**: 299, 304; **L17**: 433
Scholastics on, **E3**: 148-50
and intuitionalism, **E4**: 123, 125
on morality, **E4**: 124; **M5**: 16-17, 41; **L5**: 498; **L7**: 209
related to Stoics, **E4**: 139
on art, **E4**: 191-92; **L1**: 76-79, 86, 90
and acts, **E4**: 228; **M5**: 187-88
on concept of mean, **E4**: 245; **M5**: 126-27
philosophy of, **E5**: 8-9; **L1**: 33, 47-48; **L8**: 30-32
on metaphysics, **M2**: 14-15; **M7**: 277; **M8**: xi
on nature and experience, **M2**: 144-48; **M3**: 142; **M7**: 287-88; **M9**: 271-72, 287; **M11**: 344-45; **M12**: 125-26; **M13**: 362, 367, 368, 370n, 371, 389; **L7**: 111-12, 130; **L11**: 71-75, 83
on necessity, **M2**: 151
on noetic, **M2**: 156
on non-being, **M2**: 157
on opinion, **M2**: 173
on organism, **M2**: 178
on passion, **M2**: 186
on reality, **M2**: 220-21; **M3**: 393; **M7**: 225; **M10**: 345; **M12**: 140-41
on subject-matter, **M2**: 249; **M6**: 379
on unity, **M2**: 262-63
on vacuum, **M2**: 268
on ethics, **M3**: 48-49; **M10**: 416; **L1**: 323; **L15**: 265, 417
on man, **M3**: 89
on intelligence, **M3**: 90
attitude toward work, **M3**: 292
on species, **M4**: 5; **L4**: 130
on state and individual, **M4**: 32-33; **M5**: 120-22
on good, **M5**: 118-19, 126, 293; **M11**: 387; **M14**: 26; **L7**: 109-10, 117, 121, 271, 287
on high-mindedness, **M5**: 127n
on ideal, **M5**: 130; **M14**: 200, 201
on means and ends, **M5**: 255; **M14**: 154; **L1**: 277; **L4**: 194, 225
on intelligent action, **M5**: 278n
on justice, **M5**: 374, 408
on truth, **M6**: 33, 35n; **L1**: 123
and activity, **M6**: 361
on similarity, **M6**: 388
on evolution, **M6**: 443-44
on knowledge, **M7**: 116-17, 354-55; **M10**: 360, 368; **M11**: 342; **M12**: 143; **M14**: 130; **L4**: xv, 14, 32; **L11**: 404, 405; **L16**: 157-60
on mind, **M7**: 215

Aristotle (*continued*)
on education, **M7**: 271-72; **M9**: 261-63; **M13**: 400
on science, **M7**: 313; **L8**: 33; **L15**: 84, 93, 190, 267-68; **L17**: 352, 565
on syllogism, **M7**: 349-51
on state, **M7**: 407; **M12**: 104; **L2**: 39, 40, 238-39; **L7**: 112, 120, 130; **L14**: 400
on existence, **M8**: xi, 6n-7n
on mechanical occupation, **M9**: 264
on slavery, **M9**: 297; **M12**: 177-78, 189; **M13**: 289; **M14**: 78; **L6**: 32-33; **L13**: 287
on Plato's theory of moral virtue, **M9**: 364-65
Dewey's reply to D. Robinson on, **M10**: 100-101
on liberty, **M11**: 20
Bacon's charge against, **M12**: 96-100
on potentiality, **M12**: 112, 113; **L5**: 252, 289
on change, **M12**: 141
on excellence, **M14**: 122; **L7**: 118
on objects, **L1**: 138
on individualism, **L2**: 34; **L7**: 111-19, 132, 391
vs. Plato, **L2**: 131; **L8**: 23-24, 26
on reasoning, **L4**: x, xxi, 145n
First Philosophy of, **L4**: 12-13
on social arts, **L4**: 61
forms of, **L4**: 74
on substance, **L4**: 96
on bliss, **L4**: 220
on hypotheses, **L5**: 456
on poetry, **L6**: 17
as church philosopher, **L6**: 426
on *eudaimonia*, **L7**: 197
on friendship, **L7**: 450
attitude toward, **L8**: xivn
on universal, **L8**: 4-5; **L11**: 107
on politics, **L8**: 36; **L13**: 73, 118
Whitehead on, **L8**: 359
on esthetics, **L10**: xvii, xviii, xxv, 47, 102n, 192, 225, 231, 288-90, 293, 321, 357, 363
on method, **L11**: 128-29
on authority, **L11**: 134
Hutchins on, **L11**: 391, 393-95, 400, 407, 592-95
on taxes, **L13**: 290
Cohen on, **L14**: 387, 391-92, 394, 398
on accidental qualities, **L15**: 43
anti-naturalism of, **L15**: 46, 56, 234-35
Dubislav on, **L16**: 161n
essences of, **L16**: 180
tradition of, **L16**: 253, 388

Arithmetic. *See also* Mathematics
Fine on, **E5**: 427
teaching of, **M1**: 47; **L17**: 295
Dewey-McLellan method of, **L5**: 461
imagination in, **L17**: 246-49
attention in, **L17**: 276-77
Grube on, **L17**: 291, 563-64
errors in, **L17**: 303
Herbartians on, **L17**: 310
in Germany, **L17**: 311

Armaments
discussed at Washington Conference, **M13**: 173-74, 204-5

Armenia, **M11**: 245, 309

Armenians
in Turkey, **M15**: 132, 139-42, 144-45, 147-48

Armory exhibition (New York City), **L10**: 306-7

Arnauld, Antoine, **L12**: xi

Arnold, Matthew, **M7**: 290, 322; **L1**: 159, 362; **L6**: 289; **L7**: 170; **L9**: 36-37; **L15**: 156, 169
  on poetry, **E3**: 110-11; **L10**: 304-5, 349, 365
  sense of isolation in, **E3**: 115-17
  compared with Stoics, **E3**: 117-18
  compared with Browning, **E3**: 119-23
  on education, **M1**: 23; **M6**: 70-71; **M13**: 329
  skepticism of, **M2**: 233
  on two selves of men, **M5**: 306
  on culture, **M6**: 405-6; **M10**: 403; **M13**: 400
  on religious experience, **L9**: xiv-xv, xvii-xviii, xxiv-xxv, xxvii
  on Marcus Aurelius, **L9**: xxxi-xxxii
  on art, **L10**: 53, 355
  on life, **L10**: 342, 366
Art, **M11**: xiv; **M12**: 98, 139, 200-201, 228; **M13**: 209-10; **M14**: 111-13, 180; **L4**: 15, 21, 76, 218; **L8**: xviii, 62, 88. *See also* Esthetics; Fine art; Works of art
  freedom in, **E2**: 269-70; **L11**: 61
  related to science, **E3**: 123, 317-20; **M1**: 54; **L4**: 61, 128, 165; **L6**: 67; **L7**: 72-73; **L15**: 85-89
  purpose of, **E3**: 234-35; **L4**: 108, 119, 188, 194; **L10**: 323-25, 347-52; **L17**: 540-41
  Bosanquet on, **E4**: 190
  Plato and, **E4**: 191, 192, 196
  Plotinus on, **E4**: 192
  Christian thought on, **E4**: 192-93
  teaching of, **E5**: xciv-xcvi, 95, 337; **M1**: 52-53, 261-82; **M4**: 206-8; **L11**: 195, 503-4, 556; **L17**: 245, 286, 288-89
  children's, **M1**: 29-30; **L11**: 244, 246
  and experience and nature, **M2**: ix; **M13**: 365; **L1**: 266-94; **L6**: 331-33, 493-99; **L10**: 11-18, 25, 26
  primitive, **M2**: 48-49; **L11**: 244, 522
  ethics as, **M3**: 42
  links leisure and industry, **M3**: 293
  Santayana on, **M4**: 237-39; **M6**: 375; **M10**: 307
  F. Schiller on, **M5**: 45; **L7**: 42
  social, **M5**: 48-49; **L4**: 32, 61; **L7**: 45-47
  and individualism, **M5**: 78-80; **L5**: 89; **L7**: 72-73; **L14**: 36-38, 113-14
  attitudes toward, **M5**: 145-46
  useful vs. fine, **M7**: xxviii-xxix; **M9**: 242-44; **L10**: xi, xxxii, 33-34, 265, 343-44
  influence of, **M7**: 40-43; **L7**: 41-42, 45-46, 147-48; **L12**: 77-80; **L13**: 69-70, 169-71, 366-67
  as exemplifying ideal of interest, **M9**: 142-43, 213-14
  in education, **M9**: 246-47; **M11**: 66, 81; **L2**: xx-xxi, 111-15, 375-77; **L5**: 6-7
  Aristotle's conception of, **M9**: 262
  localism in, **M12**: 15-16
  military, **M12**: 88
  of educational engineering, **M13**: 325-26
  useful, **M13**: 362-64; **L1**:

Art (*continued*)
101-11, 119, 120, 271, 282-83, 290-91
habits as, **M14**: 15-16, 47-48, 51, 118
Turkish schools for, **M15**: 295
and judgment, **M15**: 340
Greek, **L1**: 76-81; **L4**: 73, 122, 203; **L7**: 97-98, 100, 126; **L8**: 3-4; **L10**: 31-32
as criticism of life, **L1**: 159
romantic, **L1**: 282
nature of, **L2**: 107-8; **L6**: 15, 492-94; **L10**: viii-xxxiii, 11-13, 30-41, 49, 68, 73-74, 83-91, 107-11, 118, 121, 122, 133, 138-39, 146-51, 153-57, 166, 168, 181, 187-89, 191-217, 256, 258, 264, 272, 284-85, 295-301, 327; **L13**: 358-60; **L15**: xxiii, 97-100, 313-14; **L16**: 327, 330, 366, 369-70, 372, 395-98, 417-18, 464
biological conceptions in, **L2**: 109-10
in Mexico, **L2**: 202-5, 208-9
of communication, **L2**: 349-50; **L10**: 274-75, 291
African, **L2**: 384
medicine as, **L3**: 26
gains security, **L4**: 3-4, 7, 8, 24, 69
as value, **L4**: 26, 212; **L8**: 85-86
liberal and mechanical, **L4**: 37, 60-61, 65, 214, 215
ideals in, **L4**: 211, 241
methods of, **L4**: 223, 230, 237
appreciation of, **L6**: 40, 45-46, 113
as aspect of culture, **L6**: 42
historical place of, **L6**: 43
Tate on, **L6**: 330-34, 492-501
order in, **L7**: 42
Roman, **L7**: 125-26
power of, **L8**: 348; **L10**: 9, 24, 101, 138, 204-5, 233, 235, 243, 249, 307, 315, 328
related to activity, **L10**: 53-54, 178, 189-90, 218, 227, 233, 248, 261; **L15**: 315-17
as unifying, **L10**: 142, 204, 252-53, 264, 272-75
influences on, **L10**: 163, 255, 268, 304, 319-21
variety in, **L10**: 218-49, 300-303, 307-8, 314-17
as make-believe, **L10**: 279-81, 284
as play, **L10**: 281-85
as representation, **L10**: 288-90
as mode of knowledge, **L10**: 293-95
transmits civilization, **L10**: 329-48
mysticism in, **L11**: 85
tradition of, **L11**: 117, 523-24
Abell vs. Barnes on, **L11**: 487-88
decorative, **L11**: 520-25
and religion, **L13**: 70
movement in, **L13**: 365
vision of future in, **L14**: 113-14
Jefferson on, **L14**: 208
significance of, **L14**: 255-57; **L16**: 372, 407; **L17**: 344
C. and M. Beard on, **L14**: 283-85
Rice on, **L15**: 419-24
philosophy as, **L16**: 369
Romanell on, **L16**: 466-67
Art as Experience, **M1**: xi; **M7**: xi; **M12**: xv; **M15**: x; **L12**: 372n; **L14**: x, 34, 35, 38; **L15**: 98, 509
Kaplan on, **L10**: vii-xxxiii

contributions to, **L10**: 7-8, 353, 360
Croce on, **L15**: 97, 439-43
Rice on, **L15**: 421-22
on esthetic experience, **L16**: 395-97, 465-67
"Art as Our Heritage," **L14**: xix
Artefacts
in inquiry, **L16**: 326-27
role of, **L16**: 330
Art historians, **L10**: 293
Arthur, James, **L14**: 98n
Arthurdale, W.Va.
school at, **L14**: 351, 353
Articles of Confederation, **L6**: 463, 464
Articulation, **L5**: 506
methods for achieving, in school, **L5**: 299-310
of facts and ideas, **L13**: 50
Artificiality
in education, **L13**: 15, 39-40
in German schools, **L17**: 311
Art in Education
in *Cyclopedia of Education*, **M6**: 375-79
"Art in Education—and Education in Art," **L2**: xxi
Art in Painting, The (A. Barnes), **L10**: 98, 122n, 178n, 361; **L11**: 487-88; **L17**: 128
Artisans, **M12**: 86-88, 116, 143; **L10**: 343; **L16**: 471
tradition of, **L2**: 57-58
discipline of, **L2**: 128-31
influence of mass production on, **L5**: 60
Socrates on, **L16**: 376
Artistic
interest, **E4**: 301n
vs. esthetic, **L10**: xxix, 53-61, 125, 355
achievement of, **L10**: 69, 76, 78, 141, 266
Artistic expression
teaching of, **E5**: 192-201
Artists, **L13**: 171; **L15**: 313
teachers as, **M6**: 355; **L8**: 348-49
in corporate society, **L5**: 60-61
creative process of, **L10**: xiii, xxiii, xxvii-xxxi, 33, 38, 52-58, 60, 73, 74, 80-81, 89, 92-101, 110-12, 116-17, 123, 126n, 187-88, 200, 203-10, 219, 243, 307-8, 328
criticized, **L10**: 13, 305, 315-16, 332
nature of, **L10**: 15, 21, 229-31, 303, 343-44
interests and attitudes of, **L10**: 134, 143-44, 151, 157, 163, 165, 178, 193-94, 250, 260, 263, 267-75, 284-88, 291-94, 298, 309-10, 316-17, 320-27, 337, 347
technique of, **L10**: 145-49
balance in, **L13**: 365
individuality of, **L17**: 128
Art of Henri-Matisse, The (A. Barnes), **L10**: 98n, 123n, 178n
Art of Renoir, The (A. Barnes and de Mazia), **L11**: 501
Art of Thinking, The (Dimnet), **L3**: 316-17
Art of Thought, The (Wallas), **L2**: xxii, 160, 231-34, 404
Art product
nature of, **L10**: xv-xvi, xxi-xxiii, xxix, 143, 174, 177, 181, 183, 186, 195, 208, 210, 305, 308
related to experience, **L10**: 9-12, 15, 17

Art product (*continued*)
role of, **L10**: 33-34, 55, 111-14, 127, 221, 330, 334
vs. work of art, **L10**: 167, 218
Arts and crafts
as rationalizing agencies, **M5**: 44-45
Asceticism, **M7**: 212
as end, **L7**: 203-8, 212
result of, **L7**: 448
Ascoli, Max, **L11**: 563
Ashmead, Warren G., **L9**: 353
Asia, **M12**: 227; **L15**: 61, 208, 370
as Yellow Peril, **M12**: 35
national consciousness of, **M12**: 35-37
Asia Minor, **M15**: 136, 139, 144; **L8**: 20
As I See It (N. Thomas), **L9**: 69
Aspect
as name, **L16**: 5n, 73n, 83n-84n, 259-60
Asserted universality, **L9**: 419
Assertibility. *See* Warranted assertibility
Assertion, **L12**: 109-11, 137, 283; **L16**: 40. *See also* Warranted assertion
vs. proposal of Carnap, **L9**: 304
and affirmation, **L12**: 123
and judgment, **L14**: 175
Assimilation
school causes, **M2**: 84-86
in thought, **L5**: 261
Associated Charities, **E4**: 56
Associated Press, **L11**: 127, 271
Association, **M6**: 388; **L3**: 43-44
in British psychology, **E1**: 183-84
traits of, **E2**: 83-99, 104, 106-7; **L2**: 250-51
in psychical life, **E2**: 101-3
unconscious cerebration in, **E2**: 104
and attention, **E2**: 117
in recollection, **E2**: 156, 159-60
in intellectual feeling, **E2**: 258
related to motor impulses, **E2**: 326-28
as universal fact, **L2**: 249-50, 257, 330, 348
revolt against, **L2**: 290, 296-97
economic, **L2**: 300-302
and democracy, **L2**: 325
vs. community, **L2**: 330-31
domination by, **L2**: 356
territorial and functional, **L2**: 468
of ideas, **L5**: 255-62; **L17**: 330-32
formation of, **L7**: 299, 324-25, 424-25
and individuality, **L13**: 181
Lewis on, **L16**: 37
Hume on, **L16**: 305
related to habit, **L17**: 204-6
Associationalism, **M2**: 245
and relativity of knowledge, **E1**: 19-20
Associational psychology, **L5**: 169; **L10**: 104-7
Associationism
James on, **L14**: 156, 158
Association of American Medical Colleges, **L6**: 120
Association of American Universities, **M8**: 109n; **M10**: 151n; **L6**: 120
Association of Collegiate Alumnae
reports on women, **L17**: 8-9, 553
Association of Commerce, **L5**: 372, 373

Assumption of the Virgin (Titian), **L10**: 97; **L13**: 363
As the Twig Is Bent (Welling), **L17**: 523
Astronomy, **M12**: 116-17, 122-23, 144-45, 237, 262, 264; **L15**: 268-69
  Cohen on, **L14**: 388
  rise of, **L16**: 159, 289, 338-40, 369, 414, 453, 455
  nature of, **L16**: 316, 355-57, 363-64, 372
  impact of, **L16**: 408-9
  revolution in, **L17**: 456
Asymmetry
  of terms, **L12**: 332-33
As You Like It (Shakespeare), **L10**: 102; **L17**: 563
Ataraxy
  related to moral theory, **M5**: 202
Atatürk, Kemal, **M15**: xix, 137
Atheism, **M7**: 353; **M11**: 21
  aggressive, **L9**: xvii, xxx, 36
Athens, Greece, **M12**: 86-87, 90, 258; **L2**: 125, 126; **L8**: 3, 4, 6, 20, 21; **L14**: 316; **L15**: 263-65, 266
  responsibility in, **E4**: 38-39
  community of, **E4**: 139
  art in, **L10**: 10, 13, 114-15, 252, 321, 331
  education in, **L17**: 175-77
  culture in, **L17**: 227
  morality in, **L17**: 394
Atlantic Charter, **L15**: 174-75, 509
Atlantic Monthly, **M15**: xvii, 115, 381
Atlantic Ocean, **L8**: 117
Atomic bomb, **L16**: 365
  threat of, **L15**: 199-205
Atomic individualism, **L5**: 152
Atomicity
  vs. continuity, **L14**: 134
Atomic realism, **L12**: 150-53
Atomism, **M6**: 175
  logical, **M10**: 13; **M12**: 236
  defined, **M12**: xiv
  ethical, **M14**: 167
  Greek, **L14**: 193
  Dewey opposes, **L17**: xxx
Atomistic pluralism, **M7**: 349; **M10**: 107
Atomists, **L2**: 139
  on necessity, **M2**: 151
  on non-being, **M2**: 157
  on vacuum, **M2**: 267
Atoms
  Leibniz on, **E1**: 359-60
  fission of, **L2**: 380-81
  lack individuality, **L14**: 103
Atonement, **M8**: 151
  meaning of, **E4**: 367
Attachment
  political need of, **L2**: 322, 368-69
"Attack on Western Morality, The" (Benda), **L15**: 19
Attention, **M7**: 452; **M13**: 339; **L1**: 235; **L10**: 268
  and association, **E2**: 117
  and activity, **E2**: 118-30, 181; **E4**: 93
  nature of, **E2**: 129-30; **E5**: 163; **L17**: 272-73
  division of, **E5**: 118-20
  and effort, **E5**: 163
  and interest, **E5**: 320-21; **M7**: 253-54
  and emotion, **E5**: 323
  non-voluntary, voluntary, and reflective, **M1**: 100-103; **M4**: 201-3
  in children, **M3**: 254; **L11**: 213
  importance of, **L17**: 201-2, 283

Attention (*continued*)
and habit, **L17**: 207-9
directed by teacher, **L17**: 266-67, 270-71
related to mind, **L17**: 269, 274-75
end needed for, **L17**: 271-72
in manual work, **L17**: 278-79
concentration of, **L17**: 280-81, 332
related to accuracy, **L17**: 304, 328
Attitude, **L15**: 128-29, 210. *See also* Habit
formation of, **M6**: 223; **L8**: 136-39, 164-65; **L13**: 19, 21-22, 29, 96-97, 185-86, 266, 284, 310; **L17**: 456
logic in, **M6**: 268; **L8**: 218-19
denotation of, **M13**: 4
motor-affecto, **M13**: 27
in education, **M13**: 328; **L9**: 159-60
toward race, **L7**: 66
in judgment, **L7**: 242
of corporations, **L7**: 425
change in, **L7**: 446-50; **L17**: 457, 514
importance of, **L8**: 134-35
of artist, **L8**: 348
religion vs. religious, **L9**: xxvi, 12-13, 16-20, 30-31, 56, 423-25, 429-30, 434, 436
secular vs. religious, **L9**: 44-45
scientific, **L9**: 99-100; **L13**: 271-75, 279-80
effect of education on, **L11**: 233, 550
of pupils, **L13**: 6, 35
in democracy, **L13**: 100, 153-54, 379
absolutistic, **L13**: 117
causes development, **L17**: 401
realistic, **L17**: 452
Attributes, **L12**: 259n, 296-98, 354, 357-58
in Spinoza's *Ethics*, **E1**: 11-15
Aubrey, Edwin Ewart, **L9**: 294, 426n, 435-38
Augustan Age, **L5**: 100
Augustine, Saint, **M7**: 339; **M8**: 142; **M12**: 144; **L7**: 135; **L8**: 24, 357; **L9**: 71; **L11**: xvn; **L14**: xix
on ontological argument, **M2**: 168-69
on state, **M5**: 141
on divine will, **M7**: 292-93
moral theory of, **L15**: 47, 54-55
Austen, Jane, **L10**: 176
Austin, J. L., **L3**: xix, xxxii
Austin, John, **E1**: 229, 236; **E4**: xxi, 70-90; **L3**: 326, 327; **L6**: 269, 270; **L8**: 35; **L14**: xxii, 120
Austin, Mary, **M13**: 323
"Austin's Theory of Sovereignty," **L14**: xxii
Australia
aborigines of, **M2**: 42
corroboree of, **M2**: 48-49; **L7**: 46, 56
class system of, **M5**: 26-28, 35; **L7**: 26-27, 33
customs of, **L7**: 33-34, 52, 55-56, 59, 60
Australia, from Port Macquarie to Moreton Bay (Hodgkinson), **M2**: 45n
Austria, **M15**: 93, 123, 316, 380, 394, 402
folk-psychologist school of, **M10**: 57
Poland's relation with, **M11**: xiv, 251, 262-64, 266, 268-74, 277, 278, 282, 284, 285, 289, 294, 297, 327-30

Austria-Hungary, **M11**: xii-xiii, 266, 273
Authoritarianism, **M12**: 239
Authoritative discipline, **M8**: 295
Authority, **M12**: 106-7, 160, 191-92; **M14**: 4-5, 47-48, 52, 56-58, 131, 162, 222; **L4**: 76, 110, 245; **L13**: 154
  in intellectual matters, **E3**: 125
  of state, **M5**: 31-32; **L7**: 30-31
  of group, **M5**: 55; **L7**: 50-52
  in Israel, **M5**: 93; **L7**: 86
  in Greece, **M5**: 109-17; **L7**: 99-108
  and freedom, **M9**: 314-15, 348-49; **L11**: 130-31, 136-45
  seat of, **M12**: 171
  final, **M12**: 172
  and tradition, **L2**: 58, 59; **L15**: 189-90, 366
  conflict of, **L4**: 40-59, 247
  imposition from, **L4**: 155, 182, 248, 249
  of science, **L4**: 157
  means of gaining, **L4**: 200, 201
  religious, **L4**: 203-5; **L7**: 135-37, 413; **L10**: 332; **L15**: 230-31, 235
  for values, **L4**: 210, 215-22, 225-27, 250
  Roman, **L7**: 130-34
  of law, **L7**: 182, 216, 220, 227
  moral, **L7**: 215-16, 226-27, 329-30; **L15**: 173-77, 201-2
  in marriage, **L7**: 458
  role of, in criticism, **L10**: 303-5, 309
  and individual, **L11**: 132-41; **L13**: 33-34, 295
  historical concepts of, **L11**: 133-37
  scientific vs. religious, **L11**: 454-63
  of teacher, **L13**: xiv, 58
  source of, **L13**: 8, 148; **L16**: 353, 362-63, 369, 373, 392, 400
  culture identified with, **L13**: 83-85
  of truth, **L13**: 127, 157
  methods of, **L13**: 187
  of ideas, **L13**: 258
  of printed word, **L13**: 393
  in medieval society, **L15**: 265-67
  standards provide, **L16**: 338, 453
  restricts inquiry, **L16**: 339, 455
  liberals on, **L17**: 442
  good vs. bad, **L17**: 443
"Authority and Social Change," **L11**: xvi
Autobiography (J. S. Mill), **L9**: 23
Autobiography of a Philosopher, The (G. Palmer), **L6**: 271
Autocracy
  aim of education in, **M9**: 320
Automatic arts, **L10**: 231-32
Automatism, **M7**: 203
Autonomy, **M12**: 249
  Kant on, **L7**: 155
  of logical theory, **L12**: 28-29, 158n
  industrial, **L13**: 313-14
Auto-suggestion
  related to cure, **M15**: 43, 44
Averroës
  on nature, **M2**: 147
  pantheism of, **M2**: 183, 242
Awareness, **L1**: 143
  as fact, **M4**: 125-37
  as attention, **M4**: 138-42, 314
  related to consciousness, **M7**: 80-81, 452-53; **L17**: 549
  Woodbridge on, **L17**: 549
Axiom, **L4**: xix-xx, 113, 145n; **L12**: 23-26, 401-4

Axiom (*continued*)
as postulate, **L11**: 155
as self-evident truth, **L12**: 18, 144
vs. observation, **L16**: 48
Einstein on, **L16**: 76n
as foundation, **L16**: 165n
Axis, **L15**: 207, 354
need to defeat, **L17**: 524, 525
Ayer, Alfred J., **L13**: 196-97, 402; **L14**: xv; **L16**: 166
Ayres, Clarence Edwin, **L2**: 272n; **L5**: 86; **L15**: xv; **L17**: 558
on science, **L3**: 305-10
on industrial revolution, **L9**: 50
on economics, **L15**: 89n, 108n, 359-60, 448n, 502-6
on future, **L17**: 87

Babbitt, Irving, **L5**: xxx, xxxi, 264, 265
Background
mind forms, **L10**: 269, 270
Back to Methuselah (Shaw), **L14**: 347
Backus, Burdette, **L11**: 583n
Bacon, Francis, **E1**: 48, 268, 269, 271, 275, 305; **M1**: 159; **M3**: 132n; **M4**: 254; **M6**: 175; **M7**: 120, 345; **M8**: 144; **M10**: 3; **M11**: 43; **M13**: 497, 498; **M15**: 318, 327; **L1**: 14; **L2**: 20, 389; **L3**: 3; **L5**: xxx, xxxi, 154, 264, 265; **L6**: 59, 426; **L8**: 8, 31; **L12**: 44; **L13**: 166, 402; **L15**: 13, 93; **L17**: 411
and empiricism, **E1**: 35; **L14**: 390, 392
on science, **M1**: 171; **M6**: 207, 446; **M9**: 291-92; **L7**: 144, 145; **L8**: 143; **L11**: 393; **L13**: 161-63
on controlling nature, **M5**: 154; **M7**: 390
on fallacious belief, **M6**: 198; **L8**: 131-32
realism of, **M7**: 231
system of induction of, **M7**: 240-41
on progress, **M7**: 332
on experience, **M9**: 275; **M12**: 126, 135-36; **L11**: 76; **L14**: 191; **L17**: 437, 566
on knowledge, **M9**: 301; **M12**: 95-98, 103, 108; **M13**: 310; **L11**: 141
on common law, **M11**: 28
idealism of, **M11**: 344
on truth, **M13**: 307
on ethics, **L7**: 15
on beauty, **L10**: 144, 359
on inquiry, **L11**: 52, 53; **L14**: 69
Dewey compared with, **L11**: xvn
Cohen on, **L14**: 407
Bacon, Roger, **M5**: 153; **M6**: 446; **L1**: 14, 15, 81; **L6**: 426; **L7**: 144; **L8**: xvii; **L11**: 76
Badia, Miquel y, Collection (Cooper Union Museum), **L11**: 520
Badness
as potential, **E3**: 379-80
Bagehot, Walter, **M11**: 145; **L7**: 43, 51
on cooperation, **M5**: 45n
on primitive society, **M5**: 56
Bagley, William C.
on Dewey's educational philosophy, **M8**: 414-15, 465-70
Bailey, Benjamin, **L10**: 39
Bain, Alexander, **E1**: 110; **E3**: 85; **M3**: 55; **M5**: 388; **M6**: 93, 300-301; **M10**: 417; **L1**: 158; **L2**: 7n; **L8**: 276

on mind, **E1**: 133-134, 140
theory of obligation of, **E3**: 328-30; **E4**: 330-35
on emotion, **M3**: 139
on happiness, **M5**: 242
on social good, **M5**: 261
on duty, **M5**: 321-23
on knowledge, **M6**: 112
on nature of act and thought, **M10**: 108n
G. Morris on, **M10**: 112
on pleasure, **L7**: 191-92
Baker, J. H., **E3**: 190-92
Baker, Oliver Edwin, **L6**: 361
Bakewell, Charles Montague, **M15**: 336
on Dewey's empiricism, **M3**: 168-70, 390-92
on knowledge experience, **M3**: 181-83
Bakmetiev, Boris, **L17**: 509, 572
Balance
as esthetic quality, **E5**: 202; **L10**: 20, 22, 51-52, 55, 66, 75, 120, 160-61, 177, 183-85, 189, 208, 217, 261
of sexes, **L17**: 24
lack of, **L17**: 458-59
Balance of power, **M11**: 101, 137, 392
Balch, Emily Greene, **L17**: 149-50
Baldwin, James Mark, **E4**: 187; **E5**: xiii, 350; **M2**: ix, 141n; **M10**: 71n, 74; **L16**: 20n, 43, 163, 297n
on social psychology, **E5**: lxxxvi-xciv, 385-422
on reactive consciousness, **E5**: 100-101
on effort, **E5**: 160
works on *Johnson's Cyclopaedia*, **E5**: 348-49
on Tarde's theory of society, **M7**: 236
Tarde's influence on, **M10**: 54
Baldwin, Roger N., **L9**: 206; **L15**: xxv
Baldwin, William A., **M15**: 187
Balfour, Arthur James, **M10**: 83; **M12**: 3; **M13**: 198, 202, 273
Balkan States, **M11**: 136; **M15**: 139, 143; **L6**: 461, 468n
Baltic Sea, **M11**: 266
Baltic States, **L15**: 296, 342
Balz, Albert G. A.
Dewey's reply to, **L16**: xxxiin, 5, 280-94
on doctrine of possibility, **L16**: 423-42
Balzac, Honoré de, **M5**: 145, 175-76
Banfi, Antonio, **L14**: 308
Bank of the United States v. Deveaux, **L2**: 36n
Banks, **L9**: 285
related to China, **M13**: 124, 160-61
in economic crisis, **L9**: 114-15
F. Roosevelt and, **L9**: 254, 255
moratorium on, **L9**: 254, 269
People's Lobby on crisis in, **L9**: 254-55
programs urged by, **L9**: 275
vs. congressional measures, **L9**: 288
"Baptism" (McKay), **L17**: 59-60
Barbarians
culture of, **M9**: 288-89; **L17**: 436
attitude of, toward mind, **M9**: 301
Lenin's semi-Asiatic, **L17**: 498, 569-70
Barcelona, Spain
labor conventions at, **M15**: 400
Barclay, Thomas, **M11**: 133
Bargaining power
in industry, **L7**: 392-401

Barker, Ernest, **L2**: 40, 42
Barkley, Alben W., **L6**: 346
Barnard, H. E., **L17**: 511, 519, 572, 573
Barnard, Henry, **M1**: xvii; **M3**: 230; **L9**: 167, 390; **L13**: 297
Barnes, Albert C., **L2**: 114, 115; **L6**: xii, 333, 499; **L8**: 363; **L15**: 99-100; **L17**: 128
  in Polish study, **M11**: xiv-xv, 259-60, 395, 398, 399, 401n, 403-5
  on art, **L2**: 108-10; **L10**: 98, 99, 122, 123, 178n, 205, 224-25, 358; **L11**: 487-88, 501
  contributes to *Art as Experience*, **L10**: xxxvii, 7-8, 353, 360
  interest in Russell case, **L14**: 357
Barnes, Earl, **M1**: 214
Barnes, Harry Elmer, **L2**: 40n, 42; **L5**: 382-83
Barnes, Roswell P., **L3**: 346
Barnes Foundation (Merion, Pa.), **L2**: 55n, 104n, 114, 115, 382-85; **L10**: 8, 356, 361; **L11**: 501, 505; **L14**: xxi, 357
Barnwell Address, **L6**: 99-111
Baroque art, **L10**: 157, 290
Barras, Charles M., **L17**: 555
Barrie, James Matthew, **L10**: xvii
Barry, Frederick, **L4**: 78-79, 122-23, 128n
Bartlett, A. C., **M1**: 317
Bartley, Samuel Howard, **L16**: 140n
Basal Concepts in Philosophy (Ormond), **E5**: 342, 345-46
Baseness, **E3**: 376-77
"Basis for Hope, The," **L14**: xviii
Bates, Henry M., **L6**: 120-21
Baudelaire, Charles, **E3**: 37
Bawden, H. Heath, **L15**: 305, 307
Bayer, Adam, **L9**: 361
Bayer, Herbert, **L15**: xxiii, 312
Bayle, Pierre, **E1**: 303, 421
Baylis, Charles A., **L16**: 38n
Beals, Carleton, **L11**: 313-14; **L13**: 347, 395, 404; **L15**: 493, 499
Beard, Charles A., **M5**: 419n; **M6**: xii; **L3**: 115n; **L6**: xvi, xx; **L11**: 250, 603; **L14**: 283-85
  resigns from Columbia University, **M10**: xxxiv, 165, 166
  on civics textbooks, **M10**: 194
Beard, Mary R., **L14**: 283-85
Beatification, **L10**: 157
Beati possidentes, **L9**: 205
Beauty, **L11**: 107; **L15**: 123-24; **L17**: 344
  sensuous element in, **E2**: 269
  universality of, **E2**: 270-72
  and harmony, **E2**: 273
  in art, **E4**: 190-91; **L13**: 360, 366
  Greek idea of, **L7**: 102
  quality of, **L10**: xiv, xx, xxiii, 40-41, 83, 112, 119-20, 135-36, 144, 166, 174, 189, 203, 227, 253-57, 265, 271, 289, 299, 300, 344
  function of, **L10**: 295-97
Beauty and Ugliness (Paget and Anstruther-Thomson), **L10**: 357
Beck, James Montgomery, **L2**: 179, 403
Becker, Carl L., **L14**: 371
Becker, Frank, **L17**: 527-28
Becoming
  and future, **L2**: 65-66
Beebe, William, **L16**: 147

Beers, Clifford, **L17**: 146, 562
Beethoven, Ludwig van, **L10**: 117, 212, 227; **L13**: 292, 358
Beginnings, **L1**: 83, 271
Begun, Isidore, **L9**: 320-22, 329, 337
Behavior, **M11**: 10-17; **L13**: 200, 221; **L15**: 102-3
standards in, **M6**: 223; **L8**: 165
instinctive, **M10**: 55
inference related to, **M10**: 90-97
as directed by speech, **M13**: xiv, 34
affects epistemology, **M13**: 29
coordination of, **M13**: 38
analysis of, **M13**: 39
and action, **L3**: 31-33
interaction of, **L3**: 35; **L17**: 419-20
meaning as quality of, **L3**: 36-38
conjoint, **L3**: 41-42
levels of, **L7**: 12
social, **L7**: 288-89, 302-3; **L14**: 117-18
self-interest in, **L13**: 74, 75, 140
influences on, **L13**: 193; **L17**: 427
liking and disliking as, **L13**: 202
valuations of, **L13**: 209, 237, 239, 247, 249-50; **L16**: 310, 316, 344-45, 351-52, 355
role of, in perception, **L14**: 20-21, 24-25
vs. deliberation, **L14**: 64-65, 69
determinative of experience, **L14**: 185-86
meaning of term, **L15**: 32-33
naturalist on, **L15**: 110-11
Bentley on, **L16**: xxiii
inquiry into, **L16**: 47, 73, 78-82, 101, 110, 127-30, 193n, 443, 474
as name, **L16**: 64n, 260, 447
kinds of, **L16**: 90, 133-35, 139-41, 273, 347, 472
theory of, **L16**: 94, 443
Dewey on, **L16**: 116n
characteristics of, **L16**: 135-39, 182-83
in semiotic, **L16**: 211-17, 221, 231, 235-37
C. Morris on, **L16**: 223-25
namings for, **L16**: 264-71
transactional, **L16**: 275-76, 326-28, 331, 335, 352, 473
in inquiry, **L16**: 282, 320-26, 338-39
emotional-volitional, **L16**: 312-13, 314n
intelligent, **L16**: 325, 328, 333-36, 448-51; **L17**: 417
directed, **L16**: 356
related to apprehension, **L17**: 416n
Behavior, Knowledge, Fact (A. Bentley), **L14**: 186n; **L16**: ix-x, xii, xvii, xix-xxiv, xxviii, xxxv, 318, 444
Behavior-agent
as name, **L16**: 68, 71, 259
Behavioral
sciences, **L16**: 64, 70, 122-26
event, **L16**: 69, 84-87
as name, **L16**: 260, 445
activities, **L16**: 298, 299n, 300, 303-9, 333, 448
attitudes, **L16**: 314
Behaviorism, **M13**: xiv, 39, 392; **L2**: 15, 19; **L5**: 218-28, 234-35, 483; **L16**: xv-xvi, xx, 79n
as American, **L3**: 79
Dewey's, **L3**: 370-71; **L14**: 39

Behaviorism (*continued*)
and language, **L3**: 388, 402
and consciousness, **L3**: 396-97
related to James's psychology, **L14**: 158-60, 166, 338
Behavioristic movement
influences social psychology, **M10**: 56-58
Behaviorists, **L13**: 328
Behavior-object, **L16**: 68, 71, 259
Behavior of the Lower Organisms (Jennings), **L16**: 137n
Behemoth; or, The Long Parliament (Hobbes), **M11**: 22
Being, **M12**: 260; **L16**: 371. *See also* Ontological, **L12**
Royce on, **M1**: 241, 245; **M2**: 120-37
in Greek thought, **M3**: 121; **M9**: 192; **L12**: 89, 189, 420, 517
and non-being, **M12**: 141
perfect, **M12**: 143-44; **L13**: 192
spiritual realm of, **M12**: 266
insight into, **L2**: 131
in physics, **L16**: 104
concept of, **L16**: 334-35, 358-59, 384, 397, 449-50
in mathematics, **L16**: 387
Beings
animate and inanimate, **M9**: 4-7
Belgium, **M11**: 245, 255, 309, 325; **M15**: xviiin; **L15**: 289
Germany's invasion of, **M10**: 218, 269
Belief, **M6**: 23n; **M12**: 86, 94, 217-18, 256, 261; **L8**: x, xvi, 138, 186; **L10**: 37, 340-43
and reality, **M3**: 83-100
and thought, **M6**: 184-86; **L8**: 116-22
wrong forms of, **M6**: 198-200; **L8**: 132-34, 269-71
essential to instrumentalism, **M7**: 64
vs. knowledge, **M9**: 304-5; **L4**: 15, 17, 21, 22, 66, 249, 250
Peirce on, **M10**: 74-75, 77
fundamentalism and, **M15**: 7
need for reason in, **M15**: 51
kinds of, **L4**: 6, 11
interaction of, **L4**: 29
validity of, **L4**: 32, 239
conflicts with science, **L4**: 76, 85, 86
pathology of, **L4**: 109, 181-82
integrated with conduct, **L4**: 200-205
formation of, **L4**: 209, 211, 226; **L13**: 167, 169; **L15**: 64-65, 210; **L17**: 440
function of, **L4**: 221-22
cultural context of, **L6**: 18-19
and philosophy of qualities, **L6**: 426
as fundamental of philosophy, **L6**: 428
and common sense, **L6**: 429-30
in religion, **L9**: xv-xvi, 21-25, 38-40
in Greek philosophy, **L11**: 74
effect of education on, **L11**: 550, 555-56
compartmentalization of, **L11**: 554
dual meaning of, **L12**: 15
either-or, **L13**: 5
effect of, **L13**: 246
external, **L13**: 369-70
in immortality, **L14**: 98
and warranted assertibility, **L14**: 169, 180, 182
James on, **L15**: 15-16
traditional, **L15**: 335
of pre-scientific age, **L16**: 366
assignment of, **L16**: 371
attitude toward, **L16**: 390-91

common, **L17**: 423
alternative, **L17**: 443
nationalistic vs. global, **L17**: 454-55
Belief and knowledge
nature of, **L1**: 43, 242-43, 300, 302, 314
truth of, **L1**: 93
separation of, **L1**: 315-26
"Belief in Sensation, The" (Woodbridge), **M6**: 103n
"Beliefs and Existences," **L16**: 470
Bell, Clive, **M15**: 348; **L10**: 356, 357
Bell, Daniel, **L15**: 225-26, 361
Bellamy, Edward, **L15**: xv
on new social order, **L9**: 102-6
compared with Marx, **L9**: 103-5
Benda, Julien, **L9**: 243
on morality, **L15**: xxvii, 19-26, 381-92
Benedict, Ruth, **L6**: xvi; **L14**: 193-94; **L15**: xx
Benedict, W. R., **M3**: xxii, 310
Beneke, Friedrich Eduard, **M2**: 215
Benevolence, **E3**: 309-10, 318-19; **M14**: 93
principle of, **E4**: 144
Bentham on, **M5**: 265-66
ambiguity of, **M5**: 345-47
as motive of action, **M6**: 367
as standard, **L7**: 240, 249-52, 301
Benn, Gottfried, **L2**: 124n
Benne, Kenneth D., **L15**: 510; **L17**: 88, 558
Bennett, Arnold, **M8**: 26
Benninger, Albert C., **L9**: 360
Benoit-Smullyan, Emile, **L16**: xxxiiin, 310-17
Benson, Emanuel M., **L17**: 560
criticized, **L17**: 128-29
on art exhibition, **L17**: 540-41
Bentham, Jeremy, **E1**: 229; **E4**: 72; **E5**: 352; **M2**: 36; **M6**: 392; **M7**: 212, 361; **M8**: 166; **M11**: x, 40; **M12**: 174-75, 184, 187; **M14**: 147, 207; **M15**: 59; **L1**: 323; **L2**: 214, 293n; **L4**: 146; **L8**: 35; **L13**: 173; **L14**: xxii
and law, **E4**: 85, 282-83
on moral philosophy, **E4**: 146-48; **M4**: 40; **M5**: 211, 216-17, 227-40
on motive, **E4**: 279; **L7**: 173-75
on pleasure, **E4**: 284; **M5**: 252-53, 265-68
social theory of, **E5**: 353; **M5**: 261, 269; **L11**: 28, 32, 50, 80
on ethics, **M3**: 42
on utilitarianism, **M3**: 54; **M5**: 241-42; **M6**: 367-68; **L7**: 155, 240-41
on happiness, **M5**: 244-46
on sanctions of act, **M5**: 319-20
on human dignity, **M5**: 466
as individualist, **M5**: 469
political psychology of, **M10**: 271
Mill on, **L5**: 180-81; **L7**: 244-45
ipse dixitism of, **L7**: 238, 268
contributes to liberalism, **L11**: 11-16, 284
"Bentham" (J. S. Mill), **L5**: 180
Bentley, Arthur F., **L6**: xii, xiv; **L12**: 5; **L15**: 72n, 146n; **L16**: 302n
on extrapolation and experience, **L14**: 186
collaboration with Dewey, **L16**: ix-xxxviii, 3-4, 6-7, 318-20, 443-47, 458-59

Bentley, Arthur F. (*continued*)
criticizes logics, **L16**: 8-45, 184-209, 297n
positions of, **L16**: 47n, 52, 90n, 101n, 270n, 299n, 308n
postulations of, **L16**: 48, 58, 257-58, 273-75
development of, **L16**: 51n-52n
on C. Morris, **L16**: 210-41
misunderstood, **L16**: 275-76
articles reviewed, **L16**: 276
Bentley, Charles F., **L16**: xiin
Beresford, Charles, **M12**: 60, 62
Berger, Victor Louis, **L6**: 235
Bergson, Henri, **M7**: x, xvii, 143; **M8**: 139, 140, 142, 449; **M10**: 13n, 343; **M11**: 157; **M14**: 52-53, 124, 168; **M15**: 11; **L1**: 49; **L3**: 296; **L5**: 52, 249; **L8**: 355; **L10**: xvii, 337; **L11**: xxiv, 435, 471; **L15**: 10, 51
on instinct and reason, **M6**: 130
on experience, **M7**: xii
and perception, **M7**: xiii, 3, 8, 10-12, 18-30
doctrine of, **M7**: 3, 201-4; **M12**: 221-35
on rational intuition, **M7**: 261
on "pure" memory, **M10**: 36n
on reality, **M10**: 38
compared with Spencer, **M10**: 67-70
on vitalism, **M12**: xxvi, 231, 232, 244, 246
compared with James, **M12**: xxvii-xxix, 221, 227-28, 235
on creation, **M12**: xxviii, 120, 229, 235, 242-43
scientific and mystical outlook of, **M12**: xxix, 227-28
on impulse of will, **M12**: 230-31
compared with Russell, **M12**: 236, 242-43
contribution of, **M12**: 249-50
on relation of change to knowledge, **L4**: 73-74
on morality and religion, **L11**: 428-31
Dewey's criticism of, **L11**: 431
on time, **L14**: 100-101
Hocking on, **L14**: 418
organismal theory of, **L16**: 117n
on consciousness, **L17**: 416
Berkeley, George, **E1**: 145, 269, 342; **M4**: 255; **M6**: 175, 390; **M12**: xxixn, 107-8, 241; **M13**: 385, 455; **M15**: 332; **L1**: 113, 148, 173; **L2**: 7n, 156; **L3**: 296; **L4**: 98, 113; **L6**: 17, 424; **L11**: 91; **L15**: 94
on external world, **E1**: 35
on philosophic method, **E1**: 124
on knowledge, **E1**: 372, 385-86
theory of spatial relations, **E2**: 144-45
on philosophers, **E4**: 62
on outness, **M2**: 180
idealism of, **M3**: 382; **L16**: 458
on perceived objects, **M7**: 226
condemns Gothic, **L10**: 290n
on primary and secondary qualities, **L12**: 519
Hocking on, **L14**: 422-23
vs. Newton, **L16**: 292
Berkson, Isaac B., **L15**: 510
Berle, Adolph, Jr., **L6**: xviii, xix
Berlin, Germany, **M11**: 280; **L11**: 312
Congress of 1878 at, **M15**: 390, 391
Treaty of, **M15**: 391

Berlin, University of, **M8**: 174, 177
Berman-Yurin, Konon B., **L11**: 311, 322, 602
Bernard, Claude, **L16**: 88n
Bernard, John H., **E3**: 184-85
Bernard of Chartres, **M2**: 221
Bernays, Paul, **L16**: 18, 38
Bernhardi, Friedrich von, **M8**: xxix, 155, 163n, 165, 196, 474; **M10**: 221
Bernouilli, Jacques, **E1**: 272
Bernstein, Eduard, **L15**: xxix
Bertrand Russell Case, The (Dewey and Kallen), **L14**: 357-59
Bertrand Russell Memorial Volume (Roberts), **L6**: xv
Beseler, Hans Hartwig von, **M11**: 274
Bessarabia, **L15**: 296
Bethlehem Steel Company (Bethlehem, Pa.), **L11**: 271
Between Physics and Philosophy (P. Frank), **L16**: 149n
Bias, **L2**: 80, 81, 94
  of critic, **L10**: 309, 317, 327
  of philosophy, **L10**: 325-26
Bible, **L9**: 3; **L10**: 333
  teachings of, **E4**: 111-13
  on morality, **L9**: xxviii
Bibliolatry, **L5**: 181
Big Power
  as 1932 political issue, **L6**: 150
  related to society, **L6**: 178-79
Bill of Rights, **L7**: 360; **L11**: 220, 253, 372-73; **L13**: 103, 104; **L14**: 253; **L16**: 402; **L17**: 473
Bingham, Alfred M., **L9**: 296; **L11**: 438-40
Bingham, Anne T., **L5**: 238
Binghamton, N.Y.
  books banned in, **L14**: 371, 427, 429
Biographia Literaria (Coleridge), **L10**: xxviii
Biography, **M1**: 261
  as organ of social study, **M1**: 106-7
  and art, **L10**: 320, 321
  appeal of, **L17**: 43
Biological
  as matrix of inquiry, **L12**: 30-47
  foreshadows pattern of inquiry, **L12**: 66, 110, 198-99, 244, 263-64, 385
  as name, **L16**: 260
Biological Principles (Woodger), **L16**: 117n
Biological sciences
  as division, **L16**: 63-65
  transaction used in, **L16**: 115-21
  related to semiotic, **L16**: 211-13
Biologists
  vs. psychologists, **E5**: 366-67
Biology, **M12**: 122-23, 127-28
  important to psychology, **E1**: 56
  mechanistic view in, **M8**: 3
  nature of, **M8**: 449-59; **L16**: 148-49, 357, 372, 443
  related to experience, **M10**: 6-7, 14, 24-25
  and art, **L2**: 109-10
  and social, **L2**: 243, 330-31, 357
  important to education, **L5**: 34
  related to morality, **L7**: 40-41
  organismic concept in, **L11**: 511, 512; **L14**: 35n
  effect of, **L13**: 162, 247-48, 276

Biology (*continued*)
James on, **L14**: 158-61, 165; **L15**: 13-14
related to ageing, **L14**: 344-45, 349
valuation based in, **L15**: 103, 105n, 445-47
Greek, **L15**: 268-69
post-Darwinian, **L15**: 312
study of behavior in, **L16**: 135-39
development of, **L16**: 339, 355, 393, 455; **L17**: 440
"Biophysics Symposium, A," **L16**: 121n
Bios, **L17**: 42
Biotic intuition, **L17**: 43
Birth control, **L7**: 454, 459-60
related to education, **L6**: 146-48
legislation regarding, **L6**: 388-89
Birth of Venus (Botticelli), **L10**: 174, 360
Bismarck, Otto von, **M8**: 194, 474; **M10**: 287; **M11**: 114, 170, 389; **L11**: 332
Black, Dora W., **M13**: 121n, 409-10, 494-95; **L14**: xx
Black, Max, **L16**: 186n, 210n
"Black Crook" sprite, **L17**: 14, 554
Black Hundreds, **M11**: 278
Black Mountain College (Ashville, N.C.), **L15**: xxxi
Black Sea, **M11**: 266; **M15**: 136
Blackstone, William, **L7**: 443
Blaine, Anita McCormick (Mrs. Emmons), **M2**: 67; **M3**: 273, 325, 344
Blaine, John J., **L6**: 394
Blake, William, **L9**: 25; **L10**: 209-10, 361
Blakeslee, Howard, **L11**: 127
Blame, **M14**: 17, 85, 219-20
as moral force, **L7**: 253-55
attitude toward, **L10**: 303, 351
Bland, J. O. P.
Dewey opposes, **M13**: 75
on China, **M13**: 94, 96-100
on Young China, **M13**: 98-102, 113, 229
Blanshard, Brand, **M8**: xxvi-xxvii; **L13**: xi
in Polish study, **M11**: 260, 395-400
Bliss, Henry Evelyn, **L5**: 404-6
Bliven, Bruce, **L6**: 439
Blockade
as economic sanction, **L6**: 201, 204
in WWI, **L6**: 475, 476n
Blockade and Sea Power (Parmelee), **L6**: 476n
Block universe, **M12**: 208, 220
Blocs
political, **L17**: 35-36
Blood feud, **M5**: 32, 63-64, 69, 70-71, 409; **L7**: 25n, 31-32, 59, 65, 83
as uniting factor, **M5**: 47; **L7**: 45
enforces custom, **M5**: 58-59; **L7**: 54
Blücher, Gebhard, **M8**: 177
Bluntschli, Johann Kaspar, **E1**: 236
Blut und Boden, **M8**: xxxi
Board of Education (New York City), **L9**: 332, 369
Board of Higher Education (New York City), **L14**: 241, 243
Boas, Franz, **M6**: xii; **M7**: 394; **L1**: 133, 164n; **L6**: xvi; **L7**: xiv-xv; **L15**: xx; **L17**: 404-5
Boccaccio, Giovanni, **E4**: 121
Bode, Boyd H., **M10**: 28n; **M11**: 15; **L11**: 548; **L15**: xiin, 510;

L17: 363, 371n
on knowledge experience, M3: 178-80, 398-404
pragmatism of, M10: xi
normatives of, M10: xxii
vs. Childs on education, L13: 304-5, 377-90
tribute to, L15: xxiii, 326-28
on consciousness, L17: 548
Woodbridge on, L17: 548-49
Body. *See also* Mind and body; Psycho-physical
as psycho-physiological, E1: 104
dualism of soul and, E1: 107, 112-15, 322-23; E5: 96; L7: 120-21; L16: 124n
properties of, E1: 361
related to mind, M9: 147-50, 333, 346; L1: xvii, 66, 191-225, 228, 256-57; L4: 184, 233; L10: 26-28, 267-68; L13: 332; L15: xvii-xix, 219, 365; L16: 417
inferiority of, L4: 66
cultivation of, L10: 53, 231-32, 236, 238, 284
Hocking on, L14: 421-23
Greek development of, L17: 173
school work affects, L17: 514
"Body and Mind" (Clifford), L17: 554
Boehm-Bawerk, Eugen, L15: 359, 502, 505
Boehme, Jakob, M2: 183
Boerhaave, Hermann, L14: 206
Boer War, M11: 82
Boethius, M2: 250
Bogan, William J., L17: 511, 519, 572
Bohemia, M11: xiii, 71, 101, 241, 263, 264, 285
music of, L10: 193
Bohn, William E., L17: 429, 566
Bohr, Niels Henrik David, L16: 108-9
Bois de Boulogne, Paris, L11: 322
Bolognese school of art, L10: 192
Bolsheviks, M13: 236, 237; M15: 215; L6: 125, 235, 264; L8: 52
responsible for change, M11: 96
reports about, M11: 121
in class war, M11: 164
opposition to, M11: 246
policy of, M11: 268, 270, 271, 295
Bolshevism, M11: 115; M12: 5, 19, 23, 26, 44, 66, 253-55; M15: 202, 217; L2: 117; L5: 87, 98; L6: 142, 292; L9: 76-77; L13: 132, 180, 393; L14: 313; L15: 19, 23-25, 292, 297; L17: 117, 469
Marxist, M8: 435
technical sense of, M13: 116
rumors about, M13: 233
menace of, M13: 240
related to democracy, M13: 315
in China, L2: 177
in Mexico, L2: 199, 210
on religion, L5: 356-62
class politics of, L13: 399
on history, L16: 363
claims of, L16: 375
control by, L16: 379
Bolshevist Russia (Karlgren), L3: 220
Boltzmann, Ludwig, M3: 68
Bolzano, Bernard, L16: 18
Bonar, James, E4: 214-17; L5: 172n
Boniface VIII, Bull of, M5: 138
Boodin, John E., L17: 417n, 419
Books, L15: 87-88, 362

Books (*continued*)
learning from, **E5**: 255
in school, **E5**: 265-66; **M1**: 329-30
as representatives of past, **L13**: 6
Jefferson on, **L14**: 208
investigation of, **L14**: 370-72, 427, 429
censorship of, **L14**: 373
use of, **L17**: 463-64, 503-4
Boole, George, **L16**: 185
Booth, Edwin, **L10**: 318
Borah, William E., **M13**: 216; **M15**: 94, 96, 110, 395, 405; **L2**: 171; **L5**: 352, 353; **L6**: xxin, 192, 193; **L8**: 13, 15, 16
opposed to League of Nations, **M15**: xv, 406-7
Senate resolution of, **M15**: xvi-xvii, 85-86, 92, 105-6, 108-9, 113, 117-19, 399-400, 407-8, 410, 412-17
on outlawry of war, **M15**: 88-89, 412-13; **L3**: 165, 169; **L17**: 103-4, 559
on international controversies, **M15**: 409-10, 412, 413
comments on letter to Norris, **L6**: 149, 150
and progressives, **L6**: 355, 394
on economy, **L6**: 364-67
Borchard, Edwin M., **L2**: 42n
Boring, Edwin G., **L5**: 479n; **L16**: 124n, 170
Bosanquet, Bernard, **E1**: xxv; **E3**: 143, 186; **M3**: 64; **M4**: 304, 312; **M7**: xv; **M10**: 420, 427, 428; **M12**: 157; **M15**: 337, 348; **L2**: 14, 77; **L12**: xi-xii
and new logic, **E3**: 75, 92
and moral ideas, **E3**: 93, 100
and esthetics, **E4**: 189-97
on philosophy and theology, **E5**: 10
on judgment, **M10**: 107-8
on 1910 *How We Think*, **M13**: 482
essays of, **L3**: 294, 296-98
on religious experience, **L9**: xxv
on beauty, **L10**: 174, 360
on art, **L10**: 296, 364
on interrogative propositions, **L12**: 170-71
on comparison, **L12**: 185
Carnap on, **L16**: 20n, 24n
Bosanquet, Helen (Mrs. Bernard), **M5**: 521n, 530, 531
Bosphorus, **M15**: 135, 292
Bossuet, Jacques Bénigne, **M2**: 216; **M4**: 77
Botticelli, Sandro, **L10**: 98, 174, 360
Boucher, François, **L10**: 134
Bourdeau, Jean, **L2**: 7n
Bourdon, Georges, **M8**: 191
Bourgeoisie, **L11**: 54, 59, 383; **L13**: 134
Bourget, Paul
on French literature, **E3**: 36-42
Bourne, Francis, **M11**: 73, 393
Bourne, Randolph, **M11**: 350n
disagrees with Dewey, **M11**: x, xi, 353, 354, 359-60
Bowers, Fredson, **L17**: xii
Bowne, Borden, **M5**: 237n
Bowring, John, **L14**: xxiin
Boxer Indemnity Fund, **M11**: xviii; **L2**: 174
Boxer Rebellion, **M11**: 205, 221, 223, 228, 230; **M12**: 36; **M13**: 103, 167, 245, 247, 273
Boycott
economic, **M12**: 23

and Japan, **M12**: 32-33, 39-40; **L6**: 209
and sanctions, **L6**: 201-3, 477
in China, **L6**: 205
against Latin America, **L6**: 215
and Manchuria, **L6**: 469-79
Boydston, Jo Ann, **L15**: 371n
translations by, **M7**: 113n; **L5**: 496n; **L9**: 310n
on *Collected Works*, **L17**: xi-xv
on Hook's introduction, **L17**: xxxiii-xxxiv
Boyesen, Hjalmar Hjorth, **E4**: 119
Boyle, Robert, **L2**: 142; **L11**: 393
Boys' Own Arithmetic (R. Weeks), **L2**: 386
Brackets
as symbols in logic, **L12**: 306, 406
Bracton, Henry de, **L7**: 133
Bradley, Andrew Cecil
on poetry, **L10**: 113-17, 357, 358
Bradley, Francis Herbert, **E1**: xxv; **E3**: 75, 92, 239; **E4**: xvii, xix, xxiv; **M3**: 64, 311; **M4**: xiv, 254; **M6**: xiii, 10, 94; **M7**: xiv, xv, 228; **M10**: 417; **M12**: 141; **M15**: 222; **L2**: 14; **L12**: 136n; **L14**: 33, 399
on metaphysics, **E4**: 65; **M13**: 498
and criticism of Kantian theory, **E5**: 137
on appearance and reality, **M1**: 256; **M3**: 171n; **M4**: 50-75
on This and Thisness, **M3**: 14n, 15n
on judgment, **M10**: 108
compared with Klyce, **M13**: 417-18
on identity of form, **L5**: 258-60
Hocking on, **L14**: 418
objective idealism of, **L16**: 115n
Bradshaw, Frances, **M11**: 260
Brady, James H.
on universal military training, **M10**: 383, 386-92
Brahmanism, **L6**: 321
Brailsford, Henry Noel
on China and Japan, **M13**: 173-76, 179-82
Brain
Bergson on, **M7**: 24-30, 202-4
connection of learning with, **M9**: 346-47
and mind, **L1**: 222, 224
Whitehead on, **L14**: 124
James on, **L14**: 158, 161
function of, **L15**: 14, 32-33, 75
Brameld, Theodore B. H., **L9**: 244-45; **L11**: 383n
Brandeis, Louis D., **L7**: 398; **L9**: 237-39; **L11**: 47-48, 374
Brandes, George, **E3**: 178; **M8**: 178
Brave New World (A. Huxley), **L10**: xvii
Brazil
U.S. intervention in, **L5**: 440
Break-up of China, The (Beresford), **M12**: 60, 62
Breasted, James Henry, **L9**: 37-38
Breen, Matthew B., **L9**: 373
Brehon laws, **M5**: 83; **L7**: 76
Brest-Litovsk, Treaty of, **M11**: 270-71, 275
Breughel, Pieter, the elder, **L10**: 192
Brewster, James H., **M10**: 370
Briand, Aristide, **M13**: 206, 346; **L5**: 353
on outlawry of war, **L3**: 163-68, 171, 175; **L8**: 13, 14

Briand, Aristide (*continued*)
on Pact of Paris and war, **L6**: 218-19
Bridgeport, Conn., **M7**: 466
Bridgewater, Mass., **M15**: xxiii, 158n, 170n, 180n
Bridgman, Laura, **M7**: 396; **L17**: 145, 562
Bridgman, Percy W., **L12**: 362n; **L14**: 420
Dewey praises, **L4**: xii
on operations, **L4**: xvii, 89, 90n
on observation, **L4**: 163
on concept, **L5**: 481-83
"hazes" of, **L16**: 152
on definition, **L16**: 170-71
on nature, **L16**: 192n
"Brief History of My Opinions, A" (Santayana), **L14**: 295
"Brief Studies in Realism," **M7**: 454-60
British Broadcasting Company, **L15**: 184
British empiricism, **M10**: xxv, 48, 223-25; **L5**: 173, 175
British-Japanese alliance. *See* Anglo-Japanese alliance
British Labour party. *See* Labour party (Great Britain)
British Thought and Thinkers (G. Morris), **M10**: 110
British West Indies, **L15**: 308-9
Broad, Charlie Dunbar, **L2**: 29n; **L15**: xvi
on event, **L2**: 62-68
on scientific objects, **L14**: 21n
Brodeur, Arthur G., **L11**: 530
Brodsky, Louis B., **L9**: 371-72
Brogan, Albert P., **M13**: 11n, 24n, 25n
Broglie, Louis Victor de, **L16**: 107
Bronstein, Daniel J., **L16**: 210n
Brookhart, Smith W., **L6**: 355, 394
Brookline, Mass., **E5**: xcvi
Brooklyn, N.Y., **L6**: 326
Brooks, Van Wyck, **L14**: 328
Brookwood Labor College (Katonah, N.Y.), **L5**: 331-45, 392, 506; **L6**: 327-29
Brotherston, Bruce W., **L15**: 71, 72n
Brougham, Henry Peter, **M11**: 59
Broun, Heywood, **L11**: 352, 604
Brown, G. Harrison, **L5**: 353
Brown, George A., **M8**: 466n, 469
Brown, George P., **E5**: 147
Brown, Harold Chapman, **L1**: 119n
Brown, Harry Gunnison, **L3**: 359n
Brown, Henry B., **L7**: 414
Brown, Robert, **L14**: 206
Brown, William Montgomery
spiritual development of, **L2**: 163-66
Brownell, Baker
on Santayana, **L14**: 296-300, 305
Browning, Robert, **M8**: 142; **M10**: 118; **L14**: 348
compared with Arnold, **E3**: 119-23
on art, **L10**: 286, 326-27, 352, 363, 366
criticized, **L10**: 324
Browning, William, **L11**: 530
Brownson, O. A., **M2**: 170
Bruce, Edward, **L14**: 256-57
Bruno, Giordano, **M12**: 117
on nature, **M2**: 147
pantheism of, **M2**: 183
Brunswick, Duke of, **E1**: 263, 266
Brunswik, Egon, **L16**: 125n, 144, 232n

Brusa (Bursa), Turkey, **M15**: 139-40
Brutalist
  Hegel as, **M8**: 191
Bryan, William Jennings, **M8**: 418; **M10**: 261; **M11**: 148; **M13**: 141, 498; **L6**: 231, 234
  opposes science, **M13**: 301
  in progressive movement, **M13**: 301-5
Bryant, Sophie, **E5**: 350-52
Bryce, James Bryce, **L7**: 129, 426; **L11**: 184
  on medieval church, **M5**: 138
  on sociability of Americans, **M6**: 162
  on modern democracy, **L7**: 148-49
Bryn Mawr College
  Phoebe Thorn Experimental School at, **M8**: 263
Buber, Martin, **L10**: vii
Buchanan, Scott, **L3**: 311-14
Bucharest, Treaty of, **L6**: 468n
Buchler, Justus, **L15**: 457, 466, 468; **L16**: 10n
Buddha, **M13**: 221
Buddhism, **L10**: 134
  self-denial in, **M5**: 328
  pessimistic tone of, **M7**: 296
Buell, Raymond Leslie, **L6**: 196n
  on international affairs, **L6**: xx, 200, 202, 208, 211, 220, 450-84
Buelow, Bernhard von, **M12**: 34
Buermeyer, Laurence
  on thoughts, **M13**: 61-71, 482-91
  on art, **L10**: 99n, 321n
Buffon, Georges Louis Leclerc, **L13**: 175
Bühler, Karl, **L16**: 21n, 137n, 232n, 468
Bukharin, Nikolai I.
  trial of, **L15**: xi, 338, 345-46, 348
Bukhartsev, Dmitri P., **L11**: 322, 603
Bulgaria, **M15**: 390
Bulgarians, **M15**: 140, 147
Bullitt, William, **L15**: 293-94
Bunyan, John, **M5**: 145
Burden, Samuel J., **L9**: 360-61
Bureau of Foreign and Domestic Commerce, **L6**: 353
Bureau of Labor Statistics, **L17**: 7-8, 554
Bureau of Public Information. *See* Committee on Public Information
Bureau of Railway Economics, **L6**: 370
Burgess, John William, **E4**: 73n; **L7**: 422
Burke, Edmund, **E4**: 193; **M7**: 357; **M8**: 184; **M12**: xvi; **M15**: 9
Burks, Arthur W.
  on definition, **L16**: 166, 168, 181n
Burlingame, Anson, **M11**: 228; **M13**: 167; **L2**: 174
Burlington, Vt., **L5**: 178
Burnett, Joe R.
  on Dewey's 1899-1901 writings, **M1**: ix-xxiii
Burnett, Whit, **L15**: 367n
Burns, Robert, **L13**: 358
Burr, H. S., **L16**: 121n
Burrow, Trigant, **L16**: 117n
Burt, Benjamin Chapman, **L5**: 393, 506
Burton, Ernest D., **L15**: 324
Burtt, Edwin Arthur, **L5**: 481n
Bus franchises
  in New York City, **L9**: 365-66, 385

Bush, Wendell T., **M6**: xii, 103n; **M7**: 445n; **M8**: ix; **M13**: 12n; **L5**: 500
  on experience, **M6**: 81
  on value, **M11**: 3-8, 375-87
Bush Building (New York City), **L10**: 217, 361
Business, **M12**: 102-4, 184; **L2**: 161-62; **L10**: 26, 203; **L11**: 44, 271, 277-80, 286-87. *See also* Economics; Industry
  related to morality, **M5**: 179-80, 464-65; **L7**: 260, 403-11, 414, 423-26, 429-37
  motives for, **M5**: 445-46; **L6**: 70-74, 142
  private action in, **L2**: 214-15
  and politics, **L2**: 321, 349; **L6**: 156-59, 163, 165, 177, 186
  changing concept of, **L6**: xxii; **L17**: 21
  alliance of, **L6**: 165-66
  influence of, **L7**: 373-74; **L9**: 193
  control of, **L7**: 412-13
  rate control in, **L7**: 415-17
  war's impact on, **L17**: 22
Business Week, **L9**: 252
Butler, Edward B., **M1**: 317
Butler, Joseph, **E4**: 130; **M3**: 53; **L5**: 147, 150; **L9**: xii, 422
  and conscience, **E4**: 128
  and self-regarding impulses, **E4**: 144
Butler, Nicholas Murray, **M3**: 325-26; **M4**: xvii; **L6**: 337; **L11**: 592; **L14**: xix, 374, 431
Butler, Samuel, **L7**: 379
Byrnes, James F., **L15**: 346
Byron, George Gordon, **E3**: 41; **M5**: 145
Byzantine art, **L10**: 321, 333-36
Caesar, Julius, **M8**: 194; **M10**: 237; **M15**: 33; **L7**: 23, 126, 441; **L10**: 46
Cahn, Steven M.
  on Dewey's 1938-39 writings, **L13**: ix-xviii
Caird, Edward, **E2**: xxiii; **E3**: 186; **M6**: 94; **M7**: 345; **L2**: 6; **L5**: 152
  influences Dewey, **E1**: xxv
  idealism of, **E1**: xxviii; **L16**: 115n
  on psychology, **E1**: 146, 149-50, 155-56
  on Kant, **E3**: 92, 180-84, 239; **E5**: 137
  on consciousness of things, **E4**: 22
Caird, John, **M6**: 94; **L5**: 152
Calculation, **M14**: 132, 139-45, 149; **L12**: 164, 214, 218, 277, 413, 468, 475
  and observation, **L14**: 198
Calculus of Relations, **M7**: 422
California, University of (Berkeley), **M11**: xvii, 41n; **L6**: 3n; **L11**: 530
California, University of (Los Angeles), **L5**: 289n
Caliphate, **M15**: 128-31
Calles, Plutarco Elías, **L2**: 194, 196, 199; **L3**: 160, 162
Calvin, John, **M8**: 142; **M11**: 25
Calvinism, **L14**: 406
Cambridge, University of, **M4**: 242
Camera
  vs. artist, **L10**: 89, 93
Camp, Katherine B., **E5**: 436; **M1**: 222, 325
Campanella, Tommaso, **E1**: 259
Camus, Albert, **M3**: xxiv
Candide (Voltaire), **M7**: 293

"Can Logic Be Divorced from Ontology?" (Nagel), **L5**: 203; **L16**: 16n
Canossa, **M5**: 138
"Can Peace Be Enforced?" (Levinson), **L5**: 352
"Can Teachers Stay Out of the Class Struggle?" (Childs), **L11**: 383n
Canton (Guangzhou), China, **M12**: 23, 69; **M13**: 135, 153; **L6**: 205; **L17**: 555
  British in, **M13**: 121-23
  government of, **M13**: 124-25, 129, 132, 151, 183; **L17**: 30-31
  compared with Peking, **M13**: 127-28, 134, 169
  demonstration at, **M13**: 128-29
  education in, **M13**: 129
  labor unrest in, **L17**: 31-32
  reforms in, **L17**: 32-33
  support for, **L17**: 33-34
Canton Guild, **M11**: 196
Cantril, Hadley, **L15**: 510
"Can We Choose between Values?" (Geiger), **L15**: 101
Capacity
  and self-realization, **E3**: 301-3; **E4**: 44-46, 48-50
  double meaning of word, **M9**: 46
  development of, **M9**: 123
  teaching limitation of, **M9**: 204-5
  native, in education, **L9**: 197-99
  in psychology, **L16**: 136
Capella, Martianus, **M2**: 249
Capital (Marx), **L7**: 426
Capital
  related to labor, **M9**: 323
Capitalism, **M11**: 91, 163; **M12**: xxx, 17, 102, 183-84; **M13**: 160; **L2**: 161; **L9**: 319; **L11**: xxxin, 43, 52, 57; **L13**: 390; **L15**: 359-60; **L17**: 472
  criticized, **M2**: xx-xxi
  as destroyer of group morality, **M5**: 78; **L7**: 72
  as result of science, **M9**: 292
  history of, **L7**: 142-43, 149-51
  concept of, **L7**: 375-76, 402; **L17**: 21-22
  and competition, **L7**: 376-79, 400
  problems of, **L7**: 381, 394, 403-6, 428-36; **L9**: 298
  and justice, **L7**: 406-7
  alternatives to, **L7**: 426-28
  Niebuhr on, **L9**: 73, 399-405
  Bellamy on, **L9**: 104-5
  social control of, **L9**: 208
  and F. Roosevelt's policy, **L9**: 297
  affects art, **L10**: 14
  connected with democracy, **L11**: 296; **L13**: 137, 146
  Bingham on, **L11**: 438
  Trotsky on, **L13**: 396
  collectivism in, **L14**: 92-95
  effects of, **L17**: 23
  and feudalism, **L17**: 23-24
Capitalization, **L10**: 257n
  of corporations, **M5**: 501-3
Capone, Al, **L13**: 147
Capper resolution, **L3**: 170, 433; **L6**: 471, 484
Capricious activity
  contrasted with educative activity, **M9**: 83-84, 319, 351
  as fatal to aims, **M9**: 108
  contrasted with thoughtful action, **M9**: 152-53, 161
  contrasted with continuity, **M9**: 346-47, 360

Captains Courageous (Kipling), **L5**: 395
Caravaggio, Polidoro Caldara da, **L10**: 147
Caraway, Thaddeus H., **L5**: 429
Cardanus (Geronimo Cardano), **E1**: 259
Cardozo, Benjamin Nathan, **L6**: 323
Card Players (Cézanne), **L10**: 212, 361
Care, **L16**: 247
Carings-for, **L16**: 346-47, 351-54
Carlyle, Jane Welsh, **L14**: 88
Carlyle, Thomas, **E1**: 233; **E5**: 270, 351; **M3**: 56, 289; **M10**: 175; **M14**: 125; **L2**: 217, 298, 304; **L6**: 69; **L11**: 19, 442; **L13**: 153-54; **L15**: 180, 198, 214-15
  on belief, **E3**: 110, 112
  on duty, **E3**: 321
  on industry, **M1**: 149; **M5**: 151
  on city life, **M5**: 178
  on utilitarianism, **M5**: 243, 263n; **L7**: 250-51
  on "cash nexus," **M9**: 309
  on democracy, **M13**: 330
  on society, **L7**: 327
  on art, **L10**: 296, 364
  on self-government, **L13**: 150
Carmichael, Leonard, **M7**: xxiv, xxv
Carnap, Rudolf, **L9**: 303, 304; **L14**: xiv; **L15**: 145n; **L16**: 10n
  logic of, **L16**: xxii, xxx, xxxiiin, 8, 9, 33-35, 38, 40, 116n, 193n
  on propositions, **L16**: 12, 17-32, 45
  on definition, **L16**: 132n, 165, 166n
Carnegie, Andrew, **M10**: 261
Carnegie Foundation, **M15**: 226
  1922 annual report of, **M15**: 190
Carpentry
  as introduction to physics, **M1**: 51
Carracci, **L10**: 147
Carranza, Venustiano, **L2**: 195
Carson, Edward Henry, **M11**: 120
Cartesian
  dualism, **M2**: x; **M8**: xxviii
  philosophy, **L1**: 14, 27, 255
  thinking, **L2**: 142
Cartesianism, **M9**: xxi
Cartesian-Lockean terms
  psychology expressed in, **M7**: 51
Carus, Paul, **E5**: xiii, 342n, 347; **M15**: 227; **L1**: 393-95
Carus Lectures, **L6**: 28, 310, 311
  in 1922, **L14**: xv, 413
  in 1939, **L14**: 141, 431
Carver, Thomas, **L7**: 423-24
Case, Clarence Marsh, **L6**: 451
Case. *See also* Induction, **L12**
  as representative, **L12**: 292, 427, 431-32, 435, 443-44, 473-75
Case of Leon Trotsky, The (Dewey et al.), **L11**: xxviin, 306n; **L13**: 393n; **L15**: 510
Cash nexus, **M9**: 309
Cassel, Louis, **L17**: 556
Cassel Collieries Contract, **M13**: 121-25, 410, 494; **L17**: 31, 556
Cassini protocol, **M12**: 62
Cassirer, Ernst, **L10**: xv; **L16**: 115n
Castalian, **E3**: 51n, 147n
Casuistry, **M12**: 175; **M14**: 165; **L7**: 277-78

affects moral action, **M5**: 295-98
Categorical imperative
British acceptance of, **M10**: 224
Category
as synthetic function, **E1**: 38
theories of, **E1**: 41-43; **M7**: 422
objective, **E3**: 214-19, 221
in art criticism, **L10**: 319-21
defined, **L12**: 253, 259
related to class, **L12**: 259, 271-79, 297, 341, 359, 380-81
causation as, **L12**: 453-57
physical and mental, **L17**: xxx
Catharsis, **L10**: 102n
Catholic church. *See* Roman Catholic church
Catholic World, **L15**: 50n
on Russell, **L14**: 235-36
Catlin, G. E. G., **L3**: 318, 320-23
Cato, **L7**: 128
Cattell, James McKeen, **E5**: 349; **M1**: xiii; **L7**: 454, 459; **L9**: 96n, 101
Causal forces
and state, **L2**: 242, 246-49, 251, 258, 259, 265, 269, 276
vs. causal order, **L2**: 361
Causality, **L4**: 127; **L11**: 52, 70; **L15**: 37, 85, 114
and causation, **L1**: 73, 79, 84-85, 91, 180-81, 208-9, 243
reality and, **L14**: 146
Hocking on, **L14**: 421-22
Causal nexus, **E1**: 6, 7; **M2**: 154
Causal proposition
means-consequences of, **L12**: 454-57
Causation, **M12**: 113-16, 118; **M13**: 372; **M14**: 17, 33; **L2**: 50; **L17**: 408
Leibniz on, **E1**: 319-20
in Hegel and Kant, **E3**: 137-38; **L16**: 115n
defined, **E4**: 91
teachers' use of, **M1**: 140-41
related to antecedent and consequent, **M2**: 15-16
in *Cyclopedia of Education*, **M6**: 379-81
ultimate, **M8**: 5
affected by relational theory of knowledge, **L2**: 142-43, 146
Hume's theory of, **L2**: 154
in perception, **L14**: 54, 170-71
laws of, **L14**: 179-80
Greeks on, **L14**: 195
in Santayana's philosophy, **L14**: 305
Frank on, **L16**: 149n
in science, **L16**: 410
Cause
ego as, **E4**: 91-96
vs. reason, **L13**: 17-18
terminological derivation of, **L16**: 104
child's interest in, **L17**: 286
Cause and effect, **E1**: 11; **E3**: 217; **E4**: 34-36; **M2**: 12-14; **L1**: 45, 91, 200-201, 209-10, 277, 286; **L17**: 435
of consciousness, **L1**: 233
of knowledge, **L1**: 283-84
principle of, **L13**: 56-57, 141, 229
Cavalieri, Francesco Bonaventura, **E1**: 262
Cavendish, Henry, **L14**: 397
Caylay, Arthur, **L15**: 376
Cecil, Edgar Algernon Robert, **M15**: 88, 95, 380, 406, 407

"Celebrated Jumping Frog of Calaveras County, The" (Twain), **M12**: xxixn
Cell
  nervous, **E1**: 94-95
  function of, **E1**: 96-98, 110
Cell in Development and Heredity, The (E. B. Wilson), **L16**: 117n
Cell theory, **L16**: 116-18
Celts, **M5**: 29; **L7**: 29
Censorship, **M11**: 110, 118-21, 178, 268; **L5**: 417; **L7**: 321, 329; **L11**: 253
  related to college, **L6**: 121-22
  of arts, **L10**: 13, 331, 332
  intellectual, **L14**: 371
  of textbooks, **L14**: 373
  by House Un-American Activities Committee, **L17**: 137, 560-61
Center, Function and Structure of Psychology, The (P. Hughes), **L17**: 42-43
Centered movement
  material side of, **E3**: 215-19
Center for Dewey Studies (Southern Illinois University)
  history of, **L17**: xi-xiv
Central activity
  as idea, **E5**: 97
Central High School (Philadelphia), **L6**: 99n
Central Powers, **L6**: 207-8
  future of, **M11**: 101
  in WWI, **M11**: 136, 270, 271
  on Polish question, **M11**: 268, 273, 274
Century Dictionary and Cyclopedia, The, **L16**: 137n, 155-56
Century of Progress Exposition (Chicago), **L11**: 275, 279
Ceremonies. *See also* Rituals
  role of, **L10**: xv, 330, 332
Certainty, **M12**: 91, 92; **L15**: 28, 40, 123-25
  as end of thinking, **M1**: 151-52
  love of, **M14**: 162-66
  quest for, **L4**: x, 5, 7, 16-18, 176, 185, 203, 226, 240, 243, 245
  means of attaining, **L4**: 21, 24, 28, 29, 58, 67, 163, 231
  realm of, **L4**: 41, 96, 103
  Kant on, **L4**: 49, 50
  Laplace on, **L14**: 107
Cézanne, Paul, **L10**: 361; **L13**: 361
  as artist, **L10**: xxi, xxx, 54, 98, 100, 134, 148, 192, 212-16, 239, 264
  on art, **L10**: 127, 316, 358, 365
  criticized, **L10**: 291, 306, 307
Chadbourne, Thomas L., **L5**: 441
"Challenge of Democracy to Education, The," **L11**: xvi
Challenge of Russia, The (S. Eddy), **L6**: 263-65
"Challenge to Liberal Thought," **L15**: 333
Challenge to the New Deal (A. M. Bingham and Rodman), **L9**: 296
Chamberlain, George E., **M10**: 377, 387, 392, 393
Chamberlain, Houston, **M8**: xxxi, 188n, 423
Chamberlain, John R., **L11**: 323
Chamberlain, Joseph Austin, **L17**: 498, 570
Chamberlain, Neville, **L15**: 348, 353
Chamberlain bill, **M10**: 378, 388, 389

Chamber of Commerce (U.S.), **L2**: 161; **L9**: 115, 125, 130
Champlain, Samuel de, **L8**: 173
Chance. *See also* Luck
  and necessity, **E4**: 29-36
  as causal principle, **M4**: 8-10
  belief in, **L14**: 98
Chance, Love, and Logic (C. Peirce), **M15**: xxvi, 226-28; **L2**: 28n; **L5**: 478n
Change, **L1**: 47-50, 54, 63-64, 83, 85, 94, 95, 98, 118-19, 134, 171, 236-37, 263-64; **L16**: 242, 325. *See also* Interaction, **L12**; Transformation, **L12**
  Dewey's concept of, **M10**: xxvii-xxviii
  early views on, **M12**: 112; **L17**: 456
  as law of universe, **M12**: 114
  Plato and Aristotle on, **M12**: 141
  attitude toward, **M12**: 144-46; **L10**: 325-27; **L11**: 41-42, 133, 409, 412-13
  related to duration, **M12**: 224, 228
  Darwin on, **M12**: 229
  Bergson on, **M12**: 231, 234
  Chinese student movement seeks, **M12**: 253-54
  and knowledge, **M12**: 259; **L13**: 155
  effecting of, **L4**: 3-4, 181, 186-89, 220-23, 227
  realm of, **L4**: 6, 15-17
  in science, **L4**: 66-71, 76, 80-82; **L12**: 137-38, 183; **L16**: 370
  as evil, **L4**: 82, 148, 200, 234
  regulation of, **L4**: 84, 163-71, 231, 232, 236; **L14**: 105, 113
  Newton on, **L4**: 95, 96, 114-15
  correlation of, **L4**: 103-8, 158, 197, 198, 219
  necessity for, **L7**: xiv; **L13**: 112-15, 118-19, 136, 287-88; **L17**: 463, 478
  effects of, **L7**: 177-79, 318-19, 331, 374, 444-50
  and stimulus, **L7**: 290, 292
  in nature, **L10**: 20, 22
  rhythm imposed on, **L10**: 153-54, 158-59
  in politics, **L11**: xxiii-xxiv, 274-81
  of environment, **L12**: 41
  in Greek logic, **L12**: 88-94, 212
  and negation, **L12**: 188-93
  and particulars, **L12**: 201-2, 212-13, 217, 296-97, 340, 417
  as cyclical, **L12**: 220-23, 235-36
  as vectorial, **L12**: 233-34, 237-38
  qualitative, **L12**: 453-54
  in habits, **L13**: 97, 150, 186, 291
  economic, **L13**: 290, 316, 339
  thinking related to, **L14**: 98-101; **L17**: 78-80
  classical vs. modern concept of, **L15**: 84, 87, 234, 235, 273, 312-13
  replaces immutability, **L16**: 363, 365
  physical related to moral, **L17**: 456-57
Changsha, China, **M13**: 151
Chang Shun, **M13**: 131
Chang Tso Lin, **M12**: 67, 70; **M13**: 131, 132, 134, 136, 150-51, 210
Chaplin, Charlie, **L10**: xviii

Character
nature of, **E2**: 352; **E4**: 241-42; **E5**: 78-82, 326-27; **M4**: 287-91; **M6**: 218; **M9**: 326; **M14**: 29-30; **L7**: 166-67; **L8**: 139, 159; **L17**: 298, 336-37, 347
consequences of, **E2**: 353-56; **M14**: 30, 35-36
role in morality of, **E3**: 246-47; **M5**: 234-35; **L17**: 336-37
as motive to action, **E3**: 259
failure of pleasure to unify, **E3**: 261-63
and conduct, **E3**: 343; **L7**: 168-73, 176, 193-94, 271-72
formation of, **E5**: 93, 327; **M1**: 307-8; **L7**: 14, 65
Hebrew conception of, **M5**: 101-2; **L7**: 92-94
Greek conception of, **M5**: 130-32; **L7**: 121-23
in *Cyclopedia of Education*, **M6**: 381-88, 392
education related to, **M9**: 11, 163, 195, 356, 370
intelligence and, **M9**: 363-67; **L17**: 336-38
influences affecting, **M14**: 8; **L9**: 186-93, 203-4; **L17**: 515
Mill on, **L7**: 241-42
happiness and, **L7**: 244-45
esthetic meaning of, **L10**: 247-48, 289, 292, 298
in Santayana's philosophy, **L14**: 305
volitional side of, **L17**: 338-42
feelings related to, **L17**: 343, 346
determinate, **L17**: 369
Characteristics. *See* Traits
Characterization
nature of, **L16**: 6, 133n, 145-46, 149, 152, 155
as name, **L16**: 7n, 65, 71, 260
as stage of designation, **L16**: 132, 139, 142
Characters, **L11**: xiv, 96-99, 101, 103; **L12**: 259, 341, 353, 377, 439, 447-48. *See also* Abstraction, **L12**; Universal proposition, **L12**
as condensations of belief, **M3**: 84
Characters and Events, **L14**: 13
Chardin, Jean Baptiste, **L10**: 100, 134, 192
Charity, **L13**: 317-18
and moral rules, **E4**: 56-58
and emotions, **E4**: 58-59
negative effect of, **M5**: 350
and unemployment, **L6**: 153-55
related to WWI, **L6**: 375, 406
misconception of, **L7**: 301
role of, **L7**: 382
destructiveness of, **L13**: 310
Charles Stephen, **M11**: 277, 284, 329
Charlotte, Vt., **E1**: xxiii
Charm
in art, **L10**: 130, 135-36, 145, 171, 174, 185, 296, 300, 336
Charmides (Plato), **L2**: 124, 127, 134, 138
sophrosyne in, **L2**: 131
on knowledge, **L2**: 135
Chartres, cathedral of, **L10**: 226
Chase, Daniel, **L5**: 338n, 387n, 390-92
Chase, Stuart, **L5**: xvii, 239, 240; **L6**: xvii, 329
Chastity, **M9**: 367
Chatterji, Jagadish Chandra, **L6**: 321
Cheating, **E4**: 369-70
Chekhov, Anton Pavlovich, **L10**: xviii

Chekiang (Zhejiang), China, **M13**: 104
Chelm, Poland, **M11**: 270, 273, 275
Chemistry, **M12**: 122, 217, 224; **L15**: 115-16
  teaching of, **M10**: 134-36
  terminology of, **L16**: 65
  rise of, **L16**: 339, 393, 455
  conclusions in, **L16**: 357
Ch'en Chiung-ming, **L17**: 556
  on gambling, **L17**: 31
  on labor, **L17**: 31-32
  reaction to, **L17**: 33
Chen Kwang Ming, **M13**: 122, 128, 132-34
Cherry, Richard, **M5**: 409n
Chesterton, G. K., **M6**: 11; **M13**: 217; **L15**: 54
Chiang Kai-shek, **M13**: xxiv; **L15**: 352-53
Chiaroscuro, **L10**: 209
Chicago, Ill.
  public schools of, **E5**: 423-24; **M7**: 96, 100; **L5**: 371-74
  headquarters for Polish affairs, **M11**: 242, 248, 249, 254, 256, 262, 287, 288, 293, 300-306, 310-12, 323
  political conventions in, **L6**: 235, 239, 248, 250
  League of Nations Association in, **L6**: 337
  teachers' unions in, **L9**: 328-29
  Dewey's view of, **L17**: 517-19
Chicago, Burlington and Quincy Railroad, **L6**: 371
Chicago, University of, **E4**: xvn; **E5**: xiv; **M1**: 258, 317; **M6**: 179; **L5**: 424; **L8**: 109; **L11**: 203, 453; **L14**: 4; **L15**: 321, 324; **L17**: 88, 485
  Dewey's career at, **M1**: ix-xxiii; **M3**: ix
  Veblen critical of, **M1**: xxii
  coeducation at, **M2**: 105-16
  pragmatic spirit of, **M4**: x
  Dewey and Tufts at, **M5**: ix
  Dewey and Bentley at, **L16**: xiv
  Philosophical Club, **L17**: 351n
  lecture at, **L17**: 488, 568
  training social workers at, **L17**: 517, 572-73
Chicago, University of, Department of Pedagogy, **E5**: 244, 436-47
Chicago, University of, Department of Philosophy, **M2**: 295
Chicago, University of, School of Education
  organization and curriculum of, **M2**: 67-71, 75-78; **M3**: 327-41, 344-46
  admission requirements, **M2**: 72-75
  publications, **M2**: 79
  history and philosophy of, **M3**: 273-84
  building description, **M3**: 342-44
Chicago Commercial Club, **M8**: 124, 126, 471-72
Chicago Evening Post, **E5**: 423-24
Chicago Federation of Teachers, **M10**: 170
Chicago Institute, **M2**: 67
Chicago Manual Training School, **E5**: 446-47; **M2**: 68; **M3**: 273, 275, 278, 279
Chicago Regional White House Conference on Child Health and Protection, **L17**: 511, 517, 519

Chicago school of philosophy, **M4**: 113; **M6**: 46n, 176
James's impression of, **M6**: xiii
Chicago Teachers' College, **M8**: 271
Chicago Teachers' Federation, **M8**: 472
Chicago Tribune, **M15**: 395
Child, Charles Manning, **L16**: 117n
Child
powers of, **E5**: 76-77, 121
activity of, **E5**: 91; **M1**: 210-11, 231; **L10**: 186
nature of, **E5**: 217-18, 226, 249, 451-52; **M1**: 143-44; **L17**: 238
interest of, **E5**: 227-28; **M1**: 29, 37-38, 85-86, 97-100, 201-2, 234, 340; **M6**: 205-7; **L8**: 141-43; **L17**: 223-24, 261-65, 314
imitation in, **E5**: 418-20
use of language by, **E5**: 439; **M1**: 33-36, 77-78; **L8**: 229-32
education of, **M1**: 21-24; **M2**: 273-81; **L2**: 116-22, 226-30; **L17**: 214-16, 218, 222-24, 238-39, 284, 322
development of, **M1**: 133-35; **M2**: 281-83; **L11**: 238-46, 510-14; **L17**: 238, 255-68, 284-86
mental processes and behavior of, **M6**: 190-91, 213-15, 218-20, 231, 269-70, 304, 309; **L8**: 123-24, 128, 152-53, 157, 159-61, 184-85, 219-20, 239, 262, 281-82, 286-89, 290, 298, 314
principle of selfhood in, **M7**: 342-43
and war effort, **M10**: 296-300
in Russia, **L3**: 212
society's responsibility for, **L5**: 431-33; **L6**: 137-41, 342; **L7**: 29, 30; **L17**: 24, 550-52
play of, **L10**: 281-84
needs and tendencies of, **L11**: 193-95; **L17**: 235
emotions of, **L11**: 200
related to adults, **L11**: 209, 213
effects of Depression on, **L11**: 268
and environment, **L11**: 512-13
focus on, **L13**: xii, xiii
faults of, **L17**: 237, 340
power of suggestion in, **L17**: 266, 332
attention of, **L17**: 270-83
misconception of, **L17**: 293
Child and the Curriculum, The, **M2**: xvii; **M7**: xxi, xxiv; **L11**: xviii; **L13**: xii
Child care
affects society, **L9**: 233-34
Child-centered schools, **L5**: xv-xvi, 319-25
Child development, **L3**: 330-31; **L7**: 40, 42, 70, 456
stages of, **E5**: 91, 298-99; **M1**: 225-29
instruction in, **M1**: 209-10
Dewey's interest in, **M2**: xiii
Russian study of, **L17**: 507
Childhood, **M14**: x, 5, 47, 50, 65, 85
reasoning in, **M7**: 369-76
as positive state, **M9**: 46-47, 54-55, 59
and language, **M14**: 43, 69
impulse and instinct in, **M14**: 70, 90, 106
idealization of, **M14**: 71-72
W. Hudson on, **L10**: 130-31
McKay on, **L17**: 59
importance of, **L17**: 65

play of, **L17**: 262
lies during, **L17**: 265-66
from infancy, **L17**: 268
Child labor, **M5**: 483-84; **M9**: 203; **M11**: 162, 176; **L7**: 378, 412-13; **L11**: 21
laws, **M7**: 205-6
abolition of, **M10**: 125
thirteenth conference of (1917), **M10**: 125n
contributes to illiteracy, **L5**: 316
Child Labor amendment, **L2**: 310
Child psychology, **M1**: xxi; **M9**: 180, 202, 325
distinguished from adult, **M1**: 132-33
criticism of, **M1**: 175-77
related to religious education, **M3**: 210-15
Child relief, **L5**: 431-33
Children's Bureau, **L6**: 342; **L9**: 394; **L11**: 268; **L17**: 517, 573
Children's Charter, **L6**: 92, 132, 141; **L17**: 516, 550-52
on children's welfare, **L17**: 511, 572
challenges teachers, **L17**: 512
on home influence, **L17**: 518
Children's Court (New York City), **L9**: 377
Childs, John L., **L11**: 383n; **L14**: 4; **L17**: 560
on philosophy of education, **L8**: xi-xii, 43n, 77n
vs. Bode on education, **L13**: 304-8, 377-90
on USSR, **L15**: xii, 342-43, 487-91
Child-study
principles established by, **E5**: 204-6
criticism of, **E5**: 209
related to sciences, **E5**: 210
development of interest in, **E5**: 211-21, 368-69
in educational psychology, **E5**: 445
coordination in, **M1**: 178-91
stages of, **M1**: 194-211, 213-15
Noss on, **M2**: 102-4
curriculum indebted to, **M2**: 379-82
and genetic method, **M3**: xviii, 299-304
Child-Study Monthly, **M1**: 186
Child Welfare Department, **M11**: 77
Chili faction, **M12**: 67, 70
China, **M15**: 215-18; **L6**: 353; **L11**: 184
customs of, **M5**: 23; **M11**: 215-23, 226, 231, 234; **L7**: 22-23
justice in, **M5**: 34; **L7**: 32-33
in WWI, **M11**: ix, 199-202, 229-30
education in, **M11**: xvii, 180, 200, 203, 207, 209, 231; **M13**: 112, 118-19, 228-32; **L17**: 169-71
Dewey visits, **M11**: xviii-xx, 180; **L7**: xxii-xxiii; **L14**: xx
student revolt in, **M11**: xix-xx, 186-91; **M12**: 22-27, 32, 41-51; **M13**: 101, 102, 106, 116-18, 253, 255
government in, **M11**: xix-xx, 192, 196, 199-204, 212-14, 229; **M12**: 41-50, 65-70; **M13**: xxiii, 74-76, 108-14, 129-36, 147, 150-51, 153, 182, 192, 193, 210, 495; **L17**: 29-30
foreign interests in, **M11**: 151-54, 163, 192-98, 224-40; **M12**: 22-23, 26, 28-40, 45,

China (*continued*)
58-59, 60-70, 254; **L2**: 181-84; **L6**: 209-10
Japan's relation with, **M11**: 159, 160, 168, 169, 173-80, 183, 186-91, 226, 238, 394; **M12**: xxi, 22-23, 28-40, 45, 58-59, 61-70, 254; **M13**: xxiv, 112, 162, 170, 192-93, 441-42; **L2**: 176-78; **L6**: xx, 190, 193, 203-6, 211, 452, 456, 466-67
and Paris Peace Conference, **M11**: 194, 224; **M12**: 23, 28, 32, 36, 41
and U.S., **M11**: 195-97, 207, 226-32; **M12**: 4-6, 32, 36-40, 61, 75; **M13**: 137, 157, 166-68, 409-10, 495; **L2**: 173-84; **L3**: 200, 202, 364, 429
development of, **M11**: 205-14
economics in, **M11**: 224-26, 229-30, 233; **M12**: 22-40, 59, 71-76; **M13**: 76, 93, 108-9, 124, 160-61, 181-83, 218, 494-95; **L3**: 419-20; **L6**: 202-5, 475-76
drug traffic in, **M11**: 235-40
communism in, **M12**: xxiii, 26, 253-55; **L15**: 352-53, 500
characteristics of people of, **M12**: xxiii-xxiv, 29, 35-38, 41-42, 48
bolshevism in, **M12**: 5, 19, 23, 26, 44, 46
language reform in, **M12**: 24-26
and West, **M12**: 26, 28, 34-37, 41-50, 53-54, 57
and Germany, **M12**: 26, 29-30, 37; **M13**: 141-42, 192, 202
revolution in, **M12**: 35-37, 65, 253-55
military in, **M12**: 43-44, 65-70, 73-74; **L3**: 423-28
complexity of, **M12**: 51-60
over-population of, **M12**: 53-58
and Russia, **M12**: 60-64; **M13**: 175, 233, 237; **L2**: 176-78; **L15**: 495
problems in, **M12**: 73-76; **M13**: xxiii-xxv, 73-74, 94-99, 103, 119-20, 153-54, 162, 165, 170-71, 182-88, 192, 220, 230; **L3**: 196-200, 417-18, 420-21
family system in, **M13**: xxiv, 104, 106, 110
conservatism of, **M13**: xxv, 118, 222-24
emperors in, **M13**: xxvi, 225
literary revolution in, **M13**: 109, 256
Washington Conference on, **M13**: 191-96
compared with Turkey, **L2**: 193
Crozier on, **L3**: 196-98, 417-31
illiteracy in, **L3**: 422-23
boycotts against, **L3**: 428-29
relation of Pact of Paris to, **L6**: 194
relation of League of Nations to, **L6**: 206-7, 450, 454, 457-59
and disarmament, **L6**: 460
art of, **L10**: 146, 147, 213, 315, 333-36
in WWII, **L15**: 348, 369-70
North vs. South in, **L17**: 30, 33-34
propaganda in, **L17**: 30-31
Chinese philosophy, **M13**: 226
Hocking on, **L14**: 421
Chinese Social and Political Association, **M13**: 242n

Chinese Students' Monthly, **M13**: 156
Chino-Japanese War, **M13**: 108
Chippewa Indians, **E4**: 38
Chita, USSR, **M13**: 236-37
Chivalry, **M5**: 140
Chocorua, N.H., **L11**: 465
Choctaw language, **L8**: 228
Choice, **M14**: 134-35, 144, 193, 209, 212-15; **L1**: 34-35, 51-52, 67, 80-81, 86-87, 314, 315, 320, 326, 389-92
  in volition, **E2**: 314-16
  in prudential control, **E2**: 335-37
  moral, **E2**: 348-52; **M8**: 33; **L3**: 92-97; **L7**: 166-67, 169, 171, 248, 316, 319; **L16**: 312-13
  related to character, **E2**: 354
  related to attention, **E4**: 93
  in Bergson's theory of perception, **M7**: 20-24
  and action, **L3**: 97, 101, 104; **L17**: 339
  and intellect, **L3**: 111-12
  and self, **L7**: 285-89, 307
  vs. preference, **L7**: 286; **L17**: xxv
  related to religion, **L9**: 6-8
  as passion, **L17**: xx
  consequences of, **L17**: xxxii, 476-77
Choose Life (Mandelbaum), **L9**: xxixn
Choshu clansmen (Japan), **M11**: 168, 169
Chrisman, Oscar, **L17**: 571
Christendom, **L17**: 94
Christian Century, **M15**: xxvii; **L6**: 223n; **L11**: 527
  religious discussions in, **L9**: xxi, xxiii, 223, 294, 412, 417, 435, 438
Christianity, **M11**: 121, 132, 184; **M12**: 89-90, 104-6, 143-44, 152; **L1**: 96; **L3**: 6; **L9**: 22, 32, 215, 218, 219, 223, 419-21; **L15**: 46-47, 52, 55, 61, 381, 391. *See also* Protestantism; Roman Catholic church
  and morality, **E3**: 380; **E4**: 228, 230; **M9**: 359; **L11**: 75
  as revelation, **E4**: 4-7
  soul and, **E4**: 98-99; **M7**: 341
  concepts of, **E4**: 100-102, 228, 230; **L8**: xvii, 7, 24, 31-32
  influence of, **E4**: 139-40; **M1**: xvii; **M13**: 301
  related to esthetics, **E4**: 192-93; **L10**: 37-38, 115, 296, 321, 331, 340
  in Roman Empire, **E5**: 9-11
  belief and desire in, **M3**: 89-90
  and love, **M5**: 96-97; **L7**: 88
  history of, **M5**: 103-4; **L7**: 95; **L17**: 531-33
  and life, **M5**: 103-5; **L7**: 94-96
  self-denial in, **M5**: 328; **L7**: 90
  pessimistic tone of, **M7**: 296
  related to Chinese reform, **M13**: 115
  J. Marsh on, **L5**: 178-96
  Mill on, **L5**: 181
  on human nature, **L6**: 34, 35
  church and, **L7**: 135-37, 140-41
  authority of, **L11**: 130, 134-35; **L17**: 530
  James on, **L11**: 474
  democracy related to, **L13**: 152
  on change, **L14**: 99
  social aspects of, **L14**: 286-88
  related to science, **L16**: 409
  requirement of, **L17**: 15, 17
  acknowledges industrial problem, **L17**: 19
  defense of, **L17**: 374

Christianity (*continued*)
unspirituality of, **L17**: 530
Swift on, **L17**: 537-38
Hegel on, **L17**: 565
Christians, **M15**: 108, 140-42, 147, 148
Christian Science Monitor, **M11**: 305
Christus oder Antichristus, **M15**: 330
Chung Mei service, **L17**: 30
Church, A. J.
on *Odyssey*, **E3**: 193-94
Church, Alonzo
reviews Dewey-Bentley articles, **L16**: xxxi, 276, 443-47
on Carnap, **L16**: 23n-24n
on definition, **L16**: 163-64
Church, **M13**: 304; **L13**: 148, 160, 181
and state, **E3**: 227; **M11**: 18-40; **M15**: 128, 130, 132, 205-6, 240; **L13**: 70; **L15**: 156, 281-84
medieval, **M5**: 137-39; **L2**: 32-35; **L7**: 135-37, 413
and marriage, **M5**: 514-16; **L7**: 442-43
Kant on dogmas of, **M8**: 184
influences education, **M9**: 288-89, 298
conflicts with science, **M9**: 336
authority of, **M11**: 49; **L2**: 40-41; **L4**: 61, 203, 205, 220, 225; **L16**: 362-63, 369
in U.S., **M11**: 71
important to Polish question, **M11**: 243, 249, 260, 262, 269, 277, 278, 284, 286-91, 297-311, 327, 328
controversy in, **M15**: 5-7, 11
opposed to Darwin's theories, **M15**: 47-48
and secular ethics, **M15**: 54
in Western Europe, **M15**: 128
future of, **L2**: 163-66
in Mexico, **L2**: 194-202, 208
in Russia, **L3**: 217-18
doctrine of, **L4**: 233; **L14**: 149-50; **L17**: 16-17, 19-20, 431, 437
isolation of, **L4**: 245-46
individualism of, **L5**: 77-78
Mill on, **L5**: 180-81
Coleridge on, **L5**: 190-91
Orthodox, **L5**: 355-62
urges unemployment relief, **L6**: 381-82
and philosophy, **L6**: 426
in government, **L7**: 136
in economics, **L7**: 136-37
Reformation views of, **L7**: 140-41
related to social issues, **L9**: 46, 54-55
art's relation to, **L10**: 37, 331-33; **L13**: 70
enjoins revival, **L14**: 214-15
Swift on, **L17**: 16, 537, 539
failure of, **L17**: 539
Churchill, Marlborough, **M11**: 259, 406
Churchill, Winston, **L15**: 340, 348, 509
Churchman, C. West, **L16**: 193n, 470
Churchman, **L11**: 530
Chute, Eloise, **L16**: 140n
Cicero, **M4**: 42; **M7**: 218, 295; **M11**: 19; **L4**: xxi; **L8**: 6
and Law of Nature, **E4**: 125
on reason, **L7**: 131-33
Cincinnati, Ohio
school system of, **M7**: 96
inter-denominational congress at, **L17**: 19-20, 555

CIO (Congress of Industrial Organizations), **L11**: 333; **L15**: 245, 509
Circles
as symbols in logic, **L12**: 306, 359n
Circuit
sensori-motor, **E5**: 98
organic, **E5**: 317
Circularity, **L16**: xxi, 78, 97n
in philosophy, **L14**: xiii-xiv
as name, **L16**: 62, 260-61
as procedural characteristic, **L16**: 64, 69, 70, 75, 81
Circular reasoning, **L12**: 264
Circumcision, **M5**: 61
Citizens
and politics, **L6**: 174, 182-88
and unemployment relief, **L6**: 397
teachers as, **L6**: 433-35
Dewey's faith in, **L17**: xxvi-xxix
Citizens' Committees
for Polish fundraising, **M11**: 300, 303, 310
Citizens Conference on the Crisis in Education, **L9**: 119-21, 124-25, 129, 130n
Citizenship, **M15**: 158-59; **L6**: 132, 138, 140-41; **L11**: 229, 378
defined, **M2**: 82-83
education for, **M15**: 160-61, 190; **L9**: 161-64
leisure and, **M15**: 167
Aristotle on, **L2**: 215, 321
right of, **L17**: 513
Citizens Jury on Unemployment, **L9**: 271
Citron, Alice, **L9**: 320
City Affairs Committee (New York City), **L9**: 346n
City Club (New York City), **L9**: 354
City of God (St. Augustine), **L9**: 71
Civics, **L11**: 185-86, 233-34
Civilization
compared with *Kultur*, **M8**: 168-69
conquest of nature related to, **M10**: 237-38
values in, **L9**: 57-58
Wieman on, **L9**: 415-17
art's role in, **L10**: xxxi, 16, 34, 329-52
crises in, **L11**: 131-32
teaching about, **L11**: 209-11
compared with savagery, **L13**: 22
weaknesses in, **L13**: 310
signs of, **L15**: 170-71
tradition of, **L16**: 394
threat to, **L16**: 399-400
Chinese vs. Anglo-Saxon, **L17**: 296
Civilization during the Middle Ages (G. Adams), **E4**: 200, 213
Civil liberty, **L11**: 5, 372-75
Civil rights, **M11**: 137, 264; **M12**: xxi-xxii, 9-11
types of, **M5**: 404-8
development of, **M5**: 408-23
importance of, **L14**: 93; **L16**: 402-3
Civil Service Reform Association, **L9**: 356
Civil War (U.S.), **M11**: 116, 143, 287, 337; **L8**: 57; **L9**: 176, 178; **L13**: 186; **L15**: 242, 341
and political parties, **L6**: 232, 236
and coercive force, **L6**: 463
as national crisis, **L9**: 77

Civil Works Administration, **L9**: 287
Cizek, Franz, **L2**: 55, 58
Clans
Kafir, **M5**: 25; **L7**: 24-25
of Celts, **M5**: 29; **L7**: 29
in Japan, **M11**: 168, 169
moral duties of, **L17**: 395-96
Clapp, Elsie Ripley, **L14**: 351
Clarification, **L16**: 157
as esthetic quality, **L10**: 181, 188, 199
Clark, J. B., **M5**: 485
Clark College (Worcester, Mass.), **M11**: 73n, 394
Clarke, Edward H.
on sex in education, **L17**: 7, 553
Clarke, John H., **M15**: 95; **L7**: 398
Clarke, Samuel, **M3**: 53
controversy with Leibniz, **E1**: 303, 366-68
on moral distinctions, **E4**: 127, 144
Clarkson, Thomas, **L11**: 18
Class, **L16**: 372, 419
consciousness, **M11**: xvii-xviii; **L11**: 382-86, 486; **L13**: 133-34
interests, **L8**: 67, 101
war, **L13**: 121-22, 124, 127, 134, 352-54; **L14**: 75-76
Classes, **L10**: 26. *See also* Category, **L12**; Kinds, **L12**; Species, **L12**
in rational and empirical knowledge, **M9**: 343-44
Russell on, **M10**: 96
in art, **L10**: 229, 232, 289
vs. kinds, **L11**: 102, 119n
nature of, **L11**: 106, 118-19
null-, **L11**: 121-22
ambiguity of term, **L11**: 126
Classes, social, **M12**: xv, 113, 122-23, 167, 169
in England and U.S., **E3**: 202-3
in primitive society, **M5**: 27-28; **L7**: 26-27
medieval, **M5**: 135-36; **M9**: 128; **L7**: 132, 138
in Hegel, **M9**: 65
modern, **M9**: 90, 103-4, 143, 169, 260, 265, 269, 320
Plato on, **M9**: 94-97, 102-3
in eighteenth century, **M9**: 97-98, 124-25
in conflict of applied and pure science, **M9**: 237-38
reflected in education, **M9**: 256-57; **L9**: 114, 145, 202
division into, **M14**: 5, 18, 58-59, 186-87, 208; **L10**: 252
struggle between, **L7**: 326, 385; **L11**: 52-55, 61, 342-43, 382-86, 439-40, 498
historical role of, **L11**: 56-57
privileged, **L11**: 161, 165, 168, 231, 413
Slesinger on, **L11**: 485-86
Classic art, **L10**: 304, 315
quality of, **L10**: xxxi, 9, 147, 149, 173
subject-matter of, **L10**: 192
vs. romantic, **L10**: 287-90
praised, **L10**: 351
Classic idealism
in Great Britain, **M10**: 223-25
Classicism, **M13**: 287-88
Classic philosophical tradition, **M12**: 89, 92, 93, 122, 140
doctrines of, **L4**: 7, 14-16, 21-23, 27-28, 34, 52, 57, 61-64, 103, 107, 113, 170, 171, 184, 186, 234, 240
indictment against, **L4**: 29, 57-58, 159-60

Kant furthers, **L4**: 229-30
related to culture, **L14**: 89, 313
decline of, **L16**: 369
terminology of, **L16**: 388
Classification, **M12**: 167, 176-77, 215, 263; **M14**: 92, 167; **L1**: 52, 89, 122, 136, 182, 249; **L4**: 80, 145, 200, 212; **L10**: 55, 120; **L11**: 71, 106n. *See also* Category, **L12**
educational, **M13**: 290
judging by, **M13**: 291
as enemy of democracy, **M13**: 297-98
nature of, **M13**: 358; **L12**: 295, 306-7, 340-41
of art, **M13**: 363
limits perception, **L10**: 218-21, 226-29, 252
in Aristotelian logic, **L12**: 253-54
definition as, **L16**: 166
of Dubs, **L16**: 175
Kaufmann on, **L16**: 196n
of Ogden and Richards, **L16**: 218n
"Class Struggle and the Democratic Way," **L11**: xxiiin
Claude Lorrain, **L10**: 298
Claxton, P. P., **M10**: 299
Clay, Henry, **L7**: 378
Clayton Anti-Trust Act, **L7**: 387, 418
Cleavage in Our Culture, The (Burkhardt), **L16**: 407n
Clemenceau, Georges, **M11**: 279; **M12**: 3; **M13**: 316
Clemens, Samuel L., **M12**: xxixn, 15; **L10**: 320; **L14**: xxi
Clement of Alexandria, **M2**: 153
Clergy
medieval, **L7**: 135-37
Cleveland, Grover, **L13**: 402; **L15**: 242
Cleveland, Ohio, **L8**: 13
LIPA conference at, **L6**: 239n, 246-52
Clifford, William Kingdon, **M5**: 29n; **L7**: 28n; **L17**: 11, 554
Clopton, Robert W., **M12**: 205n; **L15**: 369n
Close. *See also* Ends, **L12**
as termination, **L12**: 38, 95-96, 160, 178, 221, 385
Closed Door
related to Manchuria, **L6**: 469
"Closed Industrial State, The" (Fichte), **M8**: 175
Closed system, **L12**: 318-19, 408-9, 470-71, 481. *See also* Contingency, **L12**
Clothing
study of, **E5**: 240-41
Cluff, Benjamin, Jr., **L17**: 213, 563
Codes, moral, **M14**: 74
Cody, Sherwin, **M7**: 464
Coeducation
in western U.S. colleges, **E5**: 272
at University of Chicago, **M2**: 105-16
at Colby College, **M2**: 112
Jordan on, **M6**: 155
advantages of, **M6**: 156-63
compared with women's colleges, **M6**: 163-64
establishment of, **L17**: 7
Coercion, **L7**: 167, 217-18, 225-26. *See also* Force
as means of social control, **L11**: 45-47, 218, 379; **L13**: 82
vs. discussion, **L13**: 153
Coffin, Henry Sloane, **L15**: 356
Coghill, George Ellett, **L16**: 117n
Cognition, **M15**: 338-40, 344-45; **L11**: 73

Cognitive noting
experience as, **M10**: 34-35
Cohen, Carl
on Dewey's 1923-24 writings, **M15**: ix-xxvi
Cohen, Hermann, **L15**: xxix
Cohen, Marshall, **L9**: xxxin
Cohen, Morris R., **M15**: 226-28; **L2**: 28n; **L4**: 90n; **L6**: xiv-xv; **L14**: xiii, 154
on experience, **L1**: xi, xii, xvi
tribute to, **L3**: 361-63
on scientific method, **L6**: 299-304, 488-91
Dewey replies to, **L14**: xii, 143-50
critiques Dewey, **L14**: 379-410
logic of, **L16**: xxx, xxxi, 25, 39, 40, 184n, 187, 193-95, 209
epistemology of, **L16**: 8-10
on propositions, **L16**: 12-17, 35, 45, 208
Coherence, **L16**: 261
Cohesion
political, **L17**: 112
Coke, Edward, **M11**: 29
Colby College, **M2**: 112
Cold War, **L16**: 391, 399
Coleridge, Samuel Taylor, **E4**: 147; **M3**: 55, 56
on understanding and reason, **M2**: 260
influences J. Marsh, **L5**: 148, 178-83, 189-91
on poetry, **L10**: xx, 11, 160, 192, 353, 359-63
on esthetics, **L10**: xxviii, 198, 272
as poet, **L10**: 39, 115, 116, 322
on nature, **L10**: 218, 361
on institutions, **L11**: 18
influences Mill, **L11**: 24, 81
"Coleridge" (J. S. Mill), **L5**: 180
Colgate University, **M13**: 289
Collected Essays and Reviews (W. James), **L2**: 6-7
Collected Legal Papers (O. Holmes), **M15**: 68, 69; **L3**: 177
Collected Papers of Charles Sanders Peirce (Hartshorne and P. Weiss), **L6**: xiv, 273; **L11**: 87n, 108n, 421-24, 479-84; **L15**: 144-52
Collected Papers of Frederic William Maitland, The, **L2**: 42
Collected Works of John Dewey, 1882-1953, The
history of, **L17**: xi-xii
Collection, **L12**: 203-4, 208-9, 360-63, 409-10
Collective bargaining, **L13**: 110
Collective mind, **M10**: 60
Collectivism, **L9**: 207; **L11**: 174, 388, 485; **L15**: 215
and individualism, **L2**: 351-56; **L7**: 322, 327
Lippmann on, **L11**: 489-91, 494
private and state, **L14**: 92-97
College. *See also* Normal schools; University
health of women in, **E1**: 64-80; **L17**: 7-9
curriculum in, **E5**: 272; **L6**: 84-85, 404, 414-23, 503, 504; **L11**: 400-401, 406
preparation for, **M1**: 282-83; **L11**: 163, 172-74
role of, **M1**: 290, 309-10; **M15**: 200-201, 203-6; **L6**: 296-97
related to high school, **M1**: 291
cultural and technological, **M1**: 302

training in, **M1**: 312-13
women's, **M6**: 163-64
state of, **M6**: 471
obstacles to development of, **M15**: xxiv, 203-8
intellectual freedom in, **M15**: xxiv-xxv, 201-2, 207-11
political activity in, **L6**: 119-22
life in, **L6**: 259-62
progressive schools related to, **L9**: 156
Hutchins on, **L11**: 397-98
funding of, **L11**: 399
liberal arts, **L15**: 276-80
College of the City of New York, **L11**: 530-31; **L14**: xxi, 231, 357; **L15**: xii
College Teachers of Education, National Society of, **L17**: 138-39, 561
Collegiate Alumnae, Association of, **L17**: 8-9, 553
Collier's, **L6**: 364
Collingwood, Robin G., **L14**: 334
Collins, Anna L. P., **L6**: 433-35
Colombia, **L6**: 468-69
Colonialism, **L15**: 308-9
Colonna, Aegidius, **M5**: 138
Color
qualities of, **L10**: 21, 122, 126-29, 133, 162, 260, 344, 345
relations between, **L10**: 92-101, 141
as medium, **L10**: 146, 175-79, 184, 188, 199-207, 210-13, 230-31, 238, 281
criticism's concern with, **L10**: 312, 318
theory of, **L11**: 89, 97-98
Columbia, Mo., Elementary School
environmental study at, **M8**: 273-74
Columbia plan, **E3**: 200, 201
Columbia University, **M7**: 409; **M8**: ix, xx; **M10**: xxxiv, 164-66; **M11**: ix, xiv, 18n, 259, 398, 406; **M13**: 425; **M15**: xxiv, 193n; **L2**: 3n, 124n; **L5**: 412n; **L11**: 529; **L14**: xix, 4; **L17**: 7
philosophy of, **M4**: x
development of Dewey's thought at, **M6**: xii
academic freedom at, **L14**: 374, 431
Philosophical Club, **L17**: 374n
Graduate Department of Philosophy, **L17**: 466n
Columbia University Teachers College, **M3**: 326; **M10**: 398n; **M15**: xxiii, 184; **L3**: 251n, 253-55; **L9**: 136n; **L17**: 88
training at, **M1**: 55-56
and University Elementary School, **M1**: 329
alumni conference, **M7**: 369n
kindergarten play program at, **M8**: 278-83
Columbia War Papers, **M10**: 296n
Columbus, Christopher, **M1**: 168; **M8**: 292; **L1**: 333
as skeptic, **M6**: 185; **L8**: xvi, 117-18, 173
Colvin, Sidney
on art, **L10**: 102, 222, 357, 361
Colvin, Stephen Sheldon, **M3**: 153
on subjective idealism and psychology, **M3**: 382-89
Comédie Humaine (Balzac), **M5**: 176
Comedy, **L10**: 178, 229, 247, 285
Comenius, John Amos, **M1**: xxvii; **M6**: 423

Coming of a New Party, The (P. Douglas), **L6**: xvii, 313
Commentary, **L15**: xxv-xxvi, 210, 224, 362, 381, 388, 392
on Dewey essay, **L16**: 470-71
Commerce. *See also* Economics
in early society, **M5**: 77; **L7**: 71
Greek conception of, **M5**: 112-14; **L7**: 103-4
art's relation to, **L10**: 15, 193, 330-31, 340
Jefferson on, **L13**: 81, 102, 107
disturbance in, **L16**: 360
mechanisms of, **L16**: 370
Commerce, Association of, **L5**: 372, 373
Commerce, Bureau of Foreign and Domestic, **L6**: 353
Commercial Club of Chicago, **M8**: 124, 126, 471-72
Commercial Federation (China), **M11**: 196
Commercialism, **M13**: 306, 307, 309
Commercial subjects
in high school, **M1**: 295-99
Commission of Inquiry (American Peace Commission), **M11**: 401-3
Commission of Inquiry into the Charges Made against Leon Trotsky in the Moscow Trials, **L14**: xix-xx; **L15**: xi. *See also* American Committee for the Defense of Leon Trotsky
significance of, **L11**: xxvi-xxvii, 306-9, 318, 326-29, 331-36
formation of, **L11**: 305
preliminary report to, **L11**: 310-14
criticism of, **L11**: 315-19
findings of, **L11**: 321-26, 330-31; **L15**: 346, 351, 492-93, 499
subcommissions of, **L13**: 347-48, 395, 404
Commission on National Aid to Vocational Education, **M7**: 93-94
Commission on the Function of Philosophy in Liberal Education, **L15**: 154-55
Commission on the Teaching of the Social Studies, **L13**: 389-90
Committee for Cultural Freedom, **M9**: xiv
and Russell case, **L14**: 357
New Republic on, **L14**: 365-66
role in fostering freedom, **L14**: 367-68
Committee for Social Legislation, **L15**: 324
Committee of Forty-eight, **L6**: 235
Committee of One Hundred, **L6**: 118n, 322, 404
Committee on Dependency and Neglect, **L6**: 352
Committee on Economic Sanctions, **L6**: 456n, 471, 484
Committee on Foreign Relations, **L6**: 364-65
Committee on Labor, **L6**: 381
Committee on Manufactures, **L6**: 381
Committee on National Morale, **L15**: 353
Committee on Public Information, **M10**: 315-16; **M11**: 150, 151, 257, 394, 395
Committee on School Inquiry, **M8**: 129
Committee on Social Trends, **L9**: 133, 229-31, 235

Committee on the Socio-Economic Goals of America (NEA), **L11**: 548
Committee on Un-American Activities, **L6**: xxii
Committee on Youth Outside of Home and School, **L17**: 515
Common Faith, A, **M1**: xi; **L5**: xxx; **L9**: xi-xxxii, 293, 295, 423, 424, 426, 435, 438n, 440; **L11**: 115; **L14**: 79
  on religion vs. religious experience, **L16**: 465-66
Common good
  Rousseau on, **L13**: 149
Common interest
  nature of, **L2**: 246, 256-57
Common law, **M5**: 63; **L2**: 23-25
Common Law, The (O. Holmes), **E4**: 37, 38, 40; **M15**: 69; **L14**: xxii
Common man, **L11**: 365
  essential to democracy, **L14**: 226-27
  Cohen on, **L14**: 396
Commonplaces
  McKay on, **L17**: 58
Common qualities
  and generality, **L12**: 248-49, 261-62, 265, 268, 350
Commons, John R., **L6**: 357-58, 368; **L11**: 250; **L16**: 101n
Common sense, **M6**: 288; **M12**: 137; **M13**: 413; **L8**: 296; **L9**: 298, 312; **L12**: 56, 100-102, 118-20, 162, 264, 445, 455-56, 476-77; **L13**: 391
  and philosophy, **M10**: 39-42; **L6**: xiv, 424-25
  in act, **M13**: 13
  Klyce on, **M13**: 420
  and judgment, **M15**: 65; **L6**: 429-30
  Santayana on, **M15**: 221; **L9**: 240-41
  Lovejoy on, **M15**: 369
  empirical, **L2**: 49, 53, 54
  Peirce on, **L6**: 276-77; **L11**: 480-81
  problems in, **L12**: 71-72, 84-85, 420-22
  Trotsky on, **L13**: 392
  related to science, **L16**: xxxvii, 244-45, 252-53, 255-56, 292, 304n, 306, 451
  in Moore's logic, **L16**: 203-7
  nature of, **L16**: 242-43, 246-50, 386
"Common Sense and Science," **L16**: xxvi, 336, 450
Common-sense dualism, **M10**: 24
Common-sense knowledge
  connected with action, **M7**: 3
  compared with scientific knowledge, **L1**: 341-45
Commonweal, **L11**: 530
Commonwealth
  defined, **L7**: 133
  and law, **L7**: 397-98
Common will, **M13**: 339-40
  Rousseau on, **L13**: 149
Communication, **M9**: 7-9, 12, 225-26; **M12**: xx, xxii, 147-49, 233, 242; **M13**: 308; **L1**: 132-42, 144, 147, 149, 157-61, 187, 206-8, 213-17, 222, 272; **L3**: 51; **L4**: 36, 121, 174, 214; **L13**: xvi, 21, 324, 334. *See also* Language, **L12**
  social necessity of, **E5**: 231; **M1**: xxiii; **M15**: 239; **L2**: 253, 259-60, 273, 330, 370-72
  instinct of child, **M1**: 29

Communication (*continued*)
and knowledge, **L2**: 282-84, 345-46
related to art, **L2**: 348-50; **L10**: xxxi, 28, 110, 111, 212, 238, 242, 244, 248-49, 275, 291, 337-38, 349; **L13**: 70
effects of, **L7**: 150; **L15**: 248; **L16**: 309
in U.S., **L11**: 168-69, 261
interpersonal, **L11**: 195, 241, 417
educative power of, **L11**: 538-40
and sentences, **L12**: 174-76, 284
intelligent use of, **L13**: 90, 92
prevention of, **L13**: 323; **L14**: 89
through senses, **L13**: 366
as value in democracy, **L14**: 275-76; **L17**: 474
related to philosophy, **L14**: 325
freedom of, **L15**: 176, 179-83; **L16**: 403, 404, 406; **L17**: 86
as human trait, **L15**: 211, 266
dependability of, **L16**: 3, 4
Carnap on, **L16**: 26
inquiry into, **L16**: 126
deficiency in, **L16**: 277
Cold War affects, **L16**: 392
as social category, **L17**: 320-21
Communism, **M5**: 151; **M8**: 435; **M12**: xxiii, 26, 253-55; **L6**: xxii, 447, 464n; **L7**: 426-27; **L9**: 76-77, 298; **L11**: 598; **L13**: 131, 157, 216, 218
Marxist, **M8**: 436
contrasted with revolution, **L3**: 204, 205, 222-23
Brookwood accused of, **L5**: 331-45, 392
on religion, **L5**: 355-62
Dewey accused of, **L5**: 392
in Russia, **L6**: 263-67, 292-94
Russian vs. Western, **L9**: 91-94
reasons for denouncing, **L9**: 94-95
Bellamy on, **L9**: 103, 105
Brameld on, **L9**: 244-45
related to Teachers Union, **L9**: 338-42
on revolution, **L11**: 59
vs. fascism, **L11**: 64, 187, 495
tactics of, **L11**: 324, 333-34
on class struggle, **L11**: 331, 383, 485, 498
means and ends in, **L11**: 332; **L17**: 117
Spender on, **L11**: 497-98
and war, **L14**: 250
in U.S., **L15**: 240-46, 293, 348, 375, 488, 491
in China, **L15**: 352-53, 500
attacks democracy, **L16**: 401-5
Communist Manifesto (Marx and Engels), **L7**: 426; **L11**: 54, 59
Communist Opposition
related to unions, **L9**: 335-36, 340
Communist party, **L6**: 169-70, 235; **L9**: 69, 327, 340
factions in, **L13**: 135
members as teachers, **L17**: 136-37
enhanced, **L17**: 140
members in government, **L17**: 140, 561-62
controls unions, **L17**: 520-21
Community, **L8**: 80; **L16**: 244-45, 377
Browning on, **E3**: 120-21
related to education, **E5**: 94; **M9**: 24-26, 28, 87-89; **L9**: 183-85; **L13**: 36-37; **L14**: 351-54; **L17**: 71, 74-75, 226-27

meaning for Dewey, **M1**: xx; **M2**: xx-xxi
self-preservation of, **M5**: 62; **L7**: 57
nature of, **M9**: xi-xiii, 7; **L2**: 214-16, 300-301; **L17**: xxiv-xxv
Royce on, **M10**: 84n
communication in, **L2**: 259-60
and society, **L2**: 296, 333-34; **L8**: 53-54, 63-64, 71, 73; **L13**: 176
lack of, **L2**: 314-15, 324, 327, 350
vs. association, **L2**: 330-31
importance of local, **L2**: 367-72
Hebrew conception of, **L7**: 85, 95
moral meaning of, **L7**: 257, 335, 345, 347
art in, **L8**: 85-86; **L10**: 12-15, 87, 156, 208, 252, 330-31, 338
related to religion, **L9**: 40-42, 57-58, 431
future role of, **L11**: 540-41
self-governing, **L17**: xxvi
conflicts within, **L17**: 101, 102
state as legal organization of, **L17**: 101-4
fascism and, **L17**: 117
Greek participation in, **L17**: 172, 175, 177
Russian views on, **L17**: 504
Community Schools in Action (Clapp), **L14**: 351
Companionship, **L13**: 286
Comparative method, **L2**: 265
Comparison
in British psychology, **E1**: 183-84
in *Cyclopedia of Education*, **M6**: 388-89
defined, **L12**: 184-86
as measurement, **L12**: 202-3, 318
importance of, **L12**: 208, 212-13, 217-19, 247-48, 267, 283, 335-36, 350-51
Compensation, **M14**: 8, 24, 27, 188
Competition, **L13**: 32-33
related to individualism, **M5**: 475-78
in capitalism, **L7**: 376-79, 400
fair and unfair, **L7**: 413, 418-19
in Marxism, **L13**: 125
Hobbes on, **L13**: 140-42
destructiveness of, **L17**: 454
Complex, **L12**: 155, 481, 504
status of, **L17**: 415
in Russian schools, **L17**: 502
Complex-simple category
Russell on, **M10**: 96-97; **L16**: 200
Compossibility, **L4**: 128
Compound proposition, **L12**: 335, 340
Comprehension, **L12**: 146-47, 341, 417-18
as understanding, **L12**: 156-60
of terms, **L12**: 359-60
vs. apprehension, **L14**: 53-54
related to memory, **L17**: 328
Comprehensiveness, **E3**: 371
Compromise, **L13**: 3, 5
Compton, Betty, **L9**: 367
Compton, Karl T., **L11**: 567n, 568, 570, 573, 575-76, 579, 580
Comte, Auguste, **E4**: 214; **M6**: 366; **M11**: 26n, 43; **M12**: 85; **M14**: 93; **M15**: 11, 333; **L1**: 55, 174; **L5**: xxx, 264; **L11**: xvn, 24, 48; **L14**: 362; **L17**: 386
and moral philosophy, **E4**: 148

Comte, Auguste (*continued*)
related to political economy, **E4**: 216-17
on scientific method, **M1**: 171
interpretations of, **M2**: 36
on nature, **M2**: 143
on positivism, **M2**: 209; **M7**: 324-26
on ethics, **M3**: 56
on static and dynamic, **M6**: 424
influences Dewey, **L5**: 154
law of three stages of, **L5**: 170
on social system, **L10**: 346; **L13**: 121
on knowledge, **L16**: 97-98
Conant, James B., **L11**: 127
Conant, Levi Leonard
work of, **E5**: 355-56
psychological points of, **E5**: 356-58
Concentration, **M6**: 212; **L8**: 150-51
of attention, **L17**: 281
training of, **L17**: 302
Concept
as name, **E3**: 142-43; **L16**: 93n, 165-68, 261
related to percept, **E3**: 143-45
as mode of action, **E3**: 225
Carnap on, **L16**: 17-22, 27-29
Tarski on, **L16**: 42
Dewey on, **L16**: 55n
artificiality of, **L16**: 158, 160, 180, 192
Dubislav on, **L16**: 161n
Kaplan on, **L16**: 172
Kaufmann on, **L16**: 198
Moore on, **L16**: 205, 207
Conception, **M6**: 390-91. *See also* Hypothesis, **L12**; Operations, **L12**; Universal proposition, **L12**
as aspect of thinking, **E2**: 178-86
and judgment, **E2**: 188, 199-200; **E5**: 321, 323
of cause and effect, **E2**: 208
control of, **M6**: 256; **L8**: 259-67
nature of, **M6**: 278-81; **L8**: 216, 235-43
in education, **L8**: 238-40; **L13**: 3
operational, **L12**: 22-23, 132-33, 216, 348, 391-92, 459, 494-500
and perception, **L12**: 72-73, 162, 507-11
in history, **L12**: 232-33
and definition, **L12**: 341-42
and abstraction, **L12**: 462-64, 468
scientific, **L13**: 159, 371
Conception of conceptions
operational, **L4**: 112, 113, 116-18, 153, 176-77
empirical, **L4**: 132-33, 207
rationalistic, **L4**: 144
and laws, **L4**: 167
Conception of God, The (Royce), **M1**: 256
Conceptualism, **M7**: 360; **L11**: 112-13; **L12**: 261-62; **L16**: 158
Concern, **L16**: 246
Concessions
and extra-territoriality, **M12**: 37, 46, 65
abolition of, **M12**: 47
treaty ports in, **M12**: 71-72
Conclusion
in Spinoza, **E1**: 10
method for reaching, **M3**: 3-4; **L17**: 339, 480-81
agreement on, **L16**: 281
vs. termination, **L16**: 285
unattained by philosophy, **L16**: 294
scientific, **L16**: 355, 357, 373

Concrete, **M12**: 166, 171, 187-88; **L12**: 119, 184n, 349-51, 400
meaning of, **M6**: 286-92; **L4**: 123-25; **L8**: 293-300
in *Cyclopedia of Education*, **M6**: 391-92
Condemnation
vs. salvation, **L17**: 16-17
Condillac, Étienne Bonnot de, **M3**: 52; **M7**: 345; **M12**: 126
on sensationalism, **M2**: 246
on Locke, **L6**: 30
Condition, **L12**: 137, 169-70, 292-93, 340, 446-47, 458, 488
as category in unity, **E3**: 216-17
in logic, **L11**: 95
objective vs. internal, **L13**: 23-27
as criteria for judgment, **L15**: 139
Conditioning
perils of, **L13**: 379-80
Condorcet, Marie Jean Antoine, **M3**: 52; **M6**: 444; **L5**: xxx, 154, 264; **L8**: 31; **L13**: 162
on mathematics, **M10**: 57; **L6**: 58, 59
Conduct, **M12**: 125-26, 173; **L16**: 64n, 254, 356
well-being ideal for, **E1**: 211
meaning of, **E3**: xxxiii, 242; **E4**: 242, 371-72; **E5**: 54; **M5**: 7-8; **L4**: xiv; **L7**: 9-10, 215
motives for, **E3**: 95-96, 244, 257-58; **L4**: 25, 31, 45-47, 57, 86, 169, 170, 209-13, 216-18, 225, 249; **L7**: 242, 292, 297; **L13**: 192-93
as individualized, **E3**: 97-99; **E5**: 55-56
consequences in, **E3**: 245-46; **L7**: 249; **L17**: 399
pleasure as standard of, **E3**: 260-74
and character, **E3**: 343; **L7**: 168-73, 176, 193-94, 271-72
as referred to agent, **E4**: 228-29
related to action, **E4**: 229-31
twofold formula for, **E4**: 231-32
as impulsive, **E4**: 235
psychological view of, **E5**: 56
levels of, **M5**: 41-42; **L7**: 12, 47-48
Hebrew philosophy of, **M5**: 101; **L7**: 92-93
Greek idea of, **M5**: 110-11; **L7**: 101, 163
in *Cyclopedia of Education*, **M6**: 392
related to philosophy, **M9**: 333-34, 341-42
in morality, **M9**: 356-60
as determined by knowledge, **M9**: 364-67, 370
thinking vs. instinct in, **M15**: 65, 66
emotional factor in, **L3**: 19-20
effect of commerce on, **L3**: 20
and belief, **L4**: 200-205
study of, **L7**: ix-x, 15
as custom, **L7**: 49
continuity in, **L7**: 169-70, 172, 185, 223
legal view of, **L7**: 278
esthetic quality of, **L10**: 46, 55, 87, 202
effect on education of, **L11**: 555-56
standards of, **L13**: 5
related to habit, **L13**: 162, 292; **L17**: 431
controlling, **L17**: 310, 353
conclusions regarding, **L17**: 480

"Conduct and Experience," **L16**: 71n, 101n
Conduct of the Understanding (Locke), **M6**: 195-96, 198-200; **L8**: 129, 132-33
Confederation
  related to democracy, **L13**: 99, 100
Conference for Progressive Labor Action, **L6**: 251
Conference of Progressives, **L6**: 173-74, 355-56, 440
Conference on Curriculum for the College of Liberal Arts, **L6**: 404, 414-23, 503, 504
Conference on Educational Status of the Four- and Five-Year-Old Child, **L9**: 136n
Conference on Education and Philosophy, **L17**: 88n
Conference on Methods in Philosophy and the Sciences, **L15**: 9n; **L17**: 442n
Conference on Science, Philosophy and Religion in Their Relation to the Democratic Way of Life, **L15**: 53n
Conference on The Scientific Spirit and Democratic Faith, **L15**: 251n, 335n, 366
Conflict, **M12**: 88, 141-42, 159-61; **M14**: 30, 48, 58-59, 128, 150
  evolutionary significance of, **E4**: 210-11
  and morals, **E5**: 45-46; **L5**: 279-80; **L7**: 68-80, 103-8, 164-66
  in *Cyclopedia of Education*, **M6**: 363, 392-93
  of ends, **M12**: 174-75
  of desires, **M14**: 135; **L7**: 186-88, 190-91
  in nature, **M14**: 207
  systematic, **L7**: xxvii
  and choice, **L7**: 286-87
  individual and social, **L7**: 322-28, 385; **L16**: 412
  in Teachers Union, **L9**: 330-32
  generates art, **L10**: 23, 47, 241, 253, 272-73, 285; **L14**: 36
  and problems, **L12**: 14-15, 33-38, 123-24, 177-78, 186-87, 218-19
  of philosophies of education, **L13**: 3, 374
  class, **L13**: 100, 121-24, 127, 133-34, 352
  legislative and executive, **L13**: 111
  in democracy, **L13**: 186-87; **L17**: 472
  function of, **L13**: 233-34
  about philosophy, **L13**: 255-57
  international, **L16**: 399-406
  cause of, **L16**: 419
  effects of, **L17**: 153
  development of, **L17**: 444
Conflict of Science and Society, The (Darlington), **M12**: 262n
Conformal transference
  Whitehead on, **L14**: 134-35
Conformity, **L7**: 230, 232
  in education, **L9**: 197
Confucianism, **M11**: 164, 207; **M12**: 75; **M13**: 103, 109, 111
  vital idea in, **M13**: 114
  related to Laotze, **M13**: 221-25
  strength of, **M13**: 256
Congress. *See* United States Congress
Congressional Record, **L14**: xix
Congress of Industrial Organizations (CIO), **L11**: 333; **L15**: 245, 509

Conjunction
logical, **L12**: 333-35, 352, 425, 445, 447, 451-52, 468, 515-16
Connecticut
board of education in, **M7**: 465-66
Connection, **L12**: 276-79, 310, 329. *See also* Interaction, **L12**
in experience, **M10**: 11-12, 15-16; **L14**: 18, 20, 23
in objective idealism, **M10**: 19
as existential relation, **L12**: 57, 60, 174-75, 220
in nature, **L14**: 127-28, 137
spatio-temporal, **L15**: 5-6, 29, 163
as name, **L16**: 261
search for, **L16**: 349
involved in valuing, **L16**: 351
Connexity, **L12**: 334-35
Connotation, **L12**: 352-57
Conscience, **M11**: 123-25; **M12**: 105; **M14**: 129-31, 216
nature of, **E3**: 354; **E4**: 299; **L7**: 262-65, 272-75; **L15**: 28n, 29; **L17**: 3, 5
conventional, **E3**: 355-56
reflective, **E3**: 356-59
and sense of obligation, **E3**: 359-61
as emotional disposition, **E3**: 361-64
related to morals, **E3**: 368-71; **E4**: 292-95, 299-305; **M3**: 49; **L7**: 162-66; **L17**: xxiii
theories of, **E4**: 109, 305-10
Royce on, **E4**: 197-98
vs. consciousness, **M9**: 359, 364
related to war, **M10**: 260-64
individuality of, **L2**: 266-67; **L17**: 352
Greek symbols of, **L7**: 121-23
ego of, **L17**: 4
Conscientiousness, **E3**: 364-66
vs. Greek wisdom, **M5**: 376-77
negative aspect of, **L7**: 258-59
opposed to intuition, **L7**: 272-73
Conscientious objectors, **M10**: xxxviii, 262-64
Conscious
in thought process, **M6**: 348-50; **L8**: 342-45
in inferential function, **M10**: 66
"'Conscious' and 'Consciousness,' The Terms," **M3**: xx
Conscious control
of F. Alexander, **M11**: x, 350-55, 359-60
Consciousness, **M4**: 255; **M7**: xii; **M11**: 11-17, 51; **M14**: 46, 124-25, 128-29, 145, 221; **L1**: 71, 75, 77, 79, 87-88, 94-96, 369; **L3**: 5, 6; **L4**: 69, 181, 182, 191, 196
meaning of, **E1**: 128-31, 134-35, 137, 140, 141, 311; **E2**: 25-26; **M3**: 79-82, 154; **M4**: 91-94; **M9**: 110; **M10**: 28; **L7**: x; **L15**: 28n, 29, 50, 75, 96; **L16**: 261, 384, 457
individual and universal, **E1**: 138-42; **E2**: 7-8; **E5**: 15, 16; **M6**: 18; **L17**: 423, 428
and psychology, **E1**: 144-45; **E2**: 16, 18; **M1**: 113-22; **M7**: 48-55
and will, **E2**: 10-11, 18-25
related to emotion, **E2**: 18-20, 215-16
sensation as element of, **E2**: 34-37

Consciousness (*continued*)
related to attention, **E2**: 117; **L17**: 269
and distinction, **E2**: 128-29
as side of obligation, **E3**: 328
and habit, **E4**: 200
related to unconscious, **E5**: 53
Stanley on, **E5**: 359-62
related to belief, **M3**: 84
as experience, **M3**: 102; **M10**: 323
and knowledge, **M3**: 108-10, 175
Woodbridge on, **M3**: 178, 180; **M4**: 222-27; **L17**: 548-49
Santayana on, **M3**: 321-22
James on, **M3**: 351; **M7**: 146; **L14**: 156-57, 166
and idealism, **M3**: 385-89; **M7**: 225
as natural good, **M4**: 23-24
McGilvary on, **M4**: 143-45, 314-16
Perry on, **M6**: 477-78
Montague on, **M7**: 23n; **M10**: 326n
transsubjective reference and, **M7**: 37
related to value, **M7**: 44-46; **L16**: 348, 351
natural rights connected to, **M7**: 62
McGilvary, Perry, and Dewey debate, **M7**: 79-84, 446-60
Fechner on, **M7**: 139
as consummation of action, **M7**: 177
and mind, **M9**: 302; **L1**: 230-34
moral, **M9**: 306-10; **L17**: 3
vs. conscience, **M9**: 359, 364
as supernatural, **M10**: 25-27
Royce on, **M10**: 85-86
social, **M13**: 157; **M15**: 233-34
immediate, **M13**: 352
related to meaning, **M13**: 372; **L1**: 226-65; **L17**: 362-63, 368, 370
negative vs. constructive, **M15**: 44
related to F. Alexander's method, **M15**: 308-9, 314
isolated from nature, **L1**: xviii
problem of, **L3**: 390-92
Sellars on, **L3**: 397-98
related to art, **L10**: 30-31, 35-36, 48, 60, 79, 82, 128, 251, 265, 270, 276-78, 286
related to physical events, **L14**: 80, 82
Bergson on, **L14**: 101
flux of, **L14**: 131
Cohen on, **L14**: 385-86
as entity, **L16**: 326, 412
emotion related to, **L17**: 197, 344
importance of, **L17**: 301, 321, 323, 344, 384
classification of, **L17**: 336
related to judgment, **L17**: 366n
in apprehension, **L17**: 416n
in realism, **L17**: 417-18
Bode on, **L17**: 548
related to awareness, **L17**: 549
Consciousness, stream of, **L8**: 113-14; **L11**: 506-7
Conscription, **M10**: 263
of thought, **M10**: xxxvii, 276-80
Conscription Act (1940), **L15**: 349
Consecutiveness. *See* Orderliness
Consequences, **M14**: xv, 17-18, 33, 132; **L10**: 68, 201; **L16**: 355, 393. *See also* Ends, **L12**; Instrumental, **L12**;

Means-consequences, **L12**; Relation, **L12**
related to conduct, **E3**: 245-46; **E4**: 238, 241, 243; **L4**: 120, 125, 157-60, 164, 178, 183, 187, 190, 195-97; **L12**: 53-60; **L13**: 59; **L14**: 73, 74n
and motives, **E3**: 262; **M14**: 34-36; **L7**: 173-76, 192-93, 221-23, 249, 274, 295, 337
accidents in, **M14**: 38, 164-66, 174, 209-12
foresight of, **M14**: 142-45, 177; **L13**: 43-45, 217-18, 247
and aims, **M14**: 155-60, 168-70
important to politics, **L2**: 243-47, 250-51, 255, 260, 262, 265, 276-78, 313, 333, 358
and law, **L2**: 270-71; **L14**: 121-22
determination of, **L2**: 271-75; **L16**: 330-32
expansion of, **L2**: 314, 333, 358
individual and social, **L2**: 356
and meaning, **L3**: 408-9
of operations, **L4**: 103, 116, 149, 155
as test, **L4**: 110, 132, 230, 231, 240, 248; **L12**: 115-16, 134, 177-78, 266, 316-20, 425-27, 433-35, 455-56, 484-85
related to means, **L4**: 130, 238; **L16**: 333, 350, 448
related to values, **L4**: 207, 208, 212-22
in utilitarianism, **L7**: 156, 242-45
of impulse, **L7**: 171-72, 186-88
and self, **L7**: 285-89
and responsibility, **L7**: 304-5
as criteria for judgment, **L11**: 15; **L15**: 12-14, 139
and validity, **L12**: 20-21, 73, 80, 145, 156, 176, 193, 196-97, 224, 341-42, 399, 423-24; **L14**: 169n, 171-72, 179-80, 183
agreement of, **L12**: 25-26, 52-53, 477
and significance, **L12**: 492-93, 504-5, 526
in inquiry, **L14**: 55, 61, 184, 186-87; **L16**: 322-25, 328
potentiality understood in, **L14**: 109-10
used in philosophical method, **L14**: 138
relative to antecedents, **L14**: 146-47
as directive, **L16**: 335-39, 374, 450-51
Consequences of Pragmatism (Rorty), **L6**: xi; **L14**: xvii
Consequent conditions, **M2**: 10-11, 14-15
Conservation
as element of form, **L10**: 142-43, 149, 151, 159-61, 165, 170, 172, 176-77, 187
of nature, **L11**: xxi-xxii, 232, 251
Conservatism, **M6**: 295; **M12**: 89-90, 97, 101, 137; **M13**: 429; **M14**: 48, 76, 115; **L6**: 236; **L7**: 326, 337; **L8**: 270-71; **L13**: 86, 142, 288; **L15**: 243
related to past, **E4**: 103-4
essence of, **E4**: 132
in education, **M1**: 260-64
in China, **M13**: 118, 222-24
responds to change, **L11**: 133
in education, **L11**: 409-10

Conservatism (*continued*)
and ageing, **L14**: 343-45
and liberalism, **L17**: 430-31
genuine, **L17**: 454
Consideration, **L7**: 259
formal vs. connotative, **L9**: 303-4
Considerations upon the Reputation of T. Hobbes (Hobbes), **M11**: 22
Consistency, **M13**: 38; **L12**: 225, 506-7
definition of truth, **M6**: 33-36
totality as, **M9**: 335-36
symbols for, **L16**: 90, 93
as name, **L16**: 261
Consortium, **M12**: 22, 278
financial, **M11**: 198, 225
formation of, **M13**: 77
opposition to, **M13**: 86-90, 96, 125, 163-66, 169, 184-85
U.S. involvement with, **M13**: 90-91, 163-64
prospects for, **M13**: 92, 100, 188
railways under, **M13**: 122, 144
object of, **M13**: 124
Constable, John, **L10**: 182, 298
on art, **L10**: 274, 363
Constantinople (Istanbul), Turkey, **M15**: 128-29, 131-32, 134-35, 139, 144, 290, 418-20; **L2**: 191
Angora compared with, **M15**: 136-38
Constantinople, University of, **M15**: 292
Constituent
related to quality, **M15**: 24-25, 342-43, 345
Constitution. *See* United States Constitution
"Constitution as an Institution, The" (Llewellyn), **L16**: xii
Constitutions Modernes, Les (Dareste), **L6**: 463n
Construction, **L10**: 93
public works, **L6**: 353, 384-85, 486-87
foreign, **L6**: 365
"Construction of Good, The," **L14**: 66, 67
Constructive Conscious Control of the Individual (F. Alexander), **M15**: 308; **L6**: 315
Consumers, **L9**: 249, 286; **L10**: 15, 55-56
Russell on, **M12**: 249
compared with producers, **L9**: 64, 83-86
effect of taxes on, **L9**: 273-74, 278
purchasing power of, **L9**: 277, 280, 281
in Great Britain, **L9**: 400
Consumers' Guide, **L9**: 83
Consumers' League, National, **L3**: 280n
Consummation, **M13**: xix, xx; **L12**: 39, 41, 69, 173, 178-79, 526
Consummatory experience, **M2**: ix; **L10**: xviii, xx, 22-23, 42-44, 47, 61, 62, 142-45, 149, 160-69, 177, 262, 329; **L14**: 43, 44, 47, 48
as guide to change, **L17**: xxxiii
Consumption, **L6**: 181, 344, 353, 357, 358; **L13**: 69, 318
and production, **M15**: 251, 253, 261-63, 267-69; **L9**: 232-33
problems of, **L6**: 155, 159-62, 243-44, 486
insufficient, **L6**: 347, 348, 485
and credit, **L6**: 351, 379
and social planning, **L9**: 134

and taxes, **L9**: 259, 266, 268
of farm products, **L9**: 287
and capitalism, **L9**: 401
Contact activities, **L12**: 35-36
Contemplation, **M12**: 142; **L1**: 51, 80, 89, 98, 102, 109, 249-50, 267-68, 324
Aristotle on, **M12**: 143
in esthetics, **L10**: 257-62, 300
Contemporary American Philosophy (G. P. Adams and Montague), **L5**: 147n; **L9**: xii-xiii, 421-22
Content
in studies, **E5**: 67-68
in Baldwin, **E5**: 390-91, 393, 416
as detriment to morality, **M2**: 18-19
in *Cyclopedia of Education*, **M6**: 458-60
mathematical, **L12**: 395-96, 403
homogeneous, **L17**: 423
common, **L17**: 423-24
in experience, **L17**: 425
Contests, **L7**: 77
Context, **L16**: 166
implicit and explicit, **M6**: 348; **L6**: 11-12; **L8**: 342
symbols and, **L6**: 4-5
neglect of, **L6**: 7, 11
and unlimited extension, **L6**: 8-11, 16-17
subjectivity as, **L6**: 14-15
cultural, in philosophy, **L6**: 18-21
related to science, **L6**: 19-20
related to college life, **L6**: 261-62
for meaning, **L6**: 489; **L8**: 231-32; **L14**: 44, 85
elements of historical, **L7**: xxxii-xxxiii
importance of, **L12**: 58, 72, 138, 152-53, 223-25, 284, 287, 292-93, 338, 393-94, 423-24, 515-16, 519-20
in Santayana's thinking, **L14**: 296-97
as name, **L16**: 261
Context and Thought, **L6**: xi; **L7**: xxxiii; **L16**: 83n
Contextualism, **L14**: 85
Contiguity, **L17**: 325
association by, **L5**: 256-61; **L17**: 330-31
Continental
rationalism, **M10**: xxv
law, **L2**: 27n, 28
Contingency, **L12**: 140, 195-96, 201, 222, 225-26, 249-50, 253-54, 263, 297-300, 320, 380-81, 417n, 437-40, 451-52
defined, **E4**: 29
philosophers on, **L1**: 46-48
in nature, **L1**: 55, 81, 96, 127, 262, 269, 271, 295-96, 308-9; **L4**: 16, 184, 194, 199; **L14**: 82-83
and time, **L14**: 112
Continuation schools, **M7**: 90-91, 205; **M8**: 118
limitations of, **M8**: 401-3
Continuity, **M3**: 169-70; **M14**: 11, 160, 165, 168, 178; **L4**: 179, 183, 184, 187, 189, 192, 194. *See also* Series, **L12**
Leibniz on, **E1**: 282, 398-402, 415-18
of institutions, **E4**: 40-41
importance of, **M2**: x; **L16**: 413-14, 457
of life process, **M9**: 4-5
totality as, **M9**: 335-36
vs. dualism, **M9**: 343-49
Francke on, **M10**: 226

Continuity (*continued*)
Peirce on, **L6**: 275-76
of conduct, **L7**: 169-70, 172, 185, 223
and change, **L7**: 179
esthetic, **L10**: 142-43, 245, 327
art effects, **L10**: 329-30, 338-39
nature of, **L12**: xiv-xv, 26, 244; **L13**: 25-28, 31, 49; **L14**: 384-85; **L16**: 187n
of development, **L12**: 30-31, 38-39; **L17**: 54, 89
temporal, **L12**: 440-41, 455-56, 475
in experience, **L13**: 13, 17-20, 244, 267, 284
in nature, **L14**: 30, 108, 127-28, 137, 144-45
of inquiry, **L14**: 56, 153
vs. discreteness, **L14**: 134
Continuum of inquiry, **L12**: 16-17, 19, 143, 226, 310, 315, 480, 483-84
Peirce on, **L12**: 3
and probability, **L12**: 464-73
Contract
theory of state, **E1**: 231-32; **M12**: 104; **L7**: xviii
Pound on, **L7**: xxix
Contractualism, **L7**: xxx
Contradiction, **L12**: 183, 195-98, 343-44
Holt on, **M10**: 326n
in propositions, **L11**: 121
principle of, **L14**: 389; **L16**: 197
political, **L15**: 386
in art and philosophy, **L17**: 381
Marx on, **L17**: 444
in Russia, **L17**: 501
Contrariety, **L12**: 183, 191-93, 195
Contribution to a Bibliography of Henri Bergson, A (Mudge), **M7**: 201n
Control, **M12**: 103, 116; **M14**: 72, 97, 102, 182-84; **L1**: 63, 91, 94, 97, 112, 150, 181, 199, 208, 220, 224-25, 264-65, 315
physical, **E2**: 321-31
prudential, **E2**: 332-41
moral, **E2**: 342-56
occasions for, **M5**: 61-62; **L7**: 56-57
in Greece, **M5**: 110-17; **L7**: 100-108
by church, **M5**: 138; **L7**: 135-37
in *Cyclopedia of Education*, **M6**: 363, 365, 393-95
results in growth, **M9**: 4-5
in education, **M9**: 28, 45, 83, 350-51, 354; **L11**: 162, 165, 413
social, **M9**: 31-32, 44-45; **L1**: 104; **L7**: 57, 217-19, 321-22, 412-22; **L13**: 32-35, 82, 105, 114, 145-46, 295, 320
means of, **M9**: 38, 44-45, 49-50; **M13**: 393; **L4**: 29-30, 103, 107, 110, 170, 174, 180, 213, 214, 220-21, 226, 245; **L7**: 52-54
in Herbart's theory, **M9**: 76
vs. freedom, **M9**: 300, 314-15
power of, **M13**: 373, 375
in experience, **M13**: 380
technological, **L1**: 183
political, **L2**: 243, 246; **L13**: 126-27, 158, 317
of human nature, **L2**: 358-60
by rites, **L4**: 3, 8-9, 178, 203
by arts, **L4**: 3, 24
by intelligence, **L4**: 60-86, 132,

136, 137, 142, 197, 198, 230, 234, 236
two kinds of, **L4**: 68, 106, 228
in primitive groups, **L7**: 30-32, 36-37, 49, 65-66
of desire, **L7**: 182, 204
absolute, **L7**: 428
in inquiry, **L12**: xxi, 18-19, 109, 120n, 136, 210, 218-19, 237-38, 317, 319, 459-64
in language, **L12**: 73-75, 312-13
external, **L13**: 13, 42
public vs. private, **L13**: 107
in remembering, **L17**: 325
of ideas, **L17**: 332
of interpretation, **L17**: 353
Convention
restricts impulse, **M14**: 7, 70, 115
in Greek morals, **L7**: 95, 101-10
nature opposed to, **L7**: 97
limits art, **L10**: xviii, xxi, xxxi, 47, 156-58, 171, 193-94, 216, 245, 253, 304, 351
in language, **L12**: 51-54
of measures, **L12**: 205
of scientific postulates, **L12**: 477-80
Convention for Financial Assistance in Case of Aggression, **L6**: 476
Conversion
religious, **L9**: 426
Conviction, **L13**: 296
Cook County Normal School (Chicago), **E5**: 423; **M2**: 67; **M3**: 273, 279
Cooke, Morris L., **L17**: 70, 558
Cooking
as introduction to science, **M1**: 50-51
Cooley, Charles Horton, **L2**: 295
Cooley, Edwin G., **M7**: 101; **M8**: 126, 471
Coolidge, Calvin, **M15**: xv; **L6**: 240
Cooper, James Fenimore, **M8**: 189
Cooper, Peter, **L11**: 520
Cooperation, **L13**: 142, 325
as socializing agency, **M5**: 45-48; **L7**: 43-47; **L11**: 49; **L14**: 93-95
international, **M15**: 80-81, 380-81; **L11**: 261-64, 276; **L15**: 208-9
in industry, **L7**: 401
in business, **L11**: 44, 277-80
in science, **L11**: 51, 277-79; **L13**: 275-76
democratic, **L11**: 417, 546; **L13**: 78, 296; **L14**: 228
between philosophy and science, **L13**: 284-86
value of, **L17**: 70, 449
of school and community, **L17**: 233-34
challenge to, **L17**: 460
Cooperatives
Russell on, **M12**: 249
Cooper Union (New York City), **L14**: 312n
Cooper Union Museum for the Arts of Decoration (New York City), **L11**: 520-22, 524-25
Coordination, **L5**: 479-80
physical, **E5**: 98
development of, **E5**: 205, 307, 309; **M1**: 178-91
of theory and practice, **L17**: 69
of activities, **L17**: 153-54
Cope, Edward Drinker, **M2**: 149

Copenhagen, Denmark, **L11**: 322, 326, 330
Copernican revolution, **M13**: 375; **L4**: 78, 229-32, 235, 238, 245
Copernican theory, **M8**: xix; **M15**: 314
Copernicus, Nicholas, **M1**: 168; **M4**: 7, 305-7; **M6**: 195; **M12**: 237; **M13**: 497; **L1**: 334; **L8**: 128; **L11**: 552-53; **L16**: 340, 454
Copilowish, Irving M., **L16**: 209n
Coppage v. Kansas, **L7**: 395-97
Copula, **L12**: 224, 289, 307, 332-33
  nature of, **L12**: 128, 135-36, 311
  ambiguity of, **L12**: 138n
Corcoran, Patrick J., **L11**: 327, 333, 604
Corfu, **M15**: 123
Corn Clubs, **M8**: 268
Corneille, Pierre, **E4**: 193
Cornell, Ezra, **L11**: 173
Cornell Law Quarterly, **L14**: xxiii
Cornell University, **E5**: 434; **M10**: 165; **L17**: 8
Cornford, Francis MacDonald, **L5**: 165; **L12**: 482
Corot, Jean Baptiste Camille, **L10**: 216
Corporate Personality (Hallis), **L6**: 268-70
Corporations
  finances of, **M5**: 501-3; **L7**: 392-94
  legal personality of, **L2**: 22-43; **L13**: 112
  social responsibility of, **L2**: 354; **L7**: 425
  influence individualism, **L5**: 58-123
  vs. labor, **L7**: 379-80, 392
Correction
  of children, **L17**: 237
Correlation. *See also* Correspondence, **L12**
  in school studies, **E5**: 90, 438, 456; **M1**: 336-37
  theory of, **E5**: 230-32
  references on, **E5**: 335-36
  Russell's use of term, **M8**: 89-93
  of changes in science, **L12**: 87, 132, 141, 475-80
  functional, **L12**: 133, 164, 213, 233-34, 277
  of data, **L12**: 317
  as logical form, **L12**: 333-34
  of ideas, **L17**: 310
  value of, **L17**: 311-12
Correspondence, **L1**: 215-16; **L14**: 9
  nature of, **M6**: xiv; **M13**: 35-38
  contrasted with realism, **M6**: xx-xxi
  related to truth, **M6**: 5-6, 33-36; **M7**: 359; **L14**: 179-80, 187-88
  of words and objects, **L12**: 53, 59-60
  of facts and conceptions, **L12**: 113, 129, 133, 212-14, 218-19, 339-40
Correspondence theory
  in schools, **E5**: 253
Corroboree, **M5**: 61; **L7**: 56
  as form of art, **M2**: 48-49
Corruption, **M12**: 46-47, 66, 68-69, 74
Corry, Homer C., **L11**: 567n, 571, 574, 578

Cortical action
in perception, **M7**: 25-26
Cortissoz, Royal, **L10**: 306-7, 365
Corwin, Edward H. Lewinski, **M11**: 314
Cory, Daniel M., **L14**: 301
Cosmic process
related to ethical process, **E5**: 35-37, 53
Cosmic theism, **L17**: 94
Cosmology, **M2**: 148; **M12**: 84, 116, 119, 122, 264. *See also* Metaphysics; Ontological
Greek, **L1**: 76-81, 101-3, 137; **L14**: 192-95, 199
of Whitehead, **L11**: xiv-xv, 146-54
modern logic and ancient, **L12**: 87-88, 98, 139, 202, 341, 394, 416-18, 497-98, 526
Newton influences, **L14**: 126-28
classical, **L14**: 145
science as, **L16**: 409
Cosmopolitanism, **M9**: 97-99
Cosmos
in D'Arcy, **E5**: 27, 28
Greek conception of, **M5**: 127-28; **L7**: 118-19
man and, **L9**: 214, 217, 420-21, 435
Bentley on, **L16**: xxi-xxii
in postulations, **L16**: 80
nature of, **L16**: 82, 84n, 92, 263
as name, **L16**: 261
Costello, Harry Todd, **L15**: 454
on Dewey's judgments of practice, **M8**: xvii-xviii
on value, **M13**: 20-25
Costigan, Edward P., **L6**: 355, 356, 381, 394, 440; **L9**: 288
Costigan bill, **L6**: 387
Costigan-La Follette bill, **L6**: 227, 379, 384; **L9**: 253
Costigan-La Follette-Lewis Relief bill, **L6**: 381, 382
Costliness, **L10**: 145
Cottage School (Riverside, Ill.), **M8**: 262-63, 266, 290-91, 352
Coué, Émile, **M15**: 43-46
Coughlan, Neil, **L6**: xiin
Coughlin, Charles Edward, **L14**: 407
Coulanges, Numa Denis Fustel de. *See* Fustel de Coulanges, Numa Denis
Coulondre, Robert, **L15**: 510
Coulter, John Merle, **L5**: 296
Council of National Defense, **L6**: 393
Council of State of Poland, **M11**: 268, 269, 272-75
Counter-revolution, **L13**: 127, 135
Counting
origin and development of, **E5**: 178-80, 183-88, 190-91
uses of, **E5**: 188-89
related to measuring, **E5**: 424-26
Counts, George S., **L6**: 143, 144; **L9**: 177; **L14**: 428; **L15**: 374, 510
on Chicago schools, **L5**: 371-74
on freedom, **L6**: 142n, 445-49
on Soviet challenge to U.S., **L6**: 263-67
Courage, **M5**: 379; **L2**: 130
Courbet, Gustave, **L10**: 182, 298, 307
Course of Lectures on the Growth and Means of Train-

ing the Mental Faculty, A (Warner), **M1**: 179
Course of Study, Theory of
in *Cyclopedia of Education*, **M6**: 395-404
Courts. *See also* Seabury investigation; World Court
international, **M11**: 124-25, 129, 391
in Galicia, **M11**: 263
in England, **M11**: 389
primitive, **L7**: 57-58
labor disputes and, **L7**: 395-99
on child labor, **L7**: 412-13
on police power, **L7**: 414
on property and public interest, **L7**: 415-17, 425-26
on income tax, **L7**: 421-22
in New York City, **L9**: 348-53, 370-77
in New York State, **L9**: 376-77
Couzens, James, **L6**: 227, 355; **L9**: 288
Couzens Amendment, **L6**: 392
Covenant
in Hebrew morality, **M5**: 92
Cowan, T. A., **L16**: 193n, 470
Cowdry, Edmund Vincent, **L14**: xxiv, 341n
Cowles, Edward Spencer, **L15**: xxiii, 365
Cowley, Malcolm, **L11**: 318
Coyoacán, Mexico, **L11**: xxvi, 311; **L13**: 391, 394, 395
Cracow (Krakow), Poland, **M11**: 263, 273, 311, 313
Crafts, **L11**: 69-70, 108
Craftsmanship, **L10**: xxiii, 54, 344
Crain, Thomas C. T., **L9**: 354-55
Cram, Ralph Adams, **M11**: 73
Crane, Charles R., **M15**: 297, 419
Crane, Mrs. Charles R., **M1**: 317
Creation, **M12**: 223, 226-28, 235
as result of imagination, **L9**: 33-34
in art, **L10**: xxi, 60, 203, 279-80, 286-87, 303
"Creative Democracy—The Task Before Us," **L14**: xi
Creative Evolution (Bergson), **M7**: 202; **M12**: 226, 228-29; **L4**: 73-74; **L11**: 428
Creative Impulse in Industry, a Proposition for Educators (Marot), **M11**: 333-35
Creative Intelligence: Essays in the Pragmatic Attitude (Dewey et al.), **M10**: 3n; **L12**: 413n; **L14**: 149n, 402, 404
Creativity
Russell on, **M12**: xxix, 244, 247-48
activity as, **M14**: 99-102
method in, **L2**: 114-15
in social reconstruction, **L8**: 44, 85-86
Creator, **L16**: 104
imagination related to, **L17**: 147
A. Johnson as, **L17**: 147-48
Credit, **L6**: 187, 356, 486
control of, **L6**: 243
and consumption, **L6**: 351, 379
and foreign investments, **L6**: 364-65
and public works, **L6**: 384-85
need for, **L6**: 390
Creed
related to religion, **L9**: 22, 28-29, 56-57, 432
Creed of Mr. Hobbes Examined, The (Tenison), **M11**: 20
Creel, George, **M11**: 150, 394

Cretan art, **L10**: 333
Crime
  and politics, **L6**: 242
  Tolstoy on, **L17**: 382
  in Russia, **L17**: 499-500
  Dzerzhinskiy on, **L17**: 501, 570
Crisis, **L16**: 360
  and conduct, **M7**: 399-403
  schools during, **L17**: 138
Crisis of the Old Order, 1919-1933, The (Schlesinger), **L6**: xviin
Criterion
  as ideal, **E4**: 288-90; **L7**: 348-50
  in social philosophy, **M15**: 238-40
  of social institutions, **L7**: 344-48
Critias
  in *Charmides*, **L2**: 131-33
  affiliated with humanism, **L2**: 136-39
  compared with Nicias, **L2**: 140
Critical Philosophy of Immanuel Kant, The (E. Caird), **E3**: 92, 180-84, 239
Critical rationalism
  on idea and fact, **M1**: 244-45
Criticism, **M2**: 153; **M13**: 369, 370; **L1**: 159, 290
  French and English compared, **E3**: 36-37
  in esthetic matters, **M13**: 7
  Prall's interest in, **M13**: 8
  nature of, **M13**: 14; **L10**: xv, xvi, xxx, 16, 73, 119, 151, 193, 224, 328, 349; **L13**: 117-18; **L14**: 88-89
  of education, **M13**: 332; **L13**: 6, 14
  objectivity in, **M13**: 354; **L2**: 87-91; **L10**: 310-13
  and morals, **L1**: 297-326
  related to value, **L2**: 78, 94-97
  related to philosophy, **L5**: 141-43; **L6**: 19; **L13**: 259; **L14**: 154; **L15**: 165-69; **L16**: 377
  judicial, **L10**: 302-8
  impressionist, **L10**: 308-10, 313
  as analysis and synthesis, **L10**: 313-18
  fallacies of, **L10**: 319-21
  of governmental action, **L13**: 130
  of experience, **L13**: 255-56
  of novel, **L13**: 362
  of Dewey, **L16**: 4, 386
Critics
  preconceptions of, **L10**: 104, 114, 118, 134, 148, 203, 220, 230, 233, 247, 288, 293, 294, 331
  as judges, **L10**: 303-9, 365
  qualifications and office of, **L10**: 309-18, 321-28
Critique of Judgment (Kant), **L4**: 50; **L10**: 257
"Critique of Naturalism" (Sheldon), **L15**: 109
Critique of Practical Reason (Kant), **L4**: 48, 49; **L5**: 179; **L9**: xxx
Critique of Pure Reason (Kant), **E3**: 92; **M5**: 155; **M8**: xxix, 155; **L4**: 48, 140; **L5**: 179; **L6**: 276; **L9**: xxx; **L10**: xv
Crito (Plato), **M12**: xii
Croatians, **M11**: xiii
Croce, Benedetto, **M12**: xxx; **M15**: 348; **L10**: 271
  on esthetics, **L10**: xvii, xxii, xxvi, 188; **L15**: 97-100, 438-44
  on states of mind, **L10**: 293

Croce, Benedetto (*continued*)
on intuition, **L10**: 299, 364
vs. Dewey, **L16**: 463-64
Croker, Richard, **L9**: 353, 354
Croly, Herbert, **M11**: 404
Cromwell, Oliver, **M11**: 25, 33n
Crookshank, Francis Graham, **M15**: 223
Crothers, Samuel McChord, **M15**: 173; **L5**: 79, 85, 128
Crowd psychology, **M10**: 55; **M14**: 44
Crowther, Bosley, **L15**: 493
Crozier, William
on China, **L3**: 196-98, 417-31
Cruise, Michael J., **L9**: 356
Crusades, **M5**: 144-45; **L7**: 136, 147
Cuadrado, Augusto García, **L15**: 371
Cuba, **L15**: 20-22
U.S. intervention in, **L5**: 440-41
political situation in, **L9**: 310-11
"Cuba under President Machado" (Porter), **L9**: 310-11
Cudworth, Ralph, **E4**: 127; **M2**: 153, 156; **M3**: 53; **M11**: 34
Cue, **L16**: 147, 149, 201n
as name, **L16**: 7n, 143-45, 261
as stage of designation, **L16**: 132, 139, 142-43
"Cul-de-Sac for Realism, A" (Drake), **M10**: 439-49
Culkin, Charles W., **L9**: 356
Cullen, William, **L14**: 206
Cults, **M12**: 84, 85; **L13**: 332; **L17**: 427
Cultural lag, **L13**: 97; **L15**: 200
Cultural relativity, **L15**: xx
Culture, **M7**: xxii; **L8**: 48, 88. *See also* Common sense, **L12**
study of, **E5**: 230, 249-50; **M10**: 196-201
related to education, **M1**: 309-10; **M8**: 353-56; **M15**: 196-97; **L6**: 46, 83-84, 88-89, 421, 445
as possession of knowledge, **M7**: 116
in industrial schools, **M7**: 466-67
compared with civilization, **M8**: 168-69
Rousseau and, **M8**: 183
of Germany, **M8**: 428-29; **L13**: 84, 121
related to social efficiency theory, **M9**: 128-30
meaning of, **M9**: 267; **M13**: 400; **L4**: 141, 245; **L10**: 34, 245, 270; **L15**: 208; **L16**: 85n
and vocation, **M9**: 332
Arnold on, **M10**: 403
Western vs. Eastern, **M13**: 113
of China, **M13**: 114-15
and growth, **M13**: 404
as term, **L1**: viii, xii-xvii, 361-64
as presented by anthropology, **L1**: 42
human nature and, **L2**: 32; **L6**: xv, xvi, 37-38, 43; **L13**: 67-69, 71-74, 79, 82, 84, 86, 117, 142, 163, 184, 246-48, 273
crisis in, **L4**: 32-35, 38, 62-63, 200-211
and values, **L4**: 225; **L6**: 446; **L13**: 260; **L17**: 184
Keyserling on, **L5**: 54
and technology, **L5**: 99-123, 128-31; **L6**: 280-85
related to philosophy, **L6**:

18-21; **L8**: 29, 37, 39; **L14**: 89, 313; **L16**: 359, 404, 407-9; **L17**: 467
and environment, **L6**: 40, 445-46
and politics, **L6**: 40-48
and economics, **L6**: 43-44
Greek view of, **L6**: 46-47
and tradition, **L6**: 128-29, 143-44; **L11**: 117
Soviet challenge to, **L6**: 263-67
and law, **L7**: 364; **L13**: 85
agrarian, **L8**: 53-55, 57
as socially grounded, **L8**: 63, 80, 83
and materialism, **L8**: 70-73
art's relation to, **L8**: 85-86; **L10**: 319-21, 329-43, 347-48
related to religion, **L9**: xv, 3, 6, 38, 439-40
and need for liberty, **L9**: 89-90
Wieman on, **L9**: 415
teaching of, **L11**: 115-16, 350, 573
foundations of, **L11**: 193, 367
freedom of, **L11**: 294-95
as matrix of inquiry, **L12**: 48-65, 245, 264, 481-83
and history, **L12**: 233
influence of, **L13**: 75-77; **L14**: 15; **L16**: 380, 387, 417, 418
war as constituent of, **L13**: 164-65, 172, 180, 288-90, 311, 315
related to intellect, **L14**: 312-13
magic in, **L16**: 328
Dewey's third, **L17**: xviii-xix
Spartan idea of, **L17**: 176
differences in, **L17**: 405
in Russia, **L17**: 497-98
Culture and Culture Values
in *Cyclopedia of Education*, **M6**: 404-8
"Culture and Industry in Education," **M3**: xix
Culture-epoch theory, **E5**: xiv; **M1**: 327; **M3**: 307; **M9**: 81
in education, **E5**: 247-53; **M1**: 232, 234n
references on, **E5**: 336
in logical thought, **M1**: xiv
educators on, **M1**: xv
in *Cyclopedia of Education*, **M6**: xxiv, xxvi, 408-12
Cultus
of religion, **M5**: 34; **L7**: 33
as moralizing agent, **M5**: 94-95; **L7**: 86-87
Cumberland, Richard, **E4**: 144; **M3**: 53; **M11**: 20, 34
cummings, e. e., **L10**: xxi
Cumulation
as element of form, **L10**: 142-43, 149, 151, 159-61, 165, 170-71, 176-77, 186, 224
Cure
related to health, **M15**: 43, 44
opposed to F. Alexander's method, **M15**: 313
Curie, Marie, **M11**: 279
Curiosity, **M6**: 204-7; **L8**: 221, 299; **L10**: 66, 174
guidance of, **M6**: 216; **L8**: 154, 157-58, 292
and observation, **M6**: 329; **L8**: 315-16
defined, **L8**: 141-43, 187
lost, **L8**: 143-44
in education, **L9**: 180-81
in children, **L11**: 213
Curley, James Michael, **L9**: 262
Current History, **L9**: 311n
Current Religious Thought, **L15**: 507
Curriculum, **E5**: 89; **L9**: 143, 145, 196-97, 388-90. *See*

Curriculum (*continued*)
also School subjects
ethics of, **E4**: 55; **E5**: 76-82, 295-97; **M4**: 205-13
socially oriented, **E5**: 66-68, 383-84; **M1**: 294-99; **L9**: 167-68; **L14**: 353
form in, **E5**: 73
ideal, **E5**: 91
psychological side of, **E5**: 176
emphasis on, **E5**: 215; **L11**: 400-401, 555-56; **L13**: xii, xiii; **L17**: 76
changes in, **E5**: 268-69, 450-51; **M2**: 379-82; **M9**: 199-216, 240-58; **L9**: 148-52, 179; **L17**: 232-33, 512, 514
in college, **E5**: 272-73; **L6**: 84-85, 404, 412-23, 503, 504
references on, **E5**: 334-35
high school, **M1**: 284
overloaded, **M1**: 303-6; **L15**: 262, 278-79
of University Elementary School, **M1**: 331-32
as different from child's world, **M2**: 273-78
of University of Missouri elementary school, **M8**: 236-47
of Gary schools, **M8**: 320-28
development of, **M15**: 183-84, 187, 191-92
in Turkish education, **M15**: 281-82, 290-91
Mencken on, **L9**: 408, 409
subjects in, **L11**: 185, 394, 395, 406; **L13**: 265-66, 284; **L17**: 234, 312-21
characteristics of, **L11**: 185-89, 242
theory of, **L11**: 207-12
in Russia, **L17**: 502
Curry, John F., **L9**: 346, 347, 353
Curti, Merle, **M1**: xviin
Curzon, George Nathaniel, **M15**: 411
Cushing, Caleb, **M11**: 228
Customs, **M12**: 89, 172, 268; **M15**: 231, 246; **L1**: 164, 170; **L3**: 15-17, 20; **L16**: 292, 304-5, 359, 379. *See also* Tradition
as law, **E4**: 85-86; **M15**: 269-71; **L7**: 86; **L14**: xxi-xxii, 118-19
as binding religiously, **E4**: 132-33
Chinese, **M5**: 23; **L7**: 22
history of, **M5**: 23-26, 33-35, 37, 54-56; **L7**: 22-25, 32-34, 36, 49-52; **L13**: 51, 259, 288-89
Greek, **M5**: 24, 106; **L7**: 23-24, 97-98; **L11**: 70, 73-74; **L17**: 172, 435
marriage, **M5**: 32, 66, 100-101, 514-16; **L7**: 31, 60-61, 91-92, 129, 440
defined, **M5**: 54; **L7**: 49
taboos and ritual as, **M5**: 57-59, 66-67, 71; **L7**: 52-54, 61, 65
enforcing of, **M5**: 58-59; **L7**: 54
initiation, **M5**: 59-61; **L7**: 55-56
as reenforcers of group unity, **M5**: 65-66; **L7**: 60
of hospitality, **M5**: 68-69; **L7**: 62-63
worth of, **M5**: 69-72; **M6**: 22-23; **L7**: 54-66, 163-65, 254-55; **L17**: 86
Hebrew, **M5**: 89-99; **L7**: 82-90

and nature, **M5**: 114-17; **M6**: 23-24; **L7**: 104-8; **L13**: 86; **L17**: 99
Platonic revolt against, **M6**: 24-25
in *Cyclopedia of Education*, **M6**: 413-14
rigidity of, **M14**: 42, 74-75
and habit, **M14**: 43-50; **L7**: xxi
and morality, **M14**: 54-59
force of, **L4**: 148, 211, 212, 215-18, 248
Dewey on, **L7**: xiv, xxi, xxiii
limit art, **L10**: xxxi, 308, 351
social effects of, **L11**: 36, 133-34, 379; **L13**: 293; **L15**: 156, 158, 165
effect of education on, **L11**: 230-34
vs. ideas, **L13**: 162
and human nature, **L14**: 259-60
knowledge and, **L17**: 433-34
Cutten, George B., **M13**: 289-90, 293-94
Cutting, Bronson, **L5**: 417; **L6**: 355, 440
Cuvillier, Louis A., **L9**: 378
Cyclopedia of Education, A
Dewey's contributions to, **M6**: 359-467; **M7**: 207-365
Cynics, **E4**: 138, 263; **M5**: 387; **L2**: 134; **L8**: 26
on individualism, **M5**: 118-19; **L7**: 109-10
self-denial in, **M5**: 328
as school of philosophy, **L2**: 124, 135, 136
related to Plato, **L2**: 125, 128-30, 133
on wisdom, **L7**: 110, 203-4
Cyrenaics, **E4**: 138, 263; **L2**: 133, 138-39
on individualism, **M5**: 118-19; **L7**: 109, 110
as school of philosophy, **L2**: 124, 125, 134-37
represented by Nicias, **L2**: 131
Czarism, **M12**: 4, 61; **L3**: 225, 226; **L5**: 99; **L17**: 490
Czechoslovakia, **M15**: xviiin, 394; **L15**: 246, 289
Czechoslovaks, **M11**: xiii, 256, 264

Dairen (Dalian), China, **M11**: 238; **M12**: 31; **M13**: 144
Daladier, Édouard, **L15**: 353
Dallin, David J., **L15**: 295-98
Dalrymple, A. V., **M11**: 259, 408
Dance, **L10**: 281; **L16**: 397
in primitive society, **M5**: 48; **L7**: 45-46
Plato on, **M6**: 376-77
characteristics of, **L7**: 45-46; **L10**: 162, 200, 284, 330
as rite, **L10**: 13
as art, **L10**: 69; **L13**: 357-58
classification of, **L10**: 226, 231-32
differences in, **L13**: 361
movement in, **L13**: 365
Dane, Richard, **M13**: 95
Daniels, Jonathan, **L15**: 358
Dante Alighieri, **M10**: 359; **M12**: xxvii, 111; **L14**: 300
compared with Shakespeare, **E4**: 193
on state, **M5**: 141
topics of, **L10**: 115, 357
influences on, **L10**: 294, 322-23
praised, **L10**: 324
Dantzig (Gdansk), Poland, **M11**: 306, 326

D'Arcy, Charles
on metaphysical method in ethics, **E5**: 25-33
Dardanelles, **M11**: 136
Darden, Colgate W., **L15**: 358
Dareste de la Chavanne, François Rodolphe, **L6**: 463n
Dare the School Build a New Social Order? (Counts), **L14**: 428
Darkness at Noon (Koestler), **L15**: xi, 292, 510
Darlington, C. D., **M12**: 262n
Darrow, Karl Kelchner, **L12**: 433n; **L13**: 272
Dartmouth Eye Institute (Hanover, N.H.), **L15**: 310
Darwin, Charles, **E5**: 363, 366; **M1**: xviii; **M3**: xxiii; **M6**: 211; **M7**: 139, 354, 390-91; **M8**: 21, 142, 194; **M9**: 180; **M12**: 122, 221, 263; **M14**: 207; **M15**: 47-48; **L1**: 15; **L2**: 222; **L6**: 428; **L8**: xv, 238, 256; **L11**: 33; **L12**: 97; **L13**: 75, 120; **L14**: 385; **L15**: 312; **L16**: 74n, 117n; **L17**: 13, 40, 198, 204
on habits, **E2**: 306
on emotion, **E4**: xiv, 152-53, 159, 171; **L10**: 160
on laughter, **E4**: 155
and principle of antithesis, **E4**: 165-67
umbrella case illustration, **E4**: 184n
on optimism and pessimism, **M2**: 176
related to Spencer, **M3**: 205-9
Dewey on, **M6**: x
on science, **M6**: 279-80
on origin of species, **M6**: 444; **M12**: 208, 231
hypothesis of, **M12**: 228-29; **L16**: xxxvii, 104n, 120, 130
influence of, **L10**: xiii; **L16**: 184-85, 187n, 192, 197n, 238
on music and poetry, **L13**: 359
influences Bentley, **L16**: xvi, xxviii, xxix
on naming, **L16**: 158-59
political economy of, **L17**: 411
Darwinism
Schurman on, **M2**: 16-17
related to philosophy, **M4**: 9-14
Daszynski, Ignace, **M11**: 272, 273, 282
Data, **L12**: 149-50, 157. *See also* Facts, **L12**
control of, **M6**: 242-44, 248-49; **L8**: 248-55
vs. subject-matter, **M13**: 45n
and inference, **M13**: 47; **L14**: 172-74
defined, **M13**: 63; **L12**: 127, 153, 162, 185, 228-31, 236, 248, 288-89, 316-20, 420-22, 467-70, 477
and problems, **L4**: 79-82, 99, 107, 110, 139, 142-43, 147, 154, 158; **L12**: 167-68, 172-74, 196-97, 202, 205-6, 222, 250-51, 327, 331, 453-54; **L14**: 181
in morals, **L7**: 179
in mathematics, **L12**: 401-3
object as, **L17**: 372
Dating, **L12**: 224-25
Daughters of the American Revolution, **L11**: 576
Daumier, Honoré, **L10**: 192; **L11**: 447
David, Fritz, **L11**: 311, 322, 602
Davidson, Thomas I., **L11**: 476
Davidson, William L., **L16**: 165

Davies, Joseph E.
on Soviet purges, **L15**: xi-xii, 289-94, 338-53, 488-89, 496, 498
Davis, Helen Edna, **L5**: 398-400
Davis, Jefferson, **M13**: 74
Davis, Katharine B., **L7**: 459
Davis, Oscar, **L15**: 356
Dawes, Charles Gates, **L6**: 194
Dawn of Conscience, The (Breasted), **L9**: 37-38
Day of National Shame, **L17**: 29, 555-56
Deaf-blind, **L17**: 145
Dean, Arthur Davis, **M11**: 60, 393
De Anima (Aristotle), **L5**: 185
Death
rituals, **M5**: 65-66; **L7**: 60
primitive attitude toward, **M7**: 401
Debate
vs. argumentation, **L11**: 515
Debs, Eugene V., **L6**: 235; **L15**: 242
Debski, Alexander H., **M11**: 288, 294, 295, 396
Debts, **L6**: 360-61; **L9**: 79, 278
interallied, **L6**: 337, 364-68, 372-73
compared with school taxes, **L9**: 117
mortgage, **L9**: 249, 250, 255-57, 269-70, 277
need to reduce, **L9**: 261
national, **L9**: 281
Decision, **M6**: 263; **L8**: 215-16; **L16**: 185
logical theory related to, **M15**: 65-67
intelligent, **L17**: xxvi
consequences of, **L17**: xxxii
De Cive (Hobbes), **M11**: 22, 23, 30-31
Declaration of Independence, **M5**: 143; **M12**: xxii; **L7**: 356; **L11**: 7, 16, 167, 169, 373; **L13**: 66, 99-101, 173; **L14**: 212, 216, 218-19; **L15**: xxxi; **L17**: 437
Declarative proposition, **L12**: 162, 238-43
Decline of the West, The (Spengler), **L6**: 282; **L7**: xvi
Decorative art, **L10**: xxi, xxiv, 130-35, 146
De Corpore Politico (Hobbes), **M11**: 22, 39n
Decorum, **L10**: 202
Dedekind, Julius, **M7**: 423, 424, 440
Deduction, **M12**: 165; **L1**: 122, 152, 157, 284-85; **L4**: 113, 131; **L12**: xxiv-xxv, 18-19, 459, 470-71, 478-80, 497-98; **L13**: 352, 353; **L16**: 186n. *See also* Dialectic; Discourse, **L12**; Hypothesis, **L12**; Universal proposition, **L12**
in judgment, **E5**: 323
and induction, **M6**: 242-58; **M13**: 69, 487
in *Cyclopedia of Education*, **M6**: 414-15; **M7**: 239-45
definition of, **M13**: 63, 66, 484-85
Buermeyer on, **M13**: 66, 69
function of, **M13**: 69-70; **L8**: 263, 264
isolation of, **L8**: 265-66
Kaufmann on, **L16**: 195-98
Deed
defined, **E4**: 337-38
Defeatism, **L16**: 367-68
"Defence of Common Sense, A" (G. Moore), **L16**: 204-7

Defence of Philosophy, A (R. Perry), **L6**: 271-72
Defence of Poetry, A (Shelley), **L6**: 492
Definite article
  ambiguity of, **L11**: 123
"'Definition'" (Dewey and A. Bentley), **L16**: 443n, 447
Definition, **L1**: 122, 136, 182, 249; **L8**: 261, 265, 266; **L10**: 120
  and conceptions, **M6**: 278; **L8**: 235-45; **L12**: 341-42
  nature of, **M6**: 281-85; **L4**: 113, 114, 200, 212; **L8**: 245-47; **L11**: 105-7, 113; **L12**: 259-60, 270-71, 319-20, 338-39, 357, 404-5
  in *Cyclopedia of Education*, **M6**: 415-17
  process of, **L4**: 101, 121, 145
  in Greek philosophy, **L8**: 5
  fallacy of, **L10**: 220-21, 227, 229
  hypothetical propositions used for, **L11**: 97, 99, 101-3
  revision of, **L11**: 110-11
  in Aristotelian logic, **L12**: 91, 139-40, 239, 357
  as ideal, **L12**: 303
  accounts of, **L16**: 6, 161-71, 179-83
  Carnap on, **L16**: 29-30
  Tarski on, **L16**: 41n, 42
  vs. specification, **L16**: 63, 96
  as name, **L16**: 65-66, 71, 72, 132, 154-60, 259-62, 447
  Kaplan and Nagel on, **L16**: 172-73
  Pepper on, **L16**: 174-79
  Ogden and Richards on, **L16**: 218n
  Peirce on, **L16**: 299
  Socrates on, **L17**: 185
"Definition and Specification of Meaning" (Kaplan), **L16**: 172-73
De Foe, Daniel, **M1**: 106-7; **M4**: 194-95; **M10**: 91; **M15**: 178-79
De Garmo, Charles, **E5**: 112, 147; **L17**: 88, 559
Degas, Edgar, **L10**: xxii, 182, 192
De Generatione et Corruptione (Aristotle), **L11**: 595
De Interpretatione (Aristotle), **M10**: 101
Deism, **M2**: 182; **M7**: 293, 353
Deists, **M7**: 58, 288
Deity. *See also* God
  of Paley, **L17**: 94, 559
  Fiske on, **L17**: 95, 96
Delacroix, Eugène
  on art, **L10**: 127, 150, 204
  as artist, **L10**: 287, 307
Delaisi, Francis, **L5**: 173n
De la personnalité juridique (Saleilles), **L2**: 30n
De Legibus Naturae (Cumberland), **M11**: 34
Deliberation, **M14**: xii, xviii, 168, 171, 214; **L12**: 62-63, 163-64, 172-73, 272-73; **L15**: 105
  Hobbes on, **M5**: xivn
  in reasoning process, **M5**: 292-93
  practical, **M6**: 234; **L8**: 187-88
  nature of, **M14**: 132-38; **L7**: 272-75, 298-301; **L13**: 213
  and calculation, **M14**: 139-45
  as discovery, **M14**: 149
  and self, **L7**: 274
  in choice, **L7**: 287
  vs. muscular behavior, **L14**: 64-65, 69
de Lima, Agnes, **L15**: xxiii, 303-4

DeLisle, Joseph Nicolas, **E3**: 39
Delsarte, François, **L17**: 198, 563
Delusions, **M12**: 160
De Mazia, Violette, **L11**: 501
Democracy, **M6**: 135; **M12**: 106, 186, 198; **M14**: xxi, 45n, 48, 52; **L6**: 175-76, 413
  Dewey on, **E1**: xxxii; **M3**: xi
  status of, **E1**: 227; **L7**: 351-56
  as social organism, **E1**: 229-35
  stability of, **E1**: 237-38
  as ethical conception, **E1**: 239-40, 248; **M1**: xxi; **M2**: xx; **M5**: 424
  and aristocracy, **E1**: 243-44; **M13**: xii, 297-300
  Lowell on, **E1**: 246
  in England and U.S., **E3**: 203
  value of, **E4**: 7; **L14**: 275-79; **L15**: 270
  meaning of, **E4**: 8-9; **M13**: 315-16; **L2**: 283, 325-27; **L7**: 104; **L8**: 49, 76, 102; **L11**: 28, 117, 182, 248, 296, 368, 371, 389, 415-17, 515, 546, 550; **L13**: xvi, 151, 294-96, 305-8, 379; **L15**: 54, 174, 367-68
  origin of, **E4**: 99; **L2**: 287-90; **L7**: 333-34, 354-55; **L9**: 76; **L17**: 472-74
  related to modern life, **M1**: 128
  philosophy related to, **M3**: 73-78; **M11**: 41, 48-53; **L6**: 431
  related to education, **M3**: 229-39; **M7**: 309; **M8**: xxxiv; **M10**: 137-43; **M11**: 54-57; **L6**: 95-98, 103, 288-90; **L8**: 43-103; **L9**: 393; **L11**: 25, 161, 181-90, 235-37, 378, 385-86, 485-86, 538-39, 557-59, 579; **L13**: 17-18, 92-93, 296, 383; **L14**: 271-72; **L17**: 56, 138-39
  intelligence and, **M4**: 39-40; **L2**: xxix, 365-66; **L11**: 50-52, 56, 60-61, 219-20, 417
  Woods on, **M4**: 218-19
  science related to, **M10**: 199; **M11**: 48, 99
  and war, **M11**: xi, 108, 154, 201, 282; **L14**: 250-51, 364
  for Poles, **M11**: xiv, 260, 398, 407
  in Japan, **M11**: xvii-xviii, 154-61, 165-74, 178
  in China, **M11**: xix, 192, 196, 212-14, 229
  development of, **M11**: 99, 102, 105-6; **L7**: 148-51; **L11**: 218; **L14**: 224-30; **L15**: 177-78, 251-52, 277, 308-9; **L17**: 21, 400
  reaction against, **M11**: 110; **L11**: 64, 224-25, 288, 536-37; **L15**: 4, 6, 49, 259-60; **L16**: 360; **L17**: 47, 86, 460-61, 471
  psychology of, **M11**: 112
  public opinion in, **M11**: 118, 120-21
  and morality, **M11**: 131-32; **L7**: 348-50; **L13**: 154-57, 170, 178-79, 303
  international, **M11**: 142, 181, 198
  hero of, **M11**: 143
  economic factors in, **M11**: 335; **L6**: 244-45; **L7**: 353, 356-58, 391; **L8**: 63-64; **L13**: 114-15, 118, 305-7
  conflicts with foreign politics, **M12**: 3-7, 259, 274

Democracy (*continued*)
in labor parties, **M12**: 6
Russell on, **M12**: 239
prospects of, **M13**: 291
Carlyle on, **M13**: 330
quality of, **M13**: 330-31
means and ends of, **M13**: 338, 344; **L11**: 217-18, 298-99; **L13**: 386-88; **L17**: 461, 473
affects religious and scientific controversy, **M15**: 49-50
Lippmann on, **L2**: xxii-xxiii, 213-20
ideal, **L2**: xxviii-xxix, 327-29; **L11**: 167
in Turkey, **L2**: 190-91
alleged unity in, **L2**: 286-87
and individualism, **L2**: 289-95; **L8**: 51-54, 64, 70, 73, 75; **L14**: 113, 277
American, **L2**: 304-7; **L15**: 242, 244, 282-85, 340-41, 367-68
and experts, **L2**: 362-65
and community, **L2**: 367-68
limitations of citizens in, **L3**: xxxiii
changing perspective of, **L7**: xvi
and anarchy, **L7**: xviii
and utilitarianism, **L7**: 239-40, 315
problems of, **L7**: 359, 362-63, 365; **L13**: 87-88, 92-98, 101-3, 106-7, 112-13, 132, 135, 151, 153, 168, 176, 180, 185-86, 300
Bellamy's view of, **L9**: 103
need for interest in, **L9**: 162-63
related to Brandeis, **L9**: 238
related to Teachers Union, **L9**: 317, 318, 341, 344-45
commitment to, **L11**: 287; **L17**: 87, 453
and capitalism, **L11**: 296; **L13**: 137, 146
in Europe, **L11**: 296, 496, 528, 532
Lincoln on, **L13**: 14, 402-3
maintenance of, **L13**: 90, 106, 113, 130, 185-87, 298-99
related to Christianity, **L13**: 152
Jefferson on, **L13**: 173-79
essential, **L13**: 377-82, 386
religious values in, **L14**: 78-79
in institutions and individuals, **L14**: 92
defense of, **L14**: 262-65
totalitarianism vs., **L14**: 275-77, 293-94
C. and M. Beard on, **L14**: 284-85
social sciences related to, **L14**: 320
vs. military force, **L14**: 367-68
Hocking on, **L14**: 425-26
Addams on, **L15**: 196
inquiry in, **L15**: 231, 273-74
misapplication of term, **L15**: 248, 373
Bode on, **L15**: 327
attitude toward, **L16**: 391
responsibility of, **L16**: 400-405
participatory, **L17**: xxiv
in universities, **L17**: 71
voting in, **L17**: 86
Welling on, **L17**: 523
Democracy after the War (Hobson), **M11**: 87
Democracy and Education, **M7**: xx, xxi, xxiv; **M8**: ix, xxxii; **M11**: ix, 395, 399; **L1**: viii; **L5**: 156; **L11**: 215; **L13**: xi; **L14**: 7
Hook on, **M9**: ix-xxiv
on art, **L10**: xxvi, xxviii

Japanese translation of, **L17**: 57
Democracy and Education
in *Cyclopedia of Education*, **M6**: 417-18
"Democracy in Education," **M3**: xviii
"Democracy Is Radical," **L11**: xxivn
Democratic party, **L6**: xviii, xix, 150; **L9**: 66, 290; **L11**: 266, 526; **L15**: 239-41, 245
failure of, **L5**: 445
and economy, **L6**: 157, 158, 412, 438; **L9**: 79
and tariff bill, **L6**: 164
compared with Republican party, **L6**: 167-68, 184, 236, 248
in history, **L6**: 234
and third-party movement, **L6**: 247, 250-54
on taxation, **L9**: 260
in New York City, **L9**: 349-53, 356, 373, 379, 382, 384
and F. Roosevelt, **L9**: 400-401
Democritus, **M4**: 38; **M6**: x, 23n; **M7**: 275, 324; **M13**: 366; **M15**: 337; **L1**: 53-55, 63, 104; **L2**: 137, 138, 140; **L4**: 96; **L9**: 242; **L14**: 193, 299, 399; **L15**: 113
Demonstration, **M12**: 91. *See also* Proof; Syllogism, **L12**; Test
in *Cyclopedia of Education*, **M6**: 418-19
Bacon on, **M12**: 96, 97
of ancient science, **L1**: 121-22
as rational proof, **L12**: 242, 416-17
and description, **L12**: 352-57
Demonstratives. *See also* Singular, **L12**; This, **L12**
Dewey on, **L16**: 181n, 183n
Demoralization, **E3**: 377
De Nemours, Pierre Samuel du Pont, **L14**: 202, 213
Denmark, **M15**: 278, 304, 305, 307
Dennes, William R., **L14**: 303-5; **L15**: 461
Dennett, Mary Ware, **L17**: 127, 560
Dennett, Tyler
on education, **L11**: 588-91
Denney, Joseph Villiers, **E4**: 121
Denotata
Lewis on, **L16**: 38
Tarski on, **L16**: 42
in semiotic, **L16**: 217n, 237
C. Morris on, **L16**: 228-29
and significata, **L16**: 235
Denotation, **M13**: 389; **L1**: 16-41, 63, 75, 96, 138, 168, 226, 371-72, 375, 377, 386-87, 389-92; **L12**: 352-57
Dependence, **L4**: 244-46
as condition of growth, **M9**: 47-49
Dependency and Neglect, Committee on, **L6**: 352
Depression, economic, **L5**: xi, xxi; **L6**: xi, xvi; **L8**: 47; **L9**: 296
affects education, **L6**: xxi, xxiii, 123, 127, 129, 410-11; **L11**: 159-60, 268, 376
affects politics, **L6**: 151-52, 156-57, 236, 239-40, 324-25, 441
affects unemployment, **L6**: 153-55; **L16**: 393
production and consumption in, **L6**: 160-61, 346-47, 486-87
causes of, **L6**: 163-64
affects minorities, **L6**: 224-26

Depression, economic (*continued*)
affects health, **L6**: 342-43
legislation for, **L6**: 345, 356
People's Lobby on, **L6**: 346-54; **L9**: 261-64
Hoover's speech on, **L6**: 357-63
hoarding in, **L6**: 379-80, 386
affects character, **L9**: 190-91
economic effects of, **L9**: 267-68
demoralization in, **L11**: xi-xii, 275, 276
affects children and youth, **L11**: xix-xx, 268, 340, 353-55, 378, 555
and social planning, **L11**: 175, 339-40, 601; **L13**: 316
recurring, **L13**: 106
De rerum natura (Lucretius), **M2**: 146; **M7**: 275
Der Logische Aufbau der Welt (Carnap), **L14**: xiv
Descartes, René, **E1**: xxvii, 279, 291, 292, 303, 400; **E3**: 91; **E4**: 142, 193; **M4**: 254; **M6**: 24n, 64, 175; **M7**: 42, 51, 226; **M8**: 68, 142, 183; **M9**: xxi, 197, 303, 309; **M10**: 3, 90, 429; **M11**: 11, 43; **M12**: xiv, 108, 222, 264n; **M13**: 497, 498; **M15**: 11; **L1**: 14, 24, 27, 55, 81, 194, 255, 373; **L2**: 290; **L3**: 3; **L4**: 125; **L5**: 230, 381; **L7**: 144, 145; **L9**: 241; **L11**: xvn; **L12**: xi; **L14**: xix; **L15**: xiii, xxviii, 28, 94; **L16**: 423; **L17**: 405, 411
philosophy of, **E1**: 34, 36, 280-81
influences Leibniz, **E1**: 259, 262, 268, 271-75, 277, 415
on relation of individual to universe, **E1**: 286-87
on matter, **E1**: 356
on ontological argument, **E1**: 403; **M2**: 168-69
dualisms of, **M2**: x; **M8**: xxviii; **L10**: x, 340
on nature, **M2**: 147; **L16**: 106
on non-being, **M2**: 158
on pneuma, **M2**: 206
on rationalism, **M2**: 217
on object, **M2**: 250
on vacuum, **M2**: 268
subjective idealism of, **M3**: 382
method of analysis of, **M5**: 154
on knowledge, **M7**: 219-20; **M10**: 22; **L4**: ix, xii, xv-xvii, xx, 46, 50
and deduction, **M7**: 240-41
on good, **M8**: 23-24
presuppositions of, **L1**: 37
on sensory forms, **L1**: 108
on self and mind, **L1**: 173, 174, 177
on thinking, **L2**: 142
on science and religion, **L4**: 33-34
defines quantity, **L4**: 74
rivals Newton, **L4**: 92, 93
defines natural existence, **L4**: 113
mathematical concepts of, **L5**: 167-68; **L8**: 8, 33, 356
as skeptic, **L8**: xvi, xvii
Hocking on, **L14**: 421, 424
on vision, **L16**: 114n
on soul, **L16**: 124
on ideas, **L16**: 436, 440
Description, **L12**: 129, 131, 413-14, 462-64, 476-77. *See also* Kinds, **L12**; Traits, **L12**
Peirce on, **L11**: 93
nature of, **L11**: 99, 107
scientific, **L12**: 132-33
partial, **L12**: 240-42

and demonstration, **L12**: 352-57
as name, **L16**: 6, 146-47, 150, 262
Descriptive
judgment, **M8**: xv
definition as, **L16**: 174-79
theory, **L16**: 339, 455
end as, **L16**: 344
"Descriptive Definition, The" (S. Pepper), **L16**: 174-79
Desegregation, **L14**: xxiv
Design, **L4**: 73; **L10**: 31
vs. chance, **M4**: 8-10
as objective, **L1**: 79
artistic, **L10**: 121-22, 127, 165, 179, 236, 305, 318
Designation-event, **L16**: 142
Designations. *See also* Names
treatments of, **L16**: 6, 32, 38, 42
involved in fact, **L16**: 58-61, 66, 110
nature of, **L16**: 62, 69-70, 82-84, 93, 111, 140-44, 151-52, 165, 180
as name, **L16**: 70, 93n, 131-33, 154, 258, 262
as method of inquiry, **L16**: 81, 91, 92
as behavior, **L16**: 135, 275
related to sign, **L16**: 139, 303-5, 308
Designatum, **L13**: 204-5; **L16**: 45
meaning of term, **L15**: 142, 145-46
C. Morris on, **L16**: 9, 34-35
Carnap on, **L16**: 18-27, 32
Desirable
vs. desired, **L13**: 219
"Desirable and Emotive in Dewey's Ethics, The" (Hook), **L17**: 481
Desire, **M12**: 139-40, 143, 144; **M14**: 19, 135, 152, 162, 209; **L2**: 106; **L11**: 78, 462; **L15**: 16
nature of, **E1**: 329-30; **E4**: 267-70; **E5**: 129, 131-32; **L13**: 205-6, 217-20, 231, 238-43; **L15**: 101-5
related to pleasure, **E3**: 251-57, 268; **E4**: 202-5, 266; **E5**: 132-33; **M5**: 249-50
in Kantian theory of obligation, **E3**: 333
and reason, **E3**: 337-38; **M5**: 307-12; **L7**: 187-91; **L14**: 323-24
socialization of, **E3**: 387-88
as arousing effort, **E4**: 207; **E5**: 129
and mediated interest, **E5**: 128-29, 133
and imagery, **E5**: 320
hedonistic theory of, **M5**: 246-47; **M7**: 211
and valuation, **M8**: 35; **L13**: 205, 213, 237
habit and, **M14**: 21
control and satisfaction of, **M14**: 26-28; **L7**: 182, 204
and intelligence, **M14**: 171-81, 207; **L13**: 162, 172, 250
and purpose, **L7**: 186, 247, 308; **L13**: 42-45
and self, **L7**: 220
in esthetic experience, **L10**: 258-65, 284-85, 300, 334-36, 341, 350, 352
and effort, **L13**: 71, 313
and science, **L13**: 167, 171
vs. wish, **L13**: 205, 222
immediate, **L13**: 214, 227
related to nature, **L14**: 144-45, 384

Desired
related to desirable, **L17**: 480-84
Des Moines, Iowa, **M15**: 96
Despair, **L16**: 416
Despotism, **L17**: 231
Destiny of Man, The (J. Fiske), **L17**: 93, 559
Destruction, **L16**: 393
Detachment, **L10**: 262, 263
"Determination of Ultimate Values or Aims, The," **L13**: xvii
Determinism, **M13**: xv
and causation, **E4**: 91-95
theory of freedom in, **E4**: 344-50
in *Cyclopedia of Education*, **M6**: 419-20
economic, **L5**: 45-49; **L13**: 119
Cohen on, **L14**: 383-84
Detroit Convention (Polish National Department)
Dewey on, **M11**: xv, 259
purpose of, **M11**: xv, 284, 300-302, 310
organization of, **M11**: 242-54, 291, 302-4, 325, 328, 395, 404
decisions of, **M11**: 299, 305-6
delegates to, **M11**: 307, 312
Deussen, Paul, **E5**: 342-44
Development, **L12**: 30-31, 38-39
in *Cyclopedia of Education*, **M6**: 420-22
in educational process, **M9**: 54-58, 61, 63; **L9**: 198-200
related to culture, **M9**: 128
of individual, **L14**: 108-11
Developmental logic, **M1**: xiv
"Development of American Pragmatism, The," **L2**: xii
Devonshire, Earl of, **M11**: 22
Devotion, **L9**: 28, 219-21, 225-26
Wieman on, **L9**: 414-17, 427, 434
Dewey, Alice Chipman, **M6**: 179; **L6**: 22; **L11**: 199; **L14**: xx
Dewey, Evelyn, **M8**: xxxii, 208
Dewey, John, **L8**: 16; **L16**: 302n
biography of, **E1**: xxiii-xxiv
relation of early to later writings, **E1**: xxxv-xxxvii; **E3**: xxi-xxii
early writings of, **E3**: xxiii-xxiv; **E4**: xiii; **E5**: xiii, xx
seventieth birthday of, **L5**: xi, 418n, 497
conflicting images of, **L8**: ix-xviii
oversights of, **L11**: xxxii
eightieth birthday of, **L13**: ix; **L14**: xi
misunderstood, **L16**: 4, 275-76, 386
Collected Works of, **L17**: xi-xv
Dewey, John, Labor Research Fund, **L14**: 311
Dewey School. *See* Laboratory School, University of Chicago
Dewey School, The (Mayhew and Edwards), **M1**: 325n, 335n
"Dewey's New Logic" (B. Russell), **L14**: xiii
De Witt Clinton High School (New York City)
trial of teachers at, **M10**: 158-63, 173-77
strike of students at, **M10**: 176
Dharna, **M5**: 64; **L7**: 59
Diagnosis, **M12**: 162
Dial, **M11**: ix, xvii, 393; **M12**: 16, 278
Dialectic (M. Adler), **L3**: 311, 314-15

Dialectic, **M6**: 170; **M10**: 11, 420; **L1**: 51-54, 57, 76, 89, 107, 136, 152, 187, 202, 218-20, 234, 247, 253, 323
in medieval universities, **M5**: 141, 154
in *Cyclopedia of Education*, **M6**: 422
Platonic and Socratic, **M7**: 229-31; **L2**: 128-30
Hegelian, **M8**: 140; **L11**: 33, 51, 55, 60
idealistic, **M10**: 107
related to experience, **L5**: 487-95
inadequacy of, **L11**: 50
in Santayana's philosophy, **L14**: 297-98
Hocking on, **L14**: 424-25
Dialectical materialism, **L5**: 358; **L13**: 120, 351; **L14**: 75-76; **L15**: 24
Dialectical method, **M9**: 289, 325, 349
Dialogue, **L17**: 185
Dialogue between a Philosopher and a Student of the Common Laws of England, A (Hobbes), **M11**: 28-29
Dialogues (Plato), **M15**: 336; **L2**: ix, 124-40; **L5**: 155
Dialogus, Agricola, Germania (Tacitus), **M8**: 189
Diana of Ephesus, **L13**: 369, 404
Dianoiology, **M2**: 158
Díaz, Porfirio, **L2**: 197-200; **L3**: 159-60
Dicey, Albert Venn, **L2**: 42-43; **L11**: 17
Dick, James, **L6**: 251
Dickens, Charles, **M3**: 81; **L1**: 323; **L10**: xix-xx, 347; **L11**: 282; **L17**: 323, 325, 564
Dictatorship, **L7**: 351; **L11**: 139, 460; **L13**: xv
of proletariat, **L13**: 126-28
Mannheim on, **L14**: 293-94
rise of, **L17**: 453, 460
Dictionary of American Biography, **L6**: xivn
Dictionary of Philosophy, The (Runes), **L16**: 42-43, 163-64, 258n
Dictionary of Philosophy and Psychology (J. Baldwin), **M10**: 71n, 74; **L16**: 163, 297n
Dewey's contributions to, **M2**: ix, 141-269
Didactics
in *Cyclopedia of Education*, **M6**: 423
Diderot, Denis, **E4**: 193; **M3**: 52; **L1**: 355; **L17**: 147, 148, 430
as sensationalist, **E5**: 15
paradox of, **L10**: 86, 263
on tragedy, **L10**: 192
Die Definition (Dubislav), **L16**: 161
Die Krise der Psychologie (Bühler), **L16**: 137n
Dies, Martin, **L6**: xxii; **L14**: 370, 427
Differentiation, **L13**: 78
Difficulties, **L17**: 294
Diffidence
as motive, **L13**: 140, 142-43
Digby, Kenelm, **L14**: 399
Dilettanteism
Bourget on, **E3**: 38-39, 41
Dill, Clarence C., **L6**: 355, 394
Dilthey, Wilhelm, **L16**: xiii, xvi, 117n
Dimnet, Ernest, **L3**: 316-17
Ding-an-sich
Royce's rejection of, **M10**: 84

Dinsmore, Charles A., **L7**: 91
Diodorus of Tyre, **M2**: 186
Diogenes of Apollonia, **M2**: 162
Diplomacy, **L16**: 400
  in China, **M13**: 230, 441
  need for reform in, **M15**: 118-19
  in international disputes, **M15**: 414-15
Dirac, Paul Adrien Maurice, **L12**: 178n
Direction
  in inquiry, **L16**: 323-25
  ends provide, **L16**: 329, 331, 336, 350
  in progressive education, **L17**: 52
Directness
  in dealing with subject-matter, **M9**: 180-82
Disarmament, **L11**: 263
  and economics, **L6**: 364, 366
  and sanctions, **L6**: 459-61, 471
Discernment
  Locke's successors on, **M9**: 277
Discipline, **M12**: 139, 140, 185; **L7**: 204-5, 207, 209; **L8**: 89; **L13**: xii
  in school, **E5**: 67, 88; **M1**: 65-66; **M8**: xxxvi, 294-96; **L9**: 176-77, 179; **L17**: 343
  development of, **E5**: 119; **M1**: 308; **L13**: 6
  and interest, **E5**: 144-45; **M7**: 254, 257-58; **M9**: 131-45
  references on, **E5**: 330
  need for change in, **M1**: 11-12
  Dewey's attitude toward, **M2**: xviii
  formal, **M6**: 216; **L8**: 156-58
  related to thought, **M6**: 229-32; **L8**: 161
  in *Cyclopedia of Education*, **M6**: 423-24
  Rousseau on, **M8**: 295
  Montessori on, **M8**: 301-2
  and freedom, **M9**: 310-11; **L8**: 182-86
  in Turkish schools, **M15**: 294-95
  in Teachers Union, **L9**: 343
  misuse of, **L17**: 295
Discourse, **L1**: 74, 135-45, 152, 158-59, 206-7, 213-17
  consecutive, **M6**: 325; **L8**: 313-14
  and meaning-symbols, **L12**: 51-66, 115, 118-19, 155-57, 421
  and reasoning, **L12**: 60, 115-16, 164, 276-77, 379, 428
  controlled by situation, **L12**: 73-75, 312-13
  in Greek logic, **L12**: 98-99
Discovery, **M12**: 101-2; **L1**: 121-25, 136
  logic of, **M12**: 96-98
  moral, **M12**: 179
  in experimental method, **L4**: 146-48
  and Greek logic, **L12**: 92-93
Discovery of the Soul (Jaeger), **L17**: 10, 554
Discreteness, **L4**: 101, 140-41, 185-88
  in environment, **L14**: 30
  vs. continuity, **L14**: 134
Discrimination. *See also* Data, **L12**; Elimination, **L12**; Race discrimination; Selection, **L12**
  in judgment, **E5**: 322
  need for, **M13**: 310
  of experience, **L10**: 150, 156, 196, 251; **L13**: 17, 18
  in criticism, **L10**: 304, 309, 312-16, 319

Discussion
in terms of thinking, **M1**: 158-59
Plato on, **M1**: 161-62; **M13**: 3
vs. coercion, **L13**: 153
freedom of, **L16**: 402, 406
"Discussion of Dewey and Bentley's 'Postulations,' A" (Churchman and Cowan), **L16**: 470
Diseases of the Will, The (Ribot), **E5**: 342-43
Disfranchisement, **L6**: 226
Disinterestedness, **E3**: 385; **L7**: 201-2, 296; **L10**: 262, 263
Disjunction, **L12**: 172, 190, 193, 196, 305-7, 340, 442, 451-52. *See also* Exclusion, **L12**
Dislike, **L13**: 202, 333
Disorder
social, **L10**: 25, 26
related to esthetics, **L10**: 75
mental, **L17**: 514
Disposition, **M14**: 31
as term for feelings, **E3**: 244-45
emphasis on personal, **L7**: 241-45
as habit, **L16**: 26n
C. Morris on, **L16**: 210n, 211-12
in semiotic terminology, **L16**: 221, 231-37
meaning of, **L17**: 198
Disraeli, Benjamin, **M11**: 389
Dissemination
and social knowledge, **L2**: 345-47
and art, **L2**: 349-50
Dissent, **L13**: 127; **L15**: 297
Dissociation
connection of likeness in, **E2**: 105-6
conditions of, **E2**: 107-8
and values, **E2**: 108-14
functions of, **E2**: 115-16
distinct from attention, **E2**: 118-19
in imagination, **E2**: 169-70
in intellectual feeling, **E2**: 258
in art, **L10**: 255
Distance, **M12**: 147-48; **L12**: 35-38; **L17**: 453
Distortion
for esthetic effect, **L10**: 178
Distraction
avoidance of, **M6**: 345; **L8**: 336-37
Distribution, **L16**: 91
method of calculating, **E3**: 43-46
of power, **L7**: 347-48
of income, **L7**: 406-11, 435
justice in, **L7**: 434-36
problems in, **L9**: 250, 285
Distrust
of government, **L13**: 111
of human nature, **L13**: 152-53
of experience, **L13**: 256
Diversity
in educational capacities, **L9**: 196-99
Dividends, **L6**: 348-49, 369, 395
Divine
related to human, **E1**: 205-6
consciousness, **E3**: 23-24, 28
existence, **M8**: 7n
right of kings, **M11**: 19, 52, 170
and ideal, **L9**: xvii, 32-36
will, **L14**: xxii
Divine Comedy (Dante), **L10**: 115
Division, logical, **L12**: 340-42
Divorce, **M5**: 538-39; **L5**: 47; **L7**: 446-47
Dmowski, Roman
policies of, **M11**: 271, 275, 292, 297, 300-302, 306, 321

Dmowski, Roman (*continued*)
as Polish leader, **M11**: 277-81, 328, 405
Dobzhansky, Theodosius, **L16**: 119n
Docility, **M14**: 47, 70; **L17**: 282
Doctores scholastici, **M2**: 236
Doctrine
in religion, **L9**: xv, 18, 23-24, 436
scientific method opposed to, **L9**: 27
and supernatural, **L9**: 37
of Lenin, **L9**: 244-45
"Does 'Consciousness' Exist?" (W. James), **L14**: 156-57
"Does Reality Possess Practical Character?" **L14**: 404
Dogberry (Prentice Mulford), **L9**: 176
Dogma, **M12**: 164, 171
fatal to inquiry, **L16**: 325
political, **L16**: 362-63
in religion, **L17**: 529-30
Dogmatism, **M6**: 296; **M12**: 262-67; **M13**: 67, 308, 314; **L8**: 270-71
James on absolute, **M12**: 220
evils of, **L7**: 268, 317, 338, 343
protection against, **L17**: 443-44
Doing
in esthetics, **L10**: 50-53, 63, 75, 137, 165, 178, 218
in common sense and science, **L16**: 252-53
as goal, **L16**: 365
Doldrums, **L16**: 411
Dole, **L11**: 29
Doll's House, A (Ibsen), **M5**: 525; **M13**: 110
Domesday Book, **L7**: 138, 385
Domestic arts, **E5**: 232-33, 240-41; **M1**: 13-15, 50-51; **L17**: 234, 316-17
Dominicans, **M5**: 141
Dominion (Hobbes), **M11**: 24
Donaldson, Henry Herbert, **M9**: 123
Don't Be Afraid! (Cowles), **L15**: xxiii, 365
Dopp, Katharine Elizabeth, **M3**: 307
Dorfman, Joseph, **L6**: xixn
Dorner, Alexander, **L15**: xxiii, 312-14
"Do Things Exist?" (Boodin), **L17**: 417n
Doubt. *See also* Problem, **L12**
and thinking, **M1**: 151-52; **M6**: 188, 191, 259-60, 264-65, 296; **L8**: 121, 124, 211, 222, 271
and inference, **M6**: xviii
and inquiry, **L12**: 109-10, 123-24, 138, 162, 226; **L15**: 38-39, 80-81
in experience, **L14**: 64-65, 69, 184-86
Doughton, Robert L., **L9**: 260
Douglas, Paul H., **L5**: xvii; **L6**: xvii, xviii, 250-51, 313-14
Douglas, William O., **L14**: xxiv
Dowbor-Musnicki, Jozef, **M11**: 321
Downing, Bernard, **L9**: 365
Doyle, Arthur Conan, **L10**: xix
Doyle, William F., **L9**: 362
Drafting of the Covenant, The (D. Miller), **L6**: 473n
Drake, Durant
on empirical pluralism, **M10**: xxv
on perception, **M10**: 64-66
on realism, **M10**: 431-49
Drama, **L16**: 397
role of, **L10**: 13, 37, 330-31, 348

nature of, **L10**: 76, 118, 148, 162-63, 174, 177, 182, 185, 192, 207, 216, 238, 247-48, 257-58, 265, 298, 303, 312
Dramatic rehearsal
as deliberation, **M5**: xiii-xxxiv; **M14**: xiii, 132-33, 216
Dramatist, **L17**: 381
Dramatization
used by schools, **M8**: 286-93
Drawing, **L10**: 98-99
teaching of, **E5**: 193-201; **L17**: 287, 288-89
"Dr. Dewey Replies," **L9**: xxin, xxii-xxiii
Dreams, **M12**: 83, 148-49, 160
related to consciousness, **M10**: 25-27
neo-realists on, **M10**: 39
in esthetic theory, **L10**: 277-81, 288, 297
vs. life, **L14**: 16
Dreitzer, Ephim A., **L11**: 321, 602
Dreyfus, Alfred, **L11**: 303, 320
Driesch, Hans
on philosophy of biology, **M8**: 449-59
Drill
in teaching reading, **E5**: 263-64
overemphasis on, **L17**: 222
intelligent vs. unintelligent, **L17**: 305
Drudgery, **M6**: 351; **L8**: 346-47
Drug traffic, **M11**: 235-40
Drysdale, Alexander, **M12**: 253
Dual Empire
in eastern Europe, **M11**: 263, 277, 327
Dualism, **M2**: 142; **M3**: 311; **M14**: 8, 11, 31, 40-41, 49, 51-52, 102, 213; **M15**: xii, 361, 376; **L1**: 53-54, 102, 185-86, 353-56; **L4**: 47, 243; **L10**: x-xiii, 340; **L14**: xii; **L15**: 275, 335. *See also* Empiricism, **L12**
of material and ideal, **E5**: 164-66; **L4**: 195, 215
Cartesian, **M2**: ix; **M8**: xxviii
in *Cyclopedia of Education*, **M6**: 361, 424
related to monism, **M7**: 285; **M15**: 361, 362
and formal discipline, **M9**: 66, 70-71
educational results of, **M9**: 300
continuity vs., **M9**: 343-49
common-sense, **M10**: 24
epistemological, **M10**: 64, 66, 439-49; **M13**: 48; **M15**: 355, 358, 362, 363, 367, 370, 372; **L14**: 9-10; **L15**: 145-46, 152, 165
Dewey's rejection of, **M12**: xv, xix, 179
difficulties in, **M13**: 56
traditional and existential, **M13**: 57; **L13**: 330-31
of anticipation, **M13**: 459
vs. idealism, **M13**: 465-66
of theory and practice, **L4**: 11, 62; **L12**: 63-65, 78-80, 432-35, 455-57, 487-89, 492-93, 504-5; **L15**: 258-59
of activity, **L4**: 25-26
natural-supernatural, **L4**: 42, 246; **L15**: 200-202, 269-71; **L17**: 15
related to religion, **L9**: 49
according to Santayana, **L9**: 241-42
Whitehead on, **L11**: 148
of logic and methodology, **L12**: 12-13
mind-body, **L12**: 42-43; **L14**: 421-23; **L15**: xvii-xix, 219, 365

Dualism (*continued*)
of science and morals, **L14**: 62, 66-70
metaphysical, **L14**: 104, 145
contribution of physics to, **L14**: 126-27
in James's psychology, **L14**: 155-61, 164-67
Cohen on Dewey and, **L14**: 385-86
in philosophy, **L15**: xxii-xxiii; **L16**: 369, 371, 407-13
critique of, **L15**: xxxii-xxxiii
fact-value, **L15**: 16-17, 106, 481-82
sources of, **L15**: 157, 230
in social science, **L15**: 232-33
practical effects of, **L15**: 306
dislike for, **L16**: 115n, 423, 456
in knowledge, **L16**: 288
in judgments, **L16**: 315
normative-descriptive, **L16**: 339, 455
psychophysical, **L17**: xxix-xxx
Kantian, **L17**: xxx
cultural and vocational, **L17**: 111
Dualistic
epistemology, **M4**: 82n
realism, **M15**: 361, 362
deism, **L17**: 95, 96
Dual unionism, **L9**: 335-37
Dubislav, Walter, **L16**: 161
Dubs, Homer H.
on definition, **L16**: 167-69, 175, 181n
Ducasse, C. J., **L16**: 32, 40
logic of, **L16**: xxx, xxxi, 193n
epistemology of, **L16**: 8
on propositions, **L16**: 35-36, 45
Duggan, Stephen, **L11**: 576
Duguit, Léon, **L2**: 39, 41; **L6**: 269
Duhem, Pierre, **L14**: 22
Dulles, John Foster, **L6**: 471n
Duma
Polish question in, **M11**: 263, 267, 277-78
Dumba, Konstantin Theodor, **M11**: 294
Dunning, William Archibald, **L2**: 33n
Dunsany, Lord, **L10**: xvi
Duns Scotus, John, **L8**: xv, xvi
scholasticism of, **M2**: 241-43
philosophic system of, **M2**: 244
on subjective-objective, **M2**: 250
Cohen on, **L14**: 395
Duplicity
of subject-object structure, **L14**: 134
Du Pont, Irénée, **L9**: 89
Du Pont de Nemours, Pierre Samuel, **L14**: 202, 213
Durant, William James, **L2**: 387
Duranty, Walter, **L15**: 290, 496, 509
Duration, **L2**: 62
Bergson on, **M10**: 68-69
time and, **M12**: xxviii, 223-24
characteristics of, **M12**: 226-34
and future, **L2**: 63-74
Dürer, Albrecht, **L10**: 294
Durkheim, Émile, **L3**: 15; **L5**: 499-501
Durkheim school of collective mind, **M10**: 60
Dutch art, **L10**: 192, 239
Dutton, Samuel T., **L17**: 233
Duty, **L10**: 286, 299
and morals, **E3**: 104-9; **M9**: 360-63; **L7**: 65, 168, 181, 308
related to desire, **E3**: 337-38; **M5**: 307-12

for duty's sake, **E3**: 338-39
Sophocles on, **M5**: 131; **L7**: 122
Stoics on, **M5**: 132; **L7**: 123, 133
Kant on, **M5**: 313-18; **M8**: 162-66, 173, 474; **M10**: 226-27, 228; **L7**: 220-22
utilitarian theory of, **M5**: 318-27
in German philosophy, **M8**: 419
sense of, **L7**: xi-xii, 231-34
Romans on, **L7**: 133-34, 219, 228
social, **L7**: 217-19; **L15**: 179
justification of, **L7**: 225-31
Dworkin, Ronald, **L14**: xxiv
Dyadic terms, **L12**: 311-13
Dykhuizen, George, **L11**: xxiii, xxxi; **L14**: xx, xxi
Dynamic, **L1**: 85-86
in *Cyclopedia of Education*, **M6**: 424-25
connection, **M10**: 11-12, 16, 19
in art, **L10**: xvii, 62-63, 120-22, 166, 186, 237
Dynastic states, **L2**: 290-91
Dynnik, M., **L15**: 24n
Dzerzhinskiy, Feliks Admundovich, **L17**: 501, 570
Dzerzhinskiy, USSR, **L17**: 498, 570

Eachard, John, **M11**: 23-24
Eames, S. Morris
on Dewey's 1889-92 writings, **E3**: xxi-xxxviii
Earth, **M12**: 111, 117
East
synthesis of West and, **L17**: 35-36
Eastern Commercial Teachers Association (ECTA), **L5**: 401
Eastman, Charles
on primitive society, **M5**: 56, 61-62; **L7**: 44, 51, 57
Eastman, Max, **M7**: 149; **L17**: 58
on esthetics, **L10**: 140, 265, 359, 362
Eberhard, Johann Augustus, **E1**: 429, 430
Echoist, **L16**: 126n
Eckenstein, Lina, **M5**: 515n; **L7**: 442
Eckhart, Meister, **M2**: 183
Ecological psychology, **L16**: 125n
Ecology, **L16**: 117, 120
Economic Mind in American Civilization, The (Dorfman), **L6**: xixn
Economic Research, National Bureau of, **L6**: 343, 349, 360; **L7**: 409; **L9**: 81-82, 267, 287-88
Economics, **M14**: 11, 46, 79; **L13**: 290, 316. *See also* Business; Industry
and family, **M5**: 29-30, 46; **L7**: 28-30, 44, 444-45, 457-58
influence of, **M5**: 77-78; **M15**: 240-41, 253-54; **L7**: 71, 372
individualism in, **M5**: 77-78; **L7**: 331
among Greeks, **M5**: 112-17; **L7**: 103-8
vs. moral theory, **M5**: 179-80; **L16**: 337, 371, 452
Adam Smith's theory of, **M6**: 367-68
historic and geographical aspects of, **M9**: 223-24; **L13**: 338-39
in Japan, **M11**: xvii-xviii, 160-67, 176-79
training for, **M11**: 62-65
in U.S., **M11**: 71, 183, 185; **L11**: 168-70, 232

Economics (*continued*)
theories of, **M11**: 73-86, 89, 94, 117, 121; **M14**: 84-89, 93; **M15**: 244, 258-59, 268; **L4**: 65, 207, 218, 224-27; **L6**: xxiii, 180-81, 187-88, 409-10, 447-48
affected by League of Nations, **M11**: 125-30, 138-42, 151-52
and international relations, **M11**: 134, 136; **M15**: 125; **L6**: 178-79, 353, 364-68; **L9**: 261; **L11**: 261-64, 276
T. Roosevelt's approach to, **M11**: 148
and immigration, **M11**: 159, 241, 242
in China, **M11**: 180, 204, 205, 211, 224-27, 234; **M12**: 34-40, 47, 74; **L3**: 197, 419-20
ends of, **M12**: 177-78, 200-201
modern, **M14**: 9, 185-88; **L7**: 141-44, 149-50
acquisitiveness in, **M14**: 99-103, 147-53
and war, **M15**: 111-12; **L13**: 400
related to education, **M15**: 155-56, 195; **L6**: xxii, 104, 118-19, 123-26, 410-11; **L8**: 47, 72, 94; **L9**: 112-26, 128-30, 141-45, 183, 386-95; **L11**: 354, 519; **L13**: 386
laissez-faire, **L1**: 356-59; **L8**: 51, 57, 63-64, 73, 75; **L9**: 206, 297; **L13**: 137
Turkish struggle with, **L2**: 191-93
related to politics, **L2**: 290-93, 296-302, 306-7, 378-79; **L6**: 150, 152, 157-58, 170-74, 249, 436-37; **L7**: 355-58, 428-29; **L9**: 79, 163; **L13**: 69, 73, 101, 107, 112, 118, 129-30, 338; **L16**: 362-63, 391, 404-6
determinism in, **L2**: 309-54
in Russia, **L3**: 208-10, 221; **L6**: 263-67; **L17**: 505
laws of, **L4**: 169
and human nature, **L6**: xv, 36; **L14**: 261
monetarists on, **L6**: xix
and culture, **L6**: 43-44
related to science, **L6**: 44-45; **L9**: 97-98; **L11**: 143, 278-79; **L15**: 226-28; **L16**: 418-19
problems in, **L6**: 69-71, 74, 244, 342, 377-78; **L9**: 61, 63-64, 77, 82-83
related to tariff bill, **L6**: 164-66, 241
need for reforms in, **L6**: 174-75; **L9**: 89-90, 206-7
and minorities, **L6**: 225-30
and credit, **L6**: 243
and production, **L6**: 346-47, 358-61
Klein on, **L6**: 346-54, 485-87
Hoover on, **L6**: 357, 358
and railroads, **L6**: 368-71
and unemployment relief, **L6**: 390, 399
among Romans, **L7**: 128-30
medieval, **L7**: 136-37
and social order, **L8**: 50, 85, 86, 364; **L9**: 190-91, 208, 229, 231-35, 312; **L14**: 362
technology and, **L8**: 90, 102
George on, **L9**: 61-65
redistribution of income in, **L9**: 64, 82-83, 256, 261, 266, 288
Niebuhr on, **L9**: 71-75, 399, 404

government responsibility for, **L9**: 77, 264
crisis in, **L9**: 78-79, 113-15, 277-79, 287, 288
related to unions, **L9**: 79-80, 318-19, 333, 338-40
AAA reports on, **L9**: 83-85
producer and consumer cooperation in, **L9**: 85-86
Bellamy's view of, **L9**: 102-4
influence of citizens' committees on, **L9**: 112-13
art's relation to, **L10**: 14-16, 27, 193, 197, 265, 303, 319, 330-32, 340, 344-48, 351
affects liberalism, **L11**: 8-11, 366-67
freedom in, **L11**: 26-28, 136-40, 142-43, 249-52, 254, 258, 283, 284, 290, 365-67, 369-71, 496
structure of, **L11**: 43-44, 130, 339, 492
socialized, **L11**: 61-64, 266
and authority, **L11**: 136-37
planned, **L11**: 140-41, 144, 258
regulation of, **L11**: 168, 360, 362-63; **L13**: 105-6
and press, **L11**: 269-73
Lippmann on, **L11**: 490-94
Compton on, **L11**: 575-76
divisions in, **L13**: 114-15, 125; **L15**: 229, 237
related to democracy, **L13**: 305-7; **L17**: 472
and standard of living, **L13**: 423-24
method of intelligence applied to, **L14**: 74-75
C. and M. Beard on, **L14**: 284
related to materialism, **L14**: 319, 329, 332-33; **L15**: 60-61, 222-23, 233-35
ageing related to, **L14**: 343
Ayres on, **L15**: 89n, 108n, 359-60, 448n, 502
means-end split in, **L15**: 216-18
oppressive effects of, **L15**: 220
nature of, **L16**: 87n, 101n, 243n, 255, 353, 366, 396, 401
isolation of, **L16**: 371, 417
understanding of, **L17**: 46
of scarcity and abundance, **L17**: 444

Economic Sanctions, Committee on, **L6**: 456n, 471, 484
"Economic Situation: A Challenge to Education, The," **L6**: xxiii
Eddington, Arthur Stanley, **L5**: 483, 484; **L9**: 242; **L11**: 434, 435
on ideas, **L4**: xvii
on operations, **L4**: 89-90
on relations, **L4**: 104-5
on perception, **L4**: 191-92
Eddy, Mary Baker, **L1**: 55
Eddy, Sherwood, **L6**: 263-65
Edel, Abraham, **L14**: xxiv; **L15**: 460
on 1908 and 1932 *Ethics*, **L7**: vii-xxxv
Edinburgh, Scotland, **M11**: 237
Edinburgh, University of, **L4**: vii
Edison, Thomas Alva, **M7**: 106-8; **L8**: 233
Edman, Irwin, **L14**: 301-2; **L15**: 335n; **L17**: 466, 568
in Polish study, **M11**: 260, 396, 397, 401n
contributes to *Art as Experience*, **L10**: 7
Educating for Democracy: A Symposium, **L11**: 226n, 567n
Education (Kant), **L13**: xvii

Education, **M12**: xvi, 152, 184, 199; **M14**: 47, 50, 52, 76, 185; **L4**: 219; **L16**: 458. *See also* Elementary school; Schools; Teachers; University; Vocational education
affects health of women, **E1**: 64; **L17**: 7-9
study of, **E1**: 80; **E5**: 113, 443-47
philosophy of, **E4**: xx-xxi; **E5**: 87-91, 294-95, 328-30, 340-41, 445; **M4**: 162-63; **M7**: 297-312; **M9**: 338-42; **M10**: xxix-xxx; **M15**: xxiii; **L5**: 26-31; **L8**: 46, 48, 77-103; **L9**: 194-204, 390; **L11**: xxin; **L15**: 315, 335
theories of, **E4**: 50; **M7**: 377-86; **M9**: 78-86, 100, 125-30, 133, 209, 325, 341; **M11**: xi, 58-69, 88-92, 333-35, 348
Dewey's role in, **E5**: xvii; **M11**: ix; **L4**: vii, viii; **L6**: 414-17; **L8**: ix, xi-xii, xv; **L14**: xix; **L16**: 187
concepts of ethical in, **E5**: 75
related to society, **E5**: 84, 93-94, 213, 224-25; **M4**: 328; **M8**: 351, 353-64; **M9**: 331-32; **M15**: xxiii, 150, 158-59; **L2**: 358-59; **L6**: 96-97, 110-11, 126-27, 139-40, 143; **L8**: 58-60; **L9**: 110-11, 114, 127-28, 131-35, 145, 159-61, 167-68, 175, 180-85, 202-3, 206, 393-95; **L11**: xvii-xxiii, 25, 42, 44, 51, 170, 177, 183, 204-7, 209, 230-37, 240, 249, 252-55, 378, 382-86, 388-90, 408-14, 485-86, 550, 555-56; **L13**: 377, 381, 384-87
related to psychology, **E5**: 86, 226-29; **M1**: 135; **L9**: 150-51, 155, 179, 183, 191, 409; **L14**: 337
development of, **E5**: 214
methods of, **E5**: 232; **M3**: 307-9; **M4**: 161-62; **M10**: 142-43; **M11**: 54-57, 335, 393; **L2**: 360; **L4**: 32, 37, 201; **L6**: 100-101, 105-9, 142-45; **L9**: 178, 179, 181-82; **L11**: 162-65, 171-73, 178-80, 193-95, 202-16, 244, 343-44, 557; **L17**: 54-55, 464-65
changes in, **E5**: 257-58; **M15**: 181, 187-88, 190-91, 208-9; **L3**: 39-40, 140-41, 252; **L6**: 94-98, 109-11; **L9**: 148-50, 175-76, 390-91; **L14**: 270-72
experiment in, **E5**: 269, 288; **M7**: 387-89; **M8**: 222-35, 253; **M10**: 121-24; **L6**: 295-98
division of labor in, **E5**: 281
leaders, **E5**: 281-89
references on, **E5**: 330, 334
Harris on, **E5**: 380-82
influences on, **M1**: xvii; **M15**: 195; **L8**: 43-48, 53, 60, 65-69, 71-74, 80-82, 101-3; **L11**: 79; **L17**: 167
related to industry, **M1**: 16-17; **M3**: 285-93; **M10**: 137-43; **M15**: 162-67, 190; **L3**: 280-84; **L8**: 55-57
control of, **M1**: 18; **M8**: 123-33; **L11**: 115-16, 162, 165, 358, 413
traditional and progressive,

M1: 21-23, 264-65; **L13**: xii-xiv, 3-16, 23-24, 34, 61-62, 284, 340-41, 375-79, 383-85
related to life, **M1**: 39; **L14**: 346-47
conservatism in, **M1**: 260-61
progressive, **M1**: 262-63; **M8**: xxxii; **M9**: xv; **L3**: xxiv-xxvi, 257-68, 330-31; **L5**: xv-xvi, 319-25; **L9**: 147, 151, 153-57, 194, 198-99; **L11**: 175, 181, 190-216; **L13**: 378-79; **L15**: 303-4; **L17**: 52-56
old and new, **M1**: 265-82, 304-5
direct and indirect, **M3**: 240
tests and measurements in, **M3**: 241-48; **M15**: 182; **L3**: 260-62
related to religion, **M4**: 165-70; **L14**: 77-78
theories of mind applied to, **M4**: 181-91
moral, **M5**: 157-58; **M11**: 32-33; **L5**: 74; **L9**: 186-93; **L17**: 261
pragmatism in, **M6**: xi; **L15**: 167-68
related to science, **M6**: 69-79; **M12**: 265; **L3**: xxv, 259-61, 267-68; **L5**: xii-xiv, 3-40; **L6**: 59-60, 104-5; **L9**: 98-100, 195-98; **L11**: 34-35, 128, 186-87, 189, 200-201, 214, 503, 551-54, 556, 580
scientific and humanistic, **M6**: 70-71; **M9**: 294-98; **M10**: 181-82; **L17**: xviii-xix, 322
play and, **M6**: 308, 363; **M7**: 322-23; **L8**: 288-89; **L17**: 263, 284-85
language in, **M6**: 318-27; **L8**: 308-14
observation in, **M6**: 331-35
communication in, **M6**: 335-37; **L15**: 179-80
in *Cyclopedia of Education*, **M6**: 417-18, 425-34, 436-37
interest and effort in, **M7**: 153-97; **L6**: 88, 116-17
idealism in, **M7**: 229-33
imitation in, **M7**: 234-37
liberal, **M7**: 271-75; **M10**: 156; **L15**: 154, 276-80, 333-36, 378, 474-84
Plato's influence on, **M7**: 312-18
democracy and, **M8**: xxxiv; **L2**: 364-65; **L11**: 222-24, 385-86, 415-16, 557-59; **L13**: 17-18, 92-93, 379, 383
in Germany, **M8**: 174; **M9**: 100, 102; **M10**: 178-82; **L13**: 92, 161
Rousseau on, **M8**: 211, 213-14
Pestalozzi on, **M8**: 251-52
and leisure, **M8**: 353-56; **M15**: 167-69, 190, 194-95
purpose of, **M9**: 54-56, 77, 319-20; **M13**: 297, 320, 329, 399-405; **M14**: xx, 89-90; **L5**: xvi; **L6**: 75-89, 102, 112-13; **L9**: 147-48, 194-96; **L11**: 159-61, 167, 170, 178, 501; **L13**: 40-41, 270, 304, 376, 385; **L16**: 380; **L17**: 139, 224-25, 230-31, 294, 298, 316, 322, 337, 476
curriculum in, **M9**: 254-56; **M15**: 183-84, 187, 191-92
related to nationalism, **M10**: xxxii-xxxiii, 193-95, 203-10
current tendencies in, **M10**: 116-20
public, **M10**: 173-77; **L11**: 175, 181-82, 226-27, 229-31,

Education (*continued*)
234-37, 350-51, 579; **L15**: 281-85
in Great Britain, **M10**: 178-79, 181
universal military service as, **M10**: 183-90
and culture, **M10**: 196-201; **M15**: 196-97; **L5**: 102-3; **L6**: xxii, 46, 83-84, 421, 445-47; **L11**: 350, 573
organization in, **M10**: 397-411; **L3**: 251
in China, **M11**: xvii, 180, 200, 203, 207, 209, 231; **M13**: 231-32; **L17**: 32, 169-71
related to politics, **M11**: 32-33; **M15**: 158-63, 190; **L6**: 118-19, 188, 245, 254, 411, 437
of poor, **M11**: 77, 80
in Japan, **M11**: 157, 161, 166-72, 178, 193
of Poles, **M11**: 242, 260, 263, 265, 277, 305, 398
G. Morris's role in, **M11**: 337
F. Alexander on, **M11**: 352-55
James on, **M12**: 207; **L14**: 339
criticism of, **M12**: 248; **M13**: 293, 294, 327-28, 332, 333
hindrances to, **M13**: xv
importance of, **M13**: 228, 230-32, 283-85; **L5**: 156; **L11**: 159-61, 533
popular, **M13**: 303
beliefs about, **M13**: 318-24, 328, 402, 427-28
equipment for, **M13**: 326
Kant on, **M13**: 401; **L13**: xvii
training and, **M13**: 428
definition of, **M14**: 70; **L17**: 214, 226
individualism and, **M15**: xxiii, 170, 172-75, 180-81; **L5**: 131-43; **L7**: 364; **L8**: 43, 53-55; **L9**: 176-81, 183, 196-98, 205-7
propaganda in, **M15**: xxiv
professional, **M15**: xxiv, 193-97; **L11**: 172, 176, 188-89, 538-39
and evolution, **M15**: 50, 162; **L9**: 161-62
isolation vs. socialization in, **M15**: 176-78
theory and practice in, **M15**: 184-86, 189
role of supervisor in, **M15**: 186
finances in, **M15**: 192; **L2**: 117-20; **L9**: 115-22, 392-95; **L14**: 311
importance of thinking in, **M15**: 198-99
Turkish, **M15**: 275-77, 280-82, 290-97, 304-7
instrumentalism in, **L2**: xvii-xviii, 55-61
art, **L2**: xx-xxi, 111-15, 375-77, 382-85; **L10**: 349; **L11**: 195, 503-4, 520-25
U.S., **L2**: 115; **L6**: 90-91, 100-104; **L9**: 393, 394
problems in, **L2**: 116-22; **L8**: 263-67; **L11**: 162-63, 173-80, 231-32, 354, 357-59, 411-12, 579; **L13**: xiii, 22-23, 26-27, 36, 38, 44-45, 52-53, 55-58, 62, 264, 270, 283, 301; **L17**: 27, 110, 113, 239
quality of, **L2**: 120-23
in Mexico, **L2**: 199-205
Russell on, **L2**: 226-30
art of, **L3**: 38-39; **L5**: 6-7
in USSR, **L3**: 218-41, 247-48; **L6**: 143-45, 291-94; **L11**: 335-36, 356, 357, 509; **L15**: 373-74; **L17**: 487-510

higher, **L3**: 276-78; **L11**: 163, 172-74, 231
effects of, **L4**: 141, 217
related to economics, **L4**: 225; **L6**: xxi, xxiii, 123-25, 129, 409-11; **L9**: 112-26, 128-30, 141-45, 386-95
J. Marsh on, **L5**: 194-95
as phase of philosophy, **L5**: 289-98; **L13**: 259-60, 282
articulation in, **L5**: 299-310
workers', **L5**: 331-45
library's role in, **L5**: 404-6
practical vs. liberal, **L6**: 81-85, 88-89, 105-7; **L13**: 268, 278
universal, **L6**: 92-93, 103-4, 107, 110
emotions related to, **L6**: 114-15
imagination related to, **L6**: 115-17
and White House Conference, **L6**: 131, 135, 136
related to birth control, **L6**: 146-48
C. Gauss on, **L6**: 259-62
Nock on, **L6**: 286-90
and Brookwood Labor College, **L6**: 327-29
and citizenship, **L6**: 433-35; **L9**: 161, 163, 164
primitive customs in, **L7**: 55-56
influence of, **L7**: 149, 201, 243, 381, 410, 430, 434
institutions determine, **L7**: 363-64
related to form, **L8**: 176-82
adult, **L9**: 100, 184-85, 191; **L11**: 61, 165, 175, 176, 232, 347, 509, 519, 543; **L17**: 45-47
Mort Committee and, **L9**: 119-20, 129
union influence on, **L9**: 125-26; **L17**: 520-21
in utopian schools, **L9**: 136-40
"frills" in, **L9**: 141-46, 387-89, 406-11
activity programs related to, **L9**: 169, 173-74
success as motive for, **L9**: 177-79
subject-matter related to, **L9**: 179, 181, 182, 184-85, 196, 199-200; **L16**: 396
for *status quo*, **L9**: 181, 205, 206
Grievance Committee and, **L9**: 315-45
European, **L9**: 393, 394
Mencken criticizes, **L9**: 406-11
effect of Depression on, **L11**: 159-60, 268, 376
administration of, **L11**: 162, 165, 222-24
history of, **L11**: 172-73, 229-35, 356, 364; **L17**: 161-86
Linville's contribution to, **L11**: 380-81
Hogben on, **L11**: 391-94; **L17**: 447
Hutchins on, **L11**: 391-407, 592-97
access to, **L11**: 535
future, **L11**: 538-46
nursery and primary, **L11**: 542-43; **L17**: 177-79, 286-89
Compton on, **L11**: 568, 570
Kettering on, **L11**: 569, 570
Gilbreth on, **L11**: 569, 573-74
Henderson on, **L11**: 570
Ellis on, **L11**: 570, 576-78
Dennett on, **L11**: 588-91
artificiality in, **L13**: 15, 39-40
principles of, **L13**: 17, 61-62, 292-93, 296-98, 376

Education (*continued*)
planning in, **L13**: 36, 46-47, 68-70
Childs on, **L13**: 377-78, 381-82
Jefferson on, **L14**: 210-11; **L15**: 366
LID and, **L14**: 262-65
war related to, **L14**: 273-74, 355-56
need for new type of, **L14**: 278-79
community, **L14**: 351-54
role of, in world crisis, **L14**: 360
investigation of, **L14**: 370-72, 427, 429
Kelley on, **L15**: xxiii, 310-11
modern, **L15**: 183, 188-89, 257-65, 269-75, 308-9
medieval, **L15**: 249, 258
Greek, **L15**: 262-66; **L17**: 171-73, 175-86
Bode's contribution to, **L15**: 327-28
in Peru, **L15**: 371
Hook on, **L15**: 372
interruptions in, **L17**: 26
T. Roosevelt on, **L17**: 72
pioneer, **L17**: 72-73
population affects, **L17**: 73
Sophists influence, **L17**: 183-84
instincts applied to, **L17**: 193-95
affected by infancy, **L17**: 256-57
conception of, **L17**: 297
Spencer on, **L17**: 338
belief in, **L17**: 341, 347, 400
"Education: 1800-1939," **L14**: xix
"Education, Direct and Indirect," **M3**: xviii
Education, National Council of, **M2**: 80n; **L5**: 326n; **L6**: 142n, 445
Education, National Society for the Study of, **L9**: 169n; **L13**: 255n, 281n
Education, National Society of College Teachers of, **L17**: 138-39, 561
Education, Office of (Washington, D.C.), **L11**: 356
Educational Adaptations in a Changing Society (Malherbe), **L11**: 238n, 243n
Educational Frontier, The (Kilpatrick), **L8**: ix, xi-xii, 43n, 77n, 374n
Educational Policy in Soviet Russia (Hans and Hessen), **L6**: 291
Educational Trends, **L14**: 360-61
Educational Workers International, **L9**: 341
"Education and Social Change," **L11**: xx
Education and the Class Struggle (Slesinger), **L11**: 485-86
Education and the Good Life (B. Russell), **L2**: 226-30
Education and the Modern World (B. Russell), **L14**: 244-45
Education and the Social Crisis (Kilpatrick), **L13**: 387
"Education Cannot Lead" (T. Dennett), **L11**: 588-91
Education Development Act of 1947 (S. 2499), **L15**: 281-85
Education for Modern Man (Hook), **L15**: xxiv, 372
Education for What Is Real (E. Kelley), **L15**: 310-11

Education in the British West Indies (E. Williams), **L15**: 308-9
Education in the Soviet Union (Neilson), **L11**: 509
Education of Henry Adams, The (H. Adams), **M13**: 272; **L6**: 297
Education of Man, The (Froebel), **M7**: 383
Education Worker, **L9**: 341
Education Workers League, **L9**: 341, 342
Educators. *See* Teachers
Edwards, Anna Camp, **M1**: 325n, 335n; **L11**: 191n, 193n, 202n
Effect. *See* Cause and effect
Efficacy, **L1**: 90
Efficiency
  as constituent of character, **E5**: 78-79
  scientific, **M9**: 91
  social, **M9**: 100, 125-30
  defined, **M9**: 171-72; **L17**: 77
  movement in education, **M10**: 118-19
  as organization of force, **M10**: 247-51
  need for, **L7**: 353; **L17**: 77-78
  of production and distribution, **L13**: 311-12
  lack of intellectual, **L17**: 27
  thinking for, **L17**: 80-81
Effort, **L1**: 194
  related to will, **E4**: 253-56
  theory of, **E5**: 115-20
  in education, **E5**: 121; **M7**: 153-97, 473-74
  and desire, **E5**: 129; **L13**: 71, 313
  meaning of moral, **E5**: 135
  abnormal use of, **E5**: 136
  sensational and spiritual schools of, **E5**: 150-56
  as tension between means and ends, **E5**: 157-59
  role of self in, **E5**: 159-61
  in habits, **E5**: 162-63
  related to interest, **E5**: 166-67; **M7**: 254-56
  in *Cyclopedia of Education*, **M6**: 434-36
Egg-factories, **M12**: 73
Ego, **M7**: 291, 340, 448-49; **L1**: 173-74, 188
  as cause, **E4**: 91-96
  isolated from alter, **E5**: 403-5
  empirical and rational, **M8**: 154
  Fichte on, **M8**: 178, 187
  exaggeration of, **L16**: 384, 458
  of conscience, **L17**: 4, 352
  selecting power of, **L17**: 5
Ego-centric predicament, **M6**: 89-90, 113-22; **M7**: 79-84, 445-51, 456; **M8**: 62
Egoism, **L15**: 219, 221
  and altruism, **E3**: 285, 307-8; **L7**: 292-98
  in *Cyclopedia of Education*, **M6**: 366-69
  in children, **M9**: 28, 48-49
  as theory in individualism, **M15**: 244
Egotism, **M14**: 201; **L10**: 199
  spiritual, **M14**: 8
Egotism in German Philosophy (Santayana), **M10**: 305-9
Egypt, **M11**: 101; **L6**: 353
  British and French interests in, **L6**: 219, 468-69
  art of, **L10**: 175, 314, 330, 333-38
  mathematics in, **L17**: 237-38

Ehrlich, Henrick, **L15**: 350
Eichhorn, K. F., **M8**: 177
Eighteenth Amendment, **L6**: 250
Eighteenth Brumaire of Louis Bonaparte, The (Marx), **L17**: xxvii
Eighteenth century
  individualistic philosophy of, **M9**: 97-99, 102-3, 105
Einfühlung, **L10**: 107, 364
Einstein, Albert, **M13**: 313; **M15**: 154; **L1**: 15, 16; **L2**: 222; **L4**: 90n, 102; **L6**: 185, 488; **L8**: xvi, 208; **L10**: viii, 302; **L11**: 246; **L13**: 359-60; **L14**: 59, 398; **L16**: 61, 103
  on simultaneity, **L4**: 115-17
  transforms physics, **L16**: xxxiv, 68n, 76n, 278
  transactional approach of, **L16**: 98-99, 106-9
  on science, **L16**: 105n
Eisenhower, Dwight D., **L11**: xi
Eisler, Rudolf, **L16**: 20n, 43, 163
Eisner, Kurt, **L15**: xxix
Either-or, **L12**: 193, 343-44, 499-500; **L13**: 5-8, 14, 24, 30, 55
Élan vital, **M12**: 231, 232, 244; **L10**: xvii
Eleatic pluralism, **M10**: 32n
Eleatic school, **M13**: 364
  on non-being, **M2**: 157
  as forerunner of pantheism, **M2**: 183
Election
  of 1932, **L6**: 326
  of 1936, **L11**: 526
  of 1948, **L15**: xxvii, 239-47
  Constitution on, **L16**: 403
Electives
  in teaching philosophy, **E1**: 120-21
  in curriculum, **E5**: 332
Electoral college, **L2**: 305; **L5**: 504-5
Electricity, **L13**: 144
Elegance, **L10**: 145
Elementary Lessons in Logic (W. Jevons), **M6**: 324n, 331; **L8**: 257-58, 312n
Elementary Psychology (J. Baker), **E3**: 190-92
Elementary school, **L11**: 176, 208, 243. *See also* University Elementary School, Columbia University Teachers College
  language study in, **E5**: 254-69
  related to high school, **E5**: 274; **M1**: 300-302
  needs of child in, **E5**: 381
  need for investigation in, **E5**: 448-64
  Dewey's concern with, **M1**: xix-xx
  origin of, **M1**: 40-42
  affected by democratic movement, **M1**: 288
  aims of, **M3**: 295-96
  federal aid to, **M10**: 125-29
  science teaching in, **M10**: 131
  vocational education and, **M10**: 145-46
  problem method in, **L6**: 85-88
Elementary School of University of Chicago. *See* Laboratory School, University of Chicago
Elementary School Teacher, **M2**: 79
Elements, **L1**: 74, 115-16; **L12**: 125, 154-55, 340-41, 452-54
  mathematical, **L12**: 403-4
  as terminology, **L16**: 102, 113
Elements of Ethics (Muirhead), **E5**: 25
Elements of Jurisprudence, The (Holland), **L6**: 481n

Elements of Metaphysics, The (Deussen), **E5**: 342-44
Elements of Philosophy (Hobbes), **M11**: 31
Elements of Physiological Psychology (Ladd), **E1**: 194-204
Elgin Marbles, **L10**: 236
Elimination, **L12**: 182-83, 186, 204, 263, 317, 374, 427, 493. *See also* Exclusion; Negation, **L12**
Eliot, Charles W., **E3**: 198-99; **M10**: 250; **M15**: xvii, 191, 380; **L5**: 351; **L13**: 110, 401
Eliot, George (pseud. of Mary Ann Evans), **M3**: 56; **L7**: 198-99
  on positivism, **M2**: 209
  on happiness, **M5**: 274n
  on altruism and egoism, **M6**: 366
  on esthetic experience, **L10**: 23n-24n, 354
  other-worldliness of, **L17**: 13, 554
Eliot, T. S., **M5**: 145; **L10**: xxvi, xxxiii, 323, 366
Elizabethan Age, **L5**: 100
  drama in, **L10**: 148
Elliot, Hugh S. R., **M7**: 135-36
Elliott, John Lovejoy, **M10**: 377n; **L11**: 381
Ellis, A. Caswell, **L11**: 567n, 570, 571, 576-78
Ellis, Havelock, **M5**: 522n; **L10**: 243
Emancipation Proclamation, **L14**: 111
Embargo
  as economic sanction, **L6**: 201, 471, 475-76
  of U.S. loans to Manchuria, **L6**: 469
  leading to war, **L6**: 477-79
Emergence, **L16**: 45
  as terminology, **L16**: 121
Emergence of Man, The (Heard), **L6**: 278-79
Emergency Committee for Employment, **L6**: 374-75
Emergency Relief and Construction Act, **L6**: 397
Emergency Society for German Science and Art, **M15**: 316
Emerson, Ralph Waldo, **M3**: 56; **M4**: xxxiii, 241; **M7**: 154, 358; **M8**: 142; **M9**: xxii, 57; **M10**: 188; **M14**: 72, 100; **L2**: 207, 231, 372; **L3**: 369, 375; **L6**: 99; **L9**: xxvi; **L11**: 443, 464; **L13**: xiv; **L15**: xxxiii; **L17**: 135
  on esthetics, **E4**: 197; **L10**: 35, 354
  on compensation, **E5**: 115
  on oversoul, **M2**: 180
  philosophic concerns of, **M3**: xx-xxi
  on believing, **M3**: 99
  on logic, **M3**: 184
  on poet, **M3**: 185
  on thinker, **M3**: 187
  on idealism, **M3**: 188
  compared with transcendentalists, **M3**: 189-90
  on common man, **M3**: 190-92
  on good act, **M5**: 316
  on freedom of thought, **M5**: 399n
  on punishment reform, **M5**: 420
  Maeterlinck on, **M6**: 133
  on democracy, **M6**: 135
  on poet's name for thing, **M6**: 316; **L8**: 304
  on society, **L5**: 122
  on self-reliance, **L5**: 139

Emerson, Ralph Waldo (*cont.*)
J. Marsh influences, **L5**: 184
on abstinence, **L7**: 210
as writer, **L10**: 320
compared with Dewey, **L14**: 405, 410
Emerson School (Gary, Ind.), **M8**: 335
Émile (Rousseau), **M8**: 211; **M9**: 100n; **L6**: 495; **L8**: 37
Emmons, Nathaniel, **L17**: 564
Emotion, **M6**: 385-86; **M12**: 139, 200; **M14**: 54, 59, 175, 177-79, 181; **L1**: 174-75, 292; **L15**: 118-19
religious, **E1**: 90-92
social, **E3**: 277; **L9**: 52-55; **L15**: 223
nature of, **E4**: xiv, 170-71; **E5**: 130-31; **L4**: 220, 235; **L6**: 113-15; **L11**: 200
and charity, **E4**: 58-59
in perception and expression, **E4**: 154; **M11**: 352; **L10**: xii-xiii, xxv-xxvii, xxxi, 13, 21, 27, 29, 36, 37, 42, 44, 48-50, 56, 59, 61, 66-76, 80-84, 88, 102-4, 108, 123, 129, 135, 157, 160, 190, 207, 221, 246, 261, 264-65, 268; **L17**: 198
as laughter, **E4**: 155
ideas and, **E4**: 156-57; **L13**: 162, 169, 182; **L14**: 317
and idiopathic discharges, **E4**: 159-61
and habits, **E4**: 162-63, 187; **E5**: 93
of fear, **E4**: 164
principle of antithesis in, **E4**: 165-69
of anger, **E4**: 172-73, 183-84
involves inhibition, **E4**: 180-83
interest and, **E4**: 186-88; **E5**: 325
and action, **E5**: 93, 205, 324; **L11**: 38, 213, 244; **L17**: 196
in education, **E5**: 203; **L6**: 133-34
moral significance of, **E5**: 323-26
Stanley on, **E5**: 362-65
purpose of, **M5**: 52; **L7**: 47, 174, 269-70
Greek view of, **M5**: 101-2; **L7**: 92-93
Hebrew view of, **M5**: 102-3; **L7**: 93-94
James-Lange theory of, **M7**: xvii
James on, **M7**: 34-38; **L15**: 6-8, 17
influence of, **M7**: 397-99; **L13**: 335
Lotze on, **M8**: 24
intellect and, **M9**: 345-46; **L11**: xxix; **L16**: 249, 255; **L17**: 198-99
as guiding life, **M10**: 238-39
in motivation, **M11**: 10-16
of wartime, **M11**: 107-16, 184; **L13**: 290, 400
related to beliefs, **M11**: 132, 341, 346-47; **L15**: 16
in word usage, **L2**: 82-85
involved in response to uncertain, **L4**: x, 3, 4, 179-82
supports tradition, **L4**: 62, 234, 246
connected with imagination, **L6**: 115-16
and art, **L10**: 237-38, 242-45, 277-80, 294, 299, 308, 321, 336, 346; **L11**: 503; **L13**: 69-70
uncontrolled, **L13**: 249

Houston on, **L13**: 329-30
vs. sensation, **L13**: 333
Whitehead on, **L14**: 132-33
related to human nature, **L14**: 323-24, 332-33
in ethical judgment, **L15**: 128-36
related to instinct, **L17**: 196-97
related to consciousness, **L17**: 197
training of, **L17**: 344-46
related to well-being, **L17**: 514-15
Emotional-volitional behavior, **L16**: 312-13, 314n
Emotive, **L16**: 354
Emotivism, **L13**: xii; **L15**: xix-xxii, 107, 403
Stevenson's, **L15**: 128-36
Empathy
in esthetic theory, **L10**: 107, 108
Empedocles, **M2**: 267; **M13**: 364; **L3**: 26
Empire of the Tsars (Leroy-Beaulieu), **M11**: 277-78
Empirical
rules, **E3**: 283-84
events, **M6**: 80-85
in *Cyclopedia of Education*, **M6**: 445-51
ego, **M8**: 154
pluralism, **M10**: xxv, 64
ambiguity of term, **L12**: 17, 44
"Empirical Survey of Empiricisms, An," **L11**: xiii
Empirical thought, **M6**: 293-96
disadvantages of, **L8**: xviii, 269-71
vs. scientific, **L8**: 272-78
Empiricism, **M5**: 213; **M12**: 124, 126, 136, 213-15; **M13**: 389; **M15**: 350; **L1**: xiii, 367, 369, 373-74, 386; **L2**: 11-13; **L3**: 12-13, 53-54; **L5**: 380-81; **L13**: 121; **L15**: 94. *See also* Sensational empiricism
method of, **E1**: 35-36, 38; **L1**: 3-59, 389-92
knowledge and, **E1**: 300-301; **E5**: 15; **M12**: xiv, 259; **L4**: xi, xiii, xviii-xxii, 88, 141-42, 147, 166, 167; **L11**: 69-83, 108-9
in Green, **E3**: 20, 21
and morality, **E4**: 42, 108, 114, 264, 310; **M5**: 208-9, 279
and education, **M1**: xvii; **M9**: 277-80
functional and pragmatic, **M1**: 130n
compared with evolutionary method and intuitionalism, **M2**: 31-38
failure of, **M2**: 35; **M13**: 446; **L4**: 124-25
related to idealism, **M2**: 121
meaning of, **M2**: 245; **M9**: 233; **L4**: 63; **L8**: 268-71; **L13**: 11, 131
experience in, **M3**: 158-67; **L4**: 86; **L14**: 32
immediate, **M3**: 168-70, 390-92; **M13**: 449, 452, 474-76
radical, **M6**: 94, 100; **M7**: x, 297; **M12**: xi, 207, 217; **M13**: xvii, 353, 479; **M15**: 335
James's, **M7**: 142-48; **M13**: 448; **L15**: xxii-xxiii, 10-15
related to rationalism, **M7**: 334-35; **M9**: 343-44; **M10**: 5-23; **M12**: 126, 130; **L4**: 21, 67, 98, 204-5; **L8**: 8-9; **L12**:

Empiricism (*continued*)
17-18, 44, 78, 80, 194, 251n, 277-78, 304-5, 420, 426; **L14**: 394-95; **L16**: 92n, 148n, 284, 411
related to sensationalism, **M7**: 345
affects nature of truth, **M7**: 415
Greek, **M9**: 272-73; **L17**: 434
British, **M10**: xxv, 48, 223-25; **L5**: 173, 175; **L11**: 76-80, 82
of Hume and Kant, **M10**: 12-13
role of intelligence in, **M10**: 14
on thought, **M10**: 16, 17
experimental, **L1**: 335-36, 371; **L4**: 90
judicial, **L2**: 28
of Newton, **L4**: 92, 94, 114, 115
on conceptions, **L4**: 112, 120, 126, 132, 133
on values, **L4**: 206-8, 227-28
social applications of, **L11**: 15, 79-80
Hutchins on, **L11**: 392, 398, 400
organization of, **L13**: 6
Dewey's, **L14**: 20-21; **L16**: 465-66
and theory of time, **L14**: 99
in history of philosophy, **L14**: 142, 313; **L17**: 440-41
modern, **L14**: 190-92
of Bacon, **L14**: 390, 392
Rice on, **L15**: 436-37
Kaufmann on, **L16**: 196n
realistic, **L17**: 419
fact-finding in, **L17**: 445
Empiristic logic, **E3**: 129-32; **M3**: 63; **M10**: 335; **L12**: 107, 114, 135, 147-48, 151-52, 295, 350, 374, 389, 435, 507-11
Employment, **L10**: 345-46; **L11**: 158, 536, 538-39. *See also* Work
Enclosure
as relationship, **L12**: 463-64
Encyclopaedia and Dictionary of Education, **M13**: xv, 399n
Encyclopaedia Britannica, **L10**: 222
Encyclopaedia of the Social Sciences, **L6**: 29n; **L8**: ix, 3n, 13n, 19n; **L11**: 3; **L14**: 194n; **L15**: 232; **L17**: 125
Encyclopedia Americana, **M3**: 40n
End in Education
in *Cyclopedia of Education*, **M6**: 436-37
Ends, **M14**: xviii; **L1**: 82-99, 107, 120-21, 128, 144, 151, 159, 188, 206, 290, 303; **L2**: 106; **L12**: 41-42, 63, 120n; **L13**: 232. *See also* Aims; Ends and means; Purpose; Teleology
ideal and, **E1**: 220, 223; **E3**: 216-17
and standards, **E3**: 261; **L7**: 245-48, 281
as divine and human, **E5**: 31-33
meaning of, **E5**: 133-34; **M14**: 154-63; **L4**: 14, 17, 30, 40-47, 81, 120-23, 134, 180; **L12**: 167-69, 178; **L13**: 43
utilitarian emphasis on, **M5**: 226-27
and pleasure, **M5**: 250-51; **L7**: 191-99
values and, **M8**: 36-39; **M12**: 180; **L16**: 349-50, 353
vs. results, **M9**: 107-8

related to interest, **M9**: 134-35; **L7**: 208-12; **L17**: 293
morality of, **M10**: 83; **M12**: 175-76; **L7**: xxvi
fixed, **M12**: 119-20, 174; **L13**: 230; **L14**: 121-22; **L15**: 235
intrinsic and instrumental, **M12**: 177-79
higher, **M12**: 178
knowledge as, **M14**: 130, 149
of desire, **M14**: 172, 179
beliefs about, **L4**: 15, 29, 201, 243
formation of, **L4**: 33, 82, 119, 169, 170, 213, 239
attainment of, **L4**: 106; **L13**: 218
importance of, **L4**: 194, 195; **L13**: 350-51
in human nature, **L6**: 31-32
and good, **L7**: 181-82, 186-91
teleological theory of, **L7**: 182
and reflection, **L7**: 184-86
and success, **L7**: 202-3
and asceticism, **L7**: 203-7
personality as, **L7**: 223-24
in art, **L10**: xx, xxii, 45, 119-20, 140-44, 176-77, 201-4, 209, 230, 234, 244, 261
of inquiry, **L12**: 66-67, 145-47, 159, 219, 385; **L16**: 322-25, 328, 337, 452
in itself, **L12**: 179, 216n
in nature, **L13**: 192, 299; **L14**: 144-45
as mental state, **L13**: 223
absurdity of, **L13**: 227
appraisal of, **L13**: 229
social, **L13**: 321
as limits of histories, **L14**: 146
reconstruction of, **L14**: 149
as directive, **L16**: 329, 331
quality of, **L16**: 344, 367, 410
disagreement on, **L16**: 361
as unknown, **L17**: 96
of attention, **L17**: 272-73, 279
Russian cultural, **L17**: 499
Ends and means, **E4**: 29-32, 36; **M5**: xvi-xxvi; **M7**: 165-74; **M9**: 112-13, 333; **M12**: 121; **M14**: 23, 27-29, 184-88; **L1**: 274-77, 286, 296-97, 340-41; **L4**: 37, 124, 131, 215-16, 220, 222-27, 238, 244; **L11**: 62, 217-18, 259, 298-99, 332; **L12**: 490-91; **L13**: 188, 202, 211-16, 381, 386-87, 399; **L14**: 72-74; **L15**: 164-67, 178, 216-18, 234; **L17**: 96. *See also* Close; Consequences
in philosophy of education, **L5**: 28-33
Ends-in-view, **L15**: 70
and activity, **L13**: 209, 234-35
forming, **L13**: 213, 216, 218, 222-23, 247
appraisal of, **L13**: 226, 233, 238
ideational, **L13**: 237, 351
Enemy aliens
Poles as, **M11**: 285, 301, 322, 325, 330
Enemy of the People, An (Ibsen), **M6**: 30
Energy, **M12**: 226, 245; **L16**: 107, 116n
in children, **E5**: 120-21
as force, **M10**: 212
defined, **M10**: 246
organized in art, **L10**: xvii-xxi, xxvi, 152, 159, 161, 165-90, 195, 233-34, 238, 248
source of, **L10**: 20, 22, 30, 31, 47, 54, 60, 66, 70, 127, 260,

Energy (*continued*)
264, 284, 340, 342
of medium, **L10**: 200, 201, 209, 214, 217, 246
Santayana on, **L10**: 297
conservation of, **L13**: 123
and valuation, **L13**: 204
kinds of, **L13**: 238
waste of, **L13**: 274
need for, **L13**: 286
scientific meaning of, **L14**: 87
in Whitehead's metaphysics, **L14**: 132-33
Engelmann, George, **M8**: 459
Engels, Friedrich, **L7**: 426; **L9**: 244
Engineering, **M10**: 155-56; **L10**: 234
England. *See* Great Britain
Engle, William
interviews Dewey, **L6**: 403-7
English
jurisprudence, **L2**: 28-30, 35-36, 41-42
Parliament, **L2**: 176-77
English language, **L11**: 515
in primary education, **E5**: 254-69
experiment in, **M8**: 262-63
Enjoying
meaning of term, **L15**: 101-3
Enjoyment, **L15**: 80-83. *See also* Liking; Satisfaction
esthetic, **L2**: 108-9, 115
related to value, **L13**: 223-25, 336; **L14**: 66
value of, **L13**: 227-28
role of, in inquiry, **L14**: 43
Cohen on, **L14**: 409-10
Enjoyment of Poetry (M. Eastman), **M7**: 149; **L10**: 140, 359
Enlightenment, **M8**: 189, 194; **M10**: 18; **M12**: xiv, 107; **L7**: 145-46; **L8**: xvi, 38; **L11**: 77; **L13**: 72, 156, 160, 162, 296, 297; **L17**: 147, 468
Kant on, **M8**: 156-57, 167
French, **M8**: 183; **M13**: 421
on reason, **L2**: xiv, xxxii-xxxiii
optimism of, **L14**: 100
quality of, **L16**: 371-72
beliefs of, **L16**: 391
effect of, **L17**: 474
Russian civic, **L17**: 494
Entente Allies. *See* Allies
Entente Cordiale, **L6**: 468
Enterprise
economic, **L1**: 356-59
signification of, **L13**: 146-47
Entities
Holt on, **M6**: 473-74; **M10**: 52
Carnap on, **L16**: 20-22, 27, 28n, 32
nature of, **L16**: 45, 54, 261, 272, 303, 326, 366
as name, **L16**: 49n, 102, 104, 262
rejected, **L16**: 111, 119n, 129, 345
related to definition, **L16**: 168, 169
Cohen on, **L16**: 194-95
Russell on, **L16**: 199-203
C. Morris on, **L16**: 217
false division into, **L16**: 249, 253
in science, **L16**: 340, 454
in psychiatry, **L16**: 412
Balz on, **L16**: 439
Entombment of Christ, The (Titian), **L10**: 117, 182, 358
Environment, **M6**: 361; **M14**: 19, 38, 62, 105, 196; **L15**: 12
related to organism, **E1**: 56; **M12**: 128; **M13**: 378-79; **L1**:

211-25, 259-62; **L7**: xxvi; **L14**: 15-21, 28, 39-40, 64, 158, 161, 167, 185-86; **L16**: 103, 112, 116-26, 133, 136, 195, 417, 462
of college students, **E1**: 67-68, 74
related to individuality, **E3**: 301-3; **M7**: 393-94
man and, **E5**: 37-38, 46-47; **L11**: 502, 512-13
evolution of, **E5**: 52
Baldwin on, **E5**: 416-17
related to idea, **M4**: 83-84; **M12**: 85, 232
and morals, **M5**: 8; **L7**: 10, 340-44
in *Cyclopedia of Education*, **M6**: 437-40
related to heredity, **M7**: 286-87; **M9**: 80-81
study of, **M8**: 272-74
meaning of, **M9**: 4-5, 14-27, 32-38; **L13**: 25; **L16**: 141-42, 190, 244, 331-32
adaptation of, **M9**: 51-52
interferes with development, **M9**: 62
and experience, **M9**: 283; **M10**: 7-11; **L13**: 22-23, 273, 326-29; **L16**: 456-57
unpredictability of, **M10**: 16
control of, **M10**: 56
interaction with, **M12**: 229, 231; **L10**: xvi, 19-28, 34-35, 64-67, 70, 72, 109, 136-38, 152-56, 163, 165, 190, 217, 251-52, 257, 260, 264-69, 276, 281, 284-87, 291, 307, 317, 323, 329, 347
and meaning, **M13**: 374-75
vs. psychology, **M13**: 381
social, **M14**: 9, 15-18, 217, 219; **L6**: 40-42
harmony with, **M14**: 110, 125
influence of, **L2**: 18-21; **L7**: 456; **L9**: 188-89; **L17**: 319, 346, 423-24, 439
and artistic appreciation, **L6**: 45-46
related to health, **L6**: 140
and culture, **L6**: 445-46; **L12**: 48-50
and opportunities, **L7**: 342
religion and, **L9**: 17-19, 224-25, 227
and education, **L9**: 197, 200
as means, **L11**: 239-40
and organic activity, **L12**: 32-47
and perceived objects, **L12**: 73, 152
expansion of, **L13**: 48-49
continuity and discreteness in, **L14**: 30
in inquiry, **L16**: 97, 288-89, 327-28
in interaction and transaction, **L16**: 114, 246
as locus, **L16**: 138-40
Kantor and Dewey on, **L16**: 191-92
in semiotic, **L16**: 232, 235-37, 270
as name, **L16**: 262
Balz on, **L16**: 425-27
Epictetus, **E3**: 118; **M5**: 132; **M11**: 45; **L1**: 374; **L7**: 123, 128
Epicureanism, **M7**: 211; **M14**: 143-44, 201; **M15**: 326; **L5**: 498
Epicureans, **E4**: 263; **M2**: 81; **M7**: 275, 416; **L7**: 205; **L8**: 6, 24, 26
attributes of, **E4**: 138-39; **E5**: 9

Epicureans (*continued*)
and individual, **E4**: 230
on nature, **M2**: 145-46
on pleasures, **M5**: 118, 202; **L7**: 109
on friendship, **M5**: 123, 173-74; **L7**: 114
on wisdom, **M5**: 127; **L7**: 109, 118
theory of, **L7**: 199-202
truth underlying, **L7**: 210
Epicurus, **E4**: 139; **L15**: 418
Epimenides, **M7**: 434
Epiphenomenalism, **L14**: 303
Epiphenomenon
religious experience as, **L9**: xiv, xxiv, xxvii
Episcopalians, **M11**: 24, 25
Epistemological, **L16**: 78, 386
as name, **L16**: 262
Epistemology, **M12**: xxix, 107, 119-20, 150, 152, 227; **M15**: 350, 351; **L1**: 75, 94, 113-14, 119-20, 245-46; **L2**: xv-xvii; **L12**: 30, 69, 71-72, 94n, 113n, 387-88; **L14**: xvi
modern, **E5**: 19, 20
and science, **M3**: 93-97; **L12**: 458-65
problem of, **M3**: 119; **L14**: 44, 50, 51n; **L16**: 138, 146n, 287, 297, 303
mind in, **M6**: 18; **M9**: 302
realistic, **M6**: 111-13; **M7**: 454-60; **L14**: 188
in *Cyclopedia of Education*, **M6**: 440-42
Marvin on, **M6**: 474-75
problem of knowledge in, **M10**: 21-37
concept of neutral in, **M10**: 49-52
dualistic, **M10**: 64, 66, 439-49; **M13**: 456; **M15**: 355, 358, 362-63, 367, 370, 372; **L14**: 9-10; **L15**: 145-46, 152, 165
monistic, **M10**: 64, 66, 439-49; **M15**: 362
affected by behavior, **M13**: 29
Dewey criticizes, **M13**: 454-55; **L4**: ix-xi, xvi, xix, xx
empiricism as, **M13**: 475
and sense-perception, **L2**: 45-49, 51, 54
of James, **L4**: xviii
nature of, **L4**: 69, 192; **L15**: 91, 92
history of, **L4**: 97, 142, 144; **L14**: 45-46; **L16**: 46
types of, **L12**: 506-27; **L16**: 8-12
Cartesian and Lockean, **L14**: xix
subject vs. object in, **L14**: 178, 196-97
of Kant, **L15**: xxix, 28
positions held by, **L16**: 42, 80n, 111, 115, 137, 250, 255, 257, 258n, 269, 396
terminology of, **L16**: 129, 272, 334-35, 449-50
hostile to Peirce, **L16**: 299
of Ogden and Richards, **L16**: 300-302
Epstein, Jacob, **L10**: 175
Equality (Bellamy), **L9**: 102, 105
Equality, **L13**: 89, 296
and democracy, **E1**: 245-47; **L7**: 148; **L13**: 109-10, 388
Aristotle and Plato on, **E1**: 247-48
Rousseau on, **M13**: 298
John Adams on, **M13**: 298-99
Jefferson on, **M13**: 299
moral, **M13**: 299-300; **L7**: 257, 335, 349-50
meaning of, **L2**: 328-29; **L13**: 108

in utilitarianism, **L7**: 239
as ideal, **L7**: 346; **L11**: 167-70
as capitalistic issue, **L7**: 428
of opportunity, **L9**: 392; **L11**: 256, 416
lack of, **L11**: 29
political, **L11**: 219-20, 362, 368-71
Equational definition, **L16**: 175-78
Equilibration, **M14**: 125, 173
Equilibrium, **L16**: 391
result of tension, **L10**: xvii, 20, 23, 183-84, 261, 317
Equity, **L16**: 368; **L17**: 397
Equivalence
as basic category, **L12**: 312-18, 333, 341-42, 406-10
Erasmus, **L1**: 334
Erdmann, J. E., **E3**: 3, 185-87
Erigena, John Scotus
on visible creation, **E4**: 192-93
realism of, **M2**: 220
influences scholasticism, **M2**: 237-38
Ernst, Morris L., **L6**: xvii; **L15**: xxv; **L17**: 127, 560
Error, **L15**: 65
related to consciousness, **M10**: 25-27
neo-realists on, **M10**: 39
interpretation of, **L14**: 24-25
Erzerum, Turkey, **M15**: 290
Esch-Cummins Transportation Act, **L6**: 370, 371
Esipov, Boris Petrov, **L15**: 373-74
Espionage, **M11**: 118, 184
Essais de psychologie contemporaine (Bourget), **E3**: 36-41
Essay concerning Human Understanding, An (Locke), **E1**: 304; **M5**: 155; **M6**: 199; **L2**: xvii, 144-54; **L8**: 9, 133-34, 308; **L11**: 92; **L15**: 18
Essays, Philosophical and Psychological (Dewey et al.), **L14**: 404
Essays in Critical Realism (Lovejoy et al.), **M13**: 40, 50, 51, 58; **M15**: 27, 349, 363
Essays in Criticism (Arnold), **L9**: xxxii
Essays in Experimental Logic, **M6**: xi; **M8**: xiv, xxiii, 14n, 49n, 83n; **M13**: 56n, 57n, 58n; **L4**: ix, xx, xxii; **L8**: xiii; **L12**: 3; **L14**: xii, xv, xvi, 14, 396n, 401; **L16**: 187, 194n, 318, 444
prefatory note to, **M10**: 319
introduction to, **M10**: 320-65
note on "practical" in, **M10**: 366-69
valuation in, **M11**: 3n, 7n, 375
Essays in Philosophical Criticism (R. Haldane and Seth), **L5**: 152
Essays in Radical Empiricism (W. James), **M7**: ix, 142-48; **M10**: 50n, 51; **L14**: 156n, 166
Essays in Sociology (M. Weber), **L16**: 372-73
Essays in the Law (Pollock), **L17**: 98-100
Essays on Politics and Culture (Himmelfarb), **L9**: xxxin
Essence, **M2**: 253; **L1**: 108, 133, 136, 144-45, 149-61, 172, 200-201, 289-90, 338; **L15**: 44, 84-86, 276; **L16**: 165, 180, 287
Spinoza on, **E1**: 11-13
James on, **E4**: 46-47
Lovejoy on, **M13**: 55; **M15**: 367-68
and existence, **M13**: 373; **L5**: 197-202

Essence (*continued*)
Santayana on, **M15**: 219-22
value as, **L2**: 72
Locke on, **L2**: 145-47, 149-53
related to power, **L2**: 150-52
mind and, **L3**: 289, 292-93, 387
properties of, **L3**: 289-91; **L4**: 53, 72, 74, 112, 113, 119-20, 127-33, 241, 244; **L12**: 94
Newton on, **L4**: 96-97
role of, **L4**: 142, 154
Plato on, **L4**: 219
in esthetics, **L10**: xiv, xxi, 227, 295-99, 317n, 364
Peirce on, **L11**: 86, 92
in Greek logic, **L12**: 18, 90-91, 130, 138-40, 153, 251, 260, 357, 404, 418n; **L16**: 157
immutability of, **L14**: 99
rejected, **L16**: 102, 104,130, 346
concept restricts inquiry, **L16**: 146-47, 158, 332, 337-40, 453
Dubislav on, **L16**: 161n
Balz on, **L16**: 436-41

Esthetic
emotion, **E2**: 267-80; **L10**: 81-84, 93
interests, **M9**: 336
object, **L10**: 91, 94, 96, 140, 146, 160
value, **L10**: 95, 112, 120, 125-33, 136, 323
criticism, **L10**: 302, 319
language, **L12**: 75-76, 89, 101, 176-79, 205, 239, 372

Esthetic experience, **L14**: 34-36
nature of, **L10**: ix, xiv-xx, xxiv, xxv, xxx, 16, 19-21, 24-25, 43, 45, 103, 127-28, 140, 149-50, 180-82, 187, 199, 203, 222, 225, 250, 265, 302; **L13**: 358-68, 371
achievement of, **L10**: 58-63, 107, 143-44, 149, 178-79, 181-82, 189, 208-9, 227, 233-37, 322
uniqueness of, **L10**: 258, 276-301
role of, **L10**: 302, 321, 329-31, 342
phases of, **L16**: 395-98
Romanell on, **L16**: 463-67

Esthetic quality
of religion, **L10**: 37-38
of thought, **L10**: 45, 183
of objects, **L10**: 175-81
fused with media, **L10**: 202-3
source of, **L10**: 253, 258, 261, 264, 266
limitation of, **L10**: 345-46

Esthetics, **M15**: 22-23, 339-44, 348; **L1**: 70-82, 105, 108, 143, 186, 207, 220, 267-68, 271, 280-81, 291-92, 320; **L2**: 107, 111-13, 115; **L6**: xii
courses in, **E3**: 91, 92
and science, **E3**: 230; **M12**: 152-53; **L16**: 370
united with logic, **E3**: 235
Bosanquet on, **E4**: 189-97
nature of, **E4**: 301n; **L4**: 76, 81, 188-90, 209, 220; **L10**: xxiii, xxix, 53-63, 101, 123, 125, 344, 355; **L16**: 351-53, 356
in education, **E5**: 200, 202-3, 207
in child-study, **E5**: 215-17
of music, **M7**: 140
appreciation of, **M9**: 22
relation of environment and, **M12**: 117, 146-47, 182; **L6**: 40, 45-46; **L10**: 35
taste in, **L2**: 76
of Greeks, **L4**: 73, 74, 122, 125, 148

Tate on, **L6**: 492-501
form of, **L10**: 86, 139, 142-47, 151
need for, **L13**: 287
pragmatism and, **L14**: 34-35, 38
Dewey's, **L15**: 97-100, 439-43; **L16**: 463-64
Kantian, **L15**: 441
romantic tradition in, **L16**: 458
Esthetic theory, **L10**: 204, 302-3, 331
Dewey's, **L10**: vii-xxxiii, 7, 8, 353
construction of, **L10**: 9-18
basis for, **L10**: 53, 165
criticized, **L10**: 85, 88, 224, 278-81, 286-89, 292-301
on sense qualities, **L10**: 104-9, 121-27, 133, 136-37
on substance and form, **L10**: 112, 119
on rhythm, **L10**: 167-68, 174
on subject-matter, **L10**: 191-93
on classification, **L10**: 221, 227
fallacies in, **L10**: 250-53, 256-57, 262-65, 320n
Esthonia, **M11**: 266, 326
Estimations, **L16**: 311
Eternal, **L1**: 119; **L16**: 359, 363, 414
Eternal Values, The (Münsterberg), **M6**: 165-71
Ethereal, **L10**: 12, 17, 34-41, 196-202, 340
Ethical
postulate, **E3**: xxxiv, 320-23; **E4**: xvi, 233-34
systems, **E3**: 368
principles in education, **E5**: 60, 77-83
judgment, **M3**: 20-23, 25-26
idealism, **M3**: 156-57
Ethical Culture School (New York City), **M10**: 377n; **L15**: 251n
Ethical Import of Darwinism, The (Schurman), **M2**: 16-17
"Ethical Subject-Matter and Language," **L15**: 141n; **L16**: 356n
Ethics (1908) (Dewey and Tufts), **E2**: xxv; **E4**: xvii; **L15**: 324
Stevenson on, **M5**: ix-xxxiv
Ethics (1932) (Dewey and Tufts), **L14**: 72, 73, 379; **L15**: 324
Edel and Flower on, **L7**: vii-xxxv
Ethics (Spinoza), **E1**: 10-17; **L4**: 45
Ethics, **E1**: 408; **M12**: 172, 237; **L13**: 74; **L16**: 353
scientific, **E1**: 208-9, 212-13, 225-26
fallacy of physical, **E1**: 214-15
as conduct of man, **E1**: 219; **E4**: 60; **E5**: 420-21; **L7**: 15
theories of, **E3**: xxxii-xxxvi, 102-3, 155-58, 230, 235, 241, 290; **E4**: xiii-xvi, xviii-xix, xxii-xxiv, 42, 224-25; **E5**: 35-37, 45, 53-55; **M5**: 7; **M8**: 178; **L7**: 9; **L15**: 231-32
teaching of, **E3**: 48-49, 390-92; **E4**: 54-56, 60-61, 106-18
evolutionary, **E3**: 286-90
need for, **E4**: 53
imagination in study of, **E4**: 57-58
in moral philosophy, **E4**: 147-48
subject-matter of, **E4**: 223-24
of Stoicism, **E4**: 318
of responsibility, **E4**: 342-44
compared with politics, **E4**: 371-73

Ethics (*continued*)
Muirhead on, **E5**: 25
of method, **E5**: 293-95; **L7**: xxxii, 10-13
historical method in, **M3**: 40-58; **L17**: 351-60
psychological and social, **M3**: 59-61; **L7**: x-xi; **L9**: 235, 236; **L14**: 362
problems of, **M5**: 8-10; **L7**: xxxiii, 10-12, 180-83
in international relations, **M15**: 53, 61-62
secular, **M15**: 54
related to egoism, **M15**: 244
and anthropology, **L3**: 11-24
and individuality, **L3**: 20
reason related to, **L7**: xxiii
Russell on, **L11**: 462
relativity in, **L15**: xix-xx
of Kant, **L15**: 47, 51, 217
language of, **L15**: 127-30, 136-40
Aristotelian, **L15**: 265, 417
"Ethics and International Relations," **M15**: xiii-xiv
Ethics and Language (C. Stevenson), **L15**: xix, 127, 141; **L16**: 470
Ethics and Moral Science (Lévy-Bruhl), **L5**: 499
Ethics of Democracy, The, **M1**: xxi; **L7**: xviii
Ethnography, **L6**: 3-4
Ethnologist, **L17**: 427
Ethos, **M5**: 7, 54; **L7**: 9, 49, 151; **L17**: 110
Etiquette
in Japan and China, **M12**: 55-56
Ettinger, William L., **M15**: 190
Eucken, Rudolf, **M7**: 418; **M8**: 155, 165; **M11**: 157
Euclid, **M7**: 423-24, 439-40; **M11**: 44; **L10**: xxi; **L11**: 395
Euclidean geometry, **L4**: 13, 71, 112, 122-26, 145n; **L12**: 18, 25, 144, 148, 157-59, 394, 404, 409, 412; **L16**: 287
Eudaimonism, **M5**: 126, 212; **L7**: 117, 197
Eudemus, **M2**: 186
Euripides, **M5**: 130-31; **M7**: xxviii; **L7**: 97, 101, 121
Europe, **M15**: 120, 128; **L8**: 20, 24, 53; **L15**: 243, 245, 274
history of, **M10**: 193-95
China's relation to, **M12**: 28, 34-37, 62
intellectual revolution in, **M12**: 100-103
nationalistic movement in, **M12**: 195
on League of Nations, **M15**: 83-85
Turkey's relation to, **M15**: 129; **L2**: 192-93
education in, **M15**: 205; **L6**: 101-2, 109-10; **L9**: 393, 394
relation of U.S. to, **L2**: 167-70, 173; **L5**: 50-57
effect of WWI on, **L2**: 168-69
on sanctions, **L6**: 197, 208-9, 472-73
philosophy of, **L11**: 76-80, 155, 597
economic strife in, **L11**: 261-64
liberalism in, **L11**: 285
democracy in, **L11**: 296, 496, 528, 532
Euthydemus (Plato), **L2**: 124
Evaluation, **L13**: 209; **L16**: 311, 314, 316, 343
as judgment of practice, **L12**: 126-27, 223-24, 234-35, 455-56
of facts, **L12**: 129-30, 136
in social inquiry, **L12**: 490-91, 495-97

of hypothesis, **L13**: x
vs. valuation, **L13**: 213
theory of, **L16**: 353-57
Evangelical movement, **M13**: 303
Events, **M13**: 351; **L1**: 65, 75, 83, 92, 138, 143, 204-6, 240-46; **L4**: 170, 207, 226
related to location, **L2**: 53
and duration, **L2**: 62, 64-65
and becoming, **L2**: 65-66
acquire meaning, **L3**: 84-88, 91
important to science, **L4**: 67, 84
correlation of, **L4**: 101-7, 197-99, 216, 235
simultaneity of, **L4**: 115-17
philosophical concept of, **L6**: 9-11
selective interest as, **L6**: 14
related to propositions, **L14**: 178, 187-88
centered in organism, **L15**: 29-30, 75-79
unobservable, **L15**: 120
related to facts, **L15**: 313; **L16**: 58-61, 110-11
forms of, **L16**: 6, 62, 66-69, 83-85, 112-13, 150-51
nature of, **L16**: 69, 77, 90, 132, 168, 191, 325, 331, 414, 456
as name, **L16**: 70, 71n, 72, 93n, 148n, 259, 262
in postulations, **L16**: 81-82
Pepper on, **L16**: 177
Russell on, **L16**: 201n
Ogden and Richards on, **L16**: 302
"Events and Meanings," **L14**: xviii
"Eve of St. Agnes, The" (J. Keats), **L10**: 259
Everett, Edward, **M4**: 159
Evidence, **L8**: 120, 213, 323; **L12**: 50-51, 58, 132, 163, 183-84, 188-89, 225-26, 242, 247, 318-19, 468-70, 519-21; **L15**: xxiv. *See also* Data; Signs, **L12**
in *Cyclopedia of Education*, **M6**: 442-43
as accompanying inference, **M10**: 90
control of, **L8**: 248-51
use of, **L14**: 26
types of, **L14**: 43, 54
for valuation judgment, **L15**: 64, 68-69, 80-83, 139
Evil, **E4**: 199-200; **L10**: 351; **L13**: 233
Royce on, **M2**: 130-31
Greek treatment of, **M5**: 97; **L7**: 89
Hebrew idea of, **M5**: 103; **L7**: 94
as quasi-physical, **M5**: 409-10
in China, **M12**: 49
problem of, **M12**: 181
related to science and technology, **M12**: 274; **L16**: 364-65, 373-74, 377
perception of, **L4**: 28, 205, 212
Spencer on, **L4**: 52
associated with change, **L4**: 82, 148, 200, 234
source of, **L4**: 240, 245; **L16**: 416
war as, **L7**: 369-71
vs. good, **L9**: 31-32
Tolstoy on, **L17**: 382, 385
Evolution (J. Huxley), **L16**: 119
Evolution, **M8**: xi, 194, 198; **M10**: 240; **M14**: 196-98, 205; **L3**: 302; **L4**: 52; **L6**: 280-82, 430; **L7**: xin, 151; **L11**: 210; **L13**: 120, 121, 315; **L15**: 56-57. *See also* Darwin, Charles
and relativity of knowledge,

Evolution (*continued*)
E1: 20-21
and purposive action, **E1**: 102-3
as goal and means, **E1**: 211
and ethics, **E1**: 214; **E5**: 34-35; **L3**: 17-18, 21-22
in Leibniz, **E1**: 277-78; **M6**: 421
characteristics of, **E5**: 218; **L16**: 114n, 129, 132, 391, 413
as experimental method, **M2**: 5
compared with intuitionalism and empiricism, **M2**: 24-38
opposition to, **M2**: 56; **M15**: 48-50
Royce on, **M2**: 125-27; **M10**: 80
Spencer's theory of, **M3**: 206-9; **M10**: 14, 67-69, 98, 420-21; **L5**: 170
as principle of self-assertion, **M5**: 333-35
in *Cyclopedia of Education*, **M6**: 365, 443-45
Bergson on, **M7**: 202-4; **M12**: 228-32, 235, 237-38; **L11**: 429
problem of truth in, **M7**: 414
theory of, **M9**: 65; **M12**: 209; **L3**: 13; **L5**: 171; **L17**: 93-94
philosophical significance of, **M9**: 347
related to experience, **M10**: 14, 24-25
adapted to concept of mind, **M10**: 60
interest in, **M10**: 152, 153
sanctions automatic progress, **M10**: 238
in Aristotle, **M12**: 112-13
as educational issue, **M15**: 162; **L9**: 161-62
Heard on, **L6**: 278-79
Macintosh on, **L9**: 420-21
Mead on, **L11**: 451-52
optimism in, **L14**: 100; **L17**: 458
development through, **L14**: 108-9; **L17**: 99
Osborn on, **L16**: 116
J. Huxley on, **L16**: 119, 121n
Fiske on organic, **L17**: 96
biological conception of, **L17**: 411
Evolution and the Founders of Pragmatism (Wiener), **L17**: 50-51
Evolution of Physics, The (Einstein and Infeld), **L16**: 98n-99n
Evolution of the American Economy, The (S. Ratner et al.), **L6**: xxn
Ewer, Bernard C., **M10**: 446n
Exact, **L16**: 445-46
as name, **L16**: 259, 262
Examination. *See* Test
Examination of the Political Part of Mr. Hobbs, An (Lawson), **M11**: 19-20
Excellence, **L7**: 118
Excitation
as name, **L16**: 262-63
Excitement
as hindrance to virtue, **M5**: 367-68
related to tranquility, **L13**: 368
Excluded middle, **L5**: xxiv-xxv, 197-202, 205-7; **L12**: 344-45; **L16**: 197
Exclusion, **L12**: 90, 95, 221, 248-50, 331, 335-36, 430-31. *See also* Negation, **L12**
and inclusion, **L12**: 182-99

Exclusion act (Immigration Act of 1917), **M11**: 228; **M13**: 166
Excursions of an Evolutionist (J. Fiske), **M9**: 50n
Executiveness
training of, **L17**: 339-40, 342
in character, **L17**: 347
Exercise
as discipline, **L7**: 204-5, 207, 209
substituted for drill, **L17**: 305
Ex facto jus oritur, **L9**: 237
Exhortation
as alternative to intelligence, **L17**: 459
Existence, **M12**: 92, 223; **L2**: 65-66, 74-75. *See also* Contingency, **L12**; Generic propositions, **L12**; Particulars, **L12**
Spinoza on, **E1**: 11-14
and essence, **E1**: 129, 134-35; **M13**: 373; **L1**: 144-45, 149-61, 172; **L5**: 197-202
and unity, **E1**: 315
struggle for, **E5**: 41-42, 44-45
Aristotle on, **M8**: xi, 6n-7n
Greeks on, **M10**: 40
nature of, **M13**: 385, 386; **L16**: 6, 60, 190
Kant on, **M15**: 9-10
Santayana on, **M15**: 219; **L14**: 303-4
immediacy of, **L1**: 74-75
and logic, **L5**: 203-9
Whitehead on, **L5**: 377-78
in philosophic thought, **L6**: 11
related to experience, **L6**: 430; **L16**: 70n, 82, 110n, 111, 131-32, 383-89, 456-62
Holmes on, **L7**: 453
good vs. evil in, **L9**: 31-32, 35
and knowledge, **L9**: 56-57; **L12**: 124, 165-66
Peirce on, **L11**: 86-94
and discourse, **L12**: 60
and reference, **L12**: 61, 137-38, 187-88
and denotation, **L12**: 352-57
a-rational, **L13**: 206
potentialities as category in, **L14**: 109-10
related to designation, **L16**: 93, 141
as name, **L16**: 151-52, 257-59, 263
uniqueness of, **L17**: 355-56
value of past, **L17**: 358-59
object as, **L17**: 372
and elements, **L17**: 417
"Existence of the World as a Logical Problem, The," **M8**: ix, xix, 64n
Existential, **L16**: 424, 428, 432
defined, **L14**: 25, 26
Existential import
of propositions, **L11**: 96-97, 103, 119-22
of terms, **L11**: 100-102
Existentialism, **M12**: xxi; **L3**: xviii; **L17**: xx
Exogamy, **M5**: 66; **L7**: 60
Expansion
effect of, **L17**: 455-56
Expansion of the Common Law, The (Pollock), **M7**: 56
Expectation, **L12**: 248-50, 446-48
Expediency, **M14**: 36-37, 132, 146; **L7**: 209
Experience, **M11**: 345-47; **M12**: xi, xiv-xvi, 97, 129, 139; **M14**: 25-26, 168-69; **L2**: ix, 11-12, 16; **L8**: 83. *See also*

Experience (*continued*)
Consummatory experience; Esthetic experience
nature of, **E1**: 130-31; **L10**: 197-200, 211, 213, 217-35; **L11**: 93; **L16**: 6, 43, 284, 351-52; **L17**: 154-56, 371n
stream of, **E1**: 172-74
psychical, **E1**: 188-90; **E5**: 100-101
development of, **E1**: 191-92; **M7**: 279-81; **M13**: 352, 379-80, 394-95; **L13**: 36, 60, 380; **L17**: 312
realism and, **E1**: 192-93; **M3**: 102; **M4**: 120-24; **M10**: 25-26
unity of, **E1**: 284-86
knowledge related to, **E1**: 325-26; **M10**: 34-35, 320-65, 368; **M12**: 133-34, 213; **L4**: x-xiii, xix, xxii, 79, 84-86, 91-94, 98, 132-34, 138, 141-44, 156-59, 174-77; **L12**: 78
in Green, **E3**: 24
Hegel on, **E3**: 72
self-consciousness as category of, **E3**: 73
motor element in, **E5**: 99; **L17**: 440
in curriculum, **E5**: 174
related to consciousness, **M1**: 117-22
Royce on, **M1**: 244; **M2**: 123-24; **L9**: xxvii
art's relation to, **M2**: ix; **M13**: 362-64; **L1**: 266-67; **L6**: 331-33, 493-94, 497-99; **L10**: ix-xix, xxxi-xxxiii, 9-12, 16-25, 34-36, 90, 112-14, 122-25, 138, 150-51, 156, 189-90, 194, 210-11, 243-48, 258, 272, 275, 303-28; **L16**: 395-98, 464-67
Dewey's conception of, **M3**: xx, 114-15, 128-32; **M4**: xv-xvi; **M9**: x, 331-33; **L14**: xii, xxiv; **L16**: xxxiin
science and, **M3**: 102-6; **L9**: 24; **L11**: xiii-xiv
cognitive, **M3**: 113, 393-404; **M15**: 40-41; **L14**: 10-12, 27, 33
McGilvary on, **M4**: 151-55, 295-313
Humian doctrine of, **M6**: 4, 80
pragmatic conception of, **M6**: 4-5; **M10**: xi-xiii, 5-13; **L11**: 82-83; **L15**: 10-15, 98, 146-47
realistic and idealistic interpretations of, **M6**: 80-85
Maeterlinck on, **M6**: 132-35
meaning of, **M6**: 301; **M13**: 351-54, 369, 374, 385; **L8**: 277-78
subject-matter related to, **M6**: 336-37, 399-400; **M9**: 173-77; **L4**: 99, 100, 104, 105, 110; **L8**: 324-25
in *Cyclopedia of Education*, **M6**: 445-51
James on, **M7**: 145-48; **M10**: 50-52; **M12**: 217, 222; **L11**: 475, 477; **L14**: 18n, 21n
continuity of, **M9**: 5; **L3**: 343; **L12**: 249-50, 273, 483-85; **L13**: 13, 17-20, 244, 267; **L14**: 23
trial and error in, **M9**: 151-52, 157-58, 160, 273
and thinking, **M9**: 160-70; **L2**: 156; **L14**: 83-86; **L17**: 430-31
direct and indirect, **M9**: 240-42; **L14**: 193-98

Aristotle on, **M9**: 271-72
Plato on, **M9**: 271-72, 275-76
classic and modern notions of, **M9**: 273-85; **M12**: 106, 125-27, 132-34
medieval, **M9**: 275
and experimentation, **M9**: 280-84; **M13**: 372, 392-93
related to biology, **M10**: 6-7; **M13**: 377-81
and environment, **M10**: 7-11; **L11**: 501; **L12**: 32-47, 73-74; **L13**: 21-23, 25-26, 273, 326-28
effect of evolution on, **M10**: 14, 24-25
place of intelligence in, **M10**: 15-21
religious quality of, **M10**: 21-24; **L9**: xiv-xv, xvii-xviii, xxii-xxv, xxviii-xxix, 3-5, 8-11, 13-14, 19-20, 23-24, 26-27, 29-32, 44-45, 53-54, 220, 224, 295, 412-13, 415-17, 426, 428-30
as guide, **M12**: 124-25, 131-34
as evil, **M12**: 137-38
empiricism and, **M12**: 239; **L1**: 335; **L4**: 65-67, 155; **L5**: 175; **L14**: 32
value of, **M13**: ix-x, 328, 353; **L7**: 344; **L10**: 95, 104-10; **L13**: 26, 30, 114, 269, 284, 330, 376; **L17**: xxvi, xxvii, 280, 334-35
and education, **M13**: 294
as absolute, **M13**: 355; **L1**: 55-57; **L12**: 525
early, **M13**: 356-59
as doing and undergoing, **M13**: 360-61, 379
analysis of, **M13**: 360-64; **L7**: 146; **L14**: 138-39; **L17**: 433, 436
and nature, **M13**: 365; **L1**: xi, xviii; **L6**: 488-89; **L14**: 142-46
social, **M13**: 381-88
recognitive and projective, **M13**: 387-88
as mental, **M13**: 451-52
Kant on, **M15**: 9-10
depreciation of, **M15**: 12; **L4**: 44, 90-91, 205; **L17**: 432-33
related to law, **M15**: 69-70; **L14**: 116
and philosophy, **M15**: 332; **L1**: 3-41, 365-92; **L4**: 61-65, 79, 86, 111; **L5**: 267-78; **L6**: 20-21; **L14**: 124-26; **L17**: 429-30, 440
as term, **L1**: viii, xii-xvii, 361-64; **L16**: xxxvi, 73n, 248n, 260, 263
as personal, **L1**: 178-81
indefiniteness of, **L1**: 331-32
practical, **L2**: 3-6
and individuality, **L2**: 55-61; **L14**: 91
and dominance of foreground, **L3**: xi, 373-78, 381
varied and opposed, **L3**: 95-97
as subject of Gifford Lectures, **L4**: viii
connected with values, **L4**: 21, 22, 27, 28, 35, 201-12, 217, 222
character of, **L4**: 36, 112, 178, 181, 186-95
as means, **L4**: 87, 125
control of, **L4**: 220, 221, 234-36; **L17**: 353
and abstraction, **L5**: 7-10
related to psychology, **L5**: 228-30; **L6**: 330-32; **L17**: 187
and dialectic, **L5**: 487-95

Experience (*continued*)
Cohen on, **L6**: 488-89; **L14**: 382-85, 391-92
as epiphenomenon, **L9**: xiv, xxiv, xxvii
and formation of character, **L9**: 187
production and structure of, **L10**: 19, 26-31, 64-66, 71, 80, 81, 93, 152, 167-69, 173, 187, 251-65
ordinary vs. esthetic, **L10**: 42-63, 127-28, 140, 178-82, 222, 225, 276-301
new modes of, **L10**: 146-49, 193
culture related to, **L10**: 332-47; **L14**: 15
historical conceptions of, **L11**: 69-83; **L14**: 411-15
Locke on, **L11**: 76-80, 91-92, 94; **L17**: 438
Peirce on, **L11**: 86-94, 481
Whitehead on, **L11**: 146-49, 151-53; **L14**: 127-35
and education, **L11**: 210, 214, 504, 551-52, 556-59; **L13**: 8, 14, 27, 31, 56, 243, 264, 266-67, 296, 314, 376, 385
Hutchins on, **L11**: 393, 399
correct idea of, **L13**: 7, 11-12, 15, 31, 58
criticized, **L13**: 255-56
higher and lower, **L13**: 330-31
related to language, **L14**: xvi-xix
naturalistic theory of, **L14**: 15-16
immediate vs. mediated, **L14**: 16-19, 84-85
conditions of, **L14**: 20-21, 161
related to existence, **L14**: 30; **L16**: 383-89, 456-62
doubtful in, **L14**: 64-65, 69, 184-86
Hocking on, **L14**: 152, 417-19, 424-26
extrapolation in, **L14**: 186
actual and potential, **L14**: 189-91, 199
related to democracy, **L14**: 229-30
Otto's philosophy related to, **L14**: 289-91
moral, **L14**: 314-15; **L17**: 4-5
absolute truths vs., **L14**: 321-22
related to industry, **L14**: 345-46
lacks value in ageing, **L14**: 347
feelings related to, **L15**: 118-19; **L17**: 346
external and internal, **L17**: 155-57, 159
transfer of, **L17**: 264-65
Greek, **L17**: 435-36
Renaissance views of, **L17**: 437
"Experience, Knowledge and Value: A Rejoinder," **L14**: xi
Experience and Education, **L13**: ix, xiv, 375-76
"Experience and Existence in Dewey's Naturalistic Metaphysics" (Kahn), **L16**: 383
Experience and Nature, **M1**: xi; **M7**: xvi; **M8**: ix, x, xii; **M12**: ix; **M15**: x; **L2**: xviii; **L3**: ix, xvii; **L5**: xi, xxvii, 488, 492, 494; **L7**: xxxiv; **L14**: x, xii, xviii, 13, 14, 35n, 41, 64, 383-88, 394, 396, 408, 410, 413; **L15**: 398
Hook on, **L1**: vii-xxiii
unfinished 1948-50 introduction to, **L1**: 329-64
superseded 1925 chapter 1 in, **L1**: 365-92
E. Hall criticizes, **L3**: 82-91, 401-14

Santayana criticizes, **L3**: 367-84
Thilly criticizes, **L3**: 392-400
on esthetics, **L10**: x, xii, xviii, xxv, xxix-xxxiii, 33n; **L16**: 397-98
metaphysical in, **L16**: 383-88, 456
on experience, **L16**: 386, 458
naturalism in, **L17**: xxx
Experience and Prediction (Reichenbach), **L14**: 27n
Experiential continuum, **L13**: 13, 17, 267
Experiment, **L12**: 99-100, 115-16, 121-22, 132, 134, 151, 182, 190, 317, 420, 425-26, 455-56, 465, 502, 522
in science and psychology, **E1**: 53-55; **L8**: 67
and thinking, **E3**: 225; **L1**: xix-xxi
in laboratory schools, **E5**: 269
function of, **M6**: 240, 251, 254; **M13**: 63; **L8**: 74, 205-6, 256-58
in induction, **M13**: 65
two kinds of, **M13**: 386-87
reflection involving, **L8**: 189
failure to provide for, **L8**: 266-67
and observation, **L8**: 273
social vs. scientific, **L13**: 185
faith in, **L17**: xxvi
Experimental, **L1**: 335-36
science, **M7**: 310; **M9**: 284
naturalism, **L6**: xii
knowledge as, **L14**: 12-14
vs. absolute, **L14**: 317
Experimental College, The (Meiklejohn), **L6**: 295-98
Experimentalism, **L2**: 20; **L8**: 71, 92. *See also* Pragmatism
James on, **M12**: 220
Peirce on, **L2**: 3-5
Hocking on, **L5**: 461-76
Experimental method, **M6**: 175; **M12**: 87; **L1**: 339-40; **L13**: 131, 266. *See also* Scientific method
Dewey criticized for, **M2**: xii-xiii
nature of, **M2**: 4-5; **L2**: 361-62; **L4**: 20, 22, 29, 46, 69-76, 87-116, 121, 230-32, 247; **L8**: 94-100
impact of, **M2**: 8; **M9**: 347-49; **L4**: 5, 64, 77-86, 133-41, 144-55, 210
connected with occupations, **M9**: 209-10, 237
introduction of, **M9**: 281
in new psychology, **M10**: 58-63
in politics, **L2**: 356-61
Newton's use of, **L4**: 93-97
as model, **L4**: 158, 160, 176, 183, 185, 193, 195, 201, 204, 206, 216-22, 238, 245
applied to social sciences, **L8**: 74, 94-95, 101
in technology, **L8**: 102
Experimental school. *See* Laboratory School, University of Chicago
Experimentation, **M14**: xiii, 132-33, 150; **L15**: 37n, 88-89, 273
in *Cyclopedia of Education*, **M6**: 453-55
experience as, **M9**: 280-84
moral, **M14**: 41-42, 165, 211, 214; **L14**: 147
in art, **L10**: xxxii, 147,149, 342
Bentham on, **L11**: 13
applied to social problems, **L11**: 55-56, 58, 61, 64n, 145, 292-93, 383
imagination in, **L11**: 82

Experimentation (*continued*)
applied in education, **L11**: 194, 202-3, 206
learning by, **L11**: 238
function of, **L14**: 12-14; **L17**: 354
necessity of, **L14**: 52; **L17**: 340
history of, **L14**: 173; **L17**: 356-57
Hocking on, **L14**: 416, 425-26
physical, **L17**: 355
Experiment in Education
in *Cyclopedia of Education*, **M6**: 451-53
Experts
importance of, **L2**: 312-13, 319-20
and democracy, **L2**: 362-63
Explanation, **L4**: 145
principle of, **E3**: 224-26
in *Cyclopedia of Education*, **M6**: 455-57
defined, **L14**: 24n
of occurrences vs. things, **L14**: 112
Exploration, **M12**: 101-3
Expression, **L1**: 140, 292; **L15**: 99
nature of, **E4**: 154; **E5**: 193-94; **L10**: xxvi-xxviii, 88-89, 102-3, 145-46, 160-61, 225, 230, 270, 364
of emotions, **E4**: 168; **L15**: 131-36
motive to, **E5**: 192-93
Santayana on, **M10**: 355
artistic, **L10**: 66-87, 247-49, 275, 307, 327-31, 342
vs. statement, **L10**: 90-92, 96
medium of, **L10**: 204-5, 209, 232, 237-42, 316
through imagination, **L10**: 277, 287, 291-92, 298-99
Carnap on, **L16**: 18, 20-23, 26-27
Lewis on, **L16**: 37
Tarski on, **L16**: 40
related to impression, **L17**: 218, 220-21
Expressionism, **L10**: 303
Expression of the Emotions in Man and Animals, The (Darwin), **L10**: 160; **L17**: 198
Expressive activities
in education, **E5**: 90, 229-32
dependence on, **E5**: 226-29
Expressiveness
achievement of, **L10**: xxi, xxviii, 92, 98-101, 104-8, 123-28, 132-34, 189, 290, 292
enemies of, **L10**: 109-10
features of, **L10**: 112, 130, 145
of medium, **L10**: 200, 205, 207, 364
Extension
in Leibniz, **E1**: 356-57
as esthetic quality, **L10**: 184-88, 214, 217, 235, 246
logical, **L12**: 200, 295-96, 340-41, 357-60
of magnitudes, **L12**: 211-12
Extensive abstraction, **L12**: 411-13, 462-64
External object
in *Cyclopedia of Education*, **M6**: 457
External relations
in realism, **M6**: 138-45, 484-511
External world, **L15**: 185-86
Dewey vs. Russell on, **M8**: xx-xxv, 83-93
as problem of empiricism, **M10**: 18-21
existence of, **L1**: xvii
G. Morris on, **L5**: 152
Extra-curricular activities, **L14**: 353

Extra-territoriality, **M12**: 46-47
Extrinsic, **L16**: 349
Eyck, Jan van, **L10**: 213, 361
Ezekiel, **M5**: 100-101; **L7**: 92

Fact, Fiction, and Forecast (Goodman), **L14**: xvin
Factions, political, **L2**: 309
Factory legislation, **L7**: 377-79, 412-15, 432
Facts, **M8**: 86; **M12**: 85, 117, 135-36, 160-62, 243; **L16**: xxii, 12, 81, 113
  aspects of, **E1**: 179; **L16**: 53-55, 110, 151, 244, 261
  truths of, **E1**: 392-94, 399
  related to idea, **E3**: 84-89, 259; **M4**: 146-57; **L8**: 196-99; **L12**: 129, 133, 212-14, 218-19, 339-40
  related to thought, **E3**: 126-29
  rationality of, **E3**: 139-40
  as subject of judgment, **E3**: 231-33
  inquiry into, **E3**: 319-20; **L12**: 493-97; **L14**: 44; **L16**: 6, 66, 126, 285, 288, 325-27
  related to science, **M1**: 168-71; **L17**: 354
  world as, **M1**: 241-42
  Royce on, **M2**: 121-23
  and value, **M6**: 261; **L8**: 212-16; **L13**: 191, 249; **L14**: 323; **L15**: 16-17, 106, 481-82; **L16**: 344-45, 348, 357
  in *Cyclopedia of Education*, **M6**: 457-58
  and theories, **L2**: 238, 246; **L16**: 131-32, 283-84
  physical and social, **L2**: 240-41, 243-44; **L17**: 419
  dead, **L12**: 76, 492
  of case, **L12**: 113, 117, 185, 491
  and observation, **L12**: 114-18
  provisional, **L12**: 144-45
  as given, **L12**: 489-91
  articulation of, **L13**: 50
  classification of, **L13**: 55; **L16**: 42-44, 63, 80n, 298; **L17**: 372, 422, 446-47, 482
  vs. generalization, **L13**: 93, 96
  and inherency, **L13**: 215-16
  naturalistic conception of, **L15**: 59-60
  vs. events, **L15**: 313
  Cohen and Nagel on, **L16**: 13-16
  Carnap on, **L16**: 17, 25, 31
  Ducasse on, **L16**: 36n
  as name, **L16**: 58-61, 70, 72, 93n, 258, 263-64
  Kaplan on, **L16**: 173
  Pepper on, **L16**: 177
  Russell on, **L16**: 200, 201
  of C. Morris, **L16**: 240-41
  as analysis, **L17**: 157
  ought and is, **L17**: 351-52
  change within, **L17**: 367-68, 410
  institutional and personal, **L17**: 426
  Woodbridge on, **L17**: 548-49
"Facts and Values in History" (S. Ratner), **L6**: xviin
"Factual Space and Time of Behavior, The" (A. Bentley), **L16**: 270n
Faculties, **L16**: 93n, 111, 136
  education as training of, **M9**: 65-74, 253-54
  Herbart on, **M9**: 75-78
Failure
  in learning, **L11**: 240-41
  cause of, **L17**: 247
Fair Deal, **L5**: xx
Fairhope, Ala., **M8**: 253
  educational experiment at, **M7**: 387-89; **M8**: 222-35

Faith, **L4**: 47; **L9**: 56, 214, 432
as alternative to pessimism, **E3**: 41-42
Dewey's confession of, **M1**: xi
as skepticism, **M6**: 23
in experience, **L5**: 267-78
lack of, **L7**: 229
in human values, **L9**: xx-xxi, 57-58
as substitute for knowledge, **L9**: 14-15, 28
Locke on, **L9**: 15
moral aspect of, **L9**: 15-17, 426
Macintosh's view of, **L9**: 418, 419
in human nature, **L13**: 152, 178-79; **L17**: 86
of Enlightenment, **L13**: 160
in scientific attitude, **L13**: 275
Jefferson's democratic, **L14**: 219
in Santayana's philosophy, **L14**: 305-6
in democracy, **L17**: 87, 439, 478
reliance upon good, **L17**: 401
"Faith of a Logician, The" (M. R. Cohen), **L16**: 194n
Falkner, William, **M11**: 21n
Fallacy, **L12**: 204, 256, 263, 285, 317-18, 330, 379, 439, 472, 492, 503; **L16**: 349
philosophic, **M14**: 122-23
in art, **L10**: xxi, xxx
of classification, **L10**: 218-21, 226-29
of criticism, **L10**: 319-21
"Fallacy of the Boycott, The" (Soule), **L6**: 479n
Fallibilism, **L6**: xiv; **L12**: 46-47; **L14**: xiii
Peirce on, **L6**: 275-76; **L14**: 57n, 171
False
vs. true, **L14**: 182-83
Familiar
in art, **L10**: 145, 163, 194, 273-74, 287
lack of attention to, **L17**: 275-76
need to discover, **L17**: 277
Familiarity, **M8**: 25; **L4**: 148, 167, 174
contempt for, **M6**: 354-55; **L8**: 349-50
Family, **L1**: 163; **L13**: 177, 296
child's relation to, **E5**: 225
maternal and paternal, **M5**: 28; **L7**: 27-28; **L17**: 23-24
economic function of, **M5**: 29-31, 46; **L7**: 28-30, 44; **L9**: 233
Hebrew, **M5**: 89-97; **L7**: 82-91
in moral system, **M5**: 178-79
history of, **M5**: 510-16; **L7**: 438-43; **L17**: 23
psychological basis of, **M5**: 516-21
problems of, **M5**: 521-40; **L7**: 457-62
Pestalozzi on, **M7**: 378
in China, **M12**: 72, 253
principle, **M12**: 114-15, 188
as developer of creative impulse, **M12**: 248
materialism affects, **L5**: 47, 48, 74
Roman, **L7**: 129-30, 440-41
change in, **L7**: 374, 444-50; **L16**: 360, 371; **L17**: 24
goals of, **L7**: 438
Germanic, **L7**: 441
from social standpoint, **L7**: 452-56
effect of Depression on, **L11**: 268
and education, **L11**: 538; **L17**: 233
experience in, **L13**: 55

Fanaticism, **M12**: 176; **M14**: 157; **L15**: 58; **L16**: 350
threats of, **L17**: xxii
absolutism and, **L17**: xxiv
Fancy
vs. imagination, **L10**: xxviii, 272
development of, **L17**: 261
Fantasies, **M14**: 109, 113, 162, 188
Faraday, Michael, **L2**: xxxii, 366; **L11**: 279; **L14**: 397; **L16**: 61, 99, 278
Far East, **L8**: 7
problems of, **M13**: 81
peace of, **M13**: 82, 85, 442
coordination in respect to, **M13**: 185
political opinion in, **M13**: 259
vs. West in China, **M15**: 216
freedom in, **L13**: 80
Far Eastern Republic
and Japan, **M13**: 214
fate of, **M13**: 233
establishment of, **M13**: 235-39
and Russia, **M13**: 238, 240
Dewey on, **M13**: 239
reports about, **M13**: 241
Far Eastern Republic, The: Siberia and Japan (F. Moore, Skvirsky, and C. Smith), **M13**: 240n
Farley, Thomas M., **L9**: 356
Farmer-Labor party, **L6**: 235, 251, 254; **L9**: 297, 298
Farmers, **L2**: 316. *See also* Agriculture
in China, **M12**: 254
decline of, **L5**: 60
political organization of, **L5**: 447-49; **L6**: 172
Russian, **L6**: 265; **L17**: 503-4
economic pressures on, **L9**: 249, 250, 255-57, 269-70, 273; **L15**: 358
People's Lobby on, **L9**: 249-51
land value related to, **L9**: 250, 255, 257, 258, 262-63, 269-70
unions of, **L9**: 250, 273
situation of, **L9**: 275, 285, 307
as workers, **L11**: 160
idealization of, **L13**: 81
vs. traders, **L13**: 100, 134
Farmers and Consumers Financing Corporation, **L9**: 85
Farmers' National Educational and Cooperative Union, **L9**: 273
Farmers' Union, **L6**: 236; **L9**: 250
Farming. *See* Agriculture
Farm Land Bank (Federal Land Bank), **L6**: 386
Farm Relief Board, **L5**: 94
Fascism, **L6**: 142, 447, 464n; **L7**: 427-28; **L8**: 52; **L9**: 77-78, 93, 297, 298, 312; **L13**: 129, 151, 157, 180, 315, 317; **L15**: 175-76, 215; **L16**: 391, 401; **L17**: 469
Niebuhr on, **L9**: 401-3
adherents of, **L11**: 60, 164
vs. communism, **L11**: 64, 187, 495
danger of, **L11**: 328, 528, 536-37
Bingham on, **L11**: 440
Hutchins on, **L11**: 596
Long on, **L13**: 112
suppression in, **L13**: 316, 321; **L14**: 96
Trotsky on, **L13**: 398
denounced, **L14**: 366
virtue of, **L17**: 117
Fatalism, **M13**: 223

Fate, **L14**: 98
Fatigue, **E5**: 157
Fatigue and Impairment in Man (Bartley and Chute), **L16**: 140n
Faulkner, William, **M12**: xxvi
Fear, **M12**: 101-2; **L1**: 43; **L13**: 166, 289
  as motive, **E4**: 111-12; **L13**: 142-43; **L17**: 86
  description of, **E4**: 164
  as enemy to progress, **M13**: 425
  in school life, **M13**: 427, 428
  of Japan, **M13**: 441
Fechner, Gustav Theodor, **E4**: 195; **M2**: 149
  as founder of psychology, **M7**: 137-39
  Hocking on, **L14**: 422
Federal Bureau of Investigation, **L17**: 140
Federal Farm Board, **L5**: 433, 435
Federalist Papers, The (A. Hamilton, Madison, and Jay), **L15**: xv
Federal Land Bank, **L6**: 386
Federal Reserve Board, **L5**: 94
Federal Trade Commission, **L14**: 370
Federal Trade Commission Act, **L7**: 408-9, 418
Federation
  as governmental unit, **L2**: 377
Federation for Child Study, **M7**: 377
Federation of Women's Clubs, **L5**: 317
Feeling, **L1**: 197-99, 204, 221, 226-30, 240; **L10**: 257. *See also* Sensation
  in sensationalistic theory, **E1**: 31-32
  in consciousness, **E2**: 20-25, 215-16
  and taste and smell, **E2**: 57, 221-22
  analogy of, **E2**: 95-97
  qualitative, **E2**: 216-17, 239-55
  sensuous, **E2**: 218-27
  formal, **E2**: 228-38
  individuality of, **E2**: 254-55, 281-97
  intellectual, **E2**: 256-66
  esthetic, **E2**: 267-80
  and will, **E2**: 357-58
  Kant on, **E3**: 72
  connected with action, **E3**: 244-45, 257-58
  as end or ideal, **E4**: 264-65; **E5**: 130
  related to value, **E5**: 124-25; **L13**: 223
  isolated from function, **E5**: 227
  in psychical unity, **E5**: 313
  psychology of, **E5**: 358-67
  utilitarians on, **M5**: 229
  impotency of, **M10**: 19
  ambiguity in word, **L13**: 198-99
  related to character, **L17**: 343, 347
  related to experience, **L17**: 346
Feibleman, James, **L16**: 10n
Feigl, Herbert, **L16**: 170, 181n
Feinstone, Sol, **L14**: 311
Fellowship
  needed in education, **L14**: 278-79
  Addams on, **L15**: 198
Fénelon, François de Salignac de la Mothe, **M2**: 216
Feng Kuo Chang, **M13**: 133
Feng-shui, **M13**: 224
Fermat, Pierre de, **L14**: 397
Ferrero, Guglielmo, **L5**: 113
Ferrier, James Frederick, **M2**: 172

Ferris, Theodore R., **L17**: 545
Feti, Domenico, **L10**: 147
Feudalism, **M12**: 103-4, 113-15, 184; **M13**: 152, 283, 296, 309; **L1**: 357; **L11**: 283, 365; **L13**: 105-6; **L16**: 401
  Greek philosophy used to justify, **M4**: 35
  Germany's change from, **M8**: 185-86
  division of classes in, **M9**: 128
  effect of science on, **M9**: 292
  contrasted with individualism, **L7**: xxix
  in U.S., **L13**: 81
  in Great Britain, **L13**: 83
  breakdown of, **L15**: 213-14, 271
  education under, **L15**: 249, 258, 261, 264-66
  dualism of, **L15**: 258
  and capitalism, **L17**: 23-24
"Feudal Principle in Modern Law, A" (Pound), **L7**: xxix
Feuer, Lewis S.
  on Dewey's 1942-48 writings, **L15**: xi-xxxiv
Feuerbach, Ludwig Andreas, **L5**: 355
Feyerabend, Paul, **L8**: xiii-xiv
Fibres, nervous, **E1**: 94-95
Fichte, Johann Gottlieb, **E1**: 166, 314; **E5**: 346; **M3**: 56, 310-11; **M6**: 168; **M7**: 289, 357, 415; **M8**: 421; **M9**: 102; **M10**: 306; **L5**: 186; **L8**: 37; **L15**: 384
  idealism of, **M1**: xvii; **M7**: 138, 232, 299; **M10**: 111; **M11**: 361
  as nihilistic, **M2**: 155
  on ego, **M2**: 158; **L16**: 458
  panthelism of, **M2**: 185
  on posit, **M2**: 207
  on ethical pantheism, **M7**: 294
  and self-consciousness, **M7**: 345
  and truth, **M7**: 413
  influences Germany, **M8**: 172-82; **M10**: 221, 223, 226
  on development of humanity, **M8**: 186-89
  related to Hegel, **M8**: 191-92; **L4**: 50-51
Field, David Dudley, **M15**: 384
Field, Frederick Vanderbilt, **L15**: 352
Field
  perceptual, **L12**: 72-73, 152-53
  as name, **L16**: 67n-68n, 73n, 264
  in physics, **L16**: 107, 121n
  Einstein on, **L16**: 108
  of value, **L16**: 343-57
Fifteenth century
  revival of learning of, **M9**: 290
Fifth Symphony (Beethoven), **L10**: 117, 212, 227
Figgis, John Neville, **L2**: 39, 40
  on church-state conflict, **M11**: 18-21
  on law, **M11**: 27-28
Filmer, Robert, **M11**: 21n
Final cause, **L16**: 410. *See also* Teleology, **L12**
Final good, **M12**: xiii, xx, 172-74, 184; **L14**: 408-9
Final value, **L13**: 231, 347; **L16**: 349-50, 353, 355
Finance
  in Turkish schools, **M15**: 285-86
  and speculation, **L9**: 254
  F. Roosevelt's policy regarding, **L9**: 277-78
Fine, Henry Burchard
  on number, **E5**: xxiii-xxvii, 424-29

Fine art, **E2**: 274-77; **M12**: 152; **L1**: 271, 273, 282-83, 290-91; **L16**: 369, 397, 417. *See also* Art; Works of art
  vs. useful art, **M7**: xxviii-xxix; **M9**: 242-44; **L10**: xi, xxxii, 33-34, 265, 343-44
  compartmentalization of, **L10**: 14-17, 26, 85, 90
  quality of, **L10**: 29-30, 45, 86-87, 127, 143, 153, 155, 176-77, 232, 286
  beauty in, **L13**: 360
Finerty, John F., **L11**: 313-15, 323, 602; **L15**: 356
Finite, **L1**: 52-53, 127
  and infinite, **E3**: 227-28; **M12**: 117; **L17**: 95
  or imperfect, **M12**: 141
Finland, **M15**: 392
Fire, **M12**: 85-86, 111-12, 129, 209
Firm
  as name, **L16**: 264
First Crossing of Greenland, The (Nansen), **L5**: 395
First Philosophy, **L4**: 12-13
First principles, **L12**: 19; **L14**: 123
First Public Education Experiment Station (Obninsk, USSR), **L17**: 505
Firth, John Rupert, **L16**: 122n, 468
Fisch, Max, **L16**: xn-xin
Fischer, Kuno, **E1**: 336; **E3**: 187
Fishbein, Morris, **L17**: 518, 573
Fisher, George, **M5**: 135
Fisher, Herbert Albert L., **M11**: 59, 393
Fiske, Bradley A., **L6**: 503
Fiske, John, **E4**: 93n; **E5**: 261; **M2**: 149; **M9**: 50n; **L17**: 559
  on infancy, **E5**: 39; **M1**: 180, 339; **M5**: 519; **M7**: 246-48; **L17**: 256, 563
  as popularizer of Spencer, **L17**: 93
  on phenomena, **L17**: 93
  on cosmic theism, **L17**: 94
  teleology of, **L17**: 95, 96
  on organic evolution, **L17**: 96-97
Fitch, Robert E., **L15**: xxxiiin
Fite, Warner, **M7**: 62n
Fitness, **E5**: 40-41
Fitness of the Environment, The (L. Henderson), **M8**: 458; **L16**: 117n
Fitzpatrick, Edward A., **L17**: 67, 557
Five-year plan (USSR), **L6**: 51, 61, 65, 263, 266, 469
Fixation, **L16**: 413
Flaubert, Gustave, **E3**: 37, 39
Flemish school of art, **L10**: 192, 210
Fletcher, Duncan Upshaw, **L9**: 288
Flexibility, **L16**: 4
Flexner, Abraham, **L6**: 287
  criticizes universities, **L17**: 110-11
Flint, Robert, **E4**: 200, 213-14
Florentine school of painting, **L10**: 146, 177, 192, 315, 333
Flower, Elizabeth
  on 1908 and 1932 *Ethics*, **L7**: vii-xxxv
Flux, **M12**: 112, 141-42; **L10**: 20, 22. *See also* Change
Flynn, Elizabeth Gurley, **L15**: xxiv
Flynn, William J., **L9**: 346, 347, 362-64

Focusing
as aspect of directive action, **M9**: 30, 44-45, 68-69
Foerster, Norman, **L5**: 265
Folk
Fichte on, **M8**: 188-89
Folklore, **L13**: 165
Folk-psychologists
Austrian and German schools of, **M10**: 57
Folkways. *See also* Customs; Mores
defined, **M5**: 54; **L7**: 49
Following, **L12**: 269-71, 298-99, 313-14, 345-46, 415-18, 427-32
Foochow (Fuzhou), China, **M12**: 22, 23, 39
Food
study of, **E5**: 237-40
as stimuli, **M2**: 43
shortage, **M10**: 296
"For a New Education," **L14**: xix
Force, **L15**: 195; **L16**: 400. *See also* Coercion
in hedonistic theories of obligation, **E3**: 332
of customs, **M5**: 58-59; **L7**: 54; **L13**: 293
Hitler's doctrine of, **M8**: 425-28
Dewey's concept of, **M10**: xxviii-xxix
use of, **M10**: 21; **L11**: 294, 379; **L17**: 459
Spencer's concept of, **M10**: 68
related to violence and law, **M10**: 211-15, 244-51; **L6**: 213-14, 218, 219, 463-65
Germany's adoption of, **M10**: 220-22
coercive, for unity, **L6**: 212-13
related to sanctions, **L6**: 214-16, 450-51, 481-82
as cause, **L12**: 445-46
motives as, **L13**: 85-87
belief in, **L13**: 90-91, 145, 148
economic, **L13**: 100
impersonal, **L13**: 104
of science, **L13**: 123, 371
military, **L13**: 187, 302
rule by, **L13**: 321; **L15**: 176, 207-9
allied with truth, **L14**: 321-22
communism emphasizes, **L17**: 117
Forced Labor in Soviet Russia (Dallin and Nicolaevsky), **L15**: 295-98
Ford, Franklin, **E3**: 239; **L16**: xxvn
Ford, Henry, **L2**: 161; **L5**: 62; **L7**: 423
Foreground
consciousness as, **L10**: 270-71
Foreign Affairs, **M15**: xiii
Foreign and Domestic Commerce, Bureau of, **L6**: 353
Foreigners
in China, **M12**: 44-49, 74
Foreign intrigue
in Turkey, **M15**: 130
Foreign policy
Dewey on, **L3**: xxxi-xxxiii
C. and M. Beard on, **L14**: 283
Foreign Policy Association, **L6**: 196n, 450n
Foreign Relations, Committee on, **L6**: 364-65
Foresight, **M14**: 142-45, 164, 183-85, 195, 200, 210, 215; **L13**: 231, 237, 243; **L17**: 268
of consequences, **L13**: 43-45, 217-18, 247
of enjoyment, **L13**: 227

Foresight (*continued*)
in direction, **L17**: 52
organization in, **L17**: 52-53
lack of, **L17**: 452
Forgettery
importance of, **L17**: 333
Form, **L1**: 78, 79, 133, 177, 240, 246, 293; **L13**: 371
and content value in studies, **E5**: 67
in *Cyclopedia of Education*, **M6**: 458-60
Bradley on, **L5**: 258-60
generation of, **L10**: xx-xxiii, xxvii, 20, 29-30, 81, 86, 139-67, 188, 202, 205-6, 210, 357
related to substance in art, **L10**: 118-38, 174-76, 195, 217, 322, 325
technique's relation to, **L10**: 232-33, 306-9, 319
classic idea of, **L10**: 289, 298-300, 364; **L15**: 84-85, 276
appreciation of, **L10**: 315, 317
influences on, **L10**: 333, 343, 344
accrues in inquiry, **L12**: xx-xxi, 11-12, 29, 106, 132, 159-60
and law, **L12**: 24, 105-6, 187-88, 370-71
of material, **L12**: 159, 235, 285, 348, 429-30
abstracted, **L12**: 193
and language, **L12**: 372
mathematical, **L12**: 391-414
Formal discipline
in education, **M9**: 65-74, 253-54
interest and, **M9**: 131-45
Formalism, **E1**: xxvi; **M12**: xxiii
conceptual, **L17**: 445
neo-scholastic, **L17**: 469
Formalistic logic
and Aristotelian logic, **L12**: 88-92
transformation of, **L12**: 93, 183, 197-98, 201-2, 218, 285, 364-65
failure of, **L12**: 372-83
and social inquiry, **L12**: 502-3
Formalization of Logic (Carnap), **L16**: 30-31, 38
Formal Logic: A Scientific and Social Problem (F. Schiller), **M7**: 131-34; **L11**: 156
"Forms of Art Exhibition" (Philadelphia), **L17**: 128, 540-41, 560
Formulation. *See also* Proposition, **L12**; Symbols, **L12**
types of, **M9**: 235-36
necessity of, **L12**: 21, 25-26, 245, 249-51, 263-65, 501
Fortune, **L4**: 6, 9-10, 82, 178, 209, 241; **L15**: 333, 335-36, 474. *See also* Luck
Forward from Liberalism (Spender), **L11**: 496-98
"Forward View, The," **L11**: xviii
For-what
of attention, **L17**: 272-73
Fosdick, Raymond B., **L16**: 374, 471
Foundation, **L16**: 90, 165n
Foundation of Commercial Education (ECTA), **L5**: 401-3
Foundations of Sovereignty (Laski), **L2**: 40n
Foundations of the Nineteenth Century, The (H. Chamberlain), **M8**: 188n
Foundations of the Social Sciences (Neurath), **L16**: 187n
Foundations of the Theory of Signs (C. Morris), **L15**:

141-52, 473; **L16**: xxxii, 33-35, 224n
Founders of Modern Psychology (G. Hall), **M7**: 137-41
Founding of the German Empire by William I, The (von Sybel), **M8**: 177
Four Freedoms, **L15**: 509
Fourier, Joseph, **L15**: xvii
Four Stages of Greek Religion (G. Murray), **L5**: 165
Fourteen Points
  and League of Nations, **M11**: 135-39
Fourteenth Amendment, **L2**: 36; **L7**: 356, 395
Fox, Mary, **L9**: 271
Fragonard, Jean-Honoré, **L10**: 133
France, Anatole, **L3**: 203; **L6**: 77
France, **M11**: 19, 156, 277; **M15**: xviii, 106, 107, 109, 112, 129, 380, 411, 412; **L6**: 206, 453; **L11**: 10, 79, 520; **L13**: 348; **L14**: 277. *See also* French Revolution
  literature of, **E3**: 36-42
  language of, **E3**: 209-10
  philosophy in, **M8**: 144; **M9**: 308; **M11**: 43, 93; **M12**: xiv, 107, 222; **L17**: 438-39
  rights in, **M8**: 165-66
  Enlightenment in, **M8**: 183
  school of imitation in, **M10**: 60
  in WWI, **M10**: 219; **M11**: 100, 177, 192, 245; **L15**: 341
  on Germany, **M10**: 222-23
  and new nations, **M11**: xiii
  education in, **M11**: 58; **L17**: 492
  and U.S., **M11**: 116, 151; **M15**: 155
  publicity about, **M11**: 120
  and Alsace-Lorraine, **M11**: 136; **M12**: 60
  and League of Nations, **M11**: 140; **M15**: 85
  and Japan, **M11**: 169, 192, 198; **M12**: 35
  and China, **M11**: 190; **M13**: 202
  Poland's relation with, **M11**: 250, 251, 256, 261, 267, 268, 279-84, 293, 299, 302, 317-19, 323-28, 395
  and Paris Peace Conference, **M12**: 5, 18
  demands for concessions by, **M12**: 62
  political thought of, **M13**: 346
  interests of, in Turkey, **M15**: 132, 142, 145-46
  on nationality laws, **M15**: 388-89
  on outlawry of war, **L3**: 163, 168-69, 171, 175; **L8**: 13, 17
  and sanctions, **L6**: 197
  proposes international army, **L6**: 210
  on Egypt, **L6**: 219, 468-69
  and disarmament, **L6**: 460-61
  influences Jefferson, **L14**: 210-12
  and USSR, **L15**: 245, 347-48, 353, 494-95
  capitalist in, **L17**: 22
  on democracy, **L17**: 474
Franchise, **L6**: 226-27; **L11**: 25, 50, 51, 218, 248, 535-36. *See also* Suffrage
  denied Negroes, **L15**: 357
Franciscans, **M5**: 141
Francis of Assisi, Saint, **L14**: 102
Francis W. Parker School (Chicago), **M3**: 240n

Francis W. Parker School (*cont.*)
English experiment in, **M8**: 262-63
dramatization at, **M8**: 288-90
Francke, Kuno, **M5**: 140
on German mind, **M10**: 225-30
Franco, Francisco, **L15**: 26
Frank, Jerome, **L6**: xix; **L14**: xxiv
Frank, Philipp, **L16**: 108n, 149n
Frank, Waldo, **L5**: 72, 73
Frankel, Charles, **L13**: xvii
Frankfurter, Felix, **L6**: xix; **L9**: 237
Franklin, Benjamin, **M13**: 303; **L9**: 123; **L13**: 144; **L14**: 203-4; **L15**: xxx-xxxi
and science, **L14**: 205, 209
Jefferson on, **L14**: 223
Franklin D. Roosevelt (Freidel), **L6**: xviiin
Fraser, Alexander Campbell, **E1**: 123
Fraternity
as value in democracy, **L14**: 277
Frazier, Lynn J., **L6**: 355, 394
Frederick the Great, **M7**: 379; **M8**: 156-57, 164, 186, 474; **L14**: 399
Free assembly, **L16**: 402
Freedom, **L4**: 128, 129, 136, 199-200; **L7**: xxv; **L8**: 181; **L11**: xxi-xxii; **L15**: 56, 238. *See also* Academic freedom; Liberty
ethics of, **E1**: 41; **E4**: 341-44
democratic, **E1**: 244-45; **L14**: 227-28; **L16**: 391, 406
realization of, **E3**: 327; **M12**: 240
forms of, **E3**: 340-44; **M14**: xix, 209-15
proof of, **E4**: 95
psychology of, **E4**: 337-41
determinist and indeterminist theories of, **E4**: 344-50
and individualism, **M5**: 83-84; **L7**: 76-77
role in social order, **M5**: 390-94; **L11**: 24
of thought, **M6**: 229-32; **M12**: 8-11; **L7**: 358-66; **L11**: xxx, 47-48, 142-43, 220, 253, 270, 290, 344, 375
in Hegel, **M8**: 195
and discipline, **M9**: 310-11; **L8**: 182-86
and authority, **M9**: 314-15, 348-49; **L11**: 130-31, 136-45
American vs. German concept of, **M10**: 228
opposed to institutional control, **M11**: 18
philosophy and, **M11**: 50; **L3**: 103-4, 108-9; **L16**: 368
of expression, **M11**: 110, 184, 189; **L3**: 111-14, 136; **L6**: xxii, 121-22; **L11**: 46-48, 61, 269, 270, 272, 290
in Europe, **M11**: 136
associated with anarchy, **M11**: 216
of franchise, **M12**: 10-11
secured by vigilance, **M12**: 17-18
religious, **M12**: 105; **L3**: 124; **L7**: 77
of will, **M12**: 192; **M14**: 8-9
law and, **M12**: 198; **L14**: 247-48
internal, **M12**: 246-47
opposition to, **M14**: 61, 115-16; **L7**: 359-60; **L11**: 247-55; **L13**: 24-25, 32, 39-41, 127; **L16**: 360, 404
intellectual, **M14**: 114; **M15**: xxiv-xxv, 201-2, 207-11; **L3**: 102, 111; **L8**: 186

for teachers, **M15**: 186-87
and action, **L3**: xxvii-xxviii, 106-7; **L17**: 384
and choice, **L3**: 92-95, 105-8; **L17**: 340, 383
and liability, **L3**: 93-94
and luck, **L3**: 104-5, 107
science and, **L3**: 110-11, 123
political and economic, **L3**: 114; **L7**: 141-44; **L8**: 51; **L11**: 8-10, 26-28, 136-40, 249-52, 254, 258, 283, 284, 290, 365-67, 369-71, 496; **L13**: 67; **L15**: 216
Greeks and, **L6**: 431
and culture, **L6**: 445-49; **L11**: 294-95
Pauline conception of, **L7**: 95
nature of, **L7**: 305-6; **L11**: 532; **L13**: 9, 46, 75, 78, 144, 154
individual, **L7**: 334-35; **L13**: 80-82, 85, 102-3, 149; **L14**: 91-95; **L17**: 399
in capitalism, **L7**: 376
individual vs. collective, **L9**: 205-6; **L11**: 191-92
in esthetic theory, **L10**: xxxi, 284-86, 346
Lippmann on, **L11**: 258-59
in USSR, **L11**: 332
Russell on, **L11**: 455-56
and self-control, **L13**: 43
factors in, **L13**: 72, 97, 129, 180-81, 316
of press, **L13**: 92, 168; **L16**: 402
related to organization, **L13**: 110
problems of, **L13**: 147, 162, 185
vs. totalitarianism, **L14**: 278-79, 367-68
planning for, **L14**: 294
conditions for, **L15**: 41, 249-52
civil, **L15**: 170-83, 366-67
Aristotle on, **L15**: 265
Bode on, **L15**: 327
during Enlightenment, **L16**: 372
importance of, **L16**: 402-3
moral, **L17**: 5, 259
and responsibility, **L17**: 342-43, 462
respect for, **L17**: 473
Freedom and Culture, **M7**: xxi-xxii; **M9**: xii; **L1**: viii; **L5**: xvi; **L13**: ix, xv-xvi; **L17**: xxviii, 335n
Freedom in the Modern World (Kallen), **L3**: 92n
Freedom of Will
in *Cyclopedia of Education*, **M6**: 419, 464-66
Freeman, Edward A., **L13**: 401
Freeman, James E., **L11**: 530
Freeman, **M13**: 306
"Free Man's Worship, A" (B. Russell), **M12**: xxix; **M15**: 327
Free Poland (Washington, D.C.), **M11**: 256, 324
Free press, **L13**: 92, 168; **L16**: 402
Free Silver party, **L6**: 232
Free-Soil party, **L6**: 231
Free speech, **L6**: 124-25; **L16**: 402-3
Free verse, **L10**: 303
Free will, **M13**: xv; **L13**: 123; **L17**: 5
definition of, **M13**: 318-19
Tolstoy on, **L17**: 383
Frege, Gottlob, **M7**: 440; **L4**: x, xxi; **L14**: xiv, xv; **L16**: xviii
on mathematical number, **M10**: 95
uses definition, **L16**: 155
Dubislav on, **L16**: 161n

Frege, Gottlob (*continued*)
  Russell on, **L16**: 185, 469
Freiburg, University of, **L15**: 324
Freidel, Frank, **L6**: xviiin
Freienfels, Mueller
  describes American mind, **L5**: 51-57
French
  literature, **E3**: 36-42
  language, **E3**: 209-10
  art, **L10**: 192, 290, 319
  criticism, **L10**: 306
French Committee of Relief for Polish Sufferers, **M11**: 282-83
French Military Commission, **M11**: 320
French Philosophical Society, **L5**: 279n, 496, 497, 501, 503
French Primitives and Their Forms (A. Barnes), **L10**: 178n, 360
French Red Cross, **M11**: 250
French Revolution, **M7**: 419; **M8**: 144, 171, 183, 184, 189, 428; **M13**: 117; **L7**: 148, 349; **L8**: 31; **L11**: 7, 80-81, 368; **L13**: 84-85, 110; **L14**: 209-10, 212, 277; **L15**: 217, 252
  significance of, **E4**: 13
  as work of conservative party, **E4**: 104
  and philosophical revolution, **M8**: 176
  causes of, **M8**: 316; **L17**: 439
  excesses of, **L13**: 148
  Rousseau on, **L13**: 149
Frequency distribution, **L12**: 226
  and probability, **L12**: 465-73
Frescoes, **L10**: 226
Freud, Sigmund, **L7**: 448; **L9**: 243; **L10**: viii, xi, xxv; **L15**: xiv, xxi, xxxii
Freudian psychology, **M12**: xxvi; **L2**: 229
Freund, Ernst, **M5**: 496n; **L2**: 36n
Friedlieb, Wilhelm, **E1**: 256
Friend, The (Coleridge), **L5**: 178
Friendship, **L10**: 339
  related to society, **M5**: 121-22; **L7**: 113
  Epicureans on, **M5**: 123; **L7**: 114
  pleasure in, **L7**: 200-201
  and marriage, **L7**: 450-52
Fries, Amos Alfred, **L6**: 124, 503
Fries, Horace S., **L7**: xxx; **L16**: 470
Fries, Jakob Friedrich, **M2**: 215; **L5**: 179, 186; **L16**: 161
Friess, Horace L., **L14**: 307
Froebel, Friedrich Wilhelm, **M1**: 342; **M7**: 211, 289, 378; **M8**: xxxii, 280, 319; **M13**: 401; **L17**: 263
  influence on, **M1**: xviii
  educational principles of, **M1**: 81-85; **M6**: 308, 363, 422; **L8**: 285; **L11**: 244
  on child nature, **M1**: 235
  and activity, **M1**: 341; **M7**: 186, 232, 322; **M8**: 276-77
  compared with Herbart, **M7**: 382-83
  Rousseau's theories applied by, **M8**: 248-49
  on natural development, **M8**: 275-76; **M9**: 123
  on Absolute Whole, **M9**: 62-65, 73
"From Absolutism to Experimentalism," **M9**: ixn; **L9**: xii, xiii, xxiii
Fronczak, Francis E., **M11**: 281
Frontiers of Democracy, **L15**: 343

Fronts
unity needed among, **L17**: 130, 542-44
Frustration, **L13**: 217
Fry, Elizabeth, **L11**: 18
Fry, Roger
on art, **L10**: 92-96, 356
Fukien (Fujian), China, **M12**: 22, 23; **M13**: 128
Fulfillment. *See also* Consummatory experience
as quality of desire, **L7**: 247
Function, **M12**: xviii; **L16**: 308, 325, 334, 336. *See also* Instrumental, **L12**; Operations, **L12**
organization of, **E1**: 107-8
in individuality, **E3**: 303-4
as end of nature, **E4**: 205
moral, **E4**: 232-33
in *Cyclopedia of Education*, **M6**: 364, 365, 466-67
serial or temporal, **M13**: xviii, 378-79
consummatory, **M13**: xix, 380
induction as, **M13**: 64
distinctiveness of, **M13**: 70, 71
definition of, **M13**: 377-78
of community-life, **M13**: 382
expression as, **M13**: 419
in study of society, **M15**: 247-48
form as, **L12**: xx-xxi
biological, **L12**: 32-36
made existential, **L12**: 120, 151-52, 449-50
traits as, **L12**: 269
propositions as, **L12**: 309, 364-65
physical and logical, **L12**: 333, 410-11
laws as, **L12**: 428-32
theory as, **L12**: 468
role in cosmology, **L16**: ix
Carnap on, **L16**: 28n
as terminology, **L16**: 82n
of Cassirer, **L16**: 115n
in inquiry, **L16**: 288, 289, 322
as representative, **L16**: 298
in valuing, **L16**: 348, 356
of activity, **L17**: 154
Functional analysis
interprets experience, **L14**: 132-33, 138-39
Functionalism, **L10**: 119-20, 133, 302-3, 344-45
Functionalist, **L5**: 218-19; **L16**: 465
Functional method
as historical method, **M2**: xv
Functional psychology, **M1**: xiii, 119
Fundamentalism, **M15**: xiii
religious, **M15**: 2-7, 47; **L15**: 189
revival of, **M15**: 50-51
Fundamentals
in religion, **M15**: 3-7
in education, **L6**: 77-78, 100
Fundraising
for Dewey Research Fund, **L14**: 311
Furriers' Union, **L9**: 335
Fustel de Coulanges, Numa Denis, **M5**: 25; **L7**: 24
Future, **M12**: 106, 250; **L14**: 60-61; **L16**: 368, 377, 381
and past, **M15**: 35, 355-56; **L13**: 9
and becoming, **L2**: 65-66
in esthetics, **L10**: xx, xxxii, 24-25, 180-81, 187, 235, 239, 244, 342, 348; **L14**: 113-14
importance of, **L13**: 28, 51
preparation for, **L13**: 29
present and, **L13**: 30, 59; **L14**: 131

Future of America, The (Wells), **M8**: 476
"Future of Liberalism, The," **L11**: xxiv
"Future of the Socialist Party, The" (N. Thomas), **L9**: 66
Futurity, **L2**: 66-67

Gaius, **L2**: 35n
Galicia, **M11**: xii
  Poles in, **M11**: 262-69, 272-73, 281, 290
  future of, **M11**: 272, 273, 277, 329
  revolutionary movement in, **M11**: 288, 298
Galileo, **E1**: 275; **M1**: 168; **M4**: 7; **M6**: 24n, 64; **M7**: 226; **M9**: 303; **M11**: 31; **M13**: 497; **M15**: 47, 48; **L1**: 14, 108, 335, 336, 348; **L4**: xv, 75-78, 230; **L7**: 144, 145; **L15**: xxxii, 25; **L16**: 15, 340, 454
  on nature, **M2**: 147
  experimental method of, **M5**: 154
  on inertia, **L16**: 66-67
  changes effected by, **L16**: 98, 104-5, 158, 370
  observation of, **L16**: 130
  on philosophers, **L16**: 368
Galsworthy, John, **L10**: 190, 360
Galton, Francis
  methods of, **E3**: 43-47
  on images, **L17**: 243, 563
  on numbers, **L17**: 244
Gambling
  in Canton, **L17**: 31-32
Games, **M1**: 231
  in University Elementary School, **M1**: 82-84
  child's goals in, **M1**: 206
  and play, **M1**: 211-12
"Gaming Instinct, The" (W. I. Thomas), **M2**: 45n
Gandhi, Mohandas, **L6**: xxi, 503
Gardner, Percy
  on Greek education, **L17**: 177-80
Garfield, Harry Augustus, **M2**: 62
Garman, Charles Edward, **M4**: 217-18
Garrod, Heathcote William, **L10**: 349, 366
Gary, Ind., public schools, **M7**: 96; **M10**: 175
  vocational education in, **M8**: 120-21, 365-78
  English experiment in, **M8**: 262
  curriculum of, **M8**: 320-28
  social aims of, **M8**: 351
Gassendi, Pierre, **E1**: 275
Gauss, Christian
  on college life, **L6**: 259-62
Gauss, Karl Friedrich, **E5**: 427-28; **M7**: 424
Gay, John, **M3**: 53
Gayley, Charles Mills, **E4**: 121
Gaynor, William Jay, **M8**: 133; **L15**: 356
Gee, Wilson, **L5**: 161n
Geertz, Clifford, **L16**: xxiin
Gefühlston, **E4**: 186-88
Geiger, George Raymond, **L9**: 299, 302; **L14**: 4; **L15**: 101
  Dewey replies to, **L14**: 74-77
  on values, **L15**: 445-52
Gelb, Adhémar, **L16**: 232n
Geldart, W. M., **L2**: 22n
Gellius, Aulus, **M7**: 218
"General Confession, A" (Santayana), **L14**: 295, 298, 306n
General Education Board, **M10**: 123; **L9**: 117
Generalization, **M6**: 359, 388;

M10: 13; M12: 85, 166-67, 193; L4: 100, 108, 121, 174, 197, 249; L8: 135, 236, 249; L13: 144, 212. *See also* Generic propositions, L12; Kinds, L12
Phillips's use of term, E5: 182
and facts, M6: 246; L8: 251-52; L13: 93, 96
and educational mistakes, M6: 256-58; L8: 260, 263-64, 266
in *Cyclopedia of Education*, M7: 209-10
related to science, M9: 234-36
Locke on, M10: 12
two forms of, L12: xxv, 252, 260-62, 352, 422, 428-29
cultural origin of, L12: 49-51
use of, L12: 196-97, 201, 432-33, 491-92
Mill on, L12: 265-66
search for, L13: 123, 205
General Motors Corporation, L5: 59
General Theory of Value (R. Perry), L15: 414
Generation
as aim of science, M2: 7
Generic propositions, L11: 101-4, 119-20, 122, 124-25
character of, M3: 9-11
and universal propositions, L12: xvi-xxi, xxv-xxvi, 253-54, 351-52, 376-78, 438
Generic traits, L16: 388-89
Genesis
related to realism, M6: 483-500
Genetic classification, L12: 295
Genetic-functional method, L14: 147n
Genetic method, M3: xxiii, 299-304; M9: 222
used by Baldwin, E5: 399-400
experimental method as, M2: 4
and ethical theory, L7: xxxii
Genetic Philosophy (D. Hill), E5: 342n, 347
Genetics, L13: 158; L16: 118-19, 363
Geneva, Switzerland, M15: 141, 403
1920 Assembly at, M15: 378, 388, 393
Geneva Disarmament Conference, L6: 460
Genius
Baldwin on, E5: 410-11
"Genius of Pragmatic Empiricism, The" (Brotherston), L15: 71
Genossenschaftslehre (Gierke), L2: 39
Genteel Tradition at Bay, The (Santayana), L6: 271, 272
Gentile, Giovanni, L16: 464
Gentleman
Greek conception of, M5: 107, 110-11, 127n; L7: 98, 101, 118n
medieval ideal of, M5: 136
as class ideal, L7: 143
Gentry, George V., L16: 34n, 210n, 224n, 235n
Genung, John Franklin, L7: 90
Genus, L12: 42-43, 293
Geography, M6: 269; L8: 219-20
study of, E5: 68-70, 230; L11: 214
references on, E5: 338
Dewey's emphasis on, M1: xxi
unity of sciences in, M1: 13
social significance of, M1: 224, 230; M4: 211-12, 280-81; M9: 215-26; L17: 319
imaging power in, L17: 250-52
Geology, M12: 122; L16: 338, 453

Geometry, **L12**: 79, 97, 144, 211. *See also* Mathematics
types of, **M3**: 216-19
teaching of, **M3**: 219-28
deductive reasoning in, **L17**: 246
methods in, **L17**: 296
conception of space in, **L17**: 409
in Greece, **L17**: 434
George, Henry, **M5**: 151, 456; **M15**: 261; **L6**: xviii; **L14**: 363
tribute to, **L3**: 359-60
philosophy of, **L9**: 61-65, 299-302
on social development, **L11**: xxiv, 48, 257
as radical, **L11**: 286
George, Lloyd, **L9**: 400
"George Herbert Mead as I Knew Him," **L6**: xi-xii
George Holmes Howison Lecture, **L6**: 3-21
George Leib Harrison Foundation, **M6**: 12n
Gerard, James W., **L6**: 379
German Enigma, The (Bourdon), **M8**: 191
German language, **M8**: 153-54, 158
contrasted with French, **E3**: 209-10
German Philosophical Classics, **E1**: xxxiii
German Philosophy and Politics, **M8**: ix, 421, 470
Hook's discussion of, **M8**: xxvii-xxxi
Hocking's review of, **M8**: 473-77
German Poland, **M11**: 262-63, 265, 268, 277, 280, 285, 290
German romanticism, **L16**: 373
German Social Democracy (B. Russell), **M12**: 244
Germany, **M11**: 100, 101, 327; **M15**: xviiin, 80, 81, 109, 112, 126, 316, 390, 412; **L13**: 88, 129, 301, 315; **L14**: 365; **L15**: xi, 220, 274, 382n, 384-85, 495
education in, **E3**: 194; **M1**: xvii-xviii; **M7**: 94-97, 379; **M8**: 145; **M9**: 100, 102; **M10**: 179-81, 397-400; **M11**: 54-58, 61, 335; **L13**: 92, 161; **L17**: 310-11
philosophy of, **E4**: 42, 147-49; **M8**: 418-20, 473-77; **M9**: 309-10; **M10**: 225; **M11**: 43, 94, 337, 342, 346, 349, 374; **M12**: 90, 194, 199-200; **L2**: 7n, 27; **L3**: 131; **L5**: 148, 149, 181, 182, 190, 191, 196; **L8**: 10, 31, 37, 38; **L10**: 257n, 296; **L11**: 80; **L14**: 275, 313, 319-23, 331-32
government in, **E4**: 83; **M15**: 61
esthetics in, **E4**: 195-96; **L8**: 360-62
landholding in, **M5**: 24; **L7**: 23
psychology of, **M7**: 137-41; **M12**: 136
Kant's influence on, **M8**: xxvii-xxxi, 146-60, 197-98
literature of, **M8**: 170-71
Fichte's influence on, **M8**: 172-82
feudalism in, **M8**: 185-86
race in, **M8**: 187-88
Hegel related to, **M8**: 191-98, 430, 440-42
militarism of, **M8**: 197; **M11**: 61, 152, 158, 273, 274, 320, 324; **L6**: 460-61

technical trade training in, **M8**: 401
Hitler and, **M8**: 421-46
two-world scheme of, **M8**: 428-29
folk-psychologist school of, **M10**: 57
relation with U.S., **M10**: 158, 252, 256-59; **M11**: 114, 116, 119, 329, 388
social failure in, **M10**: 180-82
invades Belgium, **M10**: 218, 269
idealism of, **M10**: 219, 220, 222; **L3**: 131; **L13**: 149
British misunderstanding of, **M10**: 221-25
and France, **M10**: 222-23; **L13**: 148-50
mentality of, **M10**: 225-33
attitude toward, **M10**: 261, 265, 278
nationalism in, **M10**: 285-88
Santayana on, **M10**: 305-9
and WWI, **M11**: ix, xvi, xvii, 109, 135-38, 157, 161, 177-81, 192, 202, 203, 229, 230; **L6**: 207, 208, 235, 456, 475
Poland's relation with, **M11**: xv, 253, 261-78, 281, 284, 291-96, 309, 313-14, 396, 404
industry in, **M11**: xix, 104, 142, 334; **L7**: 412-13
Russia's relation with, **M11**: 115, 270, 283, 326; **L11**: 332; **L14**: 250-51
propaganda of, **M11**: 119-20, 306, 330
morality of, **M11**: 123, 131, 390
Japan's relation with, **M11**: 157-58, 161, 162, 168-72, 178, 192, 394-95; **M12**: 26, 29-30, 37
related to China, **M11**: 200, 201, 224; **M12**: 34; **M13**: 141-42, 192, 202; **L2**: 176
and Paris Peace Conference, **M12**: 5, 18
and Alsace-Lorraine, **M12**: 60
law in, **L2**: 26-27, 31n, 41
and reparations, **L6**: 179, 337, 358, 368, 372, 453
treaties with, **L6**: 461-62, 474
sanctions in, **L6**: 463
family in, **L7**: 441
Hume's influence in, **L8**: 9
as Paris Pact signatory, **L8**: 13
music of, **L10**: 193
situation in, **L11**: 277, 296, 305, 355-57, 519
church vs. state in, **L13**: 70
freedom in, **L13**: 80, 85
culture in, **L13**: 84, 89, 121
totalitarianism in, **L13**: 85, 92, 147-48, 170, 180
science in, **L13**: 159
influences Mannheim, **L14**: 293
revolution in, **L16**: 390
defeat of, **L16**: 392
capitalist in, **L17**: 22
Nazi, **L17**: 524-25, 542-43
Germany and the Next War (Bernhardi), **M8**: 155, 163n
Gerontocracy, **L2**: 284
Gerson, John, **M2**: 250
Gerson, Louis L., **M11**: 248n, 255n
Gestalt psychology, **M12**: xxvi; **L16**: 67n, 105n, 117n, 233n, 247
Gestures, **L1**: 137-39
Geulincx, Arnold, **M2**: 165-66, 217

Gibbs, Josiah Willard, **L14**: 397; **L16**: 99
G.I. Bill of Rights, **L15**: 283
Giddings, Franklin H., **L15**: xxvi
Gierke, Otto von, **L2**: 25-26, 34n, 39, 41; **L6**: 269
Gifford, Walter S., **L11**: 271, 601
Gifford Lectures
  Dewey's, **L4**: vii-ix, xi, xvi, xviii, xxii; **L14**: xviii
  syllabus for, **L4**: 253-54
  Whitehead's, **L8**: 355
Gilbert, C. B., **E5**: xcv
Gilbert, Katharine, **L15**: 97, 509
Gilbert, William, **L14**: 393, 397
Gilbert de la Porrée, **M2**: 221
Gilbreth, Lillian H., **L11**: 567n, 569, 573-74, 576
Gildersleeve, Basil, **L1**: 184
Gildersleeve, Virginia C., **L14**: 27
Gillen, Francis James, **M5**: 27n, 61n; **L7**: 26n-27n, 56
Gilson, Étienne, **L11**: 127n
Gioberti, Vincenzo, **M2**: 169-70
Giorgione, **L10**: 227
Giotto, **L2**: 114; **L8**: xvii; **L10**: 97
Given
  ambiguity of, **L12**: 127, 227n, 241, 421, 513-15
  facts as, **L12**: 489-91
Gladstone, William Ewart, **M10**: 287; **M13**: 74
Glass, Carter, **L15**: 357
Glass Banking bill, **L6**: 386
Glass-Steagall Banking bill, **L6**: 386
Glazer, Nathan, **L15**: 224-26, 229
Glorious Revolution, **L8**: 9; **L11**: 289
Glory and the Dream, The (Manchester), **L11**: xi
Glover, Katherine
  interview by, **L9**: 386-95
Gneisenau, August, **M8**: 177
Gnostics, **M2**: 203
Goal
  as ideal, **M14**: 178, 182, 187, 195, 198-99
  -object, **L16**: 228-29
God, **E4**: 3, 4, 193; **M12**: 85, 142; **M15**: 56, 330-33; **L9**: 423
  in Spinoza, **E1**: 17, 18
  existence of, **E1**: 404-5; **L9**: 9-10; **L15**: 122-23; **L17**: 93, 95
  conceptions of, **E1**: 406-8; **E4**: 8; **L9**: 439-40; **L17**: 95, 559
  as truth, **E4**: 5
  and revelation, **E4**: 6
  kingdom of, **E4**: 7, 100-101; **L14**: 287
  laws and will of, **E4**: 9, 126-27, 140
  punishment from, **E4**: 110, 114
  fear of, **E4**: 111-13
  demands imposed by, **E4**: 141
  philosophy and, **E4**: 366
  as unifying, **E5**: 30-31
  Yahweh as, **L7**: 82-84
  authority of, **L7**: 135-37; **L17**: 531
  as union of ideal and actual, **L9**: xvi-xvii, 34-36, 435-39
  a God vs. *the*, **L9**: xxi, 213-22
  as name, **L9**: xxii, 29-30, 34-36, 220-21, 294, 416, 417, 431, 435-37, 439
  good related to, **L9**: xxiii, 219-22, 224-26
  belief in, **L9**: 23, 45-46, 215-16, 220, 223-24, 228, 412-13, 415-17
  ideals related to, **L9**: 29-30,

34-36, 218-19, 225, 227-28, 294-95, 430-31
man related to, **L9**: 45-46; **L17**: 529-30
in history, **L9**: 71, 216; **L17**: 532-33
Otto on, **L9**: 214, 215, 224; **L14**: 291
Macintosh's view of, **L9**: 214, 217-19, 227-28, 419
Wieman's view of, **L9**: 214-15, 218-21, 224-28, 412-13, 427, 430-31, 438
activity allied with, **L9**: 432-34, 436
Aubrey on, **L9**: 435
as source of law, **L14**: 116, 120
Fiske on, **L17**: 94
Gödel, Kurt, **L16**: 165n
God the Invisible King (Wells), **M10**: 310-14
Godwin, William, **M13**: 400
Goebbels, Paul J., **L11**: 296
Goethe, Johann Wolfgang von, **E1**: 265, 274, 428; **E3**: 38, 321; **E4**: 194; **M5**: 145; **M6**: 444; **M7**: 289, 290; **M8**: 177; **M9**: 64; **M10**: 226, 306; **L7**: 190; **L8**: 32, 360, 361; **L10**: 321, 323, 360; **L14**: 300
objective idealism of, **M1**: xvii
on nature, **M2**: 148; **L10**: 301, 364
pantheism of, **M2**: 184
related to culture, **M6**: 406, 408-9
on art, **L10**: 285, 363
on Hamlet, **L10**: 318, 365
Goffman, Erving, **L4**: xiii-xiv
Gogh, Theo van, **L10**: 78, 91, 92, 356
Gogh, Vincent van, **L10**: xxi, 75, 78, 91-92, 306, 356
Gogol, Nikolai Vasilyevich, **L10**: xix
Golden Age, **M8**: 188; **L14**: 99-100
Golden Day, The (Mumford), **L3**: 145-47
Golden Rule, **M5**: 302; **L7**: 178, 242, 280, 281; **L13**: 74, 150
as moral rule, **E3**: 100-102
related to sanctions, **L6**: 483
Goldenweiser, Alexander, **L1**: 42n, 71-72, 164-65; **L3**: 11n
Goldschmidt, Richard, **L16**: 119n
Goldsmith, Oliver, **M5**: 192; **L7**: 171
Goldstein, Joseph, **L14**: 240, 243
Goldstein, Kurt, **L16**: 117n
Goldstein, Sidney E., **L9**: 271
Gompers, Samuel, **M10**: 146; **L5**: 342
Goncharov, N. K., **L15**: 373-74
Good, **M14**: 26, 183, 193; **L1**: 57, 80-81, 89-90, 110, 197, 279, 300-326; **L10**: 40, 202, 257, 312, 350-51; **L13**: xi-xii
and bad, **E1**: 340; **L1**: 45-46, 50, 91, 94, 295, 387-89
in Green, **E3**: 28-32, 164-65
theories of, **E3**: 249; **L4**: 30n, 42, 43, 82, 203-28, 242-45
Kant on, **E3**: 290, 296
as realized will, **E3**: 300
and morality, **E4**: 247-49; **M5**: 199-201; **L2**: 83-84, 92-94; **L5**: 281-88; **L7**: xiv, 64, 73
related to nature, **M4**: 15-30
meaning of, **M5**: 12-13; **L7**: xxxi, 265; **L13**: 212; **L15**: 42-45
Hebrew ideal of, **M5**: 103; **L7**: 94

Good (*continued*)
Plato on, **M5**: 128
in animal conduct, **M5**: 189-90
Bentham on, **M5**: 243-46
as quasi-physical, **M5**: 409-10
Descartes on, **M8**: 23-24
state and common, **M12**: xii, xx, 249; **L7**: xii, 347-48; **L13**: 149
single, **M12**: 172-73
intrinsic, **M12**: 177, 197-98
in existence, **M12**: 217; **L9**: xxii, 31-32, 35, 47
immediate, **M13**: 5
knowledge in, **M13**: 286; **L2**: 135, 136, 138
of insight, **M13**: 287
truth as, **M13**: 307
Greeks on, **M13**: 450n; **L7**: 98-99, 104, 115-17, 119-21, 287
uniqueness of, **M14**: 146-53
related to science, **L2**: 129, 132; **L16**: 364-65, 373-74, 377
qualifications of, **L4**: 12, 27-28; **L7**: 271-72
Spinoza on, **L4**: 44
compared with law, **L5**: 497-503
as central in 1908 *Ethics*, **L7**: xi
related to right, **L7**: xi, 215-17, 224-25, 229
pluralistic, **L7**: xxxi
as end, **L7**: 181-82; **L9**: 33, 36
and desire, **L7**: 186-91
and wisdom, **L7**: 191
and pleasure, **L7**: 195-96
Epicurean theory of, **L7**: 199-202
Cynics on, **L7**: 203-4
natural and moral, **L7**: 207
as objective interest, **L7**: 208-12
in utilitarianism, **L7**: 242-43
related to God, **L9**: xxiii, 219-22, 224-26
proponents of, **L9**: 33
Wieman on, **L9**: 412-14
Macintosh on, **L9**: 417-18
Cohen on, **L14**: 408-9
Goodman, Nelson, **L8**: xin; **L14**: xvi, xvii
Goodness, **M14**: 5-7, 16, 48, 157
as moral struggle, **E3**: 372-73, 378-79
in character, **E3**: 382-83; **M14**: 33-36
Goodnow, Frank Johnson, **M8**: 129, 130
Goodnow-Howe Report, **M8**: 133
Goodrich, Caspar F., **M10**: 187
Goodrich, Chauncey, **L5**: 178
Good will, **M14**: 33, 187; **L14**: 73n
Kant on, **M5**: 221-26
transcendentalists on, **M5**: 388
Gordon, Kate, **M3**: 138n
Gorgias of Leontini, **M2**: 154-55
Gorki, Maxim, **L14**: xxi
Gorski, W. O., **M11**: 308, 316
Gothic art, **L10**: 147, 226, 290, 322, 333
Goto, Shimpei, **M11**: 175, 394
Gottsched, Johann Christoph, **E4**: 193
Goudge, Thomas A., **L16**: 10n
on Peirce, **L11**: 86-94
Gouinlock, James
on Dewey's 1925-27 writings, **L2**: ix-xxxvi
Government, **L15**: 252, 366. *See also* Politics; State
democratic, **E1**: 238-39; **L11**: 25, 28, 50-52, 60, 248, 288, 296, 389; **L14**: 264-65

related to sovereignty, **E4**: 80-85, 90
related to morality, **M5**: 425-26, 428-33
ideal, **M12**: 3
Chinese, **M12**: 43-45
and public, **L2**: 216-20, 252-56, 259, 275-79, 282-83
dynastic, **L2**: 285-86
fear of, **L2**: 289, 291-93; **L13**: 111; **L16**: 402-3
related to economics, **L2**: 301-2; **L6**: 180-81, 187-88; **L13**: 102-3
related to society, **L2**: 355-56; **L14**: 93-94
need for new policies in, **L6**: 176-79
special interests and, **L6**: 183
responsibility of, to unemployed, **L6**: 350, 372-80, 386, 390, 406, 440-41; **L9**: 77, 254, 259-60, 262, 278, 283
Roman, **L7**: xxvii, 127-31
church in, **L7**: 136
functions of, **L7**: 332
and labor, **L7**: 377-79, 394-401, 412-22, 432-33
related to Depression, **L9**: 77, 79-80, 82, 264, 269, 277-78; **L11**: 268, 276
control by, **L9**: 88; **L13**: 126, 158, 317
and cultural values, **L9**: 234
actions of Cuban, **L9**: 310-11
of New York City, **L9**: 346-85
related to governed, **L11**: 11, 20-21, 221, 280, 294, 538, 549
Brandeis on, **L11**: 47-48
teaching of, **L11**: 185-86
authoritarian, **L11**: 219, 220, 223, 247, 357, 493, 495, 532
Mann on, **L11**: 226-27, 387
of Great Britain, **L11**: 265, 289, 372, 496
history of, **L11**: 283-87, 289-90, 365, 372-73
anarchist and, **L13**: 32
related to industry, **L13**: 112
Marxist theory of, **L13**: 130
Jefferson on, **L13**: 179; **L14**: 201-3, 209-18
structure of, **L14**: 224-25
international, **L15**: 194, 206-9; **L16**: 360
charges of communism in, **L17**: 140, 561-62
Tolstoy on, **L17**: 382
ideas related to, **L17**: 461
Welling on, **L17**: 523
"Government by Manipulation" (Glazer), **L15**: 224, 229
"Government Liability in Tort" (Borchard), **L2**: 42n
Goya y Lucientes, Francisco José de, **M7**: xviii; **L10**: 98, 132
GPU (Russian State Political Administration), **L11**: 328, 604; **L17**: 501, 570
Grading system
standards in, **E5**: 88; **M1**: 271
references on, **E5**: 332
criticism of, **M3**: 241-48
Graham, Stephen, **L5**: 358
Grammar, **M8**: 263; **L17**: 291, 321
"Grammar, Rhetoric, and Mr. Dewey" (Hutchins), **L11**: 592-97
Grammar school. *See* Elementary school
Grammatical
and logical, **L12**: 284-85, 308

Grand National Assembly (Turkey), **M15**: 277
Granger movement, **L6**: 232, 233
Gratian, **L7**: 137
Gray, Asa, **M4**: 9-10
Gray, J. H., **M5**: 23; **L7**: 22-23
Great Awakening, **M13**: 303
Great Britain, **M12**: xiv; **M15**: xviiin; **L3**: 170; **L6**: 179, 222, 353; **L13**: 163
sovereignty in, **E4**: 79
philosophy in, **E4**: 141-45, 147-49; **M9**: 308-9; **M11**: 43, 94, 115, 345, 349, 359; **L8**: 8-11, 38; **L11**: 76-80, 155
esthetics in, **E4**: 195-96
education in, **M10**: 178-79, 181; **M11**: 58-59; **L11**: 356; **L15**: 308-9; **L17**: 27, 232
on WWI, **M10**: 219
Germany's relation with, **M10**: 220-21, 223-25
and nationality rights, **M10**: 287
diplomacy of, **M11**: xiii, 177
industry in, **M11**: xix, 73-74, 78-85, 104; **L7**: 412-13
politics in, **M11**: 18-40, 114-15, 120, 389; **L13**: 130, 147
social upheaval in, **M11**: 87-88, 91, 393
Japan's relation with, **M11**: 113, 153-54, 169, 192; **M12**: 35, 61-63; **M13**: 77, 121, 125-26, 165, 177-79, 191, 201, 212-15, 219
related to U.S., **M11**: 116, 151; **M12**: 5, 75; **M13**: 91, 173, 179, 180, 181, 201, 207, 272, 273, 410; **M15**: 155; **L2**: 177; **L15**: 340, 354
in League of Nations, **M11**: 140, 151-52, 163
and China, **M11**: 190, 219; **L17**: 30
as world power, **M11**: 192, 196
in drug traffic, **M11**: 235-40
on Polish question, **M11**: 251, 261, 267, 279-83, 292, 293, 301, 302, 308, 328
Far East policy of, **M12**: 6; **M13**: 176, 199, 409
and Paris Peace Conference, **M12**: 18
opportunism of, **M13**: xxiv, 200
and international laws, **M15**: 106, 380, 386, 411
and Turkey, **M15**: 129, 139
on Tunis and Morocco, **M15**: 388-89
and sanctions, **L6**: 197-98
on Egypt, **L6**: 219, 468-69
and interallied debts, **L6**: 372
utilitarianism in, **L7**: 251
women in, **L7**: 443
divorce in, **L7**: 446
empiricism in, **L8**: 8-11, 38
in outlawry movement, **L8**: 13, 17
taxes in, **L9**: 284
consumers in, **L9**: 400
poetry in, **L10**: 157-58
art in, **L10**: 336
liberalism in, **L11**: xxviii, 6-15, 17-18, 282-84, 290; **L13**: 81-82, 137
Marx on, **L11**: 59n
government in, **L11**: 265, 289, 372, 496; **L15**: 251-52; **L16**: 401, 403
industrial class in, **L13**: 83, 107, 122
rebellion against, **L13**: 99-100, 102
housing in, **L13**: 313

science in, **L13**: 370
totalitarian forces in, **L15**: 182
and USSR, **L15**: 298, 342-44, 347-48, 353, 494-95
capitalist in, **L17**: 22
natural law in, **L17**: 98-99
Reform Bill of, **L17**: 492
Great Chain of Being, The (Lovejoy), **M15**: xii
"Great Community, The" (Royce), **L17**: 89, 559
Great Depression. *See* Depression, economic
Great Powers, **M15**: 139, 141, 142; **L6**: 457, 459, 466, 467, 479, 480. *See also* Allies
interested in China, **M13**: 77, 137-38, 226
and Consortium loans, **M13**: 90-91
on Open Door, **M13**: 161
agreement among, **M13**: 162-63, 212
Great Society, **L5**: xx
Lippmann on, **L2**: 218, 219, 404
and lack of community, **L2**: 296, 314-15, 324, 327, 333, 350
Great Society, The (Wallas), **L2**: 295
Great Technology, The (Rugg), **L14**: 428
Great Tradition
Nock on, **L6**: 286-89
Great Transformation, The (Polanyi), **L15**: 215, 510
Great Wall of China, **M13**: 195
Great War. *See* World War I
Greco, El, **L10**: 98, 315, 358; **L17**: 129
Greece, **M15**: 123, 132. *See also* Greeks
on responsibility of objects, **E4**: 38-39
and birth of democracy, **E4**: 99
theories of knowing in, **E4**: 125
and community welfare, **E4**: 133
conception of beauty in, **E4**: 190
landholding customs in, **M5**: 24; **L7**: 23-24
science in, **M5**: 109; **M12**: 133; **L1**: 23, 65, 203; **L7**: 100-101; **L14**: 389, 392; **L15**: 60, 268-69, 312; **L17**: 411, 434-35
class system of, **M9**: 260-63
culture and philosophy in, **M9**: 297; **L8**: 19-22, 24, 28, 30, 32, 35
authority of experience in, **M12**: 125; **L17**: 433, 435-36
on religion, **M12**: 140; **L17**: 182
Turkey's relation with, **M15**: 139-41, 144-45, 148, 402; **L2**: 191
pagan, **L3**: 6
civilization of, **L3**: 25-26; **L10**: 252, 330-33, 340
methods of inquiry in, **L3**: 66
super-empirical reality in, **L13**: 264
manual labor in, **L15**: 234, 249
education in, **L15**: 262-66; **L17**: 171-73, 175-86, 226-29
Benda on, **L15**: 386n
progress of, **L17**: 172
city-state in, **L17**: 175
subordination of individual in, **L17**: 231-32
Greek
language, **E5**: 253
literature, **M9**: 290

Greek (*continued*)
cosmology, **L1**: 76-81, 101-3, 137
Greek art, **E4**: 191; **M5**: 106-7, 109; **M12**: 133; **L4**: 203; **L7**: 97-98, 100, 126; **L10**: 231
concept of, **L10**: 10, 13, 31, 114-15, 191, 193, 298
quality of, **L10**: 147, 175, 237, 238, 252, 256, 321, 331-34, 338, 343
Greek logic
development of, **L8**: 3-6
essence in, **L12**: 18, 130, 138-40, 153, 251, 260, 357, 404, 418n
change in, **L12**: 88-94, 212
nature in, **L12**: 94-98
discourse in, **L12**: 98-99
Being in, **L12**: 189, 420, 517
Greek-medieval ontology, **L16**: 334-35, 449-50
Greek-medieval science, **L16**: 159, 337n-38n, 370, 452
Greek Orthodox church, **L5**: 355-62
Greek philosophy, **M11**: 42, 45, 51-52, 337, 342, 346; **L1**: 162; **L3**: 121; **L4**: 13, 14, 46; **L5**: 165; **L6**: 426-28; **L10**: 46, 153, 202, 231; **L11**: 6, 69-75; **L14**: 35, 146; **L15**: 48, 159, 216, 263, 265. *See also* Aristotle; Plato; Socrates
moral system of, **E4**: 138-40, 224-25; **M5**: 107-19; **L5**: 497-99; **L7**: 98-110
Christian and Roman influences on, **E5**: 9-11
on knowledge, **M3**: 121; **L4**: xiv-xvi, 17, 24, 40-44, 79, 88, 148, 164
on nature, **M4**: 35; **L4**: 43, 73, 184
on ideal, **M5**: 128-30; **L7**: 119-21
concept of personality in, **M5**: 130-32; **L7**: 121-23
on wisdom, **M5**: 375-76
on mind, **M9**: 300-301; **L1**: 163
on non-being, **M10**: 12
on existence, **M10**: 40
origin of, **M13**: xviii, 364
on experience, **L4**: 21, 22, 23
observation in, **L4**: 71-74
metaphysics of, **L4**: 96, 97
on reason, **L4**: 170
cosmology in, **L14**: 192-95, 199
characteristics of, **L14**: 316
Cohen on, **L14**: 392-93, 398-99
influence of, **L15**: 264, 312, 334, 336
nature of, **L16**: 157, 159, 271, 407, 410
vs. physics, **L16**: 303-7
Greeks, **M12**: 84-85, 87-88, 117, 118, 152; **L13**: 40
customs of, **M5**: 23-24; **L7**: 23-24
on evil, **M5**: 97-98; **L7**: 89
on emotions, **M5**: 101-2; **L7**: 92-93
group authority of, **M5**: 106, 108-17; **L7**: 97, 99-108
individuality among, **M5**: 106-7, 121-22; **L7**: 97-98, 113
on gentleman, **M5**: 107, 110-11, 127n; **L7**: 98, 101, 118n
on good, **M5**: 107-8, 113, 124-26, 128-30; **L4**: 45; **L7**: xxvii, 98-99, 104, 115-17, 119-21, 287
on propriety, **M5**: 110-11; **L7**: 101
on beauty, **M5**: 111; **L7**: 102

commerce and politics of, **M5**: 112-13; **L7**: 103-4
on problem of life, **M5**: 118-19; **L7**: 109-10
on nature, **M5**: 120-24, 128; **L7**: 111-14, 119
on character, **M5**: 130-32; **L7**: 121-23
ethical theory of, **M12**: 172
on human nature, **L6**: 32-34, 37
and culture, **L6**: 46-47
and freedom, **L6**: 431
on wisdom, **L7**: 203-4
Green, Thomas Hill, **E1**: xxv, 122, 123; **E3**: 182, 239; **E4**: xvi, xvii, 263; **E5**: 137; **M3**: 56; **M4**: 227; **M5**: 4; **M6**: 94, 392; **M8**: xxvi; **L2**: 6, 15, 147n; **L5**: 152; **L11**: xxviii, 19-20; **L12**: 156, 510; **L17**: 5
on consciousness, **E1**: 153-54
Dewey's studies of, **E3**: xxvi-xxix
character and philosophy of, **E3**: 14-35
on Kantianism, **E3**: 74, 137, 159-60
moral theory of, **E3**: 159-73; **E4**: 43, 44; **E5**: 25; **M3**: 43; **M4**: 43-44; **M5**: 208, 262-63, 385
on self, **E3**: 160-62; **E4**: 51-52, 257
and theory of sovereignty, **E4**: 70-72, 75, 76n
on judging others, **E4**: 274
contrasted with D'Arcy, **E5**: 26-28
on reality, **M4**: 50; **M6**: 109n
on psychological hedonism, **M5**: 246-47
objective idealism of, **L16**: 115n
Green, William, **L9**: 252
Greenback party, **L6**: 232, 233
Greenwich, Conn., Little School in the Woods, **M8**: 222, 266-67
Gresham's law, **L15**: 502
Grey, Edward, **M15**: 380
Grey, George, **M2**: 45n
Grief
compared with joy, **E4**: 158, 159, 168
as emotion, **E4**: 172-73
Grievance Committee. *See also* Teachers Union
address on report of, **L9**: 315-19
members of, **L9**: 320
defendants before, **L9**: 320-22, 326-30, 335-37
on unions, **L9**: 323-25, 330, 333-35
conflict in, **L9**: 330-32
and dual unionism, **L9**: 335-37
and communism, **L9**: 338-42
recommendations of, **L9**: 342-45
Griffith, Coleman R., **L16**: 63n
Grimm, Jakob, **L1**: 42
Groos, Karl, **M7**: 319
Gross, Esther S., **L9**: 320, 345
Grössler, Hermann, **E5**: 149-50
Grote, George, **M5**: 166
on Greek kinship groups, **M5**: 24; **L7**: 24
on custom, **M5**: 161, 300; **M6**: 413
on Nomos, **M6**: 17-18
Grotius, Hugo, **E3**: 91; **E4**: 216; **M11**: 34; **M15**: 55, 92; **L6**: 35; **L8**: 8, 35; **L14**: 120
and moral philosophy, **E4**: 142-43
on reason, **M3**: 51

Grotius, Hugo (*continued*)
on natural law, **M4**: 41; **M15**: 56
on sociability of man, **M6**: 366
on international laws, **M15**: 54
Ground
as used in Dewey's *Logic*, **L12**: 113-16, 119-20, 134, 140-41, 144-45, 150-51, 174-75, 181, 183-84, 188-89, 225, 230-31, 245, 250, 263-64, 266-67, 288, 304-5, 310, 332, 339-40, 422, 465, 484-85
for carings-for, **L16**: 355
Group action
of animals, **L3**: 13
of tribe, **L3**: 14
Group morality
forces which destroy, **M5**: 76-87; **L7**: 70-80
Groups
primitive, **M5**: 23-26, 61-65; **L7**: 22-25, 56-60
division of, **M5**: 26-27, 36-37, 57, 66, 82, 95; **L7**: 26-27, 35-36, 52, 60-61, 75, 87
ownership by, **M5**: 29-31, 82; **L7**: 28-30, 76, 129
political aspect of, **M5**: 31-34, 62-63; **L7**: 30-33, 57-58; **L17**: 112-13
religion of, **M5**: 34-36; **L7**: 33-35
moral significance of, **M5**: 37-39, 54-57, 106-7; **L7**: 36-37, 49-52, 97-98, 151-52, 299-300
values and defects of, **M5**: 69-72; **L7**: 63-66
conflicts of, **M5**: 74-88, 112-17; **L7**: 68-80, 103-8, 164-66, 325-27
as social concept, **M15**: 236-39
influence of economics on, **M15**: 240-41; **L7**: 71
and state, **L2**: 238-39, 252, 279-81
local, **L2**: 261
vs. individual, **L13**: 33-34, 108
ends of, **L13**: 75, 229
functional basis of, **L13**: 177
pressure of, **L13**: 206
Groves, Ernest, **L7**: 451-52
Growth, **L1**: 209-11
continuity in, **E5**: 87; **L13**: 19-20, 28, 50
stages of, **E5**: 331; **M6**: xxiv, xxvi
Baldwin on, **E5**: 403-4
related to education, **M1**: 73-80; **M9**: 46-51, 54-57; **M13**: xv-xvi, 402-5; **L9**: 195-98; **L13**: 15, 21, 30, 53, 56
related to child-study, **M1**: 133-35; **M3**: 299, 302
moral, **M5**: 10-17; **M12**: 181; **L7**: 12-14, 22
Rousseau on, **M8**: 214-17
related to environment, **M9**: 4-5, 14
habits related to, **M9**: 51-54; **L17**: 303
toward absolute goal, **M9**: 59-65
irregularity of, **M9**: 123
as requiring time, **M9**: 134
related to vocational choice, **M9**: 320-21
of knowledge, **M12**: 96-97, 185
of industry, **L7**: 141-44, 149-50
freedom needed for, **L13**: 39, 78
impulses affect, **L13**: 41
of government, **L13**: 102
importance of, **L17**: 65
prolonged infancy aids, **L17**: 256-58
play influences, **L17**: 263

Growth: A Study of Johnny and Jimmy (McGraw), **L11**: 510-14
Growth of the Brain, The (Donaldson), **M9**: 123
Grube, Wilhelm, **L17**: 291, 563-64
Grudin, Louis, **L10**: 311, 365
Guadalajara, Mexico, **L2**: 209
Guam, **M13**: 212, 215
Guardi, Francesco, **L10**: 134
Guercino, **L10**: 147
Guests
  customs regarding, **M5**: 67-68; **L7**: 62-63
Guichard, Louis, **L6**: 476n
Guidance
  education as, **M9**: 28-45
Guide to the Works of John Dewey (Boydston), **L17**: xii
Guiding principles, **L12**: 19-21, 158, 316, 336, 465
Guizot, François Pierre Guillaume, **L5**: 147
Guterman, Norbert, **L9**: 293, 423-25
Gwentian Code, **M5**: 34n; **L7**: 32n

Haack, Susan, **L6**: xvn
Habakkuk, **M5**: 102; **L7**: 94
Habit, **M14**: 19; **M15**: 265; **L1**: 235; **L8**: 87; **L12**: 146, 167, 224, 467; **L15**: 151; **L16**: 359, 364
  as function of association, **E2**: 100-104
  and emotions, **E4**: 162-63, 187; **E5**: 130-31; **M14**: 21
  related to imitation, **E4**: 198; **L17**: 308-9
  and consciousness, **E4**: 200
  need for reconstitution of, **E5**: 47-48
  and education, **E5**: 143; **M13**: 323-24
  principle of, **E5**: 307-8; **L12**: 21
  as custom, **M5**: 54, 58, 60; **L7**: xiv, xxi, 49, 53, 65
  in moral behavior, **M5**: 309-11
  formation of, **M6**: 232; **M10**: 14; **L1**: 213-15; **L8**: 89, 185-86; **L11**: 230-34, 513; **L17**: 82, 205, 298-303
  blind, **M9**: 34-35
  as expression of growth, **M9**: 51-54
  related to knowledge, **M9**: 349-50; **L4**: 69, 109, 141, 166, 183, 190, 209, 224, 246, 247, 250; **L13**: 162
  and principles, **M9**: 362-63; **M14**: 164
  Peirce on, **M10**: 77; **L11**: 107-8
  effects of, **M13**: 244, 252, 282; **L7**: 14, 185, 204, 207-9; **L12**: 19-20; **L17**: 205-6
  and meaning, **M13**: 389
  social effects of, **M14**: x-xiv; **L11**: 36, 133-34, 379
  as art or ability, **M14**: 15, 47-48, 51, 118
  related to conduct, **M14**: 15-16; **L13**: 162, 292
  and thought, **M14**: 25-26, 48-50, 121-26, 128
  nature of, **M14**: 29-31; **L13**: 18-19, 96, 108, 123, 221, 287; **L17**: 204-5
  diversity of, **M14**: 66-67
  limitations of, **M14**: 91; **L17**: 79, 299, 303
  political effects of, **L2**: 273, 341; **L9**: 234
  and individual, **L2**: 334-36; **L7**: 170-71, 205, 206
  and purpose, **L7**: 185-86

Habit (*continued*)
related to character, **L9**: 186-87
limits art, **L10**: 161, 178, 253, 273-76, 350
Greeks on, **L11**: 70, 71, 73-74; **L17**: 435
as basis of organic learning, **L12**: 38-39
Hume on, **L12**: 244, 250; **L14**: 131
inertia of, **L13**: 85
verbal, **L13**: 96
change in, **L13**: 97, 150, 186, 291; **L17**: 303
forms beliefs, **L13**: 167
in science, **L13**: 284
routine vs. intelligent, **L14**: 7
source of law in, **L14**: 118-19
James on, **L14**: 159
and human nature, **L14**: 258-60
as disposition, **L16**: 26n
in semiotic, **L16**: 233
as context, **L16**: 304-5, 329-30
and attention, **L17**: 207-9, 304
formation by animals, **L17**: 300-301
related to instinct, **L17**: 305-7, 324
Habituation, **M6**: 360; **M9**: 51-52, 57
Hadley, Arthur Twining, **M5**: 425n, 436, 503n
Haeckel, Ernst Heinrich, **M2**: 149; **M7**: 276; **M15**: 330; **L1**: 55; **L9**: 37
Hagan, James J., **L9**: 371-72
Hague, The, **M11**: 128, 130, 237, 390; **M15**: 401, 403, 415-16
Hague Conference
Second (1907), **M15**: 92, 386
First (1899), **M15**: 385
Hague Tribunal, **M15**: 93, 95, 123, 385-86, 401-2
Hahn, Lewis E.
on intuitionalism and absolutism, **E1**: xxiii-xxxviii
on Dewey's 1907-9 writings, **M4**: ix-xxxiv
on Dewey's 1916-17 writings, **M10**: ix-xxxix
Haidar Pasha (Haydarpaşa), Turkey, **M15**: 290
Hailmann, William Nicholas, **E5**: 448
Haiti, **L5**: 440
Haldane, John Scott, **E1**: xxv
vitalistic viewpoint of, **M8**: 449-59
Haldane, Richard Burdon, **E1**: xxv; **L5**: 152
Hale, Robert L., **M13**: 19n
Hale Telescope, **L16**: 374, 471
Hall, Everett W.
criticizes *Experience and Nature*, **L3**: 82-91, 401-14
Hall, Frank Haven, **L17**: 246, 563
Hall, G. Stanley, **E1**: xxv; **E2**: xxiii; **E5**: xiii; **M1**: xiii; **M3**: xxiii; **M7**: 137-41; **L11**: 243; **L17**: 507, 571
reviews Dewey's *Psychology*, **E1**: xxx-xxxii
on Dewey's system, **E2**: xxv
culture-epoch theory of, **M1**: xvn; **M6**: xxiv, xxvi
influence of German objective idealism on, **M1**: xviii
Hall, Mrs. Winfield S., **M1**: 186-87
Haller, Jozef, **M11**: 269, 275, 280
Hallgren, Mauritz A., **L6**: 439
Hallis, Frederick, **L6**: 268-70
Hallowell, Robert, **L6**: 178
Hall-Quest, Alfred L., **L13**: 375-76
Hallucination, **L13**: 335; **L15**: 65

related to consciousness, **M10**: 25-27
neo-realists on, **M10**: 39
Halsted, George Bruce
on teaching geometry, **M3**: 216-28
Hambidge, Jay, **L10**: 321
Hamilton, Alexander, **L6**: 67; **L11**: 372; **L13**: 107, 300, 403; **L14**: 203; **L15**: xiv-xv
Hamilton, Gail, **E3**: 196
Hamilton, Walton H., **L6**: xix
Hamilton, William, **E1**: 19, 49; **E3**: 191; **M2**: 154, 156, 171, 254, 261; **M3**: 62n; **M4**: 309-10
Hamlet (Shakespeare), **M5**: 28, 64; **L6**: 497; **L7**: 27, 58; **L10**: 29, 318-19; **L14**: 111
Hammurabi, **M5**: 82, 101n; **M12**: xxiii; **L7**: 75, 92n, 440
Hand, Learned, **L11**: 592
Handlin, Lilian
on Dewey's 1918-19 writings, **M11**: ix-xx
Handlin, Oscar
on Dewey's 1918-19 writings, **M11**: ix-xx
Handwriting, **M10**: 117
Hangchow (Hangzhou), China, **M11**: xviii; **M12**: 253; **M13**: 105
Hankow (Wuhan), China, **M13**: 105; **L6**: 205
Hankow-Canton railway, **M13**: 122, 124
Hankow-Hong Kong railway, **M13**: 124, 166
Hankow-Peking railway, **M11**: 231
Hanna, Marcus Alonzo, **L5**: 342
Hanover Institute (Hanover, N.H.), **L15**: 310
Hans, Nicholas, **L6**: 291-92
Hanson, Florence Curtis, **L9**: 124
Hanus Survey (Committee on School Inquiry), **M8**: 129
Happiness, **M4**: 45; **M12**: 143, 144, 182-83; **M13**: 286; **L10**: 78; **L11**: 12
and pleasure, **E2**: 253-54
individual vs. social, **E3**: 288-89
related to desire, **E4**: 265-66; **M5**: 249; **L7**: 247
as end and standard, **E4**: 282-87; **M5**: 243-46; **L7**: 245-48, 281
as eudaimonism, **M5**: 212
utilitarian concept of, **M5**: 241-43, 251-56; **L7**: 242-44
two views of, **M5**: 256-59
and social ends, **M5**: 274
private property related to, **M5**: 435-37
hedonism on, **M7**: 212
attainment of, **L7**: 156, 248; **L17**: 387-88
nature of, **L7**: 198-99, 302
and character, **L7**: 244-45
in marriage, **L7**: 452
Jefferson on, **L13**: 177-79
Tolstoy on, **L17**: 388
Hapsburg dynasty, **M11**: 273
Hara, Takashi, **M11**: 152, 164; **M13**: 87, 255, 259
Hara ministry (Japan), **M12**: 31
Hard, William, **M13**: 495
Hardenberg, Karl, **M8**: 177
Harding, Warren G., **M13**: 210, 215, 258; **M15**: xv, 85, 397, 405; **L17**: 559
and World Court, **M15**: 393, 395, 408
Hardy, Milton H., **L17**: 324, 564
Hardy, Ruth G., **L9**: 320
Hardy, Thomas, **L15**: xv
Hare, Richard, **M5**: xi

Hari-kiri, **M5**: 64; **L7**: 59
Harlan, John M., **L7**: 396
Harmony, **M6**: 420
  as goal of universe, **E1**: 217-18
  preestablished, **E1**: 295-97, 352, 430-31, 433, 434; **M2**: 212; **M7**: 276, 293; **L5**: 377
  in Leibniz's philosophy, **E1**: 411-13
  in sounds, **E2**: 63
  and beauty, **E2**: 272-73
  in *Cyclopedia of Education*, **M7**: 210-11
  natural, **M14**: 110, 115, 205
  as esthetic quality, **L10**: 20-23, 46, 50, 92, 93, 99, 120, 122, 127, 136, 153, 166, 190, 236, 244, 246, 270, 295-96, 335
Harper, William Rainey, **E5**: 433n, 442n; **L7**: vii
  on academic freedom, **M2**: 60-61
  memo on coeducation to, **M2**: 105-7
  memo on pedagogy to, **L17**: 485-86
Harrington, James, **E4**: 217; **M11**: 24n, 27
Harris, William Torrey, **E3**: xvi; **E5**: xiii, xx, 165, 173, 348; **M1**: 341, 342; **M3**: xxv; **M6**: 94; **L5**: xxii; **L17**: 88, 559
  influences Dewey, **E1**: xxiv; **L5**: 150
  on art education, **E5**: xciv-xcv
  on interest, **E5**: 147
  opposes Herbartian correlation, **E5**: 167
  and physiological psychology, **E5**: 275-77
  on educational psychology, **E5**: 372-85
  German objective idealism influences, **M1**: xviii
  and use of psycho-physical mechanism, **M1**: 142
  on James, **M6**: 101
  on coeducation, **M6**: 156
  on periods of growth, **L17**: 284, 563
  on spiritual and material wealth, **L17**: 313
Harrison, Frederic, **E3**: 125
Harrison, George Leib, **M6**: 12n
Harrison, Jane, **L5**: 165
Hart, H. L. A., **L14**: xxiv
Hart, Joseph K., **L3**: 342-45; **L6**: 420, 421
Hart, Merwin K., **L14**: 371, 373, 427-29
Hart, Robert, **M13**: 95
Harte, Bret, **M12**: 15
Hartley, David, **E4**: 145, 147; **M3**: 54-55
Hartmann, Eduard von, **E4**: 195; **M2**: 181, 184, 189; **M6**: 167; **M7**: 296
  as founder of psychology, **M7**: 137-41
Hartshorne, Charles, **L4**: 199n; **L6**: 273-77; **L11**: 87n, 108n, 421, 479, 484; **L14**: 308; **L15**: 144n-52n; **L16**: 166
Hartung, Frank E., **L16**: 307n
Harvard Teachers Association, **M1**: 258; **L6**: 112n
Harvard University, **M8**: xx, 129; **M15**: 228; **L3**: 3n, 385n; **L6**: 75n, 273; **L10**: 7; **L11**: 127, 129, 484, 488; **L15**: 351
  indebtedness to, **E3**: 198-99
  educational plan of, **E3**: 201
  Divinity School, **L17**: 135, 545-47
Harvey, George, **L9**: 379; **L14**: 239

Harvey, William, **E1**: 49; **M13**: 497; **L11**: 279; **L14**: 393, 395
Hastings, John A., **L9**: 365
Hatch, Edwin, **M9**: 288
Hatch, Roy, **L14**: 371
Hate, **L13**: 128, 152
  as antithesis of love, **E2**: 249, 293-95
  dangers of, **L13**: xv, 88
Hauriou, Maurice, **L6**: 269, 270
Havana, Cuba, **L9**: 311
Havas news service, **M11**: 151
Hawaii
  class system of, **M5**: 27; **L7**: 27
Hawley-Smoot Tariff Act, **L5**: 436; **L6**: 164-65, 172, 237, 241
Hawthorne, Nathaniel, **L10**: 320; **L11**: 442-43
Hawthorne investigation, **L5**: 238-39, 506
Hawthorne Works, Western Electric Co. (Chicago), **L5**: 506
Hay, John, **M11**: 206, 228; **M12**: 61; **M13**: 90, 167, 273, 274; **M15**: 391; **L2**: 174
Haydon, A. Eustace, **L11**: 583-84
Hayes, Carlton J. H., **M11**: 406; **L2**: 341n; **L7**: 367
Haym, Rudolf, **M8**: 192
Haynes, Fred E., **L6**: 232
Hazlitt, Henry
  critiques Ayres, **L15**: 359-60, 502-6
Hazlitt, William
  on pleasure and good, **M5**: 246, 279n; **L7**: 195
  on excitement, **M5**: 367n
  on romanticism, **L10**: 287-88, 363
Health, **M12**: 174-76, 181; **L13**: 40, 232, 311, 344; **L16**: 292
  of college women, **E1**: 64-66, 70, 77-79; **L17**: 7-9, 553
  of students in Turkey, **M15**: xxi-xxii, 293-94
  consciousness of, **M15**: 42-43; **L13**: 332
  opposed to cure, **M15**: 43, 44
  in Mexico, **L2**: 206-10
  related to schools, **L6**: 132-33; **L17**: 513-14
  mental, **L6**: 133-34, 138-40; **L17**: 514
  Depression affects, **L6**: 342-43
  and birth control, **L6**: 388
  as ideal, **L13**: 183; **L17**: xxxiii
  cause of ill, **L17**: 9
  conference on child, **L17**: 511-19
  aims, **L17**: 513
Heard, Gerald, **L6**: 278-79
Hearing, **L10**: 241-44
  sensation of, **E2**: 59-63, 224-25
  and reflex arc concept, **E5**: 100-102
Hearn, William
  on group land possession, **M5**: 29; **L7**: 28
  on early justice, **M5**: 408-9
Hearst, William Randolph
  attacks education, **L11**: 165, 344, 351, 378
  and freedom of expression, **L11**: 269
Heat
  theories of, **L16**: 98-99
Hebert, Felix, **L6**: 339
Hebrews, **M7**: 290; **L3**: 18. *See also* Jews
  customs of, **E4**: 87
  on life, **M5**: 81, 103; **L7**: 75, 94-95
  moral development of, **M5**: 89-105; **L7**: 82-97, 126

Hebrews (*continued*)
on character, **M5**: 101-2; **L7**: 92-94
theology of, **L4**: 42-46, 49, 50
prophets of, **L8**: 357
legends of, **L10**: 321
Hedonism, **M9**: 359
related to pleasure, **E3**: 249-61, 267-68, 283-84; **E4**: 267-72, 276-78; **M5**: 119, 212; **L7**: 110
Kant and, **E3**: 292-93; **L7**: 220
and theory of value, **E4**: 262-64
and happiness, **E4**: 265-66
on desire, **E4**: 267; **M5**: 246-47
and intention, **E4**: 273-74
and theory of motives, **E4**: 275-79; **M5**: 213
theory of obligation of, **E4**: 329-36
criticized, **E5**: 352-54; **L7**: 192-99, 209, 289
of Cyrenaics, **M5**: 119; **L7**: 110
universalistic, **M5**: 251-52, 261
in *Cyclopedia of Education*, **M7**: 211-13, 360
as motivation to philosophic reflection, **M15**: 325-28, 336
utilitarianism and, **L7**: 240-45, 285
Hedonistic calculus, **M14**: 142
Hedonistic paradox, **M7**: 212
Hedonistic Theories from Aristippus to Spencer (John Watson), **E5**: 350, 352-54
Hedonists, **M7**: 363; **M15**: 233-34; **L2**: 139
Hegel, Georg Wilhelm Friedrich, **E1**: xxxii, xxxiii, 420; **E3**: 91, 174; **E4**: xvi, xvii, xviii, 194, 215; **E5**: 137, 150, 400; **M3**: xxiii, 310; **M6**: 167, 444; **M7**: 289, 357, 415; **M8**: xxx-xxxi, 140, 142, 145, 176, 184-85, 421, 423, 474; **M10**: 5, 98, 306; **M11**: 43, 384; **M12**: 90, 140-41; **M14**: 214; **L1**: xvii, 37, 49; **L2**: 279; **L3**: 103, 108, 375, 388; **L5**: 148, 186; **L6**: 31; **L8**: xin, 38, 269; **L11**: xxv, 400; **L13**: 80; **L14**: xi, xiv, 29, 186, 313; **L17**: 386
influences Dewey, **E1**: xxiv-xxx, xxxvi; **E3**: xxi, xxiii-xxiv, xxvi; **L5**: xxii, 152-55
philosophy of, **E1**: 39, 153, 164-66; **E4**: 147; **E5**: 147; **M2**: x, 148; **M15**: 58, 60
negative in, **E1**: 44-45
and G. Morris, **E3**: 7, 9; **M10**: 110-13
Seth on, **E3**: 56-62, 192
compared with Kant, **E3**: 72, 134-40
on Christianity, **E3**: 187-90; **L8**: 31; **L17**: 374, 565
F. Johnson on, **E3**: 192-93
related to emotions, **E4**: 171n
on interest, **E5**: 141-42
idealism of, **M1**: xvii; **M6**: x; **M7**: 138, 227, 231-32, 299; **M13**: 418-19; **L8**: 9-11
on *Verstand*, **M1**: 156
Dewey compared with, **M2**: xv; **L16**: 426
on necessity, **M2**: 152-53
nihilism derived from, **M2**: 154
on non-being, **M2**: 158
on optimism, **M2**: 176
pantheism of, **M2**: 184
on phenomenology, **M2**: 189
on posit, **M2**: 207
on understanding and reason, **M2**: 261, 333

on ethics, **M3**: 55-56
on belief and reality, **M3**: 86n
on reason, **M4**: 43; **M9**: 309
moral theory of, **M5**: 208
dialectic of, **M6**: 170, 422; **M10**: 420; **M11**: 91; **L11**: 33, 51, 55, 60; **L13**: 119, 401; **L17**: 444
on culture, **M6**: 406, 409
and self-consciousness, **M7**: 345
and truth, **M7**: 413
on race, **M8**: 187
as realist, **M8**: 191; **M13**: 413
influences Germany, **M8**: 191-98, 430, 440-42
on Absolute Whole, **M9**: 62-65, 73
on state, **M9**: 102; **M10**: 221, 224; **M12**: 188-89, 194, 195; **L2**: 39, 40
as philosopher, **M10**: 223, 226; **M12**: 221; **L16**: xiv, xvi, 464
on logic, **M12**: 157
vs. Fichte, **L4**: 50-52
and study of mind, **L6**: 489
disciple of Plato, **L8**: 32
conceptualism of, **L8**: 361
on art, **L10**: 156
on universe, **L10**: 293
compared with Marx, **L13**: 119-21, 354
absolute spirit of, **L13**: 149
Cohen on, **L14**: 394, 398-400
Hocking on, **L14**: 422, 424
Hegelianism, **L6**: xii, xiii; **L14**: 172
Hegel's Philosophy of Mind (W. Wallace), **E5**: 342n, 343-44
Heidbreder, Edna, **M1**: xiii
Heidegger, Martin, **M3**: xxiv; **L3**: xviii; **L8**: xin; **L14**: xviii-xix
compared with Dewey, **L4**: ix, xii, xvii
Heidelberg, Germany
International Congress of Philosophy at, **M7**: 64
Heine, Heinrich, **M8**: 438; **L4**: 48
on Luther, **M8**: 146-47
on systems of thought, **M8**: 175
on German philosophy, **M8**: 176, 179-80
Heisenberg, Werner
on indeterminacy, **L4**: ix, xi, xiv, xvi, xvii, 160-63, 198; **L14**: 32, 106-7, 384
Helburn, J. W., **M13**: 72, 492-93
Helinski, T. M., **M11**: 317
Hellenic art, **L10**: 333, 334
Hellenism, **M7**: 210-11, 290; **L6**: 34
Helmholtz, Hermann Ludwig Ferdinand von, **E1**: 180, 197; **L4**: 131, 222; **L11**: 279; **L16**: 232n; **L17**: 40
as founder of psychology, **M7**: 137-41
on sensations, **L14**: 159-60
Helplessness
aids progress, **L17**: 257-58
Helvétius, Claude Adrien, **M3**: 52; **M7**: 345; **M9**: 277; **M12**: 126; **M13**: 400; **M14**: 76, 207; **L1**: 81; **L6**: 30; **L8**: 37; **L11**: 79; **L17**: 440
Henderson, Algo D., **L11**: 567, 570, 576
Henderson, Gerard Carl, **L2**: 31n, 36n
Henderson, Hanford, **M8**: 414
Henderson, Lawrence J., **M8**: 458; **L16**: 117n, 139
Hendley, Charles J., **L9**: 320, 345

Henry, Patrick, **L14**: 201
Henry VIII, **L7**: 138
Henry Sidgwick (Arthur Sidgwick and E. Sidgwick), **M4**: 242-44
Henry Street Settlement (New York City), **M7**: 205-6
Heraclitus, **M2**: 144, 151, 156; **M6**: 443; **M12**: xxvi; **M13**: 364; **M15**: 337; **L1**: 47, 49; **L3**: 26; **L5**: 495; **L14**: 101, 131; **L17**: 131
Herbart, Johann Friedrich, **E1**: 203; **E4**: 195; **E5**: xiv, 148; **M4**: 52; **M7**: 349; **L8**: 37
  on desire and will, **E5**: 137-42
  on theory of unification, **E5**: 297-98
  influence of German objective idealism on, **M1**: xviii
  on mind, **M6**: xxiv
  on formal steps of instruction, **M6**: xxvii, 338-47
  and real, **M7**: 232-33
  and interest, **M7**: 275
  and system, **M7**: 352
  compared with Froebel, **M7**: 382-83
  on theory of presentations, **M9**: 75-78, 85
  on conduct, **L17**: 310
  on correlation, **L17**: 311, 312
Herbart Society, **L17**: 88, 559
Herbert, George, **L7**: 273
Herder, Johann Gottfried von, **E4**: 195, 211; **M2**: 148, 179, 184; **M6**: 409, 444; **M8**: 194; **M9**: 64; **M10**: 226; **L8**: 32, 360
Herd instinct, **M14**: 6
Heredity, **M9**: 80-81; **L16**: 116n, 119n
  and environment, **E5**: 409-10; **M7**: 286-87
  cultural, **M4**: xxx, 156-57
  importance of, **L13**: 77
Heresy, **L13**: 127-29; **L15**: 52, 53, 58
Hermagoras, **L4**: xxi
Hermann, Ludimar, **E1**: 196
Hermitage (Leningrad), **L10**: 319
Heroes, **M8**: 193-94
Herrenwahrheit, **M7**: 433
Herrick, Charles Judson, **L16**: 117n
Herriot, Édouard, **L11**: 312
Herschberger, Ruth, **L16**: 469
Herschel, John Frederick William, **M7**: 241
Hesiod, **L10**: 331
Hesse, Mary, **L8**: xviii
Hessen, Sergei, **L6**: 291
Heterogeneity, **M13**: xxiii; **L12**: 95, 218
  and homogeneity, **L4**: 76-78, 85, 107; **L17**: 154
  in Anglo-American law, **L17**: 106
Heteronomy. *See* Autonomy; Ontological, **L12**
Hibben, John Grier, **M13**: 156, 160; **M15**: 316
Higher Learning in America, The (Hutchins), **L11**: xxii, 391-407, 592-97
High-mindedness, **M5**: 127n; **L7**: 118n
High school, **L6**: 120; **L17**: 27-28
  teaching of ethics in, **E4**: 54-61
  intermediate position of, **E5**: 270-75; **M1**: 287-302
  training of teachers by, **E5**: 275, 277
  courses needed in, **E5**: 276-80
  Germanic model of, **M1**: xvii
  Dewey's concern with, **M1**: xix
  problems relating to, **M1**: 283-84

aims of, **M3**: 296-97
teaching of sciences in, **M10**: 132, 134-36
progressive education and, **L9**: 156-57
High School of Commerce (New York City), **L9**: 315n
Hilbert, David, **M7**: 424; **L16**: 38, 155, 161n, 165n
Hill, David Jayne, **E5**: 342n, 347
Hill, Marion, **L17**: 346, 565
Hillquit, Morris, **M10**: 293; **M11**: 294, 396; **L6**: 235
Himmelfarb, Gertrude, **L9**: xxxin
Hindus, Maurice, **L5**: 358, 407-9
Hindus, **M7**: 417; **M12**: 152
group ownership by, **M5**: 29-30; **L7**: 29
Hinton, Charles Howard, **L10**: 51, 355
Hinton, James, **M14**: 81
Hippias, **L2**: 128, 129
Hippocrates, **L3**: 26; **L15**: 60
Historians, **M13**: 41
inferences of, **L13**: 99-101
Historical process
uniqueness of, **M2**: 5-6
related to morality, **M2**: 16, 20-21
"Historic Background of Corporate Legal Personality, The," **L14**: xxiii
Historicism
related to Germany, **M10**: 226
History, **M14**: 6, 78; **L1**: 42, 83-85, 90-93, 112, 118-19, 129-30, 209-11, 263; **L4**: xv, 242; **L6**: xvi, 77; **L11**: 58, 564
Green on, **E3**: 28
cycles of, **E3**: 170-73
related to social forces, **E5**: 70-72, 89, 440-41; **M1**: 230; **M4**: 192-93, 282-83; **M10**: 193-95
teaching of, **E5**: 70-74, 230; **M4**: 194-97, 208-10; **L11**: 194, 209, 214; **L17**: 318
related to child-study, **E5**: 218; **M1**: 74-75, 108-9
and culture-epoch theory, **E5**: 247-53
references on, **E5**: 337
in elementary schools, **E5**: 429-30; **M1**: 62-63, 327, 333-34
of educational systems, **E5**: 445-46
Dewey on, **M1**: xxi; **M2**: x; **L7**: xvi-xvii
bearing on ethical judgment of, **M2**: x-xv
reveals origin of ideas, **M2**: 9
biographic element in, **M4**: 194-95
economics and, **M8**: 140; **L9**: 74-75; **L11**: 168-70, 232
related to German thought, **M8**: 186
Fichte on, **M8**: 187
Herder on, **M8**: 194
study of, **M9**: 215-26
industrial, **M9**: 223-24; **L9**: 163-64
affects understanding, **M13**: 267-68, 272
and Russia, **M13**: 315; **L17**: 502-3
nature of, **M13**: 351; **L1**: 332; **L3**: 103, 321-22; **L4**: 196, 197, 211, 245; **L16**: 363, 368
and philosophy, **M13**: 353; **L14**: 312-15, 326-27
accidents in, **M14**: 9, 73, 117
of education, **M15**: 195-96; **L11**: 172-73, 229-35, 356, 364; **L13**: 5; **L17**: 161-86

History (*continued*)
and knowledge, **M15**: 374-75
modern, **L1**: 333-34
and experience, **L1**: 370; **L11**: 69-83; **L14**: xii-xiii
events as, **L2**: 64
continuity of, **L2**: 336, 347; **L10**: 338
and art, **L6**: 43; **L10**: 181, 323; **L14**: 255-56
Heard on, **L6**: 278-79
and evolution, **L6**: 280-82
of capitalism, **L7**: 142-43, 149-51
value of, **L7**: 179
related to individualism, **L7**: 331-38, 348; **L13**: 148; **L14**: 102-3, 412-13
of family, **L7**: 438-43
related to religion, **L9**: xviii-xix, xxix, xxxi, 3-6, 40-41, 43, 45, 48-49, 71, 216
politics and, **L9**: 71-72; **L15**: 175, 178, 180
communism and, **L9**: 92
of U.S. school system, **L9**: 148-50, 175-78, 390-91
Niebuhr on, **L9**: 399-400, 403-5
vs. poetry, **L10**: 288-89, 293
in criticism, **L10**: 319-21
social classes in, **L11**: 56-57, 388
concepts of authority in, **L11**: 130-37
of government, **L11**: 283-87, 289-90, 365, 372-73; **L16**: 403
and liberalism, **L11**: 291-92
logic and, **L12**: 230-38, 433-34, 440, 453-54
related to democracy, **L13**: 185
of science vs. institutions, **L13**: 277
and human nature, **L14**: 145-46; **L17**: 318
as record of habits, **L14**: 258-59
C. and M. Beard on, **L14**: 283-85
falsified, **L15**: 345-53
legal, **L17**: 106
movement of, **L17**: 230-31
imaging power in, **L17**: 252
experimentation related to, **L17**: 355
History of Aesthetics, A (B. Bosanquet), **E4**: 189-97
History of Experimental Psychology (Boring), **L5**: 479n
History of Philosophy, A (Erdmann), **E3**: 185-87
History of Philosophy, A (Windelband), **L5**: 424; **L15**: 324
History of Russian Educational Policy (Hans), **L6**: 291-92
History of the Philosophy of History (Flint), **E4**: 200, 213-14
History of the Rise and Influence of the Spirit of Rationalism in Europe (Lecky), **L11**: 456
History of the Warfare of Science with Theology in Christendom, A (A. White), **L11**: 456
History of Western Philosophy, A (B. Russell), **L16**: 203, 469
History Society, New, **L6**: 149, 503
Hitchcock, Gilbert M.
on Polish question, **M11**: 301, 302, 401-5
Hitchman Coal and Coke Co. v. Mitchell, **L7**: 398
Hitler, Adolf, **M8**: xxxi; **L11**: 190, 356, 519; **L14**: 263, 322-23, 332; **L17**: xxii, 46, 566

National Socialism of, **M8**: 421
idealistic philosophy of, **M8**: 422-46
Cohen on, **L14**: 407
U.S. sentiment toward, **L15**: xi, 244-45, 349
propaganda of, **L15**: 26, 297, 350, 367-68
Duranty on, **L15**: 290
and USSR, **L15**: 338, 340, 347-48, 352-53
sincerity of, **L17**: xxiv
Hoarding, **L6**: 379-80, 386
Hobbes, Thomas, **E1**: 275; **E3**: 91; **E4**: 142, 215, 216; **E5**: 15, 352, 353; **M2**: ix; **M4**: 254; **M6**: 24n, 64, 175; **M7**: 226; **M8**: xxvi, 65, 170; **M9**: xxii; **M10**: 62; **M12**: xiv, 130, 187-88; **M13**: ix-x, 307; **M14**: 93; **M15**: 60; **L1**: 108, 194; **L2**: 40n; **L3**: 101; **L8**: 35; **L15**: xiv, 13, 113
on government, **E1**: 229, 236
philosophy of, **E1**: 268, 271; **E4**: 127-28, 143-44; **M5**: 209; **M11**: x, 18-40
on state, **E4**: 70; **L7**: 219
on nature, **M2**: 147
on opinion, **M2**: 173
as founder of sensationalism, **M2**: 246
on ethics, **M3**: 52
on conscious, **M3**: 79n
on deliberation, **M5**: xivn
on human nature, **M5**: 339; **L6**: 36; **L13**: 82-83, 140-42, 401
on image, **M6**: 104n
on self-preservation, **M6**: 366-67
on individualism, **L7**: 153-54
Cohen on, **L14**: 382, 399
anticipates science, **L16**: 106
Hobhouse, Leonard Trelawney, **M5**: 65n; **L3**: 17-18; **L7**: 59n; **L8**: 142; **L11**: 470
on primitive society, **M5**: 56; **L7**: 51
on social institutions, **M5**: 384-85
on civil rights, **M5**: 409n, 410n
on marriage, **M5**: 513-14; **L7**: 129, 441-43
on church's attitude toward women, **M5**: 515n
on curiosity, **M6**: 205-6
Hobson, John A., **M11**: 87-88
Hoch-Smith resolution, **L6**: 371
Hocking, William Ernest, **L2**: 271; **L6**: 453n; **L14**: xiv, 382
on political philosophy in Germany, **M8**: 418-20, 473-77
on state, **L3**: 318-20, 323
on Dewey's theory of knowledge, **L5**: xxviii-xxix, 213-16, 461-76
exchange with Dewey, **L14**: xii, 150-54, 411-26
Hodgkinson, Clement, **M2**: 45n
Hodgson, Shadworth H., **M7**: 297; **L2**: 7n; **L11**: 471
exchange with Dewey, **E1**: xxvii-xxx, xli-lvii; **E2**: xxiii
psychology of, **E1**: 168-75
phenomenalism of, **M2**: 188
Hoernlé, Reinhold F. A., **M13**: 482; **L3**: 294-98
Höffding, Harald, **M5**: 232n
Hoffman, Ernst, **M8**: 178
Hofstadter, Richard, **M9**: xx
Hogben, Lancelot, **L11**: 186, 189; **L12**: 78n, 451n, 483n; **L13**: 55; **L17**: 447
on education, **L11**: 391-94
Hohenzollern dynasty, **M8**: xxviii, 164

Holbach, Paul Henri Thiry, Baron D', **M3**: 52
Holcombe, Chester, **M11**: 210, 216
Holden v. Hardy, **L7**: 397, 414
Holism
  in Dewey's philosophic system, **L14**: xi-xiii, xxiv, 29, 54
Holland, Thomas Erskine, **E4**: 79, 85-87; **L6**: 481n
Holland. *See* Netherlands
Hollinger, David A., **L6**: xivn
Hollins College, **L15**: 170n
Holmes, John Haynes, **L5**: 353; **L6**: 503; **L8**: 16
Holmes, Oliver Wendell, **M5**: 411n; **M12**: ix, 277; **L1**: xx, 312; **L6**: 214, 323; **L9**: 237; **L11**: 16, 341, 374; **L14**: xxii, xxiv; **L15**: xxx, xxxi; **L17**: 253, 346, 565
  on common law, **E4**: 37, 38, 40
  legal and social philosophy of, **E4**: 287n; **M15**: 68-69; **L3**: 177-83
  and syllogism, **M15**: 70-71
  on freedom of thought, **L7**: 358
  on unions, **L7**: 398-99
  on police power, **L7**: 414
  on existence, **L7**: 453
Holt, Edwin B., **M10**: 326n, 444, 445, 448; **L1**: 241n
  on entities, **M6**: 473-74; **M10**: 52
Holtzman, Edouard S., **L11**: 311, 312, 321-22, 602
Holy, The, **L4**: 9-10
Holy Roman Empire. *See* Roman Empire
Home
  as center of industrial occupation, **M1**: 7
  child's relation to, **M1**: 23-24; **L7**: 456; **L17**: 518
  as subject-matter in kindergarten, **M1**: 87-88
  cooperation between school and, **L17**: 233-34
  spirit of work in, **L17**: 314
Homer, **E3**: 118; **M5**: 68, 110, 115; **M8**: 292; **L2**: 128, 129; **L5**: 394; **L7**: 62, 101, 106; **L8**: 3; **L10**: 173, 232
  criticized, **L10**: 322, 324, 331
Home Rule
  in Russian Poland, **M11**: 264, 267
Homestead Acts, **L8**: 57
Home studies. *See* Domestic arts
Homo faber, **M12**: 120
Homogeneity, **L12**: 95, 211, 474; **L17**: 154
"Homogeneous America" (B. Russell), **L5**: 131
Homosexuality, **L14**: 245
Honestum, **L7**: 134
Honesty, **E4**: 108; **L7**: 142, 144, 152, 202
Hong Kong, **M11**: 238; **M13**: 129, 142
  British interests in, **M13**: 123
  assets of, **M13**: 124
  and Cassel contract, **M13**: 125
  English papers in, **L17**: 30
  opposes Canton, **L17**: 31
Honor, **M5**: 116; **L7**: 77-79, 107, 252
  as agency of individualism, **M5**: 85-87; **L7**: 77-79
Hook, Sidney, **M4**: xxxii; **M5**: xxn; **M15**: x; **L3**: xvii; **L6**: xv, xviii; **L11**: 3; **L12**: 5; **L15**: xxv, 24n, 233n, 335n; **L17**: 442
  on Dewey's 1902-3 writings, **M2**: ix-xxi

on Dewey's 1915 writings, **M8**: ix-xxxvi
on *Democracy and Education*, **M9**: ix-xxiv
on *Experience and Nature*, **L1**: vii-xxiii
on pragmatism, **L3**: 339-41
contributes to *Art as Experience*, **L10**: 7
on naturalism, **L15**: xvi, 109-26, 455, 457, 460, 463
endorsement of, **L15**: xxiv, 372
supports *Collected Works*, **L17**: xiv
on Dewey's relevance, **L17**: xvii-xxxiii
on authority, **L17**: 443
on desire, **L17**: 481
Hooker, William Jackson, **M4**: 4
Hoover, Herbert C., **M12**: 8; **M15**: 96-97; **L3**: 185; **L5**: 92, 97, 343, 434, 436; **L6**: xvi, 161, 246, 248, 323, 346, 438; **L8**: 14; **L9**: 206-7, 277
allied with business interests, **L6**: 157-58, 177
and railroads, **L6**: 165, 369
and 1932 election, **L6**: 251, 253, 326
declines to call special session, **L6**: 345
and White House Conference, **L6**: 352; **L17**: 550
keynote speech of, **L6**: 357-63
letter to, on government responsibility, **L6**: 372-73
on hoarding, **L6**: 379
and unemployment, **L6**: 386, 404, 440
on sanctions, **L6**: 472, 475
and Citizens Conference on the Crisis in Education, **L9**: 119-20, 129
and Research Committee on Social Trends, **L9**: 235
responds to Depression, **L11**: xi, 268, 339, 601
advocates laissez-faire policy, **L11**: 286, 290-91
and war, **L14**: 364
on Children's Charter, **L17**: 572
Hopkins, Harry L., **L9**: 271-72
Horace Mann Conference (Antioch College), **L11**: 567-80
Horgan, Lieutenant, **M11**: 259
Horn Scientific Expedition to Central Australia, The (B. Spencer), **M2**: 50n
Horodyski, Jan M., **M11**: 283
Hosea, **M5**: 102; **L7**: 93
Hospitality, **M5**: 68-69; **L7**: 62-63
Hostility, **L10**: 34; **L16**: 373
Hotel Center (New York City), **L11**: 321n
House, Edward M., **M11**: 248n, 255n
on Polish question, **M11**: 401-7
Housekeeping
study of, **E5**: 232-33
House of Peers (Japan), **M11**: 167
House of the Seven Gables, The (Hawthorne), **L10**: 320
House Un-American Activities Committee, **L6**: xxii; **L14**: 370
censors textbooks, **L17**: 137, 560-61
House Ways and Means Committee, **L9**: 260, 284
Housing
WWI related to problem of, **M11**: 62, 83-84, 103
Housman, A. E.
on poetry, **L10**: 192, 220, 360-61

Houston, William, **L13**: 329-30
"*How, What,* and *What For* in Social Inquiry," **L16**: xxvi, xxxvii
Howard, Blanche Willis, **E3**: 196
Howard, George E., **M5**: 514n; **L7**: 442
Howe, Frederick C., **L6**: xviii; **L17**: 71, 558
Howell, Robert B., **L6**: 394
"How Is Mind to Be Known?" **L15**: 72n
Howison, George Holmes, **L11**: 476
  on pluralism, **M2**: 204
  lecture, **L6**: 3-21
Howland School (Chicago), **M8**: 292
Howlett, Charles F., **L6**: xxin
"How to Make Our Ideas Clear" (C. Peirce), **M6**: 175; **L2**: 4; **L4**: 90n; **L16**: 33n
How We Think (1910), **E2**: xxv; **M1**: ix-x; **M7**: 383; **M12**: xviii; **M13**: 61, 63, 64, 65; **L6**: xii; **L7**: xxiii; **L12**: 3; **L16**: 318
  Dewey's theory of inquiry refined in, **M1**: xiv-xv; **M6**: xi
  psychology in, **M6**: xxiii-xxiv
  Buermeyer on, **M13**: 482-91
  importance of, **L8**: ix
How We Think (1933)
  evaluated, **L8**: ix, xi-xvii
Hsu, "Little," **M12**: 66-69
Hsu, "Old," **M12**: 66-67
Hsu Shih-chang, **M13**: 135
Huc, Évariste R., **M11**: 217
Huckleberry Finn (Twain), **L10**: 320
Hudson, Manley Ottmer
  Dewey's debate with, **M15**: xvii, 87-104
  on World Court, **M15**: 383-403
Hudson, William Henry, **L2**: 261-62
  on esthetic, **L10**: 35, 36, 354
  on childhood, **L10**: 130-31, 359
Hudson Guild, **M10**: 377n
Hughes, Charles Evans, **M13**: 171, 202, 205, 214; **M15**: 85, 380, 393, 411, 418n; **L9**: 237; **L17**: 559
  political campaign of, **M10**: xxvii, 252-55
  on international law, **M15**: 95; **L17**: 104
Hughes, Percy, **L11**: 115-17; **L12**: 276n
  on psychology, **L5**: 224; **L17**: 42-43
Hugo, Victor, **E3**: 41; **M5**: 145
Hugo of Saint Victor, **M2**: 254
Hull, Clark L., **L15**: 469; **L16**: 125n
Hullfish, H. Gordon, **L15**: 510
Hull House (Chicago), **M2**: 85, 91, 92; **L5**: 421; **L15**: 197; **L17**: 517, 573
Hulme, Thomas Ernest, **M7**: xii-xiii; **L10**: 83, 334-35
Human. *See* Man
"Human Abode of the Religious Function, The," **L9**: 294
Human association
  implications of, **M9**: 87-92
Human Conduct and the Law (Love), **L17**: 108-9
Human Enterprise, The (Otto), **L14**: 289-92
Humanism, **L9**: 224, 227, 426
  in *Cyclopedia of Education*, **M7**: 213-17, 290-91, 416
  Windelband on, **M9**: 290

described, **M9**: 297-98
as revolution in philosophy, **M12**: x
and naturalism, **M12**: 179
Cyrenaic, **L2**: 136-39
Dewey's, **L5**: xiv-xv, xxx-xxxii; **L14**: 381
modern theory of, **L5**: 73-74
science hostile to, **L5**: 113, 115
history of term, **L5**: 263-66
Santayana on, **L6**: 272
secularized, **L9**: 221-22, 421
religious, **L11**: 84-85, 583n, 584-87; **L15**: 269-70
F. Schiller on, **L11**: 156
Reiser on, **L11**: 436-37
democracy and, **L13**: 151, 170, 303
scientific, **L15**: 184-85, 376-77
Sperry on, **L17**: 545
Rafton on, **L17**: 545, 547
Humanism: Philosophical Essays (F. Schiller), **M3**: 312-18; **M6**: 176
Humanism and America (Foerster), **L5**: 265
Humanist, **L15**: xxxiii, 376
Humanist Manifesto, A, **L5**: xxx
Humanists, **L17**: 183
Humanitarianism, **L7**: 147
influence on liberalism, **L11**: xxviii, 17-18, 282-84, 365, 366
Humanities
vs. science in curriculum, **M7**: 120-27; **M9**: 236-38, 294-98
in *Cyclopedia of Education*, **M7**: 218
value of, **L17**: xviii
Humanity, **M7**: 210, 325-26; **L9**: 295; **L15**: 219
development of, **M8**: 186-89; **L14**: 145-46
philosophy related to, **M9**: 97-105; **L14**: 289-90
Kant on, **M9**: 101-2
in democracy, **L14**: 276-77
Martineau on, **L17**: 4
God related to, **L17**: 532-33
Humanity Uprooted (Hindus), **L5**: 407-9
Human Nature (Hobbes), **M11**: 22
"Human Nature," **L6**: xv, xvi
Human nature, **M6**: 420; **M15**: 246, 256; **L11**: 134, 392
related to philosophy, **M9**: 337; **L14**: 324-25, 333-34
and morals, **M14**: 4-11
alterability of, **M14**: 76-87; **L13**: 142, 287, 292
related to nature, **L1**: viii-xxiii, 349, 354; **L13**: 181
related to culture, **L6**: xv, xvi, 37-38, 43; **L13**: 84, 86, 163, 246-48, 273
and social science, **L6**: xvi, 29
concepts of, **L6**: 30-36
bibliography on, **L6**: 39
and education, **L6**: 93
sympathy in, **L7**: 238-39, 251, 270, 300
Niebuhr on, **L9**: 401
and esthetic quality, **L10**: 27, 87
constitution of, **L13**: 66, 72-79, 87-90, 96-97, 117, 134, 136, 139-40, 143, 145-47, 150-52, 286
traits of, **L13**: 68, 74-75, 91, 285, 312; **L15**: 210-12, 221
Jefferson on, **L13**: 68-69; **L14**: 203, 220
Hobbes on, **L13**: 82-83, 140-41, 401

Human nature (*continued*)
attitude toward, **L13**: 136, 152-53, 178-79
Mill on, **L13**: 138
Plato on, **L13**: 139
potentialities of, **L13**: 152-55, 318
fallacies concerning, **L13**: 184, 292-93
related to democracy, **L14**: 226-27
and social change, **L14**: 258-61
emotion and intelligence related to, **L14**: 323-24, 332-33
anti-naturalist view of, **L15**: 55, 59-61
Human Nature and Conduct, **E4**: xvi; **M1**: xii; **M5**: xi; **M12**: xvii; **M13**: xvi, xviii; **M15**: x; **L6**: xvi; **L7**: xix, xxii-xxiv; **L14**: x, 388, 401n, 407n
Murphey on, **M14**: ix-xxiii
1930 foreword to, **M14**: 228-30
moral theory in, **L5**: 501-2
on imagination, **L10**: xxviii-xxix
Human relations, **L15**: 169, 183, 212, 216
related to religion, **L9**: 40-58, 437
and imagination, **L9**: 54, 295
effects of, **L13**: 335-36
biological and cultural, **L14**: 344-49
Human Rights (UNESCO), **L16**: 471
Human rights, **M11**: 196; **L16**: 400
Humboldt, Alexander von, **M8**: 177
Humboldt, Wilhelm von, **M8**: 174, 177; **M13**: 401
Hume, David, **E1**: 19, 49, 145, 301, 342, 383; **E4**: 129, 216; **E5**: 352; **M1**: 115; **M2**: 155; **M3**: 53; **M4**: 254; **M5**: 56n, 155; **M6**: 175; **M7**: 42, 144, 223, 261; **M8**: xxvi; **M9**: xxi; **M10**: 332, 358; **M12**: 108, 127, 131; **M13**: 307, 472; **M14**: 228-29; **M15**: 9, 255, 256, 332, 344; **L1**: 32, 81, 134, 254, 373, 374; **L2**: 7n, 270; **L3**: 15, 41; **L6**: 17, 19, 424, 489; **L7**: 51n, 154; **L11**: 15, 80, 91; **L12**: 20n, 45, 153, 156, 446; **L14**: 391
on philosophic method, **E1**: 3, 36, 37, 45, 124-26
and nominalistic logic, **E1**: 59
on ideas, **E1**: 184; **M3**: 110n, 117; **M4**: 318; **L10**: xiv, 44
on knowledge, **E1**: 315, 326, 391, 392
influences Kant, **E1**: 428, 431, 434
Green on, **E3**: 19-20
on morals, **E4**: 145; **M4**: 40
on sensationalism, **E5**: 15; **M2**: 246-47; **M10**: 12-13
John Watson on, **E5**: 353
opposed to ontologism, **M2**: 169
on outness, **M2**: 180
skepticism of, **M2**: 234; **L4**: xix-xx, 113
on experience, **M3**: 132n, 134, 137; **M6**: 4, 80; **L14**: 190
and idealism, **M3**: 382; **M7**: 226
on mind, **M4**: 91n
on reason, **M5**: xiv-xv, 214; **L13**: 161
on approbation, **M5**: xxviin; **L7**: 238

and utilitarianism, **M7**: 361
on passion, **M8**: 24
theory of causation, **L2**: 154
Dewey's departure from, **L3**: 76
on mathematical truths, **L4**: 125
influence of, **L8**: 9, 35
on habit, **L12**: 244, 250; **L14**: 131
on necessity, **L13**: 120-21
pragmatism of, **L15**: 13, 16, 18, 94
on associations, **L16**: 305
Humility, **E2**: 287; **M14**: 200
Hunan, China, **M13**: 151; **L14**: xx
Hungary, **M11**: xiii, 272, 327; **M15**: 394
Hunger, **L15**: 197
Hunt, Frazier, **M13**: 346-47
Hunt, Henry T., **M11**: 259, 406
Hunt, Leigh, **E2**: 221
Hunter, Walter S., **L5**: 222n, 226
Hunting psychosis, **M2**: 42-48
Hurley, Patrick J., **L6**: 365
Hu Shih, **M11**: xviii; **M12**: xxv; **M13**: xxiii; **L11**: 127n; **L14**: xx
Huss, John, **L7**: 141
Hussein Djahid Bey, **M15**: 420
Husserl, Edmund, **L3**: xiv
Hutcheson, Francis, **E4**: 128, 144-45; **M3**: 53; **M7**: 285; **L7**: 154
Hutchins, Robert M., **L15**: 259, 267, 269
opposes Dewey on education, **L11**: xxii, 391-407, 592-97
Huxley, Aldous Leonard, **L10**: xvii
Huxley, Julian S., **L6**: 88, 279; **L11**: 344; **L15**: 184; **L16**: 119, 121n
Huxley, Thomas Henry, **E1**: xxv; **E3**: 125; **E5**: xiii; **M2**: 35, 149, 180; **M3**: x; **M4**: 4; **M7**: 276; **L5**: 147, 148; **L11**: 393; **L15**: xv
on dependence of mind on brain, **E1**: 105
on evolution and ethics, **E5**: xvi, 35-53
Huygens, Christiaan, **E1**: 262, 272; **L4**: 78; **L16**: 106
Hylozoism, **M2**: 181
Hyphenism
related to nationalism, **M10**: 205, 232, 294
Hypocrisy, **M14**: 7; **L7**: 256; **L13**: 97; **L14**: 247-48
Hypostasis, **L1**: 78, 145, 167, 251; **L9**: 221
Hypostatization, **L10**: 135; **L16**: 112, 128, 156-57, 339
significance of, **L4**: 123, 132, 174, 190, 198, 211, 244
of instruments, **L12**: 135, 173
of ends, **L12**: 178-79, 216n
Hypothecation, **M13**: 488-89
Hypothesis, **M12**: 91-92, 163; **L1**: 124, 127, 172; **L4**: 86; **L10**: 253; **L16**: 415, 417, 460. *See also* Conception, **L12**; Formulation, **L12**; Predication, **L12**; Universal proposition, **L12**
scientific, **E3**: 86-89
in action, **M6**: 240; **L8**: 205-6
and observation, **M6**: 244, 298; **L8**: 200, 202-3, 250-51, 272-73
in *Cyclopedia of Education*, **M7**: 218-21
moral, **M14**: 164-67
defined, **L4**: 63, 132, 133
concerning knowledge, **L4**:

Hypothesis (*continued*)
138, 140, 143, 144, 147, 149
verification of, **L4**: 152-55, 231; **L13**: x, 58-59; **L14**: 59-60
beliefs as, **L4**: 221-22
need for, **L4**: 247, 248; **L17**: 443
and experiment, **L8**: 74, 95; **L12**: 115-16, 132
function of, **L12**: 11, 144-45, 164-65, 173-74, 189-90, 263-65, 314-15, 485, 499; **L13**: 263; **L16**: 292-93
and symbols, **L12**: 58-59
as contingent and necessary, **L12**: 298-307
necessary for warranted assertion, **L14**: 169
vs. postulation, **L16**: 76n
in interaction and transaction, **L16**: 115
for naming, **L16**: 134-35
Maxwell on, **L16**: 277-78
for value-field, **L16**: 344-48, 351-52, 355-56
Hypothetical-deductive method, **L12**: 423-24
Hysteria, **M12**: 160

Ibsen, Henrik, **M5**: 145, 525; **M6**: 30; **L7**: 89; **L17**: 40
on ancestral curse, **M5**: 97
on spiritual selfishness, **M5**: 276n
subject-matter of, **L10**: 118, 192, 216
Idea, **L1**: 53-54, 134-35, 148-49, 177, 231-32, 263, 278; **L4**: 3, 4, 21. *See also* Possibility, **L12**
meaning of, **E1**: 176-77; **M3**: 68-72; **M4**: 83-84; **M9**: 167; **M10**: 16; **M13**: 56, 57; **L12**: 113-14, 136, 167-68, 186, 232, 288-89; **L15**: 37-38; **L16**: 264; **L17**: 440, 446
innate, **E1**: 305-9, 312; **M7**: 251-52, 286; **M8**: 159-60; **L11**: 76-77; **L17**: 430-31
related to knowledge, **E1**: 386; **E3**: 83; **L2**: 152, 154; **L4**: 137-42, 239-40; **L14**: 170
and fact, **E3**: 84-89, 259; **M4**: 146-57
related to judgment, **E3**: 231-33; **M6**: 264-66; **L8**: 221-26; **L13**: 230
related to action, **E5**: 91-92, 205; **L8**: 92; **L17**: 263, 332
in sensori-motor circuit, **E5**: 97
related to expression, **E5**: 192-95
function of, **E5**: 227; **M9**: 168-70; **L4**: xvii-xviii, 70, 87-111, 181, 182; **L13**: x, 50, 131-32; **L14**: 42-44; **L15**: 35, 176-77; **L16**: 169, 283-84, 434
fixed, **M1**: 153-56
Platonic hierarchy of, **M1**: 161
Royce on, **M1**: 241-56
environment and, **M4**: 84
McGilvary on, **M4**: 317-26
pragmatism related to, **M6**: 3-11; **M13**: 445
essential to instrumentalism, **M7**: 64
in *Cyclopedia of Education*, **M7**: 221-24
of God, **M7**: 357
ultimate, **M8**: 419
words mistaken for, **M9**: 150-51
related to German history, **M10**: 224
Locke on, **L2**: 141-42

in experience, **L2**: 156
directive office of, **L4**: 48, 224, 226, 230, 247, 248
development of, **L4**: 86-88, 91, 98, 155, 183, 214; **L13**: 45, 55, 58-59, 234, 345
theories of, **L4**: 92, 210; **L13**: 117; **L14**: 99
validity of, **L4**: 103-4, 109-12, 116, 117, 147, 154
and mathematics, **L4**: 112-35
Spinoza on, **L4**: 167
interest in, **L8**: 62-63
as hypothesis, **L8**: 95
in reflective thinking, **L8**: 196-99
in history, **L8**: 355
in art, **L10**: xi, xiii, xxii, xxxi, 13, 21, 31, 36, 56, 79, 80, 125-26, 141n, 196, 207, 246, 259, 311
quality of, **L10**: 42, 44, 216-17, 273, 277, 280, 283
child's expression of, **L11**: 213
related to symbols, **L12**: 58-59; **L16**: 429-32
in science, **L13**: 58, 249, 258, 273; **L17**: 407-8
power of, **L13**: 162; **L17**: 332, 338, 431-32
and emotions, **L13**: 162, 169, 182, 249
and opinions, **L13**: 169, 182
as end-in-view, **L13**: 216, 351
value of, **L14**: 85
Moore on, **L16**: 205, 207
abstraction in, **L16**: 285
Balz on, **L16**: 435-41
need for, **L17**: 69
automatic, **L17**: 303
correlation of, **L17**: 310
related to government, **L17**: 461
"Idea for a Universal History" (Kant), **M5**: 86-87; **M8**: 168; **L7**: 79
Ideal, **L1**: 57-58, 77, 312, 314; **L13**: 55
ethical, **E1**: 210-12, 218-19, 221-22; **E5**: 48
aristocratic, **E1**: 240-43
Green on, **E3**: xxvii-xxix, 166-68
in medieval period, **E3**: 228
vs. actual, **E3**: 259; **M12**: 153-54; **L1**: 310-11; **L7**: 13, 120-21; **L17**: 155
moral, **E3**: 368-81; **L15**: 167
abstract, **E4**: 256-62
as motive, **E4**: 287-91; **E5**: 135
D'Arcy on, **E5**: 32
conflict in, **E5**: 134
Greek, **M5**: 128-30; **L7**: 119-21, 262
influence of, **M6**: 222-23; **L8**: 90, 164-67
ultimate, **M8**: 419
Hitler on, **M8**: 430-31
conceptions of, **M12**: 139
human, **M12**: 147-48; **L13**: 183
origin of, **M12**: 215-16
in education, **M13**: 399-400, 402; **L9**: 194-96
as goal, **M14**: 178, 187, 195
stability as, **M14**: 197-98
nature of, **L4**: xx, 63, 130, 131, 215, 220; **L7**: 212, 271-75, 344-45; **L10**: 202, 324-25, 340, 350; **L17**: 66
Hegel on, **L4**: 51
formation of, **L4**: 86, 119, 134, 205, 211, 219
function of, **L4**: 166, 167, 222-27, 237; **L13**: 226; **L17**: 342
as possibility, **L4**: 239-45, 248
peace as, **L7**: 95
Hebrew-Christian, **L7**: 95-96

Ideal (*continued*)
democratic, **L7**: 348-50; **L17**: 400
related to God, **L9**: xvi-xviii, 29-30, 34-36, 227-28, 294-95, 430-31, 435-39
in religion, **L9**: 32-33, 56, 436-37
related to art, **L10**: xxii, xxxii, 31, 33, 189-90, 247, 263
matter's relation to, **L10**: 12, 34, 36, 38
Santayana on, **L10**: 144; **L14**: 297
social, **L11**: 21-22, 167-70, 297
as directive, **L12**: 179, 318-19
liberty as, **L13**: 99
utopian, **L13**: 284
vs. material, **L15**: 187, 257, 306
as name, **L16**: 264, 350
comprehensiveness of, **L17**: xxxiii, 65
Sophists and, **L17**: 184
supernatural, **L17**: 432
Idealism, **M4**: 116-17; **M7**: 348, 444; **M8**: 18, 19; **M14**: 4, 8, 38, 49, 55, 109, 114, 160, 162, 187, 208, 226; **L1**: xvii, 61-62, 64, 102, 126, 146, 150, 172, 176, 186, 219, 233, 236, 244, 245, 296, 310; **L3**: 5; **L12**: 16, 185, 207-8; **L13**: 133; **L14**: xiv; **L16**: 335; **L17**: 368, 372
Hegelian, **E1**: xxv
subjective and objective, **E1**: xlviii, 133-40; **E5**: 27-28; **M3**: 382-89; **M6**: 4; **L17**: 373
voluntaristic, **E2**: xxiv
in art, **E2**: 270
Bosanquet on, **E4**: 195
Dewey's, **M1**: x-xi; **L14**: 7-8, 62; **L16**: xiv-xv
educational influence of, **M1**: xvii-xviii
as outgrowth of consequent, **M2**: 14
related to empiricism, **M2**: 121; **M10**: 18-19; **L4**: 142
ethical, involved in pragmatism, **M3**: 156-57
naturalistic, **M3**: 319-22
related to truth, **M6**: xiv-xvi, 33-52; **M7**: 414
on real and ideal, **M6**: xvi-xvii; **L4**: 235, 240, 241, 247
related to experience, **M6**: 80-85
related to ego-centric predicament, **M6**: 113-22; **M7**: 445-51
rationalistic, **M6**: 175; **L12**: 521-24; **L17**: 365n
absolute, **M7**: xiv, 284; **M9**: 309; **M13**: 478n; **M15**: 337; **L12**: 524-26
on knowledge, **M7**: 82; **L4**: xi, xxii, 18, 151; **L16**: 288
in *Cyclopedia of Education*, **M7**: 224-33
related to Kant, **M7**: 291, 328; **M8**: 157; **L2**: 14
modern, **M7**: 294
as motive, **M7**: 418-19
ontological, **M7**: 448
realistic, **M8**: 68; **M10**: 48, 336-37; **L14**: 99
of Eucken, **M8**: 165
monistic, **M8**: 178
Hitler's appeal to, **M8**: 422-46
institutional, **M9**: 309-10
on thought, **M10**: 19-21
development of, **M10**: 24; **M11**: 344

of G. Morris, **M10**: 111-15; **L5**: 152
German, **M10**: 219, 220, 222; **L3**: 131; **L13**: 149; **L14**: 322-23, 331-32
in Great Britain, **M10**: 223-25
systems of, **M10**: 331-36; **L4**: 50-52
compared with instrumentalism, **M10**: 338-65
of U.S., **M11**: xvi, 180-85, 198, 260, 394
of Wilson, **M11**: 232
of Fichte, **M11**: 361
in theory of value, **M11**: 366-67, 375, 377
epistemological and theological, **M12**: 107-8; **M13**: 372
tragic, **M12**: 153-54
of faith, **M13**: 310
Greek, **M13**: 370-71
self-conscious, **M13**: 418
problematical, **M13**: 446
vs. dualism, **M13**: 465-66
associated with emotion, **M14**: 175-81
moral, **M14**: 199-200
practical, **L2**: 167, 171, 172; **L9**: 299
defined, **L4**: 27, 133, 186, 221
motif of, **L4**: 87, 88, 111, 113
values of, **L4**: 205-6; **L13**: 191
philosophical, **L6**: 431-32; **L15**: 3, 35, 112, 115, 146, 440-41
related to religion, **L9**: 17
related to Marx and Lenin, **L9**: 105
and social reconstruction, **L9**: 128
Niebuhr on, **L9**: 401, 403-4
influences liberalism, **L11**: 19-20
personal, **L11**: 149, 156, 423
perceptual, **L12**: 519-21
dialectic, **L13**: 119, 401
James on, **L14**: 101
in Whitehead's metaphysics, **L14**: 140
Jefferson's, **L14**: 215
of Otto, **L14**: 290
in Santayana's philosophy, **L14**: 303
Hocking on, **L14**: 417, 423
social, **L15**: 89-90, 251-53, 257
and realism, **L16**: 411; **L17**: 418
Idealism as a Philosophy (Hoernlé), **L3**: 294
Idealistic
monism, **M3**: 311
movement, **M7**: 419
dialectic, **M8**: 140; **M10**: 107
Idealists, **M6**: xiii
failure of, **L17**: 451-52
Ideality, **M12**: 140-41, 143-44
related to experience, **M3**: 141-44
Idealization
as knowledge, **E1**: 186-87; **E2**: 122
process of, **E2**: 125
imagination in, **E2**: 171-72
and feeling, **E2**: 247
intellectual and esthetic, **E2**: 268-69
three modes of, **L4**: 240-41
of impulse, **L10**: 83
of human form, **L10**: 238
of art, **L10**: 246, 296-97, 301
Idea of God as Affected by Modern Knowledge, The (J. Fiske), **L17**: 93
Idea of Value, The (Laird), **L15**: 425n
Ideation
in *Cyclopedia of Education*, **M7**: 221-24

Ideational activity, **E5**: 205
Identification
theories of, **L4**: 145-51
as stage in perception, **L10**: 30, 180, 182
Identifior, **L16**: 215-16
Identity, **L12**: 18-19, 126, 185, 229-30, 239-40, 267, 342-43, 347, 422, 427-28, 451-52, 459. *See also* Agreement, **L12**; Inclusion, **L12**
for physical moralist, **E1**: 215-17
categories of, **E1**: 376-79
Klyce on, **M13**: 418
in art, **L10**: 208, 262
principle of, **L11**: 435
"Ideology of Violence, The" (Hook), **L17**: xxviiin
Idhlozi
as aspect of individualism, **M5**: 29n
Idiopathic discharges, **E4**: 159-62
If-then proposition. *See* Hypothesis; Universal proposition, **L12**
Ignorance
and probability, **L12**: 466, 468
Socrates on, **L17**: 185
Ihering, Rudolf von, **L6**: 269-70
Ihsan Bey, **M15**: 420
Iliad (Homer), **L5**: 394; **L10**: 173, 232, 322; **L17**: 173, 226
Illiberalism, **M13**: 305; **L17**: 116
Illinois
industrial education in, **M7**: 99-103
Illinois, Northern, Teachers' Association, **M4**: 205n
Illinois, University of, **L17**: 88, 89
Illinois Society for Child-Study, **L11**: 212
Illiteracy, **M10**: 127-29
in China, **L3**: 422-23
in U.S., **L5**: 311-18
in Russia, **L17**: 493, 569
Lenin on, **L17**: 494
Ills, **M12**: 176, 181-82
Illusion, **L15**: 65
influences social institutions, **L9**: 107-8
in art, **L10**: 204-5, 279-81, 284
Illusion of Immortality, The (C. Lamont), **L11**: 425-27
"Illusory Psychology" (Hodgson), **E1**: xli-lvii
Image, **M6**: 104n
as instrument of instruction, **E5**: 92
as psychical, **E5**: 162
realized in action, **E5**: 195-97, 199
related to child play, **M1**: 198, 225, 340-41
nature of, **L10**: 280-81, 293
Imagery, **L10**: 259, 308
motor, **E5**: 194-95; **L17**: 244-45, 327
in imagination, **E5**: 315-17
movement of, **E5**: 319-21
in child, **M1**: 203-6; **L17**: 242, 246, 248
kinds of, **L17**: 242
Galton on, **L17**: 243
auditory, **L17**: 244, 327
visual, **L17**: 246, 250-51
power of, **L17**: 249-52
questioning about, **L17**: 253
lies as, **L17**: 265
Imagination, **M12**: 200-201; **M14**: 39, 113, 142, 155, 161; **L1**: 57, 77, 96, 132, 170-71, 221, 314; **L8**: 97, 115, 193; **L13**: 70; **L17**: 147

in Spinoza, **E1**: 17
and knowledge, **E2**: 168-76; **M9**: 244-46; **M12**: 121, 122
in study of ethics, **E4**: 57-58
expression of, **E5**: 199
in education, **E5**: 315-20; **M6**: 310-11; **L6**: 115-17; **L8**: 288-89; **L9**: 199
of children, **M1**: 37-38, 85-86, 99-100, 201-2, 340; **L17**: 261-64
in deliberation, **M6**: 355-56; **M14**: 133-36; **L8**: 198
free play of, **M9**: 358
reshaping power of, **M12**: 82, 139, 140-41; **L17**: 413
in philosophy, **L3**: 9-10; **L11**: 433
connected with emotion, **L6**: 115-16
as creative force, **L8**: 278, 351-52; **L9**: 33-34
related to religion, **L9**: 13-14, 17, 29-30, 54, 431, 436, 437
related to supernatural, **L9**: 47, 294-95
related to formation of character, **L9**: 186
artistic use of, **L10**: xxviii, 27, 37, 40-41, 81-82, 123, 194, 210, 246, 263, 310, 321-25
unifies esthetic elements, **L10**: 271-79, 286-87, 294-301
power in civilization, **L10**: 329, 336-42, 346-52
Greek concept of, **L11**: 71, 73
in experimentation, **L11**: 82
defined, **L11**: 210
in learning, **L11**: 241-42, 244
need for, **L16**: 363, 381
uses and development of, **L17**: 242-54, 261, 264-65, 516
in arithmetic, **L17**: 246-49

"Imagination in Arithmetic" (F. Hall), **L17**: 246
Imagism, **L10**: 238
Imitation, **M6**: 361; **M14**: 48, 70, 93
as form of habit, **E4**: 198; **L17**: 308
Baldwin on, **E5**: 389-90, 392, 414-16
in child, **E5**: 418-20
role of, **M6**: 306; **L8**: 283-84
in education, **M7**: 234-37; **L17**: 203, 308-9
in formation of mental disposition, **M9**: 38-41
in social psychology, **M10**: 54-55
French school of, **M10**: 60
in art, **L10**: xxxi, 13, 147-48, 157, 189, 225, 270, 274, 279, 288-89, 295, 304-5, 331
Immanence, **M7**: 79-80, 450
Immaturity
as condition of growth, **M9**: 46-58
Immediacy, **L1**: 74-75, 81-82, 90, 91, 94-96, 105, 146-47; **L3**: 77; **L12**: 68, 154, 227, 248. *See also* Qualities, **L12**
of knowledge, **L4**: 88, 146, 149, 150, 177
of emotions, **L4**: 180
in forming values, **L4**: 209, 214
of esthetic values, **L10**: 78, 123, 297-98
and epistemologies, **L12**: 508
Pepper on, **L16**: 178
related to experience, **L16**: 384-85, 457-58
Immediate consciousness, **M13**: 352

Immediate inference, **L12**: 321
Immediatism
F. Schiller's, **M3**: 316
Dewey's, **M3**: 390-92
Lovejoy on, **M13**: 453-54
Immigrants
illiteracy of, **M10**: 127, 129; **L5**: 313, 315
and military service, **M10**: 183-90
in U.S., **M10**: 204-6; **M11**: xiii-xvi, 228, 241-44, 255, 258-62, 285
problems of, **M11**: 130, 142, 153, 330
as political and economic question, **M11**: 159, 228
and relief funds, **M11**: 249, 250
to aid Poland, **M11**: 288
and Socialist Labor party, **L6**: 235
Immigration, **M13**: 439; **L6**: 485; **L8**: 57; **L15**: 196
restriction of, **M11**: 228; **M13**: 166; **L7**: 419-20
policies of U.S., **L2**: 178-79
Balch on, **L17**: 150
Immortality, **E4**: 367; **L11**: 425-27; **L14**: 98; **L17**: 126
Royce on, **M2**: 132-33
Immutables, **L4**: 16
related to knowledge, **L4**: 21-41, 72, 164-67, 170, 248
Newton on, **L4**: 114
and values, **L4**: 211
in Greek-medieval ontology, **L16**: 334-35, 449-50
restrict inquiry, **L16**: 337n-38n, 452
concept of, **L16**: 359, 414
in nature, **L16**: 363
in science, **L16**: 364-65, 370, 410, 413
Imperial Court (Peking), **M11**: 211, 216, 218, 221
Imperial dynasty (Japan), **M11**: 170-72, 200
Imperialism, **L11**: 55, 367
Japan on European, **M12**: 34
Russell on, **M12**: 247
in economics, **L3**: xxx
in Mexico, **L3**: 158-62
Imperial University (Tokyo), **M11**: xvii, 165, 341; **M12**: 79; **M13**: 259
Impersonal proposition, **L12**: 190-91
Implication, **L12**: 18, 57, 60, 137-38, 174-75, 220, 270-71, 276-79, 301, 310, 315-16, 329, 345-46, 374, 379, 423-24, 467-68, 470-72. *See also* Discourse, **L12**
implicit and explicit, **M13**: 416
vs. inference, **L11**: 97, 124
Implications of Social-Economic Goals for Education (NEA), **L11**: 254
Importance, **L16**: 320, 331-32
"Importance, Significance, and Meaning," **L16**: xxxvii
Impossibility
in *Dictionary of Philosophy*, **M2**: 210-12
Impression
in perception, **L10**: 150, 178, 224, 308-10
sense, **L14**: 160
related to expression, **L17**: 218, 220-21
Impressionism, **L10**: 147, 177, 256, 264, 305-7, 313, 365
Improvement of the Understanding, The (Spinoza), **L4**: 44
Improvisation, **L13**: 52
Impulse, **M14**: xxi
sensuous, **E2**: 299-309

expression of, **E2**: 317; **E4**: 236-37
motor, **E2**: 323-31
social, **E4**: 127-28
nature of, **E4**: 235-36
mediation of, **E4**: 237-43
and self, **E4**: 244; **E5**: 123-24
in ethical process, **E5**: 48
of child, **M1**: 29; **M14**: 70, 90, 106
life as, **M12**: 230-31
Russell's attitude toward, **M12**: 244-45, 247-49
as habit, **M14**: 65, 73, 75
in conduct, **M14**: 65-118
as means of reorganization, **M14**: 67, 88, 125
plasticity of, **M14**: 69
as human instinct, **M14**: 75n; **L17**: 24-25, 215, 305-6
acquisitive and competitive, **M14**: 79
classification of, **M14**: 92-104
and reason, **M14**: 136-37, 175
consequences of, **L7**: 171-72, 186-88
and will, **L7**: 190
in learning, **L11**: 239-40
and desire, **L13**: 41-46, 217, 220-21
and totalitarianism, **L13**: 70
in human nature, **L13**: 140-41
vital, **L13**: 206, 221-22, 225
formation of, **L13**: 218
related to language, **L17**: 307
negative suggestion of, **L17**: 339

Impulsion
in perception and expression, **L10**: xviii, xxvi, 64-67, 70-72, 81, 83, 87, 102-3, 167, 178, 259-63, 266, 269, 283, 291, 352

Incarnation, **M8**: 151

Inclusion, **L12**: 90, 95, 222, 249-50, 306-7, 331, 335-36. *See also* Agreement, **L12**
meaning of, **L11**: 105-7, 125
and exclusion, **L12**: 182-99
ambiguity of, **L12**: 259-60

Inclusiveness. *See* Universality

"Inclusive Philosophic Idea, The," **L3**: xx

Income
distribution of, **L6**: 243-44, 347, 350, 362-63, 386, 392, 486; **L7**: 406-11, 435; **L9**: 64, 82-83, 256, 261, 266, 278, 282, 288
in U.S., **L6**: 337-38, 343-44, 348-49, 351-52, 356, 359, 360, 364, 395-96, 485; **L7**: 404; **L9**: 252, 274, 280, 287-88
from foreign investments, **L6**: 365
tax, **L7**: 420-22
report on, **L9**: 81-82, 267, 287-88
of politicians in New York City, **L9**: 355-61

Incompatibility, **L4**: 128

Incomplete, **L17**: 65

Incubation
mental, **L8**: 345

"In Defense of a *Worthless* Theory of Value" (Prall), **M15**: 20, 21n, 338-48

Indefinables
related to definition, **L16**: 163, 166, 168, 179-80
as counterfeit, **L16**: 181-82

Indefinite article
ambiguity of, **L11**: 123

Independence
pure knowing as, **M12**: 143
social, **M12**: 185-86; **M15**: 243

Independent, **M11**: ix, 394

Indeterminacy
principle of, **L4**: ix, xv, xvi, 160-66, 198; **L14**: 32, 106-7, 384
in individual development, **L14**: 111
Indeterminate. *See also* Problem, **L12**; Situation, **L12**
possibilities, **M7**: 8
action, **M7**: 11-12
and inquiry, **L12**: 108-11, 123-24, 138, 163, 183-84, 209, 241; **L15**: 34-41
Indeterminist theory of freedom, **E4**: 344-50
India, **M11**: 101, 177, 235, 237; **M12**: 6, 35, 102; **L2**: 177, 179; **L6**: 321, 353, 503
customs of, **M5**: 29-30, 64-65, 83; **L7**: 29, 59, 76
affected by British law, **L17**: 99
Indiana
vocational education in, **M8**: 117-22
Indianapolis, Ind.
public schools of, **M8**: 255-60, 268, 340-52
Indiana State Teachers' Association, **L17**: 72n, 77n
Indiana University (Bloomington), **L16**: xiin
Indians, Mexican
education among, **L2**: 200-205
Indians, North American, **M5**: 30-31, 46, 61; **M7**: 400; **M8**: 189; **L7**: 44, 56, 61
legend of, **E4**: 38
customs of, **E4**: 86; **M5**: 66-67; **L7**: 29-30
totem group of, **M5**: 26; **L7**: 26
art of, **L10**: 333
India's Outlook on Life (Chatterji), **L6**: 321
Indifference, **L7**: 167-69; **L16**: 379
freedom of, **E3**: 342; **E4**: 91-93
Individual, **M12**: 99-100, 104-5, 108; **L1**: 22, 23, 115-18, 136-37, 162-90, 204, 296, 357
related to universals, **E1**: 169-74; **L11**: 109-10
related to universe, **E1**: 286-87
related to society, **E3**: 168-69; **E5**: 30, 94, 412-13, 417; **M12**: 190-94; **M15**: 245-46; **L2**: 271-72, 292, 299, 333-34; **L11**: 30-31, 44, 132-34, 191-93, 219, 291-92, 297
and laws, **E4**: 87
meaning of, **E4**: 99; **L15**: 49, 92
in Christianity, **E4**: 101-2
in Socratic schools, **E4**: 138-39; **E5**: 13
impulses of, **E4**: 236
in Renaissance, **E5**: 12-14
intellectual development of, **E5**: 15, 16; **L7**: 146
role in civilization of, **E5**: 20, 84
self-identity of, **E5**: 28-29
as agent in moral action, **E5**: 57
powers of, **E5**: 60-61
social nature of, **E5**: 386-87; **L2**: xxx-xxxi, 244-45, 250, 274, 290, 327-28, 330, 351-55; **L17**: 424
changing of, **M1**: xxi
psychology of, **M1**: 113-14
vs. group, **M5**: 25-26, 28n-29n, 29-30, 33, 71, 74-88, 112-17; **M9**: 311; **L2**: 247; **L7**: 25, 28n, 29, 32, 65, 68-80, 103-8, 300; **L13**:

33-34, 108
Hebrew conception of, **M5**: 100-101; **L7**: 91-92
Greek view of, **M5**: 121; **L7**: 113
Royce on, **M7**: 67-68
role of, in knowledge, **M9**: 305
state and, **M12**: 189; **L2**: 249, 282, 286, 309
James on, **M12**: 236, 250; **L11**: 473-77; **L15**: 4-5
Aristotle on, **L2**: 64
as category, **L7**: xiii, xviii, xix, xxviii-xxix, 320-28, 385; **L16**: 85n, 93n, 264
Hobbes on, **L7**: 153-54
Moral Sense writers on, **L7**: 154
influences on, **L7**: 318
worth of, **L7**: 449
liberty of, **L11**: 7-8, 76, 132-41; **L14**: 91-96
development of, **L11**: 62, 63, 187, 204, 507; **L13**: 319; **L14**: 102-3, 108-12, 412-13; **L17**: 19, 72-73, 226, 230-31, 399-401
as qualitative whole, **L12**: 74, 109-11, 125-27, 220, 283, 351-52, 441
adapting to, **L13**: 27
freedom and, **L13**: 80-81, 85, 102, 149
Mill on, **L13**: 138
in democracy, **L13**: 295
physical vs. human, **L14**: 103-8
concepts of, **L15**: 168, 218-23, 250, 313; **L16**: 118, 123n, 260
respect for, **L15**: 283
under capitalism, **L17**: 23-24
in England, **L17**: 232
opportunities for, **L17**: 400
experience of, **L17**: 437-38

Individualism, **M4**: 256-57; **M7**: 414, 435; **M11**: 375; **M14**: 7, 60, 62, 68, 210; **L9**: 57; **L13**: 138; **L16**: 243n
defined, **M5**: 75; **M8**: 161-62; **M13**: 289; **M15**: 242-44; **L2**: 296-99; **L7**: 70
historical development of, **M5**: 76-81; **L5**: 193-94; **L7**: 70-75, 331-38, 348; **L11**: 290-91, 388; **L13**: 148; **L15**: 61, 94, 231; **L17**: 461, 462
psychology of, **M5**: 81-87; **L2**: 290; **L7**: 75-80
in Hebrew morals, **M5**: 101-2; **L7**: 92-94
Greek theories of, **M5**: 108-19; **L7**: 97-110
political, **M5**: 112-17; **M12**: 104-5; **L5**: 90-98; **L7**: 103-8, 355
economic, **M5**: 112-17; **L2**: 256-57; **L7**: 103-8, 355; **L8**: 56, 63-65; **L11**: 139, 142-43, 258, 366-67; **L15**: 231
of Cynics and Cyrenaics, **M5**: 118-19; **L7**: 109-10
Plato and Aristotle on, **M5**: 120-28; **L7**: 111-19, 132, 152, 366, 391
related to business and industry, **M5**: 145-52, 469-78
modern problem of, **M5**: 204-8
of later Middle Ages, **M9**: 301
intellectual, **M9**: 306; **M13**: 434
social, **M9**: 306; **L11**: 7-8, 174
moral, **M9**: 306-10; **M12**: 104-5
in Young China, **M12**: 75
religious, **M12**: 104-5; **L17**: 19, 380, 530, 532-33
related to philosophy, **M12**: 107-8; **L14**: 92

Individualism (*continued*)
rugged, **M12**: 243; **L9**: 205-8, 231, 238; **L11**: 29-31, 270, 286, 291, 371
and experience, **L2**: 55-61
related to society, **L2**: 249, 357; **L8**: 70-71
vs. socialism, **L2**: 273-74; **L13**: 114, 146, 260; **L15**: 212-21, 274-75
in democracy, **L2**: 307-8; **L8**: 50-52
and habit, **L2**: 334-36
and collectivism, **L2**: 351-56; **L7**: 322, 327
origin of, **L2**: 389-94
influences on, **L5**: 45-49, 55-123, 128-31
old and new, **L5**: 77-89
atomic, **L5**: 152
Comte on, **L5**: 154
and theory, **L7**: xiii, xv, 299, 348-49
contrasted with feudalism, **L7**: xxix
laissez-faire, **L7**: 428; **L13**: 114, 125, 157, 182
in marriage, **L7**: 448
harm caused by, **L8**: 73, 75, 79, 81
related to Brandeis, **L9**: 238-39
failure of, **L11**: 132, 137-39; **L13**: 78, 179; **L15**: 4-5, 31, 181
metaphysical, **L13**: 248
in art, **L14**: 37-38, 113-14
in science, **L15**: 184-86
rise of, **L17**: 40
ambiguity of, **L17**: 115
T. V. Smith on, **L17**: 115-16
Individualism, Old and New, **L1**: viii; **L7**: xix, xx; **L14**: x
Kurtz on, **L5**: xvii-xxii
Individuality, **L7**: xix; **L9**: 205; **L15**: 210-12, 315
related to society, **E3**: 219-20; **L7**: 321-22; **L17**: 54
nature of, **E3**: 301-3; **E4**: 48n; **M13**: 289; **M15**: 170-71; **L4**: 117, 130, 136, 147, 163-67, 172, 174, 187-89, 192; **L7**: 69, 227; **L14**: 91-92; **L17**: 461
function in, **E3**: 303-4
in *Cyclopedia of Education*, **M7**: 237-39, 295-96, 300
Hook on Dewey's theory of, **M9**: xxi-xxiv
in eighteenth-century philosophy, **M9**: 97-99, 102-3, 105
and education, **M9**: 312-14; **M15**: xxiii, 170, 172-78, 180-81; **L5**: 131-43; **L7**: 364; **L8**: 43, 53; **L9**: 177-80, 183, 196, 198, 207
duality of association and, **M9**: 332
related to mental tests, **M13**: 292; **M15**: 181-82
misapprehensions of, **M15**: 171-72, 174-76, 178
and ethics, **L3**: 20
vs. abstract, **L4**: 109, 197-200
development of, **L7**: 70, 73, 75-79, 91-92, 99-103; **L17**: 232-33, 322, 379, 400-401
in morals, **L7**: 317-18, 348-50
related to religion, **L9**: xx, 52
related to activity programs, **L9**: 172-73
Brameld on, **L9**: 244-45
culture affects, **L13**: 77-78
freedom connected with, **L13**: 80, 102, 149, 180-81
James on, **L14**: 101
human vs. physical, **L14**: 102-14

in democracy, **L14**: 113, 277
in communism, **L17**: 117
of artists, **L17**: 128
of things, **L17**: 416-17
intelligent behavior in, **L17**: 419
"Individuality and Experience," **L2**: xvii-xviii
Individualization
in art, **L10**: 15, 73, 88, 96, 98, 113, 197, 206-9, 214, 217, 237-38, 246, 250, 253, 256, 271, 286-92, 297, 305, 316-17, 326, 327
of experience, **L10**: 78, 128, 181-82, 220
of culture, **L10**: 333, 338, 351
consciousness of, **L17**: 416
Indo-China, **M13**: 142
Indoctrination, **L13**: 341, 381, 385
in bolshevism and fascism, **L6**: 142-43
in education, **L6**: 144-45; **L9**: 178-82; **L11**: 359, 384, 415-16, 574-75
definition of, **L13**: 379-80
Induction, **M9**: 303; **M12**: 98; **L1**: 284-85; **L12**: xxiv-xxv, 266, 478-79
in judgment, **E5**: 323
in pedagogy, **E5**: 454-55
as stage of thinking, **M1**: 168
and deduction, **M6**: 242-58; **M7**: 239-45; **M13**: 69-70, 487
definition of, **M13**: 63, 483-85
Mill on, **M13**: 64-65, 483; **L16**: 158
analytic observation in, **M13**: 65, 67
hypothetical character of, **M13**: 66-68
in Greek philosophy, **M13**: 369-70; **L8**: 5
and suggestion, **M13**: 485, 488
inference in, **L8**: 255, 265
object of, **L8**: 258; **L12**: 427-28, 432-35
mathematical, **L12**: 404-6
in Aristotelian logic, **L12**: 416-17, 419n-20n
as psychological, **L12**: 419-20, 508
by enumeration, **L14**: 58-59
Indulgence
vs. sacrifice, **L7**: 189
Industrial civilization, **L3**: 142-43
philosophy in, **L3**: xxii, 126-30
affects conduct, **L3**: 20
freedom related to, **L3**: 123-24
evils of, **L3**: 124-26
Industrial Discipline and the Governmental Arts, The (Tugwell), **L8**: 364-66, 369-73
Industrial education. *See also* Vocational education
Wisconsin's system of, **M7**: 84-86, 461-68
Illinois's scheme for, **M7**: 99-103
in social view of education, **M7**: 125-27
separated from liberal education, **M9**: 259, 265-66
Dewey on, **M10**: xxx-xxxii
in democracy, **M10**: 137-43
Industrial Education, National Society for the Promotion of, **M7**: 85n
Industrialism, **L7**: viii
in China, **M13**: 221
in Japan, **M13**: 260
motives of, **M13**: 281-83, 285
Kurtz on, **L5**: xvii-xxii
affects artisan, **L5**: 60

Industrialism (*continued*)
social effects of, **L8**: 48-49, 55-61, 68-71
management and, **L8**: 64
related to production, **L13**: 319
failure of, **L14**: 96
Industrial revolution, **M13**: 330; **L5**: 270; **L7**: 149-50, 378-81, 385-87, 444-45; **L15**: 214, 252, 277, 306; **L16**: 319, 408; **L17**: 412, 455-56
affects society, **M1**: 6-7; **M5**: 149-50; **M9**: 297-98; **L11**: 10, 16, 369-70; **L14**: 341-43; **L16**: 369-71, 410
affects family, **M5**: 526-29
affects education, **M7**: 309-10
Bacon on, **M9**: 292
in China, **M13**: 105, 120
Lippmann on, **L11**: 490-92
Industry, **M11**: xvi; **L3**: 142-43; **L13**: 147, 313-14. *See also* Business; Economics
as moralizing agency, **M5**: 45-46, 78; **L7**: 43-44, 71-72
cooperation in, **M5**: 46-47; **L7**: 44
and individualism, **M5**: 145-52; **L15**: 213-14, 218
related to civilization, **M7**: xxvi-xxix
history of, **M9**: 223-24; **L11**: 10, 16, 17, 169, 228, 249, 283, 549
and vocational education, **M9**: 323-25
related to democracy, **M10**: 139-40; **L7**: 353, 356-58; **L13**: 113, 129
related to war, **M10**: 236; **M11**: 73-92; **L13**: 311; **L17**: 22-23
in China, **M11**: xix, 174, 180, 186, 190, 209, 233, 234; **M12**: 71-76, 254
education related to, **M11**: 60-65, 333-35; **M15**: 162-67, 190; **L11**: 159, 162-63, 509, 538, 546
socialization of, **M11**: 65, 102-5, 117
development of, **M11**: 70, 99, 103; **L7**: 141-44, 149-50; **L9**: 163-64, 296-97; **L13**: 69, 112, 126; **L15**: 156-57
ethics of, **M11**: 131-34; **L7**: 424-25
international effects of, **M11**: 139, 142; **L16**: 405-6
problems in, **M11**: 148; **M12**: 8; **L6**: 242-44; **L7**: 377-83, 385-87, 391-92
in Japan, **M11**: 161-67, 193, 206
labor in, **M11**: 285, 327; **M12**: 9-11, 75-76; **L7**: 178, 390-401; **L13**: 180
in Poland, **M11**: 326
guild system in, **M12**: 48, 249
science and, **M12**: 100-103; **L11**: 143, 459; **L13**: 157-59, 182, 267-68, 283, 339; **L15**: 88-89, 263, 270, 277
moral problems in, **M15**: 266-67; **L15**: 199-203
in Turkey, **M15**: 276-77
state of, **L4**: 5, 61, 64, 65, 225-26; **L6**: 359-60
methods in, **L4**: 68, 100, 173, 201, 214, 243
politics related to, **L6**: 157, 158, 161-63, 168, 172, 436
economics of, **L6**: 348-49, 366-67, 374, 395; **L7**: 387-89
nature of, **L7**: 403; **L8**: 364-66, 369-73; **L16**: 243, 360

legislation in, **L7**: 412-15, 432
social control of, **L7**: 416-17; **L13**: 114
F. Roosevelt's policy regarding, **L9**: 277-78
art's relation to, **L10**: 15, 34, 266, 286, 331, 340, 343-45
social effects of, **L11**: 251-52, 278, 536; **L17**: 24
Marx on, **L13**: 122
related to philosophy, **L14**: 318-19, 329; **L16**: 407
experience related to, **L14**: 345-46
Ayres on, **L15**: 359-60
Inequality, **E1**: 245; **M5**: 114-15; **L7**: 104-7, 396
Inertia, **L13**: 85
limits art, **L10**: 273-76, 308
study of, **L16**: 67, 105
as obstacle, **L16**: 378-79
In Fact, **L15**: 375
Infancy
language of, **E4**: 66-69
coordination in, **E5**: 310; **M1**: 178-91; **L17**: 255-60
prolongation of, **M1**: 180; **M9**: 50; **L17**: 256-57
in *Cyclopedia of Education*, **M7**: 245-48
environment related to, **L13**: 48-49
mental side of, **L17**: 256, 261
social relations during, **L17**: 260-61
transition from, **L17**: 268
Infanticide, **M2**: 28-31
Infeld, Leopold, **L16**: 98-99, 105n, 108
Inference, **L12**: 10, 51, 60-62, 115n, 133, 142, 147, 150, 160, 228, 242, 248, 310, 345-46, 475, 515. *See also* Data, **L12**; Implication, **L12**
related to observation, **E3**: 81
nature of, **E5**: 322; **L8**: 190-91, 217
stages of, **M1**: 168; **M13**: 47, 386-87
and doubt, **M6**: xviii
and proof, **M6**: 201-2; **L8**: 190-95; **L12**: 424
in *Cyclopedia of Education*, **M7**: 248-49
pragmatic notion of, **M10**: xii-xiii
related to experience, **M10**: xiii, 6, 15, 16, 19, 322-65; **L14**: 27
related to behavior, **M10**: 90-97
Russell on, **M10**: 93-97
as knowledge, **M13**: 52, 386
in reflection, **L8**: 187-90, 198
ideas in, **L8**: 221-22
and induction, **L8**: 255, 265
vs. implication, **L11**: 97, 124
mediated by universals, **L11**: 107-10, 112
and propositions, **L12**: 266-67, 294
immediate, **L12**: 321
from present to past, **L14**: 84
in inquiry, **L14**: 172-74
Inferiority, **M13**: 296
Infinitation of negative, **L12**: 193
Infinite, **M12**: 117, 118; **L1**: 52-53
Locke on, **E1**: 379-81
and finite, **E3**: 227-28; **L17**: 95
Infinity
as non-terminating, **L12**: 404-5, 409-11
Inflation
effect of, **L9**: 265-69, 275
Influence of Darwin on Philosophy, The, **M15**: 352n; **L14**:

Influence of Darwin on Philosophy, The (*continued*)
149n, 385, 401, 405n; **L16**: 470
preface to, **L17**: 39-41
Influence of Greek Ideas and Usages upon the Christian Church, The (E. Hatch), **M9**: 288
Information
and mental training, **M6**: 328-37; **L8**: 315-25
in *Cyclopedia of Education*, **M7**: 249-51
mistaken for knowledge, **M9**: 194-96
acquisition of, **L8**: 155
teaching of, **L11**: 178, 183-84
Information, Public, Committee on, **M10**: 315-16; **M11**: 150, 151, 257, 394, 395
Informational studies. *See* School subjects
Inglis Lecture on Secondary Education, **L6**: 75-89
Ingram, Marsh, **L9**: 372
Ingres, Jean Auguste Dominique, **L10**: 307
Inhaltlich, **L9**: 303
Inherent, **L13**: 215; **L15**: 42
Inhibition
in emotion, **E4**: 180-83
as function of coordination, **E5**: 308-9
awareness and organic, **M7**: 80-81, 453
nature of, **L7**: 189, 206
external vs. internal, **L13**: 41
Initiation
primitive, **M5**: 59-61; **L7**: 55-56
Initiative, **M12**: 105, 199-200; **L13**: 147
in *Cyclopedia of Education*, **M7**: 251
in education, **L9**: 196-97, 205
development of, **L17**: 343, 516
Inlander, **E3**: 148n, 192n, 193n, 195n, 197-98; **E4**: 37n, 62n
In Librum Boetii de Trinitate Expositio (Thomas Aquinas), **L11**: 595
"In Memoriam" (Tennyson), **L10**: 85
Innate faculties
Herbart's denial of, **M9**: 75-78
Innate idea, **E1**: 305-9, 312; **L11**: 76-77; **L17**: 430-31
in *Cyclopedia of Education*, **M7**: 251-52, 286
Locke's objection to, **M8**: 159-60
Inner
vs. outer, **M9**: 356-60; **L17**: 81
Innerlichkeit, **M8**: xxxi, 190, 440
Inner life, **M7**: xix-xx; **M8**: 169; **L1**: 175-78, 183, 187
Inner realm
and German spirit, **M8**: 151-60, 429
Innocent IV, Pope, **L2**: 37
on spiritual, **L2**: 33-34
Inquiry, **L2**: xii, xxi; **L13**: 86, 232, 320
and logic, **M1**: xiv; **M13**: 366; **L12**: 11-16, 25-29, 92-93, 106, 132, 158-59, 476-77; **L14**: 42-52; **L16**: 187-88, 385-86
in child, **M1**: 29
doubt and, **M1**: 166; **L12**: 109-11, 123-24, 138, 163, 183-84, 209, 226, 241
scientific, **M2**: 307; **M12**: 179, 262, 264, 266-68; **L1**: 350-53; **L2**: 49; **L13**: 135, 144, 166, 262-63, 285, 371; **L14**: 60; **L15**: 85, 228-29,

235-38; **L16**: 253-55, 316-17; **L17**: 405
reflective, **M4**: xvi-xix
Dewey's theory of, **M6**: xviii-xix; **M14**: xiii; **L16**: 192, 318-19
Dewey and Spaulding on stages of, **M6**: 146-52
importance of, **M6**: 189; **L8**: 121-22; **L13**: 222
methods of, **M12**: 89, 177, 270; **M13**: 59, 386; **L11**: 52, 53; **L16**: 91-92, 96-100, 112-15, 146-48, 152, 276-78
and knowing, **M12**: 163-64; **L14**: 63, 66-67; **L16**: 4, 72-73, 86-89, 127, 320-21, 454
development of, **M12**: 179, 265-77
and mathematics, **M12**: 237; **L12**: 391-94
nature of, **M13**: 44-47, 300; **L7**: x; **L12**: 39-42, 71-72, 84, 105, 108, 118-20, 231, 245, 279-80; **L14**: 31-34; **L16**: 258, 264, 267-68, 272, 285, 349
into meaning, **M13**: 57
social, **L2**: xxx-xxxiv, 351-72; **L17**: 448-49
naturalistic and epistemological, **L2**: 44-49, 51, 54
related to religion, **L9**: 18-19, 22-23
means-consequence relation in, **L12**: xi, 16-18, 23-24, 107-8, 381-82, 440; **L14**: 55, 61, 184-87
control in, **L12**: xxi, 120n, 136, 163, 167-88, 203, 207, 210, 218-19, 237-38, 317, 319, 440, 455, 459-64
continuum of, **L12**: 3, 19, 143, 310, 315, 464-73, 480; **L14**: 56, 153
existential matrix of, **L12**: 48-65
end of, **L12**: 66-67, 145-47, 159, 166-67, 170-71, 219, 385; **L16**: 353; **L17**: 482-83
biological, **L12**: 198-99, 244, 263-64, 385
and judgment, **L12**: 432, 462-65, 483-84
in valuation, **L13**: 221, 242-43; **L15**: 102, 108; **L16**: 313, 355
hypotheses in, **L13**: 263
subject-matter and, **L14**: 50, 147
propositions in, **L14**: 57, 174-79
Bacon on, **L14**: 69
formation of self in, **L14**: 70-73
terminates in experience, **L14**: 83-86
inference and observation in, **L14**: 171-74
warranted assertibility as end of, **L14**: 180-82
freedom of, **L15**: 25, 366; **L16**: 284, 337-40, 403, 452, 455; **L17**: 407-8, 459
indeterminateness in, **L15**: 34-41, 80-81
postulations for, **L16**: 74-77, 80-82
uses of, **L16**: 82-84, 140, 144, 286-87, 311n, 312, 399, 401
organization of, **L16**: 100-104
behavioral, **L16**: 110, 122-26, 322-26
Kaufmann on, **L16**: 195, 196n
problems in, **L16**: 281-83
efficiency of, **L16**: 288-93
mechanical appliances related to, **L16**: 327-30

Inquiry (*continued*)
Balz on, **L16**: 423-42
positive attitude of, **L17**: 274
Inquiry, Commission of (American Peace Commission), **M11**: 401-3
Inquiry into Meaning and Truth, An (B. Russell), **L14**: 168-88; **L16**: 199n, 200-202
Inquiry into the Principles of the Good Society, An (Lippmann), **L11**: 489-95
Insanity, **L15**: 65
Insecurity, **L16**: 393, 419
Inside Experience (J. Hart), **L3**: 342
Insight, **L5**: 260n
Inspiration
in art, **L10**: 71-72, 81, 271
Instinct, **M12**: 245-46; **L3**: 34; **L11**: 85, 428-30, 475, 480; **L13**: 87, 211, 287-88; **L15**: 21n
and impulse, **E5**: 77
identified with reflex arc, **E5**: 104-5
as psychical condition, **E5**: 250
as uniting force, **M5**: 51-52; **L7**: 47
Bergson on, **M6**: 130; **M7**: 202
human vs. animal, **M9**: 49-50; **L17**: 256-58
related to education, **M9**: 55; **L17**: 193-95, 222-23
in conduct, **M10**: 55; **M15**: 65, 66; **L17**: 108-9, 192-93, 215
in irrationality, **M13**: 243
in children, **M14**: 70, 90, 106; **L17**: 215
classification of, **M14**: 92-104
as source of habit, **M14**: 124; **L17**: 305-6
and social theory, **L2**: 241-44
and expression, **L10**: 65, 69, 260; **L17**: 215-16
Love on, **L17**: 108
related to emotion, **L17**: 196-97
motor character of, **L17**: 217
collecting, **L17**: 223
language as, **L17**: 313
Institute of Methods of Extracurricular Work (Moscow), **L17**: 508
Institutional idealism, **M9**: 309-10
Institutions, **M14**: 9, 58, 73; **M15**: 231
moral, **E3**: 346-49; **M5**: 207-8
continuity of, **E4**: 40-41
related to society, **E5**: 48; **M9**: 9-10; **L9**: 50, 107-8; **L14**: 96; **L17**: 426, 428, 438
and science vs. literature, **M9**: 290-91
educative value of, **M12**: 192-93; **L7**: 363-64
meet psychological needs, **M12**: 245-46
states as, **M12**: 247-48
industrial, **M12**: 249
reconstruction of, **M12**: 273; **L13**: 147; **L16**: 367
opposed to freedom, **M14**: 61, 114-16
wars as, **M14**: 79-80
economic, **M14**: 82-83, 88
legal, **M14**: 90; **L2**: 32, 246, 265
importance of, **L11**: 18
schools as, **L13**: 5-6
history of, **L13**: 51
political, **L13**: 150
self-governing, **L13**: 155
formation of, **L13**: 186
breakdown of, **L16**: 361, 366, 371, 401, 404, 407-8
authority of, **L16**: 362, 369, 376

Instruction
and formation of images, **E5**: 92
references on, **E5**: 333
Herbartian steps of, **M6**: xxvii, 338-47
standards in, **M6**: 222; **L8**: 164-65
in *Cyclopedia of Education*, **M6**: 434
by art, **L10**: 349
aims and methods of, **L13**: xiii, 6, 49
related to construction, **L17**: 219-20
Instrumental, **L1**: 80, 83, 89, 90, 96, 101-6, 116-23, 127-28, 157-60, 175, 207, 264, 275, 308. *See also* Means-consequences; Tools
values, **M9**: 247-52; **L16**: 349-50, 353
action as, **M10**: 45
material, procedural and, **L12**: 22-23, 107, 127, 139, 144, 164-68, 172-73, 229-30, 239-40, 348, 433-34
formed material and, **L12**: 383, 435-36, 468
meaning of term, **L15**: 228n
Instrumentalism, **M7**: xiv, 328, 416; **M12**: xviii, 177-78; **M15**: xii, 32n; **L2**: 3, 19, 21; **L3**: 150-51; **L4**: ix, 30n
Dewey's, **E3**: xxi-xxii; **M6**: xii, xviii-xix; **M11**: x, xvi, 360; **L5**: 157; **L14**: xvi
on truth, **M7**: 64-78, 425-29
compared with idealism and realism, **M10**: 338-65
meaning of, **M10**: 367-69; **L14**: 13-14
in China, **M11**: xx
related to valuation, **M11**: 4, 7, 376-77, 380, 383-87
as theory of knowledge, **L2**: ix-xxi; **L14**: 48-49, 172-76
in education, **L2**: xvii-xviii, xxi, 55-61
and James, **L2**: 13-15
Kurtz on, **L5**: xxiii-xxx
Hocking on, **L5**: 461-76
intention of, **L16**: 291-92
Instrumentality, **L10**: ix, 294; **L16**: 411
conception as, **L4**: 90n,154, 227
effectiveness of, **L4**: 109, 119, 193
law as, **L4**: 164, 166, 168
reflective thinking as, **L4**: 174-77
action as, **L4**: 179
experience as, **L4**: 188-91, 217
knowledge as, **L4**: 198, 200, 235, 238
value judgment as, **L4**: 214
of art, **L10**: 144-45
Instruments, **L12**: 135, 173
in scientific advance, **L12**: 388-89
Insull, Samuel, **L6**: 244
Insurance, **L13**: 313
unemployment, **L7**: 413
Insurgent America (A. M. Bingham), **L11**: 438-40
Insurgents
related to new political party, **L6**: 149-51, 161, 169, 412
and progressives conference, **L6**: 173
and prohibition, **L6**: 184
Integration
in social planning, **L9**: 230-31
of Wieman, **L9**: 432, 439
in Dewey's *Logic*, **L16**: 101n
need for, **L17**: 125
Integration Board, **L8**: 366
Intellect, **M12**: 82-83; **L2**: 105-6;

Intellect (*continued*)
L11: 394, 399, 402, 403; **L15**: 6-10
emotions and, **M9**: 345-46
Spencer and Bergson on, **M10**: 69
somnambulism of, **M12**: 160-61
related to intuition, **M12**: 227
related to culture, **L14**: 312-13
as entity, **L16**: 326, 334, 449
Intellectual
in education, **E5**: 64-66, 202-3, 256-60
history, **M9**: 224-25
individualism, **M9**: 306
in esthetics, **L10**: xiii, 21, 27, 37, 38, 44, 45, 52, 61, 76, 96, 130, 139, 187, 214, 220, 251, 254, 268, 279, 348
vs. practical, **L15**: 258-59
severance of, **L16**: 249, 255
related to valuing, **L16**: 311n, 312, 354
science as, **L16**: 364, 372
Intellectualism, **M4**: xvi; **M7**: 420, 422; **M12**: 147; **L4**: 46, 175
related to philosophy, **E1**: 34; **E5**: 15-17; **M9**: 276; **L1**: 28-29; **L16**: 381
Bradley on, **M4**: 51-75
compared with pragmatism on truth, **M6**: 3-11
and coeducation, **M6**: 159-60
Dewey opposes, **M9**: xx-xxiv
abstract, **M9**: 306-8
in Royce's philosophy, **M10**: 79-88
Intellectualization, **L8**: 201-2, 239
of art, **L10**: 123, 125, 127
Intellectuals
leadership of, **L11**: 129
Benda on, **L15**: 387-89
attitudes of, **L16**: 390-94, 409
Intellectual versus the City, The (M. White and L. White), **M1**: xxi
Intelligence, **M12**: 99-100, 108; **M14**: 10-11, 38, 207, 214; **L1**: 325-26
relation significant for, **E1**: 185
synthetic, **E1**: 189-90
Dewey and Green on, **E3**: xxix
related to science, **E3**: 125; **M10**: 130; **L9**: 98
related to morals, **E3**: 315-16; **M5**: 278-79; **L7**: 39; **L17**: 397-98
L. Ward on, **E4**: 206-9
nature of, **E5**: 397; **M12**: 134-35, 258-59; **L7**: xxiv-xxv; **L11**: xxix, 31-35, 548-49; **L16**: 333-35, 448-51; **L17**: 413-14
related to nature, **M4**: 15-30; **M7**: 62-63; **L4**: 156-77
related to society, **M4**: 36; **L2**: 231-34, 243, 329-37, 353, 360-61; **L7**: xi, 365-66; **L9**: 51-54, 107-11; **L13**: 54, 320-21; **L16**: 245, 379-80
related to democracy, **M4**: 39-40; **L2**: 365-66; **L11**: 50-52, 56, 219-20, 417; **L14**: 227, 276
pragmatic theory of, **M4**: 181-91; **M10**: xix-xx, 45
Greek conception of, **M5**: 109, 112-13; **L7**: 100, 103
during Renaissance and Enlightenment, **M5**: 153-56
evolutionary conception of, **M6**: xi
Maeterlinck on, **M6**: 129-32
related to values, **M7**: 45; **L4**: 211-12; **L13**: 256

Bergson on, **M7**: 202-4; **L11**: 428-30
idealism on, **M7**: 224-25; **M10**: 19-21
Hook on, **M9**: xx-xxi
in experience, **M9**: 333; **M10**: 15-18
and character, **M9**: 363-67
in empiricism, **M10**: 14
as directive force, **M10**: 46-48; **L4**: xviii, 60-86, 132, 136, 137, 142, 160, 166, 170-72, 175, 178, 196-98, 201, 224, 230, 234-38; **L13**: 42, 45
dependence of progress on, **M10**: 238-43
applied to justice, **M10**: 281-84
functions of, **M12**: 173-74, 226, 230; **L13**: 43, 266-69; **L17**: 458-59
development of, **M12**: 208; **L4**: 187
related to education, **M13**: 333; **L11**: 159-61, 164-65, 178, 193-95, 343-44, 559; **L13**: 53
J. Robinson on, **M13**: 422
in conduct, **M14**: 121-89
related to habits, **M14**: 121-26, 157
and desire, **M14**: 171-81
and method, **L2**: 114-15
compared with reason, **L7**: xxiii-xxiv
in judgment, **L7**: 235-37
value of, **L7**: 317; **L17**: 401, 478
and religious belief, **L9**: xx, 23-25, 38-40, 56-57, 432, 437, 438
related to art, **L10**: xvii, xxxii, 52, 66, 126n, 143, 217, 303, 312, 324, 351; **L15**: 316
applied to social problems, **L11**: xxi, xxv, xxxi, 37-38, 48-52, 55, 58-61, 64-65, 128-29, 259-60, 277, 293-94, 378-79, 564-65; **L14**: 74-77; **L15**: 41, 222, 253, 307, 378
obstacles to, **L11**: 84-85, 141-42, 144, 431, 502
authority of, **L11**: 141-45
freedom of, **L11**: 220, 344; **L13**: 39; **L15**: 175; **L17**: 473-74
vs. knowledge, **L14**: 6-7, 47-48
applied to legal questions, **L14**: 122
related to human nature, **L14**: 323-24, 332-33
for international conflict, **L16**: 399-400, 405
Socrates on, **L17**: 185-86

Intelligence in the Modern World, **L13**: 403

Intelligibility
through art, **L10**: 199, 217, 293, 295

Intensification
through art, **L10**: 246, 248, 297

Intension
logical, **L12**: 200, 292-93, 357-60

Intensity
as esthetic quality, **L10**: 159, 181, 184-88

Intensive magnitudes, **L12**: 204-6

Intention
development of, **E4**: 251-52
and will, **E4**: 273-75
utilitarians on, **M5**: 227-30
and motive, **L7**: 166-68, 173-75
goodness vs. good, **L17**: 337

Inter
as name, **L16**: 258, 264-65
Interaction, **L16**: 240
bearing on school problems, **M1**: 285-99
reveals potentiality in existence, **L1**: 129; **L14**: 109-10
social, **L1**: 134-39, 146-51, 156; **L14**: 117-18
of organism and environment, **L1**: 198-99, 215-17, 324; **L14**: 15-21, 28, 39-40, 64, 158, 161, 167, 185-86
in nature, **L1**: 207-8; **L4**: 168, 186-95, 221
necessary for knowledge, **L1**: 324; **L4**: 64, 162, 232, 236
knowing as, **L4**: xi, 86, 163, 164, 171
of external and internal, **L4**: xvi, xvii; **L13**: 24, 137
Newton on, **L4**: 115
in experimental method, **L4**: 120, 130, 142
results of, **L4**: 196-98, 207, 213, 246; **L13**: 68, 89-90
in art, **L10**: xvi, 50, 59-66, 70, 72, 126, 129, 139, 152, 156, 159, 165-68, 173, 179, 223-25, 235, 238, 251-55, 269, 276, 278, 286, 291-92, 307, 309, 313, 317, 323, 328-29, 333-34, 338
Peirce on, **L11**: 87
experience as, **L11**: 501
of child and environment, **L11**: 512-13
biological, **L12**: 31-40, 110, 199
and determination of kinds, **L12**: 111, 116-17, 133, 152-53, 164-66, 175-76, 220, 251-52, 288-89, 331-32
and causation, **L12**: 435, 440, 446-47, 452-53
principles of, **L13**: 25-27, 31, 33, 325-27
of human nature and culture, **L13**: 79, 86-87, 91, 117, 142, 184, 246-48, 273
and economics, **L13**: 115
related to science, **L16**: xxxiii-xxxiv
vs. transaction, **L16**: 4, 63, 96, 112n, 113-15, 144
nature of, **L16**: 6, 132, 135, 138, 192, 363
uses of, **L16**: 66-68, 98, 105-6, 116-21, 124
as name, **L16**: 71, 265
as stage of inquiry, **L16**: 100-104, 127-30
Balz on, **L16**: 428-29
of behavior, **L17**: 419
Interallied debts, **L6**: 364, 366-68, 372-73
Interception, **L12**: 404-5
Intercollegiate Socialist Society, **L14**: 431
Interdependence, **M13**: 382-83; **L2**: 332; **L8**: 73
physical vs. moral, **L13**: 180
global, **L17**: 453-54
Interest, **M12**: 191-92; **L1**: 130-31, 197, 235; **L13**: 194; **L17**: 423
as consciousness, **E2**: 19
related to psychical conditions, **E2**: 108; **E5**: 250
related to sensations, **E2**: 109-10, 240
of familiarity, **E2**: 110-14
and imagination, **E2**: 172-75
differentiation of, **E2**: 248; **E5**: 325
and emotion, **E2**: 292-93; **E4**: 186-88; **E5**: 113, 124-25, 129-37, 325
related to morality, **E3**: 304-6;

M9: 360-63
and self, **E3**: 306-7
as social, **E3**: 307-9; **M7**: 192-94; **M9**: 36-38; **L7**: 298-303, 336-37; **L13**: 111
scientific, **E3**: 310; **L13**: 165
in art, **E3**: 310-11; **L10**: 100, 193-95, 269, 271
and motive, **E4**: 275-76; **L7**: 290-92, 295, 298, 300
related to teacher and child, **E5**: 92-93, 142-43, 173, 175, 227-29, 260-61, 311
intellectual, **E5**: 113; **M7**: 191-92; **L6**: 88, 116-17
and attention, **E5**: 114-15, 320-21; **M13**: 339
and effort, **E5**: 114-19, 121, 131-33, 166-67
pleasure found in, **E5**: 120
psychology of, **E5**: 122-28, 137, 147-49
in Kantian and Herbartian theories, **E5**: 137-42
development of, **E5**: 144-45; **L17**: 238
in children, **E5**: 212-21; **L11**: 213; **L17**: 287, 292-93, 320
references on, **E5**: 339
Münsterberg on, **M1**: xiii-xiv
educative, **M6**: 290; **M7**: 153-97, 474-76; **M9**: 175, 183-85, 300; **L8**: 291, 297-98; **L13**: 379, 385
and observation, **M6**: 333-34; **L8**: 320-21
in *Cyclopedia of Education*, **M7**: 252-60, 275
qualities of, **M7**: 472-73; **L7**: 256-57, 296
meaning of, **M9**: 133-34; **L11**: 200, 502; **L17**: 280, 293
James on, **M13**: 364; **L14**: 160n
selective, **L6**: 14
as end, **L7**: 208-12
conflict of, **L11**: 56, 386; **L13**: 100-101, 115, 124-25, 133
in valuation, **L13**: 205-7, 217; **L15**: 67-68, 101-3; **L16**: 347-48
vs. will, **L15**: 12
Rice on, **L15**: 414-17
Interest and Effort in Education, **M7**: xxi, 469-76
Interest in Relation to Training of the Will, **E5**: xvi
Interjections
grammatical, **L15**: 132-35
Interlaken, Ind.
boys' school at, **M8**: 263-66
Intermediaries, **L12**: 316n
Intermediate school, **M1**: 43-44. *See also* Schools
Internal relations
in realism, **M6**: 138-45, 484-511
Internal Revenue, Bureau of, **L9**: 267
"Internal Social Reorganization after the War," **L13**: 315n
International Community and the Right of War, The (Sturzo), **L6**: 458n
International Conference (Peking), **L2**: 181, 184
International Congress of Arts and Science (1904), **M3**: 145-51, 352-81; **M10**: 56
International Congress of Philosophy (1926), **M7**: 64; **L3**: 3n, 385n
International court. *See* World Court
International Encyclopedia of the Social Sciences, **L6**: xxi
International Encyclopedia of Unified Science, **L13**: 271n;

International Encyclopedia of Unified Science (*continued*) **L14**: 28n; **L15**: 141n; **L16**: 187n
Internationalism, **M12**: 14, 197
lack of, in U.S., **L3**: 136-38
of modern world, **L3**: 348-53
International Journal of Ethics, **L15**: 324
International law, **L13**: 309; **L15**: 205-6
codification of, **M15**: xvi, 94, 122-26, 398-400, 407, 409-10
and World Court, **M15**: xviii, 388, 389
Great Britain and, **M15**: 106, 380, 386, 411
and Hague Tribunal, **M15**: 401-2
and outlawry of war, **M15**: 404, 414
related to Pact of Paris, **L6**: 193, 222-23
use of, **L6**: 205-6, 223, 365, 452, 454, 457-58
and foreign property, **L6**: 365
force related to, **L6**: 450-51
and non-recognition doctrine, **L6**: 470
sanctions and, **L6**: 473
International Library of Psychology, Philosophy, and Scientific Method, **L3**: 314, 315, 434
International organization
use of sanctions by, **L6**: 196, 210-11, 450-51, 461-63
Buell on, **L6**: 450-84
International Relations (Buell), **L6**: 473n
International relations, **M15**: x, xi; **L11**: 261-64, 276; **L15**: 208-9
affected by League of Nations, **M11**: 132-34; **M15**: 380-81
governed by treaties, **M11**: 135-38
economic aspects of, **M11**: 139-42
laws for, **M11**: 388-92
outlawry of war and, **M15**: xiv, 63-64, 90-91, 99, 108-21
moral problems and, **M15**: 53-54, 61-62
laws of nature and, **M15**: 54-56
influence of utilitarianism on, **M15**: 58-59
U.S. policy in, **M15**: 80-81, 88, 384, 396-97
responsibility of schools in, **M15**: 154
need for intelligence in, **L16**: 399-406
"International Supreme Court of Knowledge," **L11**: 127-29
Interpretant
meaning of term, **L15**: 142-44, 149
C. Morris on, **L16**: 9, 34-35, 45, 222
related to interpreter, **L16**: 231
in semiotic, **L16**: 234-39
Interpretation
tools of, **M6**: 264-65; **L8**: 221-24
Carnap on, **L16**: 31
Russell on, **L16**: 159-60
control of, **L17**: 353
"Interpretation of Savage Mind," **L17**: 425n
Interpreter
meaning of term, **L15**: 142-44
C. Morris on, **L16**: 9, 34-35, 222
related to interpretant, **L16**: 231
in semiotic, **L16**: 232, 234
Interrogatives, **L12**: 170-72

Interstate Commerce Commission, **L5**: 94; **L6**: 504
and railroad rates, **L6**: 368-71
Intervals, **L12**: 411, 463
esthetic function of, **L10**: 159-62, 165, 177-78, 182-83, 186, 188, 206-7, 213-16
Intervenors. *See* Thirds
Intolerance, **M13**: 308
in U.S., **M15**: 152-54
nature of, **L13**: 152-53, 277
in Germany and Italy, **L13**: 301
vs. democracy, **L14**: 277
Intrinsic
meaning of, **L13**: 216, 327; **L15**: 42-45
character, **L14**: 305
theory, applied to valuing, **L16**: 346-50
"Intrinsic Good" (B. Savery), **L15**: 42n
Introduction to Logic (Tarski), **L16**: 40n-42n
Introduction to Logic, An (Joseph), **L12**: 420n
Introduction to Metaphysics, An (Bergson), **M7**: xiii
Introduction to Semantics (Carnap), **L16**: 17-32
Introduction to the Principles of Morals and Legislation, An (Bentham), **L11**: 13
Introspection, **M12**: 192, 227; **L1**: 255-56; **L16**: 345
method of, **E1**: 53-54; **E2**: 11-15; **L15**: 27-28, 64, 68, 70, 74, 123-25, 136, 150
Harris on, **E5**: 375-76
and experience, **M1**: 118n
defined, **M13**: 392
Rice on, **L15**: 410, 428-36
Introspective psychology, **M10**: 57-58
Intuition, **M7**: 286; **M8**: 25; **M12**: 227, 234; **M14**: 26, 131; **L1**: 152, 227, 256; **L3**: 292; **L4**: 113, 146, 149, 209; **L5**: 249; **L11**: 429, 431; **L12**: 26, 28-29, 31, 93, 107, 147-48, 226-27, 498-99; **L13**: xii, 256; **L16**: 186n
meaning of, **E2**: 205-7; **E4**: 207, 308
related to knowledge, **E2**: 207-12; **E5**: 323; **L17**: 371
male and female, **E4**: 209
Bergson on, **M7**: 3, 201-2; **M10**: 38; **L14**: 101
in *Cyclopedia of Education*, **M7**: 260-61
in morality, **L7**: 238, 262, 266-68, 272-73
related to rules, **L7**: 280
in esthetics, **L10**: 40, 41, 135, 196-97, 270-71, 295-99
as empirical, **L12**: 205, 467
vs. valuing, **L13**: 194
in mathematics, **L16**: 33n
related to logic, **L16**: 192
Kaufmann on, **L16**: 195, 198
related to memory, **L17**: 334
method of, **L17**: 481
Intuitionalism, **E4**: 148; **L5**: 149, 150
compared with empiricism, **E3**: 284-85; **M2**: 31-38
and ethical theory, **E4**: 42
related to morality, **E4**: 107-8, 114, 127, 144, 310; **M5**: 208-9, 213-14, 279, 288-94
history of, **E4**: 123-31
theory of conscience in, **E4**: 305-6
compared with evolutionary method, **M2**: 24-31
and casuistry, **M5**: 295
Inukai, Ki, **L6**: 456

Invariants, **L12**: 387-88
Invention, **M12**: 101, 103, 108, 149-50, 270
  Baldwin on, **E5**: 398-99
  influences school, **E5**: 451
  affects family, **L7**: 374, 445-46
  social effect of, **L13**: 253; **L17**: 478
  as product of science, **L13**: 311-12; **L17**: 435-36
  conflict promotes, **L17**: 153, 158
Investigation, **M12**: 164-65
  of valuations, **L13**: 245
  value of, **L17**: 481-82
Investment
  political protection of, **L14**: 94
Involvement, **L12**: 57, 60n, 174-75, 220, 276-79, 310, 329. *See also* Inference, **L12**
Ipse dixit method, **M12**: 175
IQ tests, **M9**: xiii; **M13**: xiii; **M15**: 181-82; **L5**: 18
Ireland
  ancient law of, **M5**: 30, 64, 83; **L7**: 29, 59, 76
Irish, **M11**: 71, 241, 286, 293
Irkutsk, USSR, **M13**: 235
Irons, David, **E4**: 172, 177
Irrationalism, **M7**: 418; **L17**: xx, xxxii
Irrationality
  cultivation of, **M11**: 107-11
  instinct as, **M13**: 243
  of nature, **L4**: 168
Irreconcilables
  and outlawry of war, **M15**: 113, 119, 405-7
Irving, Washington, **M8**: 292
Is
  and moral conduct, **E3**: 104-9
  double meaning of, **L12**: 137-38, 289, 307
"Is a Fact a True Proposition?—A Reply" (Ducasse), **L16**: 35-36
Isaiah, **L7**: 83, 88, 90
Ishii, Kikujiro
  on Japanese-Chinese relation, **M11**: 158, 175, 394
Islam, **L14**: 406
Isocrates, **L17**: 182-84
Isolation, **L4**: 140, 163, 194, 245-46; **L10**: 253, 257
  bearing on school problems, **M1**: 285-99
  in *Cyclopedia of Education*, **M7**: 261-62
  of cultural factors, **L13**: 79
  in philosophy vs. science, **L16**: 413
  of subject-matter, **L16**: 417-19
  of logic, **L16**: 444
  in science, **L17**: 356-57
  moral consequences of, **L17**: 457
Isolation in the School (E. Young), **M1**: 269n, 272n
Isolationism, **M10**: 193-95; **M12**: xxi, 2-7; **L2**: 168, 169, 375; **L3**: 351-52; **L11**: 261-64; **L13**: xv, 186
Isolationists
  in politics, **L17**: 141, 562
  educational, **L17**: 454
Isomorphism, **L12**: 396-99, 407
Israel, Edward L., **L6**: 381
Israel, Harold E., **L16**: 170n
Israel. *See also* Hebrews
  wealth in, **M5**: 91, 103; **L7**: 84, 94
  religious law in, **M5**: 93-94, 98-99; **L7**: 86, 90-91
  politics in, **M5**: 97; **L7**: 89
Is There a God? A Conversation (Wieman, Macintosh, and

Otto), **L9**: xxi-xxiii, 213-28, 417
Iswolsky, Alexander P., **M11**: 282-83, 308, 313
Italian Letters (Goethe), **M7**: 290
Italy, **M15**: xviiin, 146; **L6**: 143-45; **L8**: 20; **L11**: 305, 355, 357; **L13**: 180, 301, 315; **L14**: 275, 365; **L15**: 179, 220, 245; **L16**: 390
in WWI, **M11**: xiii, 136, 177, 264, 274
politics in, **M11**: 120
on League of Nations, **M11**: 140
Fascist revolution in, **L7**: 427-28
art of, **L10**: 157, 256, 315, 322
Ito, Hirobumi, **M11**: 170
Itongo
as aspect of individualism, **M5**: 29n; **L7**: 28n
I Want to Be Like Stalin (Esipov and Goncharov), **L15**: 373-74

Jackman, Wilbur S., **M1**: 72
Jacks, Lawrence Pearsall, **M15**: 85
Jackson, Andrew, **M13**: 303, 305; **L17**: 347
Jackson, Robert H., **L15**: 348
Jaeger, Gustav, **L17**: 10, 554
Jamblicus, **M2**: 167
James, Alice, **L11**: 465, 466
James, Henry, **M3**: 193; **L10**: vii; **L11**: 442, 465, 467; **L17**: 40
James, Henry, Sr., **M6**: 98; **L11**: 442-45, 464-66
James, William (grandfather), **L11**: 445
James, William, **E1**: xxviii, 199; **E4**: xvii, xxiii, 159n; **E5**: xiii, 162; **M2**: ix, 297; **M3**: xxiii, xxiv, 312; **M6**: 46n, 91, 92, 94-98, 101-2; **M7**: 142; **M8**: 22, 94; **M9**: xx, xxii; **M10**: 12, 439; **M13**: xxi, 418, 488; **M15**: 226, 227, 333, 335; **L1**: 299; **L2**: 3, 40, 126, 231; **L5**: 501; **L6**: xiii, 283; **L8**: 227, 228; **L10**: 365; **L12**: 316n, 510n; **L13**: 363; **L14**: ix, x, xviii, 5, 301, 399; **L17**: xxxiii
influences Dewey, **E2**: xxvi, 5; **E4**: xiv-xv, xxiii; **M1**: xiii, xxiii; **L4**: ix, xviii; **L5**: xxii, 157-59; **L6**: xii, 500; **L10**: vii, xi-xiv, xxv
and afferent theory, **E2**: 54
on integration, **E2**: 86
meaning of essence in, **E4**: 46-47
on free will, **E4**: 94n
and ego, **E4**: 95n
on conscience, **E4**: 109
on emotions, **E4**: 153, 160-63, 170-72, 174-75, 177, 178n, 184n; **M5**: 232; **L7**: 188, 190; **L10**: 221, 361
on thought, **E4**: 157n, 183n; **M1**: 70; **M6**: 299; **L11**: xiii, 69, 82, 444, 470-77; **L16**: 51n, 468
and principle of antithesis, **E4**: 165
on affect, **E4**: 180, 182
on effort, **E5**: 152
on child-study, **E5**: 210
on philosophy and psychology at University of Chicago, **M1**: ix; **M5**: ix-x
on metaphysics, **M1**: 115; **M13**: 498; **L15**: 3-8, 456
on pluralism, **M2**: 204

James, William (*continued*)
on psychological logic, **M3**: 66
on idea, **M3**: 72; **M4**: 102-3
on belief, **M3**: 98n
on consciousness, **M3**: 102n, 123, 351; **L1**: 236
on experience, **M3**: 130; **M4**: 295-96; **M7**: xvi, 74; **M12**: 217, 222; **L1**: 18, 19, 370; **L5**: 228, 254; **L10**: 62, 125, 355, 358; **L14**: 18n, 21n; **L17**: 434, 566
on continuous transition, **M3**: 142n
Dewey on, **M4**: xx-xxii; **M13**: 479n; **L3**: 147-49
pragmatism of, **M4**: 98-115, 248-49; **M6**: xi-xii; **M7**: 326-29; **M10**: xiii, xxiii, 71, 87, 417; **M11**: 90; **M12**: 100-101; **M13**: 447-48, 457, 475; **L2**: xii-xv, 6-17, 160-62; **L3**: xv-xvi; **L4**: 90n; **L5**: xxix, 477, 478, 480n; **L8**: 11; **L10**: viii, xxiii; **L15**: xxvii-xxviii, 331; **L16**: 183n
on significance of object, **M4**: 101-2
on truth, **M4**: 103, 107-12; **M6**: xiii-xiv, xix, xxii
philosophy of, **M4**: 104; **M6**: 46n, 92, 94-97, 101-2; **M12**: ix, xxv-xxviii, 91, 205-20
on design, **M4**: 105-6
on self, **M5**: 85; **M7**: 343; **L7**: 77-79, 293
on animal conduct, **M5**: 190
on selfishness, **M5**: 341
moral theory of, **M5**: 370n; **L15**: 19-26
on psychologist's fallacy, **M5**: 525; **L10**: 128, 358
psychology of, **M6**: 93, 99; **L14**: 39, 155-67, 337-40; **L15**: 18, 39, 147, 398n; **L16**: 190
empiricism of, **M6**: 94, 100; **M7**: 142-48, 297, 324; **M12**: xi, 207, 217; **L15**: xxii-xxiii, 10-17
on reality, **M6**: 99-100
literary expression of, **M6**: 100-101; **M7**: ix-x
on knowledge, **M6**: 273n; **M12**: xxv, 208-9, 215-16; **L2**: 143n
and Royce, **M7**: xiv, 423, 427, 430-31; **M10**: xxiv, xxv, 85; **L11**: 472
on states of mind, **M7**: 33-38
and logical ideal, **M7**: 134
on individuality, **M7**: 238; **M12**: 236
on memory, **M7**: 369; **L17**: 328, 564
and instincts, **M7**: 391, 399
on "cashing in," **M10**: 44, 366-67
on neutrality, **M10**: 50-52
on behavior, **M10**: 57; **L16**: 347
and Peirce, **M10**: 72-78; **M14**: xix; **L6**: 274; **L11**: 422, 482, 483
on spatiality, **M10**: 80
and American tradition, **M11**: 53; **L3**: 117, 369-70
admired by Japanese, **M11**: 157
on instrumentalism, **M11**: 384-85
compared with Bergson, **M12**: xxx, 221, 222, 235
compared with Russell, **M12**: xxx, 236
opposes dogmatism, **M12**: 220
achievements of, **M12**: 249-50; **L2**: 158-59
on success, **M13**: 307

on concreteness, **M13**: 308, 324
on world, **M13**: 309
as meliorist, **M14**: xxi-xxii
on war, **M14**: 79-80; **L13**: 290
on stream of consciousness, **M14**: 125
on reason vs. passion, **M14**: 136
on significance of names, **L1**: 106-7
on habit, **L2**: 335; **L7**: 205, 206
Mumford criticizes, **L3**: 145-49
as Gifford Lecturer, **L4**: vii
on block universe, **L4**: 167
on seat of authority, **L4**: 227
"fringe" of, **L5**: 248n
on religion, **L5**: 267; **L10**: 79, 356; **L13**: 367
Cohen on, **L6**: xiv, 300, 489-91; **L14**: 408
on familiar and unfamiliar, **L8**: 275
on time, **L10**: 29, 354; **L14**: 100-101
on perception, **L10**: 97, 357
on variation, **L10**: 173
on sounds, **L10**: 210, 213, 361
F. Schiller's interest in, **L11**: 156
Perry on, **L11**: 441-45, 464-78
life of, **L15**: 9, 326
influences Bentley, **L16**: xxviii
on observation, **L16**: 52
double-barrelled concept of, **L16**: 53, 83n
on subject, **L16**: 88n
on semiotic, **L16**: 239
on cultural blocks, **L17**: 36, 556
James Arthur Foundation, **L14**: 98n
"Jamesian Datum, The" (A. Bentley), **L16**: xxviiin-xxixn
James-Lange theory, **E4**: 152, 169; **E5**: 360n, 363, 366; **M7**: xvii
James Lectures, **L10**: 7
Jameson, John Alexander, **E4**: 78n
Janet, Paul, **M4**: 77
Japan, **M15**: xviiin, 217, 411; **L8**: 13; **L11**: 357; **L14**: 275; **L15**: 348, 352-53, 369-70, 495; **L17**: 140, 524, 555
customs of, **M5**: 24, 64; **L7**: 23, 59
effects of WWI on, **M11**: ix, xvii-xviii, 73, 113, 157-58, 201, 202, 229, 230
political situation in, **M11**: xvii-xviii, 154-61, 165-74, 178; **M12**: 66, 68-69
Dewey in, **M11**: xvii-xviii, 395
China's relation with, **M11**: xx, 174-80, 183, 186-204, 207-8, 213, 220, 224-33, 394; **M12**: 22, 27, 29-40, 45-46, 63-68; **M13**: 77, 85, 189, 193, 202-3, 205, 255; **L2**: 176-78, 183
and U.S., **M11**: 150-55, 191, 194-95, 207, 229; **M12**: 36-37; **M13**: 79-85, 127, 173, 189, 205, 212; **M15**: 124-25; **L2**: 179-80
economics of, **M11**: 161-67, 206-7, 214; **M12**: 34-40, 74; **M13**: 82, 85, 91, 144, 258-60
diplomacy of, **M11**: 177-79, 193, 206; **M13**: 219
psychology of, **M11**: 208-9, 222
and Russia, **M11**: 230, 271; **M12**: 60-64; **M13**: 214, 237
and Germany, **M11**: 230,

Japan (*continued*)
394-95; **M12**: 26, 29-30, 34-37; **M13**: 260
in drug traffic, **M11**: 237-40
on armaments, **M12**: 22, 32-34; **M13**: 205; **L6**: 460
propaganda in, **M12**: 45, 63; **L6**: 203, 211
related to Great Britain, **M13**: 77, 91, 121, 125-26, 177-79, 191, 212-15, 219
hostile methods of, **M13**: 81, 82, 174
liberalism of, **M13**: 84, 257
blockade of, **M13**: 180
public opinion in, **M13**: 256-61
invades Manchuria and Shanghai, **L6**: xx, 190-91, 194, 204-6, 217-20
and Pact of Paris, **L6**: 193-94, 202, 204, 217-18
sanctions and, **L6**: 202-5, 216, 453-54, 456-57, 465-67, 469-70, 475-76
relation of League of Nations to, **L6**: 206-7, 450, 452, 458-59, 466
foreign interests in, **L6**: 209-10
art of, **L10**: 14, 315, 336
Japan Chronicle, **M11**: 239; **M13**: 154, 257
Japanese Kumi, **M5**: 24; **L7**: 23
Jaspers, Karl, **M3**: xxiv
Jaurès, Jean, **L15**: xxix
Jean Arnolfini and Wife (van Eyck), **L10**: 213, 361
Jeans, James Hopwood, **L9**: 242; **L11**: 435
Jefferson, Thomas, **M5**: 142; **M7**: 380; **M13**: 299, 303, 338; **L7**: 141; **L8**: 52; **L9**: 162-63; **L11**: 64, 464, 574; **L13**: 82, 108, 300, 401, 403; **L14**: xxiv; **L15**: xiv, xxvii-xxviii, xxxi, 366; **L17**: 138, 147, 473
social philosophy of, **L11**: 251, 370-71, 377
on liberalism, **L13**: 67
on human nature, **L13**: 68-69
on commerce, **L13**: 81, 107
on government, **L13**: 91, 100-102, 173-79; **L14**: 201-3, 209-19; **L17**: xxiv
on property, **L13**: 177
on happiness, **L13**: 177-79
biography and character of, **L14**: 201-9, 220-23
moral and religious philosophy of, **L14**: 203, 212-13, 215, 218-20; **L17**: xxvi
educational plan of, **L14**: 210-11
Locke influences, **L17**: 437
Jehovah, **M5**: 92-97, 100-101; **L17**: 396. *See also* Yahweh
Jellinek, Georg, **L6**: 269, 270
Jena, Germany, battle of, **M8**: 172, 180
Jena, University of, **L17**: 485, 486, 568
Jennings, Herbert Spencer, **L16**: 137
on sex and parenthood, **L7**: 460-61
Jensen, Carl Christian, **L11**: 506
Jespersen, Otto, **L1**: 72, 73
Jessup, Bertram E., **L16**: 346n
Jesus, **E4**: 5; **M5**: 103, 104; **L7**: 83, 94, 95, 136, 140; **L17**: 531, 532
and religious acts, **E4**: 4
teachings of, **E4**: 7-8, 226, 367
and moral motive, **E4**: 112
Macintosh on, **L14**: 286-88

philosophy of, **L17**: 15-16, 538-39
Tolstoy on, **L17**: 389
Jevons, Frank Byron, **M5**: 410n
on Greek education, **L17**: 177-80
Jevons, W. Stanley, **L8**: 312n
in new logic, **E3**: 75
and philosophical courses, **E3**: 90, 92
on sense of words, **M6**: 324n
on scientific observation, **M6**: 331; **L8**: 318
on experiment, **L8**: 257-58
on proper names, **L12**: 363, 364
Jewish Bride, The (Rembrandt), **L10**: 117, 358
Jews. *See also* Hebrews
customs of, **E4**: 87
as minority, **M11**: xiii, 241
rights of, **M11**: 71, 137
treatment of, **M11**: 255, 262, 264, 278-80, 306, 307
organizations of, **M11**: 285
relief fund for, **M11**: 309
in Turkey, **M15**: 140-41
in Romania, **M15**: 391
theology of, **L8**: 24; **L10**: 340
Job, Book of, **M5**: 97-98; **L7**: 89-90
John, Saint, **L17**: 531, 533, 573
John Dewey: An Intellectual Portrait (Hook), **L6**: xviii
John Dewey Labor Research Fund, **L14**: 311
John Dewey Lectures in China (Clopton and Ou), **L15**: 369n
Johns Hopkins University, **M4**: xi; **M6**: 175n; **M8**: 129; **M10**: 110; **L6**: xiii, 126; **L11**: 591
Dewey at, **L5**: 150
influences graduate schools, **L5**: 150-52
Bentley at, **L16**: xiii
Johnson, Alvin, **L8**: 3n, 13n, 19n; **L17**: 558
on fear, **L17**: 86
tribute to, **L17**: 147-48
Johnson, Edwin C., **L11**: 531; **L14**: 355
Johnson, Francis Howe, **E3**: 192-93
Johnson, Hugh S., **L9**: 280-81
Johnson, Marietta L., **M7**: 387; **M8**: 208, 414
educational experiment of, **M8**: 222-35
on physical development, **M8**: 390
Johnson, Samuel
on literature, **L10**: 85, 86, 102
Johnson, Willard, **L5**: 417n
Johnson, William Ernest, **L12**: 128n
on definition, **L16**: 166, 168, 181n
Johnson's Universal Cyclopaedia, **E4**: xviii; **E5**: 347-50
Johnstone, James, **M8**: 449-59
Joie de Vivre (Matisse), **L10**: 280
Joint Committee on Unemployment, **L9**: 81n, 253, 271-72
Jones, Henry, **M2**: 333n, 352; **M7**: 345
Jones, Lewis H., **E5**: xciv-xcvi
Jones, Richard, **E5**: xciv
Jonson, Ben, **L10**: 163, 359
Jordan, David Starr, **M6**: 155
Joseph, Horace William, **L12**: 87n, 299n, 303, 419n-20n; **L16**: 165
Joule, James Prescott, **L16**: 65, 99
Journalism
objectivity of, **L11**: 269-73

Journal of Aesthetics and Art Criticism, **L16**: 395, 463
Journal of Philosophy, **M15**: xii, 20, 27; **L14**: 16n, 387n; **L15**: xxxiii, 63, 71, 136n, 326, 331, 434, 473; **L16**: xxxi, 200, 279
Journal of Speculative Philosophy, **E1**: xxiii-xxiv, xxvi; **L5**: 150
Journal of Symbolic Logic, **L16**: xxxi, 276, 443n
Journals, **L15**: 87-88, 362
Jowett, Benjamin, **E5**: 262; **L2**: 127
Joy
 compared with grief, **E4**: 158, 168
Joyce, James, **M12**: xxvi
Juárez, Mexico, **L2**: 195
Judd, Charles H., **L17**: 513, 514, 572
Judges, **L13**: 300, 403. *See also* Courts; Critics
 for New York City, **L9**: 348-53
Judging
 as element of moral conduct, **M5**: 375
 value of, **L17**: 337-38
Judgment, **L8**: 124; **L11**: 15; **L13**: 148; **L15**: 12-14, 64-65, 139. *See also* Moral judgment; Valuation-judgment
 related to thought, **E2**: 178, 186-91; **E5**: 322-23; **M6**: 259-66; **L8**: 210-20
 and reasoning, **E2**: 199-200
 esthetic, **E2**: 277-78; **L10**: 251, 253, 257-60, 329
 as statement of action, **E3**: 230-33
 ethical, **E5**: 79-82; **M3**: xiii-xvi, 3-39; **L13**: xi
 standard related to, **E5**: 228; **M12**: 179-80; **L7**: 237-40; **L17**: 397
 and observation, **E5**: 321-22; **L13**: 87
 Royce on, **M1**: 253n
 in logic, **M2**: 296-97; **M12**: 156-57; **L2**: 17-18
 as element of character, **M6**: 382-85; **L17**: 337, 347
 in *Cyclopedia of Education*, **M7**: 262-64
 of practice, **M8**: xv-xix
 mechanism and, **M8**: 18-20
 related to value, **M8**: 23-49; **M13**: 4, 11, 14-15, 24; **M15**: xii, 20-23, 26, 231, 341; **L4**: 207-14, 217-19, 238, 249; **L6**: 428; **L7**: 216-17, 263-65, 267-68; **L16**: 353-56
 development of, **M9**: 204-5; **L8**: 221-23; **L13**: 56
 Locke's successors on, **M9**: 277
 Ueberweg on, **M10**: 86
 Dewey vs. D. Robinson on, **M10**: 98-108, 416-30
 object of, **M13**: 6, 9, 33, 44-47; **M15**: 350-52; **L7**: 188, 204; **L17**: 3, 5
 instrumental and creational, **M13**: 6, 10n
 retrospective, **M13**: 12; **M15**: 37, 350-54, 356, 358-60, 369
 nature of, **M13**: 15, 16, 19-20, 45; **L4**: x, 88, 170, 206-8, 211-12, 221, 228, 230; **L16**: 311-15; **L17**: 333
 and prejudice, **M13**: 243, 437
 scientific, **M13**: 434; **L16**: 317
 motor-affective acts and, **M15**: 21-22
 Prall on, **M15**: 23, 341-42

past, present, and future facts and, **M15**: 28-29, 37-39, 355-58, 369, 375-77; **L13**: 44
Lovejoy on, **M15**: 33, 39
subject-matter and object in, **M15**: 34
Picard on, **M15**: 339-40
Aristotle on, **L4**: xxi
and common sense, **L6**: 430
as intellectual, **L7**: 235-37
sensitivity in, **L7**: 242, 268-72
individual, **L7**: 287, 297; **L12**: 109-11, 283
of art, **L10**: 118, 174-75, 271, 302-16, 320, 323, 328
and existence, **L12**: 124, 165-66
and time, **L12**: 137
and inquiry, **L12**: 432, 462-65, 483-84; **L14**: 175
related to experience, **L14**: 153-54; **L17**: 335, 353-54
memorizing antagonistic to, **L17**: 326, 333
and choice, **L17**: 339-40
White on, **L17**: 481
Judicial empiricism, **L2**: 28
Jugo-Slavs, **M11**: 71, 263, 264
Julius Rosenthal Foundation, **L14**: 115n
Jung, Carl Gustav, **M7**: 139; **M11**: 360; **M14**: 107
Jural theory, **M5**: 207
"Juridical Persons" (Vinogradoff), **L2**: 41n
Jurisdiction, **L1**: 154-56
Jurisprudence
concept of personality in, **L6**: 268-70
on civil liberty, **L11**: 374
Pound on, **L17**: 106
Jus Naturale, **M3**: 49, 51
Jusserand, Jean Jules, **M11**: 317
Justice, **E3**: 105-7; **M14**: 17-18, 138; **L2**: 138
Plato on, **M5**: 8, 116-17, 122-23; **L7**: 10, 107-8, 113-14, 411
in primitive society, **M5**: 32, 64; **L7**: 30-33, 59
Chinese sense of, **M5**: 34; **L7**: 32-33
Hebrew idea of, **M5**: 96-97, 104; **L7**: 87-88, 96
Greek conception of, **M5**: 108, 114-17; **L7**: 99, 104-7
in industry, **M5**: 150-52
distributive and corrective, **M5**: 371-72
absolutistic notion of, **M10**: xxxviii; **L17**: xxiii
intelligence applied to, **M10**: 281-84
and property, **L2**: 292
social, **L7**: 84
in Roman law, **L7**: 130, 133
as standard, **L7**: 249-52, 279; **L17**: 397
legalistic view of, **L7**: 252
as virtue, **L7**: 259
problem of, **L7**: 406-7
in distribution of wealth, **L7**: 434-36
Justinian, Code of, **L7**: 132
Just So Stories (Kipling), **M8**: 241

Kafirs, **M5**: 65; **L7**: 60
clanship of, **M5**: 25; **L7**: 24-25
concepts of self of, **M5**: 29n; **L7**: 28n
marriage customs of, **M5**: 511-12
on women, **L7**: 439
Kahn, Sholom J.
on Dewey's metaphysics, **L16**: 383-89, 456-62

Kaizo (Japan), **M13**: 433
Kallen, Horace M., **M10**: 20n, 27n; **L2**: 159, 160; **L3**: 92n; **L11**: 563-66, 598-99; **L14**: 224n, 235n, 357n; **L17**: 444
Kalokagathos, **M5**: 107, 110; **L7**: 98, 101, 271
Kalon, **M5**: 124; **L7**: 116, 118, 238
Kandel, I. L., **L9**: 208-9
Kant, Immanuel, **E1**: 10, 19, 166, 203, 253, 271, 301, 314, 326, 379, 389, 392, 420; **E3**: 158; **E4**: xix, 52n, 106, 193, 211, 215; **E5**: 26; **M3**: 54, 310; **M4**: 42, 52, 248, 254; **M5**: 4, 155, 440, 518; **M6**: x, 392; **M7**: 51, 289; **M8**: 142, 145, 177, 419, 421, 423; **M9**: 64; **M10**: 5; **M11**: 38n, 94, 346; **M12**: xi, xxixn, 28, 197; **M15**: xiii, 348; **L1**: 55, 81, 350; **L2**: 15, 27; **L3**: 3, 7, 296; **L4**: 33; **L5**: 148, 252; **L6**: 17; **L7**: 6; **L8**: 9; **L9**: xxx, 9, 217; **L11**: 80, 403n, 480, 592; **L12**: 86, 114, 156, 189, 412, 454n, 510-11; **L13**: 84; **L14**: xi, 304-5, 331
  Dewey's criticism of, **E1**: xxvi-xxvii
  philosophic method of, **E1**: 34-47, 260, 277; **E5**: 19-20; **M2**: 153; **M7**: 425; **M12**: 136-37; **L4**: 47-50, 53, 229-31; **L6**: 269; **L16**: 115n, 458
  on self, **E1**: 152-53; **E3**: 62-74, 159, 160; **E4**: 256-57; **M5**: 328; **M7**: 342, 344-45
  apperceptive unity in, **E1**: 190
  related to mathematics, **E1**: 273
  on ideas, **E1**: 385-86; **M1**: 252
  influence of Leibniz on, **E1**: 428-34
  transcendental deduction of, **E3**: 62-74
  on experience, **E3**: 72; **M3**: 133-37; **M6**: 447; **M10**: 358; **M14**: 34, 37, 168-70; **L1**: 376; **L4**: 113; **L11**: 73, 78, 91; **L14**: 190
  courses on, **E3**: 91, 92
  and rules, **E3**: 102, 103
  and individual, **E3**: 118; **M5**: 86-87, 526; **L7**: 86-87
  compared with Hegel, **E3**: 134-38
  on knowledge, **E3**: 135-36; **E5**: 4, 14, 19, 21; **L4**: xvi, xviii, 137-45
  Caird on, **E3**: 180-83
  Mahaffy and Bernard on, **E3**: 184-85
  on good, **E3**: 290
  on desire and will, **E3**: 290-91; **E5**: 137-42; **M5**: 287-88
  theory of obligation of, **E3**: 328, 333-35; **E4**: 319-29, 331
  ethics of, **E4**: xiv, 260, 263; **M5**: 158; **L5**: 265, 503; **L15**: 47, 51, 129n, 217
  influences intuitionalism, **E4**: 129-30
  moral theory of, **E4**: 142, 145-47; **M5**: 156, 211, 213, 280-81, 387-88; **M7**: 295, 360; **M8**: 147-50; **M9**: 363-64; **L7**: 154-55, 262, 315
  and esthetics, **E4**: 194; **L10**: xii, xv, xix, 257-59, 299-300
  on judging others, **E4**: 274
  on virtue, **E4**: 352; **M14**: 122
  on synthetic judgment, **M1**: 171

and logic, **M1**: 172; **M7**: 438; **M10**: 335, 367
on reality, **M1**: 247
Royce and, **M1**: 252-53; **M10**: 80, 83, 84, 86
dualism of, **M2**: x; **L17**: xxx
on necessity, **M2**: 152
on noumenon, **M2**: 160-61
on ontology, **M2**: 168-69, 171
on opinion, **M2**: 173
on optimism, **M2**: 175
on organic, **M2**: 178
on permanence, **M2**: 187
on phenomenon, **M2**: 189-90
on phoronomy, **M2**: 202
on rationalism, **M2**: 217; **M3**: 55; **M7**: 220-21, 335
on realism, **M2**: 219
on object, **M2**: 250-52
on transcendent, **M2**: 257; **M7**: 357
on reason, **M2**: 260; **M5**: 282; **L1**: 48-49, 53; **L4**: xiii; **L7**: 146-47
Whewell and Lotze similar to, **M2**: 373n
on man's nature, **M5**: 75, 177, 339; **L7**: 69, 449
on good will, **M5**: 221-26; **M9**: 359; **L14**: 73n
on ends, **M5**: 264, 283-86, 352
on duty, **M5**: 313-18; **M8**: 162-66, 173, 474; **M10**: 226-28
on human dignity, **M5**: 466
related to dialectic, **M6**: 422
on form, **M6**: 460; **M7**: 252
idealism of, **M7**: 138, 227, 232, 291, 328; **M8**: 157; **M10**: xxv; **M12**: 108, 127; **L2**: 14
and intuition, **M7**: 261
psychological mode of thinking of, **M7**: 291
and phenomenalism, **M7**: 297
on empiricism and rationalism, **M7**: 335
on value, **M7**: 363; **L2**: 88-89
on truth, **M7**: 413, 415, 440-41
on activity, **M7**: 436
influences Germany, **M8**: xxvii-xxxi, 146-60, 197-98; **M10**: 223
on correlation, **M8**: 90
on principle of personality, **M8**: 161, 432
on civilization, **M8**: 167-71, 186-87; **L7**: 69, 79
Fichte continues work of, **M8**: 173
on church dogmas, **M8**: 184
on actual and ideal, **M8**: 430
on education, **M9**: 101-2; **M13**: 401; **L13**: xvii
on Hume's sensationalism, **M10**: 12-13, 332
and Peirce, **M10**: 71, 72, 74n, 87, 366; **L6**: 276
G. Morris on, **M10**: 112-13; **L5**: 152
Santayana on, **M10**: 306, 307
on perception, **M12**: 221; **L10**: 131
tribute to, **M15**: 8-13
on pragmatism, **L2**: 3, 4, 7n; **L14**: 11
on will, **L2**: 31n; **L17**: 403
on freedom, **L3**: 108-9; **L10**: 286n
J. Marsh on, **L5**: 179, 183, 185-89, 191
on separation of intellectual and affective, **L6**: 331
reinforces Lockean tradition, **L6**: 489
on good and law, **L7**: 155, 219-25, 229, 285
on motive, **L7**: 173

Kant, Immanuel (*continued*)
and German literary criticism, **L8**: 361
on arts, **L10**: 221
on causal necessity, **L13**: 120-21
on law, **L14**: 120
Cohen on, **L14**: 382, 394-95, 399
Hocking on, **L14**: 412, 418
epistemology of, **L15**: xxix, 28, 91-94
Croce on, **L15**: 441
Dubislav on, **L16**: 161
Kantianism, **M2**: 153
and hedonism, **E3**: 292-93
criticism of conduct in, **E3**: 293-300
Raub on, **M4**: 227-28
Kantor, Jacob R., **L16**: 130n, 468
on nervous system, **M13**: 39n
logic of, **L16**: 187, 190-92
on propositions, **L16**: 208
Kant's Critical Philosophy for English Readers (Mahaffy and J. Bernard), **E3**: 184-85
Kaplan, Abraham, **L16**: 209n
on *Art as Experience*, **L10**: vii-xxxiii
on definition, **L16**: 171-73
Kappa Delta Pi, **L13**: xiv, 375
Karlgren, Anton, **L3**: 220
"Karl Marx and the American Teacher" (Brameld), **L11**: 383n
Karma, **M5**: 100; **L7**: 91
Kato, Tomosaburo, **M13**: 194, 205, 214; **M15**: 411
Katuin, Gerald A., **M13**: 25n
Katz, David, **L16**: 232n
Kaufmann, Felix
procedures of, **L16**: 157n, 208-9
logic of, **L16**: 187, 193-98
Kay, Jean, **L14**: 240, 243
Keats, George, **L10**: 39; **L11**: 504
Keats, John, **L10**: 138, 359
on esthetics, **L10**: 26n, 38-41, 76, 149, 354, 355
technique of, **L10**: 116, 129-30, 210, 238, 259
on poetry, **L10**: 220, 262, 349, 362, 366
"Keep Out of Spain!" (*Christian Century*), **L11**: 527
Keller, Helen, **M7**: 396; **L17**: 145
Kelley, Earl C., **L15**: xxiii, 310-11
Kelley, Florence, **M5**: 466n
Kellogg, Frank B., **L5**: 353; **L8**: 13
on outlawry of war, **L3**: 163-68, 171, 175, 415
Kellogg-Briand Pact, **M15**: xviii; **L5**: 349, 353, 354; **L6**: xx, xxin; **L8**: 13, 16
power of, **L6**: 190-91, 193
connected with outlawry of war, **L6**: 191-92, 222-23
Japan's relation to, **L6**: 193-94, 202, 204, 217-18
allied with League of Nations Covenant, **L6**: 195, 222
peace-sanction and, **L6**: 219, 220
Kemal, Mustapha, **M15**: xix, 137; **L2**: 190
Kempe, Alfred Bray, **M7**: 422
"Kennetic Inquiry" (A. Bentley), **L16**: xxxvii
Kent, Mrs. William, **M1**: 317
Kepler, Johannes, **E1**: 262, 356; **M4**: 7; **M13**: 497; **L14**: 392-93, 395
Kerensky, Aleksandr F., **M11**: 270, 295; **L6**: 468
Kern, Hermann, **E5**: 150
Kerschensteiner, Georg, **M7**: 101

Kettering, Charles F., **L11**: 567n, 569, 570, 573
Key, Ellen, **L7**: 461-62
Keynes, John Maynard, **L6**: xix
Keyser, Cassius J., **M8**: 109n; **L16**: 199n
Keyserling, Hermann, **L5**: 54
Khayyám, Omar, **M1**: 256
Kiangsu (Jiangsu), China, **M12**: 71, 73
Kiao-Chou, **M8**: 169
Kidd, Benjamin
  on progress, **E4**: 200, 210-13
Kidd, Dudley
  on Kafir clanship, **M5**: 25, 29n; **L7**: 25, 28n
  on primitive morality, **M5**: 39; **L7**: 37
Kiehle, D. L., **E5**: xcv
Kiel Canal (Germany), **M15**: 390
Kierkegaard, Soren, **M3**: xi
Kilpatrick, William H., **M6**: xxvii; **L5**: xi, 419; **L8**: 43n, 77n, 374; **L11**: 548; **L13**: 377; **L14**: 4; **L15**: 326, 510
  on economics, **L13**: 387
  and progressive education, **L17**: 52-56
Kindergarten, **M6**: 422
  and child psychology, **E5**: 206-7
  beginning of, **M1**: 40
  subject-matter in, **M1**: 87-88
  play in, **M1**: 341-42
  related to activity principle, **M6**: 363, 387
  at Columbia University Teachers College, **M8**: 278-83
  at Pittsburgh School of Childhood, **M8**: 283
  at New York City Play School, **M8**: 283-86
  techniques of, **M9**: 160
  Froebelian, **M9**: 205
Kindergarten College (Chicago), **M1**: 339n
Kinds, **L11**: 99; **L12**: 196-97, 357-59
  and generic propositions, **L11**: 101-4, 122, 124
  vs. classes, **L11**: 102, 119n
  inclusion in, **L11**: 103, 105-7, 125
  and universals, **L11**: 108
  determination of, **L12**: 111, 116-17, 133, 152-53, 164-66, 175-76, 220, 251-52, 288-89, 331-32
  in Aristotelian logic, **L12**: 252-54
  induction and, **L12**: 428-32
  and probability, **L12**: 470-73
  mind and mental as, **L15**: 29
King, Irving W., **M3**: 299n
King, Martin Luther, Jr., **L6**: xxi
King, Willford I., **L7**: 408
Kingdom of God, **M8**: 187
Kingdom of Poland. *See* Russian Poland
King Lear (Shakespeare), **L11**: 86, 91, 94
King's Peace, **L2**: 265
Kinship, **M12**: 115
Kipling, Rudyard, **M8**: 241; **M10**: 403; **L5**: 73, 395; **L10**: xvii; **L15**: 20, 22
Kirkpatrick, Edwin Asbury, **M15**: 181, 182; **L3**: 276, 277
Klee, Paul, **L10**: xxiii
Klein, Julius
  on Depression, **L6**: 346-54, 485-87
Kline, Max, **L9**: 320, 345
Kluckhohn, Clyde, **M7**: xxv
Klyce, Scudder, **M10**: 324n; **M13**: 412-20
Knaap, Anthony A., **M11**: 309
Knight, Frank, **L6**: xvii

Knower, **M7**: 455-60
related to world, **M10**: 21-24; **L16**: 84n
separated from philosophy, **M10**: 46
role in self-action, **L16**: 127-28
Kaufmann on, **L16**: 197
knowledge depends on, **L16**: 288
vs. known, **L16**: 290, 424
Knowing
related to acting, **E5**: 5-6; **L16**: 331
related to consciousness, **M1**: 119n
method of, **M10**: 36-37; **L16**: 134, 319; **L17**: 410, 481
terminates in experience, **L14**: 83-86
common sense vs. scientific, **L16**: 252-55, 305-7
as inquiry, **L16**: 289, 320-22, 339, 454
as mediating, **L16**: 323-26
as intelligent behavior, **L16**: 334-37, 449-51
as goal, **L16**: 365
Knowing and the Known (Dewey and A. Bentley), **M1**: x
Dewey's theory of inquiry refined in, **M1**: xv
related to Dewey's *Logic*, **L16**: x, 55n, 77n, 92n, 116n, 160n, 268, 304n, 308n, 387, 446
writing of, **L16**: xvii, xxiv, xxvi-xxviii, 3-7, 318-20
arguments of, **L16**: xxix-xxxvii
articles constituting, **L16**: 279
criticized, **L16**: 443-47
Knowings
as natural events, **L16**: xxxiv
knowledge about, **L16**: 3-4
as observable facts, **L16**: 48-49
study of, **L16**: 55, 77, 84n
as behaviors, **L16**: 73, 273
in postulations, **L16**: 80
range of, **L16**: 82
logics on, **L16**: 185
as name, **L16**: 265
Knowings-knowns
leading names for, **L16**: 6, 46-47
as inseparable, **L16**: 52
required for knowledge, **L16**: 53
inquiry into, **L16**: 57, 74-75, 110
namings and named as, **L16**: 58, 86-89, 257-58, 261
system of, **L16**: 63, 94-97
considerations in, **L16**: 67, 275, 318
as behaviors, **L16**: 84-85, 127-30
in interaction and transaction, **L16**: 111, 114, 122-26, 273
science affects, **L16**: 252-53, 337n, 338-39, 452, 455
Knowledge, **L1**: 158, 268, 309-10, 335-36, 338, 341-45, 349; **L10**: ix; **L12**: 153-55. *See also* Ground, **L12**; Warranted assertibility, **L12**
phenomenal, **E1**: 6
ontological, **E1**: 8
and feeling, **E1**: 20-21, 23-25; **E2**: 25-26, 260
nature of, **E1**: 38, 62-63, 304, 384-402; **E2**: 10; **M1**: 130n; **M6**: xix, 111-12; **M10**: 16; **L4**: 14, 28-30, 65, 81, 144, 218-19, 224, 226, 235-39, 247; **L10**: 27, 39-41, 120, 257; **L15**: 29, 31, 36n, 88, 91-92, 157-58; **L16**: xxii,

46-47, 72, 73n, 84, 91, 131, 134, 149-50, 244, 257-58, 265, 287-88, 291-92, 314, 372; **L17**: xviii, xxxi, 371n
sources of, **E1**: 129-30, 314; **M12**: 213, 215-16; **L16**: 372
methods of, **E1**: 185-86; **E2**: 75-136, 199; **E5**: 257; **M9**: 349-54; **L16**: 96-97, 111, 277-78, 346
sensations and, **E1**: 325-26; **E2**: 29-74; **E3**: 213-14; **M9**: 346-47; **M12**: 129-31; **L1**: 199
Leibniz on, **E1**: 339
accidental and demonstrative, **E1**: 394
empirical vs. rational, **E1**: 395-402; **M9**: 343-44
as universal, **E2**: 10, 23; **L1**: 28-29; **L4**: 85, 105, 143, 175, 193, 232-35, 237-38
and consciousness, **E2**: 20, 22, 24, 25
and will, **E2**: 21, 357-58
problems of, **E2**: 75; **E5**: 4-5; **M10**: 21-37; **L2**: 141, 143, 151; **L3**: 121-22; **L4**: 96-98; **L16**: 3-4
relations in, **E2**: 75-76, 151; **E3**: 137; **L16**: 44, 55, 61
scientific, **E2**: 76-77, 202; **E3**: 228-29; **M10**: 130; **L15**: 118-19; **L16**: 152, 307, 338, 410, 453; **L17**: xxx, 372, 410
development of, **E2**: 137-38, 183-84; **L4**: 11, 30-32
perception and, **E2**: 137-53; **L2**: 141-42, 156; **L12**: 73, 458-59
stages of, **E2**: 154-76, 204-13; **M10**: 3
related to thinking, **E2**: 177-203; **M9**: 304, 336
logical, **E3**: 81-83; **M6**: 176; **L17**: 371n
in Kant, **E3**: 135-36; **L4**: 48
related to action, **E3**: 230-31; **E5**: xv, 20; **M7**: 5-6; **M9**: 345; **L1**: 285-86; **L3**: 38; **L4**: 15-20, 30-32, 38-39, 155, 164; **L8**: 86-93; **L17**: 157-59
functions of, **E5**: 21-22; **M12**: xix, 149, 150, 208-9; **L9**: 56-57; **L13**: 44-46, 376; **L16**: 378-81, 389
unification of, **M2**: 261; **L4**: 249
absolute in, **M3**: xii
as fulfillment, **M3**: 112-13, 115-18
Greek view of, **M3**: 121; **L4**: 40, 74
related to experience, **M3**: 171-83; **M10**: 34-35, 320-65, 368; **L1**: 376-77, 386; **L4**: 125; **L13**: 266-67; **L14**: 32, 83-86
theories of, **M4**: 181-91, 255-56; **M9**: 275-85; **M10**: xiv-xvi; **M11**: 342-45; **M13**: 38-41, 48, 52, 58, 310, 354-55, 370, 373; **M14**: 128; **L1**: 247-50, 378-79; **L2**: xv-xvii, 46-51; **L4**: ix-xxii, 5, 18-19, 33-36, 65, 69, 71, 145-46, 181-84; **L5**: 210-17; **L11**: 71, 73, 149, 203-4; **L12**: xxiii-xxiv; **L14**: 45-47; **L15**: 84-87, 185, 276-77
related to science, **M6**: ix; **L1**: 129-31; **L2**: 337-38, 342-43
realist-idealist controversy over, **M6**: xvii-xviii

Knowledge (*continued*)
valid, **M6**: 80-85
related to judgment, **M6**: 382-85
related to emotions, **M6**: 385-86; **M9**: 345-46; **L7**: 269-70, 280; **L14**: 317
common-sense, **M7**: 3; **L1**: 341-45
social function of, **M7**: 113-27; **L7**: 365-66; **L11**: 193; **L13**: 336; **L17**: xxvi
in *Cyclopedia of Education*, **M7**: 265-69
Locke on, **M8**: 58-60, 159-60
Fichte on, **M8**: 173
Aristotle on, **M9**: 271-72
Plato on, **M9**: 271-72, 287; **L13**: 161
classic attitude toward, **M9**: 273-75
medieval attitude toward, **M9**: 275; **M10**: 22
related to virtue, **M9**: 340
dualism between objective and subjective, **M9**: 344-45
effect of evolution on, **M9**: 347; **M10**: 14
experimental, **M9**: 347-49; **L14**: 12-14
habit and, **M9**: 349-50
related to morality, **M9**: 363-67; **M14**: 127-31; **L7**: 190, 281-83; **L14**: 62-63
orthodox view of, **M10**: xiv, 6; **M12**: 144-47, 214, 262-63
spectator theory of, **M10**: 23, 26n, 41; **M12**: 144; **L4**: x-xviii, 19, 163, 195, 232
realism on, **M10**: 26n; **M15**: 361-62
Spencer on, **M10**: 69
Bergson on, **M10**: 69; **M12**: 227
and philosophy, **M11**: x, 41-48; **L4**: 246; **L6**: 428-31; **L13**: 256, 258, 281, 320
and value, **M11**: 9; **L15**: 449-51
related to motivation, **M11**: 10-17
positive vs. traditional, **M12**: 86, 88-89
Bacon on, **M12**: 95-98, 103, 108; **L11**: 141
empirical, **M12**: 121-22; **L11**: 69-83, 108-9; **L17**: 434
related to reality, **M12**: 141-42; **L4**: 85
James on, **M12**: 216; **L15**: 11
Russell on, **M12**: 236, 238-39, 243-44, 246; **L16**: 200, 202
Costello on, **M13**: 22
instrumental, **M13**: 28, 477; **M15**: xii, 41, 349-50; **L14**: 48-49, 172-76
and communication, **M13**: 31; **L2**: 282-84, 371-72
past, present, and future facts in, **M13**: 43, 47; **M15**: 28-29, 31-32, 35, 372, 374-77; **L13**: 243
anticipatory, **M13**: 50
mediatism and immediatism in, **M13**: 51-54, 385, 392, 454; **L14**: 53-54
physical vs. psychical, **M13**: 55, 477
related to meanings, **M13**: 376; **M15**: 29-30, 364; **L17**: 362-67, 369-72
examination of, **M13**: 415-16
Klyce's approach to, **M13**: 416
revolution in, **M15**: 12-13
as knowing-process, **M15**: 16, 31-32, 373
Lamprecht on, **M15**: 27, 28, 30-31, 371-77
Lovejoy on, **M15**: 33, 35, 37, 362-63

transcendence in, **M15**: 35, 350-51, 355, 358, 372
presentative, **M15**: 40
intertemporal, **M15**: 369-70
and qualities, **L1**: 75
object of, **L1**: 87, 106-11, 120-28, 202, 324; **L4**: 17-18, 40-59, 67, 78-84, 112, 193; **L14**: 49-52, 152-53
not immediate, **L1**: 90, 109-10, 243-44, 247-48, 256
as consummatory, **L1**: 97-98
and art, **L1**: 100-131; **L10**: 293-94, 299
as acquaintance, **L1**: 247-48
as contemplation, **L1**: 249-50
and belief, **L1**: 315-26; **L4**: 15, 17, 21-24
as mode of interaction, **L1**: 324
related to temperance and courage, **L2**: 128-31, 134
of knowledge, **L2**: 132, 133, 135-42, 146; **L14**: 17-19
correlated with certainty, **L2**: 149, 153
related to ideas, **L2**: 152, 154
political, **L2**: 336-37
divided, **L2**: 344-45
as tested, **L3**: 50
and opinion, **L3**: 51; **L7**: 363
two senses of, **L3**: 57; **L17**: 366n
as subject of Gifford Lectures, **L4**: viii
related to history, **L4**: 5-7
effect of, **L4**: 52, 106, 107; **L17**: xxxii
types of, **L4**: 61, 72, 156-60, 163, 166, 168, 171, 172, 176-77; **L6**: 80-81, 88-89
attainment of, **L4**: 63-69, 72, 136-40, 229, 230; **L14**: 43, 46-47; **L17**: 358, 391
concepts of, **L4**: 76-77, 86, 103, 110-11, 200; **L16**: 53, 57, 86n, 112, 136, 147, 157-60, 162
humane, **L6**: 52, 61-62; **L16**: 374-77
understanding as, **L7**: 197
and religion, **L9**: 14-15, 18-19, 22-25, 28
rational, **L11**: 77-79, 109
Peirce on, **L11**: 86, 91-92, 107-9, 422-23, 480-81, 483-84
theoretical vs. practical, **L11**: 183-90, 215; **L15**: 90, 164
related to education, **L11**: 208; **L13**: 282, 389
Hutchins on, **L11**: 393-96, 398-99, 402-7
and inquiry, **L12**: 14-17, 28-29; **L14**: 170-71; **L16**: 88n, 126, 188, 283-84
organization of, **L13**: 55-56, 376
changes in, **L13**: 155
desire vs., **L13**: 162, 172
of human vs. non-human subject, **L13**: 250
vs. intelligence, **L14**: 6-9
and futurity, **L14**: 60-61
Whitehead on, **L14**: 132
vs. warranted assertibility, **L14**: 169
Cohen on, **L14**: 390-91, 396, 401; **L16**: 14
Hocking on, **L14**: 425
subject-matter of, **L15**: 93-96; **L16**: 127
physical vs. social, **L15**: 222-23, 251, 254, 260
natural vs. spiritual, **L15**: 268
Nagel on, **L16**: 14
Comte on, **L16**: 97-98
Hartshorne on, **L16**: 166

Knowledge (*continued*)
Lewis on, **L16**: 193n
need for, **L17**: 48, 70, 456
and custom, **L17**: 433-34
"Knowledge and Perception" (Bush), **M6**: 103n
Knowledge and Reality (B. Bosanquet), **M10**: 427
Knowledge for What? (R. Lynd), **L6**: xvii
"Knowledge of Good and Evil, The" (Royce), **E4**: 197, 199-200
Knowledge relation
ubiquity of, **M6**: 113-22
Known objects, **L5**: xxvii-xxviii
Knowns, **L16**: 265, 288, 290, 334, 449
Knox, Philander Chase, **M15**: 85, 117; **L5**: 351, 352; **L8**: 15
and outlawry of war, **M15**: 405-6, 411-12, 414
Knox-Levinson plan, **M15**: 410, 412
Kobe, Japan, **M11**: 239
Koestler, Arthur, **L15**: xi, 292, 510
Köhler, Wolfgang, **M12**: xxvi
Kokusai news service, **M11**: 151; **M13**: 87, 241
Kolchak, Aleksandr Vasilyevich, **M13**: 82, 234, 235, 237
Komsomols, **L6**: 293
KON (Polish Committee of National Defense)
policies of, **M11**: 249, 296-97, 304, 318-22, 329, 396, 400-401
accusations against, **M11**: 261, 262, 291-97, 396, 404
formation of, **M11**: 288-91
future of, **M11**: 326-28
support for, **M11**: 403, 408
Königsberg, East Prussia, **M8**: 156, 160
Konvitz, Milton R.
on Dewey's 1933-34 writings, **L9**: xi-xxxii
Koran, **M15**: 131, 132
Korea, **M12**: 6, 28, 31, 33, 62, 64; **M13**: 76, 84, 259
national interests in, **M11**: 153, 154
China's and Japan's relation with, **M11**: 169, 179, 193, 206, 210-11, 215-16, 220
poppy-growing in, **M11**: 238
North invades South, **L17**: 140, 561
Korkunov, Nikolai M., **L6**: 269
Korzybski, Alfred, **L16**: 203
Kosciusko, Thaddeus, **M11**: 269, 313
Kozicki, Stanislas, **M11**: 281
Krabbe, Hugo, **L6**: 269, 270
on law-making, **L17**: 101, 102
on sovereignty, **L17**: 103
Kraus, Arthur J., **L11**: 530-31
Krause, Karl Christian Friedrich, **M2**: 180-81
Kress, Paul, **L16**: xxiin-xxiiin, xxvi
Krestinsky, Nikolay N., **L15**: 346
Kreuger, Ivar, **L6**: 244
Krikorian, Yervant H., **L15**: xvi, 109, 462-63
Krivitsky, Walter G., **L15**: xii, 340
Krock, Arthur, **L9**: 287
Kronstadt sailors, **L13**: 400
Kropotkin, Piotr Alekseyevich, **M5**: 45n; **L3**: 13-15; **L7**: 43
Krug, Philip N., **L9**: 348
Krupskaya, Nadezhda Konstantinovna, **L3**: 243; **L17**: 494, 569
Kucharzewski, Jan, **M11**: 271, 275
Kuhn, Thomas Samuel, **L8**: xviii;

L16: xxiii
Ku Klux Klan, **M15**: 152
Kulakowski, Bronislaw D., **M11**: 294, 295, 396, 400-401
Kulaks, **L7**: 427
Kultur, **M10**: 45, 230, 233, 287; **L13**: 84, 150
compared with civilization, **M8**: 168-69
British misunderstanding of, **M10**: 221
Kumi, **L7**: 23
Kunitz, Joshua, **L17**: 571
Kuomintang, **M12**: 254
Kurtz, Paul
on Dewey's 1929-30 writings, **L5**: xi-xxxii
Kuryer Polski (Milwaukee), **M11**: 315
Kwangsi (Guangxi), China, **M13**: 122, 125; **L17**: 31, 556
Kwangtung (Guangdong), China, **M13**: 121, 122, 124, 125, 128, 132, 134
Kyoto, Japan, **M11**: 171

Laband, Paul, **L17**: 101, 559
Labor, **M14**: 86-87, 100; **L1**: 69, 71, 73, 78-79, 91, 100-103, 105, 146-47, 275-77; **L6**: 235, 236, 251, 381; **L8**: 365. *See also* Child labor; Work
in primitive society, **M5**: 44, 78; **L7**: 41, 72
attitude toward, **M5**: 145-46; **L7**: 143-44, 178, 386; **L8**: 61-62
of women and children, **M5**: 483-84, 528-31; **M11**: 162, 176; **M12**: 75; **L7**: 378, 400, 412-13
vs. leisure, **M9**: 259-70, 332
organized, **M9**: 298
related to capital, **M9**: 323; **M12**: 189
affected by WWI, **M10**: 296-97; **M11**: 84, 85, 87-88, 98, 104-5, 130, 255, 324, 330; **M12**: 20
in Japan, **M11**: xvii-xviii, 161-66, 176-77
in England, **M11**: 59, 73, 81, 87, 91
and vocational education, **M11**: 62-65
problems of, **M11**: 79-80; **M12**: 8-11; **L10**: 345-46; **L11**: 169; **L17**: 315-16
corporations vs., **M11**: 134; **L7**: 379-80, 392
management of, **M11**: 142, 333-34
in China, **M11**: 191; **M12**: 75-76, 255
European democracies and, **M12**: 6
international conventions of, **M15**: 400
laws concerning, **L2**: 277, 310; **L7**: 377-79, 394-401, 412-22, 432-33
role in politics of, **L6**: 172-73, 254-55
and Brookwood Labor College, **L6**: 327-29
and teachers, **L6**: 434-45
freedom of, **L11**: 8-10
division of, **L11**: 9, 349-51, 490-92; **L13**: 180
influence of Moscow trials on, **L11**: 327, 333-34
Dewey fund for, **L14**: 311
manual vs. intellectual, **L15**: 234, 249, 263, 277
in USSR, **L15**: 295-98; **L17**: 501-4
Labor, Bureau of Statistics of, **L17**: 7-8, 554

Labor, Committee on, **L6**: 381
Labor and Nation, **L15**: 249, 509
Laboratory
related to school, **M1**: 51-52
value of, **L17**: 67, 68-69, 221
Laboratory methods
in education, **M10**: 142-43
Laboratory School, University of Chicago, **M1**: xviii; **M3**: 275-77, 279; **M6**: 179; **L8**: 109
Dewey's work at, **E5**: xiv; **M1**: xvi, xix
purposes of, **E5**: xviii-xix, 244, 433-35, 437; **L11**: 191-92
organization of, **E5**: 224-43; **L11**: 196-200
described, **E5**: 244-46, 436-41
in university pedagogical work, **E5**: 288-89
teachers in, **E5**: 447
methods of, **L11**: 193-95, 200-201, 205-6
curriculum of, **L11**: 207-12
Labor Department, **L6**: 351
Laborers. *See* Workers
"Labor Politics and Labor Education," **L5**: 387
Labor Research Fund, **L14**: 311
Labor unions, **M10**: 207; **M13**: 429-30; **L5**: 331-45, 506; **L7**: 393-94; **L9**: 317-19; **L14**: 375; **L15**: 244-45. *See also* Teachers Union
character of, **M5**: 446-47
rights of, **M5**: 450-52
related to AAUP, **M8**: 101-2
for teachers, **M10**: ix, xxxiii-xxxiv, xxxix, 171-72
in Mexico, **L2**: 207
Holmes on, **L7**: 398-99
in economic crisis, **L9**: 79-80
related to education, **L9**: 125-26
of farmers, **L9**: 250, 273
situation of, **L9**: 333-35, 340, 341
and dual unionism, **L9**: 335-37
in Russia, **L17**: 495
Labour party (Great Britain), **M11**: 73, 81, 87, 91, 120; **L6**: 172, 246; **L9**: 289
Laches (Plato), **L2**: 124, 127, 130, 132n, 134, 139n
Ladd, George T.
on physiological psychology, **E1**: 194-204
Lafayette Escadrille, **L11**: 528
Lafferty, Theodore T., **L6**: 311-12
La Follette, Robert M., **M15**: xxivn, 317; **L6**: 381, 394; **L15**: 242
in 1924 election, **L6**: 171, 234, 356
and progressives, **L6**: 355, 440
La Follette, Suzanne C., **L11**: 314, 323; **L13**: 395, 404
on *Mission to Moscow*, **L15**: 345-55
response to, **L15**: 492-501
LaGuardia, Fiorello, **L11**: 175; **L14**: 247, 358, 431
Laidlaw, Robert W., **L11**: 530
Laidler, Harry W., **L6**: xvii, 326; **L11**: 517, 519; **L14**: 262
Laird, John, **L15**: 425n
Laisant, Charles A., **M3**: 222
Laissez-faire, **M5**: 151, 425, 432; **M7**: 58; **M10**: 240-42; **L2**: 281, 292; **L4**: 169; **L7**: 177, 328, 333; **L8**: 51, 57; **L15**: 61, 253
origin of, **L7**: 250
individualism, **L7**: 428; **L11**: 258, 366-67; **L13**: 114, 125, 157, 182

fatalism and, **L8**: 63-64
repudiation of, **L8**: 73, 75
in religion, **L9**: xx, 52, 54, 55
in social conditions, **L9**: 52, 54
in economics, **L9**: 206, 297; **L13**: 137
liberalism, **L11**: 17-19, 26, 29, 61, 63, 283-87, 289-91, 296-97, 365-67, 374; **L13**: 81-82, 134, 146; **L15**: 215-18
doctrine of, **L11**: 32, 270, 284, 291
and deductive logic, **L12**: 499
Lalande, André, **L16**: 20n, 43, 163
Lamb, Charles, **L5**: 394; **L10**: 145, 288; **L13**: 226-27
Lamb, Mary Ann, **L5**: 394
Lambeth Conference, **L7**: 460
Lammasch, Heinrich, **M15**: 402
Lamont, Corliss, **L11**: 425-27
Lamont, Thomas W., **M13**: 86, 87, 89, 96, 124
Lamprecht, Karl, **M8**: 474
Lamprecht, Sterling P., **M15**: xii, 30-32; **L14**: 306; **L15**: 459
on Dewey's theory of knowledge, **M15**: 27, 28, 371-77
Lancret, Nicolas, **L10**: 133
Land
ownership of, **M5**: 24, 29-30; **L7**: 23, 28-29; **L13**: 291
socialization of, **L11**: 256-57
tenure and taxation, **L14**: 94
discovery of new, **L17**: 455
Landman, Isaac, **L5**: 396
Land value, **L9**: 277, 290
and taxation, **L9**: 64-65, 261
and farmers, **L9**: 250, 255, 257, 258, 262-63, 269-70
in New York City, **L9**: 257-58, 265
People's Lobby on, **L9**: 263-64
U.S. Constitution and, **L9**: 266
according to George, **L9**: 301
Lane, Franklin K., **L6**: 370-71, 504
Lane School (Chicago), **M8**: 380-82
Lang, Andrew, **L14**: 193
Lange, Friedrich Albert, **M8**: 176. *See also* James-Lange theory
Langer, Susanne K., **L10**: xv; **L15**: 418-19
Langfeld, Herbert S., **L16**: 170n
Langford, Cooper Harold, **L16**: 193n, 209n
Langlois, Charles Victor, **L16**: 43
Language, **M14**: 43, 56-57, 69; **L1**: 72-73, 132-61, 198, 213-17, 222-23, 226-28, 333-34; **L4**: xiii, xviii, xix; **L8**: 282-83; **L11**: 51, 70, 515; **L12**: 21, 245, 249-51, 263-65, 501; **L13**: 96, 193-96, 236. *See also* Symbols, **L12**
of idealism, **E2**: xxiv
in spatial and temporal association, **E2**: 91-93
and mind, **E2**: 185-86; **M7**: 395-97
impulses related to, **E2**: 223-24, 307; **L17**: 307
French vs. German, **E3**: 209-10
infant, **E4**: 66-69
as tool of communication, **E5**: 90; **L2**: 82-85
in teaching drawing, **E5**: 198
study, **E5**: 254, 257, 259-60, 266, 439
references on, **E5**: 336-37
child's use of, **E5**: 439; **M1**: 33-36, 77-78
and thought, **M6**: 314-18; **L3**: 37; **L8**: 301-14; **L13**: 328,

Language (*continued*)
329; **L15**: 78-79, 211
in education, **M6**: 318-27; **M9**: 18-20; **L15**: 266; **L17**: 291
related to science, **M7**: 120-27; **M9**: 290-98; **M10**: 122; **L13**: 249; **L16**: 152
fixed by environment, **M9**: 21-22, 37-38, 43-44, 81
history of, **M9**: 291
in China, **M12**: 24
and understanding, **M13**: xiv, 355, 375, 383, 415
experience in, **M13**: 356
function of, **M13**: 384; **L3**: 36-37; **L6**: 425; **L16**: 44-45, 139-40, 148n, 182-83
related to philosophy, **L2**: 47-50; **L14**: 139, 325; **L16**: 303
and meaning, **L3**: 84, 404-8; **L12**: 82, 187-88, 214, 223, 284-86
symbols in, **L3**: 413-14; **L6**: 4-5
related to context, **L6**: 3-4
as socializing agency, **L7**: 14, 43; **L17**: 235-37, 313, 321
art of, **L10**: vii, xv, 111, 153, 219, 232, 242, 291, 331, 337-38
in logical theory, **L12**: 26-28, 45, 49-66, 105; **L16**: 207-9
esthetic, **L12**: 75-76, 89, 101, 176-79, 205, 239, 372
and definition, **L12**: 341-42
technical, **L13**: 322
theory of, **L14**: xvi-xix
Jefferson and, **L14**: 207-8
of ethics, **L15**: 127-30, 136-40
Peirce on, **L15**: 143-52; **L16**: 10
mathematics as, **L15**: 377
treatment of, **L16**: xxxiii, xxxiv, 4, 11
necessary to inquiry, **L16**: xxxvi-xxxvii, 49-50, 55, 189
Carnap on, **L16**: 25-26, 32
C. Morris on, **L16**: 33-35, 210-41
defects in, **L16**: 56n, 145-46, 275
in psychology, **L16**: 132n
nature of, **L16**: 134, 298, 309, 344, 445-46
as life-process, **L16**: 134n, 327
form of, **L16**: 143-44
Kantor on, **L16**: 191-92
Kaufmann on, **L16**: 196n
of Russell, **L16**: 199-203
as name, **L16**: 266
Language, Truth and Logic (Ayer), **L14**: xv
Language and Reality (Urban), **L15**: 425n
Lankester, Edwin Ray, **M5**: 157n
L'Année pédagogique, **M7**: 113n, 477n
Lansing, Robert, **M11**: 264, 394; **M12**: 13; **M13**: 90; **M15**: 105
Lansing-Ishii agreement, **M13**: 83, 162, 166, 191
Laotze, **L1**: 47
related to Confucianism, **M13**: 221-25
Laplace, Pierre Simon, **M8**: 8, 458; **L4**: xv, 161; **L14**: 107
Lapp, John, **M10**: 303-4
Larmor, Joseph, **L16**: 99
Larrabee, Harold A., **L15**: 462
Lashley, Karl Spencer, **L16**: 117n
Laski, Harold J., **L2**: 39, 40, 41n
Lassalle, Ferdinand, **E4**: 215; **M8**: 176
Last Puritan, The (Santayana), **L11**: 446-49
Lathrop, Julia C., **L17**: 517, 573

Latin, **M1**: 297; **L15**: 278
Latin America, **L15**: 371
  U.S. intervention in, **L6**: 209, 219, 364
  disputes in, **L6**: 215
Latins
  on feelings, **L17**: 343-44
Latvians (Letts), **M11**: 266
Laughing Horse (Willard Johnson), **L5**: 417n
Laughter, **E4**: 155, 157-58
Laurie, Simon Somerville, **E4**: 352
Lausanne, France, **M15**: 78, 402
  second conference of, **L2**: 190
Lausanne Agency, **M11**: 278-80, 283, 284, 289
Lavine, Thelma Z., **L15**: 460-61
  on *Knowing and the Known*, **L16**: ix-xxxviii
Lavoisier, Antoine Laurent, **L14**: 391, 396-97
Law, **M12**: 114-16; **L4**: 222; **L11**: 35, 53, 59-60, 374, 538; **L13**: 150, 183-84. *See also* Induction, **L12**; International law; Natural law
  and social development, **E3**: 220; **M10**: 154-55; **L2**: 357-58; **L13**: 352; **L17**: 47
  as side of obligation, **E3**: 328
  related to morality, **E3**: 349-52; **E4**: 73-75; **M5**: 180-81, 207; **L3**: 19; **L7**: xxvi; **L17**: 101, 393
  history of, **E4**: 37-41; **M1**: 158-59; **L3**: 326-29; **L8**: 8
  related to sovereignty, **E4**: 81-88
  teaching of, **M1**: 291; **L15**: 278
  logical method in, **M4**: 199-200; **M15**: 66-70, 72-75
  in primitive groups, **M5**: 61-65; **L7**: 56-60
  Greek conception of, **M5**: 106-7, 114; **L7**: 97-98, 104
  in *Cyclopedia of Education*, **M7**: 269-71
  Dewey's concept of, **M10**: xxviii; **L14**: xxi-xxiv, 115-22
  related to force, **M10**: 211-15, 244-51; **L6**: 213-14, 218, 219, 451, 463-65
  Kipling on, **M10**: 403
  authority of, **M11**: 18-40; **L7**: 182, 216, 220, 227
  and war, **M11**: 122-26, 388-92; **M15**: 92, 116-17
  and League of Nations, **M11**: 128, 129
  regulates labor, **M11**: 162, 163, 176; **L7**: 377-79, 386, 394-401, 412-22, 432-33
  in China, **M11**: 213, 219; **M12**: 41-50
  controlling drug traffic, **M11**: 236-40
  and philosophy, **M11**: 349
  reason and, **M12**: 136; **L13**: 80
  freedom and, **M12**: 198; **M15**: 202; **L13**: 109
  in international relations, **M15**: xiv, 54-56, 90-91, 94, 108-9, 111, 113-14, 122-23
  in social philosophy, **M15**: 42, 58, 62, 74-75, 234-35, 260-61, 269-71
  and outlawry of war, **M15**: 62-64, 99, 107-8; **L3**: 354-57
  rules of, **M15**: 71-72, 74-76
  and World Court, **M15**: 89, 93-94
  concept of person in, **L2**:

Law (*continued*)
22-43; **L6**: 268-70
in Mexico, **L2**: 194-96
nature of, **L2**: 268-71; **L5**: 10; **L7**: 103, 123, 152, 252; **L8**: 357; **L10**: 27, 153, 154, 286, 295, 303; **L16**: 158, 366, 379
Holmes on, **L3**: 181-82
compared with good, **L5**: 497-503
and Depression, **L6**: 345, 356, 375, 377-78, 440-41
and railroad property, **L6**: 370, 371
and birth control, **L6**: 388-89
propaganda against, **L6**: 393
of Israel, **L7**: 86, 90-91
Roman, **L7**: 130-33; **L8**: 35
of Renaissance, **L7**: 139
Kant on, **L7**: 155, 221, 229
on conduct, **L7**: 278
cultural value of, **L7**: 364
contribution of Brandeis to, **L9**: 237-39
transmits civilization, **L10**: 329, 332, 340
common, **L11**: 8-9, 11
scientific, **L11**: 9-10, 108-11, 289, 434-35; **L12**: 352, 370-71, 394-95, 428-32, 524; **L14**: 104-8; **L15**: 312-13; **L16**: 98n, 99n, 105-8, 418
Bentham on, **L11**: 12
Lippmann on, **L11**: 494-95
and forms, **L12**: 24, 105-6, 187-88, 370-71
problem of, **L13**: 82
and culture, **L13**: 85
in Marxism, **L13**: 119-20, 124
causal, **L13**: 123; **L14**: 179-80
obedience to, **L13**: 139
changes in, **L13**: 291; **L17**: 102-3
Cohen on, **L16**: 194n
Pollock on, **L17**: 98-100
Pound on, **L17**: 105-7
heterogeneity in, **L17**: 106
Law and Morals: The McNair Lectures (Pound), **L17**: 105-7
Law in the Making (C. Allen), **L3**: 326-29
Law in the Modern State (Duguit), **L2**: 41n
Lawlessness, **E3**: 375
Laws, The (Plato), **M7**: 312-14; **M15**: 19
Laws of Imitation, The (Tarde), **M10**: 53
Lawson, George
on sovereignty, **M11**: 19-20, 25-26
Lawyers, **L11**: 188
Lazarsfeld, Paul F., **L15**: xxvii
Leadership
training, **E5**: 59
political, **L6**: 128, 163, 240, 393-94
international, **L6**: 178-79
need for, **L6**: 448-49
authoritarian, **L15**: 175-76
Leading principles, **L12**: 19-21
League for Independent Political Action (LIPA), **L6**: xvii, 404, 405, 504; **L11**: xxiii
Dewey chairman of, **L5**: xvii
formation of, **L5**: 347-48; **L6**: 246
and third party, **L5**: 442-49; **L6**: 324, 438-39
goals for, **L6**: 149-52, 245, 253, 255, 324, 436-37
conference of, **L6**: 239n, 246-52
and 1932 election, **L6**: 250

political philosophy of, **L9**: 67-70
funds for, **L9**: 307-8
League for Industrial Democracy, **L6**: xvii, xviii; **L9**: 175n; **L11**: 517-19; **L14**: 262-65, 431
Discussion Outlines for, **L17**: 44-49
League of Nations, **M12**: xxi, 4, 7; **M13**: 313, 411; **M15**: xi, xviii, 100, 112, 115; **L2**: 177; **L3**: 164, 166, 169, 173-75; **L5**: 352; **L6**: xx, 453, 464; **L8**: 17; **L15**: 195
conception of, **M11**: 71, 105, 122-26
and U.S., **M11**: 71, 197, 198; **M15**: 83-86, 378-82; **L2**: 375
opposition to, **M11**: 110, 151-54, 163, 177; **M15**: xv, 405-7
importance of, **M11**: 127-42, 179, 213, 240
Levinson on, **M11**: 389
advocates of, **M15**: xvi-xvii, 81, 105, 108
international cooperation through, **M15**: 78-82, 380-81
attitude of Europe toward, **M15**: 83-85
and World Court, **M15**: 380, 386-87, 393, 395-96; **L2**: 170
and Far Eastern conflict, **L6**: 194-95, 202-3, 454; **L17**: 140
failure of, **L6**: 196, 197, 205-7, 450, 457-59, 466
use of sanctions by, **L6**: 197-200, 208-9, 471-73, 484
Council of, **L6**: 452, 453n, 466
and disarmament, **L6**: 459-61
Convention for Financial Assistance under, **L6**: 476
Balch works for, **L17**: 149
League of Nations, Covenant of, **M11**: 159; **M15**: 95, 102, 107, 116, 380, 399, 403, 405; **L6**: xx, 203, 204, 208, 467, 472; **L8**: 13; **L17**: 561
articles of, **L6**: 22, 194, 200, 201, 222, 450, 452, 453n, 455, 462, 464n, 466, 471, 480
and Pact of Paris, **L6**: 194, 195, 222
and use of sanctions, **L6**: 200, 452-54
as means for international law, **L6**: 205-6, 451-54
Japan violates, **L6**: 450, 452, 466
League of Nations Association, **L6**: 337
League to Enforce Peace, **M15**: 404, 405; **L5**: 351; **L6**: 473
Learner. *See* Students
Learning, **M12**: xv; **L1**: 213-15; **L13**: 6; **L15**: 77
psychology of, **E5**: 229
directed vs. haphazard, **M1**: 24-28
by animals, **M6**: 265; **L8**: 223
through communicated information, **M6**: 335-37; **L8**: 323-25
methods of, **M7**: xxiii; **M8**: xxxiii, 253-74; **M9**: 176, 181-82; **L5**: 412-16; **L17**: 213-25
Rousseau on, **M8**: 219-21
related to knowledge, **M9**: 156, 340
fifteenth-century revival of, **M9**: 290

Learning (*continued*)
nature of, **M9**: 344-45; **L8**: 176-77, 264; **L11**: 35, 238-42, 244; **L13**: 31, 40, 51
in and out of school, **M9**: 368-69; **L17**: 55
Bacon's three kinds of, **M12**: 95-96
by experience, **L2**: 56; **L13**: 8, 12, 20, 22, 218-19, 296
attitudes toward, **L13**: 29
aims of, **L17**: 56
physical activity in, **L17**: 217
eagerness for, **L17**: 463
books for, **L17**: 463-64
Learning to Earn (Lapp and Mote), **M10**: 303-4
Lebensanschauung, **M7**: 418
Lebensraum, **M8**: 435
Leboit, Joseph, **L9**: 320
Le Bon, Gustave, **M14**: 45n
Lecky, William E. H., **L11**: 456
Le Conte, Joseph, **M2**: 149
Lecture
as system of teaching, **E3**: 147
vs. dialogue, **L17**: 185
Lectures on the Philosophy of History (Hegel), **M8**: 193, 441
Lectures on the Relation between Law and Public Opinion in England during the Nineteenth Century (Dicey), **L11**: 17
Lednicki, Aleksander, **M11**: 295
Lee, Harold N., **L16**: 345, 470
Lee, Ivy, **L6**: 60
Lee, Vernon, **L10**: 107-9, 357
Leeds, Morris E., **L11**: 567n
Lefèvre, Edwin, **L9**: 115
Lefkowitz, Abraham, **L9**: 326, 341
Left, political, **L17**: xxiv
control by, **L16**: 362-63, 375-76
Legal
institutions, **M14**: 90; **L2**: 32, 246, 265
positivism, **L14**: xxii-xxiii
realism, **L14**: xxiii-xxiv
philosophy, **L14**: 120-21
freedom, **L14**: 247-48
Legal Foundations of Capitalism (Commons), **L16**: 101n
Legalism, **L11**: 490, 492-93
"Legal Personality," **L2**: 22
"Legal Status of War, The" (Levinson), **L5**: 352
Legends, **L9**: 40; **L10**: 321, 330
Léger, Alexis Saint-Léger, **L5**: 353
Legislation. *See* Law
Legislature, **L11**: 59-60
Lehigh University, **L6**: 49n, 311n, 419; **L17**: 527
Lehman, Herbert H., **L14**: 370
Leibniz, Gottfried Wilhelm, **E1**: 203; **M5**: 154; **M7**: 276, 324; **M8**: 167, 194; **M12**: xiv, 242; **L1**: 115n; **L2**: 70; **L4**: 125; **L5**: 377, 379, 381; **L7**: 145; **L10**: xiii; **L14**: 379, 394; **L15**: xiii, xxviii, 30
Dewey on, **E1**: xxxii-xxxv; **E4**: xiv-xv
biography of, **E1**: 255-67
philosophy of, **E1**: 268-83, 427-35
on problem of unity, **E1**: 284-98
on monads, **E1**: 292-95, 297-98, 318, 346-51, 362-63
opposes Locke, **E1**: 299-312, 321-22, 344-45, 373-83
on sensation and experience, **E1**: 313-26
on impulse and will, **E1**: 327-41

on relation of matter to spirit, **E1**: 342-54
on reality of sensible phenomena, **E1**: 355-72
on knowledge, **E1**: 384-402
theology of, **E1**: 403-13
criticized, **E1**: 414-26
and moral philosophy, **E4**: 143
on necessity, **M2**: 150, 152
on nisus, **M2**: 155
on optimism, **M2**: 175; **M7**: 293, 296
on organic, **M2**: 177-78
on rationalism, **M2**: 217; **M10**: 18
on preestablished harmony, **M6**: 420
on evolution, **M6**: 421
Santayana on, **M10**: 306, 307
on organic universe, **L10**: 208
vis viva of, **L16**: 107
insistence on simple, **L17**: 415n-16n, 565
Leipzig school of psychology, **M1**: xii-xiii
Leisure, **L1**: 76; **L4**: 4, 6; **L8**: 62, 86; **L10**: 267, 346
vs. labor, **M9**: 259-70, 332
role of, in citizenship, **M15**: 167
education and, **M15**: 167-69, 190, 194-95; **L6**: 112, 134-35
moral problems connected with, **M15**: 168-69
influence of, **L17**: 515
Lemaître, Jules, **L10**: 308, 309, 365
Lemberg, Galicia, **M11**: 263, 281
Length
as scientific unit, **L12**: 438, 475-78
Lenin, Vladimir Ilyich, **M11**: 270; **L6**: 264; **L9**: 105; **L11**: 312, 334, 592; **L13**: 90, 134, 393; **L14**: 371, 427; **L15**: 339; **L17**: 117, 502, 569
on education, **L3**: 232; **L17**: 493-94
philosophy of, **L5**: 355-58
and Dewey, **L7**: xvii
Brameld on, **L9**: 244-45
on seizure of power, **L13**: 400
internationalism of, **L15**: 291, 373-74
power of, **L17**: 491
on illiteracy, **L17**: 494
on Russian barbarism, **L17**: 498
Leningrad, USSR, **M11**: 267, 275, 295; **L10**: 319
impressions of, **L3**: 202-16
contrasted with Moscow, **L3**: 208, 216, 222-23
"Leningrad Gives the Clue," **L7**: xvii
Léon, Xavier, **L5**: 279n, 496-97, 501, 503
Leonardo da Vinci, **M12**: xii; **L1**: 124; **L10**: 177, 294; **L16**: 372
Lepley, Ray, **L15**: 63n; **L16**: 344n, 357n, 470
Lerner, Max, **L9**: 237-38
Leroy-Beaulieu, Anatole, **M11**: 277
Lesser Hippias (Plato), **L2**: 124, 127
Lessing, Gotthold Ephraim, **E1**: 265, 428; **E4**: 193, 194; **M2**: 184; **M6**: 409; **M8**: 194; **M9**: 64; **M10**: 226; **L17**: 340, 565
"Lessons from the War—in Anthropology" (M. Mead), **L14**: 431
Letters of William James, The (H. James), **L15**: 20

"Letters on the Esthetic Education of Man" (J. Schiller), **L10**: 286n
Letter to Menoeceus (Epicurus), **L15**: 418
"Letter to the Liberals" (Tolstoy), **L17**: 383
Leucippus, **M7**: 275; **M15**: 337
Leviathan (Hobbes), **M11**: 21-23, 30, 36n, 38-39; **L13**: 141, 401
Levinson, Salmon O., **M13**: 411; **M15**: xiv-xv, xvi, xviiin, 62, 92, 103, 110, 116, 119; **L2**: 171; **L6**: xx, xxin, 219, 223n; **L8**: 14, 15; **L11**: xxxin; **L17**: 559
  on outlawry of war, **M11**: 122, 125, 388-92, 403; **M15**: 105, 404-5; **L3**: 163, 353; **L5**: 349-54
  and peace-sanction, **L6**: 192
  on peace movement, **L15**: xxiii, 301-2
Levitas, Anzia Yezierska, **M11**: 260, 396
Levy, Hyman, **L15**: 507
Lévy-Bruhl, Lucien, **L3**: 15; **L5**: 499; **L15**: 382n; **L16**: 310
Lewes, George Henry, **E3**: 20; **M2**: 219; **M3**: 56; **L8**: 34
  defines science, **E1**: 185
  career of, **E1**: 207
  on human organism, **E1**: 296
Lewin, Kurt, **L16**: 125n
Lewinski-Corwin, Edward H., **M11**: 314
Lewis, C. I., **M7**: xiv; **L11**: 592, 593; **L14**: xvii; **L15**: 32-33; **L16**: 32, 209n
  Kurtz on, **L5**: xxix-xxx
  on Dewey's theory of knowledge, **L5**: 216-17, 477-86
  on philosophic method, **L5**: 235
  on deduction, **L12**: 479
  Bentley on, **L16**: xxx, xxxi
  epistemology of, **L16**: 8-10
  meanings of, **L16**: 36-38, 45
  replies to Baylis, **L16**: 38n
  logic of, **L16**: 193n
Lewis, David J., **L6**: 381
Lewis, George Cornewall
  and theory of sovereignty, **E4**: 70-73, 75, 90
Lewis, J. David, **L6**: xiii
Lewis, Mary H., **L3**: 330-31
Lewis, Sinclair, **L6**: 329; **L10**: 347
Lewis and Clark expedition, **L8**: 173
Leys, Wayne A. R.
  on Dewey's 1893-94 writings, **E4**: xiii-xxiv
Liberal arts, **L15**: 188-89
  historical meaning of, **L15**: 248-49, 257, 276-77
  curriculum of, **L15**: 278-80
Liberal arts college. *See* College
Liberal education, **L15**: 276-80, 333-36, 378, 474-84
  in *Cyclopedia of Education*, **M7**: 271-75
  vs. industrial education, **M9**: 259, 265-66
  Aristotle on, **M9**: 262
  as vocational, **M9**: 322
  meaning of, **M10**: 156
Liberal Education, Commission on the Function of Philosophy in, **L15**: 154-55
Liberalism, **M12**: 8, 19, 23, 27, 30, 48, 69-70; **M14**: 210; **L2**: 319; **L12**: 511
  of Japan, **M13**: 84, 257, 260
  allied with irrationalism, **M13**: 421, 496-99
  in religion, **M15**: 5-7; **L9**: xix,

24, 216-18, 222; **L14**: 288; **L15**: 269-70
in politics, **M15**: 396; **L6**: 184
nature of, **L3**: xxvi-xxviii, 97-101; **L13**: 316; **L14**: 150, 252-54; **L15**: 248-49
Locke on, **L3**: 97, 102; **L17**: 437
Kurtz on, **L5**: xvi-xvii
faults of, **L5**: 70, 346-48; **L11**: 63, 144, 296-97; **L15**: 168; **L16**: 375, 379; **L17**: 444
Niebuhr on, **L9**: 73-74, 400-401, 404-5
Macintosh on Dewey's view of, **L9**: 418-19
social, **L11**: xxv-xxvi, 291-95, 495
crisis in, **L11**: xxvii-xxxi, 23-37, 39
history of, **L11**: 5-22, 136, 282-85, 289-91, 364-67; **L14**: 313
utilitarianism related to, **L11**: 11-15
split in, **L11**: 21, 284-88, 374, 489
values of, **L11**: 25-41, 44-45, 65
renascent, **L11**: 41-65
future of, **L11**: 258-60
humane, **L11**: 282-88, 365-67
Lippmann on, **L11**: 489-93
Spender on, **L11**: 496-97
Jefferson on, **L13**: 67
laissez-faire, **L13**: 81-82, 134, 137, 146; **L15**: 215-18
empiricism related to, **L14**: 192
war affects, **L14**: 250
Mackay on, **L15**: 41, 399
individualism in, **L15**: 213, 231
need for principles of, **L15**: 249-50
in education, **L15**: 257, 262-65, 276-80, 333-36, 378, 483-84
publications espousing, **L15**: 362
socialism and, **L17**: 116
conservatism and, **L17**: 430-31
Liberalism and Social Action, **M9**: xii; **L1**: viii; **L5**: xvi; **L6**: xvi; **L11**: xiii, xxiv, xxvii-xxxi
"Liberalism as Faith in Intelligence" (Randall), **L11**: 359
Liberal party (Great Britain), **L11**: 496; **L17**: 134, 560
Liberals, **L11**: 5, 45, 116, 374
task of, **M13**: 496-97
faults of, **L11**: 14, 25-36, 63-64; **L15**: 242-43
and Trotsky inquiry, **L11**: 316-19, 329
"Liberating the Social Scientist," **L15**: xxvi
Liberation
of mankind, **L13**: 351-53
Libertarianism, **E4**: 91-94; **M6**: 419
Liberty, **L9**: 87-90; **L15**: 170. *See also* Freedom
Mill on, **M5**: xi
English constitutional, **M11**: 20
and law, **M11**: 39
related to philosophy, **M11**: 49-50, 349
sacrificed in war, **M11**: 184
of thought, **L2**: 277-79; **L7**: 358-66; **L13**: 316
as end in itself, **L2**: 289
and individuality, **L2**: 296-97, 355-57; **L11**: 7-8, 76, 132-41; **L13**: 321; **L14**: 91-92
concept of, **L2**: 329; **L7**: 305-8, 334; **L11**: 12, 35-36, 63, 174, 285-86, 292, 360-62, 368-71; **L13**: 80
intellectual, **L7**: 77

Liberty (*continued*)
political, **L7**: 138-40
religious, **L7**: 141; **L14**: 215
economic, **L7**: 142-43, 360; **L11**: 26-28, 136-40, 365-67, 369-71
and equality, **L7**: 349-50; **L13**: 110, 338
Cuban, **L9**: 311
civil, **L11**: 5, 372-75
of contract, **L11**: 16, 17, 26
as ideal, **L11**: 21-22, 167-70, 297; **L13**: 99
responsibilities of, **L13**: 295
Jefferson on, **L14**: 209-10
in U.S., **L14**: 365
guarantee of, **L16**: 403
Liberty League, **L11**: 26, 167, 270, 286, 290-91, 362, 489
Liberty Loans, **M11**: xvi, 327, 329
Libraries
in Turkey, **M15**: xxi, 279, 302-3, 306
role of, in education, **L5**: 404-6; **L17**: 234
Library of Living Philosophers (Schilpp), **L14**: xi, xiii, 184n, 295
Library of Philosophy
plan for series, **E3**: 185-86
Lies
as images, **L17**: 265
Life, **L15**: 353
Life, **M12**: 132, 153, 175, 185-86, 201
as Hebrew ideal, **M5**: 81, 103-4; **L7**: 75, 94-95
Greek conception of, **M5**: 118-19; **L7**: 109-10
Bergson on, **M7**: 8; **L14**: 101
thought connected with, **M8**: 143-44
renewal of, by transmission, **M9**: 4-7
as growth, **M9**: 56-57
education related to, **M9**: 254-58; **L14**: 346-47
environment and, **M12**: 128-29; **L13**: 273
moral, **M12**: 174; **L7**: 12, 462
practical, **M12**: 240
direction of, **L4**: xviii, 223-26, 244, 248-50
continuity of, **L4**: 179, 187, 188, 195
beliefs about, **L4**: 204, 218
and theory of values, **L4**: 211, 212
evils in, **L4**: 246
related to philosophy, **L6**: 431; **L16**: 319, 364-68, 381
continuity with art, **L10**: xi, xiv, xxx-xxxiii, 16, 34-35, 39, 41, 180-83, 234-37, 241-42, 247, 294, 296, 307-8, 321, 324-27, 331, 342, 348-49
nature of, **L10**: 19-30, 42-43, 51, 139, 171, 173, 177, 190, 201-2, 210-13, 260, 293; **L16**: 116, 121, 314, 370-71, 389, 464; **L17**: 385, 387
vs. dreams, **L14**: 16
modern vs. ancient, **L14**: 316-17, 327-28
transaction in, **L16**: 245-48
related to science, **L16**: 255-56, 290-92, 304-5, 317, 372-74
Tolstoy on, **L17**: 384
man's command of, **L17**: 391
Life-activities
inquiry-behavior in, **L16**: 288-89, 320-21, 325-26, 424-25, 428
as subject-matter, **L16**: 344-46

defined, **L16**: 387
indifference to, **L16**: 462
Life and Mind of John Dewey, The (Dykhuizen), **L11**: xxiii, xxxi; **L14**: xx
Life and Work of George Sylvester Morris, The (Wenley), **M10**: 109n; **M11**: 336-37
Life in College (C. Gauss), **L6**: 259-62
Life of Reason, The (Santayana), **M3**: 319-22; **M4**: 229-41; **M11**: 385; **L3**: xii, 287; **L6**: 272; **L14**: 301-3
Light, **L16**: 107-8
velocity of, **L4**: 102, 115-17, 147, 162-63
as medium, **L10**: 122, 126-27, 146-47, 175, 177, 179, 199, 206, 238, 241, 281, 305, 312, 318
Li Hung Chang, **M12**: 62
Like-mindedness, **M9**: 7, 35, 40-41
Likeness, **L8**: 255-56
Liking, **M15**: 344. *See also* Enjoyment; Satisfaction
theories of, **M13**: 5n
as preference, **M13**: 11; **L13**: 333
logical implications of, **M13**: 14
as indeterminate, **M13**: 25-26
related to value, **M15**: 20-21, 23-24, 342; **L2**: 70, 71, 80-96 passim; **L13**: 202
Prall on, **M15**: 24-25, 342-43
impulsive vs. thoughtful, **M15**: 26; **L2**: 74-77
Lillie, Frank Rattray, **L16**: 117n
Lillie, Ralph S.
on physico-chemical processes, **M8**: 3, 449-59
"Limitations of a Behavioristic Semiotic, The" (M. Black), **L16**: 210n
Limits, **L12**: 207-9, 219, 221-22, 395, 411, 471-72
Lincoln, Abraham, **E3**: 258; **M11**: 146, 147, 150; **M13**: 302, 303; **L7**: 148; **L8**: 52; **L9**: 162-63, 176; **L11**: 64, 377; **L14**: 102, 110-11
on democracy, **L13**: 14, 173, 294-95, 402-3; **L17**: 473, 476, 568
on slavery, **L17**: 454
Lincoln, cathedral of, **L10**: 226
Lindeman, Eduard C., **L6**: 329
Lindsay, Alexander Dunlop, **L2**: 32-33
Line
rhythm of, **L10**: 92-100, 236, 281
expressiveness of, **L10**: 105-8, 157, 364
as medium, **L10**: 127, 146-47, 162, 168, 172-77, 206, 209-10, 333
Linguistic Analysis of Mathematics (A. Bentley), **L16**: x-xi, xvii-xix, xxviii, 90n, 444
Linguistics
abuse of, **M6**: 318-20; **L8**: 306-8
related to value-facts, **L13**: 193-96
emotive and scientific, **L13**: 236
signs in, **L16**: 297-309
Linn, Mrs. W. R., **M1**: 317
Linnaeus, Carolus, **L16**: 120
Linville, Henry R., **L5**: 419; **L9**: 124, 326; **L11**: 380-81
Lippmann, Walter, **M10**: 185; **M11**: xii; **M13**: 290, 330; **M15**: xvii; **L1**: 229; **L2**:

Lippmann, Walter (*continued*) 308n, 404; **L6**: 198, 499n; **L7**: 74
on stereotypes, **M13**: 331
on public opinion, **M13**: 337-44
on outlawry of war, **M15**: 115-21, 404-17
on self-defense and national policy, **M15**: 117-18
on international law, **M15**: 122-24
lists causes for war, **M15**: 126, 409
on methods for democracy, **L2**: xxii-xxiii, 213-20
and omnicompetent individual, **L2**: 334
on art, **L10**: 332, 343n
on freedom, **L11**: 258-59
on good society, **L11**: 489-95
Literacy, **L11**: 51, 227, 231, 388; **L13**: 95, 168, 169; **L17**: 45
Literalists
in religion, **M15**: 5-7
Literary Guide and Rationalist Review, **L15**: 184
Literary Mind, The (M. Eastman), **L10**: 265n, 362
Literary revolution (China), **M13**: 109, 256
Literature, **L11**: 61, 506-7, 556; **L15**: 188-89; **L17**: 381
French, **E3**: 36-42
of West, **E3**: 196-98
study of, **E5**: 89, 90, 231-32, 251; **L17**: 311-12, 345
in elementary school, **M1**: 77-78, 327-28
teaching of, **M4**: 206-8; **M9**: 267
related to science, **M7**: 120-27; **M9**: 290-98
meaning of "state" in, **M8**: 169-82
and American localism, **M12**: 12-16
in Turkey, **M15**: 278-79, 301, 306
and philosophy, **L8**: 26
as art, **L8**: 360-63
esthetic nature of, **L10**: 148, 162, 174, 176, 182-86, 192-95, 200, 207-8, 212-16, 256, 258, 265, 270, 272, 287-88, 298, 300, 303-4, 320-21, 324
as medium, **L10**: 228-29, 232-35, 238, 244-49
transmits civilization, **L10**: 330, 332, 336, 342, 348; **L17**: 170, 176
Jefferson on, **L14**: 208
imaging power in, **L17**: 252-53
Russian, **L17**: 493
Literature and Dogma (Arnold), **L9**: xiv-xv, xvii-xviii, xxv
Lithuanians, **M11**: 255, 264, 266, 306, 326
Little Red School House, The (de Lima et al.), **L15**: 303-4
Little School in the Woods (Greenwich, Conn.), **M8**: 266-67
Litvinoff, Maksim M., **L15**: 291, 509
Liu Tze Shan, **M13**: 142
Live creature. *See* Organism
Living Philosophies, **L14**: 91
Livingstone, David, **M13**: 244
Livingstone, Richard W., **L11**: 592
Livonia, **M11**: 326
Li Yuan-hung, **M11**: 202
Llewellyn, Karl N., **L14**: xxiv; **L16**: xii
Lloyd George, David, **M11**: 120, 279; **M13**: 345-46
Lobbyist for the People

(B. Marsh), **L6**: xixn
Localization, **L16**: 91
of psycho-physiological functions, **E1**: 107-12
Locarno, Switzerland, **L2**: 169
Locarno Pact, **L6**: 197-98, 461n; **L8**: 13
Locatum, **L16**: 216-17
Lochner v. New York, **L7**: 415
Locke, John, **E1**: xxvii, 36, 123, 125, 131, 144, 145, 176, 254, 271, 286, 297, 299, 306, 414, 425; **E3**: 91; **E4**: 201, 216, 217; **E5**: 16, 352, 376; **M1**: 115; **M2**: ix; **M4**: 254; **M5**: 155; **M6**: 175; **M8**: 142, 356; **M10**: 223; **M12**: xiv, xxixn, 99, 108, 131-32, 167; **M13**: 307, 400; **M14**: 76; **L1**: 32, 37, 38, 177, 349, 373; **L2**: ix, xvii, 7n, 15, 48n, 51, 228; **L5**: 232n, 252; **L6**: 7, 17; **L9**: 242; **L11**: xvn, 592; **L12**: 113n, 120, 153; **L13**: 162, 173; **L14**: xix, 299; **L15**: xiii, xxxii, 13, 18; **L17**: 566
related to Leibniz, **E1**: xxxiii, 301-4
empiricism of, **E1**: 35; **M1**: xvii; **M12**: 126-27; **L4**: 92; **L5**: 173; **L8**: 9, 11; **L12**: 44, 45
on philosophy, **E1**: 124, 426-27
on perception, **E1**: 177-78
and associating activity, **E1**: 190
influence of, **E1**: 300-301; **M7**: 51, 241, 291; **M11**: 43; **L5**: 182, 183, 230
on consciousness, **E1**: 311; **M3**: 81
on knowledge, **E1**: 314, 384-92, 395; **M7**: 292; **M8**: 58-60, 159-60; **M9**: 66-67, 301; **L2**: 141-42, 146-57; **L12**: 148-50
on sensationalism, **E1**: 315-16, 342; **E5**: 15; **M2**: 246; **M9**: 276-77
on matter, **E1**: 320-21, 342-44
on space and time, **E1**: 344, 366
on qualities, **E1**: 373-74; **M6**: 23n; **L2**: 143-45; **L12**: 75; **L14**: 105
on identity, **E1**: 376
on finite and infinite, **E1**: 379-81
on essence, **E1**: 389
on intelligence, **E1**: 394
John Watson on, **E5**: 353
on opinion, **M2**: 173
on ethics, **M3**: 52-53
on idea, **M3**: 71, 117; **M4**: 318; **M7**: 222-23; **L3**: 12-13; **L4**: 147; **L10**: 44; **L12**: 519; **L17**: 430
on experience, **M3**: 131-32; **M9**: 277; **L11**: 76-80, 91-92, 94; **L14**: 190; **L17**: 430-31, 438-40
related to logic, **M3**: 139-41
on liberty, **M4**: 42; **L7**: 139, 141
on natural rights, **M5**: 142-43; **M7**: 57; **M11**: 20, 23, 25; **L2**: 289
on morals, **M5**: 290n; **M11**: 32n
on thought, **M6**: xxiii, 195-96; **M7**: 345
on education, **M6**: 195-96; **L8**: 37, 129
on belief, **M6**: 198-200; **L8**: 132-34
on language, **M6**: 321; **L8**: 308; **L12**: 284

Locke, John (*continued*)
on human nature, **M6**: 420
epistemology of, **M7**: 42; **L4**: ix, xii, xvii, 21
on reason, **M7**: 58
on innateness, **M7**: 252
as founder of utilitarianism, **M7**: 360-61
and mathematics, **M9**: 66-67; **L8**: 356
on generalization, **M10**: 12
on government, **M11**: 27n
Dewey's departure from, **L3**: 76
on liberalism, **L3**: 97, 102; **L11**: 6-9, 16; **L17**: 437-38
as disciple of Newton, **L4**: 97
on universe as organism, **L5**: 377
dualisms of, **L6**: 30; **L10**: x, 340
Kant reinforces tradition of, **L6**: 489
on power, **L7**: 205, 279
on sovereignty, **L8**: 35
on religion, **L9**: 15; **L17**: 438
Santayana on, **L9**: 240-41
vs. Jefferson, **L13**: 177
Cohen on, **L14**: 382
on intrinsic value, **L15**: 43
on final authority, **L17**: 431
"Locke and the Frontiers of Common Sense" (Santayana), **L9**: 240-41
Lockhart, Earl Granger, **L13**: 342n
Locomotion, **L2**: 53
Locus, concept of, **L1**: 154-56; **L16**: 138-40, 242
Lodge, Henry Cabot, **M13**: 212; **M15**: xv, 404; **L6**: 472-73
Loeb, Harold, **L13**: 394
Loeb, Jacques, **L16**: xiv
Logic, **M11**: 346-47; **L1**: 350; **L8**: ix, xii, xivn; **L11**: 81, 394. *See also* Aristotelian logic; Greek logic
Hegel on, **E1**: 43-44
related to philosophy, **E1**: 163-66; **E3**: 230; **L4**: 53-54
Dewey on, **E3**: xxii-xxvi; **M1**: xiv-xvi, xxiii; **M8**: xiii-xix; **L5**: xxv-xxvii; **L16**: xvn, xxxiin, 187-90, 385
dualism in, **E3**: 75-82
courses in, **E3**: 90
and scientific method, **E3**: 125-27; **M3**: 67-68; **M15**: 67-68, 72
related to thought, **E3**: 126-29; **M6**: 224-29; **L5**: 243-62; **L8**: 171-76
formal, **E3**: 127; **M2**: 304; **M3**: 62-63; **L11**: 102, 150-51, 156; **L12**: 88-93, 183, 197-98, 201-2, 218, 285, 364-65, 372-73, 502-3
empirical, **E3**: 129-32; **M3**: 63; **M10**: 335; **L12**: 107, 114, 135, 147-48, 151-52, 295, 350, 374, 389, 435, 507-11
transcendental, **E3**: 132-34, 139-40
and esthetic, **E3**: 235
Platonic, **M1**: 161-62
Socratic, **M1**: 161-62
pure, **M2**: 302; **M7**: 438-39
applied, **M2**: 303
types of, **M3**: 63-67; **M10**: 331-65; **L4**: 128-29
idealist, **M7**: xv
F. Schiller on, **M7**: 131-34; **L11**: 155-57
problem of truth in, **M7**: 414
new, **M7**: 422; **M12**: 99-100
symbolic, **M7**: 438
Russell on, **M8**: 15; **L16**: 199-203

Tarde's contribution to, **M10**: 54
Dewey vs. R. Robinson on, **M10**: 98-108, 415-30
nature of, **M12**: 84-85, 90-91, 156-58; **M15**: 65, 66; **L4**: x, xxi, xxii, 16, 69, 120
Bacon on, **M12**: 96-98
as science and art, **M12**: 157-58
in morals and politics, **M12**: 159
equivalent of syllogism, **M15**: 69-70
related to law, **M15**: 72-73, 75-77; **L14**: xxiii
related to retrospective judgments, **M15**: 359-60
Holmes on, **L3**: 180-81
explains universe, **L4**: 13, 156, 158
rational, **L4**: 112, 113
symbols in, **L4**: 123, 125; **L12**: 10, 26-27, 45-46, 306, 359n, 406
classic, **L4**: 149
and social science, **L5**: 166-72
Mill's, **L5**: 168-69
and existence, **L5**: 203-9
and ontology, **L5**: 453-60
as discipline, **L8**: x, xi, xiii-xvii, 161; **L16**: xviii, 90, 236, 287
ideas in, **L8**: 3-12, 248
method of, **L8**: 218-19
of propositions, **L11**: 95, 118-26
subject-matter of, **L11**: 108n, 112, 113; **L16**: 179-83, 320
Peirce on, **L11**: 422-23, 483; **L15**: 143, 150-52
related to inquiry, **L12**: 11-16, 25-29, 92-93, 106, 132, 158-59, 476-77; **L14**: 42-52
and metaphysics, **L12**: 30, 70-72, 286, 507-8, 516-17
ancient, **L12**: 90, 182
and history, **L12**: 230-38, 433-34, 440, 453-54
analytic and synthetic, **L14**: xii
Cohen on, **L14**: 386-90; **L16**: 193-95
Mackay on, **L15**: 393-401
defects in, **L16**: xi, 7-45, 49-50, 58, 66, 87n-88n, 102n, 104n, 112, 145-46, 157n, 192, 193n, 319
Bentley's role in, **L16**: xxiv, xxv, xxix-xxxi
terms of, **L16**: 143n, 272
positions held by, **L16**: 150, 268-69, 460-61
accounts of definition in, **L16**: 154-56, 160-62, 167-68, 174, 262
development of, **L16**: 158-60, 184-87
of Kantor, **L16**: 190-92
of Kaufmann, **L16**: 195-98
of Moore, **L16**: 203-7
related to knowledge, **L17**: 371n
Logic; or, The Morphology of Knowledge (B. Bosanquet), **M10**: 428
Logic: The Theory of Inquiry, **M1**: x; **M2**: xvi; **M6**: xi; **M8**: ix, xiv; **L2**: xiv, xxiv; **L5**: xxvii; **L6**: xiv; **L8**: xiii; **L9**: xxiv; **L11**: xiv; **L14**: x-xvii, 34, 35n, 41-46, 50, 53, 55, 56n, 59, 64, 65, 84, 169, 173-75, 180, 181n, 184-87, 386; **L15**: 36, 37, 40, 70n, 332, 393-401; **L16**: 318, 444
Dewey's theory of inquiry refined in, **M1**: xv
Nagel on, **L12**: ix-xxvii

Logic: The Theory of Inquiry (*continued*)
related to *Knowing and the Known*, **L16**: x, xxxvn, xxxvi, 55n, 77n, 92n, 116n, 160n, 268, 304n, 308n, 387, 446
Bentley's role in, **L16**: xin, xix, xxiv, xxv, xxix-xxx
on postulations, **L16**: 47n, 187-90
on object, **L16**: 68n, 267
transaction in, **L16**: 71n
on demonstratives, **L16**: 181n, 183n
Dewey discusses, **L16**: 281, 284
Balz on, **L16**: 293, 423-42
on existence, **L16**: 385, 460-62
scientific investigation in, **L17**: xxxi
Logical
empiricism, **M13**: xi; **L17**: xxx
realism, **M15**: 368; **L11**: 108n, 111-12, 149
positivism, **L3**: xviii; **L9**: 303; **L11**: 113; **L12**: 284, 512; **L13**: x; **L14**: xv; **L15**: 4, 14, 49-50; **L16**: xxxin, xxxii-xxxiii, xxxvii, 98n, 193n; **L17**: xxx
and ontological, **L12**: 30, 42-43, 91-92, 131, 178-79, 182-83, 188-89, 201, 216n, 260-61, 304-5, 357, 386-87, 394, 453-57, 497-98, 526
intension, **L12**: 200, 292-93, 357-60
extension, **L12**: 200, 295-96, 340-41, 357-60
and grammatical, **L12**: 284-85, 308
conjunction, **L12**: 333-35, 352, 425, 445, 447, 451-52, 468, 515-16
multiplication, **L12**: 336-42, 359, 438-39
meaning of term, **L14**: 175n
Logical atomism
in generalization theory, **M10**: 13
of Russell, **L16**: 104n, 159, 199, 200-202
"Logical Conditions of a Scientific Treatment of Morality," **M3**: xiii; **L15**: 153
Logical entities
three theories regarding, **M10**: 89
as logical, **M10**: 90-97
Logical form
defined, **L4**: 54, 71-73, 117
Russell on, **L12**: 157
correlation as, **L12**: 333-34
"Logical Foundations of the Unity of Science" (Carnap), **L16**: 28
"Logical Method and Law," **L14**: xxiii
Logical neutrality
compared with ontological neutrality, **M10**: 49-52
Logical theory, **M6**: 176
chaos in, **E3**: 126
as reflective process, **M2**: 300-302
related to psychology, **M2**: 309-13; **L12**: 43, 72-74, 110, 153, 285; **L14**: xvii; **L16**: 276, 443-45
value of, **M2**: 313-15
Mill's and Whewell's, **M2**: 368-75
language in, **L12**: 26-28, 45, 49-66, 105; **L16**: 101n, 269n
autonomy of, **L12**: 28-29, 158n
Logic for Use (F. Schiller), **L11**: 156
Logicians
on qualities, **L10**: 219
criticized, **L16**: 7, 8-45, 193n

on definition, **L16**: 175, 177
compared, **L16**: 207-9
"Logicians' Underlying Postulations" (A. Bentley), **L16**: 447
"Logic of Judgments of Practice, The," **M8**: ix, xiv; **M11**: 376
Logic of Modern Physics, The (P. Bridgman), **L4**: 89n; **L5**: 482n; **L16**: 192n
Logic of Relatives (C. Peirce), **L15**: 145
"Logic without Ontology" (Nagel), **L16**: 16n
Logistics, **L16**: 299n, 300, 308
Logos, **E4**: 139; **L1**: 134; **L4**: 73, 74
as hypostatized discourse, **L12**: 63-64
as middle term, **L12**: 90, 204
London, Ivan D., **L16**: 121n
London, England
Ito in, **M11**: 170
Polish question in, **M11**: 269, 279, 282-84, 290, 326
Long, Huey P., **L6**: 394; **L13**: 112
Longfellow, Henry Wadsworth, **M1**: 107; **L17**: 253
Long-run. *See* Continuum of inquiry, **L12**
Looking Backward (Bellamy), **L9**: 102, 105-6; **L15**: xv
Looking Forward: Discussion Outlines (LID)
introductions to, **L11**: 517-19; **L17**: 44-49
Lord, Robert H.
on Polish question, **M11**: 402-6
Lorentz, Hendrik Antoon, **L16**: 99
Loscalzo, Joseph V., **L9**: 360
Lotze, Rudolf Hermann, **E1**: 93; **M2**: 149; **M3**: 64; **M4**: 52, 304, 318; **M12**: 157; **L2**: 14; **L5**: 257n; **L12**: xii
and local signs, **E1**: 199
Ladd's agreement with, **E1**: 200
as intuitionalist, **E1**: 213
on logic, **E3**: 75, 92; **M2**: 302-3; **M10**: 331
Dewey criticizes, **M2**: xvi-xvii
on thought, **M2**: 317-67
similar to Kant, **M2**: 373n
as founder of psychology, **M7**: 137-38
on emotion, **M8**: 24
vs. psychology, **M10**: 362
Louis XVI, **M8**: 171
Louvre (Paris), **L10**: 14, 306n, 316, 361
Love, Mary C., **L17**: 108-9
Love, **L7**: 368, 452; **L10**: 54, 351
as feeling, **E2**: 249-50, 293
forms of, **E2**: 294-95
as moral motive, **E3**: 105-7; **E4**: 111-12; **M5**: 379
related to justice, **M5**: 372-73
related to family life, **M5**: 516-21
as moral ideal, **L7**: 88, 259
related to belief in God, **L9**: 220, 223
in teaching, **L13**: 344-45
constancy of, **L17**: 24-25
Lovejoy, Arthur Oncken, **M8**: 98, 410; **M10**: 440; **M13**: xi; **M15**: xii, xvii, 78n; **L3**: 396n, 397n; **L15**: xiv, xviii, xxxii
on pragmatism, **M13**: 40, 49, 443-81
on verification, **M13**: 42, 44, 48
on anticipatory thought, **M13**: 50
on knowledge, **M13**: 51; **M15**: 27-41, 349-70; **L14**: 46
on monistic realism, **M13**: 54
on essence, **M13**: 55

Lovejoy, Arthur Oncken (*cont.*)
on prospective judgment, **M15**: 33, 37, 39
on realism, **M15**: 35, 361-70
on U.S. joining League of Nations, **M15**: 83-86, 378-82
Lovett, Robert Morss, **L14**: 262, 431
Low, Matthew, **L15**: 350
Lowe, Robert, **L17**: 492, 568-69
Lowell, Abbott Lawrence, **M15**: vii, 380
Lowell, James Russell, **E1**: 239-40, 249; **M6**: 98
Lowie, Robert H., **L3**: 324-25
Loyalty, **M8**: 190
and right, **L7**: 233-34
allied with regimentation, **L9**: 87
Lubbock, John, **M5**: 384
Lubin, David, **M10**: 296
Lubomirski, Zdzislaw, **M11**: 275
Lucas, Robert H., **L5**: 444, 446; **L6**: 161
Luck, **L4**: 6, 9-10, 82, 178, 209, 241; **L15**: 333, 335-36, 474. *See also* Chance
primitive attitude toward, **M5**: 55-57, 68-69; **L7**: 51, 63
and freedom, **L3**: 104-5, 107
belief in, **L14**: 98
Lucretius, **M2**: 146; **M7**: 275; **L2**: 133; **L10**: xvii, 294, 323; **L14**: 193, 299, 300, 393; **L15**: xiv
"Lucy Gray" (Wordsworth), **L10**: 117, 137
Luddites, **L5**: xix
Lumholtz, Karl Sofus, **M2**: 46n
Lunacharsky, Anatoli Vasilyevich, **L3**: 218, 234; **L6**: 291
Lurye, Moissei I., **L11**: 322, 602
Lurye, Nathan L., **L11**: 322, 603
Lusitania, **M10**: 221, 242, 265, 272, 273
Lusk laws, **M13**: 426, 428, 497; **M15**: 153; **L11**: 380
Luther, Martin, **M4**: 42; **M8**: 146-47, 173, 181, 190, 191; **M10**: 308; **M11**: 25; **L1**: 334; **L14**: 400
Lutheran Protestantism, **M8**: 151
Luxembourg Palace (Paris), **L10**: 306
Luys, Jules Bernard, **E5**: 376
Lycidas (Milton), **L6**: 497; **L10**: 85
Lycurgus, **L17**: 176
Lydgate, John, **L17**: 557
Lyell, Charles, **M4**: 4; **L1**: 12
Lyman, Eugene William, **M4**: 228
Lynd, Helen Merrell, **L5**: 45
Lynd, Robert S., **L5**: 45; **L6**: xvii
Lyons, Eugene, **L15**: 353
Lyrical Ballads (Wordsworth and Coleridge), **L10**: 192
Lysis (Plato), **L2**: 124, 127

McAndrew, William, **M15**: 190; **L5**: 371, 372, 374
MacArthur, Douglas, **L11**: xi
Macaulay, Thomas B., **M7**: 240; **L2**: 298; **L8**: 10; **L15**: 23-24
Macaulay, Zachary, **L11**: 18
Macbeth (Shakespeare), **L10**: 199, 210, 289
McCarthy, Charles, **L17**: 67-69, 557
McCarthy, Joseph, **L6**: xxii; **L17**: 561-62
McClure, Matthew Thompson, Jr., **L17**: 88-89, 559
McClure's Monthly, **L17**: 346
McConn, Max, **L6**: 419
McConnell, Francis J., **L6**: 381
McCooey, John, Jr., **L9**: 380
McCooey, John H., **L9**: 346-49, 351, 352, 380

McCormick, Anne O'Hare, **L6**: 162; **L15**: 353
McCormick, James J., **L9**: 357
McDermott, John J., **L14**: xxi
on Dewey's 1935-37 writings, **L11**: xi-xxxii
on Dewey-Bentley collaboration, **L16**: xxvi, xxviin
MacDonald, Ramsay, **L2**: 176; **L5**: 359; **L6**: 194, 197
MacDonald, William, **M10**: 371-72, 451
McDougall, William, **M10**: 54, 57
McDowell, Mary E., **L17**: 517, 573
Macedonia, **M15**: 140, 144
McGeehan, John E.
and Russell case, **L14**: 231, 236-37, 240-47, 357-58
McGill, Vivian J., **L16**: 233n
McGilvary, Evander Bradley, **M4**: xxiv; **M10**: 444; **L14**: 431
exchange between Dewey and, **M4**: xxvi-xxviii; **M7**: x, 79-84
on experience and reality, **M4**: 120-24, 151-55, 295-313
on consciousness, **M4**: 143-45, 314-16
on idea, **M4**: 146-55, 317-27
on ego-centric predicament, **M7**: 445-51
on awareness, **M7**: 452-53
on "Brief Studies in Realism," **M7**: 454-60
McGoldrick, Joseph, **L9**: 113, 259
Macgowan, John, **L3**: 418
McGraw, Myrtle Byram, **L11**: 510
Mach, Ernst, **M2**: 149; **M3**: 68; **M7**: 427; **M10**: 51; **L4**: xiii; **L6**: 490
Machado, Gerardo, **L9**: 310, 311n
Machado government (Cuba), **L5**: 440
Machen, Arthur W., **L2**: 22n-23n, 37n
Machiavelli, Niccolò, **M5**: 339n; **M8**: 474; **M11**: 123; **M15**: 60; **L1**: 334; **L7**: 138; **L10**: 332
Machines
effects of, **M5**: 453-54; **M9**: 268; **L7**: 379-81, 391, 394
nature of, **L4**: 119, 129, 197
in industrial revolution, **L7**: 149-50
vs. art, **L10**: 277, 344-46
Macintosh, Douglas Clyde, **L9**: 213, 223
views God, **L9**: xxi-xxii, 214, 215, 217-19, 227-28
replies to Dewey on religion, **L9**: 417-22
on Christianity, **L14**: 286-88
MacIver, Robert M., **M6**: xii; **L6**: 482n
Mack, Robert D., **L16**: 457
McKay, Claude, **L17**: 58-60
Mackay, Donald S.
on logic, **L15**: 34-41, 393-401
Mackenzie, John Stuart, **E4**: xvii, 274, 294-95; **E5**: 25
McKenzie, William Robert
on Dewey's 1895-98 writings, **E5**: xiii-xx
McKinley, William, **M15**: 384-85
McLellan, James A., **E5**: xxiii, xxxiii-xxxiv, xlix, l, lxiii; **L5**: 461
McLennan, John, **M5**: 29; **L7**: 29
McMurry, Charles Alexander, **E5**: 147-48; **L17**: 88, 559
McMurry, Frank M., **E5**: 148; **L17**: 88, 559
McNair, John Calvin, **M8**: 138
McQuade, James A., **L9**: 357-60

Maddox, Robert J., **L6**: xxin
Madison, James, **M7**: 380; **L13**: 69; **L14**: 203; **L15**: xiv-xv
Madonna, **E5**: 216
Maeterlinck, Maurice, **M6**: 123; **L17**: 40
naturalistic mysticism of, **M6**: 125-29
on instinct and intelligence, **M6**: 129-32
on experience, **M6**: 132-35
Magic, **L1**: 44-45, 70, 77, 148, 289; **L4**: 3, 9, 32; **L16**: 78, 104, 328
belief in, **M14**: 22-23
as esthetic quality, **L10**: 200, 330
Magic Mountain, The (T. Mann), **L10**: 217
Magistrates' Courts (New York City)
investigation of, **L9**: 370-77
Magna Carta, **M11**: 20; **L10**: 329; **L11**: 372; **L13**: 81
Magnitudes
function of, in judgment, **L12**: 200-219
Magnus, Heinrich Gustav, **L6**: 317
Magyars, **M15**: 392
Mahaffy, John P., **E3**: 184-85
Mahon, William D., **L5**: 344
Mailly, Bertha H., **L9**: 306
Maine, Henry Sumner, **E4**: 37; **M4**: 31
on democracy, **E1**: 227-32
on sovereignty, **E4**: xxi, 70, 71n, 75
and customs of Jews, **E4**: 87
on primitive group life, **M5**: 26, 62, 409n; **L7**: 25, 57
Maistre, Joseph de, **M7**: 357
Maitland, Frederic W., **M5**: 65n, 409n, 411n, 412n, 416n; **L2**: 30n, 34n, 35n; **L7**: 59n
on marriage laws, **M5**: 514; **L7**: 442
on corporate legal personality, **L2**: 23, 26, 39, 41, 42
Major. *See* Premise; Syllogism, **L12**
Majority rule, **L2**: 364-65; **L7**: 355, 362; **L17**: 86
Make-believe
during childhood, **L17**: 262-63
end of, **L17**: 268
Making of Citizens, The (Merriam), **L6**: 126-27; **L17**: 112-14
Maklakoff, Vasell, **M11**: 267
Malade imaginaire, Le (Molière), **L16**: 88n
Malebranche, Nicolas, **M2**: 165-66
Malherbe, E. G., **L11**: 238n, 243n
Malinowski, Bronislaw, **M15**: 223, 224-25; **L1**: 160n, 363n; **L6**: 3-4, 12, 20-21; **L7**: 50, 52, 455; **L11**: 127n
Mallarmé, Stéphane, **L10**: xxii
Mallock, William Hurrell, **M7**: 392
Malthus, Thomas Robert, **E4**: 211; **E5**: 51; **M14**: 207; **L6**: 36, 69; **L17**: 411
Malthusian theory of population, **M12**: 56; **L17**: 411
Man, **L16**: 11, 445
as material of psychology, **E1**: 48-49
as self-conscious, **E1**: 146-47
nature of, **E1**: 149-50; **M3**: xi-xiii; **L11**: 84, 139, 246, 279, 586-87; **L13**: 258, 281, 324, 326; **L15**: 267-68
spiritual nature of, **E1**: 206-7;

E4: 5; L15: 47, 55, 233n; L17: 102
and evolution, E1: 219-21
and environment, E5: 37-38, 46-47; L17: 467
universe and, E5: 53; L9: 37-38, 214, 217, 420-21, 435; L17: 96
related to society, M5: 75, 85; L7: 69, 79; L17: 314-15, 391, 459
and nature, M9: 286-87, 290-94, 332; L10: 39, 152-55, 190, 200, 274-75, 341; L14: 127-28; L15: 57, 186, 188, 202, 255-56; L16: 74, 366
savage and civilized, M12: 81-82, 120, 128-29, 232
perfectibility of, M12: 107; L14: 100
importance of, M12: 238
Holmes on, L7: 453
related to God, L9: 45-46; L17: 529-30
in Dewey's philosophy, L9: 295
art of, L10: 31-34, 249, 250, 329-33, 335
common, L11: 282, 365; L14: 226-27, 396
beliefs of, L11: 554
rights of, L13: 148, 173-74
Otto's philosophy related to, L14: 289-92
Cohen on, L14: 382-83
scientific study of, L15: 96, 224, 227-28
Peirce on, L15: 151-52
Hook on, L15: 372
as subject-matter for philosophy, L16: 80, 319, 359-68, 377, 379-81, 412-19
Russell on, L16: 199n-200n
transactions of, L16: 243-48
concepts of educated, L17: 75-76
growth of, L17: 255-68
moral relations of, L17: 395-96
Management
vs. labor, L7: 178, 390-401
vs. ownership, L7: 424
Man and Society in an Age of Reconstruction (Mannheim), L14: 293-94
Man and Technics (Spengler), L6: 280-85
Man and the State (Hocking), L3: 318-20, 323; L6: 453n
Manchester, William, L11: xi
Manchester Guardian, L14: xxi
Manchester New College (London), L17: 3, 553
Manchoukuo, Manchuria, L6: 458
Manchu dynasty (China), M11: 200, 202, 220-22; M13: 98, 135, 225
fall of, M12: 26, 45, 65; M13: 113, 127
results of, M13: 97, 103, 183
historic parallel of, M13: 113, 147, 150, 152
efforts of, M13: 154
Manchuria, China, M12: 22, 23, 30, 31, 39, 45, 56, 63, 65, 67; M13: 143, 151, 195
national interests in, M11: 178, 204
railways of, M11: 230
drugs in, M11: 237, 238
Japan and, M13: 80, 81, 84, 91, 144, 145, 199, 259; L6: xx, 191, 194, 204, 205, 217-20, 461; L17: 140, 561
League of Nations Covenant and, L6: 450, 454, 455, 458

Manchuria, China (*continued*)
and sanctions, **L6**: 466-69
Mandarins, **M11**: 217
Mandelbaum, Bernard, **L9**: xxixn
Mandeville, Bernard, **E4**: 147
Manet, Édouard, **L10**: 148, 180, 306
Mania, **M1**: 216
Manifestation
progressive, **L17**: 154
Manifest destiny, **M10**: 240
Manipulation
as terminology, **L16**: 90n, 268
Manitou, **M7**: 400
"Manly Heart, The" (Wither), **L6**: 113
Mann, Horace, **M1**: xvii; **M2**: 97; **M7**: 380; **L9**: 167, 390, 392; **L11**: 232, 237, 545, 578; **L13**: 300; **L17**: 138
on individual growth, **M1**: 5
on education, **M1**: 260; **L11**: 181-82, 226-27, 229, 231, 388; **L13**: 297-98, 342
on democracy in schools, **M1**: 288
and origin of public schools, **M3**: 230; **L11**: 387-90, 409, 579
influences Dewey, **L11**: xvi-xvii
on government, **L11**: 226-27, 248, 387
conference, **L11**: 567-80
Mann, Thomas, **L10**: 217, 289, 317
Manners, **M9**: 22; **L13**: 37-38
Mannheim, Karl, **L14**: xxiv, 293-94
Man of sentiment, **L11**: 282
Mansel, Henry Longueville, **M2**: 154; **M3**: 62n
Man's Supreme Inheritance (F. Alexander), **M11**: 350-55, 359-60
Mantegna, Andrea, **L10**: 147
Manual of Ethics (Mackenzie), **E5**: 25
Manual of Greek Antiquities, A (Gardner and F. Jevons), **L17**: 177-80
Manual training, **M2**: 68; **M3**: 273, 275, 278, 279; **M9**: 204-7
in school, **E5**: 66, 90, 267; **M1**: 295-99, 326-27, 333-34
teaching of technique in, **E5**: 200
references on, **E5**: 337-38
Dewey's emphasis on, **M1**: xxi
as part of new education, **M1**: 6, 261-82
takes place of household occupation, **M1**: 9
social significance of, **M1**: 10, 12; **M7**: 125-27; **L17**: 316-17
related to motor activity, **M1**: 230-32
related to recapitulation theory, **M1**: 232-35
impression and expression in, **L17**: 218
value of, **L17**: 278-79, 313-14
Manual Training School (Chicago), **E5**: 446-47; **M2**: 68; **M3**: 273, 275, 278, 279
Manufacturers, National Association of, **L3**: 280-84; **L5**: 392; **L9**: 125
Manufactures, Committee on, **L6**: 381
Many-many relation, **L12**: 333-34
Many-sided interest
in *Cyclopedia of Education*, **M7**: 275
Marcantonio, Vito, **L15**: 349
Marcel, Gabriel, **M3**: xxiv

Marco Polo, **M1**: 168
Marcu, Valeriu, **L5**: 358
Marcus Aurelius, **E3**: 118; **M11**: 45; **M12**: 140; **L7**: 119, 127; **L9**: xxxi-xxxii
Marcy, Mount, **L6**: 99
Marden, Orison Swett, **L2**: 207
Margarita Teresa, **L10**: 133
Margenau, Henry, **L16**: 121n, 165-66
Marginal utility, **M15**: 264
Margins, principle of, **L17**: 63-66
Margolis, Joseph, **L16**: xxxviii
Marin, John, **L10**: 208, 361
Maritain, Jacques, **L15**: xiii, 51n
Marking system, **E5**: 88, 332; **M1**: 271; **M3**: 241-48
Marot, Helen, **M11**: 333-35, 393
Marriage
  customs of, **M5**: 30, 66, 100-101; **L7**: 31, 60-61, 91-92, 129, 440
  woman's position in, **M5**: 510-16; **L7**: 457-59
  undermining of, **L5**: 74
  church's influence on, **L7**: 441-43
  individualism in, **L7**: 448-52
  social viewpoint of, **L7**: 452-56
  Russell on, **L14**: 245-46
  free selection in, **L17**: 24
Marriage and Morals (B. Russell), **L14**: 235-41, 244
Marsh, Benjamin C., **L6**: xviii-xix, 399n, 400, 504
Marsh, James, **E1**: 112
  philosophy of, **L5**: 148, 178-96
Marshall, Alfred, **M4**: 243; **M5**: 401
Marshall, John, **E4**: 40
Marshall Plan, **L15**: 243
Mars in Civilian Disguise! (E. Johnson), **L14**: 355
Martello, Il (New York City), **L15**: xxiv
Martineau, Harriet, **L5**: 154
Martineau, James, **E4**: 238; **M6**: 392
  on religious feeling, **E1**: 91
  on motive and character, **E4**: 346-48
  retirement of, **L17**: 3, 553
Marvin, Walter T., **M6**: 473-75
Marx, Karl, **E4**: 215; **M8**: 140, 192n, 474; **M12**: 20, 26, 244; **M13**: 315; **M14**: 107, 187, 207; **L2**: xxxv, 378; **L7**: 427; **L8**: 10, 26; **L9**: 75, 91, 298; **L10**: xi; **L11**: 54, 190, 259, 293, 400; **L12**: 236; **L14**: xix, 319-20, 371, 427; **L17**: 502
  Kurtz on, **L5**: xvii, xix-xx
  predictions of, **L5**: 90-91, 367
  on religion, **L5**: 355
  Dewey and, **L7**: xvii
  writings of, **L7**: 426
  Bellamy compared with, **L9**: 103-5
  Brameld on, **L9**: 244-45
  social theory of, **L11**: 27, 33, 59, 292, 334-35, 439, 485
  compared with Hegel, **L13**: 119-21, 354, 401
  dialectic materialism of, **L13**: 120
  on British industry, **L13**: 122
  on human nature, **L13**: 134
  on philosophy, **L14**: 415
  economics of, **L15**: 60-61, 233n
  internationalism of, **L15**: 291, 373-74
  faith in working class, **L17**: xxvii-xxviii
  on contradictions, **L17**: 444
Marxism, **M8**: xxvi, 435-36; **M11**: 91, 161; **L6**: xix, 265-66; **L11**: 594; **L13**: 85,

Marxism (*continued*)
144, 184, 347, 349; **L15**: 250; **L16**: xxxviii, 254; **L17**: xxxii
in Japan, **M11**: 166
in Russia, **L3**: 205, 222-23, 245, 246; **L6**: 293
Heard on, **L6**: 279
class concept in, **L11**: 383-84, 439-40, 498; **L13**: 124-26, 128, 134, 353-54
production in, **L13**: 71, 118-19, 133
social philosophy of, **L13**: 101, 120, 122-23, 126, 132-34, 157; **L14**: 96
absolutism in, **L13**: 117
vogue of, **L13**: 119-22, 129, 131
on democracy, **L13**: 130
use of terror in, **L13**: 399
Benda on, **L15**: 385-87, 390-91
Masaccio, **L10**: 97
Masaryk, Jan, **L15**: 246
Masaryk, Thomas Garrigue, **M11**: 264
Mason, Max, **L15**: 324
Mass, **L4**: 77, 78, 89, 102, 114; **L16**: 107
in art, **L10**: 207, 212-14, 217, 236, 239
scientific concepts of, **L12**: 475-78; **L14**: 104-5
Massachusetts
vocational education in, **M8**: 463, 465
Massachusetts Bureau of Statistics of Labor
report on female health in colleges, **L17**: 7-8
Massachusetts Federation of Labor, **L5**: 506
Mass production, **L7**: 423; **L13**: 104
Matching, **L12**: 214, 217-18. *See also* Correspondence, **L12**
Material
in instruction, **E5**: 174
as factor in educational activity, **E5**: 231
value, **L7**: 212
role in art of, **L10**: xxii-xxvii, xxxii, 31, 38, 45, 68-75, 80-82, 90, 193-94, 204-5, 232-37, 243-44, 247, 272, 280-86, 290, 298, 322-23, 327, 329, 342, 345, 347; **L14**: 37
vs. spiritual, **L10**: 34; **L14**: 314, 317-18, 328-31; **L16**: 366-67; **L17**: 314-15
related to economics, **L14**: 319, 332-33
vs. ideal, **L15**: 187, 200-202, 217, 232, 235, 255, 306
assignment of, **L16**: 371, 410-11, 419
for solving problems, **L17**: 279-80
Materialism, **M3**: 311; **M8**: 18; **M12**: 107-8, 119-21, 177-78, 183-84; **M13**: 417; **L1**: 201; **L2**: 343-44; **L4**: 62, 87, 223-26; **L13**: 133; **L16**: 326n
theory of, **E1**: xxiv, 3, 4, 7, 8; **E2**: 37-42
limitations of, **E1**: 100-102; **L8**: 56, 60, 61
origin of, **M2**: 12-14
in *Cyclopedia of Education*, **M7**: 275-76
equivalent to monism, **M7**: 284
vs. spiritualism, **M13**: 264, 266, 268, 270
ideal factors of, **M13**: 270
of science, **M13**: 433; **L16**: 372, 375
compared with theism, **L2**: 9

as American philosophy, **L5**: 45-49, 55-57, 74
dialectical, **L5**: 358; **L13**: 120, 351; **L14**: 75-76; **L15**: 24
characteristics of, **L8**: 46, 71, 88; **L14**: 99
vs. naturalism, **L14**: 86-88; **L15**: 47-50, 57, 109-17, 190
psychology of, **L14**: 156
in Santayana's philosophy, **L14**: 303-4, 307
economic, **L15**: 60-61, 89, 222-23, 233-34
Sheldon on, **L15**: 454-58, 468-69
politics based on, **L16**: 362
Materialism and Empirio-Criticism (Lenin), **L7**: xvii
Materialistic-mechanistic philosophy, **L16**: 335
Materialistic reasoning, **E1**: 4-8
Material objects
in Bergson, **M12**: 222, 225-26, 228, 234
Material-physical, **L1**: 348-49
Maternal family, **M5**: 28; **L7**: 27
Mathematical
form, **M7**: 422
number, **M10**: 95
-mechanical, **L1**: 107-13, 208
physics, **L12**: 18-19, 61, 352, 395, 439
Mathematical Knowledge (M. Steiner), **L6**: xvn
Mathematical Principles of Natural Philosophy, The (Newton), **L4**: 95
Mathematics, **M12**: 158-59, 165-66, 217; **L1**: 54, 117, 128, 129, 150, 157, 201-2, 223; **L4**: 22; **L12**: 79, 84, 97, 108, 239, 285, 316, 329, 334, 350, 355, 359, 388-89. *See also* Discourse, **L12**
applied to nature, **E1**: 275, 278-79
teaching of, **E5**: 73-74; **M4**: 212, 283-84; **L8**: 204-5; **L11**: 214, 395
references on, **E5**: 337
in education, **E5**: 428-29; **M9**: 66-67
validity in, **M1**: 248
pure, **M7**: 420, 437-39; **L4**: 120-29
related to rationalism, **M10**: 18
in Russell's philosophy, **M12**: 236-39, 241-42, 244, 245; **L16**: 38, 167, 199, 201n
importance of, **L4**: xv, 46, 112, 203
function of, **L4**: 48, 67, 71, 74, 76, 78, 85, 102, 235; **L13**: 55
nature of, **L4**: 53-54; **L15**: 228, 376-77, 507-8; **L16**: 63, 98n, 109, 165n, 180, 236, 266
in Newtonian system, **L4**: 92-97, 148
in physics, **L4**: 112-17
leads to knowledge, **L4**: 156, 158, 162, 163, 166, 169, 173-76; **L16**: 258
terminology of, **L4**: 193; **L16**: 143n
methods of, **L4**: 199; **L11**: 77-78, 98, 150, 153; **L16**: 275
Descartes uses, **L5**: 167-68
related to philosophy, **L6**: xv, 425; **L14**: 333-34
Cohen on, **L6**: 302-3; **L14**: 386-87, 397
growth of, **L6**: 427
related to logic, **L8**: 5, 7, 8; **L16**: 12, 185, 189

Mathematics (*continued*)
Whitehead's philosophical, **L8**: 356; **L14**: 136-40
esthetic quality of, **L10**: xxi, 36, 89, 154, 174, 211, 321
Greek concept of, **L11**: 70, 75
and inquiry, **L12**: 391-94
symbols in, **L12**: 395-96; **L16**: 5, 69-70, 90, 110n, 148n, 159, 173, 266, 309n
data in, **L12**: 401-3
transformation in, **L12**: 406-9, 412-14
point in, **L12**: 411, 463-64
relations in, **L12**: 425-26
and probability, **L12**: 471-73
in science, **L14**: 151-52
Bentley on, **L16**: xviii-xix, xxiv, xxv
intuitionists in, **L16**: 33n
Tarski on, **L16**: 40n
definition in, **L16**: 65, 154, 167-68
of Maxwell, **L16**: 99, 278
abstraction in, **L16**: 276, 431
subject-matter of, **L16**: 284-87, 387, 460-61
on doctrine of possibility, **L16**: 432-35
operational account of, **L16**: 440
as social, **L17**: 237-38
Mathematics for the Million (Hogben), **L13**: 55
Matisse, Henri
as artist, **L10**: xxi, xxx, 123n, 134, 178, 280, 306, 356
on painting, **L10**: 89, 111, 118, 141, 358-59
Matrix
concept of universe as, **L9**: 56, 295, 431, 438-39
Matter, **M12**: 120-21, 200-201; **L1**: 65-66, 95-96, 346, 353; **L15**: 163, 202, 234
and mind, **E1**: 3-6, 8, 17; **E3**: 227-28; **M9**: 137-39, 171, 264-65, 332, 333; **L1**: 200-201, 348-49
Locke on, **E1**: 321-22, 343-45
Leibniz's theory of, **E1**: 346-59
Bergson on, **M7**: 203; **M12**: 224, 234
Aristotle and Plato on, **M7**: 292
and spirit, **L1**: 192-94
as inferior, **L4**: 4-5, 215, 216
Descartes on, **L4**: 74
meaning of, **L4**: 77, 247; **L14**: 86-87; **L16**: 266
Eddington on, **L4**: 89
esthetic, **L10**: xxi-xxiii, xxvi, xxvii, 280, 283, 292, 295, 298, 302-3, 329-30, 343
concept of, **L10**: 12, 28, 34; **L16**: 246, 358-59, 370, 414
and form, **L10**: 108-12, 120-21, 128, 136, 138, 142, 174, 195-96, 364; **L12**: 106, 132, 158-59, 285-86
critic's appreciation of, **L10**: 315, 317, 322, 325
in Aristotelian logic, **L12**: 91, 96, 418-19
in Santayana's philosophy, **L14**: 303-4
Maxwell on, **L16**: 100
Matter and Memory (Bergson), **M7**: 202
Matter and Motion (Maxwell), **L16**: 99-100, 277-78, 468
Maturity, **M13**: ix-x; **L13**: 21, 57, 219
responsibilities of, **L13**: 30, 36-37, 217
meaning of, **L13**: 218
vs. ageing, **L14**: 347-48
Maugham, Somerset, **L13**: 363

Maurer, James H., **L6**: 250, 254, 326
Maurice, Frederick Denison, **M3**: 55
Maurras, Charles, **L15**: 387, 390
Maxwell, James Clerk, **L4**: xvii, 198-99; **L10**: 202; **L11**: 279; **L16**: 61
  on transaction, **L16**: 98-100
  theory of, **L16**: 108, 277-78
  Dewey praises, **L16**: 468
May Drive, **M11**: 310, 312
May Fourth Movement, **M11**: xx, 186-91; **M12**: 41
  effects of, **M12**: 22-27; **M13**: 111, 116, 118-19
  progress of, **M12**: 51, 255; **M13**: 128
  leaders within, **M12**: 253
  background of, **M13**: xxi-xxii, 107, 110-11, 115-16
  journals of, **M13**: 116-18
  Dewey on, **M13**: 119-20
  anniversary of, **L17**: 29, 555
Mayhew, Katherine Camp, **E5**: 436; **M1**: 222, 325, 335n; **L11**: 191n, 193n, 202n
Mayr, Ernst, **L16**: 120n-21n
Mazzini, Giuseppe, **L15**: 219
Mead, George Herbert, **M4**: xx, 96n; **M5**: ix, 153n; **M10**: xxii; **M13**: 29n, 34n; **L4**: 80; **L5**: xi, 419; **L6**: 421; **L12**: 5, 413n; **L14**: 4; **L15**: xxvi, 428
  philosophy of, **E2**: xxvi; **L6**: 24-27, 307-12
  related to Dewey, **E3**: xxi; **E4**: xvi; **L6**: xi-xiv
  and emotion, **E4**: 167n
  Dewey's eulogy for, **L6**: 22-28
  writings of, **L11**: xxiv, 450-53
  at University of Chicago, **L16**: xiv
  influences Bentley, **L16**: xxviii
  "situational" of, **L16**: 101n
  on signal, **L16**: 145n
  transactional inquiries of, **L16**: 269n
Mead, Helen Castle, **L6**: 22
Mead, Henry Castle, **L6**: 26
Mead, Margaret, **L14**: 431
Mean
  Aristotle's conception of, **M5**: 126-27; **L7**: 118
Meaning, **M14**: 186; **L1**: 198, 218-23, 257-65; **L15**: 79
  in facts of consciousness, **E1**: 179
  and relationship, **E2**: 78-79
  Dewey's theory of, **E3**: xxxvi
  determination of, **M3**: 4
  Peirce on, **M6**: 46n, 175
  in thought, **M6**: 271-85; **M13**: xix, 57, 58, 374-76, 384-85, 393
  related to logic, **M7**: 132-33; **L16**: 162, 320
  nature of, **M13**: xix, 369, 372; **L8**: 127-28, 243-47, 264, 286, 301-2; **L10**: 89; **L16**: xxxiii, 32, 134, 192, 305
  nature and, **M13**: xx
  consummatory, **M13**: xx, 377
  referential and immanent, **M13**: xx-xxi, 388-89; **L3**: 89-90
  function of, **M13**: 63; **M15**: 29-30, 364-68; **L14**: xv; **L16**: 301, 331
  inner and outer, **M13**: 390
  social origin of, **M13**: 390-91
  of acts, **M14**: 105, 144
  of aims, **M14**: 179
  as relation between existents, **M15**: 363-64
  and tools, **L1**: 105, 106, 110, 113, 124-25, 129

Meaning (*continued*)
and language, **L1**: 132-61; **L3**: 84, 404-8; **L12**: 82, 187-88, 214, 223, 284-86
and truth, **L1**: 306-7; **L3**: 4-5, 8, 393; **L5**: 213-16
as quality of behavior, **L3**: 37-38
as empirical phenomena, **L3**: 50
instrumental and final, **L3**: 86-87
ambiguity in, **L3**: 87; **L12**: 359-60
in *Experience and Nature*, **L3**: 401-14
and belief, **L8**: 138
development of, **L8**: 214-15, 228-34
standardized, **L8**: 216, 235-36
and things, **L8**: 225-28
irrelevant in, **L8**: 253-54
and concrete, **L8**: 293-94
art expresses, **L10**: xxii, xxvii-xxviii, 90, 97-99, 111, 122, 126, 130, 138, 205, 237, 245-49, 263-64, 272, 307-10, 324-25, 328-29, 350
from experience, **L10**: 27, 28, 36, 38, 61, 66, 78, 80, 104
imagination's role in, **L10**: 276-79, 292-98
and signs, **L12**: 317, 324, 358n, 468
Cohen on, **L14**: 400; **L16**: 16
Hocking on, **L14**: 413
emotive, **L15**: 129n, 130-36
Nagel on, **L16**: 16
Carnap on, **L16**: 22, 23n, 30-31
C. Morris on, **L16**: 33
Lewis on, **L16**: 36-38, 45
Tarski on, **L16**: 42
Dubislav on, **L16**: 161n
Kaplan on, **L16**: 172-73
Pepper on, **L16**: 174
Kaufmann on, **L16**: 197-98
Russell on, **L16**: 200, 202
Moore on, **L16**: 207
as name, **L16**: 235, 266, 332
Woodbridge on, **L17**: 548-49
Meaning and Value of Life, The (Eucken), **M8**: 165
Meaning of Meaning, The (Ogden and Richards), **M13**: xi; **M15**: xxvi, 223-25; **L3**: 82; **L6**: 3; **L16**: 9, 218, 300-302, 470
Meaning of Truth, The (W. James), **M6**: xii, xivn; **M7**: xvi, 144; **L2**: 7, 10
"Meaning of Value, The," **L2**: xix
Meaning-relation
knowledge as, **L17**: 362, 364, 368-70, 371n
"Meanings of the Term Idea, The," **M3**: xx
Meaning-symbols. *See also* Conception, **L12**; Consequences, **L12**; Discourse, **L12**
discourse and, **L12**: 51-66, 115, 118-19, 155-57, 421
in mathematics, **L12**: 395-96
Mean proportional, **L10**: 47
Means, **M14**: 151, 172
inherent value of, **M13**: 6, 12
habits as, **M14**: 22, 24
data as, **L4**: 80
in social conditions, **L4**: 106, 220, 247
symbols as, **L4**: 121
experience as, **L4**: 123, 125, 189
in knowledge, **L4**: 154, 236, 237
development of, **L4**: 170, 171, 187

perception of, **L4**: 222-27, 244
in science, **L4**: 230
in art, **L10**: xx, xxii, 66, 69, 143-46, 176, 181, 201-4, 209, 243
vs. medium, **L10**: 261n
and action, **L10**: 278, 283; **L17**: 157
environment as, **L11**: 239-40
material and procedural, **L12**: 139, 143, 162, 168, 175, 288, 384-85, 402, 513
measurement as, **L12**: 200-202, 210
freedom as, **L13**: 39
determination of, **L13**: 56, 57, 183; **L17**: xxxiii, 292
class struggle as, **L13**: 352-53
ideas as, **L14**: 85
in inquiry, **L16**: 322-28, 336-37
nature of, **L16**: 349-50, 361, 366-67, 411
rationality as, **L17**: xx
Means and ends, **E4**: 29-32, 36; **M5**: xvi-xxvi; **M9**: 112-13, 333; **M12**: 120-21; **M14**: 23, 27-29, 188; **L8**: 84-85; **L11**: 62, 259, 332; **L12**: 490-91; **L13**: xi, 188, 202, 211-16, 228-29, 299, 381, 386-87, 399; **L14**: 72-74; **L15**: 164-67, 178, 216-18, 234
in activity, **M7**: 165-74
in independent thinking, **L2**: 57-60
in philosophy of education, **L5**: 28-33
in democracy, **L11**: 217-18, 298-99
in moral choice, **L17**: xxi
in communism, **L17**: 117
habit related to, **L17**: 206
manipulation of, **L17**: 292, 294
Means-consequences, **L1**: 101, 102, 107-15, 119, 120, 127, 128, 146-47, 189-90, 199-200, 205-6, 221, 252-53, 264, 274-77, 286, 297, 340-41, 354-56; **L16**: 333, 338, 448, 452-53
educational significance of, **M6**: 278; **L8**: 233-34, 286
as fundamental category of inquiry, **L4**: 129-30, 238; **L12**: xi, 16-18, 23-24, 107-8, 111, 381-82, 440
predicament of, **L12**: 45-46
and causal propositions, **L12**: 449-50, 454-57
in experience, **L13**: 56
Measure, **L1**: 347
in Greek morals, **M5**: 107, 108, 118, 126; **L7**: 98, 99, 109, 118
Measurement, **L4**: 90n, 163, 192; **L10**: 311, 313. *See also* Comparison, **L12**
need for study of, **E5**: 358; **L4**: 104-8
related to counting, **E5**: 424-26
temporal, **L4**: 115-16
development of, **L4**: 122-24
absent in ancient science, **L12**: 94-96, 201-2
as qualitative and numerical, **L12**: 205-19, 318, 345
Mecca Temple (New York City), **L11**: 310n
Mechanical
philosophy, **M9**: 293
in education, **M10**: 118-20
relations, **L1**: 81, 108, 111
mathematical-, **L1**: 107, 113
world, **L1**: 109-10, 208-9
reality, **L1**: 151
vs. esthetic, **L10**: 344
Mechanicalism, **L9**: 37

Mechanics, **M12**: 119
Greeks and, **M12**: 117-18
Mechanism, **M12**: 120-21, 200-201, 229-30; **L2**: 223-25; **L4**: xvii, 167, 196-98
concept of, in teaching, **M1**: 139-44
and nature, **M8**: 8; **L14**: 64
and judgment, **M8**: 18-20
in German thought, **M8**: 152-60
related to philosophy, **M13**: 417
fixed reality of, **L14**: 99
Bergson and James on, **L14**: 101
Mechanism, Life and Personality (J. Haldane), **M8**: 449
Mechanization, **M14**: 100
and habit, **M14**: 50-52, 70
Media, **L13**: xvi
Mediated experience, **M9**: 240
Mediation, **M3**: 169-70. *See also* Ground, **L12**
by ideas, **L10**: xxviii, 283
in art, **L10**: 125, 127, 137, 204
as necessary, **L12**: 190, 217-18, 248, 321, 508, 522-24
Mediatism, **M13**: 453-54, 458, 464
Medical Psychology (Lotze), **M7**: 138
Medicine, **L15**: 278
taught in college, **M1**: 291
social responsibility of, **M10**: 155
and philosophy, **L3**: 26
socialization of, **L14**: 95
advances in, **L14**: 341-42
Medieval
philosophy, **E5**: 20; **M7**: 215; **M9**: 300-302; **M11**: 342, 344; **L4**: 220; **L13**: 290
scholasticism, **M15**: 329
religion, **L10**: 37-38, 340
art, **L10**: 336
Meditation, **L10**: 269
Meditations (Descartes), **L16**: 423
Medium
nature and role of, **L10**: xxii, xxiii, xxvii, 69-70, 81-82, 91, 110, 122, 139, 162, 177, 199-209, 212, 216, 264, 277, 281, 291-92, 322-24
art as, **L10**: 111, 129, 330
artist's use of, **L10**: 151, 156
distinctive qualities of, **L10**: 218, 226, 229-38, 241, 243, 246-48
vs. means, **L10**: 261n
environment as, **L16**: 244
Megan, Charles P., **M8**: 123n
on parochial school education, **M8**: 416-17, 471-72
Megarian school of philosophy, **M7**: 349; **M10**: 90; **L2**: 124, 125, 128
Meiklejohn, Alexander
on experimental college, **L6**: 295-98
on liberal education, **L15**: 333-37, 474-86
Mein Kampf (Hitler), **M8**: 425; **L15**: 367
Meinong, Alexius, **M10**: 430; **M11**: 371; **L16**: 18
Melancholia, **M1**: 216
Meland, Bernard E.
Dewey's critique of, **L11**: xv, 84-85
on mystical naturalism, **L11**: 583-87
Melanesia, **M7**: 400
Melchizedek, **M12**: 15

Meliorism, **M7**: 294; **M12**: 181-82; **M15**: 333
Melissus, **M2**: 144
Mellon, Andrew William, **L6**: 157, 160, 179
Melting-pot metaphor, **M10**: 184, 289
Melville, Herman, **L10**: 321
Memories and Studies (W. James), **L15**: 21n
Memorizing
  opposed to understanding, **L17**: 161, 188, 326
Memory, **M6**: 263; **M12**: 80-84, 139; **L8**: 215; **L11**: 71, 73, 148
  related to perception, **E2**: 133; **M7**: 22n, 28n
  as stage of knowledge, **E2**: 154-67
  imagination in, **E2**: 169; **E5**: 318
  Cattell on, **E5**: 349
  in child, **M1**: 204-5
  organic, **M7**: 369; **L17**: 324, 329
  Bergson on, **M10**: 36n
  related to judgment, **M15**: 358-60, 369; **L17**: 333-34, 337
  expression's relation to, **L10**: 24n, 76, 95, 128, 268
  use of, **L13**: 41, 50, 51; **L17**: 325-26, 333-35
  related to psychology, **L17**: 187
  phases of, **L17**: 324-26
  varieties of, **L17**: 326-28
  motor, **L17**: 327
  educative value of, **L17**: 335
Mencius, **M13**: 225
Mencken, H. L., **L6**: 186-87
  vs. Dewey on educational "frills," **L9**: 141-46, 406-11
Mendel, Gregor Johann, **L6**: 13
Mendelism, **L13**: 158
Mendelssohn, Frans von, **L6**: 358
Menger, Karl, **L16**: 32n-33n
Meno (Plato), **L2**: 130; **L16**: 157n
Men's clubs, **M5**: 36-37; **L7**: 35
Mental, **L12**: 39-40, 42-43, 63n, 86, 107, 110, 161, 164, 185-86, 286-87, 516-21. *See also* Intellectual
  powers, **E5**: 61; **M3**: 122-24
  perspective, **E5**: 81
  and physical, **L3**: 27-29, 39-40, 45-49, 50; **L15**: xvii-xix, 87n, 110-17, 202, 219, 365
  hygiene, **L11**: 543; **L17**: 146
  knowledge of, **L15**: 27-33
  privacy of, **L15**: 64, 65, 68-79, 117-26, 136, 150, 431-34, 463, 469
  as name, **L16**: 266
Mentalism, **M6**: 4
Mental life
  emotional and rational, **M7**: 397-99
  James on, **L14**: 158-59
  balance affects, **L17**: 81
  habit and attention in, **L17**: 207
  physical activity in, **L17**: 217
  determining unit of, **L17**: 292
Mental-material
  related to concept of neutrality, **M10**: 49-52
Mercantilists, **E4**: 216
Meriam, J. L., **M8**: 414
  and University of Missouri Elementary School, **M8**: 236-47
Merion, Pa., **L14**: xxi, 357
Merit, **E3**: 381
Merriam, Charles Edward, **L6**: 126-27; **L17**: 112-13
Merrill, Jenny B., **M7**: 377n

Mersenne, Marin, **M11**: 31
Merz, John Theodore, **E1**: 262
Meta-ethical questions, **M5**: xii-xxxiv
Metaphor, **E3**: 190
Metaphysic of Morals, The (Kant), **L2**: 3
Metaphysics (Aristotle), **M15**: 336n; **L5**: 185
Metaphysics, **M12**: 89, 151, 152; **L1**: 45, 49-50, 62-63, 67, 78, 88-89, 194, 209, 308; **L13**: 222, 248; **L14**: xii; **L16**: 277. *See also* Ontological, **L12**
  and logic, **E3**: 131-32; **L12**: 30, 70-72, 286, 507-8, 516-17
  scientists on, **E3**: 141
  ethics as, **E3**: 155-56
  Bradley on, **E4**: 65; **M13**: 498
  in D'Arcy, **E5**: 31, 33
  James on, **M1**: 115; **M13**: 498; **L15**: 3-8, 456
  of Bergson, **M7**: 135-36
  in *Cyclopedia of Education*, **M7**: 276-77
  Dewey's, **M8**: x-xiii; **L1**: vii-xxiii; **L3**: x-xxi, 75-76; **L16**: 385-89, 456-62
  Aristotelian, **M8**: 79; **L15**: 234-35
  related to morals, **M15**: 15-17
  in inquiry, **M15**: 18-19, 327, 331
  in social philosophy, **M15**: 244
  systems of, **L3**: 388
  Peirce on, **L11**: 86, 89n, 93-94, 423, 482-83; **L15**: 146-47
  Hutchins on, **L11**: 395, 406-7, 596
  dialectic, **L13**: 119
  subjective and objective, **L13**: 191
  nature of, **L13**: 273-74; **L16**: 76, 104, 149, 292, 383
  materialistic vs. spiritualistic, **L14**: 86-88
  and dualism, **L14**: 104, 145
  problem of quality in, **L14**: 105
  Whitehead's, **L14**: 124-40
  rejected, **L16**: xxxiii
  of Comte, **L16**: 98
  of Russell, **L16**: 199
  Balz on, **L16**: 433-41
  of substances vs. elements, **L17**: 419
Metaphysics of Pragmatism, The (Hook), **M8**: ix; **L3**: 338
"Method" (Bawden), **L15**: 307
Method, **M12**: 165-66; **L8**: 184; **L11**: 128-29, 146, 150-54, 510-14; **L15**: 72, 307; **L16**: 336, 419, 458. *See also* Experimental method; Technique
  thought as, **E3**: 126-29; **L1**: 102-3
  in education, **E5**: 91, 205-6, 274
  related to subject-matter, **E5**: 92, 287; **M9**: 171-77, 332, 333
  psychological considerations of, **E5**: 166, 338
  and life experience, **E5**: 174
  and end, **E5**: 212
  ethics of, **E5**: 293-95
  in character training, **E5**: 327
  organization of, **E5**: 338-39
  references on, **E5**: 339
  related to evolutionary theory, **M2**: 3
  Dewey's interest in, **M5**: xii-xxxiv; **L4**: ix; **L8**: xii-xv
  as testing, **M6**: 242-53; **L8**: 248-58
  in developing abstract abilities, **M6**: 253-58; **L8**: 259-67, 299
  of animal learning, **M6**: 265; **L8**: 223

in *Cyclopedia of Education*, **M7**: 277-84
essentials of, **M9**: 159-70
as general and as individual, **M9**: 177-86
theory of, **M9**: 349-54; **L17**: 480
true, **M12**: 97
philosophy of, **M12**: 190; **L1**: 3-59
related to knowledge, **M12**: 245; **L1**: 121-24, 324-25
denotative, **L1**: 16, 61, 62, 168
in creativity, **L2**: 114-15
problem of, **L2**: 355-62; **L17**: 442
development of, **L4**: 29, 172-73, 236, 249; **L17**: 442-43, 482
supremacy of, **L4**: 160, 178-202, 222; **L14**: 65-69, 75
intelligence as, **L4**: 175-76
in social practice, **L4**: 201, 211
rationalistic and empirical, **L4**: 204-5
in morals, **L7**: 329-31, 338, 343-44, 350; **L14**: 147
united with attitude, **L8**: 136-39
logical, **L8**: 179-80, 218-19
Whitehead on, **L14**: 127-29, 136-40
Cohen on, **L14**: 386-89
hypothetico-inductive, **L15**: 63, 69, 73n
naturalistic, **L15**: 117-26
of science and common sense, **L16**: 246-50, 373
of inquiry, **L16**: 338-39, 379
for study of value, **L16**: 343-57
related to technic, **L17**: 294-97
Method of Freedom, The (Lippmann), **L11**: 258
Methodology
and logic, **L12**: 12-13
of history, **L12**: 230-31
Methodology of the Social Sciences (Kaufmann), **L16**: 157n, 195-98
Metric measurements, **L4**: 105, 108, 109, 158, 162, 192, 193
Metropolitan Tower (New York City), **L10**: 140, 359
Metternich-Winneburg, Clemens Lothar Wenzel, Fürst von, **M11**: 114; **L15**: 207-8
Mexico, **M15**: 126, 385
religion in, **L2**: 194-98, 200-201, 208
education in, **L2**: 199-205
relation of U.S. with, **L2**: 201-2, 205, 209-10; **L3**: 158-62
public health in, **L2**: 206-10
imperialism in, **L3**: 158-62
Mexico City, Mexico, **L2**: 206-8; **L11**: 310
Meyer, Adolf, **L1**: 117; **L16**: 117n
Meyer, Agnes E., **L11**: 330n
Meyer, Max, **L1**: 139n
Meyerson, Émile, **L6**: 13, 299; **L15**: xviii
Mezes, Sidney E., **M11**: 401-2
Miami, University of, **L17**: 451n
Micah, **L7**: 88
Michelangelo, **M12**: xii; **L10**: 237, 362
Michelson, Albert, **L16**: xiv
Michelson-Morley experiment, **L1**: 38; **L4**: 102, 116
Michigan, University of, **E3**: xxi-xxii, xxxvii-xxxviii; **E4**: 10; **M1**: 55; **L5**: 393, 424; **L15**: 321, 324; **L17**: 8, 213
Students' Christian Association, **E1**: 61n, 90n; **E4**: 3n, 96n, 365n, 369n

Michigan, University of (*cont.*)
courses at, **E3**: 48, 91, 92
F. Scott at, **E4**: 120-22
Dewey and Tufts at, **M5**: ix
Michigan School-Masters' Club, **E1**: 81n; **L11**: 171n
Michoud, Léon, **L2**: 26, 30
Middle Ages, **M12**: x, xiii, 106, 116, 156; **M15**: 196; **L2**: 112; **L6**: 504; **L13**: 290; **L14**: 313, 327. *See also* Feudalism; Medieval
individual in, **E4**: 213; **E5**: 11-13
universities of, **M1**: 40, 289
attitude of, toward truth, **M1**: 165
customs in, **M5**: 33, 37; **L7**: 32, 36
philosophy of, **M9**: 301; **M10**: 22, 38, 40-41; **L13**: 264
revival of interest in, **M10**: 231
German mind of, **M10**: 232
Christian supernaturalism in, **L3**: 6
human nature in, **L6**: 34-35
classes in, **L7**: 132, 138
authority and unity in, **L7**: 135-37, 413
trade in, **L7**: 142
art in, **L7**: 147
thought of, **L15**: 46, 48, 52, 155-56, 264-65, 268-69, 334, 336
intellectual authority in, **L15**: 235, 265-67
civilization in, **L17**: 228
Middle term
as logos, **L12**: 90, 204
Middletown: A Study in American Culture (H. Lynd and R. Lynd), **L5**: 45
Miles, H. E.
on industrial education, **M7**: 104-5, 461-68
Militarism, **M13**: 151
of Germany, **M11**: 61, 152, 158
of U.S., **M11**: 71
as effect of war, **M11**: 104, 388
of Japan, **M11**: 153, 160, 163, 168, 170, 173, 174, 177, 178, 193, 197; **M13**: 205, 257-61
of China, **M11**: 187-90, 194, 197-204, 212, 229, 230; **M13**: 139; **L3**: 423-28
evils of, **M13**: 163
and schools, **L3**: 346-47; **L14**: 355-56
Militarizing Our Youth (R. Barnes), **L3**: 346
Military, **L13**: 187, 302; **L15**: 220
vs. democracy, **L14**: 367-68
dictation by, **L16**: 255
operations of, **L17**: 543-44
Military Intelligence Bureau
on Polish question, **M11**: xv, 248, 259, 262, 295, 320, 396, 400, 401n, 406-7
Military training, **M10**: xxxv-xxxvii, 183-95, 296-300, 377-93; **L6**: 124
characteristics of, **M11**: 60-62, 66
in China, **M11**: 180
for Poles, **M11**: 286, 287, 324, 397
opposition to, **L17**: 122, 124
Miliukov, Paul, **M11**: 263
Mill, James, **E4**: 215, 276; **M2**: 36; **M3**: 54; **M6**: 392; **M7**: 144, 212, 345, 361; **M10**: 111; **L2**: 148; **L6**: 7; **L12**: 157, 498
and moral philosophy, **E4**: 147
and industrial democracy, **E4**: 284
on democratic government, **L2**: 293-94

Dewey's departure from, **L3**: 76
influences liberalism, **L11**: 11, 19
as empiricist, **L11**: 78, 81
Mill, John Stuart, **E3**: xxiii; **E4**: 106, 215, 217; **E5**: 352, 353; **M1**: 115; **M2**: 295; **M3**: 56; **M4**: 254; **M5**: 4, 388; **M6**: 392; **M7**: 144, 212, 357, 361; **M8**: 144; **M9**: 349; **M10**: 335; **M12**: 156; **M13**: 64, 401; **L1**: 123, 323; **L2**: 7n, 357; **L6**: 7; **L7**: 6; **L9**: xxvi, xxxi, 299; **L12**: 157, 436, 498; **L13**: 173; **L14**: xi, 186; **L15**: 13, 399, 423
important in psychology, **E1**: 49, 145
logical theory of, **E3**: 92; **M2**: 368-75; **M3**: 63; **L4**: 90n, 125, 145n; **L5**: 168-69; **L8**: 10-11; **L11**: 30, 95, 99-101, 118, 126, 128, 601; **L12**: xi, 12, 86, 160, 427n
and ethics, **E3**: 100; **E4**: xix; **M5**: xv, xxiiin
syllogism theory of, **E3**: 129-31; **L12**: 323-25
moral theory of, **E4**: 147-48, 278; **M5**: 217n, 227-40
and happiness, **E4**: 284; **M5**: 242-43, 264
on pleasure, **E4**: 284-85; **M5**: 255-56, 267-68; **L7**: 191-92, 196-97
as sensationalist, **E5**: 15
on mind, **M1**: 160; **M4**: 91
on reasoning, **M1**: 163
on laws, **M1**: 171
on judgment, **M1**: 171; **M6**: 261-62; **L8**: 213-14
opposed to intuitionalism, **M2**: 27
on analysis, **M2**: 36
on acceptance of ideas, **M2**: 58
on necessity, **M2**: 150
on positivism, **M2**: 209
on utilitarianism, **M3**: 55; **M15**: 59; **L7**: 155, 241-45
on copula, **M4**: 80n
influences Sidgwick, **M4**: 244
on liberty, **M5**: xi
social theory of, **M5**: 261, 268-70; **L11**: 11, 19, 30-32; **L13**: 138
on secondary ends, **M5**: 298-99
as democratic individualist, **M5**: 469, 536
on private property, **M5**: 495
on thought, **M6**: 195; **L8**: 128-29
on induction, **M7**: 241-42; **M13**: 65, 483, 486
G. Morris on, **M10**: 111
on British philosophy, **M10**: 224
eclipse of, **M10**: 225
political psychology of, **M10**: 271
on drawing inferences, **M10**: 342
on Bentham and Coleridge, **M15**: 59; **L5**: 180-83
denies identity of form, **L5**: 259
on wisdom, **L7**: 208, 209
on conduct, **L8**: 26
influences education, **L8**: 38
on art, **L10**: 53
life of, **L11**: 23-24, 30
empiricism of, **L11**: 80, 81; **L12**: ix, 44, 45, 147-48, 374, 389
on generalization, **L12**: 20n, 265-66
on attributes, **L12**: 150, 259n

Mill, John Stuart (*continued*)
on abstract terms, **L12**: 257-58
on connotation, **L12**: 354-55
on proper names, **L12**: 363-64
on sequence, **L12**: 437, 446
on scientific laws, **L12**: 451, 464
procedures of, **L16**: 158
on definition, **L16**: 181
compared with C. Morris, **L16**: 218n
Millay, Edna St. Vincent, **L7**: 200
Miller, David Hunter, **L6**: 473n
Miller, Herbert A., **L6**: 118, 503
Millerand, Alexandre, **M13**: 316
Millet, Jean François, **L17**: 245
Mill on the Floss, The (G. Eliot), **L10**: 23n-24n, 354
Mills, Ogden L., **L6**: 390
Milne-Edwards, Henri, **E1**: 296
Milner, Alfred, **M11**: 120
Milton, John, **M12**: xxii; **M15**: 326-27; **L6**: 497
on natural rights, **M5**: 142, 143
on sovereignty, **M11**: 27
on liberty, **L7**: 139
on power, **L7**: 207
as artist, **L10**: xxx, 85, 115, 130, 158, 294, 322-23, 357
Milwaukee, Wis., **M7**: 462
Mind, **M3**: 102; **M6**: xxiii-xxiv, 18-19; **L11**: 77, 79, 88, 156. *See also* Body; Mental
nature of, **E1**: 3-8; **M7**: 214-17; **M9**: 326; **M10**: 28; **L1**: 222; **L13**: 385; **L14**: 6, 48; **L16**: 358-59, 384, 393; **L17**: 330
existence of, **E1**: 16; **M10**: 58-60
and consciousness, **E1**: 135-37; **L1**: 230-34
activity of, **E1**: 190; **E2**: 82, 150-52, 156; **E3**: 229-30; **M7**: 195-97; **M9**: 76, 110, 356-60; **L17**: 214, 281, 305
and matter, **E1**: 320-22; **E3**: 227-28; **L1**: 200-201, 348-49, 353-54
and psychology, **E2**: 7; **M1**: 69-72; **M9**: 325; **L16**: 136
knowledge of, **E2**: 15; **L15**: 27-33, 150
memory and, **E2**: 159-60, 165-66
related to language, **E2**: 186; **M7**: 395-97; **L1**: 135
as passive, **M4**: 181-91; **M9**: 276; **L17**: 439
Dewey's theory of, **M7**: xii
states of, **M7**: 31-33
social-moral influence on, **M7**: 38-40
and art, **M7**: 40-43; **L10**: xvii, 276n, 277, 281, 291-96, 299, 301, 314
Perry on subcutaneous, **M7**: 54
realists on, **M7**: 455-60
related to social behavior, **M9**: 38, 127; **M14**: 44-46, 225-26; **L16**: 326, 334, 449
objective, **M9**: 64-65
related to education, **M9**: 76, 137-45
related to judgment, **M9**: 150-51
quality of, vs. quantity, **M9**: 179
Locke's conception of, **M9**: 277
changing historical attitudes toward, **M9**: 300-302
theories of, **M10**: 45; **M14**: 123; **L1**: 135, 207; **L17**: xxix
Spencer on, **M10**: 69
Bergson on, **M10**: 69; **M12**: 222
pure, **M12**: 143-44
role of, **M12**: 209-10; **L16**: 288, 348, 351

James on, **M12**: 222; **L14**: 156
Russell on, **M12**: 245-46
as character of events, **L1**: 65-66
Greek idea of, **L1**: 75-76, 163
and nature, **L1**: 127
as individual, **L1**: 167-74
and essence, **L3**: 289, 293, 387
Hegel on, **L6**: 489
in experience, **L10**: 28-31, 251-55, 267-72
Hocking on, **L14**: 421-23
traditional conceptions of, **L15**: 49, 50, 75, 87, 163-64, 185
as knower, **L15**: 96, 167
as source of value, **L15**: 107-8
freedom of, **L15**: 172, 175-83
relations of, **L16**: 9-11, 121, 417, 424, 464
rejected concept of, **L16**: 55, 80n, 91n, 94, 122, 146, 160
in postulates, **L16**: 78-79
Wertheimer on, **L16**: 105n
objective idealism on, **L16**: 115n
as actor, **L16**: 124
related to logic, **L16**: 162, 185, 197
related to brain, **L17**: xxx
Clifford on, **L17**: 11, 554
sensation in, **L17**: 217
related to object, **L17**: 278
closed vs. open, **L17**: 463-64
Mind, Self and Society (G. Mead), **L6**: xii; **L11**: 451; **L15**: 428; **L16**: 145n
Mind and body, **M9**: 147-50, 333, 346; **M10**: 36-37; **M14**: 24, 49, 51; **L1**: xvii, 191-225, 228, 256-57; **L2**: 104; **L4**: 184, 233; **L12**: 30; **L13**: 332
Mind and Its Place in Nature, The (Broad), **L15**: xvi
Mind in Evolution (Hobhouse), **L8**: 142
Mind in the Making, The (J. Robinson), **M13**: 421-22, 497
Mind of Primitive Man, The (Boas), **L7**: xiv; **L17**: 404-5
Ministry of Public Instruction (Turkey), **M15**: xxi, 278-83, 285-86, 296, 307, 418-20
Minneapolis, Minn., **L11**: 327, 333
Minnesota, University of, **M10**: 164
Minoan civilization, **L10**: 330
Minor. *See* Premise; Syllogism, **L12**
Minorities
in eastern Europe, **M11**: xiii, 71
protection of, **M15**: 390-92, 394
Depression affects, **L6**: 224-26
politics and, **L6**: 226-30
in Teachers Union, **L9**: 316-19, 324-28, 332, 334, 336-39
Balch on, **L17**: 150
Miró, Joan, **L10**: xxiii
Misrepresentation
in Teachers Union, **L9**: 316-18, 327, 330
in China, **L17**: 30-32
Missionaries, **M12**: 49, 57; **L6**: 203
Mission to Moscow (Davies), **L15**: xi-xii
critique of, **L15**: 289-94, 338-43, 488
Mission to Moscow (film), **L15**: xxv
critique of, **L15**: 345-55
defense of, **L15**: 492-501
Mississippi
education in, **L6**: 120

Missouri, University of, Elementary School
curriculum at, **M8**: 236-47
environmental study at, **M8**: 273-74
Mr. Hobbs's State of Nature Considered (Eachard), **M11**: 23-24
Mr. Justice Brandeis (Frankfurter), **L9**: 237-39
"Mr. Wieman and Mr. Macintosh 'Converse' with Mr. Dewey," **L9**: xxin
Mitchel, John Purroy, **M10**: 175; **M11**: 294, 396; **L17**: 68-69, 557
Mitchell, Charles E., **L9**: 254
Mitchell, Clara I., **E5**: 436; **M1**: 325
Mitchell, Wesley C., **M6**: xii; **M14**: 148n
Mitsubishi party (Japan), **M11**: 162
Mitsui party (Japan), **M11**: 162
Mitten, Arthur Allan, **L5**: 344
Mobility
social effect of, **L2**: 322
Models. *See* Patterns
Modern art, **L10**: xxx, 290, 345
Modern Democracies (Bryce), **L7**: 148-49
Modern Idea of the State, The (Krabbe), **L17**: 101-4
Modern Introduction to Logic, A (Stebbing), **L12**: 462n
Modern Man's Worship (Meland), **L11**: 583n
"Modern Philosophy," **M3**: xxv
Modern Review, **L15**: 24n
Modern Science and the Illusions of Professor Bergson (Elliot), **M7**: 135-36
Modern spirit
vs. supernaturalism, **L14**: 78
Modern State, The (MacIver), **L6**: 482n
Modern Times (Chaplin), **L10**: xviii
Modes
in Spinoza's *Ethics*, **E1**: 11, 12, 16
"Modes of Meaning, The" (C. Lewis), **L16**: 36-38
Modes of Thought (Whitehead), **L11**: xv
Modulation
in education, **L13**: 56
Mohammedanism, **M15**: 128
Molecular propositions, **M10**: 94
Moley, Raymond, **L6**: xviii
Molière, Jean Baptiste Poquelin, **L10**: 244, 362; **L16**: 88n
Molinos, Miguel de, **M2**: 216
Molotov, Viacheslev M., **L15**: 298, 347-48
Mommsen, Theodor, **M8**: 186
Monads, **M7**: 293; **M12**: 242
universal content of, **E1**: 292-95
souls as highest, **E1**: 297-98, 318
as conditions of matter, **E1**: 346-51
impenetrability of, **E1**: 362-63
Leibniz on, **L1**: 115n; **L15**: 30
Monet, Claude, **L10**: 306
Money
control of, **L6**: 73-74; **L9**: 296-97
circulation of, **L6**: 379-80
Mongolia, **M11**: 204; **M12**: 66; **M13**: 199, 235
Chinese subjugation of, **M13**: 135
Russian control of, **M13**: 195
government of, **M13**: 240-41
Monism, **M8**: 176; **M12**: 208, 211; **M13**: 313; **L2**: xiii,

8-10; **L10**: xii; **L13**: 72; **L15**: 3-4, 221
idealistic, **M3**: 311
epistemological, **M4**: 80, 82n; **M10**: 64, 66, 439-49; **M15**: 362
in *Cyclopedia of Education*, **M7**: 284-85
as dialectics, **M10**: 11
on social psychology, **M10**: 55
problems of, **L14**: 29
Monist, **E4**: xviii; **M15**: 227; **L11**: 421
Monistic
idealism, **M8**: 178
realism, **M10**: 64; **M15**: 361-62
Monopoly, economic, **L9**: 63
Monroe, James, **L14**: 203
Monroe, Paul, **M6**: 359n
Monroe Doctrine, **M11**: 193, 232; **M12**: xxi, 4; **M13**: 167, 274; **M15**: 411; **L5**: 440; **L6**: 209, 364, 473
Montagu, M. F. Ashley, **L16**: 119n
Montague, William Pepperell, **M4**: x, 133n; **M6**: xii, 473; **M7**: 23n; **M10**: 326n, 437, 445; **M13**: 445n; **L3**: 391, 392n; **L5**: 147n; **L9**: xiin; **L14**: 7
on realism, **M6**: 475-77
Montaigne, Michel Eyquem, **M2**: 233; **M7**: 295; **M9**: 301; **L11**: 77
Montenegro, **M15**: 390
Montessori, Maria, **M7**: 187, 378, 381; **M8**: xxxii; **M9**: 205; **M15**: 176
teaching methods of, **M8**: 253, 300-313; **M9**: 160
on physical development, **M8**: 390
Moody, William Vaughn, Lectureship, **L17**: 488, 568
Mooney, Thomas J., **L11**: 305, 306, 317
Moore, Addison W., **M3**: 115n; **M5**: ix; **M8**: 48; **M10**: xxii; **M13**: 450, 486; **L14**: 4; **L16**: xiv
Moore, E. C., **M1**: 325; **M8**: 129, 130; **L5**: 419
Moore, Eliakim H., **M3**: 216n
Moore, Frederick F., **M13**: 240
Moore, G. E., **M5**: xxvn; **M6**: xiii; **M7**: 422, 455; **M10**: xxvii; **M14**: 166n; **L2**: 71, 77; **L3**: xiv; **L4**: xiii; **L10**: vii; **L14**: xv; **L15**: 43
and scientific ethics, **E4**: xix, xx
on value, **M11**: 381, 383
on definition, **L16**: 166
logic of, **L16**: 187, 193, 199, 203-7
on propositions, **L16**: 208
procedures of, **L16**: 209
Moore, John Bassett, **M15**: 388, 393, 395
Moore, Merritt H., **L11**: 452
Moral, **L15**: 167
ideal, **E3**: xxviii-xxix, 163-66, 312-14, 368-71
conduct, **E3**: xxxiii-xxxiv, 315-16, 320-21, 325, 368-71
rules, **E3**: 100-103, 366-68
meaning of, **E3**: 241-42; **L15**: 236n
end, **E3**: 268-70, 315, 323-27, 340; **E5**: 131
functions, **E3**: 304-6; **E4**: 232-33
order, **E3**: 322; **E5**: 46
community, **E3**: 326-27; **L7**: 257, 335, 345, 347

Moral (*continued*)
freedom, **E3**: 340, 342-44
responsibility, **E3**: 341-42
relations, **E3**: 345-46
institutions, **E3**: 346-49
law, **E3**: 349-52, 386; **E4**: 73-75, 77; **M14**: 74
life, **E3**: 373-81; **E4**: 115-18; **L3**: 52-53; **L7**: 462
education, **E4**: 54, 55, 106-13; **E5**: 66, 75, 82-83, 88
condemnation, **E4**: 295-99
knowledge, **E4**: 308-10; **L7**: 281-83; **L16**: 377
vs. natural, **E5**: 48-49
training, **E5**: 62-65, 79-80, 119; **M4**: 269-74
personality, **M5**: 130-32
situation, **M5**: 187-95
individualism, **M9**: 306
democracy as, **L2**: 325-26; **L7**: 348-50
significance of groups, **L7**: 36-37, 49-52, 97-98, 151-52, 299-300
good, **L7**: 207
authority, **L7**: 215-16, 226-27, 329-30
re-armament, **L13**: 74
vs. material, **L15**: 60-61, 230, 255, 306
Bentley on, **L16**: xxviii
knowing as, **L16**: 253-54
subjects, **L16**: 292, 413
subject-matter, **L16**: 337-40, 452, 455
nature of, **L16**: 356, 367, 371-72, 379, 396-97, 417-18
philosophy as, **L16**: 365-66, 375-77
related to science, **L16**: 370, 378
"Moral Deficiencies as Determining Intellectual Functions" (Simmel), **E4**: 197-200
"Moral Equivalent of War, The" (W. James), **L13**: 290; **L15**: 21n
Moral Experience (Rauh), **L5**: 502
Morality
related to character, **E3**: 246-47; **L17**: 336-37
end of, **E3**: 386-88; **L17**: xxiii
motives for, **E4**: 59-60; **L7**: 64-65, 93, 164-65, 173, 209, 220-21
and children, **E4**: 115-17; **M1**: 208; **L7**: 40-41
primitive, **E4**: 132; **M5**: 43, 160-79
in Royce and Simmel, **E4**: 198-99
Socrates on, **E4**: 225; **L2**: 93
affected by history, **M2**: xi-xii, 20-21
evolution of, **M2**: 3, 16; **M4**: 219-21; **M5**: 13-14, 22; **L7**: xii-xiii, 12-14, 22; **L17**: 393, 396-401
validity of, **M2**: 20-23
infanticide as example of, **M2**: 28-31
vs. moral ideas, **M4**: 267-68
derivation of, **M5**: 7, 52; **L7**: 9, 39, 48, 163-64, 166-68, 178-80
types of, **M5**: 8; **L7**: 10, 162
genetic study of, **M5**: 8-10; **L7**: 11-12
characteristics of, **M5**: 10-17
reflective, **M5**: 41-42, 160-78; **L7**: 162-66, 235-37, 253-55
influence of arts on, **M5**: 44-45; **L7**: 41-42, 147-48
socializing agencies of, **M5**: 45-49; **L7**: 43-47
social, **M5**: 74; **M9**: 367-70;

L7: xiv, 68, 259, 308, 327
group, **M5**: 76-87; **L7**: x, xiv, 70-80, 253
science related to, **M5**: 78-80; **L7**: 72-73, 145-46, 150-51, 179-80, 282-83, 338; **L15**: 199-203, 271-75; **L17**: 351
Hebrew, **M5**: 89-105; **L7**: 82-97, 126
medieval, **M5**: 135-39
related to law, **M5**: 180-81; **L17**: 393-94
related to religion, **M5**: 181-83; **L9**: xiv, xxvii-xxviii, 16-17, 28-29; **L11**: 75; **L15**: 159, 269; **L17**: 394
related to economy, **M5**: 464-65; **L17**: 394
in *Cyclopedia of Education*, **M7**: 285-86
affected by environment, **M9**: 21-22
inner and outer, **M9**: 356-60
duty vs. interest in, **M9**: 360-63
related to intelligence, **M9**: 363-67
pragmatic rule of, **M12**: 173
as standard of judgment, **M12**: 176-77
between nations, **L2**: 376
of ends, **L7**: xxvi
terms connoting, **L7**: 152-53
Kant on, **L7**: 154-55
choice in, **L7**: 166-67, 169, 171, 190, 248, 316, 319
will in, **L7**: 175-76, 341
intuition in, **L7**: 238, 262, 266-68, 272-73
in business, **L7**: 260, 403-10, 414, 423-26, 429-37
methods for, **L7**: 329-31, 338, 343-44, 350
Arnold on, **L9**: xiv-xv, xxv
Bergson on, **L11**: 428-31
related to democracy, **L13**: 155, 178, 303; **L17**: 400
and experimentation, **L14**: 147
in Santayana's philosophy, **L14**: 300-301
introspection as tool of, **L15**: 27-28
absolutist, **L15**: 58-59, 172-81, 236, 267-68
Benda on, **L15**: 381-92
Moralization, **L17**: 359-60
Moral judgment, **M12**: 180-81; **L17**: xx, 4
subject and predicate of, **E4**: 240-46
as immediate and intuitive, **M3**: 5-6
scientific treatment of, **M3**: 6-8, 25-26
logical characteristics of, **M3**: 20-23
use of psychological and sociological analysis in, **M3**: 27-39
Sharp on, **M4**: 221-22
"Moral Life and the Construction of Values and Standards, The" (Tufts), **L7**: xxiii-xxiv, xxix
Moral Man and Immoral Society (Niebuhr), **L9**: 108
Moral philosophy
relation of ethical theory and, **E4**: 132-51
Moral pressure
as sanction, **L6**: 220-21, 455, 457, 465-67
Morals, **M12**: 152, 172, 174-77; **M14**: xiv, 33, 38, 225; **L11**: 11, 72, 75, 77-78; **L12**: 169-70, 217, 489-91
science of, **E1**: 408-9; **M14**: xvii, 5, 10-11, 18-19, 41-42,

Morals (*continued*)
154-55, 164, 167-68, 204-5, 220-22
theories of, **E3**: 170-71; **M9**: 363-70; **M14**: 204; **L14**: 232; **L17**: 3-4
and environment, **M5**: 8; **L7**: 10, 340-44
standard in, **M5**: 37-39, 75, 93, 99-100; **L7**: 12, 36-37, 69, 82, 85-86, 90-91
Kant on, **M8**: 161; **M15**: 12
Hobbes on, **M11**: x, 21, 31-40
logic of, **M11**: 9
philosophy related to, **M11**: 44; **L1**: 49-52, 121; **L4**: 48, 49, 54; **L14**: 147-50; **L17**: xxxii
politics and, **M11**: 122-26, 131-34, 152, 236; **M12**: 192-93
T. Roosevelt on, **M11**: 147-49
traditional, **M12**: 261, 272
related to science, **M12**: 265, 267-69, 272-73; **L3**: 19, 27; **L4**: 34, 81; **L5**: 156; **L13**: 171-72; **L14**: 62, 66-72
nature of, **M12**: 270-71; **L17**: 115
separated from human nature, **M14**: 6-9, 23, 31, 131
custom and, **M14**: 54-59
related to action, **M14**: 193-94; **L4**: 15, 25, 26
metaphysics related to, **M15**: 15-18; **L1**: 45
and laws of nature, **M15**: 54-56; **L4**: 194
in social philosophy, **M15**: 60-61, 238, 242-43; **L9**: 229; **L13**: 73
related to law, **M15**: 62
related to war, **M15**: 63, 111
subject-matter of, **M15**: 237-38
Greek, **L1**: 81; **L5**: 497-99
and criticism, **L1**: 304, 322
and good, **L1**: 388
anthropology and ethics and, **L3**: 11-13, 18-22
related to religion, **L3**: 19, 27; **L9**: xiv-xv, 5-6, 15-17, 28-29, 218-19, 227-28, 426
Aristotle on, **L4**: xxi
perception of, **L4**: 5, 90, 200, 240, 245
values in, **L4**: 31, 206, 209-12, 216-22, 225, 226; **L9**: 417-18
related to intelligence, **L4**: 32; **L17**: 397-99
Fichte on, **L4**: 50
knowledge related to, **L4**: 92, 149, 157, 173, 238
opposing systems of, **L5**: 281-88
study of, **L5**: 398-99
in *Human Nature and Conduct*, **L5**: 501-2
British, **L5**: 503
reflective, **L7**: 179
individuality in, **L7**: 209, 317-18, 348-50
related to progress, **L7**: 326, 328
related to production, **L7**: 374-75, 382, 385-86
education for, **L9**: 186-93
Santayana on, **L9**: 241; **L14**: 301-2, 305-8
related to art, **L10**: xxiii, xxxi, 133, 186, 193, 204, 304, 323-24, 331, 347-52
quality of, **L10**: 26, 27, 31, 46, 202
consequences and, **L14**: 73, 74n
Jefferson on, **L14**: 203, 212-13, 219-20

related to democracy, **L14**: 225, 228-30
liberalism and, **L14**: 252-53
Macintosh on, **L14**: 287-88
related to Russell case, **L14**: 358-59
influences on, **L17**: 393-94
Moral sense
in *Cyclopedia of Education*, **M7**: 285-86
Moral theory
related to moral conduct, **E3**: 93-109; **E4**: 225-27
utilitarian, **M5**: 221-40
Kantian, **M5**: 221-40; **L15**: 217
James's, **L15**: 19-26
on good, **L15**: 44-45
Christian, **L15**: 46-47, 54-55, 60
function of, **L15**: 138
compartmentalization of, **L15**: 229, 232, 235-36
More, Hannah, **L11**: 18
More, Henry, **E4**: 127, 144; **M2**: 153, 163; **M3**: 53
More, Paul Elmer, **M10**: 197; **L5**: xxx, xxxi, 264, 265; **L9**: xxxn
Mores, **M5**: 7; **L7**: 9, 12, 49
defined, **M5**: 54-55; **L7**: 49-50
authority of, **M5**: 55-56; **L7**: 50-52
enforcement of, **M5**: 57-59; **L7**: 52-54
Morgan, Arthur Ernest
on liberal arts college, **L6**: 84-85, 419-22, 503
Morgan, Barbara, **L10**: 8
Morgan, Conwy Lloyd, **L5**: 171
Morgan, John Pierpont, **M13**: 165, 217
Morgan, Joy Elmer, **L11**: 567n
Morgan, Lewis Henry, **L7**: 62
Morgan, Thomas Hunt, **L14**: 391
Morgan, Willard, **L10**: 8
Morley, John, **M8**: 160; **L17**: 430-31
Morning Notes of Adelbert Ames, Jr., The (Cantril), **L15**: 510
Morocco, **M15**: 388-89
Morphia, **M11**: 239
Morphological, **L10**: 177-78
Morrell, Ottoline, **M8**: xx; **L14**: xx
Morris, Charles W., **L7**: vii; **L16**: 10n
on signs, **L15**: 136n, 141-50, 331-32, 473
Dewey on, **L16**: xxxin, xxxii
logic of, **L16**: 8, 9, 38, 193n
semiotic of, **L16**: 32-35, 45, 210-41
Morris, George Sylvester, **E1**: xxxiii; **M3**: xxiii, xxv; **M6**: 94; **M11**: 336-37; **L5**: xxii; **L15**: xxix
influences Dewey, **E1**: xxiv; **E3**: xxi; **L5**: 152
philosophical method of, **E2**: xxiii
career of, **E3**: 3-10
as teacher, **E3**: 11-13
and esthetics, **E4**: 195-96
tribute to, **M10**: xxx, 109-15
Morris, William, **E3**: 202
Morrison, Charles Clayton, **L5**: 353; **L6**: 457n; **L8**: 16; **L9**: 216
on outlawry of war, **L3**: 348-58
Morris R. Cohen and the Scientific Ideal (Hollinger), **L6**: xivn
Morse, Wayne, **L15**: 281, 509
Mort, Paul R., **L9**: 119, 129

Mort Committee, **L9**: 119-20, 129
Mortgage debts, **L9**: 249, 250, 255-57, 269-70, 277
Mosaic form, **L10**: 322
Moscow, USSR, **L15**: 289-91, 345, 348
  contrasted with Leningrad, **L3**: 208, 216, 222-23
  impressions of, **L3**: 215-16
Moscow trials, **L11**: 306, 309-11; **L13**: 347-48, 394-95, 404; **L14**: xx
  as frame-ups, **L11**: 315, 321-25, 330-31
  Cowley on, **L11**: 318
  significance of, **L11**: 326-29, 331-36
  film depiction of, **L15**: xxv, 345-55, 492-501
  Davies on, **L15**: 338-40, 351, 353
Moses, **M5**: 82; **M12**: xxiii; **L7**: 75
Moses (Michelangelo), **L10**: 237, 362
Moslems, **M15**: 128-30, 135, 146-48; **L2**: 178
  art of, **L10**: 333, 334
Mote, Carl, **M10**: 303-4
Mother Goose, **M8**: 241
Motion. *See also* Correlation, **L12**
  primacy of, **E1**: 279-81, 283
  force as element in, **E1**: 358, 361
  characteristics of, **E2**: 30-31
  and matter, **E3**: 228
  as response, **E5**: 107-8
  laws of, **L4**: xv
  Galileo on, **L4**: 77, 78
  theories of, **L4**: 102, 107, 114-17, 120
  and science, **L12**: 212, 475-76
  absolute, **L14**: 105
  as principle, **L16**: 67, 98-99, 104-6, 370, 410, 414
Motion pictures
  influence children, **L9**: 188
Motivation, **M7**: xxii; **M11**: 10-17
  in education, **M7**: 181-82, 473-74
  social, **M7**: 379-81
  related to interest, **M9**: 131, 184
  as outgrowth of school activities, **M9**: 202-3, 213-14
  related to vocations, **M9**: 319
  in philosophy, **M15**: 14-17, 19, 325-37
Motive, **M14**: xv-xvi, 148-49, 159; **L13**: 147
  and ideal, **E2**: 315-16; **E4**: 287-91
  realization of, **E2**: 316-18
  and conduct, **E3**: 243-44, 250-51
  and consequences, **E3**: 262; **M14**: 33-36; **L7**: 173-76, 192-93, 221-23, 249, 274, 295, 337; **L13**: 85-87
  moral, **E4**: 111-13; **M5**: 69-71, 101; **M9**: 356-60; **L7**: 64-65, 93, 164-65, 173-75, 209, 220-21
    development of, **E4**: 252-53
    pleasure and, **E4**: 271-76; **L7**: 194-95
    Bentham on, **E4**: 279
    to expression, **E5**: 193
    child's, **E5**: 227-28
    as incentive, **E5**: 256; **M14**: 83-86
    Baldwin on, **E5**: 348
    and intention, **M5**: 227-30; **L7**: 166-68

nature of, **L7**: 288-92
self-love as, **L7**: 292-98, 300
profit as, **L7**: 403-6, 425, 432
inner, **L13**: 70, 74
complexity of, **L13**: 140-41, 230
for attention, **L17**: 273-75, 278, 283
taboos as, **L17**: 398
well-being as, **L17**: 427
Motor
response, **E5**: 97, 99, 101-2; **L16**: 140, 326
development, **E5**: 181; **M1**: 210-13
activities, **E5**: 205, 206
as aspect in valuing, **L16**: 354
Motor-affective relation, **M15**: 21, 22, 25, 339-40, 343, 348
Motor dispositions
in perception and expression, **L10**: 103-7, 161, 180, 260, 261
Mottoes and Commentaries of Friedrich Froebel's Mother Play, The (Froebel), **M1**: 83-84
Motz, Boleslaw, **M11**: 279, 282
Moufet, Thomas, **L16**: 147
Mount Morris Baptist Church (New York City), **L17**: 393n
Movement, **E5**: 106, 320
unified, **E3**: 128, 218
centralized, **E3**: 215-17
qualitative, **L4**: 74, 75
in art, **L10**: 29, 182, 188, 200, 207-8, 211-14, 227-28, 238, 241; **L13**: 365
in education, **L13**: 3-4
related to sensation, **L17**: 217
Movements of Thought in the Nineteenth Century (G. Mead), **L6**: xii; **L11**: 451-53
Mozart, Wolfgang Amadeus, **M7**: xviii
Mudge, Isadore Gilbert, **M7**: 201n
Mufson, Thomas, **M10**: 162
Muirhead, John Henry, **E4**: 189; **E5**: 25; **M10**: 225
Mukden (Shenyang), China, **L6**: 202, 450, 456
Mulford, Elisha, **E4**: 4
Mulford, Prentice (Dogberry), **L9**: 176
Müller, F. Max, **E5**: 342n, 343, 345
Müller, Johannes Peter, **L16**: 124n
Muller v. Oregon, **L7**: 415; **L9**: 237
Multiplication
logical, **L12**: 336-42, 359, 438-39
Mumford, Lewis
criticizes James, **L3**: xxix, 145-49
criticizes Dewey, **L3**: 146-47
Munich, Germany, **L15**: 353
Municipal Civil Service Commission (New York City), **L9**: 381, 384
Munitions, **L11**: 263
Munitz, Milton K., **L14**: 301-2
Munn v. Illinois, **L7**: 415, 426
Munro, William Bennett, **M15**: 85, 381
Münsterberg, Hugo, **M3**: xxii, 151; **M10**: 52; **L2**: 77
Dewey's disagreement with, **M1**: xiii-xiv
on scientific method, **M1**: 132
on teaching methods, **M1**: 135
on psycho-physical mechanism, **M1**: 142
on St. Louis Congress of Arts

Münsterberg, Hugo (*continued*)
and Science, **M3**: 352-73, 374-81
on will, **M6**: 167-71
Muralov, Nikolai I., **L11**: 322, 603; **L15**: 352
Murchison, Carl, **L5**: 218n
Murillo, Bartolomé Estéban, **L10**: 97
Murphey, Murray G.
on *Human Nature and Conduct*, **M14**: ix-xxiii
Murphy, Arthur E., **L6**: 307, 310; **L14**: 5, 7, 11; **L15**: 335n
Dewey replies to, **L14**: 41-52, 83-86
Murphy, Arthur H., **L9**: 372-73
Murray, Gilbert, **M15**: 380; **L1**: 104; **L5**: 165; **L6**: 34; **L8**: 24; **L10**: 296; **L15**: 184
Murray, James Edward, **L15**: 281, 509
Mursell, James L., **M13**: 32, 36
Muscles, **E5**: 162
Museums, **L11**: 521-25
art in, **L10**: 12-15, 343n
cooperation between schools and, **L17**: 234
Music, **E2**: 62-63, 275-76; **M5**: 48; **L7**: 46; **L10**: 222, 284; **L13**: 70, 359; **L16**: 397; **L17**: 309
in school, **M1**: 52-53, 261; **L17**: 288
Norton on, **M4**: 227
Plato on, **M6**: 376-77
Helmholtz on, **M7**: 140
value of, **M9**: 267
and judgment, **M15**: 22-23, 341-43
nature of, **L10**: xiii, 13, 14, 37, 45, 70, 193, 200-204, 265, 271
distinctive quality of, **L10**: 80, 102n, 111, 113, 225-27, 232-33, 237-38, 241, 243, 246-47, 300-301
rhythm in, **L10**: 160-63, 169-77, 207-8, 211-12
as spatial and temporal, **L10**: 186-89, 210, 213-16
transmits civilization, **L10**: 330-32, 336, 338
Mussolini, Benito, **L11**: 190, 259, 276, 293, 400, 601; **L13**: 294, 402; **L15**: 179, 386n
Mustapha Kemal, **M15**: xix, 137
Muste, A. J., **L5**: 331, 332, 344; **L6**: 251, 327
Muzzey, David Saville, **L14**: 371
My Heresy (W. Brown), **L2**: 164
"My Philosophy of Law," **L14**: xxii-xxiv
Mysteries of the Soul (Freienfels), **L5**: 51n
Mystical experience, **L9**: xvi, xxx, 25-28, 35, 426
Mystical naturalism, **L11**: 84-85, 583-87
"Mystical Naturalism and Religious Humanism" (Meland), **L11**: 583-87
Mysticism, **M2**: 182; **M11**: 46; **M12**: 227, 228; **L9**: 25-27; **L15**: 118-19, 122-23; **L16**: 127, 412
Catholic church and, **E4**: 125
on idea and fact, **M1**: 244-45
Royce on, **M1**: 246n
on nature, **M2**: 147
of Maeterlinck, **M6**: 125-29
in esthetic experience, **L10**: 197, 200, 297, 357
in art, **L11**: 85
Mysticism and Logic (B. Russell), **L16**: 200n, 201n

Myth, **E5**: 252; **L5**: 173n
My Vocation, By Eminent Americans (Lockhart), **L13**: 342n

Nagel, Ernest, **L6**: xviin; **L12**: 5, 293n; **L15**: xvi, 461; **L16**: 447; **L17**: xxxi
  Kurtz on Dewey's debate with, **L5**: xxiv-xxvii
  on excluded middle, **L5**: 198-99, 205-7
  on relation of logic to ontology, **L5**: 203-9, 453-60
  on logic, **L12**: ix-xxvii; **L16**: 39, 193n
  on *Theory of Valuation*, **L13**: x-xi
  responds to Sheldon, **L15**: 109-26
  Dewey on, **L16**: xin, 469
  Bentley on, **L16**: xxx, xxxi
  epistemology of, **L16**: 8-10
  on propositions, **L16**: 12-17, 35, 45
  on language, **L16**: 25, 159n
  vs. Tarski, **L16**: 40
  on Russell, **L16**: 167, 202n
  on definition, **L16**: 171, 173
  on Kantor, **L16**: 192n
  on C. Morris, **L16**: 239n
Naimska, Zofia, **M11**: 314
Naïve realism, **M7**: 456
Named, **L16**: 146, 162
  as event, **L16**: 77, 110, 132
  postulations for, **L16**: 86-89
  related to namings, **L16**: 96, 127, 180, 258
  function of, **L16**: 129, 141-42
  as name, **L16**: 266
Names
  magic in, **M7**: 396-97
  proper, **L12**: 354-55, 363-64
  search for firm, **L16**: xxxv-xxxvi, 6-7, 75n, 445-46
  Carnap on, **L16**: 19
  in logic, **L16**: 49-50, 102
  nature and function of, **L16**: 56, 113, 283, 328
  rejected status of, **L16**: 60, 111-12, 133-35, 160
  as process of designation, **L16**: 62, 307-8
  related to symbol, **L16**: 66, 173
  related to sign, **L16**: 69-70
  as name, **L16**: 72, 266
  related to description, **L16**: 146-47
  Dubislav on, **L16**: 161
  Pepper on, **L16**: 178
  related to theory of knowledge, **L16**: 257-73
  words as, **L16**: 327, 332
Namings
  nature of, **L16**: xxxvi, 47-52, 92n, 93, 104n
  as name, **L16**: 7, 266
  of Carnap, **L16**: 32
  Lewis on, **L16**: 37
  scientific and practical, **L16**: 46, 111n, 159, 307, 309
  firm, **L16**: 46, 275
  as knowings, **L16**: 57-58, 77, 96-97, 110, 127, 131-32, 257-58, 273
  experimental, **L16**: 58, 70-73
  accuracy in, **L16**: 65, 66
  function of, **L16**: 67, 113, 129, 141-42, 149
  aspects of, **L16**: 81n, 90, 180, 308
  postulations for, **L16**: 82n, 86-89
  as behavioral process, **L16**: 133-35

Namings (*continued*)
types of, **L16**: 143, 148
characterization as, **L16**: 145-46
related to description, **L16**: 146-47, 154-55
Mill on, **L16**: 158
inquiry into, **L16**: 162
Nagel on, **L16**: 173n
Nanking (Nanjing), China, **M11**: xviii, 189; **M12**: 31, 43, 253; **M13**: 112
Nansen, Fridtjof, **L5**: 395
Napoleon, **M10**: 237; **L10**: 14, 46; **L11**: 290; **L13**: 84; **L15**: 219
and Germany, **M8**: 171, 176, 189, 194
Napoleonic wars, **M9**: 100; **M11**: 58, 59, 114; **L8**: 37
Nash, Walter, **L17**: 543-44
Nathanson, Jerome, **L15**: 251n
Nation, **M11**: ix; **L6**: 328, 439; **L9**: 66, 305-6
National Advisory Council on Radio in Education, **L6**: 90n, 231n
National Association for the Advancement of Colored People, **L6**: 224; **L15**: 356
National Association of Community Chests and Councils, **L6**: 374-75
National Association of Manufacturers, **L3**: 280-84; **L5**: 392; **L9**: 125
National Association of Science Writers, **L11**: 127
National Broadcasting Company, **L6**: 341
National Bureau of Economic Research, **L6**: 343, 349, 360; **L7**: 409
on national income, **L9**: 81-82, 267, 287-88
National Civic Federation, **L5**: 342, 343
National Conference of Social Work, **M15**: 150n
National Conference on Universities and Public Service, **L17**: 67n
National Consumers' League, **L3**: 280n
National Council of Education, **M2**: 80n; **L5**: 326n; **L6**: 142n, 445
National Education Association (NEA), **M1**: 260; **M10**: 130n, 196; **M15**: 185, 192; **L5**: 299n, 317; **L6**: 123n, 445n; **L9**: 127, 167; **L11**: 217n, 247n, 345, 533-34, 548
National Grange, **L9**: 250, 273
National Industrial Recovery Act, **L9**: 160-61; **L14**: 95
Nationalism, **M13**: 249, 439; **L2**: 341; **L8**: 73-75; **L11**: 252, 459-60, 574-75; **L13**: 316; **L15**: 195, 208-9, 219, 373-74
in education, **M7**: 379; **M10**: 203-10
problems of, **M10**: 202-3; **L3**: 154-57, 351-52; **L7**: 366-71
related to nationality, **M10**: 232, 285-91, 294
development of, **L3**: 152-53
American, **L5**: 50-57
during Renaissance, **L7**: 138
power of, **L7**: 149
and patriotism, **L7**: 367-69
German, **L13**: 84, 88
and science, **L13**: 159
one-sided, **L13**: 302
value and status of, **L17**: 113

Nationalism, New, **M11**: 146
National Morale, Committee on, **L15**: 353
National Negro Conference, **M4**: 156n
National Peking University (China), **L14**: xx
National Press Club, **L11**: 319
National Recovery Administration (NRA), **L9**: 84, 280-81, 297, 387, 388
National Self Government Committee, **L11**: 516; **L17**: 523
National Service Handbook (Committee on Public Information), **M10**: 315-16
National Socialism, **M8**: xxx, 421, 432-46. *See also* Nazism
National Socialist German Workers party, **M8**: 424-26
National Society for the Promotion of Industrial Education, **M7**: 85n
National Society for the Study of Education, **L9**: 169n; **L13**: 255n, 281n
National Society of College Teachers of Education, **L17**: 138-39, 561
National Students' Union (China), **M11**: 190
Nations
  education as function of, **M9**: 99-106
  organization of, **L15**: 195-98, 204; **L16**: 400
Nativism
  in *Cyclopedia of Education*, **M7**: 286-87
Natural
  and spiritual, **E3**: 227-28
  selection, **E5**: 44, 49-50; **M4**: 9; **M8**: 21; **M12**: 229
  process, **E5**: 45
  vs. moral, **E5**: 48-49; **L16**: 372
  in *Dictionary of Philosophy*, **M2**: 141
  vs. supernatural, **L9**: 30, 37, 46-48, 294-95, 429, 434
  religion, **L9**: 43
  aristocracy, **L13**: 108
  knowings treated as, **L16**: 84-85, 91-92, 96-97
  logics, **L16**: 185-87, 192
Natural development
  Froebel on, **M8**: 275-76
  Rousseau's theory of, **M9**: 119-25
Naturalism (J. Pratt), **L15**: 453-54
Naturalism, **M7**: x-xi, 415; **L5**: 114; **L11**: 153, 554
  in *Dictionary of Philosophy*, **M2**: 142
  related to belief, **M3**: 98-99
  Dewey's, **M6**: xii; **M14**: ix-x; **L3**: 369, 374-75, 381, 383, 394; **L14**: 14-19, 381; **L15**: xii-xix, xxiii
  in *Cyclopedia of Education*, **M7**: 213-17
  and humanism, **M12**: 179
  Thilly and, **L3**: 73
  Santayana on, **L3**: 368; **L14**: 298-305; **L16**: 384, 457
  in art, **L10**: 146, 155-58, 335, 336
  mystical, **L11**: 84-85, 583-87
  and logical theory, **L12**: 26-28
  meaning of, **L14**: 63-64
  and materialism, **L14**: 86-88; **L15**: 109-15, 190
  mechanistic version of, **L14**: 143

Naturalism (*continued*)
Otto's philosophy related to, **L14**: 290-92
vs. anti-naturalism, **L15**: 46-62
method of, **L15**: 117-26
vs. supernaturalism, **L15**: 186, 200-202; **L17**: xxx
Aristotle on, **L15**: 234n
Sheldon on, **L15**: 453-72
on specification, **L16**: 152
Naturalism and the Human Spirit (Krikorian), **L15**: xvi, 109, 453-68
Naturalistic
idealism, **M3**: 319-22
philosophers, **M8**: 180
"Naturalistic Theory of Sense-Perception, A," **L2**: xv
Natural law, **M3**: 49, 51; **M5**: 205; **M7**: 56-63, 288; **M15**: 57; **L1**: 173, 357; **L2**: 291, 294, 299, 332; **L8**: 36; **L10**: 154; **L11**: 7, 10, 111-12, 552-53; **L13**: 136, 178; **L14**: xxii-xxiii
Grotius on, **M4**: 41
and morals, **M14**: 204-7
related to human nature, **L6**: 35
theory of, **L14**: 100, 115-16, 120
Pollock on, **L17**: 98-99
benefits of, **L17**: 99
Pound on, **L17**: 106
Naturalness, **L13**: 109
Natural realism
in *Dictionary of Philosophy*, **M2**: 142
Natural resources, **L6**: 351, 356, 364, 365; **L8**: 50, 51
economic advantage of, **L6**: 485
use of, **L7**: 405-6; **L13**: 388; **L17**: 451
human connection with, **L8**: 60
People's Lobby on, **L9**: 289-90
Natural rights. *See* Rights
Natural science. *See* Science
Nature, **L13**: 136, 350
ends in, **E1**: 222; **L13**: 192, 299
mechanistic view of, **E1**: 275, 278-79; **M8**: 8; **M11**: 379; **M12**: 120-21, 229-30; **M13**: 365-66
Leibniz on, **E1**: 345
in D'Arcy, **E5**: 27
related to education, **E5**: 89; **M9**: 100-101
related to science, **M2**: 4-5; **M9**: 290-94; **L13**: 163; **L16**: 372, 409
Royce on, **M2**: 124-25
in *Dictionary of Philosophy*, **M2**: 142-49
different views of, **M4**: 15-30
Greeks on, **M4**: 35; **M5**: 120-21, 123, 128; **M9**: 287, 289; **M13**: 370-71; **L1**: 80-81; **L4**: 43, 73; **L7**: 111-12, 114, 119; **L12**: 87, 94-98; **L15**: 265
social goals related to, **M5**: 55; **L7**: 39, 50; **L15**: 253, 257
convention vs., **M5**: 106, 112, 118; **L7**: 97, 103, 109
custom vs. belief in, **M6**: 23-24
Newton on, **M6**: 420; **L4**: 89, 92-96, 102, 114
in humanism and naturalism, **M7**: 214-17
classic idealism on, **M7**: 224
in *Cyclopedia of Education*, **M7**: 287-90
Pestalozzi on, **M7**: 378

Locke on, **M8**: 59
Rousseau on, **M8**: 183, 188
eighteenth-century attitude toward, **M9**: 98
vs. nurture, **M9**: 124
Socrates on, **M9**: 286; **M13**: 367
Plato on, **M9**: 286-87
Aristotle on, **M9**: 287; **L1**: 79
Windelband on, **M9**: 290
man's relation to, **M9**: 290-94, 332; **M11**: 350; **M12**: 99-100, 145-46; **L1**: viii-xxiii, 69-99, 314-15; **L11**: xxi-xxii, 84-85, 230-32, 250-51; **L15**: 96, 186, 188, 202, 255-56; **L16**: 110, 121, 366, 414, 417; **L17**: 73
Bacon's theory of, **M9**: 291-92
control of, **M10**: 206-8, 237-38; **L4**: 3, 8-9, 69, 80-84, 232; **L15**: 110-11
laws of, **M11**: 36-38; **M15**: 54-58, 233-34, 256, 258; **L7**: 131-32; **L11**: 7, 10, 111-12, 552-53
and politics, **M11**: 141, 219
theory of, **M11**: 341-45, 349; **M13**: xx, 364-65, 367, 385, 404, 433; **L1**: 81-82; **L16**: xxxvii, 82, 330, 358-59, 363
inquiry into, **M12**: 97, 100, 106, 107
and philosophy, **M12**: 110-11; **L14**: xii
poetry in, **M12**: 119
Russell on, **M12**: 240; **L16**: 199n-200n
Santayana on, **L1**: 54
stability of, **L1**: 55-68
characteristics of, **L1**: 126-27; **L2**: 47
as individualized, **L1**: 162-90
and psycho-physical, **L1**: 191-225
related to art, **L1**: 266-94; **L10**: 232-35, 238-41, 247, 269-70, 274, 281, 289-91, 296, 300, 301, 325, 327, 330, 335-37, 341
philosophies of, **L4**: xiv-xvi, 40-43, 77, 103, 108, 161, 184-86, 194-98, 204, 229-33, 236
intelligibility of, **L4**: 22, 36, 44-47, 86, 91, 156, 164, 166-72, 176, 238
as God, **L4**: 45
as source of possibilities, **L4**: 52, 212, 237, 240, 241, 244
symbolism in, **L4**: 123
and technology, **L6**: 282-83; **L13**: 69
and existence, **L6**: 430
related to experience, **L6**: 488-89; **L14**: 142-45, 414; **L16**: 384-85, 456-57
Roman conception of, **L7**: 130-31, 219
esthetic character of, **L10**: xxxiii, 20-21, 30-38, 64-66, 86, 106, 139, 144, 152-56, 166-67, 190, 200, 219
Wordsworth on, **L11**: 18-19
empiricist view of, **L11**: 79
Whitehead on, **L11**: 147-49, 151, 152; **L14**: 136-37
simplicity of, **L12**: 456
moral import of, **L13**: 108, 276
surrender of, **L13**: 123
Jefferson on, **L13**: 174
faith in, **L13**: 179
knowledge of, **L14**: 17-19
continuity in, **L14**: 30, 108,

Nature (*continued*)
126-28, 384
meaning of term, **L14**: 63-64; **L15**: 86-87
contingency in, **L14**: 82-83
Hocking on, **L14**: 152, 422-23
Cohen on, **L14**: 408; **L16**: 195
naturalists vs. anti-naturalists on, **L15**: 55, 60, 119, 463-67
vs. natural, **L16**: 74n, 97
quality of, **L16**: 75, 254, 379, 398, 412
Descartes on, **L16**: 106
Bridgman on, **L16**: 192n
Kaufmann on, **L16**: 195
as name, **L16**: 266-67, 447
Russian study of, **L17**: 502-3
"Nature and Reason in Law," **L14**: xxiii
"Nature in Experience," **L14**: x, xii
Nature of the Physical World, The (Eddington), **L4**: 90n
Nature study, **M9**: 218, 221; **M10**: 132
in school, **E5**: 199, 267; **M1**: 8-9, 261, 328; **M8**: 266-67, 269-74
child's interest in, **M1**: 97-99, 234
Naturrecht, **M3**: 51
Naval Blockade, The (Guichard), **L6**: 476n
Nazism, **M8**: xxx, 421, 426; **L11**: 296, 344, 400; **L13**: 132, 141, 150, 153, 158; **L14**: 264, 277; **L15**: xi, 196, 220, 297, 340; **L16**: xxxii
doctrine of, **M8**: 432-46
appeals by, **L13**: 88
and democracy, **L14**: 226; **L16**: 401
Mannheim and, **L14**: 293
philosophy and, **L14**: 313, 320-23, 331-32
morality of, **L15**: 175-77, 180
Davies on, **L15**: 290
Benda on, **L15**: 385
defeated, **L16**: 391
Balch reacts to, **L17**: 150
domination by, **L17**: 524
tactics of, **L17**: 525
opposes Russians, **L17**: 543
Near East, **M15**: xviii
Nearing, Scott, **M8**: 407; **M10**: 165
Necessitarian theory, **E4**: 21
Necessity, **M14**: 214-15; **L13**: 235. *See also* Contingency, **L12**; Implication, **L12**; Universal proposition, **L12**
meaning of, **E4**: 19-20, 27, 35-36, 48n
and reality, **E4**: 28-29
and chance, **E4**: 29-36
logical, **E4**: 33; **M2**: 150; **L11**: 106, 124-25; **L12**: 90, 201, 277-78, 312, 317-18, 339, 377-78, 419, 437-40, 471
in *Dictionary of Philosophy*, **M2**: 149-53
vs. freedom, **L10**: 284, 286
Aristotle on, **L10**: 288-89
Whitehead on, **L11**: 147
causal, **L13**: 120-21, 123
for valuation-propositions, **L13**: 238
Necessity of Pragmatism, The (Sleeper), **L14**: xxivn; **L16**: xxxiin
Need, **L1**: 58-59, 73-74, 194, 264, 272, 276-77; **L12**: 33-34; **L13**: 223. *See also* Conflict, **L12**
art's relation to, **L10**: 108, 235, 236, 260-61, 284-85, 291, 336, 344

function of, **L13**: 232-34
physical and non-physical, **L13**: 286-87
as constant in human nature, **L14**: 260-61
in semiotic, **L16**: 232, 239-40
"Needed—A New Politics," **L11**: xxiii
"Need for a New Social Concept, The," **M13**: 323
"Need for a Recovery of Philosophy, The," **M15**: ix, 14, 15n, 17, 18, 333; **L14**: 401
Negation, **L12**: 172, 196, 198, 305-7, 340, 442, 451-52; **L13**: 122. *See also* Comparison, **L12**; Elimination, **L12**; Exclusion, **L12**
in ancient logic, **L12**: 90, 182
change and, **L12**: 188-93
theory of, **L12**: 220-21, 263
-affirmation, **L12**: 427, 459
Negroes, **L13**: 301
national conference of, **M4**: 156n
rights of, **M5**: 32; **L7**: 31
illiteracy of, **M10**: 127-29; **L5**: 313-15
art of, **L10**: 171, 175, 236, 256, 314, 333-37
discrimination against, **L15**: 356-57
McKay on, **L17**: 59-60
Neill, Thomas P., **L15**: 50
Neilson, William Allan, **M15**: 316; **L11**: 509
Nelson, Leonard, **M8**: xxviii
Nemesis, **L7**: 106, 122
Neo-criticism
in *Dictionary of Philosophy*, **M2**: 153
Neo-Hegelianism, **M2**: x, 333; **M6**: 167; **L6**: 269
Neo-humanism
in *Cyclopedia of Education*, **M7**: 290-91
Neo-Kantian idealism, **M3**: 130, 133; **M7**: 328; **M10**: xxv; **L2**: 14
Neo-Kantianism, **E5**: 19-20; **L6**: 269
in *Dictionary of Philosophy*, **M2**: 153
Neo-Platonism, **M7**: 260, 292; **M12**: 143-44; **L8**: 24; **L9**: 25-26; **L10**: 296
in *Dictionary of Philosophy*, **M2**: 153
on noetic, **M2**: 156
on nous, **M2**: 156, 163
on non-being, **M2**: 157
on theory of One, **M2**: 167
as pantheistic, **M2**: 183
Neo-Pythagoreanism
in *Dictionary of Philosophy*, **M2**: 153
on theory of One, **M2**: 167
Neo-realism, **M7**: 223, 348; **M15**: 335
subject and object in, **M10**: 25-42
related to idealistic dialectic, **M10**: 107
classification of, **L3**: 398-400
Neo-scholasticism, **M15**: 329; **L12**: 17
Nervous activity
as process of adjustment, **E1**: 97-98
Nervous system, **L13**: 327
coordination of organs in, **E1**: 104
physiological phenomena of, **E1**: 107
functions and structures of, **E5**:

Nervous system (*continued*)
304-6, 308-9
as element of behavior, **M7**: 53
connection of learning with, **M9**: 346-47
Nescience
in *Dictionary of Philosophy*, **M2**: 153-54
Netherlands, **L10**: 117, 358; **L11**: 59n; **L15**: 245; **L16**: 403
Neurath, Otto, **L13**: x; **L16**: 10n, 187n, 469
Neutral
as logical and ontological, **M10**: 49-52
Neutral monism, **L14**: 126, 163
New Atlantis (F. Bacon), **M5**: 154; **L7**: 145
New Britain, Conn., **M7**: 466
Newcastle, Earl of, **M11**: 33n
New culture movement. *See* May Fourth Movement
New Deal, **L5**: xvii, xx; **L6**: xviii, xix, 253, 254; **L9**: 166, 259, 280-81, 296, 297; **L11**: xii, 256-57, 491; **L13**: 316; **L14**: 364
New education, **E5**: 268-69
development in, **L9**: 199-200
Mencken on, **L9**: 408-10
New Education Fellowship, **L14**: 278-79
New England, **M11**: 80, 336, 337; **L15**: 322
"New England Reformers" (Emerson), **L9**: xxvi
New England transcendentalists, **M7**: 358
New Era, **M11**: 112, 114
Newer Ideals of Peace (Addams), **L15**: 194
Newfang, Oscar, **L6**: 463n
New Guinea, **L6**: 3
New Haven Teachers Association, **L9**: 112n
New History Society, **L6**: 149, 503
New Humanist, **L11**: 84, 436, 583n
New Leader, **L15**: 295, 335n, 350; **L17**: 543
"New Leaven in Chinese Politics, The," **M12**: xxiii
New Left, **L17**: xxiv
"New Logic, The" (Menger), **L16**: 33n
Newman, John Henry, **E3**: 53; **L4**: 42, 240; **L11**: 403n, 592; **L15**: 46-47, 60
New Masses, **L15**: 352
"New Method of Presentation of the Theory of the Syllogism" (M. Black), **L16**: 186n
New Minds: New Men? (Woody), **L6**: 291-94
New Nationalism, **M11**: 146
New Organon, The (F. Bacon), **L13**: 166, 402
New pedagogy. *See* New education
New peripatetics, **M2**: 186-87
New Realists, **M6**: xiii
"New Reformation," **L8**: 357
New Republic, **M11**: ix, xvii, xviii, 404; **M12**: 5; **M13**: 421; **M15**: xiii, xvii, xixn, xxv, 115, 339n, 378; **L6**: xvii, xx, 161, 165, 439, 488; **L8**: x, 14; **L9**: 293; **L11**: 318, 530; **L14**: xviii, 365-66; **L15**: xxv
News, **L2**: 347-48
New School for Social Research (New York City), **L11**: 155n, 303n, 563n; **L15**: 9n; **L17**: 147n, 442n

Newspapers. *See* Press
New Student, **M15**: 198n
New Systematics, The (J. Huxley), **L16**: 121n
Newton, Isaac, **E1**: 272, 303; **E2**: 125; **M7**: 220, 398, 427, 428; **M8**: 10, 455; **M10**: 359; **M11**: 219; **M12**: 264n; **M13**: 311, 313; **L1**: 14, 15, 37, 38, 330, 348; **L2**: xxxii, 20, 142, 366; **L6**: 15, 428; **L7**: 145; **L8**: xvi, 28, 33; **L9**: 242; **L10**: 302; **L15**: xiii, xxxii, 235, 312; **L16**: 130, 292; **L17**: 406, 443
  importance of, **E1**: 49; **M4**: 40
  vs. Leibniz, **E1**: 262, 267
  on hypotheses, **M1**: 170-71
  on nature, **M2**: 147; **M6**: 420; **M7**: 288
  on universe, **M4**: 47
  on analysis of forces, **M5**: 154
  existence of, **M7**: 67-73
  and theory of induction, **M7**: 241
  on gravitation theory, **M7**: 354; **L8**: 243
  on primary qualities, **L12**: 120
  atomic theory of, **L12**: 130n
  contradicted, **L12**: 197, 204, 395
  scientific laws of, **L12**: 450
  on cosmology, **L14**: 126-28
  Cohen on, **L14**: 392-97
Newtonian science, **M7**: 58; **L16**: 124, 363
  nature of, **L4**: xv-xvii, 77, 78, 125, 130, 148, 153, 185; **L16**: 61, 74, 108, 286, 340, 454
  justification for, **L4**: 48
  replaces Greek science, **L4**: 79, 164
  limitations of, **L4**: 89, 161-64, 167, 169; **L16**: 89, 94
  as scientific foundation, **L4**: 92-98, 102-4, 222
  deserts empiricism, **L4**: 113-16, 120
  interactionalism of, **L16**: xxxiv, 66-67, 103, 240
  vs. transaction, **L16**: 98-100
  motion's role in, **L16**: 106, 370
  departure from, **L16**: 148, 270, 278, 414
New York (city), **L9**: 112, 121, 122, 191, 271; **L11**: 175, 268, 323, 326, 380-81, 520, 530-31; **L14**: xxi
  education in, **M7**: 205-6; **M11**: 55, 61, 393; **M13**: 426-27; **L9**: 332, 369; **L14**: 241, 243
  Polish question in, **M11**: 259, 261, 294, 311-16, 322, 396, 400, 401
  teachers' union in, **M13**: 427-30; **L17**: 520
  educational conference in, **L6**: 422
  banks in, **L9**: 114-15
  land values in, **L9**: 257-58, 265
  investigation of government of, **L9**: 346-85
New York (state)
  art education experiment in, **E5**: xciv
  court appointments in, **L6**: 323
New York Academy of Medicine, **L3**: 25n
New York Evening Post, **M11**: 305, 397
New York Globe, **M15**: 45
New York Herald Tribune, **M15**: 389; **L6**: 326, 456n, 468n, 470n; **L9**: 113; **L11**: 593; **L14**: 369
New York Journal, **M11**: 114

New York Philosophical Club, **M7**: 31n; **M8**: xx
New York State Economic Council
investigates education, **L14**: 371, 427, 429
New York Teachers Guild, **L11**: 380
New York Times, **M11**: 309; **M15**: xxiv, 190n; **L6**: 162, 422; **L9**: 287, 310, 311n; **L14**: xix, 431; **L15**: xxv, 338, 345, 351, 354, 356, 492, 499
New York Training School for Teachers, **E5**: 447
New York World, **L6**: 198
on outlawry of war, **L3**: 164-67, 174
New York World-Telegram, **L9**: 364
"Next Ten Years of the League, The" (Buell), **L6**: 458n
Nexus
in *Dictionary of Philosophy*, **M2**: 154
Nicaea, Second Council of, **L10**: 332
Nicene Creed, **L2**: 165
Nicholas, Grand Duke of Russia, **M11**: 267
Nicholas Cusanus (Nicholas of Cusa), **M2**: 147, 163-64
Nichols, Herbert, **E5**: 342, 345
Nicias, **L2**: 130-31, 135, 139
Nicolaevsky, Boris I.
on forced labor, **L15**: 295-98
Nicolson, Marjorie H., **L5**: 184
Nicomachean Ethics, The (Aristotle), **M10**: 416; **M12**: xvii; **L4**: xxi; **L11**: 595; **L15**: 417
Niebuhr, Reinhold, **M8**: 177, 186; **L5**: xvii; **L6**: 439; **L9**: 71, 73-74, 110
on illusions, **L9**: 108
on capitalism, **L9**: 399-405
on liberalism, **L9**: 404-5
Nietzsche, Friedrich Wilhelm, **E4**: xxiv; **M3**: xi; **M4**: 44; **M5**: 81, 115; **M7**: 414, 417, 420, 433; **M8**: 47, 151, 166, 423; **M10**: 226; **M11**: 156; **M15**: 330, 331; **L7**: 75, 106; **L13**: 75; **L15**: xiv, 387, 389
on sympathy, **M5**: 333n
used to justify war, **M10**: 220, 221, 223
Santayana on, **M10**: 306-8
ethics of, **L5**: 398-400
vs. Dewey, **L10**: xi, xxv
Nihilism, **L10**: xi
in *Dictionary of Philosophy*, **M2**: 154-55
Nike (*Winged Victory*), **L10**: 238
Nin, Andrés, **L11**: 324, 603-4
Nine-Power Treaty, **L6**: 192, 218, 457
Nirvana, **M2**: 155; **M14**: 122-23, 198
Nishihara loans, **L2**: 183, 403-4
Nisus
in *Dictionary of Philosophy*, **M2**: 155
Nobel Committee, **L17**: 149-50
Noble, Edmund, **L3**: 299-304; **L4**: 197n
Noble savage, **L11**: 282
Noblesse oblige, **M15**: 87-88
Noble State Bank v. Haskell, **L7**: 414
Nock, Albert Jay
on U.S. education, **L6**: 286-90
Noetic
in *Dictionary of Philosophy*, **M2**: 155-56
No Friendly Voice (Hutchins),

L11: 592
Nominal definition, **L16**: 163-64, 168, 170, 174-75, 180
Nominalism, **M7**: 348, 360; **L1**: 145-46, 148; **L2**: 7; **L11**: 89, 112; **L12**: 261-62; **L16**: 158
in *Dictionary of Philosophy*, **M2**: 156
Nomos, **L7**: 255
-physis controversy, **M6**: x
Grote on, **M6**: 17-18
Non-being, **M7**: 292; **M12**: 141; **L12**: 89, 417, 420, 521
in *Dictionary of Philosophy*, **M2**: 156-58
Greek idea of, **M10**: 12
defines realm of change, **L4**: 15-16
Non-ego
in *Dictionary of Philosophy*, **M2**: 158
Non-esthetic, **L10**: xxii, 47, 55, 107
Non-Euclidean geometry, **M7**: 423-24
Non-existential, **L16**: 429-30. *See also* Hypothesis; Idea; Possibility; Universal proposition, **L12**
Non-recognition doctrine
as international sanction, **L6**: 219-20, 467-71
Non-resistance doctrine, **M10**: 249
Non-valuable worth, **M15**: 338-39
Non-violence, **L6**: xxi
Non-Violent Coercion (Case), **L6**: 451n
Noology
in *Dictionary of Philosophy*, **M2**: 158-59
Norbeck, Peter, **L6**: 394
Norm, **L12**: 11-14, 17-18, 68, 107, 179, 498-99
in *Dictionary of Philosophy*, **M2**: 159-60
for judging behavior, **L13**: 209
Normal, **L17**: 483, 484
Normal schools, **E5**: 288. *See also* College; University
origin of, **M1**: 42
conference of instructors in, **M15**: xxiii, 158-89
in Turkey, **M15**: 286-87, 305-6
Normative, **M10**: xxii
in *Dictionary of Philosophy*, **M2**: 159-60
theory, **L16**: 338-39, 453, 455
analysis, **L17**: xix-xx, xxxi
Norris, George W., **L6**: 161; **L14**: 370
and third-party movement, **L5**: xvii, 444-49, 504-5
LIPA and, **L6**: xvii, 149-51, 436, 504
as member of progressives, **L6**: 355, 394, 440
Norris, Jean H., **L9**: 371
Norris-Sinclair bill, **L9**: 249
North American Indians. *See* Indians, North American
North American Review, **L5**: 178
"North and South" (McKay), **L17**: 58
North Carolina, University of, **M8**: 138
Northcliffe, Alfred Charles, **M11**: 120; **M13**: 177
North German Confederation, **E4**: 83
Norton, Edwin Lee, **M4**: 227
Norway, **M15**: 385; **L15**: 289
Noss, Theodore B.
on child-study, **M2**: 102-4, 379-82

Notation. *See* Symbols, **L12**
"Note on Professor Dewey's Theory of Knowledge, A" (S. Lamprecht), **M15**: 27, 28, 371-77
Notes and Queries, **L16**: 112n
Notes d'un Peintre (Matisse), **L10**: 141n
Not Guilty (Dewey, S. La Follette, et al.), **L11**: 326, 330; **L15**: 510
"Notion de personnalité morale, La" (Michoud), **L2**: 26n
Notre Dame, cathedral of, **L10**: 60
Not-self, **L17**: 155
Noumenal reality, **M12**: 92, 148, 221, 226-27
Noumenon, **M6**: 26-27
  in *Dictionary of Philosophy*, **M2**: 160-61, 189
Noun, **L16**: 346, 349n
Nous, **E4**: 130; **M13**: 369, 370; **L1**: 193
  in *Dictionary of Philosophy*, **M2**: 161-63
Novack, George, **L11**: 303, 602, 603
Novels
  criticized, **L13**: 363-64
Novelty, **L4**: 146, 151, 167
  esthetic use of, **L10**: 171-74, 178-79, 292-93, 336
  in reasoning, **L12**: 313-14
Novo-Nikolaievsk (Novosibirsk), USSR, **M13**: 234
Novum Organum (F. Bacon), **L15**: 93
Nozick, Robert, **L2**: xxxv-xxxvi
Nudes, **L10**: 101, 182
Null class, **L12**: 377-79
Nullibrists
  in *Dictionary of Philosophy*, **M2**: 163
Number, **L4**: 103, 124, 127, 193; **L12**: 201, 205, 318, 360-61, 394, 402
  theory of, **E5**: xxiii-lxxxv, 177-91; **M7**: 424, 439-40
  teaching of, **E5**: 182-83, 440; **L17**: 285-86, 302
  child's use of, **E5**: 190-91; **M1**: 77-78, 237
  interest in, **E5**: 355-56
  in *Dictionary of Philosophy*, **M2**: 163-64
  forms, **M6**: 219n; **L8**: 160n
  relations, **M6**: 289; **L8**: 297
  measurement and, **L12**: 210-19
  infinitude of, **L12**: 408-10
  Galton on, **L17**: 244
Number Concept, The (L. Conant), **E5**: 355-58
Nunn, Thomas Perry, **M4**: 148n
Nursery, **M1**: 40
Nurses, **L17**: 68
Nurture, **M7**: 286-87; **M9**: 124
Nye, Gerald P., **L6**: 347, 355, 394
Nystrom, Paul H., **L6**: 352

Oaxaca, Mexico, **L2**: 208
Obata, Yukichi, **M12**: 39-40
Obedience, **L10**: 268
  and government, **E4**: 73, 74, 88-89
  habit of, **E4**: 75
  learning value of, **E4**: 107-8
Object, **L1**: 170, 198-99, 240-41, 244-46, 257-58, 274, 297-326; **L2**: 86, 87. *See also* Thing
  absolute, **E1**: 25-29
  knowing of, **E4**: 21-26
  responsibility of, **E4**: 38-39
  and subject, **E4**: 131-35; **E5**: 26; **L4**: 97; **L10**: 251-55, 281, 284, 288; **L12**: 88-89;

L14: 132-35; **L15**: 70-72, 87, 93, 96, 165
in teaching drawing, **E5**: 197-98
in *Dictionary of Philosophy*, **M2**: 164-65
real, **M6**: 23-24
nature of, **M6**: 194, 287; **L1**: 114-18; **L4**: 89-90, 98, 99, 101-5, 107-10, 191-92, 207, 210, 214; **L8**: 127, 264, 297; **L12**: 123, 132, 513-18; **L14**: 27; **L16**: 45, 49n, 54, 55, 96, 144, 147, 225-26, 231, 288, 308, 348; **L17**: 372, 420
in neo-realism, **M10**: 25-42
and objectivism, **L1**: 182-90
well-being of, **L2**: 81-82
word reference to, **L2**: 83-84
and value, **L2**: 88-91
related to mind, **L2**: 141-42; **L5**: 246-47, 255-58; **L17**: 278
knowledge of, **L4**: xii-xvii, 123, 129, 156-59, 172-76, 230-31, 235, 236; **L5**: xxvii-xxviii; **L14**: 49-52, 67-70, 187
data substituted for, **L4**: 79-82
judgment of, **L4**: 212-13, 238, 239, 241; **L10**: 312-13, 319; **L12**: 72
and motive, **L7**: 290-91
esthetic quality of, **L10**: xxv, xxvii, 103, 120-21, 131-35, 138, 150-51, 157, 175-82, 197-98, 207, 211, 223-24, 239, 341-45
expressive, **L10**: xxviii, 88-108, 258-64, 273, 277-84, 290, 295-99
logical vs. existential, **L11**: 126
social origin of, **L12**: 49-51
and substances, **L12**: 130-33
scientific, **L14**: 20-25, 28, 61-62, 80-83, 103-5, 151-52, 196-97
natural, **L14**: 86
in James's psychology, **L14**: 155, 163-66
assumed in epistemology, **L14**: 178
of signs, **L15**: 148
as name, **L16**: xxxvi, 72, 84n, 101n, 111, 160, 259, 267
study of, **L16**: 6, 83, 149-51, 190
in triangular scheme, **L16**: 9-11, 300-302
in Peirce, **L16**: 11
Carnap on, **L16**: 22, 30, 31
C. Morris on, **L16**: 35
Tarski on, **L16**: 40, 42
as form of event, **L16**: 62, 68-69, 132
in Greek philosophy, **L16**: 159
Kantor on, **L16**: 191-92
Cohen on, **L16**: 194
Russell on, **L16**: 200-203
Moore on, **L16**: 209
in semiotic, **L16**: 214, 232
determination of, **L16**: 304-5
Object and subject
in *Cyclopedia of Education*, **M7**: 291
Objective
thought, **E3**: 136-39
reality, **E5**: 169
idealism, **M1**: xvii-xviii; **M9**: 309; **M10**: 19; **L1**: xvii; **L16**: 115n
applied to value judgment, **M8**: 32-36
relativism, **L1**: xx
vs. subjective, **L1**: 380-82; **L14**: 25-28, 189, 192-93, 196-200
reference, **L2**: xx, 78, 82-85, 87-89, 91, 94-97
conditions, **L13**: 26-27

Objective (*continued*)
as name, **L16**: 267
Objectivism
in *Dictionary of Philosophy*, **M2**: 165
"Objectivism-Subjectivism of Modern Philosophy, The," **L15**: 72n
Objectivity, **L10**: xiii, xxv, xxvii
subjectivistic definition of, **M13**: 450
in art, **L10**: 151, 156, 292
in art criticism, **L10**: 308-12, 317, 327-28
of values, **L15**: 63, 66-70
vs. subjectivity, **L15**: 64-65, 87, 165
of qualities, **L15**: 74, 76
Rice on, **L15**: 402-12, 426-34
"'Objectivity' in Value Judgments" (Rice), **L15**: 63n, 413n, 426
Object lessons, **M9**: 206, 278, 280, 344
Obligation
moral, **E3**: xxxiii-xxxiv
conflicts with pleasure, **E3**: 289
theories of, **E3**: 328-31; **E4**: 319-36
source and nature of, **E3**: 336-37, 359-61
psychology of, **E4**: 311-18
O'Brien, John P., **L9**: 383
Observation, **E5**: 322; **M12**: 160-61; **M13**: 352; **L1**: 169-70; **L12**: 22, 44; **L15**: 27, 49, 120. *See also* Data, **L12**; Experiment, **L12**
and perception, **E3**: 77-82
related to thought, **M6**: 328-35; **L8**: 252, 315-25, 351
used in education, **M6**: 331-37
for studying knowings-knowns, **L4**: xi, xiv-xviii, 67, 68, 163-67, 171; **L16**: 84n, 85, 91-92
methods of, **L4**: 114-17, 161, 162, 184; **L13**: 145, 218; **L14**: 181
in science, **L4**: 139-42, 149, 193, 230-31; **L8**: 273; **L14**: 151, 198
and reflection, **L8**: 188-89, 196-97
guided by hypothesis, **L8**: 250-51
experience as, **L11**: 76-77
related to propositions, **L11**: 101, 122-23
function of, **L12**: 76, 112-18, 136, 153, 167-68, 374-75, 379-80, 420-21, 441-42, 516-17
in inquiry, **L12**: 207-8; **L14**: 172-74; **L16**: 53, 82-83, 322-28
in history, **L12**: 230-31
significance of, **L13**: 41, 44-46, 50, 57, 91, 125, 201, 211, 285
and valuation, **L13**: 204-5; **L16**: 349, 355
centered in organism, **L15**: 75-79
influences Carnap, **L16**: 32
as criteria for namings, **L16**: 47-48, 51-52, 77, 86, 88, 267
use of, **L16**: 49-51, 55-56, 105, 111n
transactional, **L16**: 67, 90, 97, 113-15, 127-28, 352
related to postulation, **L16**: 74-75, 79, 94
superficial, **L16**: 129-30

related to memory, **L17**: 328, 329
Russian views on, **L17**: 504
Occamism
in *Dictionary of Philosophy*, **M2**: 165
Occasionalism
in *Dictionary of Philosophy*, **M2**: 165-66
Occasions of experience
Whitehead on, **L14**: 127-28, 132-34
Occidental art, **L10**: 335
Occult, **M14**: 10
Occupations, **L13**: 319
child's participation in, **E5**: 259; **M1**: xxi, 92-96
used to classify mental type, **M2**: 41-42
qualities needed in, **M5**: 43; **L7**: 41
constructive, **M6**: 312-13; **L8**: 154, 290-92
science as outgrowth of, **M9**: 208-10
changed nature of, **M9**: 284
related to education, **M9**: 318-21, 363; **L17**: 167
differentiation of, **M15**: 251-53
economic restrictions on, **M15**: 253-54
choosing, **L13**: 342-43
related to memory, **L17**: 326
Occurrence
as name, **L16**: 62, 68-72, 132, 259
Occurrent values, **L16**: 346n, 353
Octobrists, **M11**: 278; **L6**: 293
"Ode on a Grecian Urn" (J. Keats), **L10**: 40, 41, 210, 354
Odium theologicum, **L13**: 128
Odyssey (Homer), **E3**: 193-94; **M8**: 292; **L5**: 394; **L10**: 173; **L17**: 173, 226
Oedipus Tyrannos, **M7**: xix
Oersted, Hans Christian, **L5**: 179
Office. *See* Function
Officers
as agents of public, **L2**: 246-47, 256, 257, 277-78, 282
selection of, **L2**: 283-86
Of Human Bondage (Maugham), **L13**: 363
Ogburn, William Fielding, **L3**: 11n
Ogden, C. K., **M15**: xxvi, 223-25; **L1**: 160n; **L3**: 82; **L6**: 3; **L12**: 59n
theory of, **L16**: xxxii, 218n, 305
triangular scheme of, **L16**: 9, 300-302, 470
Ohio State University, **L6**: 118, 503
Oil City, Pa., **E1**: xxiii
Oken, Lorenz, **M2**: 148
Okuma, Shigenobu, **M11**: 158; **M13**: 76, 112
Olberg, Valentine P., **L11**: 312, 322, 602
Old China. *See* China
Oldham, Joseph H., **L15**: 184
Old Testament, **L2**: 165; **L14**: 288
Oligarchy, **M14**: 5
Olvany, George W., **L9**: 362
Omsk, USSR, **M13**: 82, 234, 235
"On a Certain Blindness in Human Beings" (W. James), **M12**: 206, 207
"On a Certain Vagueness in Logic" (A. Bentley), **L15**: 146n; **L16**: 297n

"On Certain Psychological Aspects of Moral Training" (Royce), **E4**: 197-99
One, **L12**: 198-99
  in *Dictionary of Philosophy*, **M2**: 166-67
"One Current Religious Problem," **L11**: xv
O'Neill, Eugene, **L10**: 185
One-to-one correspondence, **L12**: 59, 333-34, 388, 410
"One-World of Hitler's National Socialism, The," **M8**: xxx
Only, **L12**: 189-90, 239, 263, 271-72, 308, 425-27. *See also* Conjunction, **L12**; Disjunction, **L12**
"On Some Hegelisms" (W. James), **L16**: 468
"On Some Omissions of Introspective Psychology" (W. James), **L16**: 468
"On the Character of Philosophic Problems" (Carnap), **L9**: 303
"On the Function of Cognition" (W. James), **L16**: 468
"On the Nature of Things-in-Themselves" (Clifford), **L17**: 554
On the Sensations of Tone as a Physiological Basis for the Theory of Music (Helmholtz), **M7**: 139
Ontological
  idealism, **M7**: 448
  neutrality, **M10**: 49-52
  and logical, **L12**: 30, 42-43, 91-92, 131, 178-79, 182-83, 188-89, 201, 216n, 260-61, 304-5, 357, 386-87, 394, 453-57, 497-98, 526
  possibility as, **L12**: 396-401
Ontological argument
  in *Dictionary of Philosophy*, **M2**: 167-69
"Ontological Relativity" (Quine), **L14**: xv
Ontologism
  in *Dictionary of Philosophy*, **M2**: 169-70
Ontology, **M1**: 241
  in *Dictionary of Philosophy*, **M2**: 170-72
  related to logic, **L5**: xxv-xxvii, 203-9, 453-60
  vs. psychology, **L6**: 489
  modern problem of, **L14**: 197
  Cohen on, **L14**: 386-90
  vs. inquiry, **L16**: 281, 287-93, 309
  immutable in, **L16**: 334-35, 449-50
  related to science, **L16**: 337n-38n, 452
  Balz on, **L16**: 432-33, 438
Open Door, **M11**: 228, 231; **M12**: 4, 6, 34, 62, 278; **M13**: 90, 121, 191; **L2**: 174
  U.S. and, **M13**: 83, 161, 167, 174
  violation of, **M13**: 167-68, 195
  need for, **M13**: 172
  Japanese conception of, **M13**: 233
Open-mindedness, **M6**: 202; **L8**: 136-37
  in dealing with subject-matter, **M9**: 182-83
  means of evoking, **M9**: 241-42
  as moral trait, **M9**: 266
  as philosophic disposition, **M9**: 335
Open shop, **M5**: 500-501
Open universe, **L1**: xx
Operability, **L16**: 427

Operational
as name, **L16**: 267
Operationalism, **L16**: 307n
in Dewey's propositions, **L14**: xvi
defined, **L14**: 151-52
Hocking on, **L14**: 420
Operational logic, **L16**: 460
Balz on, **L16**: 435, 438-41
"Operational Principle in the Physical and Psychological Sciences, The" (Kantor), **L16**: 192n
Operations, **L4**: 18-19; **L12**: 18-19, 54, 63-64, 106. *See also* Action, **L12**; Experiment, **L12**
consequences of, **L4**: xi, 103, 110-13, 116-20, 132-34, 168, 207, 211-16, 230-32, 235-36, 241, 244, 247, 248
direction of, **L4**: xvii-xviii, 87-111, 157-60, 164, 172, 173, 176, 240
function of, **L4**: 68, 100-101, 137-39, 142, 144, 147-55, 181-85, 189, 192-94, 198, 199
physicists on, **L4**: 89, 90n
origin of, **L4**: 95, 99-100
types of, **L4**: 122-30, 146
instrumental, **L12**: 22-23, 165-66, 178, 197-98, 225-26, 251, 339-40, 396-99, 420-21, 450-51, 513-14, 526
facts and meanings as, **L12**: 116-18
combined, **L12**: 404-8
logic involves, **L16**: 190-91
vs. use, **L16**: 329-30
related to ideas, **L16**: 436
Opinion, **M13**: 59; **L1**: 124; **L2**: 345, 347; **L12**: 125; **L13**: 93, 159, 166; **L15**: 84-85
in *Dictionary of Philosophy*, **M2**: 172-74
in *Cyclopedia of Education*, **M7**: 292
and government, **L2**: 355-56
and knowledge, **L3**: 51; **L7**: 363
defined, **L4**: xx, 17, 66, 67, 76, 216
pseudo-public, **L13**: xvi
forming, **L13**: 70, 153; **L17**: 427
and habits, **L13**: 96
incompatible, **L13**: 132, 135, 144-46
and ideas, **L13**: 169, 182
in Greek philosophy, **L16**: 157n
need for enlightened public, **L17**: 46, 47
Opium, **M13**: 142, 143
Oppenheim, James, **M12**: 15-16
Oppenheimer, Franz, **L13**: 73
Opportunism
British, **M13**: 177, 200
consequences of, **L17**: xxiv
Opportunity, **L13**: 110, 295
to work, **L13**: 306, 312-13, 318
vocational, **L13**: 342
intellectual and social, **L13**: 343
equality of, **L13**: 388
for specialization, **L17**: 75
offered by peace, **L17**: 131
need for, **L17**: 400, 461
Opposites
in education, **L13**: 5, 9, 10
in economics, **L13**: 114, 125
in dialectic idealism, **L13**: 119
Opposition
square of, **L12**: 190-91

Oppression, **L13**: 68, 111, 127; **L16**: 362, 402-3
Optics (Hobbes), **M11**: 31
Optimism, **M5**: 370-71; **M8**: 19; **M12**: 181-82; **M14**: 197-200; **M15**: 326; **L14**: 100; **L16**: 391, 393
in *Dictionary of Philosophy*, **M2**: 174-77
in *Cyclopedia of Education*, **M7**: 292-94, 296
Dewey's, **L14**: 407
Or, **L12**: 336-39. *See also* Disjunction, **L12**
Oracle, **E4**: 119n
"Oration delivered before the Authorities of the City of Boston, July 4, 1842, An" (H. Mann), **L11**: 226
Order. *See also* Series, **L12**
vs. progress, **M5**: 75; **L7**: 69
in Greek morals, **M5**: 107; **L7**: 98
sequential, **L1**: 64-65, 74, 81, 84, 95, 150, 202, 213
temporal, **L1**: 92, 119
law and, **L1**: 185
inner and outer, **L1**: 215-16
esthetic, **L10**: 20, 22, 26, 31, 60, 84-87, 131-32, 153-54, 158, 161, 165-66, 170, 173-79, 186-89, 248, 283-87, 329
as logical category, **L12**: 220-21, 236-37, 374, 385, 391, 413-14, 448-49, 454, 477
Orderliness
related to reflective thinking, **M6**: 212-15; **L8**: 150-55, 174-76
Oregon
constitutional amendment in, **M15**: 153
Orestes, **M5**: 28, 64; **L7**: 27, 58
Organic
evolution, **M2**: x; **M10**: 25
in *Dictionary of Philosophy*, **M2**: 177-78
releases, **M7**: 80-81, 453
unity, **M7**: 138
memory, **M7**: 369
Organic-environmental process, **L16**: 97, 260, 270, 417, 462
designation as, **L16**: 140-42
Organicism, **L14**: 34-35, 37n
Organism, **M12**: 129; **L2**: 223-25; **L12**: 66, 109-10, 161, 187
related to experience, **E1**: 42; **L16**: 384, 456-57, 462; **L17**: 367
in Leibniz, **E1**: 277
psycho-physic, **E5**: 304-9
in *Dictionary of Philosophy*, **M2**: 178-79
in *Cyclopedia of Education*, **M6**: 437-40
behavior and nature of, **M7**: 80-81, 453; **M10**: 14, 16; **L14**: 102-3; **L16**: 112, 129-30, 133, 136, 141-42, 195, 275, 331-32, 348
related to environment, **M13**: 378-79, 381; **L2**: 105-8; **L7**: xxvi; **L10**: xv, xvi, 19-25, 34, 61, 136-38, 152, 155, 162, 165, 217; **L12**: 32-47; **L14**: 15-21, 28, 40, 64, 158, 161, 167, 185-86
complexity of, **L10**: 28-31, 59-60, 64-66, 127, 171, 173, 181, 186, 196, 231, 242-43
as force, **L10**: 251-55, 260, 267, 276, 281-85, 292, 307, 323, 345

events centered in, **L15**: 29-30, 75-79
concepts of, **L16**: 80, 87-88, 94, 127-28, 256n, 259, 267
in interaction and transaction, **L16**: 103, 114, 412, 417
evolution of, **L16**: 114n, 184
study of, **L16**: 116-26, 149, 190, 445
in semiotic, **L16**: 138-40, 144, 213-14, 228, 231-33, 236-37
Kantor and Dewey on, **L16**: 191-92
C. Morris on, **L16**: 212, 221-24
in inquiry, **L16**: 288-89, 326-28
Balz on, **L16**: 425-27
"Organismic Achievement and Environmental Probability" (Brunswik), **L16**: 144n
Organization, **M12**: 197-98; **M14**: 211-12; **L1**: 145, 196, 217-18, 230
need for, **M5**: 80; **L7**: 74; **L13**: 181, 284
social, **L2**: 214-15; **L13**: 139, 234, 236, 372, 379, 386-87; **L17**: 552
for bargaining power, **L7**: 392-93
in art, **L10**: 31, 60, 75, 87, 131, 217, 243, 316-17
of energies, **L10**: 174-83, 189-90, 195
of education, **L13**: 5, 15-16, 35, 55-58, 376; **L17**: 513
freedom related to, **L13**: 110
in war, **L13**: 289
vs. system, **L16**: 271
Kilpatrick on, **L17**: 53
influences mankind, **L17**: 393
of Russian schools, **L17**: 496-97, 501-2
in Christianity, **L17**: 531
Organization of Knowledge and the System of the Sciences, The (Bliss), **L5**: 404-6
Organon (Aristotle), **M10**: 368; **L15**: 93
Organum, **M10**: 367
Orient. *See* Far East
Oriental art, **L10**: 252, 335, 336
Origen, **M2**: 153
Origin
nature of, **M2**: 6-7
ultimate, **M8**: 3, 5-6
relativity of, **L12**: 220-21, 453-54
Original sin, **M8**: 151, 167; **L16**: 412, 414, 416
Origin and Evolution of Life, The (Osborn), **L16**: 116n
Origin of Species (Darwin), **M4**: 3, 7, 14; **M6**: x; **M12**: 208, 221; **M15**: 47; **L10**: xiii; **L11**: 33; **L12**: 97; **L16**: 120
Origin of the State, The (Lowie), **L3**: 324-25
Ormond, Alexander, **E5**: 342, 345-46
Orphanages (Turkey), **M15**: 292-93
Orr, Samuel, **L5**: 443
Orthodoxy, **M15**: xxiv, xxv
Santayana's, **L9**: 240-41, 243
Osborn, Henry Fairfield, **L16**: 116
Oshkosh, Wis., **M7**: 462
Oslo, Norway, **L11**: 312, 322, 326, 330; **L15**: 339
Ostensive definition, **L16**: 175-79, 181-83
Ostrowski, Jozef, **M11**: 275
Ostwald, Wilhelm, **M2**: 149; **M4**: 102
Osuchowski, Anthony, **M11**: 312, 397

Oswego (N.Y.) normal school pattern, **M3**: 252
Ota, **M11**: 192, 394
Othello (Shakespeare), **L17**: 12, 554
Other
 in *Dictionary of Philosophy*, **M2**: 231
 Plato on, **M7**: 292
Other-worldliness, **L17**: 13, 554
Otto, Max C., **L2**: 161, 162; **L9**: xxi, 213; **L16**: 407n; **L17**: 89
 and existence of God, **L9**: 214, 215, 224, 227
 relates philosophy to mankind, **L14**: 289-92
Ottoman Empire, **M15**: xix, 129, 139; **L2**: 192
Ou, Tsuin-Chen, **L15**: 369n
Our Changing Civilization (Randall), **L17**: 522
Our Democracy (Tufts), **L15**: 322-23, 325
Our Knowledge of the External World as a Field for Scientific Method in Philosophy (B. Russell), **M8**: 83-93
"Our National Dilemma," **M12**: xxi
Our Notions of Number and Space (Nichols and Parsons), **E5**: 342, 345
"Our Obsolete Market Mentality" (Polanyi), **L15**: 225, 361
Outcome
 attained vs. intended, **L13**: 211-12
Outer
 in moral theory, **M9**: 356-60
Outer Mongolia, **M11**: 178
Outlawry of War (Levinson), **M13**: 411
Outlawry of war, **M11**: 122-26, 388-92; **M13**: 411; **M15**: xi, xiii, xv, xvi, xvii, xviii, 101-3, 317, 398-99; **L2**: 167-72; **L5**: 349-54; **L6**: xx, 209, 218, 219, 364, 457; **L7**: 136, 370-71; **L8**: 13-18; **L17**: 559
 and international relations, **M15**: xiv, 63-64, 90-91, 99, 108-21
 relation of law to, **M15**: 62, 99, 107-8, 113-14, 116-17, 120, 127; **L3**: 354-57
 Borah on, **M15**: 88-89, 412-13; **L3**: 165
 origin of idea for, **M15**: 105, 404-6
 economic considerations of, **M15**: 111-12
 Lippmann on, **M15**: 115-18, 404-17
 France and U.S. agree on, **L3**: 163, 168-69, 171, 175
 Levinson on, **L3**: 163, 353
 as power for good, **L3**: 350-52, 354, 358; **L6**: 221-22
 opposition to, **L3**: 354, 356, 415-16
 and Pact of Paris, **L6**: 191-92, 222-23
Outlawry of War, The (Morrison), **L3**: 348; **L6**: 457n
Outlines of a Critical Theory of Ethics, **E3**: xxxii-xxxv, 239, 240; **E4**: xiii, xxii, 48n, 221; **M5**: x, xxvii; **L6**: xii, xiii
Outlines of a Philosophy of the History of Man (Herder), **M8**: 194
Outness
 in *Dictionary of Philosophy*, **M2**: 179-80

Overpopulation, **L7**: 454
Oversoul
in *Dictionary of Philosophy*, **M2**: 180
Owen, Robert, **M5**: 151; **L11**: xxviii, 18
Oxford English Dictionary, **L10**: 53, 339, 355, 366; **L11**: 105, 601; **L15**: 42, 134-35; **L16**: 137n, 155-56, 209n, 246-47, 256n, 265n, 474
Oxford University, **M7**: 133-34; **M11**: 23; **L11**: 157; **L14**: 334

Pacific Conference. *See* Washington Conference
Pacific War Council, **L17**: 544
Pacifism, **M10**: 261; **M15**: 408; **L15**: 192-94
future of, **M10**: xxxvii-xxxviii, 265-70
failure of, **M10**: 213-14
Addams on, **M10**: 266-67
in WWI, **M11**: xi-xii, xvi, 180-81
of China, **M11**: 199, 216
Pact of Paris. *See* Kellogg-Briand Pact
Paderewski, Helene
as Polish leader, **M11**: xv, 253, 257, 262, 306-18, 325, 328-29
Paderewski, Ignace Jan
as Polish leader, **M11**: xiv, xv, 256, 257, 261, 262, 279, 300, 328-29, 405-6
at Detroit Convention, **M11**: 243, 305
represents Paris Committee, **M11**: 251-54, 281, 291, 404
policies of, **M11**: 269, 271, 275, 294-96, 299, 302, 321-23
relief work of, **M11**: 282-83, 290, 310-16, 319
publicity for, **M11**: 303, 325
criticized, **M11**: 307-12, 316, 317
Dewey meets, **M11**: 401
Page-Barbour Foundation (University of Virginia), **L11**: 3
Paget, Violet, **L10**: 107-9, 357
Pain, **L13**: 74
elements of, **E1**: 330
and pleasure, **E5**: 359-62
quality of, **L13**: 333
physical, **L13**: 334
Paine, Thomas, **L9**: 298
Painters
nature of, **L10**: 52, 69, 71, 80, 81, 89, 93
technique of, **L10**: 148, 204, 239, 304
Painting, **E2**: 275; **L13**: 363; **L16**: 397
transmits civilization, **L10**: 13, 37, 332-36, 342-45
expressiveness of, **L10**: 75, 80, 91-93, 96, 107, 111, 116-18, 126-27, 157, 255-57, 260, 264, 271-74
Matisse on, **L10**: 89, 358-59
process of, **L10**: 133-34, 141, 146-47, 162, 280-81, 291-92, 312, 318-23
response to, **L10**: 150, 304-7
movements in, **L10**: 155-56, 163, 165, 287-90, 314-15
rhythm in, **L10**: 168, 174-86
distinctive traits of, **L10**: 188, 189, 219, 222, 225, 233-34, 238-39, 242, 245, 247, 300
substance of, **L10**: 191-92, 195, 199-216
Abell on, **L11**: 487-88
Barnes on, **L11**: 487-88, 501

Paléologue, Maurice, **L17**: 490, 568
Palestine, **M11**: 101
Paley, William, **M3**: 53; **M5**: 319n, 320n; **L5**: 183; **L7**: 155; **L17**: 94
Palingenesis
in *Dictionary of Philosophy*, **M2**: 180
Palladium, **E3**: 3n
Pallas Athene, **L10**: 115
Palmer, Frederick, **M12**: 11
Palmer, George Herbert, **L6**: 271
Panama, **L6**: 468-69
Panama Canal, **M15**: 411; **L6**: 468
Pan-Asianism, **M13**: xxiv, 178, 184
Pancosmism, **E1**: 18
Panentheism
in *Dictionary of Philosophy*, **M2**: 180-81
Pan-Islamism, **M15**: 130
Panlogism
in *Dictionary of Philosophy*, **M2**: 181
Royce's rejection of, **M10**: 80
Panpneumatism
in *Dictionary of Philosophy*, **M2**: 181
Panpsychic idealism, **M7**: 18n
Panpsychism, **M7**: 276, 284; **L15**: 76-77
in *Dictionary of Philosophy*, **M2**: 181
Pantheism, **E5**: 27, 28; **M8**: 176
Spinoza's, **E1**: 9-18
Green on, **E3**: 23
in *Dictionary of Philosophy*, **M2**: 181-85
in *Cyclopedia of Education*, **M7**: 284, 294, 353
of Fichte, **M8**: 178
in Germany, **M8**: 179-80
H. Torrey on, **L5**: 148
Panthelism
in *Dictionary of Philosophy*, **M2**: 185
Pantomime, **L10**: 13
Papists, **M11**: 22, 25
Paradise Lost (Milton), **M15**: 326-27; **L10**: 115, 322
Paradox, **L10**: 86, 263; **L12**: 97
of reflexive collections, **L12**: 361-63
origin of, **L12**: 380
Parallelism, **M7**: 276, 383; **L1**: 194, 205, 216, 257
Parents
instincts of, **M5**: 50-51; **L7**: 40
Jennings on, **L7**: 460-61
and teachers, **L17**: 233, 234
successful, **L17**: 513
Paris, France, **M15**: 390, 405; **L11**: 326, 330
Polish activities in, **M11**: 265, 278, 279, 282, 290, 301, 313, 402, 404
art in, **L10**: 305-6
Paris, Pact of. *See* Kellogg-Briand Pact
Paris Committee (Polish National Committee)
status of, **M11**: 251-53, 292, 299-302, 306, 326, 328, 401-4
members of, **M11**: 269, 275, 276, 280-84, 291, 316, 405
formation of, **M11**: 278-80
policies of, **M11**: 297, 317, 320-23, 326, 327, 395
Paris Peace Conference, **M12**: 5, 18; **M15**: 391; **L6**: 473. *See also* Versailles, Treaty of
preparation for, **M11**: xvi, 100, 182, 401
propaganda at, **M11**: 110

issues at, **M11**: 130, 135-38, 196, 240
publicity about, **M11**: 151
Japanese success at, **M11**: 152, 158-59, 177-80, 183, 186, 189, 198, 199, 203
Polish question at, **M11**: 246, 268, 276, 284, 293, 300, 312, 405
as menace to China, **M12**: 32
Parity
AAA report on, **L9**: 84-85
Park, Richard, **L17**: 72, 558
Parker, A. K.
letter on coeducation to, **M2**: 108-16
Parker, Alton Brooks, **L6**: 234
Parker, Francis Wayland, **M3**: 325; **M8**: 414; **L5**: 320, 374
role in education, **E5**: 423; **M2**: 67, 97-101; **M3**: 273-75, 278
school, **M3**: 240n; **M8**: 262-63, 288-90
on attention, **L17**: 278, 563
Parker, William Stanley, **L9**: 262
Parkhurst, Helen H., **L10**: 228, 362; **L11**: 244
Parliamentarianism, **L17**: 117
Parmelee, Maurice F., **L6**: 476n
Parmenides, **M2**: 144, 156, 172, 267; **M13**: 364; **L5**: 495; **L14**: 398-99
Parochial schools, **M8**: 416-17, 471-72
Parodi, Dominique
on theory of truth, **L14**: 5, 56n
Dewey replies to, **L14**: 80-83
Parousia
in *Dictionary of Philosophy*, **M2**: 185
Parsons, William E., **E5**: 342
Parthenon, **L13**: 358; **L14**: 255
as art, **L10**: 10, 113-17, 226, 231
Participants
in transaction, **L16**: 242-43
Participation, **L1**: 132, 140, 145, 158, 159, 163, 189, 248, 259-60; **L13**: 33, 43, 53
as social, **M1**: xxiii; **L4**: 169, 246
in knowledge, **L4**: 163, 195, 232
Particularism
of traditionalists, **M10**: xii-xiii
empiricism's commitment to, **M10**: 6, 12, 13
thought in, **M10**: 17
Particularity
of events, **L15**: 29-30
Particulars. *See also* Problem, **L12**
in Aristotle, **L12**: 88-89, 93-94, 183
in Mill, **L12**: 147-48
in Locke, **L12**: 149
sense-data as, **L12**: 157
change of, **L12**: 190, 201-2, 212-13, 217, 220, 296-97, 340, 417
as propositions, **L12**: 289-90
of Russell, **L16**: 199-203
Partisan armies (USSR), **M13**: 235, 236
Partisan Review, **L15**: xxiv; **L16**: 390, 471
Partisanship
evils of, **L17**: 443
pressure for, **L17**: 448
Pascal, Blaise, **M2**: 233; **M4**: 248; **L16**: 161n
Passion, **M14**: 135-38; **L10**: 85, 160. *See also* Emotion
in *Dictionary of Philosophy*, **M2**: 185-86
Plato on, **M5**: 123-24; **L7**: 114-15

Passion (*continued*)
Hume on, **M8**: 24
James on, **L7**: 188, 190
Passive
in child development, **E5**: 91
in *Dictionary of Philosophy*, **M2**: 185-86
resistance, **M10**: 249
Passivist party (Polish), **M11**: 265-67, 275, 277, 298
Passivity, **M6**: 175
and activity, **E1**: 338; **M9**: 345
evils of, **L8**: 327
of Russians, **L17**: 491-92
Past, **M12**: 201
in Dewey's theory of truth, **M6**: xxii-xxiii
knowledge of, **M13**: 469-70; **L10**: 304, 327; **L11**: 52-53; **L13**: 6, 44; **L15**: 333, 336; **L17**: 456
involved in perception, **L10**: xx, xxiv, xxxii, 23-25, 30, 78, 180-81, 187, 276, 283, 287-88
art conveys, **L10**: 235-36, 239, 244-45, 330, 340-43, 348
and future, **L13**: 9
and present, **L13**: 9, 51-53, 57, 97; **L14**: 84, 131, 135
related to philosophy, **L14**: 312-15; **L16**: 361-62, 382
Chinese idea of, **L17**: 172
Past and Present (T. Carlyle), **M5**: 151
Pasteur, Louis, **L6**: 45; **L11**: 279; **L14**: 342; **L17**: 40
Pater, Walter, **L17**: 11
humanism of, **L5**: xxx, 263-64
on esthetics, **L10**: 37-38, 233, 288, 354, 362-63
Paternal family, **M5**: 28; **L7**: 27
Paternalism, **M12**: 75; **L2**: 274
Pathology
of beliefs, **L4**: 181
Patriotism, **L3**: 154; **L7**: 367-69; **L17**: 455
Fichte on, **M8**: 187
Japanese, **M13**: 257, 258
in education, **L9**: 161
in U.S., **L14**: 250
Patterns
of experience, **L10**: 22, 31, 50, 155
esthetic use of, **L10**: 93, 122, 178-79, 327, 330
Patterns of Culture (R. Benedict), **L6**: xvi
Patton, George, **L11**: xi
Paul, Francis J., **M10**: 161
Paul, Saint, **E1**: 114-15; **M2**: 141, 203; **M4**: 42; **M5**: 104, 297; **L7**: 95, 279; **L15**: 47, 54-55; **L17**: 532, 533
Paulsen, Friedrich, **M15**: 337
Pauses. *See* Intervals
Pavlov, Ivan Petrovich, **M13**: xiv; **L6**: 319
on signal, **L16**: 69, 139-40, 144
Pawlowski, Wenzel A., **M11**: 316
Pax Romana, **M15**: 61; **L6**: 221-22
Peace, **M15**: 380, 396; **L6**: xx, xxin, 198; **L11**: 252; **L13**: 303; **L16**: 365, 372, 391, 400
movement, **M10**: 213-14, 260
means for achieving, **M11**: ix, xii, 119, 135-38, 142, 150-51, 404; **L6**: 211-13, 220-23, 454, 461-62; **L15**: 301-2; **L17**: 396
education for, **M11**: 67-69
ideals, **M11**: 112, 181-83; **L7**: 95; **L17**: 529
enforcement of, **M11**: 127, 129, 130
U.S. responsibility for, **M15**: 87

Pact of Paris related to, **L6**: 190-95
and sanctions, **L6**: 483-84
and war, **L7**: 369-71
conditions for, **L15**: 171, 192-98, 206-9
after WWII, **L15**: 342-44, 368-70
opportunity offered by, **L17**: 131
assurance of, **L17**: 453, 462
Peace and Bread in Time of War (Addams), **L15**: 192-98
Peace Conference. *See* Paris Peace Conference
Peace Mobilization, American, **L15**: 348
Peace Pact. *See* Kellogg-Briand Pact
Peace-sanction, **L6**: 192, 219, 220
Pearl, Raymond, **L14**: 391
Pearl Harbor, Hawaii, **M8**: xxx; **L6**: xx; **L15**: 349
Pearson, Karl, **L4**: xiii; **L6**: 490
Peasantry, **E3**: 178-79
"Pedagogics of the Kindergarten" (Froebel), **M1**: 341
Pedagogy, **M4**: 158; **M15**: 173
Baker on, **E3**: 191
as discipline, **E5**: 280-89, 433, 446
principles in, **E5**: 443-45, 453-54
in Dewey's writings, **M1**: xix
Kant's treatise on, **M9**: 101
disrepute of, **M9**: 176-77
related to psychology and ethics, **L17**: 485
department of, **L17**: 486
"Pedagogy as a University Discipline," **L11**: 202n, 203
Pedantry
in *Cyclopedia of Education*, **M7**: 294-95
Pedology, **L17**: 571
Russian study of, **L17**: 507
Peiping (Beijing), China, **L6**: 205. *See also* Peking
Peirce, Benjamin, **M3**: 65
Peirce, Charles Sanders, **M3**: xxiv; **M4**: 100; **M7**: 422, 423; **M8**: x, xxiii; **M9**: xx, xxi; **M10**: xiii; **M12**: x; **M13**: 307, 393; **M14**: xii, xix, xxii; **M15**: xxvi, 226-28; **L1**: xvii; **L3**: xvii; **L5**: 215; **L6**: xii-xiv; **L8**: xiv, xvi, 11; **L11**: xiv, xvi, xxiv; **L12**: x, xii, xv, 5; **L14**: x, xiii, xiv, xviii, 5, 390; **L15**: 72, 273; **L17**: 51
compared with Dewey, **E3**: xxii-xxiii; **M1**: xvi; **L4**: ix, xviii; **L10**: vii, viii, xii, xiii, xvi, xxviii; **L14**: 387
response to, **E4**: 19
on Hegelian system, **M2**: x
on tychism, **M2**: 259
on continuity, **M3**: 19n-20n; **L12**: 3, 17n
on logic, **M3**: 66; **L16**: 187
on experience, **M3**: 130; **L14**: 21n
on pragmatism, **M6**: xi; **M7**: 326-27; **M10**: 71-78, 87, 366; **L2**: xii-xiv, 3-7, 28-29; **L5**: 477-79; **L11**: 421-24; **L16**: 33, 183n
on truth, **M6**: xxii; **L12**: 343n; **L14**: 56-57; **L16**: 459
on meaning, **M6**: 46n; **M10**: 73-74; **L16**: 174n
"How to Make Our Ideas Clear," **M6**: 175
on practical, **M10**: xxiii, xxv
on fixation of belief, **M10**: 74-75, 77
influences Royce, **M10**: 84n

Peirce, Charles Sanders (*cont.*)
on conceptions, **L4**: 90n, 117
on reality, **L5**: 470
philosophy of, **L6**: 273-77, 425
compared with Mead, **L6**: 309
on knowledge, **L11**: 86, 91-92, 107-9, 422-23, 480-81, 483-84
metaphysics of, **L11**: 86-94, 423, 482-83
psychology of, **L11**: 93, 481
writings of, **L11**: 479-80
on guiding principles, **L12**: 19-21, 158
on fallibilism, **L12**: 46-47; **L14**: 171
on abstract, **L12**: 462-63
on form and method, **L12**: 464-65
on effect of social factor on science, **L12**: 484n
on signs, **L15**: 136n, 141-52, 331; **L16**: 51, 297-99
C. Morris on, **L15**: 473
as forerunner, **L16**: xxviii, xxix, 193-94, 238-39, 299n
epistemology of, **L16**: 8-11
development of, **L16**: 10n, 51n
on interpretant, **L16**: 34n
on precept, **L16**: 66
on observation, **L16**: 88n
"Peirce's Theory of Linguistic Signs, Thought, and Meaning," **L15**: 331; **L16**: 239n
Pei-Yang party (China), **M12**: 66
Peking (Beijing), China, **M12**: 23, 25, 27, 30, 39, 43, 56, 61, 205n; **M13**: 72, 105, 122, 139, 153, 210, 495; **L2**: 181, 184; **L6**: 205; **L14**: xx, xxi
Dewey and, **M11**: xviii; **M13**: 136-37
Japanese students in, **M11**: 173
student revolt in, **M11**: 187-89; **L17**: 29, 555
protests sent to, **M11**: 194, 224
Imperial Court at, **M11**: 211, 216
police of, **M12**: 26, 42, 44
government in, **M12**: 67-68; **M13**: 130, 131, 134-35; **L17**: 33
bolshevism in, **M12**: 253, 254
Bland in, **M13**: 100-101
schools in, **M13**: 112, 116
Lamont in, **M13**: 124
opposes Canton, **M13**: 125, 127-28
revolutionary movement against, **M13**: 132, 151
foreign support of, **M13**: 136, 154
effect of consortium on, **M13**: 169
teachers' strike in, **L17**: 30, 556
Peking University, **M12**: 23, 41-43
revolt at, **M11**: 186-91
Pellegrini, Angelo M., **L11**: 515
Penal measures. *See* Punishment
Pendennis, **L10**: 289
Penmanship, **L17**: 286
Pennsylvania
Polish activities in, **M11**: 293, 303, 318
Pennsylvania, University of, **M10**: 165
Pennsylvania Museum of Art (Philadelphia)
art exhibition at, **L17**: 128-29, 560
Penrose, Boies, **M11**: 287, 396
Peoples Church (Chicago), **L11**: 274n
People's Houses
as Russian centers, **L17**: 494
People's Lobby, **L6**: xvii-xix, 322, 335, 400, 404, 440, 504

registration of, **L5**: 429-30
on national income, **L5**: 431
on child relief, **L5**: 432-33
on unemployment, **L5**: 434-39; **L6**: 339-40, 372-80, 384, 390-91; **L9**: 253
related to taxation, **L6**: 337-38, 344, 392; **L9**: 256-60, 266, 273-74, 282-84
on special session, **L6**: 345, 355-56; **L9**: 269-70
on Depression, **L6**: 346-54; **L9**: 261-64
queries Hoover, **L6**: 357-63
on interallied debts, **L6**: 364-67
criticizes Interstate Commerce Commission, **L6**: 368-71
criticizes F. Roosevelt, **L6**: 395-96
on needs of farmers, **L9**: 249-51
urges solution to banking crisis, **L9**: 254-55
lists programs for Congress, **L9**: 276, 287-88
urges appraisal of New Deal, **L9**: 280-81
advocates public ownership program, **L9**: 285-86
advocates socialization system, **L9**: 289-90
People's Lobby Bulletin, **L6**: xviii, 341-83, 386-94, 397-98; **L9**: 249-90
People's party, **L6**: 233-34
Pepper, Claude, **L15**: 281, 509
Pepper, Stephen C., **M15**: 347; **L14**: 5, 306; **L16**: 42n
exchange with Dewey, **L14**: 15, 34-38
on truth, **L16**: 83n
on definition, **L16**: 171, 174-79, 181n
on C. Morris, **L16**: 239n
on value, **L16**: 343
Percept
related to concept, **E3**: 143-45, 218-19
as name, **L16**: 93n, 267-68
Perception, **M3**: 137-41; **M7**: xiii; **M8**: 87; **L1**: 85, 143, 230-31, 233, 235, 239, 240-44, 250-55, 259, 283, 339; **L11**: 71, 421; **L16**: 140
agreement of, **E1**: 35-36
interpreted, **E1**: 54; **L4**: viii, xvii, 229, 231, 235
in consciousness, **E1**: 173
in Locke, **E1**: 177-78
as meaning, **E1**: 180-81
Leibniz on, **E1**: 317
in knowledge, **E2**: 137-53; **L4**: xxii, 66, 136, 137, 140-43, 213, 214
memory in, **E2**: 154-57, 164-66
temporal, **E2**: 161-64; **L10**: 179-80, 187-88
imagination in, **E2**: 168-69
and conception, **E2**: 180; **E3**: 77-82; **E5**: 321; **L12**: 72-73, 162, 507-11
impulses in, **E2**: 302-3
Dewey's views of, **E3**: xxv
achievement of, **E5**: 154-55; **L10**: 30, 48, 328
in animals, **M6**: 194; **L8**: 129
Bergson's theory of, **M7**: 3, 8, 10-12, 18-30; **M12**: 225
rational, **M7**: 260-61
McGilvary on, **M7**: 454-60
relativity in, **M10**: 29-30
Drake's theory of, **M10**: 64-66
and classification, **M12**: 215
Russell ignores, **M12**: 239
nature of, **M12**: 242; **L4**: 72,

Perception (*continued*)
113, 165, 184, 192, 221, 239; **L10**: 29, 53-58, 113, 118, 126, 129, 134-35, 157-58, 222-24, 229, 239, 258-63, 276, 294, 299; **L16**: 232n, 307n, 331; **L17**: 425
Klyce on, **M13**: 418
and epistemology, **L2**: 45, 51; **L12**: 518-20
subject-matter of, **L4**: 73, 80, 97, 98; **L10**: 154
artistic, **L10**: 38, 40-41, 93-96, 100, 103-4, 107, 140-42, 181-82, 195-96, 204-5, 216; **L16**: 352, 398
rhythms of, **L10**: 161, 165-68, 174
limitations on, **L10**: 194, 208, 230; **L17**: 420
supplies material for judgment, **L10**: 302-4
Santayana on, **L11**: 78, 92
privacy of, **L11**: 461-62
psychological theory of, **L12**: 152-53
not directly cognitive, **L12**: 458-59, 476-77
behavior's role in, **L14**: 20-21, 24-25
and observational propositions, **L14**: 54, 170-71
James on, **L14**: 160-61
Ames on, **L15**: 310-11
Langer on, **L15**: 419
Rice on, **L15**: 431-34
Wertheimer on, **L16**: 106n
characteristic of cue, **L16**: 143-44
in inquiry, **L16**: 322-25, 328
of dramatist, **L17**: 381
"Perception and Epistemology" (Woodbridge), **M6**: 103n
Perception-manipulation
as name, **L16**: 90, 258, 268
Perceptual, **L16**: 11
Perfectibility
human, **L13**: 160
Perfection, **M14**: 122-23
Periclean Age, **L5**: 100
Pericles, **L11**: 6; **L17**: 177
Peril
escape from, **L4**: x, 26, 226, 243
attitude toward, **L4**: 3-20, 62
source of, **L4**: 27, 67, 178, 187, 194
Periodicity, **L12**: 220-21, 407-8
Peripatetic philosophy, **L4**: 75-78
Peripatetics
in *Dictionary of Philosophy*, **M2**: 186-87
on pneuma, **M2**: 205
Permanence
in *Dictionary of Philosophy*, **M2**: 187
attitude toward, **L10**: 325-27
related to knowings-knowns, **L16**: 85, 160
essential to Aristotle, **L16**: 157
Permanent Court of Arbitration. *See* Hague Tribunal
Permanent Court of International Justice. *See* World Court
Perry, Arthur, **M10**: 174
Perry, Harry C., **L9**: 356
Perry, Ralph Barton, **M6**: 473; **M10**: 440; **M13**: 11n, 12, 20, 22; **M15**: 335, 339, 343; **L1**: 365; **L2**: xx, 80; **L3**: 396; **L5**: xi, 419; **L15**: 414, 420
on ego-centric predicament, **M6**: 89-90, 113, 117n; **M7**: 79-80, 445-51
on consciousness, **M6**: 477-78
on James, **M7**: x, 144, 148; **L11**: 441-45, 464-78

on subcutaneous mind, **M7**: 54
on value judgments, **M11**: 3-7, 361-77, 381-83
defines value, **L2**: 86, 90, 92
on philosophy, **L6**: 271-72
Perry Movement
and mathematics, **M3**: 227
Perseity
in *Dictionary of Philosophy*, **M2**: 187-88
Persia, **M15**: 136
art of, **L10**: 256, 314, 336
Person, **L12**: 87-89, 109-10, 517-18
vs. thing, **M2**: 127n
as legal conception, **L2**: 22-43
defined, **L14**: 27-28; **L15**: 49
judgment of, **L17**: 3
Personal
idealism, **M7**: 418
identity, **L14**: 156-57, 165-66
Personalism, **L15**: 221
Personality, **M12**: 105-6, 188, 199-200; **L11**: 504, 568; **L13**: 26; **L15**: 174, 316-17
in democracy, **E1**: 244
in aristocracy, **E1**: 246
Baldwin on, **E5**: 387-89, 393-95, 397-98, 417-18
concept of, in teaching, **M1**: 139
in adolescence, **M1**: 216
Greek conception of, **M5**: 130-32; **L7**: 121-23
in *Cyclopedia of Education*, **M7**: 295-96
Kant on, **M8**: 161, 432
Hitler's reverence for, **M8**: 431-32
related to law, **L6**: 268-70
as end, **L7**: 223-24
development of, **L11**: 221, 538-40, 544, 548; **L17**: 77
primacy of, **L13**: 149
respect for, **L13**: 385
theory of, **L14**: 40
Martineau on, **L17**: 4
"Personality of Associations, The" (Laski), **L2**: 40n
Personification, **L17**: 254, 320
Personnel Research Federation, **L5**: 236n
Perspective
in art, **L10**: 146, 147
philosophical, **L14**: 141-42, 154
Persuasion, **M12**: 96-97; **L13**: 153
role of, **L16**: 356-57, 380
reasonableness of, **L17**: xx-xxi
Peru, **L15**: 371, 510
Pessimism, **M2**: 174-76; **M5**: 370-71; **M12**: 181-82, 240; **M14**: 37, 53, 198-99; **M15**: 256, 326; **L15**: 59
in *Cyclopedia of Education*, **M7**: 296-97
toward science, **L16**: 365, 373, 393
Pestalozzi, Johann Heinrich, **E5**: xiv; **M7**: 115, 185, 289; **M8**: xxxii, 275, 319, 356; **M9**: 99, 123, 206; **M13**: 401
educational theories of, **M1**: xvii, 260; **M7**: 378-79, 381-82; **M8**: 251-52
on games, **M1**: 342
on stages of growth, **M6**: xxiv, xxvi
applies Rousseau's theories, **M8**: 248-49
on social development, **M8**: 249-50
on sense perception, **L17**: 217
Peter of Spain, **M2**: 222
Peter the Great, **L3**: 203
Petrograd (Leningrad), USSR, **M11**: 267, 275, 295. *See also* Leningrad

Pfleiderer, Edmund, **M8**: 190
Phaedo (Plato), **L2**: 133
Phänomenologie des Geistes (Hegel), **M7**: 413
Phantom Public, The (Lippmann), **L2**: xxii, xxiii, 213-20
Phariseeism, **M12**: 180-81; **L7**: 278
Pharisees
  Tolstoy on, **L17**: 385-86, 565
Phase
  in *Dictionary of Philosophy*, **M2**: 188
  as name, **L16**: 5n, 59, 73n, 259, 268
Pheidias, **L10**: 147, 175
Phelps, Elizabeth Stuart, **L17**: 12-13, 554
Phenomenal, **L1**: 55, 60, 95, 126
  reality, **M12**: 92-93, 148, 221, 226-27
Phenomenalism, **M13**: 417; **L4**: 154; **L15**: 4
  in *Dictionary of Philosophy*, **M2**: 188
  in *Cyclopedia of Education*, **M7**: 297
  growth of, **M10**: 24
  vs. pragmatism, **M10**: 73
Phenomenology, **L11**: 86, 434
  in *Dictionary of Philosophy*, **M2**: 188-89
Phenomenon, **L4**: 48, 49, 118, 193; **L10**: 299
  mental and material, **E1**: 5, 7; **L17**: 422-23
  Kant's theory of, **E1**: 41
  in *Dictionary of Philosophy*, **M2**: 189-90
  Plato on, **M6**: 26-27
  nature of, **L4**: 40, 73, 74, 77-84, 113-16, 148, 205, 240
  laws of, **L4**: 161, 165
  abstraction of, **L16**: 103n; **L17**: 95
  Einstein on, **L16**: 108
  C. Morris on, **L16**: 212n
  as name, **L16**: 268
Phidias, **M7**: xxviii
Philadelphia, Pa.
  Polish study in, **M11**: xiv, xv, 242, 259, 260, 287, 292, 303, 306, 312, 318, 320, 396-99, 403-7
  morphia in, **M11**: 239
"Philadelphia Martyr, The" (*New York Times*), **M8**: 407
Philanthropy, **L13**: 75
  related to school, **M7**: 379-80
Philebus (Plato), **L2**: 133n
Philippines, **L15**: 20-22, 309
Philipson, Raphael, **L9**: 320, 345
Phillips, Daniel Edward
  on psychology of number, **E5**: xxviii-lxxxv, 177-91
Phillips, Harry Irving, **M15**: 45
Philo, **M2**: 206
Philology, **E3**: 174; **M8**: 186
"Philosopher as Poet and Critic, The" (Rice), **L14**: 300-301
Philosophers
  as social beings, **E4**: 62-63
  rivalry of, **L2**: 124-26
  as part of history, **L3**: 4
  oppositions of, **L10**: 27, 38, 88
  on intuition, **L10**: 40, 41, 196
  vs. artists, **L10**: 80, 262
  on classification, **L10**: 230
  nature of, **L10**: 253-54, 270, 273, 308
  positions of, **L16**: 137, 163-64, 281, 402
  situation of, **L16**: 250, 286, 294, 368, 377-78

Dewey's conception of, **L17**: xx, 85
related to scientists, **L17**: 406
Philosophes, **L14**: 205, 209
Philosophical Club (Columbia University), **M10**: 89n
Philosophical Club (New York City), **M8**: xx
"Philosophical Conceptions and Practical Results" (W. James), **M6**: 175-76; **L5**: 480n
Philosophical Essays (B. Russell), **M8**: 22n
Philosophical Investigations (Wittgenstein), **L6**: xi
Philosophical Review, **L5**: 424; **L14**: xxiii; **L15**: 326
Philosophical Rudiments (Hobbes), **M11**: 23, 24, 30-31
Philosophical Union (University of California), **M11**: 41n
Philosophic Approach to Communism, A (Brameld), **L9**: 244-45
Philosophic method
Kant's, **E1**: 37-40
dialectic in, **E1**: 45-46
Locke on, **E1**: 124
"Philosophy," **L8**: ix
Philosophy, **M15**: x-xiii, 323-24; **L4**: viii; **L10**: 156, 257n; **L13**: 320. *See also* Classic philosophical tradition; Greek philosophy
test of, **E1**: 9-10
history of, **E1**: 34; **E3**: 90-91; **E4**: 63-64; **E5**: 6, 9; **M2**: ix; **M9**: 339-40; **M12**: 82, 89-90, 93-94, 136-37, 227, 258, 264, 270-73; **L1**: 330-64; **L4**: xix, 203; **L5**: 149, 162-66; **L11**: 69-83; **L14**: 3, 4, 98-101, 142, 313; **L15**: 3, 86-87, 90, 93-94, 269, 274
teaching and study of, **E1**: 116-21; **E3**: 49-50, 90; **E4**: 62-65; **M1**: ix; **M6**: 136-37; **L5**: 150-52; **L11**: 395, 406; **L15**: 10
English, **E1**: 144-45; **L5**: 173
characteristics of, **E1**: 152; **M9**: 333-37; **M10**: 3-5, 38-42, 240- 42; **M12**: 218, 220, 239-40, 256-57, 262, 267; **M13**: 364-70; **M15**: 28; **L6**: xiv, xv, 424-25; **L14**: xiii-xiv, 39, 141-42, 154, 323; **L15**: 46-55, 61-62; **L16**: 243n, 244, 345, 381, 455, 458, 464
related to science, **E1**: 158, 233-34; **E2**: 202; **E3**: 211-12, 227; **E5**: 14; **M11**: 31-35, 41-48; **M12**: 205-6, 260-76; **M15**: 15, 16, 325, 331-32, 335-37; **L1**: 349-53, 366-69; **L2**: 224-25; **L3**: 25-27, 115, 118-21; **L4**: ix, xvii, 76-77, 103, 111; **L6**: 19-20, 425-29, 489; **L12**: 41-42, 82-83; **L13**: 258, 284; **L14**: 316-19, 329-31; **L16**: 149n, 340, 371, 425; **L17**: 402-14, 468
related to social sciences, **E1**: 227-30; **E4**: 214-17; **L5**: xxii-xxiii, 159, 161-77; **L14**: 312-15, 326-27
abstractions in, **E3**: 148-49; **L10**: 127
defined, **E3**: 211; **E4**: 365; **L6**: 428-29; **L13**: 255-56, 258-60; **L14**: 381
related to psychology, **E3**: 228; **M1**: 121-30; **M10**: 362; **L5**:

Philosophy (*continued*)
158-59; **L17**: 43
types of, E3: 230; **M9**: 293; **M13**: xvii, 352-54, 375-76; **L1**: 46-47; **L3**: 12-13, 53-54; **L6**: xii, xiii, 269, 321; **L13**: 257, 269, 281-82; **L14**: xvii, xix
Scotch school of, **E4**: 129; **M7**: 201; **L5**: 148, 149, 182, 183; **L12**: 68
related to morals, **E4**: 143; **M15**: 15, 18; **L14**: 148-50
positions of, **E4**: 366-67; **M11**: 10-11; **L4**: 195-98, 205-6; **L6**: 425-26; **L10**: 40, 120-21, 136; **L14**: 147n; **L16**: 42, 250, 269, 330
medieval, **E5**: 20; **M7**: 215; **M9**: 300-302; **M11**: 342, 344; **L4**: 220; **L13**: 290
method of, **E5**: 22; **L1**: 3-59; **L4**: 63-64, 69
role of, **E5**: 23-24; **M11**: x, xvii; **M12**: xi-xii, 89-91, 93, 143-44, 149-51, 260, 270-77; **L1**: ix; **L8**: 19-39; **L14**: 89, 136-40; **L15**: 15-17, 154-69; **L17**: 409, 466-67
in *Dictionary of Philosophy*, **M2**: 190-202
related to democracy, **M3**: 73-78; **M11**: 43-45, 48-53
true problem of, **M3**: 171; **M15**: 14-15, 333-34; **L4**: xviii, 37, 61-62, 134-35, 201-4, 216, 246-50; **L5**: 174-77
literature's relation to, **M3**: 186-87; **L8**: 360-63; **L10**: 323-26; **L17**: 381
pragmatism's relation to, **M4**: 257; **M10**: xv-xxxix
metaphysical problem of, **M8**: 3, 449; **M15**: 18-19, 327, 331; **L4**: 239; **L16**: 292, 383-88
related to social conditions, **M8**: 144; **M11**: 342-45, 348-49, 398; **L3**: xxi-xxii, xxviii, 7-9; **L6**: 18-21; **L9**: 236; **L11**: 130, 258; **L15**: 274-75
German, **M8**: 176, 179-80, 183; **M9**: 309-10; **L2**: 27; **L5**: 148, 149, 181, 182, 190, 191, 196
European, **M8**: 200-204; **M11**: 94; **L11**: 76-80, 155, 597
American, **M8**: 200-204; **L3**: 9-10, 116-18, 120; **L5**: 45-49
related to education, **M9**: 338-41; **L5**: 289-98; **L6**: xxii, xxiii; **L8**: 77-103; **L9**: 194-204, 390; **L11**: 177, 203-4
a priori and *a posteriori* in, **M10**: 14; **L13**: 268-69
related to intelligence, **M10**: 46-48; **M12**: 258
Dewey's place in, **M11**: ix, x, xx, 404; **L4**: ix, x, xix; **L8**: ix-xviii; **L10**: vii-viii; **L16**: 187, 319-20
in Japan, **M11**: 156-57
reconstruction in, **M12**: x, xix, 77-201, 256-77
future of, **M12**: 94, 107, 266, 270, 272, 275-77; **L5**: 159-60; **L16**: xxxvii-xxxviii, 358-69, 375-77, 380-82, 404, 407-19; **L17**: 467, 469
criticized, **M12**: 237, 257-58
and religion, **M12**: 237-38, 264-66; **L4**: 13, 42-44
value of, **M13**: 314, 353
experiential, **M13**: 359-60; **L1**:

331-32, 365-92; **L4**: 66, 79; **L5**: 267-78; **L10**: 42, 44, 337-38; **L14**: 123-26, 138; **L16**: 397-98; **L17**: 429-41
modern, **M13**: 372-73; **L1**: 107, 109, 121, 162, 174, 354-56, 361-64; **L4**: 20, 21-40, 53-55, 58-59, 83-86, 105, 156, 163-64, 175, 176, 226-28; **L14**: 8-12, 190-95, 199-200, 315-17, 327
motivation in, **M15**: 14, 15, 17, 19, 325-31
problems in, **M15**: 17-19; **L11**: 115, 433, 436, 451; **L16**: 255, 289-90, 294
scholastic, **M15**: 421-22; **L5**: 166
Cartesian, **L1**: 14, 27, 255
false, **L1**: 51; **L17**: 382-83
as criticism, **L1**: 298-300, 302, 304-26; **L6**: 19
Holmes on, **L1**: 312-13
schools of, **L2**: 124, 125, 134-37; **L3**: 116, 131
totalitarian, **L2**: 379; **L14**: 275, 313, 317-23, 330-31
related to other fields, **L3**: 3, 4, 8, 46; **L5**: 141-43
contempt for, **L3**: 4
on knowledge and action, **L4**: 4-7, 11, 12, 16-20, 136, 140, 149, 154, 238
peripatetic, **L4**: 75-78
on conceptions, **L4**: 87-89, 112, 113, 117, 120
Dewey's, **L5**: xi, 148-50, 152-55; **L9**: 295; **L14**: ix-x, xxiii, xxiv; **L17**: 85
J. Marsh's, **L5**: 178-96
related to context, **L6**: 5-10, 14-17, 20-21
related to law, **L6**: 268-70
Perry on, **L6**: 271-72
and knowledge, **L6**: 428-31
and idealism, **L6**: 431-32
and communism, **L9**: 92, 244-45
and esthetics, **L10**: ix-xvii, xxxii-xxxiii, 126, 153, 203, 274, 278-79, 288-301
dualisms in, **L10**: 165, 340; **L14**: 167, 421-23; **L15**: 145-46, 152, 165, 201-2, 230, 275, 306, 336, 365; **L16**: 246-49, 339
related to art, **L10**: 191; **L16**: 464
Whitehead on, **L11**: 147, 150-51
Hutchins on, **L11**: 406, 596-97
James on, **L11**: 470-73; **L15**: 6-8
Peirce on, **L11**: 480-81
and logic, **L12**: 10, 15-16, 71-72
subject-matter of, **L14**: 148-50
related to human nature, **L14**: 289-90, 324-25, 333-34
Cohen on, **L14**: 394-95, 398-410
Marx on, **L14**: 415
Chinese, **L14**: 421
state of, **L15**: 14, 87, 162, 305-7, 313, 335
Tufts's place in, **L15**: 322-25
Bode's place in, **L15**: 326-27
Sheldon on, **L15**: 470-72
terminology of, **L16**: 266, 332, 334, 449-50
conception of, **L17**: xix, 387, 466
revision of, **L17**: 40, 467-68
Kilpatrick on, **L17**: 53
Philosophy: An Introduction (Randall and Buchler), **L15**: 457, 466, 468
"Philosophy and American National Life," **M3**: xi

Philosophy and Civilization, **L6**: 53n, 493, 500; **L14**: 383n
"Philosophy and Democracy," **L17**: xix
Philosophy and Phenomenological Research, **L16**: 279
Philosophy and Political Economy in Some of Their Historical Relations (Bonar), **E4**: 214-17; **L5**: 172n
"Philosophy and Public Policy" (Hook), **L17**: xxn
Philosophy and the Concepts of Modern Science (Reiser), **L11**: 432-37
Philosophy in American Education (Blanshard et al.), **L15**: 154-56
Philosophy in a New Key (Langer), **L15**: 418
Philosophy in Liberal Education, Commission on the Function of, **L15**: 154-55
Philosophy of art. *See* Esthetic theory
Philosophy of Bertrand Russell, The (Schilpp), **L16**: 202n, 204n
Philosophy of Biology, The (Johnstone), **M8**: 449-59
Philosophy of education
  in *Cyclopedia of Education*, **M7**: 297-312
  as source of science of education, **L5**: 26-31
  means and ends in, **L5**: 28-31
Philosophy of George Santayana, The (Schilpp), **L14**: 295-308
Philosophy of Henry George, The (Geiger), **L9**: 299
Philosophy of John Dewey, The (McDermott), **L14**: xxi
Philosophy of John Dewey, The (Schilpp), **L11**: xvn; **L14**: xii, xiii, 418n
Philosophy of John Stuart Mill, The (Marshall Cohen), **L9**: xxxin
"Philosophy of Logical Atomism, The" (B. Russell), **L16**: 200-202
Philosophy of Logics (Haack), **L6**: xvn
Philosophy of Right (Hegel), **M8**: 192, 193
Philosophy of Science, **L16**: 279
Philosophy of the Act, The (G. Mead), **L6**: xii
Philosophy of the Present, The (G. Mead), **L6**: xii, 307
Philosophy of the Spirit (Croce), **M12**: xxx
Phoebe Thorn Experimental School (Bryn Mawr College), **M8**: 263
Phoronomy
  in *Dictionary of Philosophy*, **M2**: 202-3
Photographs, **L10**: xxi, xxx, 8, 157, 200
Phronesis, **L2**: 132n, 135
Phusis, **L12**: 88
Physical, **L16**: 344, 352
  vs. psychical, **E1**: 94-98, 100, 103, 179; **M9**: 356-60; **L15**: 230, 306
  vs. ideal, **E3**: 228
  and action, **E3**: 229-30
  education, **M1**: 50
  concept of, in experience, **M7**: 146
  conditioning, **M11**: 60-63, 77, 103, 350-60
  defined, **L4**: 17, 52, 98, 149, 173-76, 190-93, 215
  in perception, **L10**: 220, 223,

235, 251, 254, 277, 340-41
and mental, **L12**: 42-43; **L15**: xvii-xix, 87n, 112-17, 202, 219, 365
in Aristotle, **L12**: 88
as name, **L16**: 268
Physical development
Rousseau on, **M8**: 214-17
importance of, **M8**: 389-90
Physical energy
F. Alexander's control of, **L6**: 315-20
Physical-material, **L1**: 348-49
Physical science. *See* Science
"Physical Science and Philosophy" (R. Tolman), **L16**: 103n
Physicians, **L13**: 331-32, 336
Physico-chemical science, **M8**: 3-5, 449-59
Physics (Aristotle), **L11**: 395
Physics, **M12**: 122-23, 217, 239, 262, 264; **L11**: 60, 149, 434, 461; **L13**: 272; **L15**: 305. *See also* Newton, Isaac
scientific habit of mind formed by, **M4**: 199-200
teaching of, **M10**: 134-36
mathematical, **L12**: 18-19, 61, 352, 395, 439
field theory in, **L14**: 28-29; **L16**: 121n, 264
influences Whitehead, **L14**: 131, 135
atomicity in, **L14**: 134
Cohen on, **L14**: 384-85; **L16**: 194
Bentley on, **L16**: xviii
uses transaction, **L16**: xxxiv, 96-100, 104-9, 121, 139
as discipline, **L16**: 63, 116n, 126
rise of, **L16**: 65-67, 289, 338-40, 355, 369, 453, 455
Einstein on, **L16**: 68n, 76n
techniques of, **L16**: 125, 148-49, 366, 372
principles of, **L16**: 165n, 316, 363, 414
vs. Greek philosophy, **L16**: 303-7
impact of, **L16**: 408-10
imaging power in, **L17**: 251-52
as subject-matter, **L17**: 467
Physiocrats, **M15**: 256
Physiological
science, **L16**: 64, 70
vs. behavioral, **L16**: 136-37, 270
as name, **L16**: 268
activities, **L16**: 288, 304
Physiological Optics (Helmholtz), **M7**: 139
Physiological psychology
as new science, **E1**: xxxii, 195
errors of, **E1**: 52
facts of, **E1**: 94-98
misconceptions concerning, **E1**: 194-95
criticism of Ladd's, **E1**: 200-203
course in, **E3**: 91
Dewey's work in, **M1**: xi-xiv
Physiology
and psychical events, **E1**: 52
importance to psychology, **E1**: 55-56, 94
educational, **E5**: 443
method in, **L16**: 63, 126-27, 326, 356-57, 366-67, 378-79
subject-matter of, **L16**: 88, 271, 309
uses transaction and interaction, **L16**: 110, 116-18, 138
as discipline, **L16**: 122-23, 221n, 344, 412

Physiology (*continued*)
study of behavior in, **L16**: 135-39
rise of, **L16**: 289, 292, 338, 340, 368-69, 375-76, 414, 453
Piancastelli, Giovanni, Collection (Cooper Union Museum), **L11**: 520
Piatt, Donald A., **L14**: 3, 4, 14, 23-24
Picard, Maurice, **M13**: 4n, 5n, 7n, 12n, 20n; **L2**: 80
on worth and value, **M15**: 338-40, 343-47
Picasso, Pablo, **L10**: xx; **L17**: 129
Picture
as object, **E5**: 198-99
Pierce, Arthur Henry, **M4**: 228
Pillon, François Thomas, **M2**: 153; **L15**: 20
Pilsudski, Joseph
as Polish leader, **M11**: 269, 273-75, 288, 291, 293, 295, 313, 327
Piltz, Erasme, **M11**: 280-81
Pinchot, Gifford, **L9**: 286
Pindar, **M5**: 116; **L7**: 107
Pinkevitch, Albert P., **L17**: 570
on Russian education, **L17**: 492, 569
Pioneers
conditions of, **L2**: 304-5
group in Russia, **L6**: 266, 293
value of, **L17**: 317
Pious Fund, **M15**: 385
Pistrak, Moisei Mikhailovich, L3: 247-48
Pitkin, Walter Boughton, **M4**: 295; **M6**: 473, 478-80
Pitney, Mahlon, **L7**: 396
Pittsburgh, Pa., **M11**: 288, 305
Pittsburgh School of Childhood kindergarten, **M8**: 283
Pity, **L13**: 289
Place of Industries in Elementary Education, The (Dopp), **M3**: 307-9
Plan. *See also* Design
ends-in-view as, **L13**: 238
Planck, Max, **L12**: 461; **L16**: 99
Planning
in education, **L13**: 36, 46-47, 68-70
social, **L13**: 321, 388
in inquiry, **L16**: 329-30, 336
responsibility for, **L17**: 452
attitude toward, **L17**: 457, 459
Plan of Organization of the University Primary School, **L11**: 204
Plastic arts, **L10**: 98, 122, 134, 242
Plasticity, **M6**: 361
as condition of growth, **M9**: 49-50, 51n, 54
in human nature, **L13**: 68, 292
Plato, **E1**: xxxiii, 257, 314; **E3**: 91; **E4**: 130, 171n, 215-16; **E5**: 141, 212-14; **M3**: 310; **M4**: 16, 20; **M5**: 182; **M6**: x; **M7**: 299, 306; **M8**: 68, 207, 275; **M10**: 90, 364; **M11**: 12, 34, 46; **M12**: xii, xxvii, xxixn, 26, 187, 197, 221; **M13**: 3, 362, 364; **M14**: 37; **M15**: 19, 184, 335-37; **L1**: 104, 192; **L2**: ix, 70, 71, 165; **L3**: 295; **L5**: 252, 289, 297; **L6**: 297; **L7**: 163; **L9**: xiii; **L11**: xxii, xxvi, 107, 538; **L13**: 401; **L14**: x, 140, 299; **L16**: 157n; **L17**: 173, 402, 403-4, 406. *See also* Neo-Platonism
on state, **E1**: xxxii, 239-41, 247-48; **M5**: 122-23, 128,

426; **M7**: 406-7; **M8**: 144; **L7**: 113-14, 120
matter of, **E1**: 166
cosmology of, **E1**: 281-82; **L14**: 193
on mathematics, **E1**: 281-82; **M9**: 268; **L1**: 37
compared with Leibniz, **E1**: 339-40, 364
G. Morris on, **E3**: 8
ideas of, **E3**: 226; **M7**: 221-22, 230; **L1**: 53-55; **L10**: 293, 298, 300
Laws of, **E4**: 38-39
conception of good, **E4**: 124; **M5**: 118-19, 125, 128; **M7**: 292; **L2**: 129n, 132n; **L7**: 109-10, 117, 119
moral system of, **E4**: 136-37; **M4**: 31-32; **M5**: 131-32, 165; **L5**: 497-99, 502-3; **L7**: 10, 122-23, 209; **L17**: 177
on ethics, **E4**: 138; **M3**: 46-48; **M14**: 55-56
on relation of citizen to community, **E4**: 139
on art and esthetics, **E4**: 191, 192, 196; **M5**: 45, 107; **M6**: 376-77; **L1**: 77, 78, 90, 166; **L7**: 42, 98; **L10**: vii, x, xvii, xx, xxii, xxviii, 13, 31, 295-300, 321, 331-32, 363-64
on reason, **E4**: 327n; **M2**: 260; **M5**: 123-24; **M7**: 260-61; **M9**: 271-72, 275, 276; **L7**: 114-15
on virtue, **E4**: 353; **M4**: 170-71; **M5**: 439; **M9**: 364-65; **L2**: 130-31, 135-38
on discussion, **M1**: 161-62
on man and nature, **M2**: 145; **M9**: 286-87
on necessity, **M2**: 151
on noetic, **M2**: 156
on non-being, **M2**: 157; **M6**: 104n; **L3**: 288
on noumena and phenomena, **M2**: 160; **M6**: 26-27
on nous, **M2**: 162
on theory of One, **M2**: 166-67
on opinion, **M2**: 172-73; **M7**: 292; **L7**: 363
on optimism, **M2**: 174-75
on organism, **M2**: 178
on reality, **M2**: 219; **M7**: 225; **M12**: 140-41
on subject, **M2**: 249
on vacuum, **M2**: 268
on experience, **M3**: 141n; **M9**: 271-72, 275, 276; **M11**: 345; **M12**: 125, 132-33; **L11**: 70-75
on classes, **M4**: 33; **M9**: xiv; **L10**: 252
on justice, **M5**: 8, 114-17; **L7**: 10, 107-8, 411
on hospitality, **M5**: 68; **L7**: 63
on propriety, **M5**: 110; **L7**: 101-2
on inequality, **M5**: 114-15; **L7**: 105-7
on life, **M5**: 118-19; **L5**: 291-92; **L7**: 109-10
on individualism, **M5**: 120, 123-28; **L7**: 111, 114-19, 152, 366
on pleasure, **M5**: 125; **L7**: 116-17
on self, **M5**: 131-32; **L7**: 122-23
on guilt of objects, **M5**: 411n
on truth, **M6**: 15, 24-25, 31-32; **M7**: 359
educational philosophy of, **M6**: 308, 363, 386; **M9**: 94-97,

Plato (*continued*)
102, 105, 127, 318-19; **M13**: 400; **L8**: 37, 285; **L17**: 263
on similarity, **M6**: 388
on change, **M6**: 443-44; **M12**: 141; **L12**: 189
in *Cyclopedia of Education*, **M7**: 312-18
on play, **M7**: 322
on original traits, **M7**: 393
on knowledge, **M9**: 203, 287; **L4**: ix, x, 214; **L7**: 363; **L13**: 161; **L17**: xxv-xxvi
and Aristotle, **M12**: 87, 89, 90
dramatic sense of, **M12**: 88
social thought of, **M12**: 133-34; **L11**: 563, 564
fundamental point of, **M13**: 17
and Socrates, **M13**: 367-68
on soul, **M14**: 94
Socratic Dialogues of, **L2**: ix, 124-40
adapts to Athens, **L3**: 6
structure of, **L4**: xxi, 13, 74; **L5**: 154-55
influence of, **L5**: 184, 377, 381
on slaves, **L6**: 431; **L13**: 43; **L17**: 315
on love, **L7**: 452
and Dewey, **L8**: xviii; **L13**: xvii-xviii
opposes Sophists, **L8**: 4-5, 21
evolution of doctrines of, **L8**: 22-24, 26, 30, 32
on economics, **L8**: 36
Whitehead on, **L8**: 356-59
Hutchins on, **L11**: 391, 393, 394, 401, 405, 407, 592, 593
on human nature, **L13**: 139-40, 143
"seven notions" of, **L14**: 136-37
Cohen on, **L14**: 398-99
on artisans, **L16**: 471
on growth and reform, **L17**: 183
compared with Tolstoy, **L17**: 386
particular and universal of, **L17**: 420
Platonic idealism, **M5**: 129; **M11**: 342; **M14**: 200-201; **L4**: xx, 112, 120, 125, 145, 219; **L7**: 120, 262
affects education, **M7**: 229-31
Platonic philosophy, **E5**: 8-9; **M1**: xi; **M2**: 81, 195-96
Platonic transcendentalism, **M7**: 201
Play, **M1**: 231; **M14**: 110-13
psychologists on, **E5**: 206
related to work, **E5**: 229; **M9**: 212-13, 325; **L8**: 287-88, 346-48
educational value of, **M1**: 82-84; **M8**: 278-83; **L8**: 153-54, 181, 289; **L17**: 263, 284-85
significance of, **M1**: 194-210; **L8**: 284-85, 289, 394; **L11**: 209, 244-45
vs. games, **M1**: 211-12; **L17**: 268, 285
defined, **M1**: 339-40
as thought activity, **M6**: 307-13
Froebel on, **M6**: 308
Plato on, **M6**: 308, 363
in *Cyclopedia of Education*, **M7**: 318-24
imagination in, **M9**: 245; **L17**: 263-64
art as, **L10**: 281-86, 295
Play School (New York City), **M8**: 272-73, 283-86
Pleasure, **M14**: 109-10, 139-42,

172; **L13**: 74; **L15**: 417-18, 423
as criterion, **E3**: 250-51, 272-73; **E4**: 276-81
related to desire, **E3**: 251-57, 268; **E4**: 264-69; **M5**: 249-50
and motive, **E3**: 252; **E4**: 271-76
as standard of conduct, **E3**: 260-74
quality of, **E3**: 270-73; **E4**: 284; **L7**: 244-45
private, **E3**: 276-83
in hedonism, **E3**: 283-84; **L7**: 191-99
vs. obligation, **E3**: 289
esthetic, **E4**: 190-91
two types of, **E5**: 120; **M7**: 158-59
theories of, **E5**: 136-37
among Hebrews, **M5**: 103; **L7**: 94
Plato on, **M5**: 125; **L7**: 116
in Greek theory, **M5**: 125-28; **L7**: 116-18
Epicurean doctrine of, **L7**: 200-202
in utilitarianism, **L7**: 240-44
Plenty, **L9**: 81
vs. poverty, **L9**: 61-62
Plenum
in *Dictionary of Philosophy*, **M2**: 203
Pleroma
in *Dictionary of Philosophy*, **M2**: 203
Plexus
in *Dictionary of Philosophy*, **M2**: 203
Plotinus, **M12**: 140
on art, **E4**: 192
on nature, **M2**: 146
on theory of One, **M2**: 167
on opinion, **M2**: 173
on parousia, **M2**: 185
on esthetics, **L10**: xxii, 296
Pluralism, **M12**: 196-97, 207, 211, 236-37, 243; **M14**: xxi; **L2**: xiii, 8-9; **L5**: 502, 503; **L12**: 524; **L13**: 131; **L15**: 221
in *Dictionary of Philosophy*, **M2**: 203-4
in *Cyclopedia of Education*, **M7**: 285, 324
atomistic, **M7**: 349; **M10**: 107; **L14**: 29
empirical, **M10**: xxv, 64
eleatic, **M10**: 32n
in social psychology, **M10**: 56
political, **L2**: 280-81
in science, **L13**: 123
James's, **L15**: 3-6
in religion, **L16**: 394
of values, **L17**: xxii
Pluralism of ultimates, **M10**: 11
Pluralistic
universe, **M12**: 208
realism, **M15**: 361-62, 372, 376
good, **L7**: xxxi
Pluralistic Universe, A (W. James), **M7**: 144; **L5**: 157; **L15**: 5
Pluralists, **L10**: xii
Plurality
in *Dictionary of Philosophy*, **M2**: 205
of causes, **L12**: 451-52
Pneuma
in *Dictionary of Philosophy*, **M2**: 205-6
Pneumatology
in *Dictionary of Philosophy*, **M2**: 206
Podolsky, B., **L16**: 109

Poe, Edgar Allan
on art, **L10**: 80-81, 198, 356, 360, 366
Poetesses, Academy of, **E3**: 195-96
Poetry, **M12**: 15, 83, 84, 139, 201, 228, 234; **L1**: 96, 143, 159, 270, 305; **L10**: 39, 83; **L13**: 359; **L15**: 376
and association, **E2**: 96
as ideal, **E2**: 276
forms of, **E2**: 277
related to science and philosophy, **E3**: xxxv-xxxvii, 17, 112-13; **M3**: 186-87; **L6**: 492-93
reflects life, **E3**: 113
Hebrew, **M5**: 103; **L7**: 94, 126
Dewey's, **M10**: ix
distinctive qualities of, **L10**: xx, xxii, xxix, 11, 220, 222, 228, 233-34, 237-38, 244-47, 257, 271, 285, 288-89, 293-94, 300, 318, 326-27
creation of, **L10**: 70-76, 91, 113-16
substance of, **L10**: 154, 192-96
movements in, **L10**: 155, 158, 303
influences on, **L10**: 157, 304, 312, 320-24
rhythm in, **L10**: 160, 169-70, 174, 177-78, 186, 207, 214, 216
spatial and temporal in, **L10**: 188
role of, **L10**: 330-31, 342, 348-51
in Santayana's philosophy, **L14**: 297-99
Poets
nature of, **L10**: 70, 80, 262, 272, 293, 298, 362
philosophy of, **L10**: 323, 326-27, 349, 350
attacks on, **L10**: 331
Poincaré, Jules Henri, **M3**: 68; **L12**: 405; **L14**: 386
Poincaré, Raymond, **M15**: 411
Point
in mathematics, **L12**: 411, 463
Pointillism, **L10**: 127
Pointing. *See also* This, **L12**
at and out, **L12**: 127, 150-51, 242
Poland, **M15**: xviiin, 390-92, 394
persecution in, **M10**: 288; **L11**: 530
future of, **M11**: xiii, xiv, 101, 136, 242, 246-47, 250-53, 263-77, 286, 287, 298, 300, 320, 325-28, 400, 405-6
partitions of, **M11**: xiv, xv, 255, 262-67, 271
patriotism in, **M11**: 222
relief funds for, **M11**: 245-46, 250, 286, 290, 309-19
army of, **M11**: 250, 268-69, 273-74, 283, 288, 292, 294, 305-6, 321
represented by Paris Committee, **M11**: 251-53, 278-84, 299-302, 328
economic conditions in, **M11**: 263-66
on border dispute, **L6**: 461-62
music of, **L10**: 193
occupied, **L15**: 295-96, 342, 347, 350, 352
Polanyi, Karl, **L15**: 215, 225, 361, 510
Polarity, **L5**: 179; **L10**: 161
Poles
rights of, **M11**: 71
in WWI, **M11**: 242, 319-25, 330, 395

dissension among, **M11**: 245-62, 284, 286, 296, 298, 300, 303-22, 327, 329, 405
Americanization of, **M11**: 290, 328
Police power, **L7**: 394, 414
Polish Activist party, **M11**: 265, 275, 298
Polish Army Corps, First, **M11**: 321
Polish Associated Press, **M11**: 251, 256-57, 295, 302, 325-28
Polish Catholic church, **M11**: 305
Polish Central Relief Committee, **M11**: 312-13
Polish Committee of National Defense. *See* KON
Polish Democrats, Union of, **M11**: 279, 282
Polish Falcons, Alliance of, **M11**: 287-88, 313, 322
Polish Legions, **M11**: 269, 273-75, 305, 313, 321, 325
Polish Military Commission, **M11**: 300, 308, 311, 315, 317, 322-23
Polish National Alliance, **M11**: 242, 286-89, 296, 312, 322, 403
Polish National Army, **M11**: 256, 257, 301, 310-12, 317-25, 395, 397
Polish National Committee. *See* Paris Committee
Polish National Council, **M11**: xv, 267, 269, 272, 279, 289-90, 313
Polish National Democratic party
policies of, **M11**: 267, 269, 275, 289, 291, 301, 306, 308, 320, 321
forms Paris Committee, **M11**: 277-84
status of, **M11**: 326-27
Polish National Department, **M11**: 242-43, 248-49, 279, 290-91, 296-97, 301-5, 395
Polish Parliamentary Club, **M11**: 272-73, 280
Polish Passivist party, **M11**: 265-67, 275, 277, 298
Polish press, **M11**: 290
reports of, **M11**: 244, 248, 249, 284, 303, 310, 317-22
in Poland, **M11**: 280, 281
in U.S. election, **M11**: 287
management of, **M11**: 305
Polish Press Bureau, **M11**: 251, 256-57, 295, 302, 325-28
Polish Progressives, **M11**: 267
Polish Roman Catholic Alliance, **M11**: 242, 286-89, 296, 303, 312
Polish Sanitary Commission, **M11**: 315
Polish Socialist party, **M11**: 262, 265-67, 272, 273, 396
Polish study
discussed, **M11**: xiv-xvi, 395, 398-408
Dewey on, **M11**: 242, 259-62, 306, 318
Polish Victims' Relief Fund, **M11**: 290, 300, 308, 309, 312
Polish White Cross, **M11**: 250, 306, 316-19, 329
Polish Women's League, **M11**: 314, 316
Polish Young Men's Alliance, **M11**: 288
Political
interest, **E5**: 212
rights, **M5**: 423-24
psychology, **M10**: 271
theories, **L2**: 238-39, 241, 288

Political (*continued*)
pluralism, **L2**: 280-81
attachment, **L2**: 322, 368-69
apathy, **L3**: 135
institutions, **L6**: 126-27; **L17**: 167
Political History of Poland, The (Corwin), **M11**: 314
Political Ideals (B. Russell), **M12**: 244
"Political Interference in Higher Education and Research," **L6**: xxii
Political Myths and Economic Realities (Delaisi), **L5**: 173n
Political parties, **L2**: 309-11; **L11**: xxiii, 50-51, 266, 274-75, 412, 496, 526; **L14**: 203; **L15**: 242, 244
state of, **L6**: 149-52, 156-61
business alliance with, **L6**: 156-59, 163-65, 177
and third-party program, **L6**: 167-73, 185-86, 324-25
related to Congress, **L6**: 227, 250
history of, **L6**: 231-40, 313-14
British, **L6**: 246
Farmer-Labor, **L6**: 251, 254
Political science, **M15**: 234-35; **L9**: 299-300; **L14**: 362
and philosophy, **E4**: 214-17
teaching of, **E5**: 279
psychology as, **M1**: xii
Catlin on, **L3**: 321-23
Bentley's role in, **L16**: xxv
Political Theories, Ancient and Mediaeval (Dunning), **L2**: 33n
Political Theories of the Middle Age (Gierke), **L2**: 26
Politics (Aristotle), **L4**: xxi; **L7**: 132; **L14**: 394
Politics, **M12**: 151-52; **M15**: ix, xi, xxiv; **L15**: 159, 170, 229; **L17**: 35-36
as art, **E3**: 206-8; **L10**: 31, 286, 291, 319, 321, 323, 329, 331-32, 348, 351
morals and, **E4**: 371-73; **M12**: 192-93; **L17**: 101
constituent groups in, **M5**: 31-34, 62-63; **L6**: 172-75, 355-56, 392-94, 440; **L7**: 30-33, 57-58; **L17**: 112
in Israel, **M5**: 97; **L7**: 89
beliefs about, **M5**: 112-17; **L4**: 5, 136, 200, 207, 218, 221; **L7**: 103-8
characteristics of, **M8**: 144; **M11**: x, 9, 21; **L2**: 356-61; **L6**: xvi, 128, 448-49; **L9**: 74-75, 312; **L10**: 26; **L11**: xxx, 51, 219-20, 362, 368-71; **L13**: 136; **L14**: 74-76; **L16**: 360, 366, 369, 390-91, 396-97, 417-18; **L17**: 44, 47, 112-13, 117-18
philosophy related to, **M10**: 3-4; **M11**: 42-53, 344, 349
and democracy, **M10**: 137-38
in China, **M11**: xix-xx, 174, 177, 186, 190-96, 205, 206, 212, 215-29; **M12**: 28-40, 65-70, 73-74
Hobbes on, **M11**: 18-40
as social science, **M11**: 31-35, 89, 93-97; **L4**: 15, 81, 169, 194, 225, 226; **L9**: 71-72; **L14**: 362
related to education, **M11**: 54-57; **M15**: 158-59, 190; **L6**: xxiii, 118-21, 411, 437; **L9**: 406-8

affected by war, **M11**: 70-72, 98-106; **M15**: 100, 106, 112, 119-20
in New York City and State, **M11**: 94, 394; **L9**: 346-85
international, **M11**: 127-30, 133; **M13**: 90, 161-62, 210; **L15**: 195, 219-20
European, **M11**: 137; **M13**: 164-66, 345
T. Roosevelt's role in, **M11**: 146-49
in Japan, **M11**: 152-67, 171, 174, 177
of Polish question, **M11**: 261-62, 287, 297, 298, 307, 311-12, 322, 326, 398-408
problems in, **M12**: 66-69, 74; **L6**: 438; **L7**: 352-58; **L13**: 82, 107
change in, **M12**: 103-6; **L9**: 296, 298; **L11**: xxiii-xxiv, 274-81; **L16**: 319, 370
as career, **M13**: 314
propaganda in, **M13**: 330-31
in Turkey, **M15**: 128-30
individualism and, **M15**: 243; **L7**: 331
related to culture, **M15**: 271; **L6**: 40-48; **L9**: 231, 234-35; **L14**: 343
liberalism in, **M15**: 396
importance of consequences to, **L2**: 243-47, 250-51, 255, 260, 262, 265, 276-78, 313, 333
related to economics, **L2**: 290-326 passim, 332, 344, 348-49, 378-79; **L6**: 150-52, 156-58, 161-63, 170-71, 236, 239-40, 249, 324-25, 441; **L9**: 163, 360-61; **L13**: 69, 101, 112, 129-30, 338; **L14**: 94
political parties and, **L6**: 156-61, 246-55, 403-6, 412-13, 436-39; **L9**: 66, 79, 80, 297
and citizenry, **L6**: 174, 182-88; **L15**: 246-47
and prohibition, **L6**: 183-84, 249-50
and minorities, **L6**: 224-30
and crime, **L6**: 242
and 1932 election, **L6**: 326
and liberty, **L7**: 138-40
Dewey's role in, **L8**: x-xii, xviii
LIPA and, **L9**: 67-70, 307
power of, **L9**: 76-77; **L13**: 75, 102; **L16**: 243n, 255
unions and, **L9**: 318-19, 333-34, 338, 339
Niebuhr on, **L9**: 399-401
attitude toward, **L11**: 189, 233
Aristotle on, **L13**: 73, 118
campaigns in, **L13**: 294
of bolshevism, **L13**: 399
Jefferson on, **L14**: 211-13, 217-18
LID and, **L14**: 262-65
C. and M. Beard on, **L14**: 284
movements in, **L15**: 156-57, 177-78, 213, 217; **L16**: 362-63, 375, 404-7
T. V. Smith on, **L17**: 115-18
"Politics and Culture," **L6**: xvi
Pollak, Walter, **L6**: 323
Pollock, Frederick, **M5**: 65n; **M7**: 56; **M12**: ix; **M15**: 55; **L7**: 59n, 442
on legal and judicial matters, **M5**: 409n, 411n, 412n, 416n, 424n, 514n
on law of nature, **L17**: 98-100

Poll tax, **L15**: 357
Polyadic terms, **L12**: 311-12
Polygamy, **L17**: 25
Polynesia, **M7**: 400; **L10**: 337
Polytheism, **M7**: 353; **L9**: 294
Pomponatius, **M2**: 187
Poor Richard's Almanack (Franklin), **L15**: xxx
Pope, Arthur Upham, **L11**: 488
  on Soviet situation, **L15**: 351-55, 492-501
Popocrats, **L6**: 231
Popper, Karl, **L4**: xv
Popular Front, **L13**: 132
Popular Science Monthly, **M15**: 227
Population
  in U.S., **L6**: 361
  age make-up of, **L14**: 342
  growth of, **L17**: 73
  Malthus on, **L17**: 411
Populist party, **L6**: 231-34
Populus, **L2**: 246
Pornography, **L10**: 101, 182
Port Arthur (Lüshun), China, **M13**: 145
Porter, Russell, **L9**: 310-11
Porto Rico, **L15**: 20-22
Port Royal *Logic*, **M2**: 217
Portsmouth, Treaty of, **M12**: 38-39, 62-63; **M13**: 492
Posen (Poznan), Poland, **M11**: 280, 283, 396
Po-shan (Boshan), China, **M12**: 37-38
Posit
  in *Dictionary of Philosophy*, **M2**: 207-8
Position
  in art, **L10**: 216-17, 312
Position of Foreign Corporations in American Constitutional Law, The (G. Henderson), **L2**: 31n
Positive, **L1**: 172-73; **L16**: 97-98
  law, **E4**: 73-75, 83
  in *Dictionary of Philosophy*, **M2**: 208
  stress on, **L17**: 267
Positive proposition. *See also* Agreement, **L12**; Comparison, **L12**; Conjunction, **L12**
  in Aristotle, **L12**: 90
Positivism, **M2**: 142; **M15**: 333; **L12**: 511-12; **L16**: 310
  on relativity of knowledge, **E1**: 19
  in *Dictionary of Philosophy*, **M2**: 208-10
  in *Cyclopedia of Education*, **M7**: 324-26, 415
  agnostic, **M10**: 38
  revolt against, **L16**: xiv-xv, xxxiiin
Possession
  connected with enjoyment, **L13**: 224-25
  importance of, **L17**: 63-64
Possibility (Buchanan), **L3**: 311
Possibility, **L4**: xx; **L12**: 113-15, 134, 264-65, 269-70, 279, 288-89, 301-2, 338-39, 341, 392, 423, 436
  in *Dictionary of Philosophy*, **M2**: 210-12
  in Bergson's theory of perception, **M7**: 15-16
  esthetic, metaphysical, scientific, **L3**: 312-13
  defined, **L4**: 239-48
  pure, **L12**: 10, 54-55
  as ontological, **L12**: 396-401
  of human values, **L13**: 263
  use of, **L16**: 282-83
  Balz on, **L16**: 423-42

Possible
in *Dictionary of Philosophy*, **M2**: 210-12
Post, Albert, **L7**: 58
Postimpressionism, **L10**: xx, 307, 314, 365
Post-Kantian idealism, **M7**: 291
Postulates, **M10**: 84; **L14**: 123
axiom as, **L11**: 155
and logic, **L12**: 23-26
and mathematics, **L12**: 401-4
scientific, **L12**: 477-80
vs. postulations, **L16**: 75-80
of Lewis, **L16**: 193n
arbitrary, **L16**: 306-7, 333, 448
for value, **L16**: 343
Postulational method, **L16**: 3, 4
"Postulation for Behavioral Inquiry" (A. Bentley), **L16**: 47n
Postulations
of Dewey and Bentley, **L16**: 47n, 48, 58, 187-90, 257-58, 273-75
role in inquiry, **L16**: 74-79
for behavioral events, **L16**: 80-85, 333, 448
for namings and named, **L16**: 86-90
orientation for, **L16**: 92-94
in logic, **L16**: 184-87
of Kantor, **L16**: 190-92
in mathematics, **L16**: 287
Potentiality, **M12**: 112, 113; **L1**: 51, 102, 109, 143, 147, 192-93, 201, 282; **L2**: 47-48; **L11**: 110; **L12**: 94n, 111, 132, 164, 238, 288-89, 332, 385-88, 476. *See also* Interaction, **L12**; Kinds, **L12**
vs. actualization, **E1**: 319; **L16**: 434-35
role and nature of, **M7**: 16-18; **L16**: 282-83, 427-28, 460-61
Peirce on, **L11**: 86-89, 481-82
as category of existence, **L14**: 109-10
related to possibility, **L16**: 424-26
Potocki, Count, **M11**: 318
Pound, Roscoe, **M7**: 56; **M15**: 70; **L7**: xxix; **L17**: 100, 102, 106
Poussin, Nicolas, **L10**: 115, 256
Poverty, **L3**: 359; **L9**: 81; **L15**: 252
in Leningrad, **L3**: 206
vs. plenty, **L9**: 61-62
abolition of, **L17**: 453
Powell, Thomas Reed, **L11**: 603
Power, **L6**: 150, 178-79; **L13**: 54, 86, 109, 140, 143; **L17**: 293, 309
concept of, **M10**: xxviii, 48, 246; **L13**: 68, 74-75, 91, 285, 312
will to, **M14**: 97-99
spiritual, **L2**: 33-34
Locke on, **L2**: 141, 146-48, 150-52; **L7**: 205, 279
state as, **L7**: 149; **L13**: 128; **L16**: 402-3
Milton on, **L7**: 207
distribution of, **L7**: 347-48; **L17**: 115-16
politics and, **L9**: 76-77; **L13**: 75, 102; **L15**: 177-78
in social affairs, **L9**: 109
purchasing, **L9**: 277, 280, 281
of media, **L13**: xvi
freedom as, **L13**: 41
of habits, **L13**: 96, 162
of laborers, **L13**: 107
quality of, **L13**: 128, 163, 180, 321
of rabblerouser, **L13**: 176

Power (*continued*)
over nature, **L13**: 179-80, 350
of prediction, **L13**: 243
of art, **L13**: 367
Lenin on, **L13**: 400
increase of, **L17**: 292-93
of ideas, **L17**: 332, 338
Power: A New Social Analysis (B. Russell), **L13**: 160n, 402
Power Trust, **L6**: 118
Practical
activity in teaching, **E5**: 182-83; **M8**: 391-95
interest, as source of child-study, **E5**: 212-15
pragmatism on, **M10**: xxiii-xxv
vs. esthetic, **L10**: 26-27, 45-47, 61, 265-68, 351
vs. intellectual, **L15**: 258-59
Practicalism, **M10**: 87
Practical judgment
nature of, **M8**: 14-23
and value judgment, **M8**: 23-49
reply to D. Robinson on, **M10**: 98-108
Practice, **L1**: 70; **L10**: xii; **L17**: 408. *See also* Experiment, **L12**; Operations, **L12**
vs. theory, **M9**: 142, 235-37, 269, 271-81, 300, 303, 316, 329, 333, 340, 346; **L1**: 237-38, 267, 269-70; **L7**: xxxiii-xxxiv; **L12**: 63-65, 78-80, 432-35, 455-57, 487-89, 492-93, 504-5; **L15**: 190, 228-29; **L17**: 67-69, 85
political, **L1**: 171
and recognition, **L1**: 247
related to knowledge, **L4**: ix, x, xiii, xvi, xvii, xix, 157, 163, 204, 223-27
depreciated, **L4**: 4-7, 11, 14, 16, 22, 24, 28, 30, 41, 56, 58, 65, 69, 85, 171
meaning of, **L4**: 25-26
modes of, **L4**: 203
experimental method in, **L4**: 219
educational value of, **L5**: 16-23
in forming habits, **L7**: 204
related to logical theory, **L16**: 92n, 134n, 190
in inquiry, **L16**: 323-24
related to repetition, **L17**: 304-5
deviation of moral, **L17**: 398-99
Pragmatic, **L16**: 183n
defined, **M10**: xi-xiii, 5-13; **L12**: 4
Peirce on, **M10**: 366
method, **M13**: 27
knowing, **M14**: 127-31
C. Morris on, **L15**: 142-43
as name, **L16**: 268
Pragmaticism
Peirce and James on, **M7**: 327; **M10**: 72-78
Pragmatisch, **M10**: 72
Pragmatism (W. James), **M4**: 98; **M7**: 144; **M10**: 417; **M15**: 335; **L2**: 161; **L5**: 157, 478n; **L11**: 82, 465; **L15**: 11, 12, 19
Pragmatism, **M7**: x, xi, 416, 444; **M8**: 152; **M9**: 353-54; **M11**: xi, 361, 376, 383; **M15**: 226, 227, 333-34, 357-60, 368-69; **L5**: 497, 503; **L8**: x; **L13**: 131; **L14**: xviii; **L15**: xxvii-xxviii, 3-6
Dewey's, **M2**: xvi-xvii; **M4**: xi-xii; **M6**: xi; **M10**: ix-xxxix; **L4**: vii-ix, xvii-xix, xxii

on intelligence and knowledge, **M3**: 153-56; **M4**: 61n, 128-32, 181-91; **M10**: 21, 45
ethical idealism involved in, **M3**: 156-57
F. Schiller's, **M3**: 317-18; **L11**: 156
James's, **M4**: 98-115; **M6**: 94-97; **M10**: 71; **M12**: x, 100-101, 205, 212, 217, 219, 227, 246; **L2**: xiii-xiv, 6-11, 13-17, 160-62; **L5**: xxix, 477-79, 480n; **L8**: 11-12; **L14**: 160; **L15**: 12-13
on science and morals, **M4**: 132-33; **M10**: 14
disputed, **M4**: 245-49; **L3**: 145-47; **L15**: 19-26
movement of, **M4**: 253-57; **M6**: xi-xii; **M13**: 307, 445-46; **L16**: xxxvii-xxxviii; **L17**: 51
in education, **M6**: xi; **L15**: 167-68
and theory of truth, **M6**: 3-11, 33-52
perception of, **M6**: 86-90; **M10**: 42-44
affects philosophy, **M6**: 175-76; **M10**: xxv-xxxix
related to experience, **M6**: 447; **L11**: 82-83
in *Cyclopedia of Education*, **M7**: 326-30
Russell on, **M8**: 22-23
on reality, **M10**: 39
Peirce's, **M10**: 71-78, 87; **L2**: xii-xiii, 6-9, 28-29; **L4**: 117; **L5**: 477-79; **L11**: 421-24; **L15**: 142; **L16**: 238, 239n
theory of, **M10**: 366-67; **M13**: 477-81; **L3**: 25; **L4**: xiii, 30n, 90n; **L11**: 565-66; **L14**: 55; **L15**: 97-98, 161-63; **L17**: 39-40
and instrumentalism, **M10**: 367-69; **L3**: 340-41
Lovejoy on, **M13**: 40, 49, 443-81
American, **M13**: 306-10; **L2**: 3-21; **L14**: 12-13
Santayana on, **L3**: 370, 382-83
Hocking on, **L5**: 461-76
Lewis on, **L5**: 477-86
on esthetics, **L10**: vii-xi, xiv, xvii, xxiii, xxxii-xxxiii; **L14**: 34-35, 38
on social problems, **L11**: 563, 564
attributed to Kant, **L14**: 11
C. Morris's, **L15**: 331-32; **L16**: 33-35
in Dewey-Bentley collaboration, **L16**: xxv, xxviii-xxix
Stein on, **L17**: 39
Wiener on, **L17**: 50-51
Pragmatism and Pragmaticism (C. Peirce), **L11**: 421-24
"Pragmatism of Peirce, The," **L6**: xiv
Praise, **L10**: 303, 315, 351
Praktisch, **M10**: 72
Prall, David Wight, **M13**: 8, 11n, 12, 20, 22; **M15**: xii; **L2**: xix-xx
on value, **M15**: 20-26, 338-48; **L2**: 69-77, 82, 83, 85-86, 393-402
on judgment, **M15**: 23, 341-42
Pratt, Caroline, **M8**: 272-73, 283-86
Pratt, Carroll C., **L16**: 170n
Pratt, James Bissett, **M4**: xx; **L3**: 396, 397; **L15**: 454

Pratt Institute (New York City), **E5**: xcvi, 436
Praxagoras, **M2**: 205
Prayer, **L9**: 433-34
Precedent, **L7**: 275, 329-30. *See also* Tradition
Precept, **L16**: 66, 299
Preceptorial system (Princeton University), **L11**: 591, 605
Preconceptions
  limit esthetic experience, **L10**: 118, 165, 204, 293, 299
Predestination, **L13**: 292
Predeterminism, **E4**: 94n; **M8**: 18
Predicables, **L12**: 94, 139-41
Predication, **L5**: 252-55; **L12**: 96, 127-30, 134-35, 139-41, 151, 168, 239-40, 252, 273-75, 284-85, 307-9
Prediction, **L8**: 208-9; **L12**: 113-14, 450-51, 468-69; **L13**: 243; **L15**: 138-39
Preestablished harmony, **M7**: 276, 293; **L5**: 377
  in *Dictionary of Philosophy*, **M2**: 212
Preface to Logic, A (M. R. Cohen), **L16**: 184n, 194
Preface to Morals, A (Lippmann), **L6**: 499n; **L10**: 332n
Preference, **L7**: 286
Prehension, **L14**: 132
Prejudice, **M6**: 185, 201, 262; **M12**: 238, 268; **M13**: xxvii-xxviii, 174; **L3**: 185; **L4**: 211, 212; **L7**: 267-68; **L8**: 116, 136, 214; **L13**: xv, 88, 153; **L14**: 367. *See also* Race discrimination
  Yellow Peril as, **M7**: 407
  factors in, **M13**: 243-51, 253, 437, 439, 440
  effects of, **M13**: 251, 261
  alleviation of, **M13**: 251-54, 439; **L9**: 203-4
  in Teachers Union, **L9**: 316-18, 322, 326
  countered by art, **L10**: xxxi, 101, 328, 337
  regarding Chinese government, **L17**: 30
Preliminary Commission of Inquiry. *See* Commission of Inquiry into the Charges Made against Leon Trotsky in the Moscow Trials
Prelude, The (Wordsworth), **L10**: 138, 169-70, 359, 360
Premise, **L1**: 283-84
  nature of, **M15**: 65-66; **L12**: 145, 166-67, 310-11, 322-23, 420
  supplied by syllogism, **M15**: 70
  in law, **M15**: 71-72
  and logical principles, **L12**: 21, 158-59
  in Aristotle, **L12**: 90
  vs. observation, **L16**: 48
Preparation, **M13**: 402-3
  meaning of, **L13**: 28-30
  inflexible, **L13**: 36
Preparatory-stimulus, **L16**: 233
  C. Morris on, **L16**: 210n, 211, 213, 220
Presbyterians, **M11**: 22-25
Presence
  Royce on, **M10**: 80
Present
  importance of living in, **M9**: 59-61, 79, 81-82, 320
  involved in perception, **L10**: xx, xxiv, 78, 128, 181, 276-77, 283, 287-88, 327, 342, 348
  and past, **L13**: 9, 51-53, 57, 97; **L14**: 84, 131, 135
  and future, **L13**: 30, 59
Presentation
  Herbart's theory of, **M9**: 75-78

as act of knowing, **M10**: 36-37
Presentationism
in *Dictionary of Philosophy*, **M2**: 213
Presentative realism, **M7**: 82-83, 454-60; **M10**: 26n, 41
Present-Day Thinkers and the New Scholasticism (Zybura), **L2**: 388n
President's Organization on Unemployment Relief, **L6**: 374
President's Research Committee on Social Trends, **L9**: 133, 229-31, 235
Pre-Socratics, **M2**: 150; **L8**: 32
Press, **L2**: 219; **L11**: 269-73, 307, 343-44. *See also* Publicity
reports social issues, **M11**: 87, 88, 159
reports WWI, **M11**: 114, 119
regulation of, **M11**: 118-21
anti-Americanism in, **M11**: 150-55, 177, 179
reports peace conference, **M11**: 151, 159, 199, 203
opposes League of Nations, **M11**: 163
reports on Japan, **M11**: 166
reports on Siberia, **M11**: 167
reports on China, **M11**: 191, 228, 239
reports Polish question, **M11**: 243-44, 248-49, 256, 268, 277, 280-84, 287, 290, 297, 300, 301, 303, 305, 308-10, 315, 317-22, 397
influence of, **L13**: 92, 168; **L16**: 402
Press Club, National, **L11**: 319
Preyer, William, **M3**: 299
child psychology of, **M1**: 175-77, 186-87
Price, Richard, **E4**: 123, 128, 129; **M3**: 53
Price system, **M15**: 262, 264
Pride, **E2**: 287; **L4**: 245-46
Priestley, Joseph, **M7**: 276; **L14**: 205; **L15**: xxx
Primary
in *Dictionary of Philosophy*, **M2**: 213
Primary school. *See* Elementary school
Prime Ministers and Presidents (Sherrill), **M13**: 345-46
Prime numbers, **M7**: 439-40
Primer of Philosophy (Carus), **E5**: 342, 347
Primitive. *See also* Postulates, **L12**
credulity, **E3**: 85
mind, **M1**: 155; **M2**: 39-40, 43
man, **M1**: 234; **M2**: 46n; **M5**: 28n; **M12**: 81-82, 128-29, 180-81, 246; **L7**: 28n
woman, **M2**: 46; **L7**: 27, 30, 31, 438-44
in *Dictionary of Philosophy*, **M2**: 213
art, **L10**: 200, 330-31, 336
propositions, **L12**: 151, 157-58, 314-15, 403-4
esthetic element in, **L16**: 397
Bentley vs. Church on, **L16**: 445-46
Boas on, **L17**: 404-5
Primitive life, **M1**: 31-32, 223; **M5**: 27n, 36-37, 48-49; **M14**: 68, 72, 74; **L3**: 11, 14, 17-18, 335-37; **L7**: 26n-27n, 35-36, 45-47; **L13**: 22, 291
justice in, **M5**: 31-34, 64; **L7**: 30-33, 59
commerce in, **M5**: 77; **L7**: 71
crises in, **M7**: 399-402
beliefs of, **L4**: 3, 10-12
compared with modern, **L4**: 8-9, 81
impotency of, **L4**: 26, 203, 226

Primitive life (*continued*)
desire for knowledge of, **L4**: 30
Primitive Man as Philosopher (Radin), **L3**: 335
Primogeniture, **L13**: 81
Primordial
in *Dictionary of Philosophy*, **M2**: 213
Primum mobile
in *Dictionary of Philosophy*, **M2**: 213
Princeton University, **L11**: 591, 605
Principia Mathematica (B. Russell and Whitehead), **L5**: 483; **L14**: xiv, xv; **L16**: xviii
Principle
in *Dictionary of Philosophy*, **M2**: 214
Principles, **M12**: 106, 126, 173, 240-41, 243; **M14**: 4
and tendencies, **M14**: 36-37
nature of, **M14**: 164-69; **L7**: 232, 275-83, 330
vs. rules, **L7**: xxv, 276-80
derived from habits, **L11**: 107-8
Hutchins on, **L11**: 395, 400, 406-7, 596
eternal, **L11**: 405, 407
first, **L12**: 19; **L14**: 123
leading, **L12**: 19-21, 158, 316, 336, 465
authoritative, **L16**: 338, 453
Principles of Behavior (Hull), **L16**: 125n
Principles of Literary Criticism (Richards), **L6**: 499
Principles of Philosophy (C. Peirce), **L6**: 273-77
Principles of Philosophy, The (Descartes), **M8**: 24
Principles of Physiological Psychology (Wundt), **M7**: 140, 141
Principles of Political Economy (J. S. Mill), **L11**: 601
Principles of Psychology, The (W. James), **M1**: xxiii, 321; **M6**: 273n, 299; **M7**: 142; **M10**: 50, 53; **M12**: xxv, 205, 214; **L2**: xiii, 15-16; **L5**: xxii, 157-59; **L8**: 227, 228, 275; **L11**: xiii, 69, 82; **L12**: 510n; **L13**: 363; **L14**: x, 155-67; **L15**: 11, 12, 18; **L17**: 434
Principles of Social Reconstruction (B. Russell), **M12**: 244; **L14**: 236
Principles of Sociology, The (H. Spencer), **M2**: 39-40
Principles of Systematic Psychology (Griffith), **L16**: 63n
Pringle, Henry Fowles, **L17**: 524, 573
Pringle, R. W., **M1**: xv; **M6**: xxv
Prinkipo (Büyükada), Turkey, **L11**: 311
Printing
affects education, **M9**: 189
Prior Analytics (Aristotle), **L8**: xivn
Pritchett, Henry Smith, **M15**: 190
Privacy, **L1**: 148, 171, 181, 187; **L15**: 30-31
Private, **L2**: 245; **L16**: 170n
Privilege, **L7**: 347-48
Privy Council, **M11**: 168
Prizing, **L13**: 195
variants of, **L13**: 203, 208
appraising related to, **L13**: 213
meaning of term, **L15**: 101-5
related to valuing, **L16**: 311-12, 347-52
as subject-matter, **L16**: 315-16
in judgment, **L16**: 354-55
Probability, **M12**: 91; **L12**: 222n, 225-26, 255, 318-19, 379,

389, 408-9, 426-27. *See also* Contingency, **L12**
Condorcet on, **M10**: 57
as nature of experience, **L4**: 6, 21
theory of, **L4**: 162, 165, 166, 198-99
and frequency distribution, **L12**: 465-73
of distribution of kinds, **L12**: 470-73
in science, **L13**: 123; **L14**: 106-7, 111
and induction, **L14**: 58
Problem, **M12**: xviii
in reflective thought, **E5**: 34
related to child's interest, **E5**: 145
nature of, **M6**: 190, 191, 236; **L8**: 121, 123, 201-2; **L12**: 193-94
in *Cyclopedia of Education*, **M7**: 330-31
important in philosophy, **L4**: 67, 80-84, 98, 99, 107, 139-44, 147, 151, 152, 155, 200; **L16**: 255, 290, 294, 407
resolution of, **L4**: 158, 159, 172, 173, 176-89, 194, 195; **L17**: 150, 279-80, 317-18, 469
in art, **L10**: 21, 143
and conflict, **L12**: 14-15, 33-38, 177-78, 186-87, 218-19
in common sense and science, **L12**: 71-72, 84-85, 420-22; **L13**: 376
formation of, **L12**: 111-15, 123-24; **L13**: 249, 283
and data, **L12**: 127, 167-68, 172-74, 196-97, 202, 205-6, 222, 250-51, 327, 331, 420, 453-54
and existential propositions, **L12**: 288, 299-300, 373-74, 422-23, 445-46
epistemological, **L12**: 456-57
in inquiry, **L12**: 487-89, 492-506; **L16**: 281-83, 325
as stimulus to thinking, **L13**: 52-53
regarding freedom, **L13**: 147, 162, 185
troubles as, **L13**: 233
artificial, **L13**: 273-74
subject-matter of, **L16**: 285, 288, 301
treatment of, **L16**: 291
identifying, **L17**: 85, 274, 446
self-set, **L17**: 446-47
Problematic situation
as basis of inquiry, **L12**: 3, 41-42, 231, 245, 279-80
in mathematics, **L12**: 401-2
Problem of China, The (B. Russell), **M15**: 215-18
Problem of Conduct, The (Taylor), **M11**: 10
"Problem of Counterfactual Conditionals, The" (Goodman), **L14**: xvi
Problems of Ageing (Cowdry), **L14**: xxiv, 341
Problems of Men, **L15**: xxviii, xxix, 153
Proceedings of the Sixth International Congress of Philosophy, **L14**: 382, 400
Proceedings of the Tenth International Congress of Philosophy, **L16**: 358n
Procès de Socrate, Le (Sorel), **L15**: 387
Process, **M12**: 260
of education, **E5**: 91
study of, **E5**: 231, 257-58
emphasis on, **E5**: 232

Process (*continued*)
nature of, **E5**: 251; **M2**: x, 17; **L1**: 333; **L7**: x
in *Cyclopedia of Education*, **M7**: 331
and product, **M14**: 99-100
in study of society, **M15**: 247, 248, 254
economic and biologic, **M15**: 248-51
as name, **L16**: 268
Process and Reality (Whitehead), **M12**: xxx; **L5**: 375-81; **L6**: 301; **L8**: 355, 358; **L11**: 147n; **L14**: 136n
Process of Government, The (A. Bentley), **L16**: xii, xv-xvi, xix, xxviii, 101n, 318
Proclus, **M2**: 167
Procrastination, **L17**: 297
Procrustes, **M12**: 220
Prodicus, **L2**: 132
Produce, **L16**: 230
Producer
compared with consumer, **L9**: 64, 83-86
artist as, **L10**: 15, 55-56, 60, 127-28, 265-66
Product, **L16**: 190
related to act, **L16**: 155-57, 160
Kantor on, **L16**: 191-92
Production, **M12**: 183; **L9**: 134, 289; **L13**: 104
and consumption, **L6**: 160-61; **L9**: 232-33
and politics, **L6**: 161-63
control of, **L6**: 341-42, 354; **L7**: 431; **L11**: 46, 278, 367; **L13**: 319
and economics, **L6**: 346-47, 358-61
problems of, **L7**: 374-75, 382, 385-86, 389-90; **L13**: 320
industrial, **L7**: 423; **L15**: 89
and distribution, **L9**: 250, 285
farm, **L9**: 287
artistic, **L10**: 280, 285, 294, 344-47
social effects of, **L11**: 28, 54, 57, 62, 522-24
improvement in, **L11**: 52, 159, 208, 365
in Marxism, **L13**: 71, 118-19, 133
machine vs. power, **L13**: 159
efficiency of, **L13**: 311-12
government restriction of, **L14**: 94
purpose of, **L17**: 21
Productive Thinking (Wertheimer), **L16**: 7n, 76n, 102n, 105, 109n
Professionalism, **M15**: 42
in education, **M15**: xxiv, 193-97
Professional school, **L11**: 172, 176, 188-89, 191-216, 538-39
vocational education's effect on, **M10**: 151-57
Profit, **L6**: 395
as business motive, **L6**: 73-74; **L7**: 403-6, 425, 431-32
defects of, **L7**: 433-34, 436-37
related to unemployment, **L9**: 65, 289
Pro-Germanism, **M10**: 261, 265, 278
Progress, **M12**: 103, 106, 146, 200-201; **M14**: 9, 19-20, 67-68, 73, 75n, 182
Kidd on, **E4**: 210-12
in Renaissance, **E5**: 13
nature of, **M5**: 75; **M10**: 234-36; **M14**: 194-99; **L7**: 69; **L17**: 153
in *Cyclopedia of Education*,

M7: 331-33
concept of, **M10**: xxvii-xxviii
intelligence applied to, **M10**: 238-43
Bacon and, **M12**: 97, 98
economic and moral, **M12**: 151-52; **L7**: 326, 328
in science, **M14**: 104
prospect for, **L14**: 112-13
indefinite, **L17**: 439

Progress and Poverty (H. George), **L3**: 359; **L9**: 61-62, 300

Progressive education, **M8**: xxxii; **M9**: xv; **L3**: xxiv-xxvi, 257-68, 330-31; **L9**: 147, 151, 153-57, 194, 198; **L11**: 175, 181, 190-216; **L13**: 378-79; **L15**: 303-4
Kurtz on, **L5**: xv-xvi
evaluation of, **L5**: 319-25
foresight and planning in, **L17**: 52
Kilpatrick and, **L17**: 52-56
origin of, **L17**: 55

Progressive Education Association, **L3**: 257n; **L11**: 181n, 593; **L17**: 558

Progressive integration, **L9**: 432, 439

Progressive party, **M11**: 146, 149, 267; **L6**: xvii, 175, 393-94, 405
conference of, **L6**: 173-74, 355-56, 440-41
and Revenue bill, **L6**: 392

Progressives
in Teachers Union, **L9**: 323, 324, 335, 337, 340, 342

Progressivism, **L6**: 234-35
reception of, **L13**: 17, 18
weakness of, **L13**: 100-101

Progress of the Human Mind (Condorcet), **M10**: 57

Prohibition, **M15**: 101; **L2**: 317-18; **L3**: 184-85; **L6**: 65, 231, 239
and politics, **L6**: 183-84, 249-50

Projection
psychological, **M10**: 314
in esthetic vision, **L10**: 254-55

Project method
in USSR, **L17**: 54-55

Projects
educative, **L8**: 291-92

Prokofiev, Sergei Sergeyevich, **L10**: xxi

Prolegomena to Ethics (T. Green), **E3**: 17, 21-24; **E5**: 25; **L17**: 5

Proletarian art, **L10**: 194, 303, 319, 332n, 346-47

Proletariat, **L11**: 5, 60; **L13**: 126, 133-34
Communists on, **L11**: 331, 383, 498

Promised Land, The (Antin), **M10**: 184

Promise of American Politics, The (T. V. Smith), **L17**: 115-18

Promotion
school, **E5**: 88, 332-33; **M1**: 271

Proof, **M12**: 91; **L4**: 98, 247; **L8**: 182; **L12**: 352-57, 416-17. *See also* Consequences; Test
as type of thinking, **M1**: 163
as ideal, **L4**: xx, 113, 133, 242
of reflective thought, **L4**: 88, 90, 145-47
determination of, **L12**: 112-18
Mill's theory of, **L12**: 147, 389
nature of, **L12**: 160, 228-29, 242, 316-17, 323-24,

Proof (*continued*)
454-55, 479-80
and inference, **L12**: 424
in logics, **L16**: 187
Propaganda, **M13**: 331; **L2**: 348-49; **L6**: 130, 216, 322; **L7**: 360-61; **L11**: 51, 344, 576-78; **L13**: 145, 167-68, 297, 301; **L15**: 345, 352-53. *See also* Press
dangers of, **M11**: 108, 110; **L6**: 178
during WWI, **M11**: 118-20, 150, 151, 257, 395, 408; **L13**: 289; **L14**: 364
opposing U.S., **M11**: 153, 329
in Germany, **M11**: 158, 268, 394; **L15**: 26, 297, 350, 367
in Japan, **M11**: 178-79, 194, 195; **L6**: 203, 211
in China, **M11**: 189; **L3**: 199-200; **L17**: 30-31
about Polish question, **M11**: 245, 249, 268, 286, 306, 311, 330
in U.S., **M12**: 6, 32-33
student, **M12**: 69
in education, **M15**: xxiv; **L6**: 434; **L14**: 373
for League of Nations, **M15**: 81, 105
for outlawry of war, **M15**: 408
in Russia, **L3**: 221-22, 237, 249; **L17**: 495
opposing legislation, **L6**: 393
use of radio for, **L9**: 309
in art, **L10**: 186
effect of, **L13**: 89-90, 95, 96
and totalitarianism, **L14**: 275
for military projects, **L14**: 355-56
science used in, **L16**: 393
exposure to, **L17**: 45, 46
Proper names, **L12**: 354, 363-64. *See also* Singular; This, **L12**
Properties
as predicable, **L12**: 140-41
logics on, **L16**: 162, 164
Cohen on, **L16**: 194-95
Kaufmann on, **L16**: 198
C. Morris on, **L16**: 217
in semiotic, **L16**: 219, 238
produce stimuli, **L16**: 225-26
nature of, **L16**: 278, 346, 356
Property, **M12**: 183-84, 188; **M14**: 82-83, 169
in *Dictionary of Philosophy*, **M2**: 215
in primitive groups, **M5**: 29-31, 50, 82; **L7**: 28-30, 76, 129
related to happiness, **M5**: 435-37
social aspects of, **M5**: 439-43
ownership and use of, **M5**: 492-95
in Germany, **M8**: 174-75
and individualism, **L2**: 274
and government, **L2**: 292-93
and capitalism, **L6**: 364-65, 368; **L7**: 375, 394, 429
and medieval church, **L7**: 136-37
courts on, **L7**: 415-17, 425-26
private, **L11**: 7, 8, 53-54, 549
significance of, **L13**: 104, 291
Jefferson and Locke on, **L13**: 177
physical vs. psychological, **L15**: 112-17
sacredness of, **L17**: 398
Prophets
as moralizing agents, **M5**: 90-91, 96-97, 100-101, 104; **L7**: 83, 87-88, 91-92, 95
Proportion
esthetic, **L10**: 76, 202, 296

Proposals
vs. assertions, **L9**: 304
Proposition, **L10**: 139; **L14**: xvi. *See also* Universal proposition, **L12**; Valuation-judgment
Dewey on, **M6**: xv-xvi; **L16**: 188-89, 208
in *Cyclopedia of Education*, **M7**: 333-34
Peirce on, **M10**: 73-74
Russell on, **M10**: 415; **L16**: 38, 200-202
hypothetical, **L11**: 95-97, 99, 101-4, 118-20, 122, 124, 126; **L12**: 298-305
singular, **L11**: 101-3, 122-23; **L12**: 249, 255-56, 267-68, 290-93
generic, **L11**: 101-4, 119-20, 124-25
existential, **L11**: 103; **L12**: 373-74, 422-23, 445-46; **L14**: 61
general, **L11**: 118-23
nature of, **L12**: 24-25, 114-18, 309, 364-65; **L13**: 211, 321; **L14**: 178, 187-88; **L16**: xxxiii, 11-12, 192, 353, 446
positive, **L12**: 90
and symbols, **L12**: 123, 137-39, 207n, 214, 245, 261, 340, 423-24
operational, **L12**: 144, 167-68, 182, 197-98, 204, 206, 219, 231; **L14**: 181
simple, **L12**: 150-53, 335, 340
primitive, **L12**: 151, 157-58, 314-15, 403-4
declarative, **L12**: 162-64, 238-43
and sentence, **L12**: 174, 284-89
impersonal, **L12**: 190-91
contrary, **L12**: 191-92
subcontrary, **L12**: 193-94
subalternate, **L12**: 194-95
contradictory, **L12**: 196-98
particular, **L12**: 289-90
disjunctive, **L12**: 305-7
relational, **L12**: 307-9
compound, **L12**: 335, 340
reflexive, **L12**: 360-63
causal, **L12**: 449-50, 454-57
about valuations, **L13**: 201-2, 212-13, 217-18, 242-43, 246
matter-of-fact, **L13**: 208
appraisal of, **L13**: 222, 237
scientific, **L13**: 236
grounded, **L13**: 242
instrumental character of, **L14**: 46-47, 57, 174-79, 182-83
observational, **L14**: 54, 170-71
verification of, **L14**: 55, 59
Cohen and Nagel on, **L16**: 13-17
Carnap on, **L16**: 17-32
treatments of, **L16**: 32, 208-9
Ducasse on, **L16**: 35-36
Tarski on, **L16**: 40
logics on, **L16**: 45, 162
status of, **L16**: 180
Lewis on, **L16**: 193n
Kaufmann on, **L16**: 196-98
Moore on, **L16**: 203-7
as name, **L16**: 268
forming, **L17**: 482-83
de facto, **L17**: 483-84
Propositional function, **L11**: 122
"Propositions, Truth, and the Ultimate Criterion of Truth" (Ducasse), **L16**: 36n
"Propositions, Warranted Assertibility, and Truth," **L14**: x, xv-xvi
Propriety, **M5**: 107, 110-11; **L7**: 98, 101-2; **L10**: 202

Proprioceptor nerves, **L15**: 78
Prose, **L10**: 91, 244-46
Prosser, C. A., **M7**: 465
Protagoras (Plato), **L2**: 127, 130n, 133, 134
Protagoras, **E4**: 134; **M2**: 245; **M3**: 383; **M4**: 20; **M5**: 8; **M11**: 12; **L2**: 135; **L5**: 264; **L7**: 10, 163; **L8**: xin; **L17**: 177
Protestantism, **M8**: 151, 184-85; **M9**: 301; **M11**: 24, 26n, 123-24, 286; **M12**: 105; **M15**: 47, 318; **L2**: 163, 166; **L8**: 357; **L11**: 116, 474; **L15**: 95-96, 189, 216; **L17**: 438
  vs. Roman Catholicism, **M7**: 216; **L9**: 45-46
  as movement, **L7**: 140-41
  and family, **L7**: 443
  in art, **L10**: 115, 322
  and individualism, **L17**: 19, 380
Protestant Reformation, **M7**: 134; **M8**: 155; **M9**: 291; **L1**: 334; **L7**: 75, 140-41, 145, 443; **L16**: 408
Proudhon, Pierre Joseph, **M12**: 188
Proust, Marcel, **L10**: xvii
Providence
  related to politics, **L6**: 157, 158, 240
Prudence, **E3**: 306-7
Prussian
  philosophy, **M11**: xvii
  education, **M11**: 54-57, 61; **L17**: 27
  science, **M11**: 99
  nationalism, **M11**: 110
  Silesia, **M11**: 286
  future, **M11**: 326
  state, **M12**: 188-89, 195
Prussianism, **M10**: 159, 179
Prussian Poland, **M11**: xiv, 266, 281
Pseudo-idealism, **M13**: 418
Pseudo-intellectualism, **M13**: 418
Pseudo-time, **M12**: 223-24
Psyche, **M1**: xiii; **L5**: 158; **L16**: 122, 124
Psychiatry, **L5**: 35-36, 238; **L16**: 412
Psychical
  vs. physical, **E1**: 94-98, 100, 103, 179; **M9**: 356-60
  as form of action, **E3**: 230
  related to educational psychology, **E5**: 173-74, 309-19
  Sidgwick on, **M4**: 244
  distance, **L10**: xxix, 262-63
Psychical states, **M7**: xvii
  nature of, **M7**: 34-38
  treatment of, in psychology, **M7**: 50-55
Psychic Factor, The (Van Norden), **E5**: 342, 345
Psychic Factors of Civilization, The (L. Ward), **E4**: 200-210
Psychoanalysis, **M14**: 27, 61, 93, 106, 173
Psychoanalytic art criticism, **L10**: viii, 319-20
Psycho-epistemology, **M15**: 17-19
Psychological
  point of view, **E2**: xxiii; **E5**: xvii-xviii, 169-70
  science, **E3**: 228; **E5**: 94, 377
  ethics, **E5**: 54-55
  process, **E5**: 85, 294
  factors, **E5**: 165, 224, 229
  in *Johnson's Cyclopaedia*, **E5**: 347-50
  Conant on, **E5**: 356-58
  analysis, **M3**: 27-32
  Royce on, **M7**: 66-67, 72

adaptation, **L2**: 223-25
ecology, **L16**: 125n
"Psychological Atomism" (Münsterberg), **M10**: 52
Psychological Review, **L17**: 548
Psychologic Foundations of Education (Harris), **E5**: 372-85
Psychologies of 1930 (Murchison), **L5**: 218n
Psychologism
in *Dictionary of Philosophy*, **M2**: 215
Psychologists, **M12**: 210; **L10**: xi, 27, 73, 210
vs. biologists, **E5**: 366-67
on sign, **L16**: 137n, 212
on habit, **L17**: 204-5
Psychologist's fallacy, **M1**: 118; **L10**: 128-29, 358; **L14**: 164
Psychology, **E1**: xxiv; **E2**: 5; **E4**: xviii; **L6**: xii, xiii
Schneider on, **E2**: xxiii-xxvi
Psychology (W. James), **M7**: 327, 369
Psychology, **M12**: 157-58; **L1**: 42, 181-84, 224, 231, 242, 252, 284, 319-20, 365; **L3**: 9; **L4**: 27; **L10**: 346, 364; **L11**: 14, 461; **L13**: 162, 222, 247; **L14**: 379; **L16**: 4, 105n, 117n, 233n
Dewey's use of, **E1**: xxx-xxxi; **E2**: xxiii, xxvi; **M1**: xi-xiii, 119n, 130n; **M10**: xxxiv-xxxv; **M11**: ix; **L4**: x; **L7**: x, xxii; **L14**: 38-41
physiological, **E1**: xxxii, 52, 94-98, 194-95, 200-203; **E3**: 91; **M1**: xi-xiv
old and new, **E1**: 48-51, 58-60; **E2**: xxiii, xxiv; **M1**: 68-72; **M10**: 58-63; **M12**: 128, 206, 209; **M14**: 95, 102, 107-8; **L5**: 237-38; **L11**: 83, 187, 434, 506, 511
teaching and study of, **E1**: 82-88; **E3**: 90; **E5**: 277-80; **M1**: ix; **M2**: 56-57; **L17**: 14, 187
related to philosophy, **E1**: 122-25, 144-67, 174-75, 183-84; **E2**: 3, 4; **E5**: 22-23; **M1**: 121-22; **M10**: 362; **M12**: 205; **L4**: xiii-xiv, xvi; **L6**: 489; **L14**: 11
task of, **E1**: 130-31; **M13**: 392
related to logic, **E1**: 174-75; **M2**: 309-13; **L12**: 28-29, 43, 72-74, 110, 153, 285; **L14**: xvii; **L16**: xxxiin, 167, 193n, 276, 443-45
as science, **E2**: 3, 7-17, 25-26; **E4**: 200-202; **E5**: 22-23; **M14**: 35, 104, 221-22; **L4**: viii; **L8**: xi, xv-xvii; **L17**: 43
related to perception, **E2**: 140-41; **L15**: 310-11
methods and subject-matter of, **E2**: 362-63; **M10**: 314; **L5**: 410-11; **L12**: 419-20, 508; **L16**: 63, 67, 78, 82n, 122-26, 136, 269, 275
Scotch, **E3**: 191-92
mechanistic, **E5**: xvi
educational, **E5**: 77, 372-85, 443, 445, 446; **M9**: x-xii, 33, 202, 325; **L5**: 31-36; **L9**: 150-51, 155, 179, 183, 191, 409; **L11**: 203-4, 580
concepts in, **E5**: 96; **M12**: 245-46; **L6**: xii, 7, 37; **L13**: 329
Van Norden on, **E5**: 345
of feeling, **E5**: 358-67
rational, **E5**: 376; **M1**: 128n
in mathematics, **E5**: 428-29

Psychology (*continued*)
schools of, **M1**: xii; **L5**: 34-35, 222-30
child, **M1**: xxi, 132-33, 175-77; **M3**: 210-15; **M9**: 180, 202, 325
individual vs. social, **M1**: 113-14; **M10**: 55
analytic, **M1**: 120-22; **L17**: 422
dynamic, **M1**: 130n
social, **M1**: 131, 146-50; **M8**: 178; **M10**: xxxiv-xxxv, 53-58; **M14**: 3, 44-46, 60-62, 95, 102, 107-8; **L2**: 458-59; **L5**: 238; **L14**: 40; **L17**: 54, 422-28
Witmer on, **M2**: 118
as method of ethics, **M3**: 59-61
in 1910 *How We Think*, **M6**: xxiii-xxiv
James's, **M6**: 93, 99; **M12**: 221; **L4**: xviii; **L5**: 158-59; **L14**: 39, 155-67, 337-40; **L15**: 10-15, 18, 39, 147, 398n
behavioristic, **M7**: 52-55, 390-408; **M13**: 39; **L5**: 218-28, 234-35, 483
associational, **M7**: 136; **L5**: 169; **L10**: 104-7; **L11**: 32, 76-81
in Germany, **M7**: 137-41
concepts of, **M7**: 414
introspective, **M10**: 57-58; **L5**: 230-33
of war, **M10**: 271-80; **M11**: xvi-xvii, 107-16, 120, 360
of Japan and China, **M11**: xviii-xix, 174-76, 195, 206-12
of motivation, **M11**: 10-17
of industry, **M11**: 333-35
sensationalistic, **M11**: 345, 346; **L5**: 169
of crowd, **M12**: 53-58
malicious, **M12**: 126-27; **L9**: 241
evolutionary hypothesis of, **M12**: 208-9
Bergson's, **M12**: 221
as basis of Russell's theories, **M12**: 245
defects in, **M12**: 259; **L16**: 88n, 149, 247, 249, 366
and environment, **M13**: 381
of meaning, **M13**: 393
related to morals, **M14**: 10-11, 66; **L9**: 241
of habit, **L2**: 273, 334-36
of individualism, **L2**: 290
of private consciousness, **L2**: 297
related to religion, **L4**: 244; **L9**: 3, 57
of work, **L5**: 236-42
experimental, **L5**: 238
functional, **L5**: 479
of experience, **L6**: 330-32
related to esthetics, **L10**: 37, 80, 109, 127, 199, 252-53, 260-67
Peirce's, **L11**: 93, 481; **L15**: 150
related to ageing, **L14**: 343-44, 348-50
dualism in, **L15**: 365
as basis for values, **L15**: 445-47
Bentley on, **L16**: xx, xxv
positions held by, **L16**: 83n, 111, 115, 243n
terminology of, **L16**: 93n, 132n, 266, 270, 307, 347
of Kantor, **L16**: 190-91
divisions of, **L17**: 42, 54
Hughes on, **L17**: 42-43
Psychology and Life (Münsterberg), **M1**: 135
Psychology and Logic (Kantor), **L16**: 190-92

"Psychology and Philosophic Method," **M1**: xii
"Psychology and Social Practice," **M1**: xii
Psychology of Child Development, The (I. King), **M3**: 299n
Psychology of Number, The (Dewey and McLellan), **E5**: xxiii-xxvii, xxxiii-xxxiv, l-li, lxiii
Psycho-physical, **L1**: 134-35, 190, 198, 201-6, 239, 264
  parallelism, **M7**: 136
  dualism, **M15**: 367; **L17**: xxix-xxx
Psycho-physic organism, **E5**: 304-9
Psycho-physics, **M7**: 139
Ptolemaic theory, **M8**: xix; **M15**: 48, 314
Ptolemy, **L8**: 34, 128; **L14**: 393
Pubescence, **M1**: 215-17
Public
  attitudes of, **M5**: 57; **L7**: 52; **L16**: 393, 408, 410
  welfare, **L2**: 167
  Lippmann on, **L2**: 213-20
  and private, **L2**: 243-47, 265-68; **L7**: 336-37
  government and, **L2**: 252-56, 275-79, 283
  and political agencies, **L2**: 257, 259-60, 277
  designation of, **L2**: 260-75; **L7**: xx
  and ownership, **L2**: 273-74
  inchoate, **L2**: 303
  education of, **L2**: 305-6
  eclipse of, **L2**: 307, 311, 316-17, 320, 351
  problem of, **L2**: 313, 330, 351, 365, 370
  publicity and, **L2**: 339-42, 371-72
  Bridgman on, **L16**: 170n
Public agency and control
  ethical aspects of, **M5**: 480-504
Public and Its Problems, The, **E4**: xxii; **M1**: xxi; **M9**: xii; **L5**: xvi; **L7**: xv, xix; **L13**: 176; **L17**: xxiv
  Gouinlock on, **L2**: xix, xxiii-xxxv
  1946 introduction to, **L2**: 375-81
Publications, **M12**: 5, 10, 73; **L15**: 87-88, 362
  in U.S., **M12**: 12-14
  Chinese language reform in, **M12**: 24
  suppression of, **M12**: 46, 69
Public Buildings Administration, **L14**: 255-57
Public Education Association, **M10**: 144n
Public Information, Committee on, **M10**: 15-16; **M11**: 150, 151, 257, 394, 395
Publicity. *See also* Press
  Baldwin on, **E5**: 395-97
  as deterrent, **M5**: 465-66
  T. Roosevelt's use of, **M11**: 145
  about U.S., **M11**: 150-55
  for Polish affairs, **M11**: 255-59, 306, 309-12, 325-28
  about Washington Conference, **M13**: 171-72, 197, 203-6, 209
  and business, **M13**: 285
  and public, **L2**: 339-42, 371-72
Public Opinion (Lippmann), **M13**: 337-44
Public opinion, **L2**: 345-46
  on Far East treaties, **M13**: 85

Public opinion (*continued*)
Japanese vs. Chinese, **M13**: 256
control of, **M13**: 330
analysis of, **M13**: 339-40
effect of press on, **M13**: 340-41
Dewey on, **M13**: 343-44
Public schools. *See* Schools
Public School 26 (Indianapolis)
social settlement work at, **M8**: 340-52
Public School 45 (Indianapolis)
learning by doing at, **M8**: 255-60
Public works, **L6**: 379, 384-85, 396, 404
program for, **L6**: 353, 486-87
Public Works Administration, **L9**: 286
Puerto Rico, **L15**: 20-22
Puffendorf, Samuel, **E1**: 408; **E4**: 143
Pugnacity, **L13**: 289
Punch, **M15**: 208
Punishment, **L10**: 351
Bain on, **E3**: 329
related to morality, **E4**: 110-11, 114; **M5**: 94; **L7**: 86
reform in, **M5**: 420-21
force related to, **M10**: 248
Tolstoy on, **L17**: 382
Pupils. *See* Students
Pure
in *Dictionary of Philosophy*, **M2**: 215
mathematics, **M7**: 420, 437-39; **L4**: 120-29
logic, **M7**: 438-39
thought, **M8**: 143-44; **L4**: 67, 112, 113, 120
reason, **M12**: 124-25, 217, 235, 238, 240, 243; **M14**: 25; **L10**: 257; **L12**: 18, 31, 64, 78, 92; **L13**: 256; **L16**: 386
Purists, **L16**: 310
Puritan Evangelicism, **M11**: 336
Puritanism, **M5**: 328; **M13**: 277, 278, 303, 306; **M14**: 6, 109; **L6**: 271; **L7**: 143-44, 204, 278; **L11**: 446
Purpose, **M12**: 245; **L8**: 84. *See also* Aims; Ends
regulates thinking, **M6**: 189; **L8**: 122-23, 125-26
in art, **M13**: 363; **L10**: 31, 56, 61, 65, 68, 120-22, 235, 268, 278, 280-83, 298, 323, 334, 350, 352
defined, **L4**: 180-81, 195, 250
change of, **L4**: 186
in nature, **L4**: 196-97, 200, 201
beliefs about, **L4**: 203-5
and habit, **L7**: 185-86
and desire, **L7**: 186, 247, 308
formation of, **L13**: 43-46, 87, 223, 258, 376
in education, **L17**: 54
theory of, **L17**: 96
Purpose of History, The (Woodbridge), **M15**: 375
Purposive Evolution (Noble), **L3**: 299-304; **L4**: 197n
Purposiveness
as animal characteristic, **L16**: 136
Putilov, Aleksei Ivanovich, **L17**: 490-91, 568
Putnam, Hilary, **L14**: xvin
Pyatakov, Yuri L., **L11**: 311, 312, 322, 603; **L15**: 338-39
Pyramidal forms, **L10**: 184
Pyrrho, **L4**: x, xix, xx
Pyrrhonism, **L8**: xvii
Pythagoras, **M4**: 37; **L3**: 26; **L4**: 74; **L14**: 392, 425

Pythagoreans, **M2**: 153, 163, 167, 267; **M7**: 313; **L8**: 26

Quadrivium, **M7**: 314
Qualification, **L16**: 474
Qualitative
and common sense, **L12**: 69-72
science and, **L12**: 71, 248-49
situations as, **L12**: 74-76, 190-91, 350-51, 364-65, 441
as individual, **L12**: 201-2, 211, 218-19, 525
"Qualitative Thought," **M7**: xviiin; **L6**: 332, 495; **L10**: 126n, 197n
Qualities, **L1**: 75, 81-82, 86-87, 89, 92-96, 107-8, 115, 120, 133, 198-99, 202-6, 226-27, 253; **L3**: 85; **L6**: 426; **L12**: 519
primary, secondary, tertiary, **M6**: x, 20-21; **L4**: 97, 98, 191; **L14**: 25-28
quaternary, **M6**: 21
related to values, **M7**: 45; **L4**: 207, 212-14
constituent related to, **M15**: 24-25, 342-43, 345
Locke on, **L2**: 143-46, 154, 156-57
related to power, **L2**: 150
in science, **L4**: 43, 99, 105-6, 127, 239; **L12**: 83-84, 119-20, 151-52, 215-16; **L14**: 80-83
static, **L4**: 101
control of, **L4**: 110
subjectivity of, **L4**: 185-91, 220
and common sense, **L6**: 430
as material for art, **L10**: xiii, 45, 52, 55, 56, 80, 99, 101, 104, 131-32, 174, 196-97, 211, 217-20, 227-28, 239, 280, 297, 341
sensory, **L10**: xxviii, 107, 126-28, 263-64; **L14**: 162
judgment of, **L10**: 312, 319
as signs, **L12**: 76-77, 132, 149-50, 240, 248-49, 252, 268-69, 475
and change, **L12**: 136-37, 295-96
and magnitude, **L12**: 207
common, **L12**: 248-49, 261-62, 265, 268, 350
unique, **L12**: 294-95, 319, 350-51
immediate, **L15**: 29-32, 66-70
indeterminateness as, **L15**: 39, 40
intrinsic, **L15**: 42-44
objectivity of, **L15**: 74, 76
logics on, **L16**: 162
Quality
Peirce on, **L11**: xiv, 86-94
nature of, **L11**: 95-101
in universals, **L11**: 107, 113
of experience, **L13**: 12-13
inherent, **L13**: 214-15
significance of, **L13**: 330
relational treatment of, **L14**: 22
in nature, **L14**: 63-64, 144-45
metaphysical status of, **L14**: 105
sensible, **L14**: 171
Quantity, **E5**: 189-90; **L4**: 74, 108; **L10**: 311
concepts of, **L8**: 261
as accident, **L12**: 94, 201
role of, in science, **L16**: 370-71
Quantum mechanics, **L15**: 305
Quarrel, **L13**: 140
Queens County, N.Y., **L9**: 346, 350-53, 360-61, 378
Quest for Being (Hook), **M8**: xiv

Quest for Certainty, The, **M1**: xi; **M5**: xi; **M8**: ix; **M12**: ix; **M15**: x; **L3**: ix; **L5**: 460, 471n, 473, 475n, 486n, 490, 491, 494; **L6**: 496; **L7**: xxiv; **L8**: ix; **L10**: xviii, 323n; **L12**: xxi; **L14**: x, xviii, 7, 9, 10, 21-22, 25-26, 30, 35, 48-49, 51, 52, 65-67, 69, 147n, 148, 395n; **L15**: 400
  Toulmin on, **L4**: vii-xxii
  Kurtz on, **L5**: xi, xxv, xxvii
Questioning
  art of, **M6**: 339, 342; **L8**: 331-32, 335
Quest of the Ages, The (Haydon), **L11**: 583-84
Quick, Herbert, **L9**: 262-63
Quietism
  in *Dictionary of Philosophy*, **M2**: 216
Quincy, Mass.
  educational experiment at, **M2**: 97, 101
Quine, Willard V., **L4**: xviii; **L14**: xv, xvii; **L16**: 18, 49-50, 150
Quis custodiet ipsos custodes, **L6**: 481-82

Rabbi Ben Ezra (R. Browning), **L14**: 348
Rabelais, François, **M7**: 295
Race, **L16**: 372
  development, **E5**: 248-50
  in Germany, **M8**: 187-88
  attitude toward, **M11**: 222-23; **L7**: 66
  cultural factors in, **M13**: 438-39
  differences in, **L13**: 76
  relations, **L15**: 171, 196
Race discrimination, **L13**: xv, 153; **L15**: 282, 356-57. *See also* Prejudice
  affects Japanese-U.S. relations, **M11**: 151-54, 172, 222
  discussed at peace conference, **M11**: 158, 159
  U.S. accused of, **M11**: 177
Racine, Wis., **M7**: 461, 462
Radcliffe College, **L17**: 7, 553
Radek, Karl B., **L11**: 312, 318, 322, 603
  trial of, **L15**: 338, 345-47
Radford, William, **L5**: xv
Radical empiricism, **M7**: x, 297; **M12**: xi, 207, 217; **M15**: 335
  James's, **M6**: 94, 100; **M7**: 142-48
Radicalism, **E4**: 103-4; **M12**: 89-90, 137, 239, 255; **M13**: 429; **M14**: 115-16; **L7**: 337; **L13**: 142, 291-92
  aided by reactionaryism, **M12**: 10-11, 19-20
  Dewey's, **M14**: xxii
  in U.S., **L9**: 297, 298
  ends of, **L11**: xii, 298-99
  and liberalism, **L11**: 287, 293
  sources of, **L13**: 86
Radin, Paul, **L3**: 335-37
Radio
  Dewey's broadcasts over, **L6**: 90-98, 231-38, 341-44; **L9**: 61-65, 81-86, 309; **L11**: 158-61, 167-70, 256-57, 261-64, 326-29
  related to political convention, **L6**: 248-49
Radio in Education, National Advisory Council on, **L6**: 90n, 231n
Radio Manufacturers' Association, **L6**: 346
Rafton, Harold Robert, **L17**: 560
  on religion at Harvard, **L17**: 135, 545-47
Railroads, **M12**: 29-30, 37, 61,

65, 72-74; **L6**: 166, 233, 356, 361
and government, **L2**: 318
cases involving, **L6**: 165, 370-71, 504
economics of, **L6**: 368-71
Railway Economics, Bureau of, **L6**: 370
Ramus, Petrus, **L8**: xvii
Randall, John H., Jr., **L11**: 359; **L14**: 4, 6, 8, 75n, 88; **L17**: 522
on naturalism, **L15**: 457, 464-68
Rand School of Social Science (New York City), **L6**: 40n; **L9**: 305-6; **L15**: 378; **L17**: 429n
Rank, **M12**: 115-16
Rank and File Group
in Teachers Union, **L9**: 323-29, 334-37, 340-42
Ranke, Leopold von, **M8**: 186
Raphael, **L10**: 117, 315, 335
Raskob, John J., **L6**: 158, 161
Rasquin, Almon G., **L9**: 348
Rates
control of, **L7**: 415-17
Ratiocination, **L1**: 152, 165
Ratio idea
and series idea, **E5**: 184-85, 188-91
related to number, **E5**: 426-27
Rational, **L12**: 26
idealism, **M6**: 175; **M7**: 227
perception, **M7**: 260-61
deism, **M7**: 293
ego, **M8**: 154
knowledge, **M9**: 343-44
and empirical, **L12**: 17-18, 44, 78, 80, 194, 251n, 277-78, 304-5, 420, 426
Rationalism, **E4**: 263; **M4**: 323n; **M5**: 213-14; **M12**: xiv, 129-31; **L1**: 372; **L8**: 8, 21, 359; **L11**: 77-79, 109, 146, 147, 150; **L12**: 114, 134, 142, 162, 436, 497, 508-13; **L13**: 123; **L15**: 94; **L17**: 446. *See also A priori*, **L12**
on feelings and objects, **E4**: 264
on knowledge, **E5**: 15; **L4**: 137, 144
and sensationalism, **E5**: 16-18; **L4**: 91, 92; **L16**: 334-35
role of, **E5**: 21
on idea and fact, **M1**: 244-45
in *Dictionary of Philosophy*, **M2**: 216-18
transcendental, **M4**: 181-91; **L2**: 77
in *Cyclopedia of Education*, **M7**: 334-35, 357
and individualism, **M9**: 307-8
particular and general in, **M9**: 352-53
continental, **M10**: xxv
vs. empiricism, **M10**: 5-23; **L4**: 21, 67, 98; **L14**: 394-95; **L16**: 92n, 148n, 284, 411
effect of Kantianism on, **M10**: 13
on thought, **M10**: 16, 17
related to mathematics, **M10**: 18
rigidity of, **M12**: 135-36
in Russell's philosophy, **M12**: 239
faults of, **L4**: 92, 211; **L14**: 151
logic of, **L4**: 112-15, 123-24, 132, 133, 204-6
reaction against, **L8**: xiii, xiv; **L13**: 169; **L14**: 387
Piatt on, **L14**: 23-24
James on, **L14**: 156, 158
formalistic, **L17**: 445
study of, **L17**: 546

Rationality, **L17**: xviii, xx, xxii
emotion influences, **M7**: 397-99
in esthetics, **L10**: 174, 176, 263
freedom and, **L13**: 80
reasonable vs. arbitrary, **L13**: 225-26
need for, **L16**: 314; **L17**: 15, 17, 538
of Dewey's philosophy, **L17**: xxxii
"Rationality, Activity and Faith" (W. James), **L11**: 473
Rationalization, **M12**: 135, 138; **M13**: 421
as stage of moral development, **M5**: 15; **L7**: 13
as response to change, **L11**: 41-42
Ratner, Joseph, **L5**: 217; **L12**: 5, 405n; **L14**: 4
on new introduction to *Experience and Nature*, **L1**: 329-30, 361
contributes to Dewey's work, **L10**: 7; **L16**: 5
on Dewey's theory of knowledge, **L14**: 6, 48
edits Dewey's typescript, **L16**: 448
Ratner, Sidney
on Dewey's 1931-32 writings, **L6**: xi-xxiii
on Dewey-Bentley collaboration, **L16**: xvn, xvi, xixn, xxvii, xxxvn-xxxvin
Ratzel, Friedrich, **M13**: 311
Raub, William Longstreth, **M4**: 227-28
Rauh, Frédéric, **L5**: 502
Raup, R. Bruce, **L11**: 385
"Raven, The" (Poe), **L10**: 80
Rawls, John, **L2**: xxxv-xxxvi
Reaching
related to seeing, **E5**: 98
Reaction, **M14**: 109
elements in, **L13**: 333
as name, **L16**: 90, 269
Maxwell on, **L16**: 100
Osborn on, **L16**: 116n
C. Morris on, **L16**: 220-21
Reactionaries, **L11**: xii, 63
use of force by, **L11**: 294, 379
respond to change, **L11**: 409, 412-13
criticize education, **L15**: 257-61, 264, 269-75
Reactionaryism, **M12**: 5, 10-11, 17-21
Reading
as tool, **E5**: 255-57
teaching of, **E5**: 262-66; **M10**: 117; **L11**: 213, 240; **L17**: 329-30
in Greece, **L17**: 180
skills, **L17**: 188
oral, **L17**: 219
mechanical vs. spiritual, **L17**: 304, 306
imitation in, **L17**: 308-9
social value of, **L17**: 321
in Russia, **L17**: 494, 495
Reading circles
in Turkey, **M15**: 278, 287, 301-2
Readjustments
in school, **E5**: 453
Real
object, **M6**: 23-24
time, **M10**: 68-69
conceptions of, **M12**: 139
and ideal, **M12**: 153-54; **L1**: 310-11
meaning of term, **L14**: 25-26
definition, **L16**: 163-70, 175, 180

Real Business of Living, The (Tufts), **L15**: 322, 325
Realism, **M4**: 116-17; **M7**: 223, 348, 360, 422; **M10**: xxv, 107; **M14**: 123-24, 176, 206; **M15**: 335, 337; **L1**: 62, 127, 166, 233, 260, 285; **L3**: 398-400; **L14**: xiii, xiv
  transfigured, **E1**: 132-33
  naturalistic, **M1**: 130n
  on idea and fact, **M1**: 244-45
  in *Dictionary of Philosophy*, **M2**: 218-23
  on correspondence, **M6**: xiv, xx-xxi
  related to truth, **M6**: xiv-xvi, 33-52
  vs. idealism, **M6**: xvi-xvii, 80-85, 113-22; **M10**: 48, 336-37; **L4**: 235; **L16**: 411; **L17**: 418
  naïve vs. presentative, **M6**: 103-11; **M13**: 459
  epistemological, **M6**: 111-13; **M13**: 372; **L14**: 188; **L15**: 146
  external and internal relations in, **M6**: 138-45, 484-511
  Montague on, **M6**: 475-77
  Pitkin on, **M6**: 478-80
  Spaulding on, **M6**: 480-511
  on knowledge, **M7**: 82-83; **M10**: 26n; **L4**: xi, 18, 53; **L16**: 288
  in education, **M7**: 229-33
  and ego-centric predicament, **M7**: 445-51
  McGilvary on, **M7**: 454-60
  analytic, **M8**: 68; **M10**: 90; **M13**: 419
  growth of, **M10**: 24
  in experience, **M10**: 25-26
  monistic, dualistic, pluralistic, **M10**: 64; **M13**: 54, 55, 460-61; **M15**: 361-62
  compared with instrumentalism, **M10**: 338-65
  Drake on, **M10**: 431-39
  logical, **M15**: 368; **L11**: 108n, 111-12, 149
  school of, **L3**: 385-88
  on sense data, **L4**: 141, 142
  nature of, **L4**: 147, 191, 219; **L14**: 99; **L17**: 454
  on values, **L4**: 206; **L13**: 191
  political, **L9**: 404-5
  religious, **L9**: 422
  knowledge in, **L12**: 16, 261
  atomic, **L12**: 150-53
  apprehension in, **L12**: 168, 493-94
  theories of, **L12**: 513-18
  Dewey's relation to, **L14**: 7-8, 383
  social, **L15**: 253
  on word and thing, **L16**: 158
"Realism without Monism or Dualism," **M15**: 27, 349n, 371
Realistic
  idealism, **M8**: 68; **L14**: 290
  art, **L10**: 157, 279, 288
Realists, **M6**: xiii; **M8**: 191; **M11**: 267, 275
  failure of, **L17**: 451-52
Reality, **M2**: 296; **M4**: 254; **M13**: 413; **M15**: 18; **L1**: 52, 53, 56-57, 60, 112-13, 119-20, 126, 325, 344, 372; **L10**: 284, 292
  order and harmony of, **E1**: 292
  concepts of, **E1**: 321; **E4**: xiv; **M11**: 342; **L13**: 255; **L16**: 151, 181, 255, 358-59, 414-15
  related to experience, **M1**:

Reality (*continued*)
126-30; **M3**: 102; **M4**: 120-24
vs. belief, **M3**: 83-100
attitude of scientist toward, **M3**: 102-6
absolute, **M3**: 124; **M12**: 92, 94
Bradley on, **M4**: 50-75
McGilvary on, **M4**: 297-313
James on, **M6**: 99-100
related to knowledge and action, **M7**: 5-6
Pestalozzi on, **M7**: 378-79
ultimate, **M10**: 38-42; **M12**: 140-44; **L14**: 314-15; **L17**: 17
related to pragmatism, **M10**: 39
related to philosophy, **M10**: 46; **M11**: 42, 47, 50, 51, 364; **L14**: 289-91; **L15**: 156-62
Spencer on, **M10**: 67-68
Peirce on, **M10**: 75-78; **L5**: 470
and democracy, **M11**: 48
Bush on, **M11**: 375-78
noumenal vs. phenomenal, **M12**: 92
super-empirical, **L13**: 264
withdrawal from, **L13**: 328
and appearance, **L14**: 25, 26, 196-97; **L17**: 367n
and time, **L14**: 98-101
and causality, **L14**: 146
and thought, **L14**: 152-53
Hocking on, **L14**: 415-20, 423
relations of, **L16**: 43, 44, 286, 359
rejected, **L16**: 102, 111
as name, **L16**: 104, 258, 269
Einstein and Bohr on, **L16**: 108-9
Hartshorne on, **L16**: 166
Moore on, **L16**: 203
and self, **L17**: 155-56
Realize
McGilvary on, **M4**: 300
Realm of Essence, The (Santayana), **L3**: 287-93
Realpolitik, **M8**: 419, 475
Reals
in *Dictionary of Philosophy*, **M2**: 223-24
as name, **L16**: xxxvi, 269
in postulates, **L16**: 78-79
rejected, **L16**: 82n, 83, 89, 94
in interaction, **L16**: 114, 127
vs. terms, **L16**: 159
organized, **L16**: 261
Reason, **M12**: 97, 127, 179; **M15**: 56-58; **L1**: 61, 98, 263, 324-25; **L13**: 139; **L15**: 12, 90-91, 307
Kant's theory of, **E1**: 34-35, 40-41; **E3**: 333; **L7**: 146-47, 222-23
nature of, **E1**: 45; **M9**: 275-85; **M11**: 345-47; **L4**: 227; **L7**: xxiii; **L11**: 565-66; **L13**: 91; **L16**: 312, 326, 355, 386
principle of sufficient, **E1**: 282, 415-18
connected with freedom, **E1**: 337-38
truths of, **E1**: 392, 398-402
related to sense, **E3**: 227-28, 333-35; **L17**: 157
related to knowledge, **E5**: 5, 6; **M9**: 353; **L4**: 71, 72, 136, 140, 154
in judgment, **E5**: 323
and understanding, **M2**: 259-61
Grotius on, **M3**: 51
Greeks on, **M4**: 35; **M5**: 108-12, 118-19, 123-28; **M9**: 260-63; **L7**: 99-103, 109-10, 114-19

Santayana on, **M4**: 233-34
Plato on, **M5**: 123-24; **M9**: 271-72, 275; **L7**: 114-15
Bergson on, **M6**: 130
Locke on, **M7**: 57, 58
Fichte's formula for, **M8**: 173, 188
absolute, **M8**: 188; **L13**: 148-49
Aristotle on, **M9**: 271-72; **L4**: 145n
attitudes toward, **M9**: 273-75
related to action, **M9**: 340; **L17**: 383
rationalism on, **M10**: 12
related to experience, **M10**: 15-18; **M12**: 134
idealism on, **M10**: 19-21
perception of, **M12**: 124; **L4**: 35, 44, 231, 235; **L7**: 217; **L11**: 7, 9, 17, 20, 72-76, 282, 403; **L14**: 191-92
and intelligence, **M12**: 134-35; **L7**: xxiv-xxv
pure, **M12**: 217, 235, 238, 240, 243; **M14**: 25; **L12**: 18, 31, 64, 78, 92; **L13**: 256
as element in change, **M12**: 259
of J. Robinson, **M13**: 421
in belief, **M15**: 51
and science, **L2**: 221-25; **L7**: 145; **L16**: 365, 409
and state, **L2**: 248
and law, **L2**: 270-72
debates about, **L4**: x, xiii, xix-xxii; **L6**: 304, 488-91
forming of, **L4**: 14, 40-43
function of, **L4**: 21, 22, 28, 43, 88, 90, 169-70, 205, 229-30, 235, 241; **L7**: 386, 401
related to morals, **L4**: 47, 49; **L7**: 13, 41-43, 64, 146, 155
J. Marsh on, **L5**: 183, 185-89
related to law, **L7**: 130-33; **L13**: 80
and desire, **L7**: 187, 191; **L14**: 323-24
related to esthetics, **L10**: xii, 39-41, 257-58, 263, 265, 278, 293-99, 324-25, 337, 342, 348
Hogben on, **L11**: 391-92
Hutchins on, **L11**: 391-92, 402, 404-5
vs. cause, **L13**: 17-18
Hume on, **L13**: 161
in Enlightenment, **L14**: 100; **L16**: 372
Cohen on, **L16**: 195
value of, **L17**: 334-35

Reasonableness, **M14**: 48-49, 55, 134-38, 149

Reason and Goodness (Blanshard), **L13**: xi

Reason and Nature (M. R. Cohen), **L6**: xiv-xv, 299-304, 488

"Reason and Nature" (Hook), **L6**: xvn

"Reason and Violence—Some Truths and Myths about John Dewey" (Hook), **L17**: xxviiin

Reason in Art (Santayana), **M11**: 385; **L10**: 231n

Reasoning, **L11**: 215. *See also* Discourse, **L12**; Meaning-symbols, **L12**; Symbols, **L12**
and meaning, **E1**: 180-81
as aspect of thinking, **E2**: 178, 192-201; **M1**: 163
and knowledge, **M6**: 239-41; **L8**: 203-5
in childhood, **M7**: 369-76
defined, **M13**: 64n; **L17**: 253
and reflection, **M13**: 487-88

Reasoning (*continued*)
intellectual and affective, **L2**: 105-7
control of, **L8**: 259-67
as ordered discourse, **L12**: 60, 115-16, 164, 276-77, 379, 428
by disjunction, **L12**: 193
circular, **L12**: 264
novelty in, **L12**: 313-14
image needed for, **L17**: 246, 253-54
Rebellion, **M14**: 114
Recapitulation theory
of education, **E5**: 248; **M1**: xv; **M9**: 78-82, 209
in logical thought, **M1**: xiv
related to manual training, **M1**: 232-35
Recent Social Trends in the United States (President's Research Committee), **L9**: 229-36
Receptivity, **L10**: 51-52, 58-59; **L14**: 118
Recht, **L17**: 102
Reciprocity, **L14**: 118; **L16**: 115n
Recitation
conduct of, **E5**: 339; **L8**: 333-37
in education, **M1**: 33-35; **M3**: 347
in training thought, **M6**: 338-47
Rousseau on, **M8**: 228
negative aspects of, **L8**: 154-55; **L17**: 282
false ideas about, **L8**: 326-27
functions of, **L8**: 327-33, 340-41
teacher's role in, **L8**: 337-40
power of, **L17**: 313, 342
Recognition, **M8**: 25; **L1**: 247-48; **L12**: 154-55
desire for, **M5**: 85-86; **L7**: 78
as cognition, **L4**: 148
vs. perception, **L10**: xxiv, 29, 58-59, 118, 150, 180, 182, 258, 261, 263, 279
value of, **L17**: 68
Recollection
vs. perception, **M7**: 8
as mediated, **L12**: 223-27
Reconciliation, **L10**: 190
Reconstruction, **M3**: 169-70
in religion, **E4**: 97, 99-100, 103, 105
of society, **M5**: 87-88; **L7**: xi, xix, 80
of education, **M9**: 82-86, 325, 341; **M11**: xi, 58-69, 88-92, 333-35, 348; **L9**: 393-95
after WWI, **L13**: 314
of experience, **L13**: 380
Reconstruction Finance Corporation, **L6**: 386, 397-98; **L9**: 125, 253, 262, 286; **L11**: 286, 339
Reconstruction in Philosophy, **M11**: ix, xvii, 341-49; **M12**: ix-x, xiv, xviii, xx-xxi; **M13**: xviii; **M15**: x; **L7**: xviii, xix, xxi-xxii; **L8**: ix; **L10**: ix, xxxii; **L11**: 596-97; **L14**: x, 386-89, 394-96, 398, 401-2, 405, 408-9
anticipated in New Psychology, **E1**: xxxi
1948 introduction to, **M12**: 256-77
reason in, **L7**: xxiv-xxv
Reconstruction in philosophy, **M12**: x, xix
historical factors of, **M12**: 95

problems of, **M12**: 103-4, 260, 265-77
as essential, **M12**: 108
scientific factor in, **M12**: 110
function of, **M12**: 137-38
in moral conceptions, **M12**: 172
social philosophy and, **M12**: 187
intelligence in, **M12**: 258
Recreation, **L16**: 366
importance of, **M2**: 91-92
in Russia, **L3**: 214
affects character, **L9**: 191-92
in art, **L10**: 60, 66, 113
Recurrence
esthetic, **L10**: 175
nature of, **L12**: 246-52
Red-baiting
and Teachers Union, **L9**: 316, 322, 326, 330, 339-41
Red Cross, **M11**: 231, 393
involved in Polish question, **M11**: xvi, 250, 316-19, 327, 329
French, **M11**: 250
Redintegration, **E2**: 88
Rediscovery of America, The (W. Frank), **L5**: 72
Reductio ad absurdum, **L12**: 301, 503
Reductionism, **L14**: xiii; **L15**: 231n
Reductive fallacy, **L10**: 319-20
Reed, Charles L., **L5**: 506
Reenforcement
as esthetic quality, **L10**: 103, 151, 165, 172, 181, 186, 235
Rees, J. R., **L14**: 245
Reference, **M13**: 380
existential, **L12**: 59-60, 80, 137-38, 174-75, 188, 254-55, 283-84, 313, 353-54, 374-75, 378, 411-14, 417, 423-24, 475, 513-14, 517-18
of signs, **L15**: 132-35, 148, 150
as name, **L16**: 269, 303n, 308
References
on history of education, **L17**: 162-64, 169, 174-75, 181, 186
on psychology for teachers, **L17**: 188-90, 192, 196, 200, 204, 207
Referent
Ogden and Richards on, **L16**: 300-302
determination of, **L16**: 303-5, 308
Reflection, **L1**: 303-4, 340-41, 387-89; **L13**: 285; **L16**: 320
involved in logical theory, **M2**: 300-302
in pragmatism, **M10**: xvii-xix; **M13**: 480, 486-90
related to experience, **M10**: 322-65, 368
as instrumental, **M13**: 27
in representation, **M13**: 51
stages of, **M13**: 58, 445, 490-91
philosophic, **M13**: 413
and cognitive process, **M15**: 338-39
as reconstructive, **L7**: xi
development of, **L7**: xiii, xxiii
and ends, **L7**: 184-86
in esthetics, **L10**: 21, 151, 198, 263-64, 269, 295, 297, 316
observation and memory as, **L13**: 41
meaning of, **L13**: 59
free, **L13**: 321
Reflections on Violence (Sorel), **L15**: 387

Reflective
approbation, **E4**: 292-95
interest, **E5**: 311
inquiry, **M4**: xvi, xviii-xix
morality, **L7**: 162-66, 235-37, 253-55
Reflective thinking, **M2**: 298-300; **L12**: 28-29; **L16**: 339. *See also* Inquiry, **L12**
nature of, **L4**: 88, 90, 112, 117, 174-77; **L8**: 114-15, 117-20, 171-76, 193-95
role of, **L4**: 98, 137, 144-50, 206-9
analysis of, **L8**: xii-xviii, 196-209
vs. belief, **L8**: 116-17
phases of, **L8**: 120-23, 200-208
as educational aim, **L8**: 125-39, 176-82
illustrations of, **L8**: 187-90
judgment in, **L8**: 210-20
control of, **L8**: 344-45
Reflex action
in perception, **M7**: 25-26
Reflex arc, **E3**: 212-14; **M1**: xiii; **L6**: xii, 9
as concept in psychology, **E5**: xviii-xix, 96-109
unit, **E5**: 305
"Reflex Arc Concept in Psychology, The," **M6**: xi; **L5**: 479; **L7**: ix; **L14**: xii; **L16**: 101n, 221n
Reflexes, **L11**: 513
Reflexive proposition, **L12**: 360-63
Reform, **M12**: 182, 183, 192
meaning of, **L7**: 251
monetary, **L9**: 296-97
in Canton, **L17**: 32-33
as stimulus, **L17**: 66
Reformation, **M5**: 82; **M7**: 134; **M8**: 155; **M9**: 291; **L1**: 334; **L7**: 75, 140-41, 145, 443; **L16**: 408
Reform Bill of 1867 (Great Britain), **L17**: 492, 568-69
Refugees, **L17**: 150
Regency
governs Poland, **M11**: 268-71, 274-77, 292-95
Regeneration, **M2**: 180
Regimentation
allied with loyalty, **L9**: 87
in government, **L9**: 88
economic, **L9**: 89-90, 206-7
Reichenbach, Hans, **L13**: ix; **L14**: 5, 15, 61
Dewey replies to, **L14**: 19-28, 58-59
on theory of knowledge, **L14**: 63
Reid, Herbert A., **L11**: 487
Reid, John R., **L16**: 169, 175
Reid, Thomas, **E1**: 271; **E3**: 191; **M2**: 180; **L12**: 68
Reify
in *Dictionary of Philosophy*, **M2**: 224
Rein, Wilhelm, **L17**: 568
Reinsch, Paul Samuel, **L3**: 200
Reiser, Oliver L.
on science and philosophy, **L11**: 432-37
Relation, **L2**: 156-57; **L8**: 225-26, 264; **L15**: 79n. *See also* Connection
as ideal, **E1**: 185-86
principles of, **E5**: 246; **L4**: 164, 165
in *Dictionary of Philosophy*, **M2**: 224-30
internal and external, **M10**: 12n

of Brogan, **M13**: 25n
discovery of, **L2**: 141-43; **L4**: 67, 74, 82, 84, 144, 214, 216, 219, 235, 239
substances in, **L2**: 144-46
connection as distinct from, **L2**: 148, 149
as scientific subject-matter, **L4**: 74, 197-99; **L12**: 119
measurement of, **L4**: 100-107
formal, **L4**: 118, 119
vs. individuality, **L4**: 189, 190, 193
necessary to value, **L4**: 207, 212-13
as interaction, **L10**: 31, 155-57
in art, **L10**: 106-7, 121, 139, 142, 158, 205-6, 216-17, 287; **L14**: 37-38
ambiguity of term, **L12**: 60-62, 328-29, 397-99
in Greek logic, **L12**: 96
of meanings, **L12**: 115-16, 137-38
whole-part, **L12**: 203-6
propositions as, **L12**: 307-9
terms as, **L12**: 332-33, 347-48
mathematical, **L12**: 391-414, 425-26
empirical vs. rational, **L14**: 20, 23
Carnap on, **L16**: 30
Tarski on, **L16**: 41-42
as name, **L16**: 93n, 140n, 102, 269
inter-cultural, **L17**: 35
philosophical, **L17**: 36

Relational theory
applied to valuing, **L16**: 348-51
in physics, **L16**: 363

"Relation of Sense Data to Physics, The" (B. Russell), **M8**: xx

"Relation of Theory to Practice in Education, The," **M3**: xvii

Relationship, **L12**: 396-401, 407, 463
human, **L7**: xxviii; **L13**: 335-36

Relativism, **M7**: 435; **M10**: 24; **M13**: 417; **L1**: xx; **L7**: 336; **L15**: 162-63

Relativity, **L1**: 347
of knowledge, **E1**: 19-22; **M4**: 133-34
of feeling, **E1**: 22-25, 29, 31-33
in perception, **M10**: 29-30
theory of, **L4**: 102, 116, 117; **L13**: 158; **L15**: 235, 305, 507; **L16**: xxxiv, 76n, 286, 340, 414, 454
in history, **L11**: 291-92

Relativity in Man and Society (A. Bentley), **L16**: 318

Relevance, **L12**: 115, 235. *See also* Data, **L12**
of Dewey, **L17**: xvii-xxxiii

Relief
farmers' need for, **L9**: 249-51
government role in, **L9**: 253-54, 259-60, 268, 271-72

Religion, **M11**: 337; **M12**: 139, 200, 201; **M14**: 6-7, 180-81, 226-27; **L1**: 41, 133; **L8**: xvii, 45; **L11**: xv, 283, 549; **L15**: 171, 334. *See also* Christianity; Church; Protestantism; Roman Catholic church
Green on, **E3**: 34-35
course in, **E3**: 91
Hegel's philosophy of, **E3**: 187-90
fundamentals of, **E4**: 3, 5-6, 365; **M10**: 22; **M15**: 3-7; **L9**: xv-xvi, 3-8, 23, 27,

Religion (*continued*)
45-46, 215-16, 220, 221, 228, 414-17, 423; **L13**: 71
conflicts with science, **E4**: 6, 15; **M12**: 264-66; **L3**: 19, 27; **L4**: 33-34, 247; **L9**: xv-xvi, 3, 22-23, 27, 37, 42-43, 221, 418-20; **L11**: 135, 141-42, 552; **L13**: 123, 152, 182; **L15**: 56, 93, 157, 184-85, 189, 271-72, 376-77, 507-8; **L16**: 371, 408-9, 418; **L17**: 13-14, 412
redirection of, **E4**: 96-105; **L4**: 242-48
and society, **E4**: 211; **M5**: 81; **M11**: x, 21; **M13**: 257; **L2**: 261-62, 266, 340-42; **L5**: 71-72; **L7**: 74-75; **L9**: xviii-xix, 3, 6, 38-42, 43-46, 53-58, 295, 424, 427, 428, 431
in D'Arcy, **E5**: 30-31
in Baldwin, **E5**: 408-9
related to education, **M4**: 165-75; **L17**: 167
Santayana on, **M4**: 236-37; **M10**: 311; **L9**: 13
philosophy's relation to, **M4**: 257; **M11**: 44, 51, 341, 344, 349, 383; **M12**: 237-38; **L4**: 13, 42-44, 54, 61-62; **L8**: 25-26
primitive, **M5**: 34-36; **M15**: 240; **L4**: 3, 9-12; **L7**: 33-35, 50
quality of, **M5**: 84; **M15**: 42, 43; **L2**: 223; **L4**: 128, 186, 188, 194, 200, 203-7, 216, 219-21, 226, 233, 234, 238; **L7**: 77; **L9**: xiv, xxiv, 43; **L10**: xv, 12, 13, 26, 36-38, 79, 114-15, 274-75; **L16**: 396-97, 417, 471; **L17**: 16, 375, 533
Greek, **M5**: 108-10, 129; **L7**: 99-101, 120-22
morality's relation to, **M5**: 181-83; **L7**: 74-75, 82, 85-86, 90, 92-95; **L9**: xxvii-xxviii, 5-6, 16-17, 28-29
medieval, **M9**: 301; **L7**: 135-37
controversies and wars in, **M11**: 58; **M15**: x, xiii, 47-50; **L2**: 163-66; **L15**: 51-52
in U.S., **M11**: 124, 241
in Japan, **M11**: 170-72
in China, **M11**: 211
of Poles, **M11**: 260, 263, 277, 285-87, 398
development of, **M12**: 105-6; **L1**: 43-45; **L7**: 140-41; **L9**: xv, xviii-xix, xxix, xxxi, 3-6, 40-41, 43, 45, 48-49, 216; **L14**: 77-80; **L17**: 93, 379
related to art and esthetics, **M12**: 248; **L9**: 17, 29-30, 54, 431, 436, 437; **L10**: 157, 199, 296, 329-32, 338, 340, 350; **L13**: 70, 169-70
in Turkey, **M15**: 128-30, 132
in Mexico, **L2**: 194-201, 208
guides conduct, **L4**: 25, 31, 46, 57, 86; **L9**: 12-13
environment and, **L4**: 45, 186; **L9**: 17-19, 224-25, 227
two-realm scheme in, **L4**: 47, 76, 186
Kant's relation to, **L4**: 48, 49
authority of, **L4**: 52; **L15**: 230-31, 235
Kurtz on, **L5**: xxxi-xxxii
attitude toward, **L5**: 47-49; **L13**: xv; **L16**: 390-94
Dewey's view of, **L5**: 149-50, 153-54; **L9**: xii-xiii, xxiii-xxiv

Russian treatment of, **L5**: 355-62
Whitehead on, **L8**: 357-58
vs. religious experience, **L9**: xi-xii, xiv-xv, xxvi, 4, 12-13, 16-17, 19-20, 29-31, 56, 423-25, 429-30, 434, 436; **L16**: 465-66
supernatural in, **L9**: xvi-xviii, xx, xxviii-xxix, 3-5, 25, 27, 30-32, 44-45, 53-54, 295, 428-30; **L17**: 378, 427
liberalism in, **L9**: xix, 24, 216-18, 222
laissez-faire in, **L9**: xx, 52, 54, 55
symbolism in, **L9**: 5, 28-29, 215
adaptation related to, **L9**: 11-14
and knowledge, **L9**: 14-15, 18-19, 21-25, 28, 38-39, 56-57
Otto on, **L9**: 214, 215
Macintosh on, **L9**: 421-22
Guterman on, **L9**: 423-25
Wieman on, **L9**: 426-34
function of, **L9**: 434; **L17**: 529
humanism in, **L11**: 84-85, 583n, 584-87; **L15**: 269-70
problem in, **L11**: 115-17
Lamont on, **L11**: 425-27
Bergson on, **L11**: 428-31
Reiser on, **L11**: 435, 436
Russell on, **L11**: 455-56, 459-60
James on, **L11**: 474-76; **L13**: 367
Jefferson on, **L14**: 215, 218-19
Cohen on, **L14**: 406
heresy in, **L15**: 53, 58
freedom of, **L15**: 172-75, 183; **L16**: 402
source of individualism, **L15**: 212-17
subsidy for, **L15**: 282-85
impact of, **L16**: 243, 254-55, 407; **L17**: 530
universality of, **L17**: 374-77
ethical factor of, **L17**: 375-76
at Harvard, **L17**: 545-47

Religion and Science (B. Russell), **L11**: xxiv, 454-63
Religion in the Post-War World (Ferris), **L17**: 545
Religion Today and Tomorrow (Macintosh), **L14**: 286
Religious
education, **M3**: 210-15
art, **L10**: 134, 146, 156, 191-92, 256, 319-22
Religious Aspect of Philosophy, The (Royce), **M6**: xivn; **M10**: 82-83
Religious experience
as epiphenomenon, **L9**: xiv, xxiv
Arnold on, **L9**: xiv-xv, xvii-xviii, xxiv-xxv, xxvii
Bosanquet on, **L9**: xxv
Royce on, **L9**: xxviii
concept of, **L9**: xxviii-xxix, 3-4, 8-11, 13-14, 23-24, 26, 426
vs. religion, **L9**: 4, 8-9, 29
Macintosh on, **L9**: 418
Remains of the Rev. James Marsh, The (J. Torrey), **L5**: 195
"Remarks at a Peace Banquet" (W. James), **L15**: 21n
Rembrandt, **M5**: 145; **L10**: 60, 98, 117, 209-10, 286, 355, 358
Remembering
compared with reminiscencing, **L17**: 325
related to thinking, **L17**: 326, 332-33

Reminiscence, **L1**: 273
defined, **M13**: 42; **L17**: 325
development of, **M13**: 43
Lovejoy on, **M13**: 53
Renaissance, **M9**: 290; **M12**: xii, 95-96; **M15**: 196; **L1**: 334; **L5**: 166; **L8**: 25, 30, 32; **L16**: 408
individual in, **E5**: 13; **L17**: 437
freedom of thought in, **M1**: 167
schools of, **M1**: 289
philosophy, **M7**: 215-16
nationalism during, **L7**: 138
law in, **L7**: 139
liberty and religion in, **L7**: 140-41; **L9**: xix
economic development in, **L7**: 141-44
science in, **L7**: 144
art in, **L7**: 147-48; **L10**: 146, 256, 332-34
Renaissance of Physics, The (Darrow), **L13**: 272
Renan, Ernest, **E3**: 37, 39
and Dewey, **E3**: xxv-xxvi; **E4**: xix-xx
on science and civilization, **E3**: 174-79; **E4**: 11-18
Rendt, David S., **L9**: 346-48, 351
Renoir, Pierre Auguste, **L10**: 101, 133-34, 172, 182, 305-6, 359; **L11**: 501; **L13**: 361
Renouvier, Charles Bernard, **M2**: 153; **M7**: 297
Rent
socialization of, **L11**: xxiv, 256-57
Renunciation
Tolstoy teaches, **L17**: 389, 390
Reorganization
after WWI, **L13**: 309, 312-15
Repetition
evils of, **L17**: 205, 220-21, 301-2, 328
related to habits, **L17**: 299-300, 304, 307
value of, **L17**: 304-5
"Reply to Criticisms" (B. Russell), **L16**: 200-202
"Reply to John Dewey, A" (Meiklejohn), **L15**: 333
"Reply to My Critics, A" (G. Moore), **L16**: 204-7
Report and Recommendation upon Turkish Education, **M15**: xixn, xx-xxiii
Representation, **L12**: 58, 118, 121, 177, 292, 432, 473-75, 516-20
function of, **M13**: 50-52, 456n, 464
Lovejoy on, **M13**: 53
esthetic vs. cognitive, **M13**: 54
meaning as, **M13**: 58
in art, **L10**: 88-89, 92-96, 99, 107, 189, 200, 204-5, 225-27, 258, 288, 292, 295, 319, 356; **L14**: 37
determination of, **L16**: 301
behavioral, **L16**: 473-74
Representation and Form (Abell), **L11**: 487-88
Representatives
words as, **L16**: 297-99
Republic, The (Plato), **E1**: 239-41; **M7**: 312-14; **M8**: 144; **M9**: 286; **M12**: xxvii; **M15**: 19; **L2**: 129-38; **L8**: 23, 37; **L11**: 72
Republicanism, **M13**: 140, 151
Republican party, **L6**: xviii, 405, 412; **L9**: 290; **L11**: 526; **L15**: 239-42, 245
Poles vote for, **M11**: 242, 287, 396
identified with prosperity, **L5**: 91-92
failure of, **L5**: 444-47

blocs in, **L6**: 152, 235-36
related to industry, **L6**: 157, 158, 168, 172
compared with Democratic party, **L6**: 167-68, 184, 236, 248
and third-party program, **L6**: 185, 247, 250-51, 254, 504
related to minorities, **L6**: 227-29
history of, **L6**: 231-34, 240
in New York City, **L9**: 349-53, 355, 379, 382, 384
Res, **M7**: 37; **M10**: 322, 323, 345
Research, **M12**: 100, 102
in Russia, **L17**: 507
Research in the Social Sciences (Gee), **L5**: 161n
Resistance
esthetic role of, **L10**: 21, 22, 29-31, 51, 59, 65-67, 71, 143, 152, 154, 159-66, 171, 184, 187, 265, 267, 286, 341-42; **L14**: 36-37
Resources. *See also* Natural resources
use of, **L13**: 388
Respectability, **L7**: 253
Response, **L12**: 36-38
and stimulus, **E1**: 106; **E5**: 98, 100-109; **M9**: 29-30, 52, 67-68
centrality of, **E5**: 359-60
effective, **M9**: 161
three types of, **M13**: 37-38
as name, **L16**: 90, 269
C. Morris on, **L16**: 213, 220-23
-disposition, **L16**: 231-35
in semiotic, **L16**: 239-40
Responsibility, **M12**: 173; **M14**: xv, 18, 216-17; **L8**: 137-38; **L14**: 17n, 402-6
ethics of, **E4**: 342-44
collective, **M5**: 32-33, 46-47, 62, 63; **L7**: 31-33, 44-46, 57, 58
individual, **M5**: 33-34, 100; **L7**: 32, 91-92, 300
in social order, **M5**: 390-94
in dealing with subject-matter, **M9**: 185-86
basis of, **M9**: 346-47
as prospective, **L7**: xxv
nature of, **L7**: 303-4
and consequences, **L7**: 304-5
and freedom, **L7**: 305-6; **L17**: 342-43, 462
for labor conditions, **L7**: 378-79; **L13**: 317
of education, **L13**: 26-27
active, **L13**: 277
intellectual, **L17**: 80
for children, **L17**: 518
Responsiveness
training in, **E5**: 82, 202-3
in art, **L13**: 366-67
Rests. *See* Intervals
Result, **L16**: 344
"Results of Child-Study Applied to Education," **L11**: 212n, 213-14
Resuscitation
Tolstoy on, **L17**: 386
Retention
nature of, **E2**: 78, 130-35, 247
and experience, **M13**: 352
Retirement, **L11**: 529
Retreat from Reason, The (Hogben), **L11**: 186, 391-96; **L12**: 451n; **L17**: 447
Retribution
in wartime, **M10**: 281-84
Retrospection
in education, **M9**: 78-82
in knowledge, **M13**: 467-72
"Return to Normalcy," **L13**: 315

Reuter news service, **M11**: 151; **M13**: 241

Revcoms (USSR revolutionary committees), **M13**: 235

Revelation
- conditions of, **E4**: 4-7
- in art, **L10**: 274

Revenue Act, **L9**: 259, 260, 274, 282

Revenue bill (1932), **L6**: 385, 392

Reverence
- religious, **M5**: 34-35, 55, 131; **L7**: 33, 50, 122
- for ancestors, **M5**: 36, 61; **L7**: 34-35, 56
- for duty, **M5**: 71; **L7**: 65

Reverie, **L1**: 27, 69, 77, 98, 174-75, 220, 235, 257-59
- in esthetics, **L10**: 224, 277-80, 295
- important in understanding nature, **L14**: 144-45, 384

Review
- as educational method, **L8**: 267

Revival
- enjoined by church, **L14**: 214-15

Revolt against Dualism, The (Lovejoy), **L15**: xviii

Revolution, **L11**: 5, 7, 170; **L13**: 86, 135; **L16**: 370, 390. *See also* French Revolution; Industrial revolution; Russian Revolution
- vs. revolutionary, **E4**: 83
- Marxist theory of, **M12**: 20; **L11**: 59, 334-35, 439, 485
- in China, **M12**: 65, 253, 255; **M13**: 135, 183
- of thought, **M12**: 110, 114
- Dewey describes, **L7**: xvii
- American, **L7**: 148-50; **L15**: 217, 252
- Glorious (1688), **L8**: 9; **L11**: 289
- as process, **L9**: 77; **L13**: 100, 127, 339; **L14**: 76; **L17**: xxvii-xxviii
- Brameld's view of, **L9**: 245
- political, **L9**: 296, 298; **L15**: 174, 252
- Niebuhr on, **L9**: 402-3
- of 1800, **L14**: 214, 216
- effects of, **L16**: 319, 401, 408, 410
- Paléologue on, **L17**: 490
- Putilov on, **L17**: 568

"Revolutions in Science" (Santayana), **L9**: 242-43

Reymond, Du Bois, **E1**: 196

Reynolds, Joshua
- on art, **L10**: 191-92, 289-90, 304, 360, 363, 365

Rhadamanthus, **M5**: 63; **L7**: 58

Rhetoric (Aristotle), **L4**: xxi

Rhetoric, **L10**: 331; **L11**: 394

Rhode, Paul P., **M11**: 289, 301, 396

Rhodes, Cecil J., **L15**: xxvii, 20, 26

Rhythm
- qualities of, **E2**: 161-63; **L10**: 20-22, 25, 29, 31, 41, 62-63, 93, 103, 142, 165, 169-89, 222, 232, 236, 241
- related to series concept, **E5**: 181-82, 202
- in primitive society, **M5**: 48-49; **L7**: 46
- of intellectual progress, **M6**: 274, 349; **L8**: 227-28, 345
- essential property of form, **L10**: 151-61
- misconception of, **L10**: 167-68, 174-75, 180
- determined by medium, **L10**:

206-7, 217, 246
Greeks on, **L17**: 176
Ribera, José, **L10**: 147
Ribot, Théodule, **E5**: 342n
Ricardo, David, **L6**: 36, 69
Rice, Philip Blair, **L15**: xviii-xix, xxi; **L16**: 351n, 470
on Santayana, **L14**: 300-301
on value, **L15**: 63-64, 402-26, 431-37
Dewey critiques, **L15**: 66-71, 73n, 75-83
on objectivity vs. subjectivity, **L15**: 74-75, 426-34
Rice riots, **M11**: xvii-xviii, 165, 177
Richard B. Westbrook Free Lectureship Foundation, **L6**: 424
Richards, I. A., **M15**: xxvi, 223-25; **L1**: 160n; **L3**: 82; **L6**: 3, 494, 499; **L12**: 59n
on beautiful, **L10**: 255, 362
on linguistics, **L16**: xxxii, 218n, 305
triangular scheme of, **L16**: 9, 300-302, 470
Rickert, Heinrich, **M11**: 361
Rickover, Hyman George, **L5**: xv
Ridicule, **M5**: 57; **L7**: 52
Rieber, Clara, **L9**: 320, 321
Riehl, Wilhelm Heinrich, **M5**: 530-31
Rifle practice, **L17**: 121, 560
Right, **M14**: xv; **L16**: 376
and duty, **M12**: 198
authority of, **M14**: 222-25
in moral theory, **L5**: 281-88
and good, **L7**: xi
interpretation of, **L7**: xxviii
Tufts on, **L7**: xxix-xxx
as basic concept, **L7**: 214-17, 308
Kantian theory of, **L7**: 221-22
justification of, **L7**: 224-31
and loyalty, **L7**: 233-34
Right-and-duty-bearing unit, **L2**: 23, 25-27, 29
Righteousness, **M5**: 99-100; **L7**: 90-91
Rights, **M11**: 196; **L15**: 179; **L16**: 400. *See also* Civil rights
natural, **E1**: 410-11; **M5**: 143-44; **M7**: 57; **M11**: 20, 23, 25; **L2**: 289, 294, 299; **L3**: 99-100; **L7**: 138-40, 143, 331-32, 334; **L9**: 301-2; **L11**: xxvii, 7, 15, 26, 289, 373, 598; **L13**: 85, 136, 174, 178; **L14**: 212-13; **L16**: 402-3
defined, **M5**: 12-13; **L9**: 89
Negro, **M5**: 32; **L7**: 31
types of, **M5**: 394-402
voting, **M5**: 423-24
French principle of, **M8**: 165-66
of man, **M8**: 166; **L13**: 148, 173-74
of minorities, **M11**: 71
British theory of, **L6**: 35-36
of children, **L7**: 29, 30
development of, **L7**: 31-32, 75-77, 131-33
labor, **L7**: 395-96
divine, **L11**: 549
federal vs. states', **L13**: 175
personal vs. property, **L13**: 177-78
Rignano, Eugenio, **L6**: 330-31; **L14**: 64n
on reasoning, **L2**: 105-6
on thinking, **L12**: 34-35
Riichiro, Hoashi, **L17**: 57, 557
Rijksmuseum (Amsterdam), **L10**: 117, 358
"Rime of the Ancient Mariner, The" (Coleridge), **L10**: 115, 116, 322

Rip Van Winkle, **M8**: 292
Rise of American Civilization, The (C. Beard and M. Beard), **L14**: 283
Rising Temper of the East, The (F. Hunt), **M13**: 345-47
Ritchie, David G., **M11**: 25
Rites, **M14**: 227
 role of, **L9**: 40-41, 427; **L10**: v, 330, 332
Ritter, William Emerson, **L16**: 117n
Rituals, **L10**: xv, 330, 332
 enforce customs, **M5**: 58, 66-67, 95; **L7**: 53, 61, 87
 death, **M5**: 65; **L7**: 60
Rivera, Diego, **L11**: 311
Riverside, Ill., Cottage School
 grammar experiment at, **M8**: 262-63
 nature study at, **M8**: 266
 dramatization at, **M8**: 290-91
 social ideals of, **M8**: 352
Roads to Freedom (B. Russell), **M12**: 244
Robbins, Hayes, **M5**: 464n
Robert Elsmere (Mrs. H. Ward), **E3**: 14
Roberts, George W., **L6**: xvn
Robert Schalkenbach Foundation, **L3**: 359n; **L9**: 61n
Robertson, George Croom, **E2**: xxiii; **M11**: 21-22, 30
Robins, Raymond, **L5**: 353; **L8**: 16
Robinson, Daniel Sommer, **M13**: 11n, 12; **M15**: xii
 Dewey's reply to, **M10**: 98-108
 on logic, **M10**: 415-30
 on philosophic reflection, **M15**: 14-19, 323-37
Robinson, James Harvey, **M5**: 419n; **M6**: xii; **M13**: 421-22, 497-99; **M15**: 192; **L2**: 217; **L6**: xvi; **L17**: 517, 572
 at curriculum conference, **L6**: 414-19, 504
Robinson Crusoe (De Foe), **M1**: 106-7; **M4**: 194-95; **M10**: 91; **M15**: 178-79
Rockefeller Foundation, **L15**: 154
Rodbertus, Karl Johann, **M8**: 176
Rodin, Auguste, **L17**: 40
Rodman, Selden, **L9**: 296
 on Trotsky, **L13**: 347-48, 391-400
Roentgen, Wilhelm C., **L11**: 279; **L16**: 99
Rolland, Romain, **L6**: 272
Rollins College
 curriculum conference at, **L6**: 404, 414-23, 503, 504
Roman
 law, **E5**: 10; **L2**: 31n, 35, 41
 school of painting, **L10**: 191, 192, 304, 315, 333
 civilization, **L10**: 330, 332, 340
 education, **L17**: 228
Roman Catholic church, **E4**: 142; **M7**: 216; **M8**: 416; **M11**: 73; **M15**: 142, 146, 318; **L4**: 57; **L11**: 116; **L13**: 148
 and mysticism, **E4**: 125
 doctrine of, **E4**: 126; **L15**: xii-xiii, 46-47, 50-55, 95, 189, 235
 structure and ethics of, **E4**: 141; **M11**: 24
 important to Polish question, **M11**: xv, 242, 278, 286-89, 296, 297, 303, 305, 312, 328
 in Mexico, **L2**: 194-98, 200-202, 208
 vs. Protestantism, **L9**: 45-46; **L17**: 438

restricts artists, **L10**: 332
schools of, **L15**: 284-85
in political spectrum, **L16**: 375
Romanell, Patrick
on esthetic experience, **L16**: 395-98, 463-67
Roman Empire, **E4**: 130, 138; **M15**: 135-36, 385; **L10**: 331; **L15**: 207
anarchy in, **E4**: 83
and birth of democracy, **E4**: 99
and development of intuitionalism, **E4**: 124-26
influences moral philosophy, **E4**: 140-41
Romania, **M11**: xiii, 137, 307; **M15**: 390, 391
Romantic
school of philosophy, **M7**: 419
art, **L10**: xxvi, 149, 173, 287, 315, 336
Romanticism, **M8**: 18, 198; **M14**: 7-8, 53, 72, 97, 114, 176; **L1**: 49, 97, 177, 178, 187, 282; **L8**: 38, 361; **L11**: xxviii, 18-19, 80-81
Bourget on, **E3**: 40-42
related to will, **M10**: 229-30
and Middle Ages, **M10**: 231
vs. classicism, **M13**: 287-88
economic theory and, **L6**: 69-70, 74
of negations, **L13**: 122
Weber reflects, **L16**: 373
Dewey charged with, **L16**: 384-85, 457-58
Romantic School in Germany, The (Brandes), **M8**: 178
Rome, Italy, **M11**: 121, 170, 264, 290; **L8**: 6, 24, 32
slavery in, **M5**: 78; **L7**: 72, 128-29, 132-33
moral contributions of, **L7**: xxvii, 130-34, 219, 228
ancient society of, **L7**: 125-30
family in, **L7**: 129-30, 440-41
Romeo and Juliet (Shakespeare), **L17**: 325, 564
Romm, Vladimir, **L11**: 311, 322, 603
Roosevelt, Franklin D., **L6**: xvi, xviii, xix, 323, 326, 405; **L9**: 260, 289; **L11**: 526; **L14**: 284; **L15**: 244, 340, 345, 509; **L17**: 566
as presidential candidate, **L6**: 248, 251, 253
criticized, **L6**: 395-96
policies of, **L9**: 78-79, 254, 255, 277-80, 287, 288, 296-97
letters to, **L9**: 265-66, 269-70, 273-74, 277-78
related to Seabury investigation, **L9**: 355, 356, 369
and Democratic party, **L9**: 400-401
on fear, **L17**: 476, 568
Roosevelt, Theodore, **M7**: 115; **M10**: 186, 254, 290; **M12**: 63; **M13**: 302, 498; **M15**: 404; **L6**: 229, 231, 234, 472
tribute to, **M11**: xix, 143-49
on WWI, **M11**: 127
on China, **M11**: 199
on education, **L17**: 72
Roosevelt Corollary, **L6**: 473
Root, Elihu, **M10**: 164, 279; **M15**: 406, 407
principles of, **M13**: 198, 207, 215
and World Court, **M15**: 386, 387, 393
and diplomacy, **M15**: 415
Rorty, Richard, **L4**: xiin; **L6**: xi; **L14**: xvii

Rorty, Richard (*continued*)
on Dewey's 1933 writings, **L8**: ix-xviii
Roscelin, **M2**: 221
Rosch, Eleanor, **L4**: xiii
Rosen, N., **L16**: 109
Rosenberg, Alfred, **M8**: 439
Rosenheck, Charles, **L11**: 530
Rosenkranz, Johann Karl Friedrich, **E4**: 195
Rosenthal, Henry M., **L14**: 307
Rosenthal, Julius, **L14**: 115n
Rosmer, Alfred, **L11**: 323
Ross, Edward Alsworth, **M5**: 465; **M10**: 54; **L11**: 323
Ross, Ralph
on Dewey's 1912-14 writings, **M7**: ix-xxix
on Dewey's 1920 writings, **M12**: ix-xx
on Dewey's 1921-22 writings, **M13**: ix-xxix
Rouen, cathedral of, **L10**: 224
Roumania, **M11**: xiii, 137, 307; **M15**: 390, 391
Round Table, **L6**: 198
Rousseau, Henri (le Douanier), **L10**: 239
Rousseau, Jean Jacques, **E3**: 91; **E4**: 62, 214; **M4**: 248; **M5**: 142; **M7**: 293, 377; **M8**: xxxii, 275, 356, 389; **M11**: 27n; **M12**: xxiv; **M13**: 298, 400; **M15**: 9, 244; **L2**: 31n, 332; **L6**: 495; **L7**: 155, 326; **L8**: 26, 37; **L9**: 195; **L11**: 282; **L13**: 156; **L14**: xxii; **L17**: 230, 430, 501
on theory of sovereignty, **E4**: 76n, 89, 90, 146
influence of, **E4**: 193-94; **M8**: 222, 248-49; **L10**: 193
and economic forces, **E4**: 216-17
on education, **M1**: xvii, 288; **M8**: 211, 213-14, 219-21, 228; **M9**: 119-25
on nature, **M2**: 148; **M7**: 288-89; **M8**: 183, 188
on optimism, **M2**: 175
on natural rights, **M5**: 143
on goodness of man, **M5**: 205
related to culture, **M6**: 405-6, 408-9
Kant on, **M8**: 168
on physical growth, **M8**: 214-17
on senses, **M8**: 217-18
on discipline, **M8**: 295
on social conditions, **M9**: 65
Plato's influence on, **M9**: 97
on citizen, **M9**: 100n
on consciousness, **M14**: 125
on primitive simplicity, **M14**: 197
on liberty, **L7**: 139, 359-60
on arts and sciences, **L13**: 84
political writings of, **L13**: 149
on law, **L14**: 120
on habits, **L17**: 298, 299, 303, 564
on feelings, **L17**: 390
Tolstoy compared with, **L17**: 391
Routine, **M14**: 48, 52, 74, 146-47, 159; **L1**: 270-71; **L13**: 13-14, 361-62
habit and, **M14**: 32, 50, 71, 164
vs. philosophy, **L13**: 259
Royce, Josiah, **E4**: xxiii; **M3**: 311; **M4**: 254; **M6**: xiii, xiv; **M7**: x, xii, 228; **M8**: xx; **M15**: 319, 329; **L1**: 174, 176; **L2**: 19, 126; **L5**: 477; **L6**: xiii; **L11**: 472, 476; **L14**: 301; **L17**: 366n, 559, 565
on morality, **E4**: xvii, 199-200; **M5**: 370n

on conscience, **E4**: 197-98
on Being, **M1**: 242-56; **M2**: 120-37
on meaning, **M2**: 360n-61n
on logic, **M3**: 65
and absolute truth, **M7**: xiv-xvi, 413-44
Dewey criticizes, **M7**: xvii, 64-78
voluntarism and intellectualism in, **M7**: 418, 423, 435, 444; **M10**: xxiv, 79-88
on Kant, **M10**: 80
on religion and philosophy, **M10**: 82-83; **M15**: 19, 328; **L9**: xxvii; **L15**: 168-69
influences on, **M10**: 84n, 85
on Santayana, **M15**: 219
on hedonic motivation, **M15**: 325-26
Rozwadowski, Jan J., **M11**: 281
Rubens, Peter Paul, **L10**: 210
Rubinow, I. M., **L7**: 432
Rucker, Darnell
on Dewey's 1903-6 writings, **M3**: ix-xxv
Ruehle, Otto, **L11**: 312, 314, 323; **L13**: 395, 404
Rugg, Harold
investigation of, **L14**: 371, 373
textbooks of, **L14**: 427-29
Rugged individualism, **M12**: 243; **L9**: 205-8, 231, 238; **L11**: 29-31, 270, 286, 291, 371
Ruhr, Germany, **M15**: xviiin, 78, 109, 123; **L6**: 453
Rulers. *See* Government; Officers
Rules, **L13**: 5, 166
of conduct, **M12**: 174
in science of education, **L5**: 14-15
and principles, **L7**: xxv, 276-80
restrict art, **L10**: 208, 229-30, 283, 304-5, 308, 313, 317, 332n
need for, **L13**: 32, 139, 209-10, 242
maintenance of, **L13**: 82
as products of interaction, **L13**: 86
propositions as, **L13**: 211, 321
Kaufmann on, **L16**: 196, 198
Rules for the Direction of Mind (Descartes), **M10**: 90
Rumford, Benjamin Thompson, **L16**: 65, 99
Runes, Dagobert D., **L16**: 42n, 163-64, 258n
Ruskin, John, **M12**: 71; **L5**: 105; **L11**: 19
and esthetics, **E4**: 195-96
on industrial civilization, **M1**: 149
Russell, Bertrand, **M6**: xiii; **M7**: xiv, 455; **M8**: xiv; **M10**: xxiii; **M12**: 235; **M13**: 258; **M15**: xxv-xxvi, 327; **L1**: 54; **L2**: 13n, 71, 77; **L3**: xiv-xv, 298; **L5**: 483; **L6**: xv, 428; **L9**: 91; **L10**: vii, xiii, xiv; **L13**: ix, 401-2; **L14**: 5, 19, 30n, 34n, 306, 402; **L15**: xii-xiii, xxxiii, 509; **L16**: 469
on truth, **M6**: xx; **M7**: 440-41
contradiction of, **M7**: 414
logic of, **M7**: 422; **M8**: 15; **M10**: 415; **L4**: xxi; **L12**: 157; **L15**: 395-98; **L16**: 90n, 104n, 147, 159-60, 187, 193, 199-204
Dewey's relation with, **M8**: xx; **L11**: xxiv, 460-63; **L14**: x-xiii, xvii, xx-xxi, 12-15, 29-34, 44, 52-58, 168-88, 399; **L16**: xxxiin
on external world, **M8**: xx-

Russell, Bertrand (*continued*) xxv, 83-93; **M13**: 447
on pragmatism, **M8**: 22-23
on sense perception, **M8**: 58, 60-63; **L4**: xiii
on inferential function, **M10**: 93-97
on time, **M10**: 100, 422
on value judgments, **M11**: 364, 371
on philosophy, **M12**: xxvii, 236, 239; **L6**: 425
on impulse and instinct, **M12**: xxix, 244-46
compared with Bergson and James, **M12**: xxx, 236, 242-43
philosophy of, **M12**: 235-50; **L14**: xiv-xv
on psychology, **M12**: 236
on philosophy and political concepts, **M12**: 237-41, 247-49, 288
contributions of, **M12**: 249-50
positions of, **M13**: 306; **M15**: 198; **L1**: xi, xvi; **L16**: xviii, 167, 186n, 189n, 208
on China, **M15**: 215-18
on education, **L2**: 226-30
terminology of, **L4**: xviii; **L16**: 38
on America, **L5**: 130-31; **L17**: 50, 557
on religion and science, **L11**: 454-61; **L13**: 160
court case of, **L14**: xxi, xxiv, 236-48, 357-59, 369
on sexual ethics, **L14**: 231-35, 238-45
on Santayana, **L14**: 308
writings of, **L14**: 371
on morality, **L15**: 159-60
influences Carnap, **L16**: 18
procedure of, **L16**: 165n, 185, 209
Russell, William Fletcher, **L3**: 251n
Russia. *See* Union of Soviet Socialist Republics
Russian art, **L10**: 321
Russian Poland (Kingdom of Poland)
conditions in, **M11**: 263-67, 281, 290
German occupation of, **M11**: 268, 278
future of, **M11**: 272, 273, 277, 329
as place of origin, **M11**: 285, 322
Russian Revolution, **M12**: xxi, 254; **L3**: 204, 205, 217; **L11**: 288, 312, 323-25; **L13**: 126. *See also* Bolsheviks
effects of, **M11**: ix, 98; **L17**: 22
affects Polish question, **M11**: 262, 264, 269-74, 278, 282, 298
understanding of, **L5**: 409; **L17**: 490-91
Russo-Japanese war, **M11**: 156
effects of, **M11**: 113, 150-53, 207
peace terms of, **M11**: 159-60; **L2**: 176
Ruthenians, **M11**: xiii, 255
Ryan, John A., **L6**: 381
Rykov, Aleksey I., **L15**: 338
Ryle, Gilbert, **M6**: xvi; **L10**: vii; **L16**: 209n

Sabin, Henry, **E5**: xcv
Sacco-Vanzetti case, **L3**: xxix; **L11**: 303, 306, 317, 328
Fuller report on, **L3**: 186-95

Sacred
days, **M5**: 66-67; **L7**: 61
secular invades, **L16**: 408
Sacrifice
vs. indulgence, **L7**: 189
Saghalien (Sakhalin), USSR, **M13**: 258
Sainte-Beuve, Charles Augustin, **E3**: 36
St. German, Christopher, **M7**: 56
Saint Joan (Shaw), **M15**: 128
St. John's College (Annapolis)
curriculum of, **L15**: 335-36, 476-84
St. Louis, Mo., **M15**: 395; **L13**: 323n
Congress of Arts and Science at (1904), **M3**: 145-51, 352-73, 374-81; **M10**: 56
Saint Louis University, **M15**: 318n, 421
St. Paul decision, **L6**: 165, 504
Saintsbury, George Edward Bateman, **L5**: 263
Saint Sophia (Hagia Sophia), **L10**: 224
Salaries
of teachers, **L9**: 116-17
Saleilles, Raymond, **L2**: 30n
Salmasius, Claudius, **M11**: 27n
Salter, William M., **E3**: 93, 109
Salvation
vs. condemnation, **L17**: 16-17
Same
in *Dictionary of Philosophy*, **M2**: 231
Sample, **L12**: 474-75. *See also* Case, **L12**
Sanctification, **M8**: 151
Sanctions
international, **L6**: xx, 196, 207-11, 450-51, 462-65
Pact of Paris and, **L6**: 192, 219, 220
relation of League of Nations to, **L6**: 196-200, 450, 466, 484
Europe vs. U.S. regarding, **L6**: 197-98, 208-9, 472-73
effects of, **L6**: 199, 455, 474-77
economic vs. military, **L6**: 200-202, 456n, 458-59
related to war, **L6**: 201-2, 453-58, 477-79
in Japan, **L6**: 203-4
force in relation to, **L6**: 214-16, 481-82
non-recognition doctrine as, **L6**: 219-20, 467-71
moral pressure as, **L6**: 220-21, 455, 465-67
vs. outlawry of war, **L6**: 221-22
and disarmament, **L6**: 459-61, 471
in Switzerland, **L6**: 463
opposition to, **L6**: 464, 471-83
in moral theory, **L7**: 226
Sand, George, **E5**: 367
San Domingo, **M15**: 386
Sanford, Edmund Clark, **M11**: 85, 394
Sanger, Margaret, **L15**: xxiv
Sanity, **L10**: 198
San Jose State Normal School, **L17**: 63
Santayana, George, **M2**: xiv; **M3**: 118; **M5**: 410n; **M7**: ix, x; **M8**: xxvi; **M9**: xxi; **M15**: xxvi, 248, 329, 334, 348; **L1**: 24, 54, 177, 369; **L2**: 19, 126, 367; **L4**: 191; **L6**: 271, 421; **L7**: 211; **L12**: 75; **L13**: ix; **L14**: 5, 193, 400; **L15**: xiv, 28-29, 423

Santayana, George (*continued*)
style of, **M3**: xxii; **M4**: 229-30; **L3**: 290, 293
on experience, **M3**: 103n; **L10**: 23, 354; **L16**: 384-85
natural idealism of, **M3**: 144n, 319-22
philosophy of, **M4**: 232-33; **L3**: 288, 290-91; **L9**: 240-43; **L14**: 295-308
on reason, **M4**: 233-41
on tertiary qualities, **M6**: 20-21
on art and esthetics, **M6**: 375; **L9**: 13; **L10**: xvii, xx, 231n
on German philosophy, **M10**: 305-9
on religion, **M10**: 311; **L9**: 13
on expression, **M10**: 355
on value, **M11**: 384, 385; **L2**: 70-72, 74, 80, 92, 94
positions of, **M12**: 127; **M13**: 58, 59; **L6**: 272; **L17**: xxvi
on essence, **M15**: 219-22; **L10**: 297, 364; **L16**: 146n
Dewey's relationship with, **L3**: xi-xv, 73-81; **L14**: 15-19
criticizes Dewey, **L3**: 75, 76, 367-84; **L14**: 10n; **L16**: 456-58
and American scene, **L3**: 117
Thilly on, **L3**: 398
on nature, **L10**: 144, 359
on costliness, **L10**: 145, 359
on perception, **L10**: 161, 359; **L11**: 78, 92
criticizes writers, **L10**: 324, 366
on Greek civilization, **L10**: 332-33, 366
fiction of, **L11**: 446-49
skepticism of, **L14**: 11, 302
"Santayana's Materialism" (Dennes), **L14**: 303-4
"Santayana's Philosophical Inheritance" (Sullivan), **L14**: 300
"Santayana's Theory of Value" (S. Pepper), **L14**: 306
Sargent, John Singer, **L10**: 54
Sartre, Jean-Paul, **M3**: xii, xxiv; **L14**: xix; **L15**: xxxiii
Satisfaction, **M14**: 97, 109-10, 122-23, 146, 197; **L1**: 158-59, 194, 197. *See also* Consequences, **L12**; Enjoyment; Liking
defined, **L4**: 207-8; **L16**: 165
related to value, **L4**: 212, 214; **L15**: 66-72
as objective, **L4**: 241; **L12**: 33-35
influence of, **L13**: 88-89
interpretation of, **L13**: 223
in inquiry, **L14**: 56, 183
Tarski on, **L16**: 42
Satsuma clansmen (Japan), **M11**: 168, 169
Saturday Evening Post, **L9**: 115, 117
Savage mind, **M2**: 39-40, 43
Savages, **M12**: 81-82, 128-29, 180-81, 246; **M14**: 68, 72, 74; **L13**: 22, 291. *See also* Primitive life
Savery, Barnett, **L15**: 42n
Savery, William
exchange with Dewey, **L14**: 5, 30n, 59-62, 86-88
Savigny, Friedrich Karl von, **L2**: 41
Savings
in U.S., **L6**: 359
Scale, **L12**: 191, 213-15
Scaliger, Joseph Justus, **M2**: 187
Scaliger, Julius Caesar, **E4**: 193
Scandinavia, **L15**: 245
Scepticism. *See* Skepticism
Scepticism and Animal Faith (Santayana), **M15**: xxvi, 219-22; **L14**: 301-2

Schaarschmidt, C., **E1**: 302
Schaefer-Simmern, Henry, **L15**: xxiii
on art, **L15**: 315-17
Schaeffer, Nathan C., **E5**: xciv
Schalkenbach, Robert, Foundation, **L3**: 359n; **L9**: 61n
Schall, Thomas D., **L6**: 394
Schapiro, Meyer, **L10**: 7
Scharnhorst, Gerhard, **M8**: 163, 177, 474
Schasler, Max Alexander Friedrich, **E4**: 195
Schaub, Edward L., **L14**: 5, 306
Dewey replies to, **L14**: 77-80
Schelling, Friedrich Wilhelm Joseph von, **M1**: 40; **M2**: 148, 179, 184; **M3**: 310; **M6**: 168; **M7**: 138, 357; **M8**: 180n, 438; **L3**: 375; **L5**: 148
Schematism
in *Dictionary of Philosophy*, **M2**: 235-36
Scherer, Wilhelm, **L8**: 362
Schiller, F. C. S., **M3**: xxii; **M4**: xxi; **M7**: x, 131-34, 289, 318, 327; **M12**: x; **L5**: xxxi, 264; **L11**: 422, 444; **L14**: 295
on humanism, **M3**: 312-22; **M6**: 176
on art and morality, **M5**: 45; **L7**: 42
on truth, **M6**: xiii-xiv, xxii
related to culture, **M6**: 406
on judgment, **M10**: 417, 418
on value judgments, **M11**: 361
logic of, **L11**: 155-57
Schiller, Johann Christoph Friedrich von, **E4**: 194; **M2**: 148; **M8**: 177; **M9**: 64; **M10**: 226; **L7**: 42; **L8**: 360
on poetry, **L10**: 195-96, 360
on art, **L10**: 286n
Schilpp, Paul Arthur, **L11**: xvn; **L13**: ix; **L14**: xi-xiii, 184n, 295, 306, 418n; **L16**: 202n, 204n
Schinz, Albert
on pragmatism, **M4**: 245-49
Schleiden, Matthias Jakob, **L16**: 117
Schleiermacher, Friedrich, **E5**: 137; **M8**: 145, 177; **L4**: 244
Schlesinger, Arthur M., Jr., **L6**: xviin
Schmoller, Gustav, **M8**: 474; **L16**: xiii
Schneersohn, Fischel, **L5**: 410-11
Schneider, Herbert W., **E4**: xxii; **L2**: 32n; **L4**: viii; **L6**: xii; **L11**: 3; **L15**: 466-67
on Dewey's *Psychology*, **E2**: xxiii-xxvi
on value, **M11**: 375, 376
on 1908 and 1932 *Ethics*, **L7**: viiin
on Dewey-Bentley collaboration, **L16**: xxxvin
Schneider, Herman, **L17**: 70, 557
Schnitte, **M7**: 440
Scholar, **M8**: 173; **L13**: 345
Scholarship, **L8**: 163; **L10**: 37
Scholastici, **M2**: 237
Scholasticism, **M7**: 360; **M12**: 96; **M15**: 318-19, 329; **L1**: 32, 192; **L5**: 166; **L11**: 72, 480; **L12**: 17
thought in, **E3**: 128-29; **M2**: 186; **M7**: 350-51
evolution of, **E3**: 148-51
on moral law, **E4**: 125-27
on nature, **M2**: 142-43, 145, 147
in *Dictionary of Philosophy*, **M2**: 236-44
methods of, in schools, **M9**: 289, 352

Scholasticism (*continued*)
attitudes toward, **L2**: 388-89
in Santayana's philosophy, **L14**: 298-99
creates synthesis, **L16**: 360
Scholastics, **M7**: 352
School and Society, **M1**: xviii-xix, 317; **M5**: 158n; **M7**: xxi, xxiv, xxv, 380; **L6**: 409; **L11**: xviii
School and Society in Chicago (Counts), **L5**: 371-74
"School as Social Centre, The," **M2**: xvii
School Citizens Committee, **L11**: 516
School Inquiry, Committee on, **M8**: 129
School of Childhood kindergarten (Pittsburgh), **M8**: 283
School of Education Parents' Association (Chicago), **M3**: 273n
School Review, **M2**: 79
Schools, **L6**: 90. *See also* Curriculum; Elementary school; High school; Progressive education; Teachers; Vocational education
social function of, **E5**: 57-59, 61-62, 86-87, 206, 269, 285-86, 329-33, 437-38, 450; **M1**: 46-47, 287-99; **M2**: 80-93; **M4**: 269-74; **M10**: 196-201, 203-10; **M15**: 150-51, 154-57; **L5**: 326-30, 371-74; **L9**: 127-28, 142-44, 167-68, 183-85, 192-93, 200-204, 207-8; **L11**: 179, 188, 192, 193, 204-5, 211, 234-37, 254-55, 345-47, 408-14, 541, 557-59; **L17**: 237, 239, 315
aims of, **E5**: 58, 60, 225, 292-93; **M2**: 90; **L8**: 53-54, 156-67, 300; **L13**: 4-8, 169, 385; **L17**: 71, 138-39, 240, 476
problems of, **E5**: 59-60, 80-81, 292-93; **L7**: 364-65
community and, **E5**: 62-63, 75-76, 87-88, 224-25, 232, 438; **L6**: 242; **L13**: 22-23; **L14**: 351-54; **L17**: 74-75
affect character, **E5**: 66-68, 76-82, 89, 383-84, 448-49; **M4**: 205-13; **L9**: 187-89, 192, 203-4
grading system of, **E5**: 88, 332-33; **M1**: 271; **M3**: 241-48
as institutions, **E5**: 224-25, 300-301; **M1**: 287-90
organization and administration of, **E5**: 244-45, 330, 443-45; **M1**: 267-68, 283; **M3**: 229-39; **M8**: 129; **M9**: 104, 171, 368; **M10**: 303-4, 397-411; **L9**: 183-85, 192-93; **L11**: 222-24, 345-47; **L17**: 514, 515
change in, **E5**: 269, 450-52; **M1**: 5-20; **M8**: 317-20; **L6**: 131-36, 433-35; **L16**: 371; **L17**: 73-74, 113
faults of, **E5**: 273; **L5**: 102-3; **L9**: 406-11; **L11**: 163-66, 268, 342-43, 377-78, 389, 502, 574-75; **L13**: 57; **L17**: 239, 463
Harris on, **E5**: 380-82
history of, **M1**: 42-44; **M8**: 314-16; **L6**: 91-94; **L11**: 181, 248, 364, 535; **L14**: 339
Dewey's attitude toward, **M2**: xvii-xviii
free expression and, **M3**: 234-39
and training of thought, **M6**: 216-23

public, **M7**: xxvi; **M9**: 26, 100, 265; **L11**: 350-51, 356-59, 376, 387-90, 416, 579; **L15**: 281-82, 284-85
continuation, **M7**: 90-91, 205; **M8**: 118, 401-3
Gary, **M7**: 96; **M8**: 120-21, 262, 320-38, 351, 365-78
Chicago, **M8**: 124-27, 260-62, 269-71, 351-52
Indianapolis, **M8**: 255-60, 268, 340-52
methods of, **M8**: 286-93; **L8**: 88-89; **L14**: 373; **L17**: 75, 242
discipline in, **M8**: 294-96
parochial, **M8**: 416-17, 471-72
experimental, **M10**: 121-24; **L8**: 239, 266-67
and militarism, **M10**: 191-95, 296-300; **L3**: 346-47; **L14**: 355-56; **L17**: 121, 122, 124
articulation in, **L5**: 299-310
child-centered, **L5**: 319-25
economics of, **L9**: 112-26, 128-30, 141-46, 183, 185, 386-95
enrollment in, **L9**: 118-19, 386-87
private, **L9**: 129-30, 145
utopian, **L9**: 136-40
Cuban, **L9**: 311
and democracy, **L13**: 92-93, 296, 299, 302, 307, 379, 382
pressures on, **L13**: 264-65
natural vs. repressive, **L17**: 216-17, 237, 239
home and, **L17**: 233-34, 314-15, 341
related to outside agencies, **L17**: 234, 515-16
Schools, Turkish
health in, **M15**: xxi, 293-94
system of, **M15**: xxi-xxii, 288-93, 295-96, 305-7
aims of, **M15**: 276-78
literature in, **M15**: 278-79, 301-2, 306
Ministry of Public Instruction and, **M15**: 278-83, 285-86, 296, 307
teachers in, **M15**: 283-88
discipline in, **M15**: 294-95
equipment in, **M15**: 302-3
physical structure of, **M15**: 303-4, 306
Schools of To-Morrow, **M8**: ix, 414
Hook on, **M8**: xxxi-xxxvi
Bagley reviews, **M8**: 466-70
School subjects
imagination stimulated by, **M6**: 216-17; **L8**: 351
nature of, **M6**: 220-22; **L8**: 161-64
methods of teaching, **M6**: 255-58, 266-70; **L8**: 72, 178-80, 204-5, 219-20, 233-34, 263-67, 341
and occupations, **M6**: 312-13; **L8**: 290-91
and observation, **M6**: 331-33; **L8**: 319-22
and thought, **L8**: 149
concepts in, **L8**: 261-62
Schopenhauer, Arthur, **E3**: 39, 165; **E4**: 195, 201; **M3**: xi, 310, 382; **M5**: x, 81; **M6**: 167; **M7**: 296; **M10**: 69, 306-8; **M11**: 43; **M15**: 326, 330; **L3**: 296, 297; **L7**: 75; **L10**: 293
as nihilistic, **M2**: 155
on pessimism, **M2**: 176-77
on palingenesis, **M2**: 180
panthelism of, **M2**: 185
on solipsism, **M3**: 385

Schopenhauer, Arthur (*cont.*)
esthetic theory of, **L10**: 235, 243, 299-301, 362, 364
Schopenhauerism
in *Dictionary of Philosophy*, **M2**: 244
Schücking, Walther, **M15**: 390
Schulz, George M. S., **L9**: 372, 373
Schurman, Jacob Gould, **E5**: 433-34
on Darwinism, **M2**: 16-17
on university teachers, **M10**: 165-66
Schurtz, Heinrich, **M5**: 37; **L7**: 35
Schutz, Alfred, **L16**: xxiii
Schütze, Martin, **L8**: 360-63; **L10**: 320n, 365
Schuyler, George S., **L6**: 226
Schwab, Charles M., **M11**: 73, 87, 393; **L9**: 63
Schwann, Theodor, **L16**: 117
Science, **E5**: 424, 430; **M12**: xiii, 87-88, 92-93, 99; **L10**: 267; **L11**: 60. *See also* Deduction, **L12**; Experiment; Induction, **L12**; Technology
basis of, **E1**: 101; **M13**: 311-12, 433, 434; **L4**: xiv-xvii, 89, 92-105, 110, 111, 125, 147-48, 163, 194, 195, 222
related to ethics and morals, **E1**: 208-9, 212-13, 225-26; **E3**: 104-9, 311-12; **E4**: 148-49; **M12**: 178-79; **M15**: 12; **L3**: 19, 27; **L5**: 156; **L7**: xxxiv-xxxv, 179-80, 282-83, 338; **L13**: 171-72; **L14**: 61-62, 66-70; **L15**: 127-28, 136-39, 186-87, 458; **L17**: 351, 458
characteristics of, **E1**: 223-25; **E2**: 76-77; **M9**: 232-39; **M12**: 218; **L1**: 234; **L8**: 62, 85; **L10**: 37, 100, 187-88, 197, 210-11, 220, 253, 291, 298; **L14**: 151-52; **L15**: 7, 156, 160, 186, 227, 235-36, 237n; **L16**: xxi-xxii, xxxiii, xxxvi, 300, 316-17, 397; **L17**: 407-8, 546
and psychology, **E2**: 3, 9; **E5**: 377; **L13**: 247-48, 276; **L17**: 420-21
physical, **E2**: 11; **L1**: 346-47, 352-53; **L2**: 47-48, 51, 54, 347, 359-60; **L6**: xvi-xvii, 65-66; **L13**: 182-83, 229, 276
and philosophy, **E2**: 202; **E3**: xxvi, xxxv-xxxvii, 211-12; **E5**: 14; **M9**: 334-35, 339; **M10**: 3-4, 39-42; **M11**: 41-48, 341-47; **M12**: 205-6, 260-66; **M15**: 15, 16, 234, 325, 331-32, 335-37; **L1**: 366-69, 376; **L3**: x, 9, 10, 25, 115, 118-19, 121; **L4**: ix-xxii, 22-24, 40-49, 53, 57, 58, 235, 247; **L6**: 19-20, 425-29, 489; **L12**: 41-42, 82-83; **L14**: 316-19, 329-31; **L16**: 157, 359, 410-11, 415, 419, 425; **L17**: 406-7
Green on, **E3**: xxvii, 17
Taine on, **E3**: 40
related to art and esthetics, **E3**: 123, 317-20; **E5**: 95; **M12**: xx, 152-53; **L1**: 107, 266-70, 275-76, 286; **L2**: 106-8, 111-13; **L4**: 61, 128, 165; **L7**: 72-73; **L10**: ix, xiii, xiv, xxxiii, 33n, 90-91, 126, 143-44, 148-49, 153-54, 174, 202-3, 274, 279, 285-86, 322-23, 340-44, 348; **L14**: 113; **L15**: 85-89, 98

Renan on, **E3**: 177-78; **E4**: 11-18
concepts and laws in, **E3**: 228; **E4**: 91; **M2**: 5; **M12**: 114-17, 228, 262-63; **M13**: 372; **M15**: 48; **L3**: 110; **L5**: 10-12, 14-15; **L11**: 9-10, 12, 97-99, 108-11, 149, 289, 434-35, 511; **L12**: 352, 370-71, 394-95, 428-32, 524; **L14**: 59-60, 87, 104-8, 111; **L15**: 312-13
social and political effects of, **E3**: 317-20; **M10**: 199, 236; **M11**: 33-35, 67-70, 98-99, 103, 142; **L3**: 111; **L5**: 113-23; **L6**: 49-63, 417-19; **L7**: 352; **L8**: 46, 59-61, 68-71; **L9**: 96-97, 100, 101, 108-10; **L11**: xiii-xvi, 48-49, 53, 58, 81-82, 141-45, 186-87, 189-90, 277-79, 343, 457-60, 563-64; **L13**: 53, 54, 58, 85, 156, 159-60, 165, 167, 171-72, 192, 250, 262, 269, 274-75, 278-79, 371; **L15**: 17, 158, 166-67, 184-86, 199-203, 251, 260, 273-74; **L16**: 255, 290-92, 319, 364-68, 372-74, 377; **L17**: xix, xxv-xxvi, xxxi, 238, 411-12
religion's relation to, **E4**: 6, 15; **M12**: 264-66; **M15**: x, xiii, 47-50; **L3**: 19, 27; **L4**: 33-34, 204, 206, 242, 243, 247; **L9**: xv-xvi, 3, 22-23, 27, 37, 42-43, 221, 418-20; **L13**: 123, 152, 182; **L14**: 78-79; **L15**: 157, 230, 272; **L17**: 13-14, 17, 412, 546-47
and truth, **E4**: 102-3; **M6**: ix; **L3**: 307; **L11**: 277, 551
history of, **E5**: 14; **M6**: 312; **M10**: 240; **M11**: x-xii, 78, 236; **M12**: xiv, 86, 110; **M13**: 284; **L4**: 71-76, 141, 199; **L8**: 290; **L11**: 24-25, 70, 74-75, 79, 117, 135, 141-42, 275-76, 455, 552-53; **L13**: 117, 143-44, 170, 181-82, 263-66, 275, 277, 299, 370; **L15**: 28, 84, 85, 90-96, 213, 268-69, 305, 307; **L16**: 340, 346, 349, 369-71, 375, 380, 417, 454-55, 460; **L17**: 411
and individualism, **E5**: 20; **M5**: 78-80; **L5**: 88-89; **L7**: 72-73
perception of, **E5**: 21-22; **M5**: 109-10; **M9**: 196-99; **M11**: 390; **M15**: 44; **L3**: 308, 310; **L4**: 13-15, 17, 18, 22, 153, 157; **L7**: 100-101; **L8**: 66, 67; **L15**: 253-54
teaching of, **E5**: 89, 90, 230, 440; **M1**: 303-6; **M6**: 69-79; **M9**: 227-29, 267, 294-98; **M10**: 130-36, 181-82; **L11**: 34-35, 128, 186-87, 189, 200-201, 214, 503, 551-54, 556, 580; **L14**: 267-70; **L15**: 257-62, 278-80, 479-80; **L17**: 311-12
related to experience, **E5**: 90; **M12**: 134; **L1**: 105-31; **L17**: 434-35
interest of child in, **E5**: 220-21, 246; **M1**: 63-64, 227, 328, 333-34
references on, **E5**: 338
classic and modern, **M1**: 170-71, 303, 305, 310; **M12**: 96; **L1**: 338-40; **L4**: 32-38, 159, 169, 219, 248-50
and epistemology, **M3**: 93-97
Santayana on, **M4**: 239-41; **L9**: 241-43; **L14**: 302-3

Science (*continued*)
impact of, **M5**: 78-79; **M13**: 433-36; **L2**: 142, 145, 150; **L7**: 72-73, 144-46, 150-51, 366; **L13**: xvi, 57-59, 93, 94, 160, 163-67, 275, 281, 284-85, 369; **L16**: 405, 407, 413-14, 452
related to knowledge, **M6**: ix; **M13**: 415; **L1**: 123-24, 128-31; **L2**: 337-38, 342-43; **L15**: 31, 32; **L17**: 372
value of, **M6**: 70-71; **M12**: 178-79, 265; **L17**: xvii-xviii, 414, 458
Bacon on, **M6**: 207, 446; **M9**: 291-92
Darwin on, **M6**: 279-80
observation in, **M6**: 331; **L8**: 318-19; **L14**: 150-53
Bergson on, **M7**: 3; **M12**: 226-27
related to humanities, **M7**: 120-27
and sense perception, **M8**: 60-63
in Germany, **M8**: 149; **M15**: 316; **L13**: 159
vs. language and literature, **M9**: 290-98; **M10**: 122; **L6**: 492-93
conquest of nature by, **M10**: 237-38
ability for, **M11**: 80-81
as discipline, **M11**: 93-95; **L8**: x, xv, xvii, xviii
in Japan, **M11**: 160-61, 193, 206
and industry, **M12**: 100-103; **L13**: 157-59, 182, 267, 283, 339; **L15**: 86, 263, 270-71, 277
natural, **M12**: 103, 106, 178-79, 260-61, 265-67, 270-77; **M13**: 270-71; **L13**: 389; **L15**: 186-87, 458
method and subject-matter of, **M12**: 238; **M15**: 311-13; **L2**: 361; **L4**: 21-22, 30, 58-59, 63-86, 182, 211; **L6**: 15-16; **L13**: 131, 266; **L14**: 194-98; **L16**: 62-64, 70, 103n, 191, 250-56, 312, 338-39, 386
attitude toward, **M13**: 301; **L4**: xvi, 153, 176, 186, 238; **L15**: 48, 55-58, 188-91, 255-56, 267, 271, 366; **L16**: 309, 376-78, 390-94, 409, 416-19
related to education, **M13**: 321, 333; **L5**: xii-xiv, 3-40; **L6**: 104-8; **L9**: 98-100, 195-98
J. Robinson on, **M13**: 422
and culture, **M15**: 11; **L3**: 306, 308; **L5**: 106-7; **L14**: 8-10, 100; **L17**: 405
and social science, **M15**: 235-36; **L2**: 47-48, 51, 54, 347, 359-60; **L6**: xvi-xvii, 65-66; **L16**: x, 313
in Austria, **M15**: 316
objects of, **L1**: 111-19, 126-27, 130, 131; **L14**: 20-25, 28, 80-83, 151-52, 196-97
pure and applied, **L1**: 128-30; **L2**: 342-45, 443-44; **L4**: 65, 68; **L6**: 431; **L13**: 54-55, 211, 261, 267-68, 272, 282-83, 320; **L15**: 190, 228
experimental, **L1**: 319; **L8**: 67-69, 102; **L17**: 355
change in, **L1**: 330; **L12**: 87, 132, 137-38, 141, 183; **L17**: 468
reason and, **L2**: 221-25
Holmes on, **L3**: 181-82
related to values, **L4**: 20, 76, 206, 209, 226, 227

and real, **L4**: 173-77, 196, 198-200
Kurtz on, **L5**: xx-xxi
Comte on, **L5**: 154
J. Marsh on, **L5**: 179
and economics, **L6**: 44-45; **L9**: 97-98; **L13**: 69; **L17**: 412
Cohen on, **L6**: 299-303; **L14**: 389, 392-98; **L16**: 194
abstraction in, **L8**: 295; **L16**: 285-86
Hogben on, **L11**: 391-94; **L12**: 483n
Hutchins on, **L11**: 404-7, 594-95
Peirce on, **L11**: 422, 423, 481, 483-84
Reiser on, **L11**: 432-35
Bingham on, **L11**: 438
authority of, **L11**: 454-63
Russell on, **L11**: 455-61
and qualitative, **L12**: 71, 248-49
and teleology, **L12**: 81-86, 96-97, 177-78
ancient, **L12**: 94-96, 201-2
and qualities, **L12**: 119-20, 151-52, 215-16
and practical, **L12**: 163, 175-76, 180-81
units of, **L12**: 212, 475-78
and singular, **L12**: 432-34, 443-45
understanding of, **L13**: 135, 258, 268, 271, 273
in Great Britain, **L13**: 370
important to Dewey, **L14**: xiii, xiv
Franklin and, **L14**: 205, 209
Jefferson on, **L14**: 205-6, 209
fund for, **L14**: 311
Hocking on, **L14**: 416-17
Ayres on, **L15**: 359-60
Bentley on, **L16**: xxviii, 319
related to common sense, **L16**: xxxvii, 244-45, 249
related to logic, **L16**: 45, 146-47, 160
naming in, **L16**: 46, 148-49, 159
as systematic inquiry, **L16**: 91, 303-7, 336, 337n-38n
Einstein on, **L16**: 105n
as transaction, **L16**: 111, 242-43
as name, **L16**: 111n, 269
as specification, **L16**: 150-52, 180, 270
definition in, **L16**: 167-68
Kaufmann on, **L16**: 195-98
semiotic as, **L16**: 211-13, 241
Maxwell on, **L16**: 277-78
judgments in, **L16**: 355-57
related to facts, **L17**: 13, 294, 352, 354
Fiske on, **L17**: 94
accumulation in, **L17**: 357-58
Tolstoy on, **L17**: 386-87
in Russian schools, **L17**: 502
Science: The False Messiah (Ayres), **L3**: 305
"Science and Faith at the Moscow Trials" (H. Loeb), **L13**: 394
Science and Method of Politics, The (Catlin), **L3**: 321-23
Science and Philosophy and Other Essays (B. Bosanquet), **L3**: 294, 297
"Science and Society," **L6**: xvi
Science and the Modern World (Whitehead), **L2**: 221-25; **L5**: 265n; **L14**: 130
"Science as Subject-Matter and as Method," **L17**: xvii-xviii, xxi

Science of education
system in, **L5**: 10-13
rules in, **L5**: 14-15
practices in, **L5**: 16-23
content of, **L5**: 24-26
philosophy of education and, **L5**: 26-31
psychology and, **L5**: 31-36
sociology and, **L5**: 36-38
Science Writers, National Association of, **L11**: 127
Scientific
applied to education, **E1**: 64; **E5**: 258
hypotheses, **E3**: 86-89
laws, **E3**: 136
interest, **E3**: 315-17; **E5**: 217-18
definition of, **M3**: xiv, 3-5, 37
knowledge, **L1**: 341-45
Scientific Habit of Thought, The (Barry), **L4**: 79n
Scientific inquiry. *See* Inquiry
Scientific judgment
compared with moral judgment, **M3**: 6-8
nature of, **M3**: 8-20
Scientific method, **E3**: 92, 126; **E5**: 209; **M1**: 171; **M5**: 156-57; **L1**: 365; **L4**: xvi, xviii, 57, 182; **L10**: 341-43; **L11**: 81-82, 151, 155, 157, 433; **L15**: 85; **L17**: 448. *See also* Experimental method
nature of, **M6**: 251-53; **L8**: xi, 226, 253-58; **L14**: 65-66; **L16**: 3, 84, 102, 386
vs. empirical thought, **M6**: 296-301; **L8**: 268-78
in *Cyclopedia of Education*, **M7**: 335-39
in philosophy, **M11**: x, xvi, xviii, 31-32, 351
in education, **M11**: 57
in Polish study, **M11**: 260, 395
in industry, **M11**: 334, 335
Cohen on, **L6**: 299-304, 488-91
applied to human affairs, **L11**: 17, 51-54, 128, 175, 211; **L15**: 60, 102, 158, 161, 164-65, 255-56, 258, 272-75
consensus produced through, **L11**: 48, 142
vs. epistemology, **L12**: 458-65
vs. prescientific method, **L14**: 12
for valuation, **L14**: 51
limits of, **L15**: 117-26
Sheldon on, **L15**: 454, 459-72
as model, **L16**: 48, 50, 55, 65, 66, 72-75, 80, 127, 257-58, 314n, 362-63
Scientific Research and Social Needs (J. Huxley), **L11**: 344
Scientific revolution, **L16**: 289, 292, 319, 337n-38n, 340, 369, 408, 454
impact of, **L4**: 22, 41, 69, 74-78, 204
origin of, **L4**: 72, 117, 206
Scientific Thought (Broad), **L2**: 29; **L14**: 21n
Scientism, **L17**: xviii
Scientists, **L13**: 271-72, 376
vs. artists, **L10**: 21, 52, 80
nature of, **L10**: 44, 267, 270, 308
effect of science on, **L13**: 370-71
work of, **L17**: 356-57
related to philosopher, **L17**: 406
Scientists Are Human (D. Watson), **L13**: 369-72
Scotch psychology, **E3**: 190-92
Scotch school of philosophy, **E4**:

129; **M7**: 201; **L5**: 148, 149, 182, 183; **L12**: 68
Scotism, **M2**: 186, 187
in *Dictionary of Philosophy*, **M2**: 244
Scott, Fred Newton, **E3**: 92; **E4**: 119-22
Scott, Geoffrey, **L10**: 133n
Scott, Walter, **M10**: 310; **L10**: 176, 287
Scotten, Robert M.
on Dewey's visit to Turkey, **M15**: 418-20
Scotus Erigena, **M2**: 183, 205
Scribes
Tolstoy on, **L17**: 386-87, 565
Scripta Mathematica (Keyser), **L16**: 199n
Scriptures, **L9**: xxviii-xxix, 3
Sculpture, **L16**: 397
nature of, **L10**: 13, 37, 111, 147, 162, 200, 256, 270, 318-21
rhythm in, **L10**: 174-75, 180, 182, 222-25
spatial and temporal in, **L10**: 189
distinguishing traits of, **L10**: 231, 234-38, 241-42, 245, 300
transmits civilization, **L10**: 331-36
Seabury, Samuel, **L9**: 348, 354-55, 358, 362, 367-70, 380
Seabury investigation, **L9**: 346, 362, 364
origin of, **L9**: 354-55
F. Roosevelt and, **L9**: 355, 356, 369
recommendations of, **L9**: 377, 380-85
significance of, **L9**: 377-80
Seager, Henry R.
social legislation of, **M5**: 505-9
Search for Order, The (Wiebe), **L16**: ix
Seasons
rituals of, **M5**: 66-67; **L7**: 61
Secondary school. *See* High school
Second Coming, **L13**: 85
Second Reich, **M8**: xxxi
Second Twenty Years at Hull-House, The (Addams), **L15**: 509
Secret societies
among primitive people, **M5**: 37; **L7**: 35-36
Sectarianism, **L14**: 78
Section of Fine Arts (Public Buildings Administration), **L14**: 256-57
Secular humanism. *See* Humanism
Secularism, **L1**: 356; **L9**: xviii-xix, 43-46, 55-56
"Secularizing a Theocracy," **M15**: xx
Security, **L13**: 320
role of, **L4**: x, 149, 181
search for, **L4**: 3-20, 26, 163, 203, 231, 234-37; **L13**: 106, 140, 318
attainment of, **L4**: 24, 29-30, 32, 44, 136, 245
locus of, **L4**: 41, 194
and international armies, **L6**: 210, 457
economic, **L6**: 448
and sanctions, **L6**: 459, 465
in industry, **L7**: 381-83, 390-92, 412-15, 431-36
compatible with freedom, **L11**: 532

Security (*continued*)
threat to, **L15**: 199
supernaturalism provides, **L16**: 392
as child's birthright, **L17**: 518
Sedgwick, Adam, **M6**: 279; **L8**: 238
Seebohm, Frederic, **M5**: 63; **L7**: 58
on tribal solidarity, **M5**: 34; **L7**: 32-33
on wergeld, **M5**: 58-59; **L7**: 54
Sefa Bey, **M15**: 419
Seguin, Edouard, **M8**: 303
Seignobos, Michel Jean Charles, **L16**: 43
Selby, Clarence J., **L17**: 145
Selden, Charles A., **L5**: 359
Seldes, George, **L15**: 375
Selected Poems of Claude McKay (M. Eastman), **L17**: 58-60
Selected Writings (G. Mead), **L6**: xiiin
Selection. *See also* Data, **L12**
in social life, **E5**: 49-53
omitted from logic, **M7**: 132-33
necessity for, **L12**: 126, 129-33, 136, 151-52, 184, 203, 231-32, 267, 318-19, 364-65, 374, 391, 420, 455, 462, 470, 491, 493-94, 499-502, 519-21
basis of, **L17**: 301
Selection-rejection
related to life-processes, **L16**: 344-47, 354
Selectivity
in art, **L10**: 75, 100-101, 131, 151, 188-90, 193, 211, 243, 283, 298
Self, **M6**: 175; **M7**: 403-5; **M14**: 16, 40, 61-62, 82, 95-97, 150, 201-2; **L1**: 173-74, 179-80, 188-90
as subject of psychology, **E1**: 150-53; **E2**: 9
as consciousness, **E2**: 7-8
as individual, **E2**: 8; **E5**: 31
and feeling, **E2**: 21-22, 216, 254-55
growth of, **E2**: 77, 78
in adjustment, **E2**: 125-26
and perception, **E2**: 150-51; **L10**: 168, 180, 225, 251-57, 262, 269, 278, 281, 284-87, 334
and memory, **E2**: 164-66
and intuition, **E2**: 206, 209-11
actual and ideal, **E2**: 254; **E4**: 52-53, 256-57
and harmony, **E2**: 273
as will, **E2**: 311-12, 318-19, 357
Green on, **E3**: xxviii, 23, 24, 160-62
Seth on, **E3**: 56-62, 64-68
transcendental, **E3**: 56-74; **E5**: 31
in Kant, **E3**: 62-74
and desire, **E3**: 161-63; **L7**: 220
unity of, **E3**: 169; **E5**: 26; **L13**: 323; **L17**: 155
social, **E3**: 335-36; **M5**: 16, 85; **L7**: 14, 78-79; **L17**: 4, 59
and universality, **E5**: 27
use of, **E5**: 28; **L13**: 328
and impulse, **E5**: 123-24
moral and ethical, **E5**: 396-97, 406-8, 421
projective, **E5**: 404-5, 418
Baldwin on, **E5**: 404-8, 421-22
Royce on, **M2**: 127-29
theories of, **M5**: 28-29; **L7**: 28, 285-86; **L15**: 49, 50, 94
Kafirs on, **M5**: 28n-29n; **L7**: 28n

Greek conception of, **M5**: 130-32; **L7**: 121-23
in *Cyclopedia of Education*, **M7**: 339-43, 357
relation of things and, **M7**: 454-55
Fichte on, **M8**: 187
as knowing, **M9**: 180-81
related to interest, **M9**: 361-62
Dewey on, **M14**: xi
primacy of, **L5**: 72n
and habit, **L7**: 170-71, 205
and choice, **L7**: 274, 285-89, 297, 307
and action, **L7**: 288-90, 292, 306
static and dynamic, **L7**: 306-8
nature of, **L11**: 84-85, 452-53, 586; **L16**: 248, 288, 384
in literature, **L11**: 506-7
absolute, **L13**: 148-49
formation of, in inquiry, **L14**: 70-73
James on, **L14**: 164-66
Hocking on, **L14**: 411-12
as name, **L16**: 269
and reality, **L17**: 155-56

Self-action
as name, **L16**: xxxiii-xxxiv, 71, 269
vs. transaction, **L16**: 4, 96, 144
nature of, **L16**: 66-68, 132, 135
as stage of inquiry, **L16**: 100-104, 108, 112, 123-24, 127-30
uses of, **L16**: 104-5, 138
replaced, **L16**: 114-15
traces of, **L16**: 116, 121

Self-activity, **E5**: 374-75
as ultimate educational ideal, **M7**: 183
influences on, **M7**: 185-87
related to physical activity, **M9**: 311

Self-assertion, **E5**: 42-46
tendencies toward, **M5**: 81-86; **L7**: 75-78
criticism of, **M5**: 332-37

Self-consciousness, **E1**: 160; **E2**: 16; **E5**: 26-27; **L17**: 4
during adolescence, **M1**: 216
in *Cyclopedia of Education*, **M7**: 343-45

Self-control, **E5**: 43; **L13**: 12
meaning of, **L13**: 41-42
and freedom, **L13**: 43
Greek idea of, **L17**: 172
need for, **L17**: 343

Self-creation, **M12**: xxvii, 223
Self-criticism, **L13**: 276-77
Self-deception, **M14**: 105-6, 173-74
Self-defense
vs. defensive war, **L6**: 223, 457-58
need for, **L17**: 525
Self-delusion, **M12**: 160-61
Self-denial, **M5**: 80; **L7**: 74
criticism of, **M5**: 328-32
Self-determination, **E5**: 29, 374
Self-development, **E5**: 400
Self-discipline, **M5**: 80; **L7**: 74
Self-education
in Russia, **L17**: 495-96
Self-evidence, **L1**: 73, 93, 106; **L12**: 18, 25, 144, 148, 157-59, 404; **L15**: 28
Self-expression, **M6**: 225; **L8**: 180
vs. expression, **L10**: xxvi, 15, 68, 112, 288
Self-government, **L13**: 66, 95, 114, 147, 177
in China, **M13**: 129, 150
Marxist, **L13**: 101

Self-government (*continued*)
means for, **L13**: 103, 104
Jefferson on, **L13**: 107, 175
Rousseau on, **L13**: 149
Carlyle on, **L13**: 150
importance and complexity of, **L13**: 155
Self Government and Politics in School (Welling), **L11**: 516
Selfhood, **M7**: 295
Self-hypnosis, **M15**: 45
Self-interest, **M12**: 191-92
as motivation, **M6**: 367; **L7**: 292-98, 300; **L13**: 147
doctrines of, **M9**: 308-9; **L7**: 332
and success, **L7**: 202
consequences of, **L7**: 295, 322
in behavior, **L13**: 74, 75, 140
in Marxism, **L13**: 132-33
Selfishness, **E3**: 375-76
Kant on, **M5**: 280; **L7**: 220
for self-preservation, **L7**: 153-54
nature of, **L7**: 226, 294-96
Self-love, **M6**: 367; **M14**: 21, 92-97, 202
Self-mastery, **L2**: 138
Self-negation, **E5**: 43
Self-preservation, **M6**: 366-67
of community, **M5**: 62; **L7**: 57
supported by environment, **M10**: 7-8
Hobbes on, **L7**: 153-54
Self-realization, **L7**: 302
Dewey on, **E2**: xxv; **E4**: xvii; **M5**: xii-xxxiv
concept of, **E4**: 42-44, 52-53, 246
Self-relation, **L2**: 131, 133
"Self-Reliance" (Emerson), **L5**: 139
Self-respect, **L7**: 297
Self-sacrifice, **L7**: 189
Self-satisfaction, **E3**: 327
Seligman, Edwin R. A., **M8**: 410; **L8**: 3n, 13n, 19n; **L17**: 125, 560
Sellars, Roy Wood, **M4**: xx; **M7**: x; **L3**: 397-98; **L16**: 79n, 209n
Semantical definition, **L16**: 164, 169
"Semantic Conception of Truth, The" (Tarski), **L16**: 40-42
Semanticists, **L16**: 299n
Semantics
C. Morris on, **L15**: 142-45, 150; **L16**: 33-35
Carnap on, **L16**: 18, 29n, 30-32
logicians on, **L16**: 38-39
nature of, **L16**: 155, 160, 171, 300, 446
terminology of, **L16**: 272
Sembrich, Marcella, **M11**: 313-14
Seminal reasons
in *Dictionary of Philosophy*, **M2**: 244-45
Semiosis, **L15**: 142
nature of, **L16**: 9, 217, 222-23
as sign-process, **L16**: 211-13
problem of, **L16**: 230-35, 270
terminology of, **L16**: 236-40
Semiotic
of C. Morris, **L16**: 33-35, 210-41
disposition in, **L16**: 221, 231-37
Semitic totem group, **M5**: 26; **L7**: 26
Senate. *See* United States Senate
Seneca, **M5**: 132; **L7**: 123, 131, 132
Sensa
and observational propositions, **L14**: 170-71
Sensation, **E3**: 213, 214; **M4**:

118-19, 150; **M12**: xiv, 128, 132; **L1**: 246, 339; **L11**: 71, 73, 77, 78, 83; **L12**: 91-92, 147-49, 418-19; **L15**: 49, 84, 85, 90-91. *See also* Feeling; Sensori-motor
and knowledge, **E1**: 19, 21-22, 125-28; **E3**: 213-14; **E5**: 5, 6, 15-16, 18, 21; **M14**: 132; **L4**: 136, 138, 154, 206
analyzed by experiment, **E1**: 54
and stimulus, **E1**: 106-7; **E2**: 30-34, 37-43; **E5**: 97, 99, 106-7, 439
theories of, **E1**: 180-83, 186-88, 313-19, 324-25, 342; **L13**: 93; **L16**: 103
characteristics of, **E2**: 29, 31, 43-45; **E5**: 96-97
as element in consciousness, **E2**: 34-37
differentiation of, **E2**: 45-47
of pressure, **E2**: 49
of place, **E2**: 51-52
muscular, **E2**: 53-55, 142, 143
of senses, **E2**: 56-68, 144
of temperature, **E2**: 68-70
organic, **E2**: 70-72
interest in, **E2**: 109-10
psychology of, **E4**: 201-2
and idea, **E5**: 96
related to mental state, **M7**: 34
James on, **M10**: 50; **L14**: 159-63
and experience, **M12**: 129; **M14**: 25, 140; **L14**: 125, 191, 197; **L16**: 245, 263
relativity of, **M12**: 130-31
in art, **L10**: xxvii-xxviii, 27, 250, 259-60
vs. emotion, **L13**: 333
related to physical events, **L14**: 80-81
as terminology, **L16**: 93n
in vision, **L16**: 114n
related to movement, **L17**: 217, 301
as psychical, **L17**: 424
Sensational empiricism, **E3**: 18; **M3**: 158n; **M6**: 175; **M7**: xvi; **M9**: 276; **L5**: 149, 152; **L10**: 136, 293, 364; **L14**: 99; **L16**: 335
on knowledge, **L4**: 88, 137, 141, 144, 145n
failure of, **L4**: 90, 125; **L16**: 326
on sensory qualities, **L4**: 91, 92
vs. rationalism, **L4**: 98
reaction to, **L4**: 210
Sensationalism, **M6**: 175; **M7**: 144; **L5**: 169, 479; **L15**: 10-11
and relativity of feeling, **E1**: 22-25, 29, 31-33
in empirical logic, **E3**: 131-32
in *Dictionary of Philosophy*, **M2**: 245-47
in *Cyclopedia of Education*, **M7**: 345-46
Locke's theory of, **M9**: 276-77
of Helvétius, **M9**: 277
related to education, **M9**: 277-80
affected by particular and general, **M9**: 352-53
Hume on, **M10**: 12-13
Sensationalists, **L1**: 149
Sensation-image, **M10**: 65
Sense, **M8**: 87; **L10**: 154. *See also* Sensation
experience, **E1**: 370
and self, **E3**: 73-74
and reason, **E3**: 227-28, 333-35; **L17**: 157
training, **M1**: 93-96; **M6**: 289-90, 330; **L8**: 297, 317

Sense (*continued*)
illusions, **M8**: 53-54
object, **M8**: 58, 86
Rousseau on, **M8**: 217-18
and meaning, **L1**: 144, 198, 200-207, 221, 246-47
qualities, **L2**: 45, 47, 54; **L10**: 22, 104-9, 122, 319
role of, **L4**: xix, 113, 114, 125, 184, 239
Dewey on, **L4**: xx
attitude toward, **L4**: 67, 71-73
as source of ideas, **L4**: 91-94, 98, 99, 101
J. Marsh on, **L5**: 185-89
esthetic role of, **L10**: xxi-xxii, xxiv-xxviii, 24-28, 36-40, 55, 56, 180, 221-23, 244, 263-65
in esthetic experience, **L10**: 278, 294-99; **L13**: 366
impression, **L14**: 160
appeal to, **L17**: 17-18
Sense data, **M8**: 84; **L5**: 158, 175; **L12**: 149-50, 153, 157
concepts of, **L4**: xiii; **L16**: xxxiii, 192, 334-35
character of, **L4**: 53, 90
function of, **L4**: 137-43, 150, 156, 158
esthetic value of, **L10**: 112, 120-33, 136, 203, 257
Cohen and Nagel on, **L16**: 15, 195
Kaufmann vs. Dewey on, **L16**: 196n
Russell on, **L16**: 201n
Moore on, **L16**: 203-7
Sense of Beauty, The (Santayana), **M11**: 385; **L10**: 364
Sense-organs, **L2**: 47-48; **L14**: 171
as media, **L10**: 28, 31, 58, 199-201
convey qualities, **L10**: 123, 127-28, 131, 220, 239-46, 254-55
Sense perception, **E5**: 5, 226-27, 317-18; **M7**: 260-61; **M11**: 345; **M12**: 259; **L1**: 250-55, 339; **L8**: 8, 12; **L12**: 290, 418-19
and science, **M8**: 60-63; **L16**: 306-7
nature of, **L2**: 44-54; **L17**: 251
structure of, **L17**: 424-25
Senses and the Intellect, The (Bain), **M6**: 300-301; **L8**: 276
Sensitivity, **L1**: 196-97, 223; **L13**: 19
esthetic, **L10**: 203, 269-70, 287, 308, 313-14, 327-28
art affects, **L13**: 366
D. Watson on, **L13**: 371
Sensori-motor
apparatus, **E5**: 96; **M7**: 27-29
circuit, **E5**: 97, 109
process, **E5**: 103
coordinations, **E5**: 205; **M2**: 43-48
Sensory, **M8**: 85, 86
quales, **E5**: 97-98, 108, 156
related to motor and perceptional, **L16**: 140, 307n, 326
in inquiry, **L16**: 329
Sensualism
in *Dictionary of Philosophy*, **M2**: 247
Sentence, **M6**: 325-26; **L8**: 232, 313-14. *See also* Language, **L12**
and proposition, **L12**: 174, 284-89
Carnap on, **L16**: 17, 18, 21-27, 31
Tarski on, **L16**: 39-40
as name, **L16**: 269
Sentiency, **L1**: 199, 204, 205
Sentimentalism, **E5**: 93; **M12**: 121; **M14**: 17

"Sentiment of Rationality, The" (W. James), **L11**: 473
Sequence, **L12**: 437
Serbia, **M10**: 269, 288; **M11**: xiii, 245, 255; **M15**: 93, 123, 140
Serenity
  in art, **L10**: 165-66
Serfdom, **L17**: 503
Series, **L1**: 192-93, 206-7, 212-13
  idea in number sense, **E5**: 177-85, 188-91
  parts in, **E5**: 191
  organic, **L12**: 36-37, 41-42, 56, 385
  in Greek logic, **L12**: 212-13
  temporal, **L12**: 224-25, 245, 316-17, 330
Service
  esteem for, **M9**: 323
  in industry, **L7**: 424-25
Seth, Andrew, **E1**: xxv; **E2**: xxiii; **E3**: 186
  on Hegel, **E1**: 164-65; **E3**: 56-62, 192
  on self, **E3**: 64-68
  on philosophy, **M2**: 191-92
Settled, **L12**: 15-16, 123-25, 186, 189, 220
Seven Philosophical Problems (Hobbes), **M11**: 21
Seventy Times Seven (Jensen), **L11**: 506-8
Seward, William H., **M11**: 206
Sewing
  teaching of, **M1**: 13-15
Sex, **M14**: 93, 104, 106-7, 114; **L10**: 194, 243
  and psycho-physic activity, **M2**: 43
  in coeducation, **M2**: 115-16
  groups based on, **M5**: 36; **L7**: 35, 52, 60-61, 75, 87
  in primitive societies, **M5**: 36-37; **L7**: 35-36
  in family life, **M5**: 49-50
  as agency of individualism, **M5**: 82; **L7**: 75
  attitude toward, **L7**: 447
  significance of, **L7**: 447-48
  and marriage, **L7**: 450-52, 458-59
  Jennings on, **L7**: 460-61
  information about, **L17**: 127
Sex in Education (E. Clarke), **L17**: 7, 553
Sex Side of Life, The (M. Dennett), **L17**: 127, 560
Sextus Empiricus, **L4**: x, xix, xx
Sexual ethics
  Russell on, **L14**: 232-35, 238-46
Seyda, Marjan
  on Polish question, **M11**: 276, 280, 283-84, 301, 302, 323
Shaftesbury, Anthony Ashley Cooper, 3d earl of, **E4**: 128, 144, 147; **M3**: 53; **M7**: 285; **M15**: 9; **L7**: 154, 238; **L11**: 18
Shakespeare, William, **E1**: 48; **M3**: 69; **M5**: 28, 64, 94n, 145, 182, 215; **M6**: 193; **M7**: 277; **M8**: 191; **M12**: xiii, 134; **M13**: 30-31; **M15**: 332; **L3**: 5, 61; **L5**: 394; **L6**: 497; **L7**: 27, 43, 58, 147; **L8**: 126; **L9**: 225; **L10**: xxx, 289; **L11**: 86, 91, 94; **L13**: 358; **L14**: 98, 111; **L15**: 87; **L17**: 12, 554, 557
  on ethical postulate, **E3**: 322
  compared with Dante, **E4**: 193
  as poet, **L10**: 29, 102, 130, 148, 163, 178, 194, 199, 209-10, 354
  attitude of, **L10**: 39, 41
  on judgment, **L10**: 303, 365

Shakespeare, William (*continued*)
criticized, **L10**: 318-19, 324-25, 351, 365
on ages of man, **L17**: 255, 563
memory in, **L17**: 325, 564
"Shall We Join the League of Nations?" (Lovejoy), **M15**: xvii
"Shall We Use the Class Dynamic?" (Raup), **L11**: 385-86
Shaman, **L9**: 26
Shanghai, China, **M12**: 5, 31, 71-72, 74, 253, 255; **M13**: 72, 89, 105, 108, 122, 124, 144, 180; **L6**: 207
Dewey visits, **M11**: xviii
revolt in, **M11**: 189, 196
drugs in, **M11**: 236, 239, 240
Japan invades, **L6**: xx, 190, 205-6
and Pact of Paris, **L6**: 194
sanctions related to, **L6**: 202, 450, 456n, 457
Shank, George H., **M13**: 410, 494-95
Shantung (Shandong), China, **M12**: 22, 23, 68; **M13**: 80, 91, 199, 211; **M15**: 126
issue of, **M11**: 158; **M12**: 37
Japan's control of, **M11**: 186, 189, 194, 198, 224, 232; **M12**: 28-40; **M13**: 192
China claims, **M11**: 201, 203
drugs in, **M11**: 238
and Versailles Treaty, **M13**: 73, 202
diplomatic position of, **M13**: 77, 85, 144-45, 201-3
economic question in, **M13**: 81, 123, 142-43
Shape
artistic use of, **L10**: xxi-xxii, 21, 99, 107-9, 119-22, 231-32, 333, 345, 357, 364
Share-the-Work
committee, **L9**: 252-53
campaign, **L9**: 307
Sharp, Frank Chapman
on moral judgment, **M4**: 221-22
Shatsky, Stanislav, **L6**: 292; **L17**: 505, 571
experimental programs of, **L3**: 247-48, 433
Shaw, George Bernard, **M15**: 128; **L2**: 227; **L7**: 409-10; **L14**: 95, 347
Sheboygan, Wis., **M7**: 461-62
Sheffield, Alfred Dwight, **L5**: 412n, 414
Shelburne Essays (P. More), **L9**: xxxn
Sheldon, Wilmon Henry
on value, **M11**: 375, 377, 382
on naturalism, **L15**: xvi, 453-72
response to, **L15**: 109-26
Shelley, Percy Bysshe, **E3**: 123; **M5**: 145; **M11**: 384; **L1**: 369; **L6**: 492-93; **L10**: 116, 326
on poetry, **L10**: 294, 347-51, 363, 366
Sheppard, Morris, **L6**: 394
Sherman Anti-Trust Act, **L5**: 59; **L7**: 417, 430; **L9**: 281
Sherrill, Charles Hitchcock, **M13**: 345-47
Sherrington, Charles Scott, **L3**: 35; **L15**: xvii-xviii
Sherwood, Russell T., **L9**: 366-68
Shestov, Alexei A., **L11**: 322, 603
Shibusawa, Eiichi, **M11**: 231-32, 395
Shintoism, **M11**: 170, 171
Shiplacoff, Abraham I., **L5**: 443
Shipler, Guy Emery, **L11**: 530
Shipstead, Henrik, **L6**: 355, 394

Shorey, Paul, **L11**: 592
"Short Catechism concerning Truth, A," **L8**: xn
"Shortening the Years of Elementary Schooling" (Soldan), **M3**: 294-98
Short Study of Ethics, A (D'Arcy), **E5**: 25-33
Shotwell, James T.
  criticizes outlawry of war, **L3**: 163n, 168-72, 415-16
Shouse, Jouett, **L9**: 89
Shu Shi Chang, **M13**: 131
Shuster, George N., **L11**: 530
Siberia, USSR, **L6**: 458
  intervention in, **M11**: 120, 151-54, 163, 167, 178, 199
  recruiting in, **M11**: 306
  diplomatic and strategic importance of, **M12**: 64; **M13**: 79-82, 84, 85, 91, 233-37, 241
Sic et Non (Abelard), **M5**: 141
Sidgwick, Alfred, **M3**: 65; **M10**: 352n
Sidgwick, Arthur, **M4**: 242
Sidgwick, Eleanor M., **M4**: 242
Sidgwick, Henry, **E3**: 93; **E4**: 42; **M3**: 55; **M4**: 11; **M5**: 4; **L7**: 6
  memoir of, **M4**: 242-49
  on good, **M5**: 237n
  on happiness theory, **M5**: 243n
  on religious sanctions, **M5**: 320n
Sidney, Philip, **E4**: 121, 193
Sidorsky, David
  on Dewey's 1927-28 writings, **L3**: ix-xxxiii
Siems-Carey Company, **M11**: 231, 395
Sienkiewicz, Henryk, **M11**: 312, 397
Sight, **E5**: 106
  as element of knowledge, **E2**: 63-68, 225-26
Signals, **L1**: 139-42, 213-14
  nature of, **L16**: 6, 93, 141, 275, 309n
  as process of designation, **L16**: 62, 131
  as stage of sign, **L16**: 69-70, 139-40, 474
  as name, **L16**: 72, 270
  postulations for, **L16**: 84, 90
  forms of, **L16**: 110n, 143-47, 261
  C. Morris on, **L16**: 225
Sign-behavior, **L16**: 212n, 223-24
Sign-events, **L16**: 21n
Sign-family, **L16**: 226
Significance, **E1**: 178-79; **L15**: xxii-xxiii, 15-16; **L16**: 320, 331-32
Significant Paragraphs from Henry George's "Progress and Poverty" (H. G. Brown), **L3**: 359n
Signification, **L1**: 200, 202, 207. *See also* Meaning
  C. Morris on, **L16**: 210n, 227
  modes of, **L16**: 234, 236
Significatum
  C. Morris on, **L16**: 213, 216-17, 227
  in semiotic, **L16**: 232-37
Signifying
  function of, **M6**: 187; **L8**: 119-20
  C. Morris on, **L16**: 214-18
Sign-process, **L16**: 137, 144, 183
  as semiosis, **L16**: 211-13
  C. Morris on, **L16**: 212n, 220n, 226
  factors in, **L16**: 232-33
  in semiotic, **L16**: 237, 270

Signs, **L13**: 198-200, 248n. *See also* Evidence, **L12**
and sensations, **E2**: 52, 142-44
linguistic, **M6**: 192, 314-20; **L8**: 127-28, 166, 297, 301-5; **L16**: xxxii, 297-309
nature of, **M13**: 383, 389; **L4**: 203; **L13**: 197; **L16**: 5, 6, 62, 86n, 225, 332
data as, **L4**: 80, 140, 143
numbers as, **L4**: 103-4
role of, **L4**: 106, 189, 237
judgment of, **L4**: 170
as qualities, **L4**: 191, 193; **L12**: 76-77, 132, 149-50, 240, 248-49, 252, 268-69, 475
artificial, **L8**: 126, 302-3
in art, **L10**: xiii, 89-91, 97, 220
and meanings, **L12**: 57, 317, 324, 358n, 468
and consequences, **L12**: 504-5
and epistemology, **L12**: 515-16, 519-20
theory of, **L15**: 131-36, 141-52, 473
in triadic relation, **L16**: 9-11
Peirce on, **L16**: 11, 51
Carnap on, **L16**: 22, 23n, 26-27, 29n, 31
Cohen and Nagel on, **L16**: 25
behavioral, **L16**: 69-70, 134-39, 473-74
as name, **L16**: 72, 91, 270
Dubislav on, **L16**: 161n
C. Morris on, **L16**: 210-20
in semiotic, **L16**: 229-31, 236-37
status of, **L16**: 235-36
in inquiry, **L16**: 322-25
Signs, Language and Behavior (C. Morris), **L15**: 473; **L16**: 210-41
Sign vehicle
C. Morris on, **L16**: 9, 34-35, 45, 226-27
vs. sign, **L16**: 134
Sigwart, Christoph, **E3**: 75, 92; **M3**: 64; **L12**: xii, 188
Sikorski, Wladyslaw, **L15**: 295
Silbermann, Jesse, **L9**: 372-73
Silesia, **M11**: 266, 286
Silhouettes, **L10**: 184
Simeon Stylites, Saint, **M10**: 249
Similarity, **M6**: 388; **L12**: 185-86. *See also* Comparison, **L12**
association by, **L5**: 256-61; **L17**: 330-31
Simkhovitch, Vladimir G., **L15**: xxvi
Simmel, Georg, **L16**: xiii, xvi, 120n
on intellectual and moral, **E4**: 197-200
Simmons, Duane B., **M5**: 24
Simonds, Frank H., **L6**: 468n
Simple proposition, **L12**: 150-53, 335, 340
Simples
of Russell, **L16**: 199-202
Simplification
in education, **L13**: 14-15
evaluated, **L13**: 116
classes of, **L13**: 117
Marxist, **L13**: 119
of human nature, **L13**: 137-38
Simultaneity, **L4**: 115-16
Sin
in Hebrew morality, **M5**: 94; **L7**: 86
as part of cultus, **M5**: 95; **L7**: 87
aspects of, **M5**: 100; **L7**: 91
Sincerity, **M5**: 101; **L7**: 93; **L17**: xxiv
Singapore, **M11**: 238; **L2**: 176

Singer, Edgar A., Jr., **M11**: 13
Singular, **L12**: xvi, 351-52. *See also* This, **L12**
concept of, **L12**: 72-73, 126, 129, 196, 201, 209, 220, 242, 247
propositions, **L12**: 249, 255-56, 267-68, 290-93
and science, **L12**: 432-34, 443-45
Singularism
in *Dictionary of Philosophy*, **M2**: 247
Sino-Japanese conflict. *See* China; Japan
Sisto, J. A., **L9**: 366
Sisyphus, **M8**: 64
Situation, **M7**: xviii. *See also* Individual, **L12**; Qualitative, **L12**
related to knowledge, **M6**: xvii-xviii
in judgments of practice, **M8**: xv-xvi
function of, in thought, **L5**: 246-52, 256-62
problematic vs. unified, **L11**: 152, 215; **L14**: 44, 46, 56, 69-72, 76, 81n; **L15**: 36-41, 69-71, 72n
as end of inquiry, **L12**: xx, xxii, 108-9, 163, 167-68, 203, 207, 220, 440, 455-56, 466-67; **L14**: 43, 47-48, 83-85
defined, **L12**: 72; **L13**: 32
formation of, **L13**: 24
related to interaction, **L13**: 25-26, 33
concept of, **L14**: 28-34
indeterminate, **L14**: 180-81, 184-87
doubtful, **L14**: 183-87
Mackay on, **L15**: 393-401
Rice on, **L15**: 431-32
as name, **L16**: 6, 43, 71, 270
as form of event, **L16**: 62, 68-69, 132
Dewey on, **L16**: 92n-93n, 281-82
uniqueness of, **L17**: xxiii
Situational
of Mead, **L16**: 101n
Situs, **L2**: 52-54
Sixteenth Amendment, **L7**: 420
"Sixth Meditation" (Descartes), **M8**: 23
Skepticism, **E1**: 61, 62; **M10**: 38; **M12**: 220; **M13**: 68, 486; **M15**: 326; **L1**: 378, 383; **L9**: xx; **L11**: 79; **L15**: 63
intuitionalism as, **M2**: 28
in *Dictionary of Philosophy*, **M2**: 231-34
nature of, **M6**: 23; **L4**: 176, 182; **L17**: 13, 17
Dewey on, **L4**: x, xix-xxii; **L8**: xvi-xvii
of Hume, **L4**: 113
sources of, **L4**: 154, 155; **L14**: 199
Santayana on, **L9**: 242, 243; **L14**: 11, 302
misconception about, **L17**: xxi
regarding Christianity, **L17**: 530
Skeptics, **E4**: 230; **E5**: 9; **M5**: 127, 202; **L7**: 118; **L8**: 6, 24
Sketch Book of Geoffrey Crayon, Gent., The (Irving), **M8**: 292
Skill
related to child, **M1**: 213-15, 227; **L17**: 286, 293
studies, **M6**: 220; **L8**: 162
transfer of, **M9**: 69-70
limitations of, **M9**: 83-84, 264-65, 320, 349-50

Skill (*continued*)
and thinking, **M9**: 159
modes of, **M9**: 267-68
of artist, **L10**: 87, 145, 269, 291, 333
role in inquiry, **L16**: 327-31
technical, **L16**: 362
need for, **L17**: 77-78
command of, **L17**: 296
overemphasis on, **L17**: 514-15
Skinner, B. F., **M7**: xxiii; **M13**: xiv
on definition, **L16**: 167, 170-71
on logic, **L16**: 183n
praised, **L16**: 447
Skipped intermediaries, **L12**: 316n
Skirmunt, Constantine, **M11**: 281
Sklavenwahrheit, **M7**: 433
Skvirsky, Boris E., **M13**: 240n
Slavery, **M13**: 289; **L15**: 277, 309; **L17**: 315, 503
ideology of, **M5**: 76; **L7**: 76; **L15**: 163-64, 173, 234
Roman, **M5**: 78; **L7**: 72, 128-29, 132-33
Aristotle on, **M9**: 261-62; **L13**: 287
of Greek social system, **M9**: 297
economic wastefulness of, **M9**: 318
origins of, **L3**: 20
Plato on, **L13**: 43
Slavs, **M5**: 25n, 62, 83; **M11**: xiii, 325, 326; **L7**: 25n, 57, 76
group ownership of, **M5**: 30; **L7**: 29
Sleeper, Ralph W.
on Dewey's 1939-41 writings, **L14**: ix-xxiv
on Dewey's logic, **L16**: xxxiin
Slesinger, Zalmen, **L11**: 485-86
Slovaks, **M11**: xiii
Smedley, F. W., **M1**: 325
Smell
as element of knowledge, **E2**: 56-57
and taste, **E2**: 59, 221-22
Smiley, W. H., **E5**: xcvi
Smirnov, Ivan N., **L11**: 321, 602
Smith, Adam, **E4**: 142, 215; **M3**: 53; **M5**: 155; **M7**: 332, 361; **M13**: 281; **M15**: 255, 256; **L2**: 244, 291; **L4**: xxi; **L7**: 154, 238, 411; **L12**: 498; **L13**: 73, 126
moral philosophy of, **E4**: 145; **M5**: 150
on commerce, **M4**: 38-41
on conscience, **M5**: 132; **L7**: 123
as individualist, **M5**: 469, 472
economic theory of, **M6**: 367-68; **L7**: 143, 403
influences liberalism, **L11**: 9-12, 283
Smith, Alfred E., **L5**: 336; **L6**: 158
Dewey supports, **L3**: 184-85
Smith, Arthur, **M5**: 70; **L7**: 64
Smith, C. H., **M13**: 240n
Smith, H. B., **E3**: 3
Smith, Henry Preserved, **M5**: 102; **L7**: 93
Smith, J. Allan, **L9**: 365
Smith, James Allen, **M5**: 496n
Smith, John M. P., **L7**: 83
Smith, Munroe, **M5**: 496n, 497
Smith, Payson, **L11**: 567n, 572, 577-79
Smith, Richard L., **L6**: xiii
Smith, Sydney, **M3**: 53
Smith, Theobald, **L14**: 397
Smith, Thomas Vernor, **L2**: 327n; **L15**: 321n
political philosophy of, **L17**: 115-18

Smith, William Robertson, **M5**: 33, 35n, 410n; **L7**: 32, 33n
Smith College, **E3**: 110n; **M6**: 3n; **M11**: 70n; **L17**: 7, 8
Smoot-Hawley Tariff Act, **L5**: 436; **L6**: 164-65, 172, 237, 241
Smullyan, Arthur Francis, **L16**: 210n
  reviews Dewey-Bentley articles, **L16**: xxxi, 276, 443-47
Smulski, John F.
  as Polish leader, **M11**: 256, 257, 261, 280, 287, 299-306, 309, 328, 395
  policies of, **M11**: 269, 295, 296, 322
Smyth, Herbert C., **M10**: 161
Snedden, David
  on vocational education, **M8**: 411-13, 460-65
Snobbery, **L13**: 167
Snow, C. P., **L17**: xviii
"Snow-Bound" (Whittier), **L17**: 252, 253
Sociability, **M6**: 162, 366; **L13**: 34-35; **L17**: 427
Social, **L13**: 26
  satisfaction, **E3**: 320-22, 327
  influence on duty, **E3**: 339
  life, **E5**: 13, 14, 89, 249; **L17**: 75-76, 405
  ethics, **E5**: 22, 23, 54-55, 279-80
  role in education, **E5**: 68-69, 85, 214, 220-21, 229, 255-56, 451; **L17**: 226-41, 170
  imagination, **E5**: 72
  values, **E5**: 76
  related to psychological, **E5**: 85-86
  heritage, **E5**: 90
  communication, **E5**: 230; **L17**: 320-22
  progress, **E5**: 300, 411-12
  sanctions, **E5**: 390-91
  development, **M8**: 249-50
  vs. individual, **M9**: 306; **L2**: xxx-xxxi, 244-45, 250, 274, 290, 330, 351-55; **L7**: xiii, xviii, xix, xxviii-xxix, 320-28, 385
  predestination, **M9**: 327, 328
  absolutism, **M13**: 314, 316
  commitment, **M14**: xxii
  phenomena, **M15**: 231-32, 235
  action, **L1**: 149
  compact, **L1**: 169
  consequences, **L1**: 199
  reform, **L1**: 307-8, 323; **L16**: 381
  and biological, **L2**: 243, 330-31, 357
  as principle of philosophical reflection, **L3**: 41-54
  tools, **L5**: 36-37
  institutions, **L7**: 344-48, 452-56; **L9**: 50
  attitude, **L7**: 446-50
  influences inquiry, **L12**: 26-28
  inquiries into, **L12**: 487-506; **L16**: 316-17
  examples of, **L13**: 86, 200
  nature of, **L13**: 338-40; **L16**: 123n, 244, 260, 304-5
  meaning of term, **L14**: 117; **L15**: 92, 210-12, 221, 224
  responsibility, **L14**: 402-6
  conflict, **L14**: 403
  as name, **L16**: 85n, 93n, 270
  spirit, **L17**: 75, 232-33, 235, 237, 241
  language as, **L17**: 235, 236-37, 313
  arithmetic as, **L17**: 237-38

Social (*continued*)
subject-matter, **L17**: 449
in Russia, **L17**: 502
Social and Ethical Interpretations in Mental Development (J. Baldwin), **E5**: lxxxvi-xciv, 385-422
"Social as a Category," **L5**: 175n; **L7**: xx
Social behavior, **L7**: 288-89, 302-3
interaction in, **E5**: 422; **L1**: 134-39, 146-51, 156; **L14**: 117-18
educators influence, **L14**: 360-61
Social change, **L5**: xiv; **L13**: 118-19, 287; **L15**: 248-53, 257, 273
through violence, **M10**: 244; **L11**: xxi, 45-46, 55-56, 58-61, 65, 170, 259-60, 266, 287-88, 293-94, 378-79
history of, **L11**: xxx, 11, 19, 30-32, 168-70, 228, 235, 409
mediated by liberalism, **L11**: 5, 36-37, 41-65
conditions of, **L11**: 26-27, 57-59, 131-34, 136-42, 144, 259, 383-86, 414, 493, 522-24; **L14**: 76, 96
technology related to, **L11**: 143, 186-89, 261, 277-79, 457-60
education related to, **L11**: 189-90
effects of, **L11**: 251-52, 278, 360, 362, 409, 519, 536
Slesinger on, **L11**: 485-86
human nature related to, **L14**: 258-61
Social contract theory, **E1**: 231
Social control, **M5**: 62; **L7**: 57, 217-19, 321-22, 412-22
related to social science, **L6**: xvi-xvii, 65-66
of economics, **L6**: 437
democratic vs. authoritarian, **L11**: 218-21, 223
effects of, **L11**: 223-24, 287, 362, 367, 379
Social-Darwinism, **M9**: xxii
Social Democratic party, **L9**: 289
Social efficiency theory of education, **M9**: 100, 125-30
Social environment, **E5**: 67
moral significance of, **M5**: 16, 38-39, 45-49, 110; **L7**: 14, 37, 43-47, 101, 222, 233-34, 283, 314-20, 330-31, 340-44
problems of, **L7**: 351-58
Social Evolution (B. Kidd), **E4**: 200, 210-13
Social Frontier, **L13**: 304, 403
Dewey's articles in, **L11**: xiii, xvi, 339, 340, 342, 370, 377, 380, 382, 383, 386, 399, 592, 593
Social Ideas of American Educators, The (Curti), **M1**: xvn
Socialism, **M5**: 151-52, 470-71; **M10**: 261; **M12**: xxx, 247, 249; **M15**: 245; **L6**: xviii; **L9**: 76-77
basis of, **E4**: 211; **M5**: 486; **L7**: 426
criticized, **M2**: xx-xxi
Fichte on, **M8**: 175
involved with Polish question, **M11**: xv, 251, 262, 265-67, 270-73, 277, 282, 287, 293-94, 326, 396
in industry, **M11**: 83, 102, 104
nature of, **M11**: 84, 117, 120; **L11**: 61-64, 492; **L13**: 131, 135
in Japan, **M11**: 165

vs. bolshevism, **M11**: 246
international, **M13**: 254
prediction for, **L5**: xx
vs. individualism, **L5**: 80; **L13**: 113-14, 146, 260; **L15**: 212-15, 218-21, 274-75
public vs. capitalistic, **L5**: 90-98
related to Russia, **L6**: 264; **L7**: 427; **L17**: 497-98
on equal distribution, **L7**: 409-10
U.S. attitude toward, **L7**: 428-30
vs. fascism, **L9**: 402-3
Lippmann on, **L11**: 489-90, 493
ultimate vs. utopian, **L13**: 120
as collectivist movement, **L14**: 92-95
and liberalism, **L17**: 116
Lenin on, **L17**: 493

Socialist Call, **L13**: 392
Socialist Labor party, **L6**: 235
Socialist party, **L6**: xix, 169-70, 235, 250, 254, 326; **L9**: 66-69; **L11**: xxiii
Socialists, **L6**: 231, 232, 237; **L13**: 113, 114, 132; **L14**: 365-66
Sociality, **L13**: 78, 163
Socialization, **L2**: 279; **L11**: xxiv, 188, 240, 256-57, 265-66
as stage of moral development, **M5**: 15-16; **L7**: 13-14
Social Legislation, Committee for, **L15**: 324
Social movements
influence philosophy, **L14**: 312-13, 326
Social order, **E3**: 219-20; **L15**: 209, 213, 277
reconstruction of, **M11**: xii, 73-92, 98-99, 102-6, 112-14; **L6**: 94-95; **L7**: xix, 80
explanations of, **M11**: 19, 71, 93-97
and philosophy, **M11**: 43-45, 48, 51-52, 342-45, 348-49
as international bond, **M11**: 123-26
prophet of, **M11**: 148
in Japan, **M11**: 166
in China, **M11**: 220
education related to, **L6**: xxii, 123-24; **L9**: 127, 131-32, 134-35, 159, 167-68, 182-85, 192-93, 206-9
measure of, **L6**: 40-42
and economics, **L6**: 244; **L9**: 208, 229, 231, 232, 234-35, 312
in Russia, **L6**: 263-67
related to legal system, **L6**: 268-70; **L14**: 117-22
churches lag in, **L9**: 46, 54-55
Bellamy on, **L9**: 102-6
and history, **L9**: 205
Brandeis on, **L9**: 237
development of new, **L9**: 297; **L11**: 168, 281, 550
Niebuhr on, **L9**: 402-4
problems of, **L11**: 15, 23-25, 28, 32, 38-41, 50, 54, 64, 79-82, 227-37, 249, 297, 357, 517
Spencer on, **L11**: 16, 29, 33

Social Phases of Education (Dutton), **L17**: 233
Social philosophy
Dewey's work in, **M1**: xii, xxi
reconstruction of, **M12**: 187-88
law in, **M15**: 42, 58, 62, 74-75, 234-35, 260-61, 269-71
morals in, **M15**: 60-61, 238, 242-43

Social philosophy (*continued*)
related to social phenomena, **M15**: 231-32, 259-60
subject-matter of, **M15**: 233
contrasted with social science, **M15**: 234
problems in, **M15**: 237, 240-41
function of criterion in, **M15**: 238-40
individualism defined in, **M15**: 242-44
economic, **M15**: 254-57
psychological and actual wants in, **M15**: 263-66
Social planning, **L6**: 29; **L11**: 174-75, 204-7, 209, 389-90; **L15**: 223, 249-50, 254
and freedom, **L6**: 447-48; **L14**: 294
need for, **L9**: 133-34, 230-32
characteristics of, **L13**: 388-90
Social Problems (H. George), **L9**: 62-63
Social problems, **L11**: 42-44, 53-54, 57, 115-16, 158, 160, 165-66, 484, 563-65; **L15**: 41, 170-83, 203, 222, 253, 261, 264, 307, 378
intelligence applied to, **L14**: 74-76
related to ageing, **L14**: 341-50
Cohen on, **L14**: 402-10
Social psychology, **M1**: 113-14, 131, 146-50; **M8**: 178; **M14**: 3, 44-46, 60-62, 95, 102, 107-8; **L2**: 458-59; **L5**: 238; **L14**: 40
Dewey on, **M10**: xxxiv-xxxv
development of, **M10**: 53-54; **L17**: 54, 422-28
conceptions of, **M10**: 55-56
task of, **M10**: 56-58
"Social Realities *versus* Police Court Fictions," **L14**: xxi
Social relations, **L17**: 260-61
supernatural and, **L9**: xix, 49-50, 52, 53-55
Brameld on, **L9**: 244-45
psychology of, **L14**: 40
Social Religion (Macintosh), **L14**: 286-88
Social science, **E5**: 94; **M11**: 89-93; **L3**: 9; **L11**: 33-36, 392, 394, 406, 555-56, 563-64, 571, 595; **L15**: xxvi, 224
value for psychology, **E1**: 57-58
need for, **M7**: 406-8; **L6**: 67-68
related to philosophy, **M15**: 234; **L3**: 46; **L5**: 159, 161-77; **L14**: 330
vs. science, **M15**: 235-36; **L15**: 161, 166-67, 228-29, 235-38
in Mill's logic, **L5**: 168-69
central issue of, **L5**: 174-77
significance of human nature in, **L6**: xvi, 29
development of, **L6**: 52, 59-61, 447-48
physical vs. social facts in, **L6**: 64-65
cause and effect in, **L6**: 66-67
history of, **L9**: 71-75
affects law, **L14**: xxiv
technology influences, **L14**: 318-19
related to democracy, **L14**: 320
interdependence of subjects in, **L14**: 362-63
Cohen on, **L14**: 385, 407
prejudgment in, **L15**: 226-28
methods of, **L15**: 231, 235
dualism in, **L15**: 232-33
Bentley on, **L16**: xviii, xxiii
Dewey's role in, **L16**: 187
value-judgments in, **L16**: 310-15

inquiry in, **L16**: 340, 454
backward state of, **L16**: 413-16
"Social Science and Social Control," **L6**: xvi, xvii
Social Sciences and Their Interrelations, The (Ogburn and Goldenweiser), **L3**: 11n
Social service, **M11**: 60-63, 66, 76, 393
Social settlement, **M5**: 150; **L17**: 517, 573
at Indianapolis Public School 26, **M8**: 340-52
"Social Significance of Academic Freedom, The," **L11**: xxin
Social Statics (H. Spencer), **M3**: 201-4; **L11**: 16
Social struggle
Niebuhr's views on, **L9**: 399-405
Social studies
teaching of, **L11**: 184-86
Commission on the Teaching of the, **L13**: 389-90
"Social Thought of Mr. Justice Brandeis, The" (Lerner), **L9**: 237-38
Social trends
President's Research Committee on, **L9**: 133, 229-31, 235
conflict in, **L9**: 234-35
Social unity
as creed of National Socialism, **M8**: 432-46
Social Work, National Conference of, **M15**: 150n
Social workers
training of, **L17**: 517, 572-73
Society, **M12**: 103-4, 194. *See also* Greece; Primitive life
conception of, **E1**: 236-37; **M2**: 81; **L15**: 168, 221
Green on, **E3**: 27-29
and moral ends, **E5**: 57; **M9**: 367-70; **L7**: 298-302, 436; **L9**: 431
and art, **E5**: 214; **L6**: 493-99; **L10**: xi, xxxi, 13, 26-28, 33, 110, 245, 251-52, 266, 285, 303, 320, 324, 329-31, 337, 344-47, 351
industrial, **E5**: 258-60; **M15**: 257-58; **L14**: 341-43
Baldwin on, **E5**: 412-14, 417
changing of, **M1**: xx-xxiii; **L7**: 176-78
nature of, **M5**: 37; **L7**: 35-36, 323-24
Kant on, **M5**: 75, 86-87; **L7**: 69, 79
and economics, **M5**: 77; **L6**: xxii; **L7**: 71; **L9**: 61-62, 286
Cynics and Cyrenaics on, **M5**: 118-19; **L7**: 109-10
individual related to, **M5**: 121-22; **M12**: 185-88; **M15**: 245-46; **L7**: 113; **L11**: 30-31, 44, 132-34, 191-93, 219, 291-92, 297; **L14**: 17n; **L17**: 4
status in, **M6**: 214; **L8**: 152
adjustments to, **M6**: 304; **L8**: 282-83
related to imitation, **M7**: 234-37
philosophy related to, **M8**: 144; **M12**: 151, 190; **L4**: 136, 149; **L15**: 163-64; **L16**: 381
in German literature, **M8**: 170-71
related to education, **M8**: 351, 356-64; **L5**: 371-74; **L6**: xxiii, 93-98, 102-4, 108-11, 126-27, 143, 260-61; **L9**: 127-28, 132, 133, 142-44, 151-52, 175, 180, 183-85, 200-204, 207-8; **L11**: xviii-xix, 211, 340-42, 344-47, 537, 541, 547, 557-59

Society (*continued*)
welfare of, **M12**: 182-83; **L11**: 7-9, 174, 373-75
evils of, **M12**: 183-84
theories about, **M12**: 187-88; **M15**: 244-45; **L17**: 101
groupings in, **M12**: 196-97
defined, **M15**: 239; **L5**: 82-83
study of, **M15**: 247-48; **L7**: 328; **L9**: 229-30, 235, 236; **L11**: xxv-xxvi, 55-56, 58, 61, 64n, 145, 292-93, 383
and state, **L2**: 251-54, 278-81, 327-29; **L6**: 177-79
and community, **L2**: 296, 333-34; **L13**: 176
knowledge of, **L4**: xiv, xvi, 158, 168, 170, 174, 216-18
direction of, **L4**: xiv, 212, 219, 220, 238, 249
condition of, **L4**: 62, 200-201, 227, 244
related to science, **L4**: 157, 159, 166, 172, 173; **L6**: 49-63, 417-19; **L9**: 96-97, 100, 101, 108-10
values of, **L4**: 207, 225, 226, 248, 249
religion related to, **L5**: 71-72; **L9**: xviii-xix, 6, 38-42, 44-45, 52-56, 295, 424, 427, 428
Emerson on, **L5**: 122
and children, **L6**: 137-41, 342; **L9**: 233-34
responsible for unemployment relief, **L6**: 153-55, 381-82, 397-400, 436
and politics, **L6**: 188; **L9**: 94-95, 231, 234-35
history of, **L6**: 278-79
stationary vs. progressive, **L7**: x-xi; **L11**: 549-50
demands of, **L7**: 224-25
utilitarianism and, **L7**: 251-52
Carlyle on, **L7**: 327
freedom in, **L7**: 349-50; **L15**: 6, 170-72, 175-83
intelligence related to, **L7**: 365-66; **L9**: 51-53, 107-11
Dewey's role in, **L8**: x-xii
influences of, **L8**: 134-35; **L9**: 191
laissez-faire in, **L9**: 52, 54
George on, **L9**: 65, 300-301; **L11**: xxiv, 48, 257
Kandel on, **L9**: 208-9
structure of, **L11**: xvii-xxiii, 31, 130-31, 182-83, 228-29, 252-55, 258, 361, 370-71, 563
opposing forces in, **L11**: 46-47, 177, 227, 339-40, 342-43, 378, 409-14
classless, **L11**: 60, 383, 497
Reiser on, **L11**: 432-33
Bingham on, **L11**: 438-40
Lippmann on, **L11**: 489-95
Corry on, **L11**: 574
Mill on, **L13**: 138
management of, **L13**: 315
planned vs. planning, **L13**: 321
critique of, **L14**: 14
international, **L15**: 204-5
universities reflect, **L17**: 110
Tolstoy on, **L17**: 382
Society for Ethical Culture (New York City), **M7**: 377; **L13**: 294n
Socio-cultural, **L16**: 309, 392, 394
Socio-Economic Goals of America, Committee on the, **L11**: 548

Sociological
analysis, **M3**: 32-39
motivation, **M15**: 14-15, 17, 19, 325, 331-35
art criticism, **L10**: 320
Sociology, **M11**: 56, 89-90, 398, 407
and psychology, **E4**: 200-201; **E5**: 402
educational, **E5**: 85, 224, 280, 443-45
used by Baldwin, **E5**: 386
teaching of, **M2**: 56-57
important to science of education, **L5**: 36-38
Dewey's philosophy compared with, **L5**: 499-501
related to social conditions, **L9**: 229
Comte's idea of, **L13**: 121
characteristics of, **L16**: 63, 88n, 149, 417, 443
positions held by, **L16**: 82n, 83n, 111, 115
inquiry in, **L16**: 122-26
Sociology and Political Theory (H. Barnes), **L2**: 40
Socius, **E5**: 397; **M10**: 53
Socrates, **E3**: 170, 171, 226; **E4**: 98, 228; **E5**: 24; **M5**: 87, 112, 118; **M7**: 306; **M8**: xxvi; **M10**: 34; **M12**: xii, xxvii, 87, 89; **M14**: 37; **M15**: 70, 336; **L2**: 128; **L5**: 289, 297; **L7**: 80, 103, 109; **L8**: 26, 32; **L11**: xxvi; **L14**: xix, 102, 390; **L15**: 24, 25, 169
on good, **E4**: 124; **M5**: 200; **L2**: 132-33; **L5**: 291
and moral philosophy, **E4**: 134-36, 138, 198, 225
and knowledge of self, **E5**: 6-8
on realism, **M2**: 219
on ethics, **M3**: 45-46
on conduct, **M5**: 10, 111; **L7**: 15, 101, 163
on wisdom, **M5**: 375; **L2**: 130
and foundation of dialectic, **M6**: 422
on knowledge, **M7**: 265-66; **M9**: 197, 364
nature of truth in, **M7**: 416
on nature and man, **M9**: 286
rational discourse of, **M13**: 367
on custom, **M14**: 56
and rational morality, **L2**: 93
as center of *Dialogues*, **L2**: 124-26
criticized, **L2**: 126-27
and virtue, **L2**: 130n
and soul, **L2**: 131-32, 137-39
and comparison of *Protagoras* and *Charmides*, **L2**: 133-35, 138
discovers induction and definition, **L8**: 4-5
on philosophy, **L8**: 21; **L16**: 319, 365, 376-77
on politics and morals as art, **L10**: 31
on artisans, **L16**: 471
distinguishing features of, **L17**: 184-85
significance of, **L17**: 185-86
Socratic Dialogues (Plato), **M15**: 336; **L2**: ix, 124-40; **L5**: 155
Socratic school of philosophy, **M1**: 161
Soddy, Frederick, **L13**: 165
Sokolnikov, Grigory Y., **L15**: 346
Sokols (Alliance of Polish Falcons), **M11**: 287-88, 313, 322
Soldan, Frank Louis, **E5**: xciv; **M3**: 294

S. O. Levinson and the Pact of Paris (Stoner), **M15**: xvn, xviiin; **L6**: xxin; **L15**: 301-2
Solidity
  Locke on, **E1**: 342-44
  Leibniz on, **E1**: 359
  tactile, **E5**: 430
Soliloquy, **L1**: 135, 137
Solipsism, **M1**: 130n; **L15**: 76
  and speech, **M13**: 35-36
Solon, **M12**: xxiii; **L15**: xxx
Solow, Herbert, **L11**: 602
Solution
  subject-matter of, **L16**: 282-83
  abstraction in, **L16**: 285
  in inquiry, **L16**: 291
  of Ogden and Richards, **L16**: 301-2
Some, **L12**: 183, 193-95, 200, 208, 336. *See also* Particulars, **L12**
"Some Logical Considerations concerning the Mental" (C. Lewis), **L15**: 32
"Some Reflections on the Use of Language in the Natural Sciences" (Nagel), **L16**: 173
"Some Stages of Logical Thought," **M1**: xiv; **M6**: xi; **L14**: xvi
Some Turns of Thought in Modern Philosophy (Santayana), **L9**: 240-43
Song, **L10**: 222, 226, 231-32, 284, 330, 332; **L16**: 397; **L17**: 309
  force of, **M5**: 48; **L13**: 70
Song of Hiawatha, The (Longfellow), **M1**: 107
"Songs for Jamaica" (McKay), **L17**: 58-59
Sonnino, Sidney, **M12**: 3
Sons of the American Revolution, **L17**: 561
Sophia (Electress of Hanover), **E1**: 266
Sophia Charlotte (Queen of Prussia), **E1**: 266
Sophists, **E4**: 224, 225; **M7**: 305-6, 416; **M9**: 339-40; **M12**: 87, 88; **L1**: 104; **L2**: 124n, 140; **L8**: 3, 4, 21
  influence of, **E4**: 133-35; **L17**: 183-84
  on ideas, **M1**: 159
  on thinking, **M1**: 161
  on nature, **M2**: 145
  skepticism of, **M2**: 232
  on characterizations, **L16**: 145
  meaning of, **L17**: 184
  Socrates as one of, **L17**: 184-85
Sophocles, **E4**: 225
  on nature, **M2**: 145
  on group significance, **M5**: 38, 106-7; **L7**: 37, 97-98
  on political authority, **M5**: 112, 131; **L7**: 103, 122
  on moral personality, **M5**: 130, 131; **L7**: 121-22
Sophrosyne
  in *Charmides*, **L2**: 131-32
  as supreme virtue, **L2**: 137
  defined, **L2**: 138, 139
Sorel, Georges, **L3**: 369; **L15**: 387
Sorley, William Ritchie, **M3**: 42
Sorokin, Pitirim, **L14**: 328, 431
Sosnowski, George J., **M11**: 294, 396
Soul, **M12**: 247; **M14**: 60, 68, 96, 123; **L1**: 193, 223-24; **L10**: 28, 252; **L15**: 75, 95
  related to body, **E1**: 107, 112-15, 322-23; **M5**: 129-30; **L7**: 120-21
  Leibniz on, **E1**: 297-98, 311, 318, 338
  and Christianity, **E4**: 98-99; **M7**: 341

-substance, **M1**: 130n
conception of, **M10**: 22; **L16**: 124, 136, 326, 334, 449; **L17**: 172
Aristotle on, **M10**: 109
Socrates on, **L2**: 131-32, 137-39
Freienfels on, **L5**: 51n
James on, **L14**: 156
ignoring of, **L17**: 10-11
renascence of, **L17**: 11-14
Phelps on, **L17**: 12-13
existence of, **L17**: 17
Soule, George, **L6**: 180, 479n
Sound
as element of knowledge, **E2**: 60-63
sensation of, **E5**: 100-101
as medium, **L10**: 178-80, 260, 291
distinctive quality of, **L10**: 200, 203, 205, 210, 213, 230, 239-46
Source Book in Ancient Philosophy (Bakewell), **M15**: 336
Sources of a Science of Education, The, **L5**: xii-xiv
Souriau, Paul, **L14**: 157
South Africa, **L9**: 203
South African Education Conference, **L9**: 194n
Southern Association of Colleges and Secondary Schools, **L6**: 120
Southern Illinois University (Carbondale), **L16**: xiin
supports *Collected Works*, **L17**: xi-xv
Southern Manchurian Railway, **M12**: 30
South Sea islands art, **L10**: 333
South Side Academy (Chicago), **M2**: 68; **M3**: 277
Southwestern Normal School (California, Pa.), **M2**: 379n
Sovereignty (P. Ward), **L3**: 92
Sovereignty, **M12**: 39, 197
theory of, **E1**: 235-36; **E4**: 70-90; **M11**: 18-40; **L8**: 35
Dewey on, **L14**: xxii-xxiii
as source of law, **L14**: 120-21; **L17**: 102
elimination of, **L17**: 101
international political, **L17**: 103
national, **L17**: 455
Soviet Challenge to America, The (Counts), **L6**: 263, 265-67
Soviet Union. *See* Union of Soviet Socialist Republics
Space, **M12**: 147-49, 214, 224, 228, 260, 261; **L12**: 217-18, 238-39, 311, 441
Locke on, **E1**: 344, 366
Leibniz on, **E1**: 364-69
perception of, **L4**: 75, 78; **L14**: 103
theories of, **L4**: 77, 102, 107, 113-17, 120, 127
as medium, **L10**: xxi, 29, 30, 179, 184, 206, 210-17, 255, 281
absolute, **L14**: 105
terms referring to, **L14**: 170-71
Space, Time and Deity (S. Alexander), **M12**: xxx
Space-time, **E3**: 74; **L1**: 215, 347; **L15**: 5-6, 29, 111-12, 116, 163
in theory of perception, **M7**: 11
in art, **L10**: 187-88, 210-14
context for inquiry, **L12**: 475-80; **L16**: 300, 306-9, 329, 338-40, 453-55
nature of, **L16**: 4, 51-52, 83n, 128, 138-39, 148, 281, 359, 387
Cohen and Nagel on, **L16**: 15, 194-95
related to knowings-knowns, **L16**: 47, 85, 335

Space-time (*continued*)
in event and designation, **L16**: 59, 68-69, 89, 92
in interaction and transaction, **L16**: 66-68, 113, 278
characteristic of subject-matters, **L16**: 83, 92-94, 417
characteristic of namings-named, **L16**: 86-87
in science, **L16**: 98n, 106, 286, 363, 370, 414
Frank on, **L16**: 149n
Mill on, **L16**: 158
Moore on, **L16**: 207
C. Morris on, **L16**: 216
as name, **L16**: 270
context for valuing, **L16**: 316, 345-48, 352
Spahr, Charles B., **M5**: 488
Spain, **M11**: 101, 140, 255; **L11**: 324, 327, 527-28
Spanish-American War, **M10**: 260; **L15**: 20-22; **L17**: 573
Spargo, John, **M5**: 486
Sparta, Greece, **L8**: 20; **L10**: 321; **L17**: 176, 231
Spatial
relationships, **M12**: 222-24
in art, **L10**: xxiii, 168, 187-89, 222-26, 236
Spatiality, **M10**: 80
Spaulding, Edward Gleason, **M6**: 473; **L3**: 389
on external relations, **M6**: 143-45
on inquiry process, **M6**: 146-52
on realism, **M6**: 480-511
Specialist
importance of, **L17**: 75, 320, 449
learned, **L17**: 75-76
and ethnologist, **L17**: 427
Specialization, **E3**: 319-20
in science, **L13**: 275-76
Species, **M13**: 369; **L1**: 162, 177; **L10**: 301; **L12**: 91-92, 130, 139-40, 172, 182-83, 254, 260, 294-95, 416-17; **L16**: 413. *See also* Kinds, **L12**
history of term, **M4**: 4-8
integral part of, **M4**: 8-9
of Aristotle, **L10**: 289-90, 293
Specification
as name, **L16**: xxxv, 62-63, 71, 181, 270
nature of, **L16**: 6, 72, 96-97, 171, 269, 273, 278
as naming procedure, **L16**: 7n, 65-66, 142, 154
as form of designation, **L16**: 69, 111, 131-32, 139
related to definition, **L16**: 133n, 174, 180
as method of inquiry, **L16**: 146-53
Kaplan on, **L16**: 172-73
accuracy in, **L16**: 257, 263-64
namings for, **L16**: 259, 261, 271
Specimen, **L12**: 432, 435-36, 474-75. *See also* Case, **L12**
Spectator theory of knowledge, **M10**: 23, 26n, 41
disputed, **L4**: x-xiii, xviii, 163, 195
origin of, **L4**: xiv-xv, 19
modified, **L4**: xvi, 232
Speculation, **L16**: 423
in *Dictionary of Philosophy*, **M2**: 247-48
related to farmers, **L9**: 250, 256-57
problems caused by, **L9**: 254
land, **L9**: 265

Speculations (Hulme), **L10**: 83, 334-35
Speech, **L1**: 134, 135, 141-44, 217, 230. *See also* Language
function of, **M6**: 305; **M13**: 38, 276-79; **L8**: 282-83; **L16**: 329
as intellectual tool, **M6**: 318-27; **L8**: 306-14
freedom of, **M12**: 9-11, 21; **L3**: 111-14, 136; **L7**: 358-62
and action, **M13**: xiv, 29-35
esthetic nature of, **L10**: 73, 111, 129, 153, 174, 242, 245, 337-38
colloquial, **L16**: 249
transformed, **L16**: 328
Greek idea of, **L17**: 173
beginnings of, **L17**: 259, 307
Speer, William W., **L17**: 328, 564
Spelling
methods for learning, **L17**: 327-28
Spencer, Herbert, **E3**: 100; **E4**: xviii, 106, 201; **E5**: xiii, 352, 353; **M4**: 43, 47; **M5**: 4, 55, 70, 388, 461; **M6**: 93, 167, 392; **M7**: 58, 141, 276; **M8**: 10n, 142, 194; **M9**: 229; **M12**: 213-14, 221, 232, 237; **M13**: 311, 402-3; **M14**: 122, 205; **M15**: 11, 256, 333; **L1**: 44, 49, 215, 216; **L2**: 16, 275, 284; **L3**: 299, 300; **L4**: 52-53; **L6**: 428; **L7**: 6, 50, 250, 292; **L8**: 26, 38; **L13**: 107, 121; **L14**: 399; **L15**: xv; **L17**: 93, 386, 405, 559, 563
influence of, **E1**: xxvi, 145; **E5**: 47
on relativity of feeling, **E1**: 22, 30
on absolute object, **E1**: 24, 25
on sensations, **E1**: 183, 185
on science, **E1**: 224, 342, 376; **M6**: 74; **M7**: 121
Green on, **E3**: 20-21
on ethics, **E3**: 239; **M3**: 56
on duty, **E3**: 330-31; **E4**: 333-36; **M5**: 323-25
moral theory of, **E4**: 129; **M2**: 33; **M5**: 190-91, 208, 212
on pleasure, **E4**: 285-86
on evolution, **E5**: 47; **M6**: 365, 444; **M10**: 14, 98, 420-21; **M11**: 373; **L5**: 170; **L14**: 100; **L17**: 154
on primitive mind, **M2**: 39-40
and philosophy of nature, **M2**: 149; **M3**: 200-203
on organism, **M2**: 179
philosophical system of, **M2**: 184; **M3**: xx-xxii, 193-209; **L14**: 193
on positivism, **M2**: 209
on realism, **M2**: 219
on knowledge, **M2**: 261; **M7**: 335
theory of unknowable, **M4**: xiii, 12; **M7**: 297; **L17**: 94-95
on universe, **M4**: 23
on goodness, **M5**: 215
on happiness theory, **M5**: 243n, 263n
on esthetics, **M5**: 337n; **L10**: 119, 358
on freedom, **M5**: 350n
on competition, **M5**: 476
on altruism and egoism, **M6**: 366-68
on education, **M6**: 434; **L17**: 338, 564
and theory of play, **M7**: 318-19
on utilitarianism, **M7**: 361
compared with Bergson, **M10**: 67-70

Spencer, Herbert (*continued*)
on government, **M11**: 104
advises Japan, **M11**: 170
social theory of, **L11**: 16, 29, 33; **L14**: 96
psychology of, **L14**: 158
Fiske compared with, **L17**: 94
Spencer, Ichabod, Lectures, **M7**: 390-408
Spencer, Walter Baldwin, **M2**: 50n; **M5**: 27n, 61; **L7**: 26n-27n, 56
Spender, Stephen, **L11**: 496-98
Spengler, Oswald, **M8**: 423; **L6**: 280-85; **L7**: xvi
Spenser, Edmund, **L10**: 285, 363
Sperry, Willard L., **L17**: 545
Speusippus, **M2**: 167; **M7**: 313
Speyer School (Chicago), **M8**: 292
Spinoza, Benedict, **M3**: 310; **M5**: 81, 357; **M7**: 293-94; **M8**: 194; **M9**: xxi; **M10**: 5; **M12**: xiv, 140; **M14**: 200-201, 214; **M15**: 60, 221, 335; **L1**: 54, 55, 81, 162, 373; **L2**: 70; **L3**: xiii, 295; **L5**: 381; **L7**: 75, 303; **L8**: 8, 26, 32, 35; **L9**: 11, 240, 241, 243; **L12**: 488; **L14**: 299, 304, 399; **L15**: xiii, xxviii, 46, 415-16
pantheism of, **E1**: xxiv-xxv, 9-18, 166; **M2**: 184
on reason, **E1**: 45, 339; **M2**: 152, 217
on nature, **E1**: 222; **M2**: 147; **M3**: 90
relation of Leibniz and, **E1**: 263, 271, 273, 277, 377, 415, 419, 425, 426
on relation of individual to universe, **E1**: 286-87, 291-92
realism of, **M2**: 168-69; **M10**: 29; **L1**: 255
on good, **M5**: 368n
on knowledge, **L1**: 27
on truth, **L1**: 32
presuppositions of, **L1**: 37
theology of, **L1**: 310, 312
on freedom, **L3**: 101-3
significance of, **L4**: 43-46
vs. Hegel, **L4**: 51
philosophy of, **L4**: 113, 167, 230, 244
and mind, **L6**: 489
on emotion, **L10**: xxv
Spirit, **M12**: 200, 245, 249; **L1**: 65, 192-94, 223-24
absolute, **M8**: 430; **L13**: 148-49
in esthetics, **L10**: 26, 28, 296, 297, 299
nature of, **L16**: 124n, 358-59
in doctrine, **L16**: 326, 335
authority of, **L16**: 362
disbelief in, **L17**: 17
social, **L17**: 75
in evolution, **L17**: 93-94
of teacher, **L17**: 341
in Russia, **L17**: 497, 510
Spirit of Modern Philosophy, The (Royce), **M15**: 326, 328; **L9**: xxvii
Spiritual, **L15**: 48
in medieval church, **E3**: 227-28
world, **M12**: 225-26, 234
vs. material, **M13**: 264-66, 268, 270; **L14**: 314, 317-18, 328-31; **L15**: 200-202, 217, 230, 232, 235; **L16**: 366-67
power, **L2**: 33-34
esthetic quality of, **L10**: xiii-xiv, 12, 17, 34-41, 83, 196-99, 202, 340
assignment of, **L16**: 371
Spontaneity
in Leibniz, **E1**: 336-37
in art, **L10**: 76-79, 144, 284-87
vs. voluntary, **L17**: 4

Sport, **L10**: 69; **L16**: 366
Sportsmanship Brotherhood, **L5**: 390-92
Sprachtheorie (Bühler), **L16**: 468
Spring (Botticelli), **L10**: 174, 360
Square
  in cognitive style, **L10**: xii
  of opposition, **L12**: 183
Stability
  of relationships and ideals, **L3**: 22-23
  esthetic, **L10**: 22, 25
  and social change, **L11**: 131-34, 136-40, 144
Stahl, Georg Ernst, **L14**: 206
Staley, Ellis J., **L9**: 369
Stalin, Joseph V., **M8**: 435; **L14**: xx; **L15**: 26, 296, 386
  vs. Trotsky, **L11**: 312, 334, 598; **L13**: 393-94, 398
  methods of, **L11**: 331-32
  purges of, **L15**: xi-xiii, 338-40, 343, 345, 493-97, 500
  defenders of, **L15**: 244-45, 290-93, 340-42, 375
  Davies on, **L15**: 290-91
  collaborates with Hitler, **L15**: 340, 347-48, 352-53
  Childs on, **L15**: 487-88
Stalinists, **L13**: 349, 396
Stalinski, John, **M11**: 295, 396
Stammler, Rudolf, **L6**: 269
Stamp, Josiah, **L7**: 381
Standard, **M12**: 179-80. *See also* Norm
  and pleasure, **E3**: 260-74; **M5**: 125-26; **L7**: 117-18
  for action, **E3**: 325-26
  related to ideal and motive, **E4**: 287-91
  moral, **M5**: 13, 37-39, 75, 89, 91-92, 99-100; **M14**: 54-58, 74-75, 165; **L7**: 12, 36-37, 69, 82, 85-86, 90-91
  custom as, **M5**: 63; **L7**: 58, 64-66
  reason and nature as, **M5**: 117-25; **L7**: 108-16, 130-33
  of living, **M5**: 507-9; **L13**: 311, 313, 423-24
  in instruction, **M6**: 222; **L8**: 164-65
  in value judgment, **M8**: 39-46; **L1**: 317-18
  source of, **L4**: 35, 44, 205, 211, 221-22
  development of, **L4**: 130, 134, 149, 190, 203-5
  as principle of judgment, **L7**: 237-40
  in utilitarianism, **L7**: 240-45
  and ends, **L7**: 245-48, 281
  significance of, **L7**: 246, 255, 265
  justice and benevolence in, **L7**: 249-52, 279, 301
  for art, **L10**: 310-13
  as authoritative, **L16**: 338-39, 453
  variety of, **L17**: 396-97
Standard Dictionary of the English Language, A, **L16**: 155-56
Standardization
  in education, **M10**: 118-20
Standardized material, **L12**: 22-23, 115-16, 129, 170, 172-73, 245, 293, 382-83, 427n, 475-80
Standards of American Legislation (Freund), **L2**: 36
Standard Statistics Company, **L6**: 348
Stanley, Hiram Miner
  on psychology of feeling, **E5**: 358-67

"Star Spangled Banner, The" (M. Hill), **L17**: 346, *565*
State, **L1**: 168-69, 357; **L16**: 400. *See also* Government
and church, **E3**: 227; **M11**: 18-40; **L13**: 70; **L15**: 156, 281-84
defined, **M2**: 81
primitive group as, **M5**: 31-34; **L7**: 30-31
moral value of, **M5**: 104-5, 389-90; **L7**: 95-96
Aristotle on, **M5**: 120-21, 128; **M12**: 104; **L2**: 39, 40; **L7**: 112, 120, 130
ancient conceptions of, **M5**: 120-23, 141; **L7**: 111-14
Plato on, **M5**: 122; **L7**: 113-14, 120
growth of, **M7**: 406-8
Kant on, **M8**: 161
in German thought, **M8**: 169-82; **M10**: 227-28
support of education, **M9**: 99-106
organic character of, **M9**: 100-101
Hegel on, **M10**: 224; **L2**: 39, 40
adulation of, **M10**: 227-28; **L2**: 39, 40
Tolstoians on, **M10**: 244, 248
as power, **M10**: 245; **L2**: 35; **L13**: 128, 147
and nationalism, **M10**: 285; **L7**: 138, 366-71
American, **M10**: 400-404; **L5**: 193-94
theories of, **M12**: 104-5, 116; **L3**: 318-20
individual and, **M12**: 188-89
modern conception of, **M12**: 194
importance of, **M12**: 195-97
Russell on, **M12**: 247-49
relation between groups and, **L2**: xxiv-xxviii, 40, 238-39, 252, 279-81
personality of, **L2**: 32n, 33n, 38, 41-42
and causal forces, **L2**: 242, 246-51, 258, 259, 265, 269, 276
and society, **L2**: 327-29
as ideal, **L2**: 377
origin of, **L3**: 324-25
Mill on, **L5**: 180-81
Roman views of, **L7**: 130-34
Hobbes on, **L7**: 219
political balance in, **L14**: 93-95
bound by law, **L17**: 101
State Conference of Normal School Instructors, **M15**: 158n, 170n, 180n
State Department. *See* United States Department of State
"State in Recent Political Theory, The" (Lindsay), **L2**: 33n
Statement
vs. expression, **L10**: xxviii, 91, 96
"Statement on Academic Freedom," **L14**: xix
Statesman's Manual, The (Coleridge), **L5**: 178
States' rights, **L11**: 168-69
Static, **M6**: 424; **L1**: 55, 85-86
Statistics
in social psychology, **M10**: 56-57
and scientific law, **L14**: 106
Statue of Condillac
in *Dictionary of Philosophy*, **M2**: 248
Status quo
related to education, **L6**:

125-26; **L9**: 181, 205, 206
related to peace, **L6**: 454
related to disarmament, **L6**: 459-60
in social relations, **L9**: 51
Stearns, Alfred E., **M15**: 190
Stebbing, L. Susan, **L12**: 27n, 462n
on general propositions, **L11**: 118-23
on experience, **L12**: 482n
Stein, Karl, **M8**: 174, 177
Stein, Leo, **L2**: 113-15
on art, **L10**: 162, 209, 359, 361
Stein, Ludwig, **L17**: 39, 40, 556
Steiner, Celestine J., **M15**: 318, 421, 422
Steiner, Mark, **L6**: xvn
Steinthal, Heymann, **M3**: 67
Stendhal (pseud. of Marie Henri Beyle), **E3**: 37
Stephen, Leslie, **M5**: 388
on ethics, **E3**: 239; **M3**: 43
and conduciveness, **E4**: 286
on pleasure, **M5**: 250
on sympathy, **M5**: 340n
on character, **L7**: 172-73
Stereotypes, **M13**: 331, 339
Sterling, John, **M3**: 55
Sterrett, J. MacBride, **E3**: 187-90
Stevens, Frederick W., **M13**: 86, 88, 164
Stevens, Stanley S., **L16**: 220n
Stevenson, Charles L., **M15**: x; **L16**: 357, 470
on Dewey's 1908 *Ethics*, **M5**: ix-xxxiv
ethics of, **L15**: xix-xxii, 127-41
Stevenson, Matilda Coxe, **M5**: 67; **L7**: 61
Stevenson, Robert Louis, **M10**: 310; **L9**: 199
Stevenson Act, **L5**: 441
Stewart, Cora Wilson, **L5**: 316
Stewart, Dugald, **L12**: 68
Stillingfleet, Edward, **L2**: 146n, 153
Stimson, Henry L., **L6**: 192, 193, 219, 469
Stimulation, **E5**: 308
Stimulus
formation of, **E1**: 103-6
extra-organic, **E2**: 31-33
physiological, **E2**: 32-34
in sensation, **E2**: 37-43
in smell, **E2**: 56
in taste, **E2**: 58
in hearing, **E2**: 59
in sight, **E2**: 63-64
in feeling, **E2**: 219-20
in motor impulses, **E2**: 325-26
and control, **E5**: 88
in child's consciousness, **E5**: 180-81
function of, **M9**: 29-31; **M13**: 33; **L7**: 290
to speech, **M13**: 29-30
in relation to perception, **L1**: 250-55
vs. motive, **L7**: 289-90
as name, **L16**: 90, 270-71
as sign, **L16**: 140n, 214, 219-21, 225
C. Morris on, **L16**: 212-15
related to object, **L16**: 213, 219, 231-32
in semiotic, **L16**: 235-40
Stimulus and response, **E5**: 96, 100-109; **M6**: 361; **M9**: 51n, 67-69; **M14**: 121, 139-40, 144; **L12**: 36-38
in *Cyclopedia of Education*, **M7**: 346-47
in activities, **M12**: 208, 209
theory of, **L3**: 33-35

Stimulus and response (*cont.*)
psychology of, **L5**: 34-35, 222-28
Stipulation
and postulate, **L12**: 24-25
Stirling, Brents, **L11**: 515
Stirling, James Hutchison, **M2**: 180
Stirner, Max, **M10**: 306
Stock Exchange, **L9**: 288
Stockholm, Sweden, **M11**: 192, 293, 394
Stock market
1929 crash of, **L5**: xi, xvii, 97
Stoicism, **E4**: 216, 263; **M9**: 335; **M11**: 45; **M15**: 326
and intuitionalism, **E4**: 125
attributes of, **E4**: 138-39
and individual, **E4**: 230
ethics of, **E4**: 318; **L7**: 109-10
Stoics, **E5**: 9; **M2**: 81; **M5**: 387; **M7**: 288, 416; **L5**: 497, 498; **L8**: 6, 26; **L10**: x, xxv; **L11**: 134; **L13**: 136
on nature, **M2**: 146; **L7**: 50, 114, 119, 130-31
on necessity, **M2**: 151-52
on concept of universe, **M2**: 179, 183, 205-6; **M5**: 173
on subject, **M2**: 249
cosmopolitanism of, **M5**: 118, 123; **L7**: 109, 132
ethics of, **M5**: 118-19; **L7**: 109-10
on wisdom, **M5**: 127; **L7**: 118
moral theory of, **M5**: 131-32, 202, 205, 328; **L7**: 123
on human nature, **L6**: 33-34
influence Romans, **L7**: 130-34
on duty, **L7**: 133-34
Stolberg, Benjamin, **L11**: 314, 323; **L13**: 395, 404
Stoner, John E., **M15**: xvn, xviiin; **L6**: xxin; **L15**: 301-2
Stories
important to children, **M8**: 241-42
telling of, **L16**: 397
Story, Joseph, **E4**: 40
Story of Philosophy, The (Durant), **L2**: 387
Story of the Odyssey, The (A. J. Church), **E3**: 193-94
Stout, George Frederick, **M1**: 242; **L8**: 307
Strachey, John, **L13**: 131
Strato, **M2**: 186
Strauss, David Friedrich, **E1**: 228, 242
Strayer, George D., **M15**: 190
Stream of consciousness, **M12**: xxvi, xxviii, 210-12, 222; **L10**: 303; **L11**: 506-7
"Stream of Thought, The" (W. James), **L14**: 156
Strike
by students, **M10**: 176
force related to, **M10**: 244, 247
of Peking teachers, **L17**: 30, 556
Strong, C. A., **M15**: 363; **L14**: 308
Strong, Charles H., **M15**: 100, 102, 383, 401
Strong, Josiah, **L17**: 555
Structuralism, **M13**: xix
Structuralists, **L5**: 218-21
Structure, **L1**: 64-66; **L4**: xxi, 242; **L16**: 105n
modification of, **E5**: 50, 249
and function, **E5**: 96; **L4**: 118-19, 129-31
Structure of Science, The (Nagel), **L6**: xviin
"Struggle for Immortality, The" (Phelps), **L17**: 12-13, 554

Struik, Dirk Jan, **L15**: 507
Stuart, Henry Waldgrave, **M3**: 27n, 138n; **M13**: 25n; **M14**: 151n; **L14**: 5, 81n
  Dewey replies to, **L14**: 62-74
Student movement. *See* May Fourth Movement
Students, **L11**: 376, 516, 557, 572
  on moral experiences, **E4**: 106-13
  strike in high school, **M10**: 176
  in China, **M11**: xix-xx, 173, 186-91; **M12**: 22-27, 41-51, 253, 255; **L3**: 197
  in Turkey, **M15**: xxi-xxii, 293-94
  participation by, **L13**: 6, 35, 43, 53
  freedom of, **L13**: 9
  science and, **L13**: 54, 55
  differing capacities of, **L17**: 54
  directions to, **L17**: 161-62, 165, 187-88
Students' Christian Association (University of Michigan), **E1**: 61n, 90n; **E4**: 3n, 96n, 365n, 369n
Students' Union, National (China), **M11**: 190
Studies
  selection of, **E5**: 167, 266-68, 439
  as psychologically determined, **E5**: 167-76
  elementary school, **E5**: 245-46
Studies in Character (Bryant), **E5**: 350-52
Studies in Education (E. Barnes), **M1**: 214
Studies in Hegel's Philosophy of Religion (Sterrett), **E3**: 187-90
Studies in Logical Theory (Dewey et al.), **M1**: ix; **M4**: 78, 296; **M14**: xiii; **L2**: 15; **L12**: 3; **L14**: x, xii, xv, 6, 12, 50; **L16**: 187, 444; **L17**: 373
Studies in Philosophy (Lafferty), **L6**: 311
Studies in Psycho-Expedition (Schneersohn), **L5**: 410-11
Studies in the Evolutionary Psychology of Feeling (Stanley), **E5**: 358-67
Studies in the History of Ideas (Columbia University), **M11**: 18n; **L2**: 3n, 124n; **L11**: 69n
Studies in the Nature of Facts (S. Pepper et al.), **L16**: 42n
Studies of Childhood (Sully), **E5**: 367-72
Study
  habits of, **L8**: 330-32
  aids to, **L17**: 165-69, 170, 174-75, 181-86, 191-93, 195-209
Study of Ethics, The: A Syllabus, **E4**: xiii-xviii, xxii-xxiv; **L7**: x; **L10**: 355
Stuhr Museum of the Prairie Pioneer (Grand Island, Neb.), **L16**: xiin
Stull, DeForest, **L14**: 371
Stumpf, Carl, **E4**: 195; **L11**: 470
Sturzo, Luigi, **L6**: 458n
Subalternation, **L12**: 183, 194-95
Subcommission of Inquiry. *See* Commission of Inquiry into the Charges Made against Leon Trotsky in the Moscow Trials
Subconscious, **M4**: 228; **L1**: 227, 228, 239. *See also* Unconscious
  conscious control and, **M15**: 45

Subconscious (*continued*)
in art, **L10**: 71, 76-80, 118, 143, 155, 159, 161, 279
Subcontraries, **L12**: 183, 193-94, 205
Subimplication, **L12**: 321
Subject. *See also* Data, **L12**; Existence, **L12**
and object, **E1**: 131-35; **E5**: 26; **L4**: 97; **L10**: 251-55, 281, 284, 288; **L12**: 88-89; **L14**: 132-35; **L15**: 70-72, 87, 93, 96, 165; **L16**: 111, 290, 297, 334-35, 449-50
as mode of experience, **E5**: 169-74
in *Dictionary of Philosophy*, **M2**: 248-52
in *Cyclopedia of Education*, **M7**: 291, 347-49
in neo-realism, **M10**: 25-42
and subjectivism, **L1**: 22-26, 85, 135-36, 168-90, 315
meaning of term, **L14**: 27, 39; **L15**: 49; **L17**: 419
as knower, **L14**: 67-70, 187
in James's psychology, **L14**: 155-67
assumed in epistemology, **L14**: 178, 196-97
as name, **L16**: xxxvi, 271
role and nature of, **L16**: 288, 348, 384
Subjective, **L12**: 40, 110. *See also* Mental, **L12**
meaning of, **E3**: 219, 221; **L14**: 19-20
and objective, **E3**: 223; **L1**: 380-82; **L14**: 25-28, 39, 189, 192-93, 196-200
applied to value judgment, **M8**: 32-36
probability as, **L12**: 465-69
as name, **L16**: 271
Subjective idealism, **E1**: xlviii, 133-40; **E5**: 27-28; **M3**: 382-89; **M6**: 4
Subjectivism, **M10**: 25-42; **M13**: 417; **M14**: 16, 20, 23, 38-39, 140; **M15**: 358; **L17**: 366, 419
and pragmatism, **M1**: 130n; **M4**: 125, 245-46; **M13**: 449, 468
in *Dictionary of Philosophy*, **M2**: 252
defined, **M8**: 162; **M9**: 302
essence of, **M13**: 49
in public opinion, **M13**: 342
elimination of, **M13**: 419
and subject, **L1**: 22-26, 85, 135-36, 168-90, 315
problem of, **L14**: 11, 17-19
in philosophy, **L14**: 39
in moral theory, **L14**: 73
Subjectivistic
psychology, **L16**: 347
relativism, **L17**: xxi
Subjectivity, **E1**: 28
in knowledge, **M4**: 255
Dewey opposes, **L4**: xix, xxii
of Kant, **L4**: 49, 229
in logic, **L4**: 171
of modern thought, **L4**: 185-86, 191, 193, 196, 206, 219-23
as context in philosophy, **L6**: 14-15
in art, **L10**: xiii, 151, 280, 288, 290, 292, 308, 309, 327
vs. objectivity, **L15**: 64-65, 74-75, 87, 165
and values, **L15**: 69-70
Rice on, **L15**: 426-34
Subject-matter, **M7**: 445-46; **L8**: 72, 234; **L12**: 122
social, **E5**: 89; **L13**: 338; **L17**: 449

choice and organization of, **E5**: 126-27, 171, 333-38, 441; **M6**: 400-404; **L13**: 7-9, 35, 51, 52, 55, 56, 108, 376, 396; **L16**: 259, 277, 371, 396-97; **L17**: 469
and method, **E5**: 164-66, 287; **M9**: 180-85, 332, 333
psychology of, **E5**: 166, 175
related to child, **E5**: 174, 266-68; **M2**: 281-88; **L17**: 224-25
development of, **E5**: 274; **M9**: 366-67
Harris on, **E5**: 381-82
misapplication of, **M2**: 288-91
significance of, **M6**: 396-99
related to experience, **M6**: 399-400; **M13**: 381-82, 392-94
in education, **M8**: 395-99; **M9**: 242; **M15**: 187; **L6**: xxii, 78-80, 83; **L9**: 179, 181, 182, 184-85, 196, 199
Herbart on, **M9**: 75-78
related to mind, **M9**: 137-45
philosophy related to, **M9**: 334; **M13**: 52; **L14**: 148-50; **L16**: 358-61, 365, 381, 411, 415-19, 464
related to judgment, **M13**: 9-11; **M15**: 352-54
vs. object, **M13**: 43-47; **M15**: 34, 38, 350-54
of science and common sense, **M13**: 388; **L6**: 15-16; **L13**: 53-54, 271, 284; **L14**: 194-99; **L16**: 246-53, 290-92, 305-9, 312-17, 334, 386, 449
role in inquiry, **M15**: 38, 353-55; **L14**: 50, 147; **L16**: 6, 88, 140, 187, 282-83, 288, 335, 337
nature of, **M15**: 39, 70, 351; **L6**: 14, 16-17; **L12**: 513; **L13**: 340-41; **L16**: 48-49, 82-84, 92-93, 115, 127, 144, 180, 285, 308, 323-24, 458
substance's relation to, **L10**: xxvii, 113-18, 134, 154
attitude toward, **L10**: 54, 60, 70, 71, 74, 76, 115, 191-95, 230, 357
important to art, **L10**: 80, 85-86, 94, 95, 100, 109, 142, 156, 159, 175-76, 183, 256, 258, 261-63, 280, 287, 290, 332n
for criticism, **L10**: 302, 307-11, 314, 322
problems of, **L13**: 28, 31
form of, **L13**: 48, 49, 59; **L16**: 62-64, 338-39, 356-57, 370; **L17**: 416n
of propositions, **L14**: 181
namings for, **L16**: 46, 258
behavioral, **L16**: 122, 344-45
of logic, **L16**: 188, 320
Kantor on, **L16**: 191
as name, **L16**: 271
of mathematics, **L16**: 284-87
of valuings, **L16**: 311, 343
Dewey's vs. Bentley's, **L16**: 318-19
"Subject-Matter of Metaphysical Inquiry, The," **M8**: ix-xi
Sublimation, **M14**: 98, 108, 113-14, 135
Subordination, **L10**: 103
Subsistence, **L17**: 417
Substance, **L1**: 94-96, 126, 135-36, 263, 346; **L4**: 242; **L12**: 86-89, 130-33, 247-48, 285. *See also* Object, **L12**
in Spinoza's *Ethics*, **E1**: 10-11, 14-16
character of, **E1**: 124, 322-24;

Substance (*continued*)
L16: 108, 115n; **L17**: 95
as category, **E1**: 373, 375-76
in *Dictionary of Philosophy*, **M2**: 252-53
Locke on, **L2**: 144-46
constitutes reality, **L4**: 96, 97, 102, 103
in Newtonian system, **L4**: 148, 164, 165
of art, **L10**: xxvii, 195, 205, 210-14, 217
form's relation to, **L10**: 111-18, 128-29, 133-34, 142, 154, 158, 175-76, 232-33, 322, 332-33
as name, **L16**: 104, 271-72
"Substance, Power and Quality in Locke," **L2**: xvii
Substantiality theory (Substantialism)
in *Dictionary of Philosophy*, **M2**: 253-54
Substitution. *See also* Equivalence, **L12**
in science, **L1**: 115
Subsumption, **L12**: 417, 429, 497
Success, **M12**: 182; **M14**: 7, 174; **L7**: 50-51, 236
qualities needed for, **M5**: 80; **L7**: 74; **L17**: 278, 326-27
James on, **M13**: 307
proof of, **M13**: 309
as end, **L7**: 202-3
nature of, **L7**: 209; **L17**: 301
as motive for education, **L9**: 177-79
affects character, **L9**: 190-91
habits formed through, **L17**: 300-301, 304, 307
Succession, **L12**: 33, 330, 445
origin of, **E5**: 181
Royce on, **M10**: 80-81
Sudeten, **M11**: xiii; **L15**: 289
Suffering, **M5**: 94, 97; **L7**: 89, 90; **L10**: 47-50
Suffrage, **M5**: 423-24; **M6**: 153-54; **M7**: 409; **M11**: 167; **L6**: 186, 226-27; **L9**: 381-82; **L11**: 25, 50, 51, 218, 248, 535-36; **L15**: 357; **L16**: 403; **L17**: 44, 47
Suggestion, **L10**: 253. *See also* Formulation, **L12**
as phase of thinking, **M6**: 186, 239; **L8**: 118-19, 123, 197, 200-202
nature of, **M6**: 207-12; **L8**: 144-49, 157
idea as, **M6**: 264; **L8**: 221-24
and experience, **M13**: 66-67, 485-88
inadequacy of, **L12**: 146-47, 224, 228, 251-52, 275, 300-301, 312, 321-22, 428-29, 462, 492
power of, **L17**: 266, 284, 363
negative, **L17**: 267
Sui Generis
in *Dictionary of Philosophy*, **M2**: 254
Sullivan, Celestine J., Jr., **L14**: 300
Sully, James
child psychology of, **E5**: 367-72; **M1**: 196-97
Sultanate, **M15**: xx, 129
Summa Theologica (Thomas Aquinas), **L11**: 595
Summing Up, The (Maugham), **L13**: 363
Summists
in *Dictionary of Philosophy*, **M2**: 254-55
Summum bonum, **M12**: xiii, xx, 172-74; **L14**: 408-9
Sumner, Charles, **M11**: 388; **L5**: 350

Sumner, William Graham, **M14**: 55; **L1**: 42; **L7**: 49, 51, 53, 151
on primitive society, **M5**: 54-58; **L7**: 49, 51, 53
on moral conceptions, **M5**: 163-64, 176, 355n, 370n
Sunday, William Ashley, **M10**: 313
Sun Yat Sen, **M12**: 58, 69, 254; **L3**: 423, 427
election of, **M13**: xxii, 127, 131; **L17**: 29, 555
as leader, **M13**: xxiii, 122, 132; **L17**: 33
views of, **M13**: 130, 135-36; **L17**: 31-32
and Anfu Club, **M13**: 135
vs. England, **M13**: 494; **L17**: 30
Superior, Wis., **M7**: 462-63
Superiority, **M13**: 296; **L13**: 84
Supernatural, **M12**: 105-6; **L1**: 52, 71-72, 104, 127, 130, 134; **L4**: 9-10, 184; **L9**: xxx, 36; **L10**: 37, 337; **L12**: 31-32, 47, 49; **L13**: 123; **L15**: xxxi-xxxii, 269
nature of, **M7**: 211; **L14**: 78; **L16**: 409-12
attitude toward, **M9**: 290; **L16**: 392, 394, 416; **L17**: 458
consciousness as, **M10**: 25-27
related to religion, **L9**: xvi-xviii, xx, xxviii-xxix, 3-5, 25, 27, 30-32, 44-45, 53-54, 295, 428-30
compared with natural, **L9**: 30, 37, 46-48, 294-95, 429, 434; **L14**: 64; **L15**: 46-61, 186, 200-202, 463-64
and social relations, **L9**: 38, 49-55
related to imagination, **L9**: 47, 294-95
vs. secularism, **L15**: 155-56, 160
power of, **L17**: 431-32
related to moral, **L17**: 545
related to science, **L17**: 546-47
Superstition, **M13**: 224, 435; **M15**: 330; **L1**: 45, 63, 70, 129, 201, 279, 287; **L8**: 131; **L13**: 76; **L17**: 398
Supply and demand, **M5**: 455-56
Suppression, **L11**: 218-19; **L16**: 362
of liberties, **L13**: 316, 321
dangers of, **L17**: 477
"Supremacy of Method, The," **L14**: 65, 66, 69
Supreme Court. *See* United States Supreme Court
Supreme Court and Sovereign States, The (Warren), **L6**: 463n
Supreme National Committee (Poland), **M11**: 313
Survey, **M7**: 387
Survey of Child Psychiatry, A (Rees), **L14**: 245
Survival, **L7**: 39; **L17**: xxiii
Survival of fittest, **E5**: 38-39
Susceptibility, **L1**: 197
Suspense
value of, **M6**: 191, 332; **L8**: 124, 320-21, 332
esthetic purpose of, **L10**: xx, 165, 166, 174
Sussex, **M10**: 265
Sutherland, Alexander, **M5**: 50, 409n
Suzzallo, Henry
on education, **M4**: 328-31; **M7**: 469-71
Swammerdam, Jan, **E1**: 272, 276

Swan, Mrs. Joseph R., **L5**: 418, 419
Swann, William Francis Gray, **L16**: 106n
Sweet, Henry, **M12**: 11
Swift, H. S.
  on man's spiritual nature, **L17**: 15-17, 537-39
Swift, Jonathan, **E3**: 208; **M10**: 119; **M11**: 122
Switzerland, **M15**: 307
  Polish activities in, **M11**: 261, 278, 281, 290, 293, 312, 313
  sanctions in, **L6**: 463
Sybel, Heinrich von, **M8**: 177, 178
Syllabus of Certain Topics of Logic (C. Peirce), **L16**: 10
Syllogism, **L8**: 171-73; **L11**: 101; **L12**: 90, 93, 100, 417; **L16**: 270
  theory in Mill, **E3**: 129-31
  in *Cyclopedia of Education*, **M7**: 349-51
  nature of, **M15**: 69-71; **L12**: 321-26
Symbolic
  period, **E5**: 310-11
  logic, **M7**: 438; **L16**: 194, 199
  formalists, **L16**: xxxin
  knowledge, **L16**: 258, 261
Symbolic Interaction, **L6**: xiii
Symboling, **L16**: 84, 90, 132n
Symbolism, **L1**: 72, 288-90; **L15**: 418; **L16**: 301
Symbolization, **L2**: 79
  of words, **L2**: 83-84
  nature of, **L16**: 171, 183, 264
  as name, **L16**: 181, 259, 271
Symbols, **L3**: 90; **L13**: 13, 322. *See also* Signs
  value of, **E5**: 92
  social import of, **E5**: 260; **L2**: 323-24, 330-31, 371; **L9**: 301
  child's use of, **E5**: 260-61; **L11**: 241-42, 245-46
  as ideas, **M4**: 95; **L16**: 430, 432, 435-36
  and language, **M6**: 314-20; **L6**: 4-5; **L12**: 53-54
  nature and use of, **M9**: 23, 230-31, 278-79; **L10**: 36, 45, 52, 89; **L12**: xiv; **L16**: 6, 76n, 110n, 159, 275, 309n, 414
  Froebel on, **M9**: 62-64, 73-74
  Herbart's relation to, **M9**: 76-77
  dependent on imagination, **M9**: 245-46
  in meaning, **L3**: 413-14; **L16**: 174
  designate operations, **L4**: 120-29, 132, 158, 173, 186, 200, 230
  in religion, **L4**: 234; **L9**: 28-29, 215
  in art, **L10**: xiii, xv, 97, 156, 198, 317
  in science, **L10**: 154, 202-3; **L16**: 149n
  in politics, **L11**: xxx, 51
  and logic, **L11**: 112, 122-23; **L12**: 10, 26-27, 45-46; **L16**: 191
  defined, **L12**: 57-60
  need for, **L12**: 80, 114, 118, 218; **L17**: 321
  and propositions, **L12**: 123, 137-39, 207n, 214, 245, 261, 340, 423-24
  in mathematics, **L16**: 5, 148n, 173, 180, 266
  Peirce on, **L16**: 10
  Cohen and Nagel on, **L16**: 14, 194-95
  Lewis on, **L16**: 36-38

as process of designation, **L16**: 62, 90, 93, 131, 152
as name, **L16**: 66, 72, 271, 446
as genera of sign, **L16**: 69-70, 139, 225
in nominal definition, **L16**: 175-78
Russell on, **L16**: 199-203
in triangular scheme, **L16**: 300-301
related to potentialities, **L16**: 428-29
Balz on, **L16**: 437-41
Symmetry
as esthetic quality, **L10**: 168, 183-89, 222, 296
of terms, **L12**: 332-33
Symonds, John Addington, **L17**: 11
Sympathetic resentment, **M5**: 71; **L7**: 65
Sympathy, **L10**: 317, 324; **L11**: 11, 282
as feeling, **E2**: 283-87
as socialization factor, **M5**: 16, 38, 48; **L7**: 14, 37, 45-46
and art, **M5**: 48; **L7**: 45, 147
moral concept of, **M5**: 150, 272-73, 302-3
in human nature, **L7**: 238-39, 251, 270, 300; **L13**: 74, 78, 147, 150, 289
Mill and Bentham on, **L7**: 243-44
in teacher, **L13**: 345
reliance upon, **L17**: 401
"Symposium on Operationism" (Boring et al.), **L16**: 170-71
Symptoms, **L13**: 197-98, 248n
Syncretism
in *Dictionary of Philosophy*, **M2**: 255
Synechism, **M10**: 74; **L10**: xiii; **L14**: x
Syntactical definition, **L16**: 164, 169
Syntactics
C. Morris on, **L15**: 142-45; **L16**: 33-35
nature of, **L16**: 90, 93, 155, 160
Syntax, **L16**: 31, 202, 309
Synthesis, **M14**: 128-29; **L13**: 56-57; **L16**: 418; **L17**: 159
as key to knowledge, **E1**: 36-37
in philosophic method, **E1**: 40; **L16**: 115n
and analysis, **E3**: 78-80; **M6**: 281; **L8**: 242-43; **L17**: 158
related to thought, **M6**: 266-70
in experiment, **M6**: 298-99; **L8**: 273-74
in *Cyclopedia of Education*, **M6**: 370-75
in judgment, **L8**: 216-20; **L10**: 313, 317-18, 325
in art, **L10**: 342
scholasticism creates, **L16**: 360
self as, **L17**: 156
in Russian schools, **L17**: 502
Syracuse University, **L17**: 8
Syria, **M15**: 136
Syski, Alexander, **M11**: 295, 301, 396
System
educational, **E5**: 444; **L17**: 171
in *Dictionary of Philosophy*, **M2**: 255-56
in *Cyclopedia of Education*, **M7**: 351-52
in science, **L5**: 10-13
two forms of, **L12**: 55-56, 301, 312, 315, 333-34, 421, 468, 478-79
and inference, **L12**: 294
organism and environment as, **L16**: 191
as name, **L16**: 271
Systematization, **E2**: 201

System of Ethics, A (Paulsen), **M15**: 337
System of Logic, Ratiocinative and Inductive, A (J. S. Mill), **M7**: 241; **L5**: 168, 169; **L11**: 30, 99n, 128; **L12**: 510; **L13**: 138; **L16**: 158n, 218n
Szechuan (Sichuan), China, **M13**: 87

Taboo, **M8**: 190
  enforces customs, **M5**: 57; **L7**: 52-53
  in inquiry, **L16**: 337, 452
  as motive, **L17**: 398
  for savages, **L17**: 399
Tabula rasa, **M9**: 277; **L14**: 192
  Leibniz rejects, **E1**: 310
  in *Dictionary of Philosophy*, **M2**: 256
Tacitus, **M8**: 189; **L11**: 460
Taft, William Howard, **M11**: 206; **M13**: 303; **M15**: xvii, 380, 404; **L6**: 472; **L7**: 398, 421
Taft-Hartley Labor Act, **L15**: 245
Taine, Hippolyte Adolphe, **E3**: 37, 39-40; **M8**: 144; **L10**: 334, 366
Taiping rebellion, **M13**: 113
Talbot, Anna Hedges, **M11**: 64, 393
Talbot, Winthrop, **L5**: 316
Tales from Shakespeare (C. Lamb and M. Lamb), **L5**: 394
Talks to Teachers on Psychology (W. James), **L14**: 337-40
Talleyrand, Charles Maurice de, **M9**: 89
Talmud, **L9**: xxixn
Tammany Hall, **M11**: 94, 243, 394; **L6**: 384; **L9**: 353-55, 362, 369, 372, 379, 382, 384, 385
Tammany Society, **L9**: 354
Taney, Roger Brooke, **M5**: 32; **L7**: 31
Tang Shao Yi, **M13**: 130, 132
Tantalus, **M8**: 64
Taoism, **L10**: 134. *See also* Laotze
Tarde, Gabriel de, **M7**: 234, 236
  and logic, **M10**: 53-54
  on mind, **M10**: 59
Tariffs, **L2**: 317; **L5**: 436; **L6**: 183, 338, 350, 353, 356, 366; **L11**: 261; **L14**: 94
  bill regulating, **L6**: 164-65, 172, 237, 241
  on farm products, **L9**: 249, 250
Tarski, Alfred
  Bentley on, **L16**: xxx
  positions of, **L16**: 8, 45, 132n, 165, 193n
  terminology of, **L16**: 39-42
Tartars, **M13**: 225
Taste, **L4**: 26, 209, 210
  sense of, **E2**: 58-59
  and smell, **E2**: 59, 221-22
  esthetic, **E2**: 278-79; **L2**: 76; **L17**: 516
  consumer, **L7**: 433
Tate, Allen
  on arts, **L6**: 330-34, 492-501
Tautology, **L12**: 313
Tawney, G. A., **M15**: 374n
Tawney, Richard, **L7**: 411, 436-37
Taxation and Democracy in America (S. Ratner), **L6**: xxn
Taxes, **L6**: 241, 395-96; **L8**: 47, 54; **L11**: 265-67; **L14**: 94
  distribution of, **L6**: 179, 337-38, 345, 356, 386, 387; **L9**: 249, 254, 256
  income, **L6**: 343-44; **L7**: 420-22

for unemployment relief, **L6**: 381-82
and Couzens Amendment, **L6**: 392
and land value, **L9**: 64-65
related to education, **L9**: 115-22, 146, 394-95, 407-8, 410-11
changes in, **L9**: 146, 256-58, 282-84
and consumption, **L9**: 259, 266, 268, 273-74, 278
Democratic platform on, **L9**: 260
and farmers, **L9**: 273
and Constitution, **L9**: 282
in Great Britain, **L9**: 284
George on, **L9**: 300, 301
in New York City, **L9**: 378
Aristotle on, **L13**: 290
poll, **L15**: 357
Taxicabs, **L9**: 366
Taxonomy, **L12**: 172, 253, 295; **L16**: 120
Taylor, Alfred Edward, **M11**: 10-12
Tcheka, **L17**: 501, 570
"Teacher and the Public, The," **L11**: xixn
Teachers, **M15**: ix, xi; **L11**: 162, 268, 529; **L14**: 360-61
social responsibility of, **E5**: 95; **L6**: 129-30, 136; **L9**: 134-35, 167, 206-9; **L11**: xviii-xix, 340-42, 344, 537, 547; **L13**: 389; **L14**: 360-61; **L17**: 512, 516
success of, **E5**: 459-60
at University Elementary School, **M1**: 65, 317
authority of, **M1**: 272-74; **M3**: 230-34; **L13**: xiv, 33-34, 58
professionalism of, **M1**: 274-76; **M7**: 109-12; **L9**: 116-17
role and duties of, **M6**: 217-20; **L5**: 23-24, 326-30; **L8**: xiv, xv, 59-60, 73-74, 155, 158-61, 181, 337-38, 348-49, 352; **L9**: 123-24; **L11**: 158-60, 485-86; **L13**: 6, 13, 21-23, 26-27, 30, 35-37, 41, 46-47, 49, 53, 54, 59, 283, 332, 342, 344-45, 381, 386-87; **L17**: 216, 223-25, 316, 342
participation by, **M6**: 341-43; **L8**: 334-36; **L11**: 222-24, 345, 358; **L17**: 53, 54
education of, **M6**: 343-45; **L8**: 144, 338-40; **L9**: 183, 185; **L11**: 389, 544-45, 580
organization of, **M10**: ix, xxxiii-xxxiv, xxxix, 168-72; **L5**: 331-33, 336, 401; **L9**: 182-83, 328-29, 332; **L11**: 236, 348-52, 359, 380, 533; **L14**: 375
trial of, **M10**: 158-63, 173-77
vs. university government, **M10**: 164-67
in Turkey, **M15**: xxi-xxii, 283-88
importance of, **M15**: xxiii-xxiv, 157, 161-63, 166, 169, 182-84, 186-89
as citizens, **L2**: 115-23; **L6**: 433-35; **L14**: 352-53
quality and kinds of, **L6**: 131-32; **L13**: 50-51, 307, 390
Mencken on, **L9**: 407-11
at Laboratory School, **L11**: 196-200
status of, **L11**: 348-49; **L13**: 343; **L17**: 179-80
freedom of, **L11**: 376, 378
knowledge of, **L13**: 50, 345

Teachers (*continued*)
psychology for, **L14**: 337-40; **L17**: 187-209
in China, **L17**: 30, 556
Communists as, **L17**: 136-37
and parent, **L17**: 233, 234
Russian, **L17**: 495
Teachers College. *See* Columbia University Teachers College
Teachers' League (New York City), **M7**: 109n
Teachers Union (New York City), **M13**: 428-30; **L11**: 349-52, 380. *See also* Grievance Committee
organization of, **L9**: 315, 317, 320-21, 323-25, 329, 341-43
communism related to, **L9**: 316, 322, 326, 330, 338-42
groups in, **L9**: 316-19, 323-29, 332, 334-39, 340-42
and politics, **L9**: 317-19, 338, 339, 341, 344-45
need for unity in, **L9**: 324, 337-38, 343-44
conflict in, **L9**: 330-32
functions of, **L9**: 332-33, 338
Teacher training, **E5**: 275-77, 281, 447; **L2**: 204; **L9**: 164-66, 168; **L11**: 389, 544-45, 580; **L17**: 138-39
methods of, **M3**: 249-72
Teaching, **L10**: 267, 349
methods of, **M4**: 275-78; **L6**: 85-88, 109; **L11**: 199, 213, 215, 222-23, 240-41, 557-59, 580; **L13**: 31; **L17**: 81-82, 166, 266-67, 270, 273, 276-77, 341, 514
philosophy associated with, **M10**: 3-4
experiment in, **L6**: 295-98
as profession, **L11**: 540-46; **L13**: 342-46
Teagle, Walter C., **L9**: 252
Technic. *See* Technique
Technical, **L16**: 367-68, 378
school, **M1**: 42
terms, **M6**: 325; **L8**: 312-13
trade training, **M8**: 401
studies, **L17**: 310-22
Technique
in imagination and expression, **E5**: 192-200
in interest, **E5**: 228
relativity of, **L10**: 87, 145-49, 203, 209, 232, 306-8, 315, 319, 332n, 333
introduction of, **L17**: 288-90, 296
related to method, **L17**: 294-97
of social communication, **L17**: 320-22
Technocracy, **L9**: 62, 105, 296, 297, 312; **L14**: 95-96
Technological art, **L10**: xxxii, 33, 53, 121-22, 146, 151, 153, 176, 181, 231, 347
Technology, **L3**: 142-43; **L15**: xxviii
in useful arts, **L1**: 101-11, 119, 120, 271, 282-83, 290-91
and science, **L1**: 119, 128-31; **L12**: 77-80, 98-99, 132, 150-51, 210-11, 388-89, 430-31, 481-86; **L15**: 88-90, 270, 359-60
methods of, **L2**: 378; **L4**: xvi, 68, 107, 201, 214, 218, 221, 226, 249; **L11**: 275-76; **L15**: 158, 306-7; **L16**: 393
social effects of, **L4**: 61, 65; **L5**: 99-123, 128-31; **L6**: 280-85; **L8**: 45, 60, 61, 67-71, 90; **L11**: 42, 53-54, 57-58, 62-63, 143, 261, 343, 457-60
nature of, **L5**: 88-89; **L6**: 282-83; **L11**: 162-63; **L14**:

110; **L15**: 253-54; **L16**: 405
in Greece, **L14**: 195
influences social science, **L14**: 318-19
problems of, **L15**: 190-91, 199-203, 223
attacks on, **L15**: 190-91, 255-56
teaching of, **L15**: 257-64, 279
Teleology, **M12**: 229-31; **M13**: 364-65; **L1**: 83, 208, 210, 264, 279. *See also* Consequences, **L12**; Ends, **L12**
theory of, **M5**: 207; **L7**: 182; **L14**: 99
and science, **M9**: 293; **L12**: 81-86, 96-97, 177-78
popular, **L1**: 87-89
event as, **L12**: 232-33, 454-56
Telos, **M13**: 369
Temperance, **M5**: 364-65
Temperature, sense of, **E2**: 68-70
Temporal
succession, **M2**: 123-24
in art, **L10**: xxiii, 168, 187-89, 210-14, 217, 222-26, 238
Temptation, **L7**: 164, 168-69; **L13**: 366
Tenacity, **M10**: 75, 77
Tendency, **M14**: xvi-xvii, 36-37; **L1**: 279-80
native, **L8**: 140-55
vs. classification, **L10**: 227-29, 233, 246, 287
Tenenbaum, Samuel, **L17**: 52
Tenison, Thomas, **M11**: 20
Tennessee Valley Authority, **L11**: 257
Tennyson, Alfred Lord, **M5**: 81; **M7**: 443; **L7**: 75; **L10**: 85, 197, 360; **L13**: 19; **L17**: 204
Tension, **L16**: 360-61. *See also* Conflict, **L12**
as feature of emotion, **E5**: 131
esthetic result of, **L10**: xxvii, 20, 21, 29, 66, 143, 149, 159-67, 184, 187
Tenure
academic, **M8**: 106-8
Ten-year plan (USSR), **L6**: 51, 61
Terauchi ministry (Japan), **M11**: 152; **M12**: 31
Tercentenary Conference in Arts and Sciences (Harvard University), **L11**: 127
Terence, **L7**: 131; **L14**: 204; **L17**: 395, 565
Term, **E5**: 149; **L11**: 97-98, 100-102
in *Cyclopedia of Education*, **M7**: 352-53
defined, **M10**: 351n, 356-57; **L12**: 347
concrete and abstract, **L12**: 119, 257-58, 349-52, 400
and words, **L12**: 284-86
dyadic and polyadic, **L12**: 311-12
transposition of, **L12**: 320-21
relational, **L12**: 327-29, 334-35
symmetry of, **L12**: 332-33
denotative-connotative, **L12**: 352-57
in extension and intension, **L12**: 357-60
in comprehension, **L12**: 359-60
collective, **L12**: 360-63
logics on, **L16**: 19, 21, 27-29, 37, 39-42, 162, 172, 189, 217-18, 240-41
as name, **L16**: 143, 180, 271-72
vs. reals, **L16**: 159
related to definition, **L16**: 168, 171
Terminists, **M2**: 165
Terminology, **M12**: 91
for knowings-knowns, **L16**: 6-7, 46-73, 96-97, 274

Terminology (*continued*)
of Tarski, **L16**: 39-42
uses of, **L16**: 93n, 129, 332, 386, 447
in transaction, **L16**: 102, 113, 121
of semiotic, **L16**: 236-40
"Terminology for Knowings and Knowns, A" (Dewey and A. Bentley), **L16**: 302n, 308n
Terror, **L13**: 399
Terror in Cuba (Révolutionnaires cubains), **L9**: 310-11
Tess of the D'Urbervilles (T. Hardy), **L15**: xv
Test, **E5**: 332. *See also* Consequences, **L12**; Ground, **L12**; Proof, **L12**
uses of, **E5**: 89; **M13**: 292, 490; **L16**: 4, 48, 292, 322, 355
of knowledge, **L3**: 50; **L4**: 83, 136
in education, **L3**: 260-62
of reflective thought, **L4**: 88, 210
of ideas, **L4**: 90n, 91, 92, 103-4, 109-12, 132-33, 142, 147
of operations, **L4**: 100, 128, 149, 150
of essences, **L4**: 129
of hypothesis, **L4**: 152, 231, 247, 248; **L8**: 205-6, 322
of beliefs, **L4**: 221, 222, 239
of values, **L4**: 236, 239
limits art, **L10**: 304, 314
Testing, **L13**: 58-59, 285
and inference, **M6**: 201-2; **L8**: 187-95
method as, **M6**: 243; **L8**: 248-51
consequences of, **M13**: 291
two kinds of, **L8**: 192-93
Textbooks. *See also* Books
role in learning, **E3**: 147
criticized, **M10**: 194
investigated, **L14**: 370-72, 427-29
censored, **L14**: 373
Thackeray, William Makepeace, **M5**: 145
Thales, **L15**: xxx, xxxi
Thayer, H. S.
on Dewey's 1910-11 writings, **M6**: ix-xxviii
Thayer, V. T.
on Dewey's 1910-11 writings, **M6**: ix-xxviii
Theaetetus (Plato), **M11**: 12; **M15**: 335-37; **L2**: 124, 130, 133n; **L16**: 157n, 471
"Their Morals and Ours" (L. Trotsky), **L13**: 349
Theism, **M2**: 182; **L2**: 9
in *Cyclopedia of Education*, **M7**: 353
Theocracy, **M15**: 128; **L2**: 261-62, 266, 285
Theodicy (Leibniz), **E1**: 303; **M7**: 293
Theodore Roosevelt: An Autobiography, **L17**: 72
Theodorus, **M15**: 336; **L7**: 110
Theofel, John, **L9**: 346, 347, 360, 361, 378, 379
testimony of, **L9**: 348-53
Theology, **M15**: x; **L15**: 159. *See also* Religion
nature of, **E1**: 209; **L4**: 42, 61, 186, 220; **L16**: 410, 412
history of, **M9**: 291; **L15**: 269, 334
related to philosophy, **M10**: 3; **M15**: 325, 328-31; **L4**: 12, 23
related to experience, **M10**: 21-24
vs. science, **M15**: xiii, 47-50; **L15**: 56, 93, 157, 184-85,

189, 230, 271-72; **L16**: 372-73, 409; **L17**: 17
as topic of Gifford Lectures, **L4**: vii, viii
teaching of, **L5**: 148-50
Jefferson's, **L14**: 218-19
Macintosh's, **L14**: 286-88
Theophrastus, **M2**: 186
Theory, **L10**: xii, 16, 220, 351. *See also* Esthetic theory
depreciation of, **M6**: 288; **L8**: 295-96
validity of, **M12**: 169-70
growth of, **M12**: 219
role of facts in, **L2**: 246; **L16**: 325, 327
and knowledge, **L3**: 51
and individualism, **L7**: xiii, xv, 299, 348-49
as function, **L12**: 468
verification of, **L14**: 59-60
necessary for warranted assertion, **L14**: 169
role of, in observation, **L14**: 172-74
terminology for, **L16**: 46-73
abstraction in, **L16**: 285-86
as hypothesis, **L16**: 292-93
in inquiry, **L16**: 323-24, 328
fallacy in, **L16**: 349-50
Theory and practice, **E3**: 227; **M12**: 160-63; **M14**: 50, 188; **L4**: ix, xiv, xvi, xvii, 4-5, 11, 18, 24, 56, 62, 134, 154, 223-27; **L7**: xxxiii-xxxiv; **L8**: 87, 89-90; **L12**: 63-65, 78-80, 432-35, 455-57, 487-89, 492-93, 504-5; **L15**: 190, 228-29; **L17**: 67-69, 85
in *Cyclopedia of Education*, **M7**: 354-56
Theory of Economic Progress, The (Ayres), **L15**: 108n, 359-60, 502-6
Theory of Education in the United States, The (Nock), **L6**: 286-90
Theory of Justice, A (Rawls), **L2**: xxxv
Theory of Moral Sentiments, The (Adam Smith), **M5**: 155
Theory of Poetry, The (Abercrombie), **L10**: 72n, 247, 355
Theory of Valuation, **M13**: xi; **L7**: xxxi, xxxii; **L13**: ix-xii; **L14**: 28n; **L15**: 421
These Russians (W. White), **L6**: 263, 267
Theses on Freedom (National Council of Education), **L6**: 445n
Thibet (Xizang), China, **M13**: 195
Thilly, Frank
and naturalism, **L3**: 73
criticizes *Experience and Nature*, **L3**: 392-400
criticizes Santayana, **L3**: 398
Thing. *See also* Object
vs. person, **M2**: 127n; **M7**: 454-55
and meaning, **M6**: 272; **L8**: 225-28
qualities of, **M9**: 150-51; **L13**: 214-15; **L16**: 175
as name, **L16**: 49n, 73n, 155-58, 272, 345n, 346
function of, **L16**: 66-67, 102n, 133-34
concepts of, **L16**: 113-14, 162, 182, 298, 331, 337
in transaction, **L16**: 243-44, 247
signs for, **L16**: 304-5, 328
as means and ends, **L16**: 323, 325, 349-50
Thing-in-itself, **M2**: 160-61, 189; **M6**: 4; **M7**: 297; **M8**: 190
Thinking. *See* Thought

Third party, **L9**: 297
  and Norris, **L6**: 149-51, 436, 504
  need for, **L6**: 156-61, 246-55, 403, 404; **L9**: 79, 80
  program for, **L6**: 167-73, 324-25, 408, 412-13
  problems facing, **L6**: 182-89
  in political history, **L6**: 237-38
  and LIPA, **L6**: 324, 438-39
  members of, **L6**: 406, 437
Third Reich, **M8**: xxx
Thirds, **L16**: 49, 133, 234n
  in postulates, **L16**: 78-79
This, **L1**: 264; **L12**: 73, 126, 150-51, 189-90, 240-41, 246, 249-50, 291-92, 351-52, 360-63, 468. *See also* Selection, **L12**; Singular, **L12**
This and *the*, **L4**: 189-92
"This Hour of Bewilderment" (I. Lee), **L6**: 60
This Is My Best (W. Burnett), **L15**: 367n
Thomas, Elmer, **L6**: 355, 394
Thomas, Norman, **L5**: xvii; **L6**: xvii, 250, 254, 255, 326; **L9**: 66-67, 69; **L11**: xxiii, 526; **L14**: 365-66; **L15**: xxv
Thomas, Wendelin, **L11**: 323
Thomas, William I., **M2**: 45n, 51n; **M5**: 522n; **M10**: 56; **L15**: xxvi; **L16**: xiv
Thomas Aquinas, Saint, **M8**: 142; **M12**: 111, 140; **L1**: 55, 192; **L2**: 33, 34; **L4**: xxi; **L6**: 19; **L7**: 137; **L13**: 58, 268
  scholasticism of, **M2**: 240
  on seminal reasons, **M2**: 244-45
  on state, **M5**: 141
  significance of, **L11**: xvn, xxii, 401; **L14**: 395
  Hutchins on, **L11**: 391, 393, 394, 400, 407, 592-94
  on knowledge, **L11**: 404, 405
  on Christian love, **L15**: xiii, 52
Thomasius, Christian, **E4**: 143, 146
Thomism
  on perseity, **M2**: 187
  in *Dictionary of Philosophy*, **M2**: 256
Thompson, Dorothy, **L15**: 353
Thompson, Helen Bradford, **M4**: 304n; **L7**: xix
Thompson, Ralph, **L15**: 338
Thompson, William Hale, **L5**: 371, 372
Thoreau, Henry David, **M5**: 437; **M9**: xxii; **L9**: xxvi; **L10**: 320
Thorez, Maurice, **L15**: 391
Thorndike, Edward Lee, **M10**: 54, 57
Thorwaldsen, Albert Bertel, **L10**: 147
Thought, **E4**: 156-57; **M8**: 175; **M12**: xxix, 147; **M14**: 71, 77; **L1**: xvii-xxi, 60-63, 98-99, 103, 126-27, 132, 171-72, 178-80, 212-13, 227, 228, 269, 283, 326, 340-41; **L11**: 215; **L13**: 362; **L15**: 37n. *See also* Inquiry, **L12**; Reflective thinking; Training of thought
  unity of, **E1**: 105; **E5**: 313-14
  knowledge related to, **E2**: 177-203; **E5**: 5; **M9**: 304, 336
  logic related to, **E3**: 126-30; **M6**: 224-29; **M12**: 157-58
  related to experience, **E3**: 151-52; **M6**: 353-56; **M8**: 143-44; **M9**: 146-58; **M10**: 6, 15-18, 322-65; **L14**: 414-15

history of, **E3**: 224-30; **M1**: 161, 167; **L3**: 4; **L4**: 87-92, 121-26, 136, 203, 220
and action, **E5**: 10-12, 195; **M6**: 304-13; **M7**: 176-83; **M10**: 108n; **L3**: 51-52; **L4**: 99, 101, 108-10, 129-30, 133-35, 178, 185, 199, 213; **L17**: 263
influences on, **E5**: 316, 318; **M14**: 177, 179; **L8**: 130-35
function of, **M1**: xii-xiii; **M6**: 192-95; **M12**: xxii, 122-23, 134-35, 248-49; **L4**: xviii, 90, 117, 210, 227, 231-41, 250; **L7**: 42-43, 190, 316
origin of, **M1**: 93-96; **M12**: xvii-xviii, 159-60; **L13**: 52-53; **L15**: 78-79, 211
process of, **M1**: 151-52, 168; **M2**: xvi-xvii; **M6**: 188-91, 212-15, 266-70, 350-56; **M10**: 80-81; **M15**: 71; **L8**: 139; **L13**: 91
as discussion, **M1**: 158-59; **M6**: 335-37
antecedents of, **M2**: 317-36
data of, **M2**: 337-50
objects of, **M2**: 351-67
Bradley on, **M4**: 60-64
meaning of, **M6**: 182-88; **L2**: 142; **L4**: xiii, xix, xxii, 4-7, 179-84, 194, 206; **L8**: 113-18; **L17**: 77
curiosity and, **M6**: 204-7
role of suggestion in, **M6**: 207-12
freedom of, **M6**: 229-32; **M10**: xxxvii, 276-80; **L3**: 111-14, 136; **L7**: 358-66; **L11**: xxx, 47-48, 142-43, 220, 270, 290, 344, 375
analysis of, **M6**: 234-41
induction and deduction in, **M6**: 242-58
related to judgment, **M6**: 259-66; **M15**: 356, 359, 369
meaning and understanding in, **M6**: 271-85
concrete and abstract, **M6**: 286-92
empirical, **M6**: 292-96
science related to, **M6**: 296-301; **M15**: 210-11; **L2**: 221-25; **L13**: 369-70; **L14**: 150-53
language and, **M6**: 314-27; **L3**: 37; **L12**: 54; **L13**: 328-29; **L16**: 134
and observation, **M6**: 328-35; **L8**: 252
unconscious and conscious, **M6**: 348-50
Bergson on, **M7**: 203; **M10**: 69
in education, **M7**: 473-74; **M9**: 159-70; **M15**: 198-99, 207-10
as pure, **M8**: 143-44; **L4**: 67, 112, 113, 120
nature of, **M9**: 166, 179-80, 312; **M12**: 163-64; **M14**: 127, 137; **M15**: 65, 66; **L3**: 316-17; **L6**: 12-13; **L8**: 118-24; **L10**: 21, 25, 27, 36, 38, 44-47, 52, 125-26, 137, 161, 183; **L16**: 308
idealism on, **M10**: 19-21
as subject for philosophy, **M10**: 69; **L8**: x, xii, xv, xvii, xviii
modern, **M12**: 95, 107-9
need for, **M14**: xii-xiii, 125, 140; **L14**: 361; **L17**: 48, 77-79, 82, 441
habits and, **M14**: 25, 49, 121-23
impulse and, **M14**: 118, 153; **L13**: 41-42

Thought (*continued*)
and value, **M15**: 26; **L2**: 69, 71, 73, 74, 393-402
epistemological and naturalistic, **L2**: 45-51
social, **L2**: 231-34
James on, **L5**: 158
types of, **L5**: 243; **L6**: 128
qualitative, **L5**: 243-62; **L6**: 332, 495
related to environment, **L6**: 4-5, 11-12; **L13**: 327-28
affective, **L6**: 330, 332, 493, 496, 498
Dewey's, **L7**: ix-x
as inhibitory, **L7**: 189; **L10**: 154, 165
formal vs. actual, **L8**: 171-76
in esthetic experience, **L10**: xii-xiii, 66, 80, 120, 253, 258-59, 264, 278, 351-52
Trotsky on, **L13**: 397
apart, **L14**: x-xvii, xxii
Greek, **L14**: 192
Peirce on, **L15**: 146, 149-51; **L16**: 51
in triangular scheme, **L16**: 301-2
Thought and Character of William James, The (R. Perry), **L11**: 441-45, 464-78
Thrace, **L2**: 139
"Three Contemporary Philosophers," **M12**: xxx
"Three Independent Factors in Morals," **L7**: xxvi
Three Lectures on the Vedanta Philosophy (F. Müller), **E5**: 342n, 343, 345
Three Philosophical Poets (Santayana), **L14**: 300
"Tick-tock" theory, **L10**: 168, 171
Tientsin (Tianjin), China, **M11**: 189; **M12**: 23, 30, 31, 47; **M13**: 101, 144; **L6**: 205
Tigert, John J., **M15**: 190
Tilden, Samuel J., **E1**: 234-35; **L2**: 365
Tildsley, John L., **M10**: 160, 161; **M11**: 55, 393
Tillich, Paul, **L14**: xix
Time, **L15**: 353
Time, **M8**: 15; **M12**: xxviii, 214, 223, 241, 260, 261; **M15**: 267; **L1**: 63, 91, 95, 325; **L4**: 151; **L13**: 187; **L15**: 145. *See also* Series, **L12**; Space-time; Temporal; Transformation, **L12**
Leibniz and Locke on, **E1**: 344-45, 364-69
unity and difference in, **E2**: 166
fallacy regarding, **M2**: 10-11
Bergson on, **M7**: 11, 202-4; **M10**: 68-69
Dewey's reply to D. Robinson on, **M10**: 99-101
important to China, **M13**: xxvi, 154, 170, 189, 223
and judgment, **M13**: 13; **L12**: 137
and race prejudice, **M13**: 252-54
eternal and temporal, **L1**: 60, 92, 274
role of, **L4**: 76, 78, 81, 189, 217
relations involving, **L4**: 102, 107, 116, 206, 230, 231
theories of, **L4**: 113-17, 120
attentiveness to, **L7**: x
in esthetic experience, **L10**: xxi, 29-30, 62-63, 70-71, 179-81, 186-89, 305, 309-10, 316
and organic behavior, **L12**: 50-51
measurement of, **L12**: 217-19
continuum, **L12**: 441-45, 448-52, 476-80
history of, **L14**: 98-101

and individuality, **L14**: 102-14
Whitehead on, **L14**: 131-33
"Time, Meaning and Transcendence" (Lovejoy), **M15**: 27, 349-70
"Time and Individuality," **L14**: x
Time and Its Mysteries, **L14**: 98n
Times (London), **M13**: 177
Tintern Abbey, **L10**: 91, 155
Tintoretto, **L10**: 98, 147, 304, 315, 316
Titchener, Edward Bradford, **M1**: xiii; **M7**: 141
Titian, **L13**: 363
technique of, **L10**: 97, 98, 117, 133, 147, 182, 213, 319, 357, 358
Titles
function in art, **L10**: xxx, 116-17
Tlaxcala, Mexico, **L2**: 203
Tocqueville, Alexis de, **L2**: 364; **L11**: 592
Toennies, Ferdinand, **M11**: 21-22
Tokugawa Shogunate (Japan), **M11**: 168, 169; **M13**: 113
Tokyo, Japan, **M11**: 150, 152, 161, 166, 179; **M13**: 219, 255
Dewey in, **M11**: xvii, 341
Toland, John, **M2**: 184
Tolerance, **L7**: 231; **L13**: 277
religious, **M12**: 105; **L2**: 266-67; **L15**: 172-75, 183
negative idea of, **L17**: 379
Locke on, **L17**: 438
attack on, **L17**: 460
Tolman, Edward C., **L16**: 144n, 238-40
Tolman, Richard C., **L16**: 103n
Tolstoians
on violence, **M10**: 212-13, 244, 248
Tolstoy, Leo, **M1**: 149; **M5**: 145; **M8**: 290; **M14**: 197, 214; **L7**: 326; **L17**: 565
on man's relation to universe, **M3**: 85n
on freedom, **M11**: 49-50
influences Russian education, **L3**: 225, 235; **L17**: 501, 570
ethics of, **L5**: 398-400
as artist, **L10**: 110, 194, 204, 305, 357, 360, 365; **L17**: 381, 388
on science, **L16**: 372; **L17**: 386-87
on government, **L17**: 382, 383
on meaning of life, **L17**: 382, 385
on truth, **L17**: 384
on happiness, **L17**: 388
as mystic and ascetic, **L17**: 389
on knowledge and conduct, **L17**: 391
related to modern thought, **L17**: 391-92
Tolstoy and Nietzsche (H. Davis), **L5**: 398-400
Tongues of Men, The (Firth), **L16**: 122n, 468
Tools. *See also* Instrumental; Means-consequences
related to intelligence, **M7**: 188
function of, **M14**: 168; **L4**: 119, 123, 132, 217, 221-23
defined, **L1**: 73, 101-2, 104, 105
and science, **L1**: 110, 128-29, 134; **L4**: 68, 70-73, 99-100, 185, 186, 200
nature of, **L1**: 121, 189; **L4**: 8, 10, 176, 193
language as, **L1**: 134, 146-47
and meaning, **L1**: 145-46, 227-28, 261
value of, **L4**: 108-9, 152-53, 238; **L16**: 133-34, 304-5, 329

Tools (*continued*)
of thought, **L4**: 122, 166
knowledge as, **L4**: 149, 150
in inquiry, **L16**: 126, 326-27
Topics (Aristotle), **L4**: x, xix, xxi
Torrey, H. A. P., **M3**: xxv; **L5**: xxii; **L15**: xxix, xxxiii
influences Dewey, **E1**: xxiii-xxiv; **L5**: 148-50
Torrey, Joseph, **L5**: 195
Totalitarianism, **L13**: xv, 141, 156, 168, 176, 185, 187; **L15**: 17, 59
features of, **L13**: 70-71, 160; **L15**: 176-77
rise of, **L13**: 73, 170; **L14**: 91-92, 95; **L17**: 460
German, **L13**: 80, 85, 92, 147-48, 180; **L16**: 390
evils of, **L13**: 87-88; **L17**: 469
challenge issued by, **L13**: 116, 151
Russian, **L13**: 129
contemporary, **L13**: 149
philosophy of, **L14**: 113, 275, 313, 317-20, 323, 330-31
vs. democracy, **L14**: 275-77, 293-94; **L15**: 4, 6, 248; **L17**: 472-73
vs. freedom, **L14**: 278-79, 367-68; **L15**: 171-72, 178, 182, 252, 366
related to Russell case, **L14**: 358
in Europe, **L14**: 365; **L16**: 390
collective, **L15**: 215-18, 246
on education, **L17**: 477-78
Totality
of response, **M9**: 335-36
in art, **L10**: 197, 324, 326
freedom created by, **L17**: 154
Totem group, **M5**: 26, 35; **L7**: 26, 33
Totemism, **M2**: 49-50
Touch, **E2**: 222
passive, **E2**: 48-52
active, **E2**: 55-56
and spatial relations, **E2**: 143-45
Toulmin, Stephen, **L14**: xviii
on *The Quest for Certainty*, **L4**: vii-xxii
"Toward a Perspective Realism" (McGilvary), **L14**: 431
To-what
of attention, **L17**: 272-73
Tractatus Logico-Philosophicus (Wittgenstein), **L14**: xv
Tracy, Frederick, **E4**: 66-67, 69
Trade, **L10**: 197, 344
in Middle Ages, **L7**: 142
European, **L11**: 261-64
as transaction, **L16**: 242-43
Trade education. *See* Vocational education
Trade unions. *See* Labor unions
Trade Union Unity League, **L9**: 341
Tradition, **M12**: 87-89, 268; **L11**: 117, 132-34; **L12**: 55-56, 68, 83, 264; **L15**: 100, 185, 204; **L16**: 380. *See also* Customs
in *Cyclopedia of Education*, **M7**: 356-57
revolt against, **M9**: 271-72, 303; **L2**: 288-89
authority and, **L2**: 58, 59
influence of, **L2**: 166; **L6**: 128-29, 142-44; **L8**: 52; **L13**: 102, 260-61, 293, 299; **L17**: 459
European, **L2**: 172
and morals, **L3**: 11
tribal, **L3**: 13-14
emotion supports, **L4**: 62, 234, 246
Nock on, **L6**: 286-89

related to education, **L6**: 446-47; **L9**: 175; **L17**: 167
as restrictive, **L8**: 44, 67, 78; **L10**: 304, 306, 327
regulates action, **L8**: 87, 90
vs. science, **L8**: 95; **L14**: 8, 10
artistic use of, **L10**: 163, 165, 251, 269-70, 275, 314-16, 336, 340
operation in context of, **L16**: 329-30
"Tradition, Metaphysics, and Morals," **M15**: 32n
Traditionalists, **M15**: 5-7
Tragedy, **L10**: xviii, 101-2, 178, 192, 198, 216, 247
"Tragic Philosophy" (Santayana), **L14**: 306
Training
vs. education, **M9**: 16-20; **L13**: 292
Training for Group Experience (Sheffield), **L5**: 412-16
Training of thought
reasons for, **M6**: 195-203; **L8**: 129-30
and school conditions, **M6**: 216-23; **L8**: 156-67
recitation methods in, **M6**: 338-47; **L8**: 326-41
resources in, **L8**: 140-55
and activity, **L8**: 281-92
language in, **L8**: 301-14
observation and information in, **L8**: 315-25
Traits, **M8**: 4; **L12**: 259, 269, 341, 353, 377, 386-87, 425-26, 439, 447-48, 451-52. *See also* Kinds, **L12**
Tranquility, **L13**: 368
Trans
as name, **L16**: 258, 272
Transaction, **L15**: 102
important to Dewey, **M6**: xxv-xxvi; **L16**: xxviii, 192
as name, **L16**: xxxiii-xxxiv, 71, 265n, 272
vs. interaction, **L16**: 4, 63, 112-15, 144
importance of, **L16**: 6, 66-68, 96-97, 111, 275, 278
establishment of, **L16**: 77, 131, 153
role of naming in, **L16**: 86-89, 127-30, 135, 260-61, 264, 270
used in science, **L16**: 98-100, 106-9, 115-21
as level of inquiry, **L16**: 100-104, 146
uses of, **L16**: 110, 144, 149, 160, 309
necessary for behavioral inquiries, **L16**: 122-26
aspects of, **L16**: 132, 242-44, 303n, 305, 308, 472-73
sign, signal, and designation as, **L16**: 138-42
in life, **L16**: 246-48, 255-56
Transactional, **L16**: 94, 348
point of view, **L16**: 3-4
behavior, **L16**: 275-76, 326-28, 331, 335, 352, 473
valuing, **L16**: 355
"Transactions as Known and Named" (Dewey and A. Bentley), **L16**: 459
Transcendence, **M7**: 37, 79-80, 450; **M15**: 35, 350-51, 355, 358, 372
in knowledge experience, **M3**: 173
attitude toward, **M6**: 4-7
and judgment, **M13**: 48

Transcendent
in *Dictionary of Philosophy*, **M2**: 257-58
Transcendental
logic, **E1**: 37-38
deduction, **E1**: 41, 43, 44
theory of rationalism, **M4**: 181-91
Transcendentalism, **M5**: 213-14; **M7**: 201; **M14**: 38, 40, 57; **L1**: 41, 134, 174, 282; **L5**: 184, 196; **L9**: 43
vs. empiricism, **E1**: 122
in *Dictionary of Philosophy*, **M2**: 258
in *Cyclopedia of Education*, **M7**: 357-58
German, **L2**: 7n
defects of, **L4**: 48, 207, 210
values determined by, **L4**: 63, 205, 206, 227
in Santayana's philosophy, **L14**: 307
Transfer
of experience, **L17**: 264-65
Transfigured realism, **E1**: 132-33
Transformation
by environment, **L12**: 34-35, 48-51
needed for conclusion, **L12**: 108, 121, 124-25, 137-38, 226-28, 238, 245, 287, 320-21, 420, 428, 440, 477, 484-85, 492
in mathematics, **L12**: 391-94, 401, 406-7, 409, 412-14
by inquiry, **L14**: 63, 66-67, 84
Transient
in *Dictionary of Philosophy*, **M2**: 258-59
Transition, **L14**: 80-81; **L17**: 40, 268
Transitivity, **L12**: 327, 329-32
Transitoriness, **M12**: 140-41
Transmission, **M9**: 6-9, 12, 331
of culture, **M10**: 196-201; **L10**: 329-48
Transportation, **L11**: 168-69, 261
Transposition of terms, **L12**: 320-21
Transsubjective reference, **M7**: 37
Transylvania, **M15**: 390, 392
Travel, **M12**: 101
Treason, **M10**: 292-95
Treatise Concerning the Principles of Human Knowledge, A (Berkeley), **E1**: 372
Treatise of Human Nature, A (Hume), **M5**: 155; **M8**: 24n; **L15**: 18
Treaty ports, **M12**: 37, 71-72
Treitschke, Heinrich von, **M8**: 423; **M10**: 221
Trendelenburg, Friedrich Adolf, **E3**: 3, 6-7; **L5**: 152
Tresca, Carlo, **L11**: 323; **L15**: xxiv-xxv
Treue, **M8**: 190
Triadic relation, **L10**: 111; **L16**: 9-11, 34-35, 39, 49, 58, 157-60, 300-302
Trieste, Italy, **M10**: 290
Trinitarians, **L10**: xii
Trotsky, Leon, **L11**: 303, 306; **L13**: 349, 404; **L14**: xix-xx, 366, 371, 427; **L15**: xi, 346, 352, 497, 510. *See also* Moscow trials
defense of, **L5**: xix; **L11**: xxvi-xxvii, 307-9, 310n, 324, 598-99
charges against, **L11**: 305, 307-8, 315-19, 321-23, 326-30, 333-34, 604; **L13**: 347-48
testimony of, **L11**: 310-13

beliefs of, **L11**: 318, 319, 323, 334-35; **L13**: 350-52, 354, 391-400
Trotsky, Leon Sedov, **L11**: 307-9, 312, 321-22, 326, 330, 602
Trotsky, Natalia I. Sedov-, **L11**: 312
Trotskyism, **L11**: 324, 327
Trotter, Wilfred, **M10**: 276
Troubled Philosopher: John Dewey and the Struggle for World Peace (Howlett), **L6**: xxin
Troubles, **M12**: 159-61; **L13**: 233
Troy, **L10**: 330
Troyanovsky, Alexander A., **L11**: 316, 319-20; **L15**: 293
True vs. false, **L14**: 182-83
Truman, Harry S., **L15**: xxvii, 240; **L17**: 562
Trusts, **L7**: 417
Truth, **M6**: 176; **M7**: xiv, 132-33; **M11**: 42; **L4**: 47, 55; **L8**: x, xi; **L10**: 40-41, 257, 271, 297; **L13**: x, 125, 132; **L15**: xxii-xxiii, 28. *See also* Validity; Warranted assertibility, **L12**
discovery of, **E1**: 34-35; **M12**: 235
varieties of, **E1**: 326; **M8**: 59; **M12**: 97, 98, 213; **L5**: 464-72; **L13**: 58, 321
conceptions of, **E1**: 395; **M6**: xiv-xvi; **M12**: 168-72, 174-75, 206-7; **L2**: 6-8, 11, 12, 16; **L14**: 5, 55-58, 71, 179-80; **L16**: 48, 78, 112, 314n; **L17**: 65, 272-73
and science, **E4**: 101-3; **M6**: ix, 28-31; **L3**: 307; **L11**: 277, 551; **L14**: 60; **L17**: 436
related to religion, **E4**: 101-3; **L9**: xv-xvi, 23, 27, 423; **L17**: 538
standard of, **E4**: 366; **E5**: 19
absolute vs. pragmatic, **E5**: 16; **M3**: 118; **M4**: 256; **M6**: xxii-xxiii, 3-11, 31, 37-52; **M7**: xv; **L13**: 131, 257; **L15**: 24-26
in Aristotle, **M1**: 164-65
mathematical, **M1**: 247; **L13**: 154
correspondence theory of, **M2**: xvii; **M6**: 33-36; **M8**: xix-xx; **L14**: 187-88
Dewey on, **M4**: xiv-xv; **M6**: xiii-xvi, xix-xx
Bradley on, **M4**: 54, 64-70
intellectualist theory of, **M4**: 76-77
attitude toward, **M6**: 12-16, 21-22; **M13**: 22, 306, 308, 481
Plato on, **M6**: 15, 24-25, 31-32
de facto and *de jure* views of, **M6**: 25-27
and consistency, **M6**: 33-36; **M13**: 38
objective conception of, **M6**: 52-68
instrumentalism on, **M7**: 64-78, 424-29
in *Cyclopedia of Education*, **M7**: 358-59
and warranted assertibility, **M8**: xviii-xix; **L14**: 85, 168-69, 176, 182
Peirce on, **M10**: 75-78; **L12**: 343n; **L15**: 273; **L16**: 459
Royce on, **M10**: 79, 81
James's theory of, **M12**: 217-20
Bacon on, **M13**: 307
vs. meaning, **M13**: 354; **L3**:

Truth (*continued*)
4-5, 8, 393; **L5**: 181, 213-16; **L14**: 400
in logic, **L11**: 155-57; **L12**: 18, 144; **L16**: 31, 36, 40-42, 45, 203, 206
authority of, **L13**: 127, 157
social, **L13**: 154; **L17**: 436
self-evident, **L13**: 173-74, 214; **L14**: 169n, 171-72
allied with force, **L14**: 321-22
moral, **L15**: 58, 178
related to fact, **L16**: 13-16, 43, 44
as name, **L16**: 272
"Truth, Reality, and Behavioral Fact" (A. Bentley), **L15**: 72n
"Truth and Knowledge of the Truth" (Nagel), **L16**: 17n
Tsarism, **M12**: 4, 61; **L3**: 225, 226; **L5**: 99; **L17**: 490
Tsinan (Jinan), China, **M12**: 29-32, 37; **M13**: 139-40, 144
Tsing Hua College (Peking), **M11**: xviii
Tsingtao (Qingdao), China, **M11**: 187, 225, 238; **M12**: 29, 30, 32-33; **M13**: 141-44
Tsuin-chen Ou, **M12**: 205n
Tuan Chi-jui, **M11**: 201, 202; **M12**: 66-67, 69; **M13**: 133
Tuchuns (China), **M11**: 203, 204; **M13**: 98, 130, 150
Tucker, Abraham, **M5**: 320n; **L16**: 256n
Tufts, James Hayden, **M4**: xxviii; **M10**: xxii, xxvii; **L7**: vii; **L14**: 4, 72, 73, 379
at University of Chicago, **E3**: xxi; **L16**: xiv
on moral evolution, **M4**: 219-21; **L7**: xix, xxix-xxx
on reward, **M5**: 488-89
tributes to, **L5**: 424-25; **L15**: xxiii, 321-25, 510
on intelligence and reason, **L7**: xxiv
Tugwell, Rexford G., **L6**: xvii-xix
on education, **L8**: 74-75
on industry, **L8**: 364-66, 369-73
Tukhachevsky, Marshal Mikhail N., **L15**: xi, 346, 352, 495-96
Tunis, **M15**: 388-89
Turczynowicz, Laura de Gozdawa, **M11**: 315
Turkey, **M15**: xi
educational system in, **M15**: xix-xx, 275-97, 301-7
Dewey visits, **M15**: xix-xx, 418-20
Ministry of Public Instruction in, **M15**: xxi, 278-83, 285-86, 296, 307, 418-20
libraries in, **M15**: xxi, 279, 302-3, 306
religion and politics in, **M15**: 128-30, 132; **L2**: 189-93
foreign schools in, **M15**: 132, 144-49
construction in, **M15**: 136-37
minority problems in, **M15**: 139-43
foreign relations of, **M15**: 149, 402; **L6**: 468n
reading circles in, **M15**: 278, 287, 301-2
orphanages in, **M15**: 292-93
Twain, Mark (pseud. of Samuel L. Clemens), **M12**: xxixn, 15; **L10**: 320; **L14**: xxi
Twentieth Century Fund, **L6**: 471, 484
Twenty-one Demands, **M11**: 187,

193, 194; **M12**: 22, 30-31, 61; **M13**: 130, 199, 211; **L6**: 206; **L15**: 370
cancelled, **M13**: 85
treaties connected with, **M13**: 85, 145-46, 167, 192
opposed, **M13**: 136
commemorated, **M13**: 140
signed, **L17**: 29, 555-56
"Two Basic Issues in the Problem of Meaning and of Truth" (Burtt), **L5**: 481n
Two Cultures, The (Snow), **L17**: xviii
Two Expeditions (G. Grey), **M2**: 45n
Two Sources of Morality and Religion, The (Bergson), **L11**: 428-31
Tychism
in *Dictionary of Philosophy*, **M2**: 259
Tydings, Millard E., **L17**: 562
Tyler, H. W., **M10**: 372
Tylor, Edward B., **M5**: 411n; **L1**: 42; **L14**: 193
Tyndall, John, **E1**: 105; **M2**: 149
Types of Ethical Theory (J. Martineau), **L17**: 3
"Types of Philosophic Thought," **M13**: xvi-xxi
"Types of Value Judgments" (Rice), **L15**: 73n

Ubication
in *Dictionary of Philosophy*, **M2**: 259
Uchida, Yasuya, **M11**: 175, 177, 394; **M13**: 346
Uebermensch, **M7**: 414
Ueberweg, Friedrich, **E3**: 3-4, 186; **M10**: 86
Uexküll, Jakob von, **L16**: 117n
Ugliness, **L13**: 360
esthetic use of, **L10**: xx, 101, 120, 178, 208, 235-36
Ukraine, USSR, **M11**: 101, 263-66, 270-75, 326; **L11**: 509
Ulpian, **L7**: 129, 133
Ultimate
traits, **M8**: 3-4
origins, **M8**: 3-6
causation, **M8**: 5
ideals, **M8**: 419
ideas, **M8**: 419
reality, **M10**: 38-42
Ultimates, **L16**: 168, 179, 181-82
Ulysses, **L7**: 45
Umbrian art, **L10**: 304
Umwertung aller Werte, **M7**: 414
Un-American Activities, Committee on, **L6**: xxii; **L14**: 370; **L17**: 137, 560-61
Uncertainty, **L10**: xxxiii, 41, 50, 72; **L16**: 375
importance of, **M6**: 188; **L8**: 121-22
perception of, **L4**: x, 3, 4, 31, 53, 240, 246
locus of, **L4**: 178-85, 188, 194, 199, 212
principle of, **L14**: 32, 106-7, 384
as outcome, **L16**: 360-61, 367, 370, 381
Unconditional. *See* Universal proposition, **L12**
Unconscious, **L15**: 16. *See also* Subconscious
experience, **M3**: 179-80
in thought process, **M6**: 348-50; **L8**: 342-45
as entity, **L16**: 412
Underconsumption, **L6**: 347, 348, 485-86

Undergoing, **M10**: 8-9
Understanding, **L10**: xxxiii, 274; **L12**: 505; **L13**: 144; **L16**: 376, 399
  in thought, **M6**: 271-74
  and language, **M13**: xiv, 355, 375, 383
  importance of, **M13**: 263-64, 268-69, 439; **L3**: 342-43; **L13**: 94
  difficulties in, **M13**: 264-66
  history and, **M13**: 267-68, 272, 273
  J. Marsh on, **L5**: 183, 185-89
  as knowing, **L7**: 197
  creation of, **L8**: 221-47
  as comprehension, **L12**: 156-60
  growth in, **L13**: 21, 56
  related to senses, **L14**: 197
  vs. memorizing, **L17**: 161, 188
Understanding and Reason
  in *Dictionary of Philosophy*, **M2**: 259-61
Undertaking, **L13**: 146
Undeterminism, **E4**: 92
Unearned increment, **M5**: 503-4
Unemployment, **M11**: xii, 75-76, 83, 87-88; **L6**: 337-38, 341-42, 360, 361, 367, 411-12; **L9**: 61, 64, 256, 275, 333; **L13**: 105
  consequences of, **L5**: 67-68; **L9**: 270, 307; **L11**: 275
  People's Lobby on, **L5**: 434-39; **L9**: 253
  government responsibility for, **L6**: xviii-xix, 160, 350, 372-80, 386, 390, 406, 440-41; **L9**: 77, 254, 259-60, 262, 278, 283
  social responsibility for, **L6**: 153-55, 179, 381-82, 397-400, 436
  insurance, **L6**: 339-40, 362, 404; **L7**: 413
  special session regarding, **L6**: 344, 345, 352, 355-58
  prevention of, **L7**: 382-83, 432-33
  related to profit motive, **L9**: 65, 289
  in April 1930, **L9**: 252-53
  relief for, **L9**: 271-72; **L11**: 257, 266-67, 601
  suppressed facts about, **L11**: 270-71
  of youth, **L11**: 340, 353-54
  evils of, **L13**: 310-11, 317-18
  cause of, **L16**: 393
Unemployment, Joint Committee on, **L9**: 81n, 253, 271-72
Unemployment Relief, President's Organization on, **L6**: 374
UNESCO (United Nations Educational, Scientific, and Cultural Organization), **L16**: 399-405, 471
Unesthetic, **L10**: 46, 47, 84, 156, 202, 267
Unfolding of Artistic Activity, The (Schaefer-Simmern), **L15**: xxiii, 315-17
Unification
  Herbartian theory of, **E5**: 297-98
  aspects of, **M13**: 412-13, 415, 417
  of ideal ends, **L9**: 294
  Guterman on, **L9**: 424-25
  of desire and purpose, **L9**: 432
  as function of judgment, **L10**: 304, 313, 317-18
  as esthetic function, **L10**: 326
  nature of, **L12**: 523

moral, **L17**: 453-55
Unification of Knowledge
in *Dictionary of Philosophy*, **M2**: 261
Uniformity, **L4**: 130, 166; **L5**: 170-71; **L13**: 89
in morals, **L3**: 23
artificial, **L13**: 39
in education, **L13**: 40
of Communist thought, **L13**: 131-32, 218
Union Labor Life Insurance Company, **L5**: 387-89
Union of Polish Democrats, **M11**: 279, 282
Union of Soviet Socialist Republics (USSR), **M13**: 113, 238, 240, 316; **M15**: 80, 81, 139, 141, 215, 392, 412; **L2**: 177-78, 378, 379; **L6**: 180, 235; **L8**: 62; **L11**: xxvi, 262, 322; **L13**: 128, 130, 180, 315, 317, 394; **L14**: 323, 365; **L17**: 130, 140, 557. *See also* Russian Revolution
Poland's relation to, **M11**: xiv, xv, 262-84, 288-95, 298, 306-9, 313, 321, 326, 327
as world power, **M11**: 101, 135, 136, 192, 199, 224; **M13**: 175-76; **L6**: 206-7, 458; **L17**: 542, 543
government of, **M11**: 115, 120, 191, 263, 269, 280, 298; **L11**: 296, 328; **L14**: 275-76, 320; **L15**: 220, 297
and Germany, **M11**: 115, 270; **L14**: 250-51
and Japan, **M11**: 177, 178, 192, 230; **M13**: 214
Jews of, **M11**: 241, 264, 278
immigrants from, **M11**: 241, 285
tsarist, **M12**: 4; **L3**: 225, 226; **L5**: 99
foreign relations of, **M12**: 6, 60-64; **L6**: 468; **L11**: 328, 332; **L15**: 239-40, 244-46, 298, 342-44, 347-50, 353, 355, 373, 488-91, 494-95; **L16**: 392, 401
Siberian situation in, **M12**: 64
Dewey's impressions of, **L3**: 202-7, 250; **L5**: xix
economics in, **L3**: 208-10, 221; **L17**: 495, 502-3, 505
life in, **L3**: 212-14, 230-32, 243-45, 247; **L17**: 491-92, 496-97, 507, 509
religion in, **L3**: 217-18; **L5**: 355-62; **L7**: 90; **L13**: 70
education in, **L3**: 218-41, 247-48; **L6**: 143-45, 291-94; **L11**: 335-36, 356, 357, 509; **L15**: 373-74; **L17**: 54, 489, 493-510
propaganda in, **L3**: 221-22, 237, 249
Third International in, **L3**: 250
socialism and communism in, **L5**: 87, 98; **L6**: 263, 267, 292-94; **L7**: 426-27; **L9**: 91-94; **L13**: 126, 347, 349, 353-54; **L15**: 215; **L17**: xxxii
five-year plan in, **L5**: 237; **L6**: 51, 61, 65, 263, 266, 469
Hindus on, **L5**: 407-9
ten-year plan in, **L6**: 51, 61
and sanctions, **L6**: 199, 201, 469, 475
U.S. attitude toward, **L6**: 263-67, 322; **L11**: 316, 493, 495; **L15**: 289-93, 296-97, 375; **L17**: 509
Trotsky's relationship with, **L11**: 307-8, 318, 323

Union of Soviet Socialist Republics (*continued*)
history of, **L13**: 129, 134, 151; **L17**: 510
science in, **L13**: 157; **L17**: 507
purges of, **L15**: xi-xii, 338-40, 345-47, 352, 493-97, 500
Wallace on, **L15**: 243-45
in WWII, **L15**: 340, 342, 347-48, 352-53, 494-98
effect of war on, **L16**: 391; **L17**: 492
Tolstoy on, **L17**: 383
criminal colony in, **L17**: 499-501
Union party, **L11**: 526
Unions. *See* Labor unions
Union Teacher, **L9**: 324
Union Theological Seminary, **L15**: 356
Unique Function of Education in American Democracy, The (NEA), **L11**: 250
Unitarianism
in *Dictionary of Philosophy*, **M2**: 261
Unitarians
Laymen's League, **M15**: xvii, 87n, 100, 383
related to minority problems, **M15**: 390-92
"United, We Shall Stand," **L11**: xixn
United Nations, **L15**: 244, 369; **L16**: 360; **L17**: 140, 149, 542, 561
Charter of, **L6**: xxi
Relief and Rehabilitation Administration, **L15**: 197, 509
War Council, **L17**: 543
United Nations Educational, Scientific, and Cultural Organization (UNESCO), **L16**: 399-405, 471
United States (U.S.), **M15**: 126, 278, 284
government and politics in, **E4**: 77-79; **M12**: xxii; **L7**: 352-54, 428-30; **L8**: 13, 14, 16, 17, 50; **L9**: 297, 298, 402-3; **L11**: 7-8, 15-16, 18, 46-48, 60, 167, 169, 220, 253, 285-86, 372-74, 377, 589; **L14**: 203; **L15**: xxvii, 182, 239-47, 293, 348, 375, 488, 491; **L17**: 44
law in, **E4**: 86; **L2**: 36
quality of life in, **E5**: 59-60; **M11**: 131, 374; **L3**: 134-36, 138-40, 144; **L5**: 50-57, 130-31; **L6**: 94-95; **L7**: 446; **L11**: 59n, 266, 297, 357, 517, 535-36
education in, **M10**: 125-29; **M11**: 54-57, 60-69, 335; **L2**: 115; **L3**: 140-41; **L5**: 311-18; **L6**: 100-104, 109-10; **L8**: 43-47, 53-55, 75, 83, 102-3; **L9**: 393-94; **L11**: 172-73, 229-35, 356-59, 364, 535; **L15**: 274, 281-85, 309
in WWI, **M11**: ix-xiii, xvi-xvii, 88, 104, 107-21, 126, 127, 137-38, 142, 180-85, 200-202, 229, 282, 298, 319, 329, 394
immigration in, **M11**: xiii-xvi, 228, 241-47, 284-330; **M13**: 439; **L2**: 178-79; **L7**: 419-20
economy of, **M11**: xvi, xix, 78; **L2**: 161; **L3**: 142-43; **L7**: 404, 412-13; **L8**: 55-58, 60-65; **L9**: 284; **L11**: 232, 262-67
Far Eastern policy of, **M11**: xviii, 176-79, 186, 190-98, 201-2, 209, 226-34, 150-60,

164, 176-79, 194-95, 394; **M12**: 4-6, 32, 36-40, 61, 75; **M13**: xxiii, 79-85, 91, 102, 136-37, 156-58, 161, 163-64, 167-70, 178, 184, 189, 199, 202, 230-32, 261, 409-10; **M15**: 124-25; **L2**: 173-74, 176-84; **L3**: 200, 202, 364, 429; **L6**: 202-3, 216, 457-59, 469
foreign relations of, **M11**: 70-72, 127, 129, 132, 246, 279; **M12**: xxi-xxii, 3-7, 32, 36-37, 61; **M15**: xviii, 87, 88, 384, 396-97, 411; **L3**: 136-38, 351-52; **L5**: 440-41; **L6**: 209, 219, 364; **L11**: 247-48, 328, 527-28; **L15**: 298, 340-44, 354-55, 371, 373, 488-91, 494
Civil War of, **M11**: 116, 143, 287, 337; **L6**: 232, 236, 463; **L8**: 57; **L9**: 77, 176, 178; **L13**: 186; **L15**: 242, 341
and League of Nations, **M11**: 123, 128, 140, 151, 163; **M15**: xvi, 78-79, 81; **L2**: 375; **L6**: 197, 222
T. Roosevelt as representative of, **M11**: 143-49
in drug traffic, **M11**: 236-40
on Polish question, **M11**: 246, 250-58, 272, 279-82, 293, 296-300, 302, 305-7, 314-30, 400, 403, 404
James on, **M12**: 220; **L2**: 158-62
as world power, **M13**: 164, 173, 174; **L14**: 368; **L15**: 194, 196; **L16**: 402, 405-6; **L17**: 131, 140
and Europe, **M13**: 164-66; **M15**: 155; **L2**: 170
and Great Britain, **M13**: 165, 178, 180, 181, 218, 272, 273; **M15**: 155; **L2**: 177
thought in, **M13**: 306-10; **L2**: 18-21
and World Court, **M15**: 96-97, 385, 393-96, 402-3
schools of, in Turkey, **M15**: 144, 146-49
on outlawry of war, **L2**: 167-72; **L3**: 163, 168-69, 171, 175
and Mexico, **L2**: 198, 201, 205, 209-10; **L3**: 158-62
democracy in, **L2**: 304-7; **L8**: 49-55, 64, 76; **L15**: 367-68; **L16**: 401
history of, **L6**: 99-100; **L11**: 230, 232-33, 248-49, 387-89; **L13**: 81
on sanctions, **L6**: 197-98, 208-9, 463-64, 472-73, 480, 483-84
attitude toward USSR, **L6**: 263-67; **L11**: 316, 326-29, 333-34, 493, 495
Niebuhr on, **L9**: 399-400
ideals of, **L11**: 167-70, 247-55, 261, 535, 536, 547
C. and M. Beard on, **L14**: 283-85
in WWII, **L14**: 364; **L15**: 192-93, 349, 369-70
in Spanish-American War, **L15**: 20-22
propaganda in, **L15**: 345, 352-53
"United States and Central American Revolutions, The" (Buell), **L6**: 468n
United States Army
vs. Polish National Army, **M11**: 242, 245, 321-25

United States Bureau of Internal Revenue, **L9**: 267
United States Chamber of Commerce, **L2**: 161; **L9**: 115, 125, 130
United States Congress, **M11**: 239, 402; **M15**: xv, 101; **L9**: 81n, 162, 254, 267, 275; **L15**: 281-85, 349
  and immigration, **M15**: 124
  and World Court, **M15**: 393, 398, 415-17
  and unemployment relief, **L6**: xviii-xix, 160, 339, 381, 384-87, 397-98; **L9**: 272
  membership of, **L6**: 163, 169, 393-94, 438-39
  and politics, **L6**: 227, 235-37, 250, 326
  and economics, **L6**: 342, 353; **L9**: 256, 266, 270, 288
  special session of, **L6**: 344, 345, 352, 355-58, 375
  and sanctions, **L6**: 472
  on child labor, **L7**: 413
  and farmers, **L9**: 249, 250, 273
  People's Lobby and, **L9**: 276
  letter to, on New Deal, **L9**: 280-81
United States Constitution, **M11**: 88; **M12**: xxii; **M15**: 159-61; **L6**: 176, 356, 393, 463, 464; **L7**: 352, 354, 358-59; **L8**: 14; **L13**: 99, 130, 175; **L14**: xxiv, 219; **L15**: xv, 172, 357
  Fourteenth Amendment, **L7**: 356, 395
  Bill of Rights, **L7**: 360; **L11**: 220, 253, 372-73; **L13**: 103, 104; **L14**: 253; **L16**: 402; **L17**: 473
  Sixteenth Amendment, **L7**: 420
  amending, **L7**: 426
  and liberty, **L9**: 87
  adoption of, **L9**: 161, 162
  related to education, **L9**: 181, 206
  and land value, **L9**: 266
  and taxation, **L9**: 282
  vs. Declaration of Independence, **L13**: 100
  Jefferson on, **L14**: 215-16
  on suffrage, **L16**: 403
United States Department of Agriculture, **L6**: 361; **L9**: 85
United States Department of Education, **L9**: 393-94
United States Department of Labor, **L6**: 351
United States Department of State, **M12**: 253n; **M13**: 86, 90, 160, 167, 201, 202, 211, 212, 410; **L2**: 181; **L8**: 13
  on Polish question, **M11**: 251-52, 259, 306, 400
  and Mexico, **L2**: 210
  charge of Communists in, **L17**: 140, 561-62
United States Federal Trade Commission, **L7**: 408-9, 418; **L14**: 370
United States House of Representatives, **L6**: xxii; **L9**: 260, 284; **L14**: 370; **L17**: 137, 560-61
United States of the World, The (Newfang), **L6**: 463n
United States Senate, **M11**: 251, 301-2; **M15**: 85, 397, 405-6, 411, 414, 417; **L6**: 173, 339, 458; **L8**: 14-16
  on universal military training, **M10**: xxxv-xxxvii, 377-93
  Committee on Banking and Currency, **L9**: 288
  on international law, **L17**: 103
  Foreign Relations Committee, **L17**: 562

United States Steel Corporation, **L5**: 59
United States Supreme Court, **M15**: xvi, 398, 406, 408, 415, 416; **L2**: 179; **L6**: 323, 463-64; **L7**: 395, 415, 418, 421, 426; **L8**: 15; **L9**: 238, 266, 282; **L15**: 356-58
 World Court modeled on, **M15**: 92-93
 on railroads, **L6**: 371, 504
United States War Department, **L6**: 118-19, 125
 on Polish question, **M11**: xv, 248, 251-52, 257, 259, 262, 295, 320, 396, 400, 401n, 406-7
Units, **L12**: 205, 217-19, 363, 475-80
Unity, **M12**: 141-42, 211; **L1**: 60
 spiritual nature of, **E1**: 289-91; **L9**: xvi-xvii, 29-30, 431, 436; **L17**: 529-30, 532-33
 concept of, **E1**: 291-92; **E3**: 173; **L13**: 324-25; **L16**: 169, 175, 281, 363
 and existence, **E1**: 315
 organic, **E1**: 377; **L9**: 220-21, 226, 414-17
 Green on, **E3**: 163-64, 169
 of action, **E3**: 214; **L17**: 157, 450
 as centered movement, **E3**: 215-19
 social, **E3**: 219-22
 in Dewey's work, **E5**: xiv-xv
 Being as, **M1**: 250
 in *Dictionary of Philosophy*, **M2**: 261-63
 absolute, **M8**: 172
 political, **L9**: 74-75; **L17**: 130, 542-43
 in Teachers Union, **L9**: 324, 337-38, 343-44
 as esthetic quality, **L10**: xxxii, 43-49, 54, 63, 76, 78, 87, 98, 105, 122, 137-38, 141-42, 166, 186, 188, 195-96, 199, 204, 206, 233-37, 253, 257, 264, 272, 278, 297, 332, 340, 343, 351-52
 search for, **L13**: 332-33
 lack of, **L13**: 340
 of universe, **L17**: 93-94
 of self, **L17**: 155-57, 449, 516, 566
Universal, **L1**: 96, 119, 122, 147-48, 241, 249, 325; **L4**: 16
 in Kantianism, **E3**: 294-98
 Royce on, **M1**: 251
 judgment, **M1**: 253n
 in *Dictionary of Philosophy*, **M2**: 263-65
 in *Cyclopedia of Education*, **M7**: 360
 vs. particular, **M9**: 352-53
 nature of, **L4**: 113, 124, 129, 130, 136, 145
Universalism, **E5**: 12; **L1**: 168
Universality, **M12**: 116, 213, 260, 263; **M14**: 168-70
 in social unity, **E3**: 219-20
 of art, **L10**: 73-74, 88, 112, 114, 190, 193-94, 219-20, 237, 256, 288-92, 326
 of qualities, **L11**: 86-89
 of philosophical subject-matter, **L16**: 358-61, 381, 411-12, 418
 of religion, **L17**: 374-77, 379
 of science, **L17**: 546
Universal military training, **M10**: xxxv-xxxvii, 183-90, 377-93. *See also* Military training
Universal postulate
 in *Dictionary of Philosophy*, **M2**: 265

Universal proposition, **L11**: 96-97, 99-104, 119, 120, 124, 125. *See also* Operations, **L12**; Possibility, **L12**
singular and, **L12**: xvi, 351-52
generic and, **L12**: xvi-xxi, xxv-xxvi, 253-54, 351-52, 376-78, 438
Aristotelian, **L12**: 90, 139-40, 183
concrete, **L12**: 184n
abstract, **L12**: 254-57, 259, 261, 394-96
hypothetical, **L12**: 300-305
disjunctive, **L12**: 305-7
Universals
and characters, **L11**: 97-99, 103
described, **L11**: 107-8
related to individual, **L11**: 109-10
theories of, **L11**: 111-13
in Santayana's philosophy, **L14**: 296-97
Cohen on, **L14**: 388
Universe (Klyce), **M13**: 412-20
Universe, **M7**: 357; **L2**: 13; **L13**: 255
relation of self to, **E1**: 148-49; **L9**: 14, 37-38
in *Dictionary of Philosophy*, **M2**: 265
closed conception of, **M12**: 110-12, 260
as continuous process, **M12**: 113, 226-28, 235
pluralistic and block, **M12**: 208, 212, 220-21
philosophy on, **M12**: 237-38
matrix concept of, **L9**: 56-57, 295, 431, 438-39
and organic unity, **L9**: 220-21, 226, 415
as source of values, **L9**: 438
Universitas, **L2**: 26, 33
Universities: American, English, German (Flexner), **L17**: 110-11
Universities and Public Service, National Conference on, **L17**: 67n
University, **M15**: 205-6; **L17**: 537. *See also* College; Normal schools
expectations of, **E3**: 51-55
changes in, **E3**: 199-202
extension, **E3**: 203-6
role of, **E3**: 277-80
role in school reorganization, **E5**: 283-84
medieval, **M1**: 40; **M5**: 153, 157
modern, **M5**: 141
vocational education's effect on, **M10**: 151-57
teachers vs. university government, **M10**: 164-67
Dewey at, **M11**: ix, xvii, 165, 180, 341, 406
criticized, **M11**: 32-33; **L17**: 110-11
in Japan, **M11**: 165, 173
in China, **M11**: 180, 186-91
related to war, **L14**: 273-74
Russell case affects, **L14**: 358-59
University Elementary School, Columbia University Teachers College
description of, **M1**: ix, 56-66, 268, 317-20, 325-34
philosophy of, **M1**: 81-84, 92-96, 333-36
organization of, **M1**: 225-29, 330-34
University of the Air, **L9**: 61n, 309

University Primary School. *See* Laboratory School, University of Chicago
Unknowable, **L17**: 95
in *Dictionary of Philosophy*, **M2**: 266
"Unlearner, The" (C. Hinton), **L10**: 51, 355
Unlikeness, **M6**: 250; **L8**: 255-56
Unlimited extension
fallacy of, **L6**: 8-11, 16-17
Unreality, **L1**: 56-57
Unselfishness, **M9**: 362
Unthinkable
in *Dictionary of Philosophy*, **M2**: 266-67
Upanishads, **M7**: 417
Urban, Wilbur M., **L15**: 425n
on value judgments, **M11**: 370-76
Urbanization, **L11**: 55, 56, 208, 249
Urga (Ulan Bator), China, **M13**: 240
Urvolk, **M8**: 188, 189
Use, **L1**: 50, 90-91, 128-30, 271-72
of art product, **L10**: 33-34, 120-22, 153, 234-37
vs. esthetics, **L10**: 144
influences on, **L10**: 265-67
adaptation to, **L10**: 344-45
-enjoyment, **L16**: 307
significance of, **L16**: 329-30, 380
vs. absolute, **L16**: 338, 453
Useful art
vs. fine art, **L10**: x, xxxii, 33-34, 265, 277, 343-44
Use of the Self, The (F. Alexander), **L6**: 315
Ushenko, Andrew Paul, **L16**: 209n
Usury, **L7**: 136, 142; **L13**: 290; **L16**: 370
Utah, University of, **M8**: 409-10
Utah State Insane Asylum (Provo), **L17**: 324, 325, 564
Utensils, **L10**: 265-66, 330
Uterhart, Henry A., **M11**: 259, 302, 396, 406
Utilitarianism (J. S. Mill), **L15**: 423
Utilitarianism, **E3**: 91; **E4**: xix, 145, 263; **M4**: 40-41; **M7**: 212; **M9**: 359; **M11**: x, 348; **M12**: 182-85; **M14**: 37-38, 132, 147, 149, 153-54, 200-201; **M15**: 233-34; **L1**: 69; **L2**: 292; **L4**: 25, 205; **L10**: 202; **L13**: 144-45
criticized, **E3**: 274-76
evolutionary, **E3**: 283-90
moral theory of, **E4**: 42, 147-48; **M5**: 158, 226-40
influences intuitionalism, **E4**: 128-29
concept of happiness, **E4**: 282; **M5**: 251-56
of Bentham, **M5**: 241-42; **M6**: 367-68
on rules, **M5**: 298-303
theory of duty, **M5**: 318-27
in *Cyclopedia of Education*, **M7**: 360-62
on deliberation, **M14**: 139-45
formation of, **M15**: 57-58
in international affairs, **M15**: 58-61
and natural rights, **M15**: 244
conception of, **L7**: 155-56, 288
value of, **L7**: 175
standard in, **L7**: 237-40
confused with hedonism, **L7**: 240-45, 285
Carlyle on, **L7**: 250-51

Utilitarianism (*continued*)
and society, **L7**: 251-52, 315; **L11**: 11-15
Pollock on, **L17**: 99-100
Utilities, public, **L9**: 286
Utility, **M12**: 170, 227; **L4**: 32
meaning of, **M6**: 310; **M9**: 267; **L4**: 118, 123; **L8**: 288-89
of experienced objects, **L4**: 84-85, 177, 190
principle of, **L11**: 12-13, 16, 28, 50, 284
"Utility of Religion" (J. S. Mill), **L9**: xxxi
Utopia, **M8**: 18, 19; **L9**: 102
education in, **L9**: 136-40
Baconian, **L14**: 407
Utrillo, Maurice, **L10**: 298

Vacuum
in *Dictionary of Philosophy*, **M2**: 267-68
in education, **L9**: 127-28, 199-200
in politics, **L9**: 288
Vague
as name, **L16**: 47n, 73n, 272
Vagueness
consequences of, **M6**: 282; **L8**: 243-44
in propositions, **L14**: 176-77
"Vagueness in Logic" (A. Bentley), **L16**: xxx
Validity, **L1**: 35, 93, 123-24, 128, 129, 136, 219, 234-35, 304-5, 307; **L4**: 79, 112, 117, 157, 196, 230. *See also* Truth
Royce on, **M1**: 248-56
application of, **M2**: 20-31
determination of, **M3**: 4; **L4**: 59, 116, 132
in knowledge experience, **M3**: 176-77
in *Cyclopedia of Education*, **M7**: 362
of values, **L4**: 34, 210, 213
of ideas, **L4**: 48, 88, 90, 98, 103-4, 154
and consequences, **L12**: 20-21, 73, 80, 145, 156, 176, 193, 196-97, 224, 318-20, 341-42, 399, 423-24
defined, **L12**: 287
testing of, **L14**: 61
Valid knowledge
related to empirical events, **M6**: 80-85
Valley of Fear, The (A. Doyle), **L10**: xix
Valuation, **M7**: 45; **L1**: 313, 320-21
conditions of, **M9**: 242-44; **M13**: 26; **L14**: 51; **L15**: 101, 104-6
and values, **M13**: xi, 10, 25; **L16**: 310, 314, 316
subject-matter of, **M13**: 19; **L15**: 66, 68, 80-81
in social philosophy, **M15**: 231-32, 256-57, 263-64
and judgment, **M15**: 341-42
Marx on, **L13**: 120
theories about, **L13**: 193, 219, 221, 243
as appraisal, **L13**: 195, 209-11, 213, 216, 223-24
and desiring, **L13**: 204, 206-7, 217, 237, 240, 336, 348
nature of, **L13**: 204, 212, 218; **L14**: 28; **L16**: 311, 317, 355
problems of, **L13**: 225, 240-41, 245-48
moral, **L14**: 71
"Valuation and Experimental Knowledge," **M15**: 338, 340n, 341, 344

Valuation-judgment, **M15**: 25, 234, 343, 344
 character of, **M13**: 15; **L15**: 73n, 102-7
 definition of, **M13**: 16, 19
 object of, **M13**: 17
 evidence for, **L15**: 80-83, 139
 Rice on, **L15**: 407-12, 431-37
"Valuation Judgments and Immediate Quality," **L15**: 413n, 426
Valuation-proposition, **L15**: 106
Value, **L1**: 286-87; **L11**: 461, 462; **L12**: 83, 101
 and hedonism, **E4**: 262-64
 as subjective, **E5**: 124
 Hebrew conception of, **M5**: 96, 101-2; **L7**: 88, 93-94
 Greek conception of, **M5**: 106-8; **L7**: 97-99
 Dewey, Perry, Urban, and Bush debate, **M11**: 3-9, 361-87
 and logical empiricists, **M13**: xi
 and taste, **M13**: xi-xii
 meaning of, **M13**: 3-7, 18; **M15**: 20; **L1**: 295-326; **L2**: xviii-xx, 69-97
 and interest, **M13**: 11n; **L13**: 194
 and liking, **M13**: 12n; **M15**: 25-26; **L2**: 70, 71, 80, 82, 83, 87, 89-91, 95-96
 as object, **M13**: 20-22
 in economic theories, **M15**: 268
 Picard on, **M15**: 338-39
 and affecto-motor theory, **M15**: 339-40, 343, 344
 dyadic relation as, **M15**: 345
 thought and, **L2**: 69, 71, 73, 74, 393-402
 ambiguity of term, **L2**: 69-71, 82
 ideational factor in, **L2**: 88-89, 92-96
 spiritual, **L4**: 206, 209, 226, 227; **L9**: xix, xxiv-xxv, 29-30, 47-49, 57-58, 225, 232, 423-25, 430-31
 concern with, **L7**: xxxi
 sense of, **L7**: 266
 Wieman on, **L9**: 413-17
 nature of, **L16**: 311, 313, 315, 359
 field of, **L16**: 343-57
 intellectual vs. emotional, **L17**: 158
Value: A Cooperative Inquiry (Lepley), **L16**: 344n, 351, 357n, 470
"Value, Objective Reference and Criticism," **L2**: xx
Value and Destiny of the Individual, The (B. Bosanquet), **M15**: 337; **L9**: xxv
"Value and Fact" (Vivas), **L15**: 404, 406
"Value and Thought-Process" (Prall), **L2**: xix
"Value and Worth" (Picard), **M15**: 338, 340
Value-conceptions, **L13**: 192
Value-expressions, **L13**: 200, 236-37
Value judgment, **L2**: 78-79, 91-92, 96-97; **L16**: 312-15, 356-57
 practical judgment and, **M8**: 23-49
 objectivity of, **M8**: 32-36; **L15**: 63-68, 71
 choice in, **M8**: 33; **M13**: 24
 desire in, **M8**: 35
 end in, **M8**: 36-39
 standard in, **M8**: 39-46
 D. Robinson on, **M10**: 416-30
 analysis of, **L17**: xxxi

"Value Judgments and the Social Sciences" (Benoit-Smullyan), **L16**: xxxiiin, 310
Value-proposition, **L13**: 237-38
Value-quality, **M15**: 20, 21, 24, 25
Values
educational, **E5**: 334; **M7**: 362-65; **M9**: 252-58; **L8**: 79, 83-84, 90-91; **L9**: 173-74; **L13**: 270, 375
problem of, **M7**: 44-46; **L7**: 165; **L13**: 192
intrinsic vs. instrumental, **M9**: 247-52; **M15**: 339, 345-46; **L13**: 215-16; **L17**: xxiii
and valuation, **M13**: ix, 23-25
and judgment, **M13**: 11-12, 16; **M15**: xii, 20-21; **L7**: 216-17, 263-65, 267-68
esthetic, **M13**: 17; **M15**: 347; **L8**: 86; **L10**: xx, xxii, xxxii, 16, 73, 122n, 123, 146, 156, 177-78, 186, 189-90, 193, 199, 203, 211, 225, 228, 233-35, 238, 244-45
beliefs about, **M13**: 19n; **L4**: 15, 18, 40-48, 56-59, 201; **L13**: 191
series of, **M13**: 20
immanent meanings as, **M13**: 380
of object, **M15**: 26; **L10**: 101
criticism and, **L2**: 78-97; **L10**: 310-12
knowledge's relation to, **L4**: 20, 105, 106, 237, 238; **L8**: 91, 97, 102; **L14**: 47
security of, **L4**: 23-38, 106-7, 241, 243, 247
realm of, **L4**: 52-54, 63, 76, 110, 186
development of, **L4**: 83-86, 136, 155, 203-28
as possibilities, **L4**: 240-43
search for, **L4**: 248-50
and culture, **L6**: 446; **L9**: 234
ideal and material, **L7**: 212, 271-72; **L10**: 297; **L17**: 458-59
in experience, **L7**: 344; **L10**: 26, 36, 38, 76-80, 103, 142, 254, 261, 272, 283, 291, 339, 341, 346-49
social, **L9**: 301; **L14**: 149; **L15**: 54, 108, 173, 205; **L17**: 428
imagination's role in, **L10**: 276-77
confusion of, **L10**: 321-24; **L17**: 359
need for, **L13**: 71, 134
estimate of, **L13**: 87, 143
science related to, **L13**: 171-72; **L14**: 9; **L15**: 7, 160
nature of, **L13**: 194-95, 225; **L15**: 63-72, 82, 103-5, 163-64
as feeling, **L13**: 223
final, **L13**: 227, 236, 241; **L14**: 77; **L15**: xx-xxii
of ends, **L13**: 232
etymology of, **L13**: 242
vs. facts, **L13**: 249; **L14**: 323; **L15**: 16-17, 106, 481-82
in democracy, **L13**: 379; **L14**: 275-79
vs. enjoyments, **L14**: 66
in nature, **L14**: 144-45
philosophical treatment of, **L15**: 49, 159-60
basis of, **L15**: 59, 126, 445-47
questions concerning, **L15**: 101-2, 107-8
Rice on, **L15**: 402-26, 431-37

Geiger on, **L15**: 445-52
pluralism of, **L17**: xxii-xxiii
waste of, **L17**: 451
Values, Immediate and Contributory (Picard), **M15**: 345n
"Values, Valuations, and Social Facts," **L16**: xxxiiin
Value-situation, **M15**: 24, 342-43
Valuing, **M15**: xii, 25-26; **L13**: 194; **L15**: 73n, 103-5
conditions and consequences of, **L16**: 6, 343-57
nature of, **L16**: 310-17
Van Liew, Charles Cecil, **E5**: 247
Van Norden, Charles, **E5**: 342, 345
Vare machine (Philadelphia), **M11**: 287, 396
Variation
in rhythm, **L10**: 29, 169-79
in repetition, **L17**: 304
Varieties of Religious Experience, The (W. James), **M7**: 399; **L11**: 474-75
Variety, **L10**: 166, 230
Vasconcelos, José, **L2**: 203
Vassar College, **L17**: 8
Vassif Bey, **M15**: 418, 419
Veblen, Thorstein, **L5**: 102; **L7**: 379; **L11**: 271; **L15**: xxvi
at University of Chicago, **M1**: xxii; **L16**: xiv
on property, **M5**: 437
on leisure, **M5**: 460-61, 528-29
on Germany, **M11**: 54-55
Vedic philosophy, **L6**: 321
Vehm, **M5**: 37; **L7**: 36
Velásquez, Diego Rodríguez de Silva y, **L10**: 133
Venetian school of painting, **L10**: 146-47, 192, 210, 315-16, 319
Venn, John, **M3**: 63n; **M6**: 194
on logic, **E3**: xxiv, 75-82; **E4**: 22-25
Vera causa, **L12**: 106, 162, 370
Verbs
temporal, **L12**: 137-38, 224, 332-33
Verification, **E3**: xxiv-xxv; **M12**: 169-70; **L12**: 159-60, 433-34, 512; **L15**: 63, 69-72, 117-26. *See also* Consequences, **L12**; Hypothesis, **L12**; Test
analysis of, **E3**: 83-89
view of, **M1**: 130n; **M4**: 85
and truth, **M4**: 67; **M6**: xix-xx, 7-8; **M13**: 23-24
necessity of, **M13**: 20
existence of, **M13**: 22
and thought, **M13**: 41
Lovejoy on, **M13**: 42, 471-73
vs. meaning of past, **M13**: 43-44
indirect, **M13**: 48
as confrontation, **L14**: 55, 59-60
Verkhne-Udinsk (Ulan-Ude), USSR, **M13**: 235, 237
Vermont, **M11**: xvii
Vermont, University of, **M3**: 73n; **M6**: 471n; **L5**: 178n, 191, 420
Dewey at, **L5**: xxii, 147-50
education at, **L14**: 266-70
Vernacular, **M12**: 25-26
Vernunft, **M8**: 184, 441
Versailles, Treaty of, **M8**: xxx, 427; **M11**: 136-37, 173, 194, 197, 224, 232-33; **M12**: 23, 28, 36, 41; **M13**: 179, 201, 206, 208, 213, 274, 313; **M15**: xviii, 79-81, 91, 101,

Versailles, Treaty of (*continued*) 105, 116, 123, 317, 378, 388, 403; **L5**: 352; **L6**: xx, 194, 197, 474; **L14**: 274. *See also* Paris Peace Conference
and China, **M13**: 73, 110, 145, 166, 202, 210; **L17**: 555
disillusionment following, **M13**: 146, 156, 160, 261
connected with League of Nations, **M15**: 84-85
connected with World Court, **M15**: 96, 113, 390
Verstand, **M1**: 156; **M8**: 184, 441
Vesalius, Andreas, **M13**: 497
Vevey, Switzerland, **M11**: 312, 316
Vice, **M5**: 175-76, 359. *See also* Virtue
Victorian era, **L5**: 277; **L10**: 336; **L13**: 362; **L17**: 457
Victory of Samothrace, **L10**: 238
Viedt, Ernst, **E5**: 150
Vienna, Austria, **M11**: 273; **L15**: 367
Vienna Circle, **L3**: xvii-xviii; **L13**: x; **L16**: xxxii
Vigilance, **L17**: 461, 462
Village cottage reading room (USSR), **L17**: 494, 495
Villard, Oswald Garrison, **L5**: xvii; **L6**: xvii, 329
Vinogradoff, Paul, **L2**: 41n; **L3**: 326; **L6**: 270
Violence, **L8**: 99; **L10**: 186; **L13**: 293
in classroom, **M8**: xxxvi
Dewey's concept of, **M10**: xxviii
related to force and law, **M10**: 211-15
Tolstoians on, **M10**: 212-13, 244, 248
energy as, **M10**: 246
as means for social change, **L11**: xxi, 45-46, 55-56, 58-61, 65, 170, 259-60, 266, 287-88, 293-94, 378-79
Bolshevist justification for, **L17**: 117
Virchow, Rudolf, **M12**: xiii
Virgil, **E3**: 118; **L2**: 165
Virginia
constitution of, **L15**: 357
Virginia, University of, **L11**: 3; **L14**: 204-5, 207, 221
Virtue, **L7**: xi-xii; **L15**: 46-47
as wisdom, **M5**: 127; **L7**: 118
related to knowledge, **M9**: 340
Socratic-Platonic teaching on, **M9**: 364-65; **L2**: 130, 131, 135, 137-38; **L17**: 185
conceptions of, **M9**: 367-68; **L7**: xxx, 94, 237, 253, 255-60, 306
prudence as, **L7**: 195-96
Mann on, **L11**: 227, 388
speculative vs. practical, **L11**: 404-5
as intelligence, **L17**: xxi
Virtues, **M4**: 170-71; **M5**: 212, 359, 362; **M12**: 173-74; **M14**: xvi
defined, **E3**: 382-83
cardinal, **E3**: 383-84
statement of, **E4**: 351-53
classification of, **E4**: 353-62
Vis aestimativa, **M8**: 24
Vishniak, Mark, **L15**: 386
Vision, **E5**: 106; **M12**: 91, 206; **L4**: xvii
perception in, **E2**: 144-50
as knowledge, **L4**: x, 19, 157, 162, 170, 195
artistic, **L10**: xxx, 57, 92-95, 98, 140-41, 163, 165, 241-42, 273, 287, 294, 307, 310, 316
theories of, **L16**: 114n, 124

Visual, **M8**: 85, 86
language, **E5**: 198
Vitalism, **M12**: xxvi, 231, 232, 244, 246; **L2**: 224
Vital principle
in biological sciences, **L16**: 115-16
Vivas, Eliseo, **L14**: 301, 303, 305; **L15**: 404-6
Vladeck, Baruch Charney, **L5**: 443; **L6**: 326
Vladivostok, USSR, **M13**: 235, 239, 258
Vocabulaire (Lalande), **L16**: 43, 163
Vocabulary
in education, **M6**: 321-25
development of, **L8**: 309-10; **L17**: 259
precision of, **L8**: 311-13
Vocation. *See also* Occupations
meaning of, **M9**: 316-18
place of, in education, **M9**: 318-21
and culture dualism, **M9**: 322
Vocational education, **M7**: xxvii, 379; **M8**: xxxv, 117-22, 365-87, 411-13, 460-65; **M11**: 60-69; **M15**: 165-66, 195; **L5**: 401-3; **L6**: 105-6, 132, 288-89; **L9**: 145-46; **L11**: 188-89, 234-35, 350, 392-93; **L15**: 258-59, 264, 279-80, 482-84. *See also* Industrial education
related to activity principle, **M6**: 363-64
policy of, **M7**: 85-105; **M9**: 266, 316
in New York City, **M7**: 205-6
aims of, **M9**: 318-21
and industry, **M9**: 323-24
reorganization of, **M9**: 325-29
Dewey on, **M10**: xxx-xxxii
in public education, **M10**: 144-50
affects university, **M10**: 151-57
need for, **M10**: 303-4
James on, **L14**: 339
Vocational Education, Commission on National Aid to, **M7**: 93-94
Vocational Education Association of the Middle West, **M11**: 58n
Vocational guidance, **L17**: 512-13
Volapük, **E3**: 208, 209
Volga River, **M15**: 215
Volition, **L17**: 4. *See also* Will
Volitional
training in education, **E5**: 202-3
consciousness and action, **E5**: 361
Volks-geist, **M8**: 178; **M10**: 60
Volks-seele, **M8**: 178
Volstead Act, **L6**: 184
Voltaire, François Marie Arouet de, **E4**: 193; **M7**: 293; **M10**: 18; **M15**: 89, 205, 385; **L7**: 146; **L17**: 430
on optimism, **M2**: 175
on sensationalism, **M2**: 246
on reason, **M5**: 155
on lawyers, **M5**: 180
Volume
esthetic, **L10**: 186-88, 216, 217, 312
Voluntarism, **M1**: xiv, xvii; **M3**: 317; **L11**: 156
Royce on, **M7**: 418, 423, 435, 444; **M10**: 79-88
Voluntary, **L17**: 4, 200-203
act, **M5**: 188-89, 210-20
Vorstellungen, **M9**: 75
Voting, **M5**: 423-24; **M7**: 409; **M11**: 167. *See also* Suffrage

Voting (*continued*)
in New York City, **L9**: 381-82
Vyshinsky, Andrei Y., **L11**: 308-9, 311, 323, 326, 330, 603; **L13**: 398; **L15**: 24n

Wage earners. *See* Workers
Wages, **L7**: 387-89; **L13**: 313
Wagner, Adolf, **L16**: xiii
Wagner, Richard, **M5**: 145; **M8**: 438; **L13**: 358
Wagner, Robert F., **L6**: 339, 384-85
Wagner Construction bill, **L6**: 387
Wagner Free Institute of Science (Philadelphia), **L6**: 424
Wagner Relief bill, **L6**: 384, 387; **L9**: 253
Walden (Thoreau), **L9**: xxvi; **L10**: 320
Wales
kin groups of, **M5**: 34, 62-63; **L7**: 33, 57-58
customs of, **M5**: 58-59; **L7**: 54
Walker, James J., **L9**: 346, 364-70
Walker, Janet Allen, **L9**: 367
Walker, W. H., **L9**: 368
Wallace, Alfred Russel, **M6**: 444
Wallace, Henry A.
candidacy of, **L15**: xxvii, 239-45
Wallace, William, **E1**: xxv; **E3**: 186; **E5**: 342n, 343-44; **L5**: 152
Wallas, Graham, **M10**: 54; **L2**: xxii, 160, 231-34, 295, 404; **L11**: 13-14
Waller, Odell, **L15**: xxiv, 356-58, 510
Wallis, John, **E1**: 262; **M11**: 32
Walsemann, A., **E5**: 149
Walsh, Thomas James, **L6**: 161; **L8**: 16; **L14**: 370
Wants
of self, **E3**: 161-63
socially conditioned, **L2**: 299-300
War, **M12**: 196-97; **L6**: 322. *See also* Outlawry of war; World War I; World War II
positive aspects of, **M5**: 45, 80-81; **L7**: 74; **L17**: 457
as unifying factor, **M5**: 47-48, 63, 67; **L7**: 45, 58, 61-62; **L17**: 542-44
Germany's justification for, **M8**: 197
characteristics of, **M10**: 211-15, 244-59; **L15**: 171, 220
illusions about, **M10**: 217
Spanish-American, **M10**: 260; **L15**: 20-22; **L17**: 573
psychology of, **M12**: 9, 11; **L2**: 190; **L13**: 290, 400
effects of, **M13**: 259-60; **L11**: 6, 252, 459; **L17**: 24, 25, 453-55, 457
related to human nature, **M14**: 78-82, 88; **L13**: 164-65, 172, 180, 288-90, 314-15
judicial substitute for, **M15**: xvi, 89, 92, 116-17, 119-20, 407-8, 414
as moral problem, **M15**: 63; **L7**: 164-65, 178, 320-21
system, **M15**: 90, 95, 98-99, 113, 397, 412
politics and, **M15**: 100, 106; **L2**: 284-85
related to economics, **M15**: 107; **L6**: 365-66; **L13**: 310-11
causes of, **M15**: 111-12, 125-26, 409; **L11**: 27, 58-59, 363, 367; **L16**: 400; **L17**: 438

prevention of, **M15**: 124
modern, **L2**: 376-78
Wright on, **L6**: xxi
related to sanctions, **L6**: 201-2, 215-16, 453-58, 477-79
national vs. international, **L6**: 207-8, 465
defensive, **L6**: 210, 218-19, 223
evils of, **L7**: 369-71; **L17**: 48, 451
resisters, **L7**: 370
threat of, **L11**: 276, 328, 517; **L14**: 364; **L15**: 204-5
study of, **L13**: 262; **L14**: 320, 330, 431
education related to, **L14**: 273-74, 355-56; **L17**: 26-28
philosophical lesson of, **L14**: 312, 315, 324, 334
and democracy, **L14**: 364; **L17**: 123
James on, **L15**: 21n
religious, **L15**: 51-52
abolition of, **L15**: 192-94, 251-52
science in, **L16**: 393
"War and a Code of Law," **M15**: xvii
Ward, Mrs. Humphry, **E3**: 14
Ward, James, **E1**: 199; **E2**: xxiii; **E3**: 186; **L3**: 296; **L11**: 471
Ward, James F.
on Dewey-Bentley collaboration, **L16**: xiin, xivn, xxvi-xxvii
Ward, Lester F., **M6**: 266n
on contributions of psychology to sociology, **E4**: xv, 200-210
Ward, Nathaniel, **M11**: 32
Ward, Paul, **L3**: 92
War Department. *See* United States War Department
War Industries Board, **M11**: 118
Warner, Francis, **M1**: 179
Warner Brothers Pictures, Inc., **L15**: 353
War Policies Commission, **L6**: 365
Warranted assertibility, **M8**: xviii-xix
as end of inquiry, **L12**: xx, 15-18, 29, 108, 122, 142, 146, 156-61, 173, 195-96, 260-61, 328; **L14**: 180-82
meaning of, **L14**: 168-69
Warranted assertion, **L16**: 187-88
as truth, **L14**: 85, 169, 176; **L16**: 272
in postulations, **L16**: 87
Warren, Charles, **L6**: 463n
Warsaw, Poland, **M11**: 272, 275, 279, 281, 294
War Trade Board, **M11**: 311
Washington, George, **M11**: 70, 150
Washington, D.C., **M11**: 119, 203; **M15**: 150n; **L6**: 224n; **L9**: 124, 125, 129, 260, 285, 287, 307; **L11**: 530
Polish question in, **M11**: 246-47, 251, 253, 256, 259, 261, 295, 297, 301, 302, 317, 325, 400, 406, 407
political situation in, **L6**: 162-63, 166
Washington Conference, **M15**: 78, 381, 405, 407
issues of, **M13**: 145-46, 156, 166, 173, 181, 186, 442, 495
effect of, **M13**: 157-59, 172, 212
and Great Britain, **M13**: 165, 273
and China, **M13**: 167, 181, 191-96, 209-11, 228

Washington Conference (*continued*)
on armaments, **M13**: 173-74, 204
Dewey on, **M13**: 186-89, 197, 208, 214-16, 440-42
publicity regarding, **M13**: 197-98, 203
Japan on, **M13**: 205, 206, 214, 257-58
U.S. and, **M13**: 206, 261, 495
Washington (D.C.) Dance Association, **L13**: 357, 404
Waste
prevention of, **L7**: 431-32
of human values, **L17**: 451
Watson, David Lindsay, **L13**: 369-71
Watson, Goodwin, **L11**: 535
Watson, James, **L6**: 339
Watson, John, **E5**: 350; **L5**: 152
criticizes hedonism, **E5**: 352-54
Watson, John B.
behaviorism of, **M11**: 13-14; **M13**: xiii, xiv; **L2**: 15; **L16**: 79n
Watt, James, **L11**: 169
Watteau, Antoine, **L10**: 133
Way beyond "Art," The—The Work of Herbert Bayer (Dorner), **L15**: xxiii, 312-14
Way Out of Educational Confusion, The, **L6**: xxi
Ways and Means Committee, **L9**: 260, 284
Ways of Worldmaking (Goodman), **L14**: xvi
Wealth, **M12**: 101-3, 151-52
in Israel, **M5**: 91, 103; **L7**: 84, 94
in Greece, **M5**: 112-17, 124-25; **L7**: 103-7, 115-16
moral principles concerning, **M5**: 460-67; **L7**: 136-37
in Rome, **L7**: 128-30
increase of, **L7**: 149-50, 404
corporate, **L7**: 392-94
distribution of, **L7**: 407-11
spiritual and material, **L17**: 313
Weaving
social significance of, **M1**: 13-15; **L17**: 316-17
Weber, Ernst Heinrich, **E1**: 198; **E2**: 49-51; **L1**: 236
Weber, Max, **M7**: 138
compared with Bentley, **L16**: xviin
sociology of, **L16**: xxiii
on science, **L16**: 372-73
Weber's law, **E2**: 49-51; **L1**: 236
Webster's New International Dictionary of the English Language, **L16**: 155-56
Wedda, Joseph, **M11**: 256, 257, 295, 395, 401n
Weekly Review of the Far East, **L17**: 29
Weeks, J. H., **L3**: 82
Weeks, Raymond, **L2**: 386
Weigel, Erhard, **E1**: 259
Weight, **E5**: 430
Weihaiwei (Weihai), China, **M13**: 125
Weimar Republic, **L14**: 293
Weismann, August, **E4**: 188, 210, 212
Weiss, Albert Paul, **L3**: 395-96
Weiss, Paul, **L11**: 87n, 108n, 421, 479, 484; **L15**: 144n-52n
on Peirce, **L6**: 273-77
Weitz, Morris, **L16**: 166
Welch, William Henry, **L17**: 146, 562
Welfare
Bentham on, **L7**: 240
public, **L9**: 275, 286
social, **L13**: 159, 164
child, **L17**: 512, 518

Well-being
emotions related to, **L17**: 514-15
Welles, Sumner, **L15**: 349
Wellesley College, **L17**: 7, 8
Welling, Richard, **L11**: 516; **L17**: 523
Wells, H. G., **M8**: 476; **M11**: 82, 115; **M15**: 46; **L6**: 88, 94; **L14**: 95; **L17**: 45, 48, 557
on theology, **M10**: 310-14
on U.S., **M13**: 74
on Anglo-Japanese alliance, **M13**: 219
world history of, **M13**: 311
on state-mindedness, **M13**: 313
Weltanschauung, **M7**: 418; **M8**: 169, 426, 427; **M15**: 325; **L14**: x
Wenley, Robert Mark, **M10**: 109n; **M11**: 336-37
Wergeld, **M5**: 34, 58, 64; **L7**: 33, 54, 59
Wertheimer, Max, **M12**: xxvi; **L16**: 99n
positions of, **L16**: 7n, 102n, 106n
on science, **L16**: 67n, 76n, 105, 109n
Wesley, John, **L11**: 283
West
China's relation with, **M12**: 26, 41-50, 57; **M15**: 215-18
attitude of, toward Asia, **M12**: 35
synthesis of East and, **L17**: 35-36
Westbrook, Richard B., Free Lectureship Foundation, **L6**: 424
West Chester Normal School (Pa.), **L3**: 279, 434
Westermarck, Edward Alexander, **M5**: 65; **M11**: 362; **M14**: 54-55; **L3**: 15-16; **L5**: 286; **L7**: 59
on hospitality, **M5**: 68; **L7**: 62-63
on sympathetic resentment, **M5**: 71; **L7**: 65
on civil rights, **M5**: 409n, 410n
on guilt of animals, **M5**: 411
on insanity plea, **M5**: 414n
Western Rate Advance Case, **L6**: 371, 504
Weston, John C., **L9**: 374-75
Weyl, Hermann, **L16**: 165n
Whalen, John, **M10**: 160, 176
Wharton, Francis, **E4**: 86
"What Are Definitions?" (J. Reid), **L16**: 169
"What Are Universals?" **L11**: xiv
What I Believe (B. Russell), **L16**: 199n
"What Is an Emotion?" (W. James), **L16**: 468
"What Is It to Be a Linguistic Sign or Name?" **L16**: xxxii, 472-74
What Is Reality? (F. Johnson), **E3**: 192-93
"What Is Sociology's Job?" (Glazer), **L15**: 225
What Is the Communist Opposition? (Wolfe), **L9**: 335
"What Kind of Realism?" (Drake), **M10**: 431-38
"What Outlawry of War Is Not," **M15**: xvii
"What Pragmatism Is" (C. Peirce), **L5**: 478n
"What Pragmatism Means for the Social Sciences" (Kallen), **L11**: 563-66
Wheeler, Burton K., **L6**: 161, 355, 365, 394, 440

Wheeler-La Guardia bill, **L5**: 432-33
When the Prussians Came to Poland (Turczynowicz), **M11**: 315
"Where Love Is, There God Is Also" (Tolstoy), **M8**: 290
Whewell, William, **M1**: 160; **M2**: 295; **M7**: 241; **L4**: xxi; **L11**: 403n, 592
  on logical theory, **M2**: 368-75
Whig party, **L15**: 242
Whipple, Guy Montrose, **L13**: 255n
Whistler, James Abbott McNeill, **L10**: 172
White, Andrew D., **L11**: 456
White, James C., **M11**: 256, 295, 302, 325, 401n
White, Lucia, **M1**: xxi
White, Morton G., **M1**: xxi; **M14**: xxii
  on logic, **L17**: 480-84
White, William C., **L6**: 263, 267
White Cross, Polish, **M11**: 250, 306, 316-19, 329
Whitehead, Alfred North, **M12**: xxx; **L2**: 29n; **L5**: 483; **L6**: 274-75, 301, 312; **L9**: 420, 435, 438; **L14**: 5, 327; **L16**: xviii
  philosophy of, applied to art, **L2**: 111, 113, 114
  on science, **L2**: 221-25; **L12**: 388n
  as humanist, **L5**: 265
  philosophic system of, **L5**: 375-81
  on social change, **L6**: 53-54
  and creative advance, **L8**: 355-56
  reveres Plato, **L8**: 356-59
  cosmology of, **L11**: xiv-xv, 146-54
  Reiser on, **L11**: 435
  on Dewey, **L13**: ix
  on change, **L14**: 101
  Dewey critiques, **L14**: 124-40
  on experience, **L14**: 127-35, 189-90
  Hocking on, **L14**: 421-23
  on language, **L16**: 50
  organismal theory of, **L16**: 117n
"Whitehead's Philosophy," **L11**: xiv-xv
White House Conference on Child Health and Protection, **L6**: 92, 131-36, 139, 141, 352; **L17**: 511-12, 550-52, 572
Whither Mankind: A Panorama of Modern Civilization (C. Beard), **L3**: 115n
Whitman, Charles Otis, **L16**: 117n
Whitman, Walt, **M6**: 135; **M12**: 15, 207; **L2**: 350
Whittaker, Edmund, **L15**: 507
Whittier, John Greenleaf, **L17**: 252
Whole. *See also* Individual, **L12**; Situation, **L12**
  absolute, **M7**: 187; **M9**: 62-65, 73
  qualitative, **M9**: 206-7; **L12**: 89, 218-19, 469-70
  -heartedness, **L7**: 256; **L8**: 137
  -part relation, **L12**: 203-6
  related to elements, **L17**: 153-56
Wholeness, **E3**: 384; **L13**: 323
Whyte, A. Gowan, **L15**: 509
Wiebe, Robert H., **L16**: ix

Wieman, Henry Nelson, **L9**: xxi, 213, 435, 437
  vs. Dewey on religion, **L9**: xxii-xxiii, 214-15, 218-28, 294-95, 412-17, 426-34, 438-40
Wiener, Philip Paul, **L17**: 50-51
Wigmore, John H., **M5**: 24; **M10**: 372, 373
Wilberforce, William, **L11**: 18
Wilbur, Ray Lyman, **L9**: 119-20
Wild boys (USSR), **L17**: 505, 571
Wilkins, Mary, **M12**: 15
Wilkinson, Cyril H., **L11**: 592
Will, **E5**: 202-3, 361; **M8**: 419; **L10**: 257; **L11**: 20, 78, 84; **L15**: 12; **L17**: 4
  doctrine of, **E1**: 327-28
  nature of, **E1**: 330-32; **E2**: 328-30, 358, 362-63; **E3**: 214; **E5**: 314; **M9**: 134-35, 140, 144-45; **M10**: 245; **L2**: 30-31; **L4**: 171, 180, 186, 199
  freedom of, **E1**: 333-34; **E4**: 91-92, 94; **M6**: 419, 464-66; **M9**: 175; **M14**: 8-9; **L3**: 93-94
  as aspect of consciousness, **E2**: 10-11, 18-20, 22-26
  and feeling, **E2**: 21
  in perception, **E2**: 151
  and sense impulses, **E2**: 299-300
  training of, **E2**: 309-10; **E4**: 249-50; **E5**: 118, 146; **L17**: 340-42
  elements of, **E2**: 310-11, 314-16, 319-20
  and self, **E2**: 311-12, 318-19, 357-58
  realizing activity of, **E2**: 320, 358-59; **E3**: 300
  in physical control, **E2**: 329-31; **M14**: 24
  in morals, **E2**: 344-45, 359-60; **L7**: 175-76, 341
  and character, **E2**: 352, 353; **L17**: 338
  and religion, **E2**: 360-62; **L4**: 42; **L17**: 16
  Kant on, **E3**: 290-91; **L4**: 47; **L14**: 73n
  cause of, **E4**: 91-93; **L17**: 200-204
  in D'Arcy, **E5**: 29
  Münsterberg on, **M1**: xiii; **M6**: 167-71
  divine, **M7**: 292-93; **M10**: 45
  Royce on, **M10**: 82-84
  compared with *Wille*, **M10**: 229-30
  James on, **M12**: 209, 217-18
  Bergson on, **M12**: 230-32
  free, **M13**: xv, 318-19; **L13**: 123; **L17**: 5, 383
  and habits, **M14**: 21, 32-34, 178
  to power, **M14**: 97-99
  and government, **L2**: 248, 259-60, 269, 278
  common, **L2**: 331; **L13**: 149
  related to values, **L4**: 214
  in knowledge, **L7**: 190, 281
  revolutionary, **L9**: 424-25
  esthetic function of, **L10**: 79, 84, 160, 299-301
  social, **L13**: 296
  spirit in, **L17**: 14
Willard, Louis H., **L9**: 363-64
Willcox, Walter Francis, **M4**: 218
Willcox, William G., **M10**: 159
Wille, **M10**: 229-30
William, Maurice, **M14**: 187n
William II, **M10**: 229

William E. Borah and American Foreign Policy (Maddox), **L6**: xxin
William Heard Kilpatrick: Trail Blazer in Education (Tenenbaum), **L17**: 52-56
William H. Kilpatrick Award for Distinguished Service in Philosophy of Education, **L15**: 326, 510
"William James as Empiricist," **L15**: xxii
William James Lectures, **L10**: 7
William of Champeaux, **M2**: 221
William of Occam, **M2**: 165, 222, 250
Williams, Donald, **L15**: 456-57
Williams, Eric, **L15**: xxiii, 308-9
Williams, J. A., **L17**: 145
Williams, S. G., **E5**: xcvi
William Vaughn Moody Lectureship, **L17**: 488, 568
Willkie, Wendell L., **L17**: 453
Will to Believe, The (W. James), **M7**: 142, 327; **M12**: 217; **L5**: 157
Willy-Nicky letters, **M12**: 61
Wilson, Dudley, **L9**: 360-61
Wilson, Edmund, **L15**: xxv
Wilson, Edmund Beecher, **L16**: 117n
Wilson, Woodrow, **M8**: 418; **M10**: xxxvii, 102, 158, 193, 260, 261; **M12**: 13, 29, 39; **M13**: 180, 213, 274; **M15**: 78, 81, 95, 105, 116, 404, 405; **L2**: 295-96; **L6**: 208, 234; **L11**: 591, 605; **L15**: 195, 242
- and Hughes campaign, **M10**: 252-55
- during WWI, **M10**: 265-66, 275; **M11**: 201, 268
- principles of, **M11**: xiii, xiv, 109, 146, 158, 184, 232, 260; **M13**: 253, 316
- on League of Nations, **M11**: 128-29
- Fourteen Points of, **M11**: 135, 138, 139
- foreign reaction to, **M11**: 151, 152, 177, 207
- plans for peace, **M11**: 181, 183, 190, 401-4
- on Polish question, **M11**: 242, 250-53, 272, 276, 279, 296, 298, 299, 316-17, 401n, 402, 405, 407
- on China, **M13**: 115, 126, 166, 210

Winckelmann, Johann Joachim, **E4**: 193; **M7**: 290
Windelband, Wilhelm, **M7**: 216; **M9**: 290; **L1**: 118; **L5**: 424; **L7**: 110; **L15**: 324
Winds of Doctrine (Santayana), **M15**: 329
Winged Victory, The (*Nike*; *Victory of Samothrace*), **L10**: 238
Winter Institute of Arts and Sciences (Coral Gables, Fla.), **L17**: 451n
Wirt, William Albert, **M8**: 262, 320
Wirth, Arthur, **M1**: xix
Wisconsin
- industrial education in, **M7**: 84-86, 461-68

Wisconsin, University of, **L15**: 3n, 335, 475; **L17**: 8, 89
- educational experiment at, **L6**: 295-98

Wisdom, **L1**: 53
- among Hebrews, **M5**: 97-98; **L7**: 89-90

attaining, **M5**: 111; **L7**: 102, 208, 209
Epicurean theory of, **M5**: 118; **L7**: 109, 199-202
Cynics on, **M5**: 119; **L7**: 110, 203-4
as supreme virtue, **M5**: 375-76; **L7**: 117-18
love of, **L1**: 50, 305-6, 308
and courage, **L2**: 130
and good, **L7**: 191
defined, **L7**: 210; **L17**: xix
philosophy as search for, **L15**: 159-60; **L16**: 365, 376, 378, 388-89
needed, **L16**: 319
Wise, Stephen S., **L6**: 381, 503
Wise man, **M5**: 127
Withdrawal, **L13**: 328-29
Wither, George, **L6**: 113
With-which
of attention, **L17**: 276
Witmer, Lightner, **M2**: 119
Wittgenstein, Ludwig, **M6**: xvi; **M8**: xiii; **L6**: xi; **L10**: vii; **L16**: 18
compared with Dewey, **L4**: ix, xii-xiv, xvii-xix; **L14**: xv-xix; **L17**: xxx-xxxi
Wolfe, Bertram D., **L9**: 320, 321, 335
Wolff, Christian von, **E1**: 34
systematizes Leibniz's ideas, **E1**: 265, 345-46
epigenesis theory of, **E1**: 278
and moral philosophy, **E4**: 143
on ontology, **M2**: 170-71
on optimism, **M2**: 175
on rationalism, **M2**: 217
Wolfman, Joseph, **L9**: 374
Woll, Matthew, **L5**: 338n, 390n; **L6**: 322, 404
accuses Brookwood of communism, **L5**: 340-45
and Union Labor Life Insurance Co., **L5**: 387-89
accuses Dewey of communism, **L5**: 392
Wolna Polska, **M11**: 309
Women
health of college, **E1**: 64-66, 70, 77-79; **L17**: 7-9
in primitive society, **M2**: 46; **L7**: 27, 30, 31, 438-44
as laborers, **M5**: 483-84, 528-31; **M11**: 162, 176; **M12**: 75; **L7**: 378, 400, 412-13
in marriage customs, **M5**: 511-16
suffrage for, **M6**: 153-54; **M7**: 409; **L6**: 186
education of, **M6**: 163-64; **M11**: 62, 66; **M12**: 55, 75; **L17**: 7
Aristotle's classification of, **M9**: 261-62
as philosophers, **M11**: 45
in China, **M11**: 196; **M12**: 48-49
Polish, **M11**: 314-19
as teachers, **L2**: 115-22, 204
social status of, **L4**: 7-8; **L7**: 129-30; **L17**: 24-25
Kafir, **L7**: 439
modern problems of, **L7**: 444-50, 461-62
economic interests of, **L7**: 457-58; **L17**: 24
sex life of, **L7**: 458-59
cooperate for peace, **L17**: 149-50
Women's Court (New York City), **L9**: 374-76
Women's International League for Peace and Freedom, **L17**: 149

Wonder, **L10**: xxxiii, 144, 274
Wood, Charles W., **M13**: 425
Wood, John S., **L17**: 137, 560
Wood, Leonard, **M10**: 184
Woodbridge, F. J. E., **M4**: x, xvii; **M6**: 103n; **M8**: x, 9, 54, 55; **M10**: 443; **M15**: 375; **L3**: 390, 391; **L4**: viii; **L14**: 7; **L17**: 371n
  on pragmatism, **M3**: 153
  on experience, **M3**: 171-77, 393-97, 400-402
  on consciousness, **M3**: 178, 180; **M4**: xxviii-xxix, 81n, 222-27; **L17**: 364-66
  influences Dewey, **M6**: xii
  on Dewey's theory of knowledge, **L5**: xxvii-xxviii, 210-13, 487-95
  on knowledge and existence, **L17**: 361, 370
  on fact, **L17**: 363, 366
  answers Bode, **L17**: 548-49
Woodger, J. H., **L16**: 117n, 165, 166n
Woodrow Wilson and the Rebirth of Poland, 1914–1920 (L. Gerson), **M11**: 248n, 255n
Woods, Robert Archey, **M4**: 218-19
Woodward, Frederic, **L15**: 321n
Woodworking, **E5**: 233-37, 243
Woodworth, Robert Sessions, **M4**: 228; **L5**: 223
Woody, Thomas
  on Soviet education, **L6**: 291-94
Woolf, S. J.
  interviews Dewey, **L6**: 408-13
  influence of, **L17**: 526, 573
Woolsey, Theodore Dwight, **M11**: 390
Worcester, Bishop of, **E1**: 373
Words, **L13**: 13; **L15**: 248-49. *See also* Language; Signs; Speech
  function of, **M1**: 152-53; **L10**: 219-20, 244-47, 343, 348
  meaning of, **M6**: 194, 282; **L8**: 127-28, 225, 231-33, 303-5; **L12**: 291-93, 303-4; **L13**: 323, 365
  Locke on, **M6**: 321
  W. Jevons on, **M6**: 324n
  mistaken for ideas, **M9**: 150-51
  Klyce on, **M10**: 324n; **M13**: 414-17
  as medium, **L10**: 22, 72n, 73, 80, 81, 89, 119, 200, 203, 209, 232, 273, 324
  and symbols, **L12**: 53-54, 57-60
  and terms, **L12**: 284-86
  invention of, **L13**: 324
  nature of, **L13**: 393; **L16**: 44-45, 69, 155-57, 162, 166, 168, 180, 346
  Tarski on, **L16**: 42
  vague, **L16**: 47, 49n, 56n, 68n, 73n, 75n, 84, 259, 265
  in triangular scheme, **L16**: 49, 58, 157-60, 300
  rejected view of, **L16**: 104, 112, 134
  Pepper on, **L16**: 175, 177
  Russell on, **L16**: 202-3
  Moore on, **L16**: 209
  as name, **L16**: 273, 327, 332
  as sign, **L16**: 298-300
  adjectival, **L16**: 346
Wordsworth, William, **E3**: 123; **M6**: 205; **L8**: 141
  on poetry, **L10**: 75, 294, 322, 355, 363, 365
  as poet, **L10**: 91, 137, 155, 158-59, 169-70, 192,

359, 360
poetry of, **L10**: 117, 138, 245, 279, 359, 363
on nature, **L11**: 18-19
influences Mill, **L11**: 81
Work, **M12**: 48, 75, 160, 183, 249; **L10**: 266, 345-46; **L11**: 158, 536, 538-39; **L15**: 182, 201-2, 263. *See also* Labor
vs. drudgery, **E5**: 125-28
related to play, **E5**: 197, 229; **M1**: 199-202, 339-40; **M7**: 320-21; **M9**: 212-13, 325; **L8**: 287-88; **L10**: 283-86
teaching about, **M1**: 222-23
as rationalizing agency, **M5**: 43-44; **L7**: 41
cooperation in, **M5**: 46-47; **L7**: 43-44
as thought activity, **M6**: 307-13
significance of, **M6**: 350-51; **L8**: 285-89, 346-48
types of, **M7**: 189-91
as curse, **L4**: 4, 12
psychology of, **L5**: 236-42
Clay on, **L7**: 378
art's relation to, **L10**: 231, 346
right to, **L13**: 306, 312-13, 318
need for, **L13**: 309-10
spirit of, **L17**: 314-15
retreat from, **L17**: 469
Russian view of, **L17**: 502
Workers
protection of, **M5**: 505-7
emancipation of, **L2**: 296-97
education of, **L5**: 331-45
defined, **L11**: 158
relations among, **L11**: 159-61
regimentation of, **L11**: 252, 258-59, 294-95
power of, **L13**: 107
Workers' Education Bureau of America, **L5**: 506
Working Man's Programme, The (Lasalle), **M8**: 176
Works of art, **L16**: 396
nature and meaning of, **L10**: xv-xvi, xxii, xxiii, xxvi-xxxi, 35, 43, 52, 54, 58, 61, 69-73, 76-79, 85-90, 99, 101, 104, 110-12, 121-23, 126, 128, 132-33, 140, 144, 149-51, 165-67, 175-76, 182-86, 195-99, 208-13, 218, 223, 230, 233, 235, 250, 258, 260-65, 271-72, 275
esthetic theory based on, **L10**: 9-10, 15-18
operation of, **L10**: 186-90, 277-300
judgment of, **L10**: 302-3, 308-13, 317-22, 328
transmit civilization, **L10**: 332-37, 347-48
Works of Jeremy Bentham, The (Bowring), **L14**: xxii
World, **M12**: 217, 225, 238; **L16**: 128, 360
-determination, **E5**: 29
in *Dictionary of Philosophy*, **M2**: 269
Dewey vs. Russell on external, **M8**: xx-xxv, 83-93
mind and, **M9**: 302-5
as problem of empiricism, **M10**: 18-21
knower outside, **M10**: 21-24
noumenal and phenomenal, **M12**: 92-93, 221, 226-27
conceptions of, **M12**: 101, 110-11, 114-16, 145, 226, 260; **L1**: xvii
affects education, **L17**: 228-30
World and the Individual, The (Royce), **M1**: x-xi, 241-56;

World and the Individual, The (*continued*)
M2: 120-37; **M10**: 85; **L11**: 472
World Court, **M13**: 411; **M15**: xi, 85, 114, 116, 122, 125-26, 405-7; **L2**: 170; **L6**: 223, 452; **L8**: 17
U.S. relations with, **M15**: xv-xviii, 95, 383-403, 415-17
law related to, **M15**: 89-91, 93-94, 123-24, 389
plan for, **M15**: 92-93, 386-87
and Treaty of Versailles, **M15**: 96, 113, 390
historical position of, **M15**: 108, 385-86
connected with League of Nations, **M15**: 380, 386-87, 393, 395-96
convening of, **M15**: 388-89
and minority treaties, **M15**: 391-92
World Fellowship of Faiths, First International Assembly of the, **L11**: 274n
World Politics in Modern Civilization (H. Barnes), **L5**: 382-83
World Tomorrow, **L6**: 439, 458n
World Views and Their Ethical Implications (W. Benedict), **M3**: 310-11
World War I (WWI), **M7**: xxiv; **M8**: xxvii-xxxi; **M10**: 158; **M12**: 35, 65, 238, 256; **M15**: 50, 58, 126, 141, 383; **L2**: 314-16; **L5**: 349-51, 382-83; **L6**: xx, 198; **L7**: 453; **L11**: 375, 517; **L13**: 180; **L14**: 249, 273, 364; **L15**: 192-93, 323, 341, 382n; **L17**: 573
attitude toward, **M10**: xxxix, 256-59, 265-66, 275, 292-95; **L17**: 149
education affected by, **M10**: 178-82; **M11**: xi, 54, 58-69
nationalism during, **M10**: 202-10; **M12**: 195; **L6**: 124
justification for, **M10**: 218-21, 223, 230
unpreparedness for, **M10**: 220
effect of science on, **M10**: 236
conscience related to, **M10**: 260-64
psychology of, **M10**: 271-80; **M11**: xvi-xvii, 107-16, 120, 360; **M12**: 4, 153; **L2**: 168; **L7**: xvi; **L16**: 390, 392
related to justice, **M10**: 281-84
children and, **M10**: 296-300; **L6**: 342
international effects of, **M11**: ix-x, xvii-xviii, 70-72, 153, 154, 161, 165, 173, 176, 186, 192, 267, 268-69; **M15**: 129
Dewey's response to, **M11**: x-xii, xx
pacifism in, **M11**: xi-xii, xvi, 180-81
social and political effects of, **M11**: xi-xii, 73-92, 98-106, 117-21, 393; **M12**: 4, 19-20; **L6**: 235, 240
alliances in, **M11**: xiii, 230, 394-95
goals of, **M11**: 126, 132, 180-85, 325, 389, 390
and League of Nations, **M11**: 127-30
economic effects of, **M11**: 134, 255, 324, 330; **L6**: 241, 337, 364-68, 372-73
conclusion of, **M11**: 180-85, 365

Polish question in, **M11**: 278, 279, 282, 293, 296-99, 306, 309, 319, 326-29
relief work in, **M11**: 286, 291
lessons of, **M12**: 153-54; **L17**: 459-60
influences Russell, **M12**: 236, 244, 247-48
and Germany, **L6**: 207, 235
and sanctions, **L6**: 208, 456, 467, 473, 477
related to charity, **L6**: 375, 406
cause of, **L6**: 451
and blockades, **L6**: 475, 476n
as victory for democracy, **L16**: 401
World War II (WWII), **M8**: xxx; **L6**: xx-xxi; **L11**: xxxi; **L13**: xv, 309, 316; **L15**: 302, 323; **L17**: 454-55, 471
economics and, **L6**: xix
significance of, **L14**: 249-51
causes of, **L15**: 61-62, 171-72, 196, 256
U.S. in, **L15**: 192-93, 349, 369-70
compared with WWI, **L15**: 193
veterans of, **L15**: 283
USSR in, **L15**: 340, 342, 347-48, 352-53, 494-98
peace after, **L15**: 342-44, 368-70
China in, **L15**: 348, 369-70
affects beliefs, **L16**: 390, 392
Wormser, I. Maurice, **L7**: 425
Worship
defined, **E4**: 3
of ancestors, **M5**: 35; **L7**: 34-35
of Yahweh, **M5**: 92-93, 97; **L7**: 87, 89
object of, **L9**: 5, 9, 28, 29, 36, 221

Wörterbuch der Philosophischen Begriffe (Eisler), **L16**: 43, 163
Worth, **M13**: 26-27
non-valuable, **M15**: 338-39
triadic relation as, **M15**: 345-47
of individual, **L7**: 449
Wren, Christopher, **L17**: 148, 562
Wright, Carroll Davidson, **L17**: 8, 554
Wright, Chauncey, **M6**: 99
Wright, Quincy, **L6**: xxi
Wright, Sewall, **L16**: 119n
Writers, **L10**: 74, 81, 162
Writing
affects education, **M9**: 189
teaching of, **L11**: 213; **L17**: 291-92
Wrongdoing, **L17**: 397
Wronski, Thaddeus, **M11**: 310-11
Wuchang uprising (China), **L17**: 555
Wundt, Wilhelm, **E3**: 75, 92; **E4**: 153n; **E5**: xiii; **M2**: 149; **M3**: 64; **L3**: 16-17; **L5**: 225; **L17**: 11
psychology of, **E1**: xxx, 196, 202-3; **M1**: xii-xiii; **M7**: 137-41
on stimuli, **E1**: 99-100
on function, **E1**: 110-11
on association, **E1**: 184-85
on impulses, **E2**: 306-7
James on, **L11**: 470-71
Wu Pei Fu, **M12**: 70; **M13**: 127n, 151-52
Wyclif (Wycliffe), John, **M5**: 141; **L7**: 140-41

Xenocrates, **M2**: 167
Xenophanes, **M2**: 144
Xenophon, **M5**: 182; **L7**: 101n

Yagoda, Genrikh G., **L15**: 345-46, 348
Yahweh, **M5**: 92-97; **L7**: 82-87, 89. *See also* Jehovah
Yale University, **E1**: 119; **L15**: 324
Yangtze region (China), **M12**: 30, 46, 62
Yangtze River (Chang Jiang), **M13**: xxiv, 127, 132, 178; **L6**: 190, 191, 205
Yellow Man's Burden, **M13**: 80
Yellow Peril, **M7**: 407; **M12**: 35; **M13**: xxvii, 249
Yezierska, Anzia, **M11**: 260, 396
Yokohama, Japan, **M11**: 166
Yokohama Specie Bank, **M13**: 85, 87, 160
Young, Ella Flagg, **M3**: 263n; **M6**: 179; **M10**: 390; **L8**: 109
  on school, **M1**: 269n, 272n; **M10**: 380; **M15**: 188; **L5**: 307, 372, 374; **L11**: 195, 199
Young, Owen D., **L7**: 424
Young, Robert, **M13**: 154
Young, Stark, **M15**: 339n
Young China
  features of, **M12**: 25, 49, 50, 59, 75; **M13**: 111, 113-14, 229-30
  attitude toward, **M12**: 53-54, 59; **M13**: 94, 98, 113, 120, 229
  origin of term, **M13**: 98-99, 108
Young John Dewey (Coughlan), **L6**: xiin
Young Men's Christian Association, **M15**: 147, 217
Youth
  Russell on, **M15**: 198
  character of, **L9**: 186-93; **L17**: 463
  effect of Depression on, **L11**: xix-xx, 340, 353-55, 378, 555
  opportunities of, **L17**: 462
  education of, **L17**: 462-63, 476
  Russian, **L17**: 505
"Youth in a Confused World," **L11**: xxn
Youth Outside of Home and School, Committee on, **L17**: 515
Yüan Shih-k'ai, **M11**: 200, 202; **M12**: 65, 66, 69, 254; **M13**: 88, 99, 130, 133, 151, 169; **L17**: 555
Yugo-Slavs, **M11**: 71, 263, 264

Zakopane, Poland, **M11**: 288
Zamora, Francisco, **L11**: 323
Zamoyski, Maurice, **M11**: 279, 281
Zekeria Bey, **M15**: 420
Zelenko, Aleksandr Ustinovich, **L17**: 507-8, 571
Zeller, Eduard, **M7**: 137-38
Zeno of Elea, **L12**: 97; **L14**: 398
Zero, **L12**: 408-9
Zionism, **M10**: 291
Zirkle, Raymond E., **L16**: 121n
Zitron, Abraham, **L9**: 320
Zola, Émile, **M3**: 193-94; **L11**: 320
Zöllner, Johann Karl Friedrich, **M3**: 163, 165n, 391
Zook, George, **L9**: 387
Zuñi Indians, **M5**: 66-67; **L7**: 61
Zybura, John S., **L2**: 388n